Higher Education in Portugal 1974–2009

Guy Neave • Alberto Amaral
Editors

Higher Education in Portugal 1974-2009

A Nation, a Generation

Centro de Investigação de
Políticas do Ensino Superior

Editors
Guy Neave
Centro de Investigação de
Politicas do Ensino Superior (CIPES)
Rua 1 de Dezembro 399
4450-227 Matosinhos
Portugal
guy.r.neave@gmail.com

Alberto Amaral
A3ES
Praça de Alvalade
6-5 Frente
1700-036 Lisbon
Portugal
alberto.amaral@a3es.pt

ISBN 978-94-007-2134-0   e-ISBN 978-94-007-2135-7
DOI 10.1007/978-94-007-2135-7
Springer Dordrecht Heidelberg London New York

Library of Congress Control Number: 2011944022

© Springer Science+Business Media B.V. 2012
No part of this work may be reproduced, stored in a retrieval system, or transmitted in any form or by any means, electronic, mechanical, photocopying, microfilming, recording or otherwise, without written permission from the Publisher, with the exception of any material supplied specifically for the purpose of being entered and executed on a computer system, for exclusive use by the purchaser of the work.

Printed on acid-free paper

Springer is part of Springer Science+Business Media (www.springer.com)

Preface

CIPES was established in 1998. From the outset, its mission is to engage in scholarly research, advance critical thought and forward informed understanding about the vital issues of policy that higher education faces both nationally and internationally. CIPES was initially set up as a research centre of the Foundation of Portuguese Universities (FUP). In 2006, it became a private association founded by the Universities of Aveiro and Porto.

Under the leadership of its founding Director, our colleague Alberto Amaral, CIPES set itself the task to become a centre of reference for higher education research in Portugal and abroad. At the national level, CIPES' aim is to strengthen and to spur on public debate on issues in higher education and to remedy a situation made no better by the relative paucity of policy studies of any kind in Portugal.

After its initial period of growth, CIPES consolidated its research team into becoming one of the largest research centres specialised in the domain of higher education. From the first, CIPES placed major weight upon having a visible and tangible international presence. Central to this strategy has been CIPES' participation as Founding Associate in the European Consortium for Higher Education Data Development and Analysis (HEDDA) together with similar centres and groups from the UK, Finland, Norway, France, the Netherlands, Germany and the Czech Republic. CIPES has also been highly active in EUREDOCS – the European Network of Doctoral Students in Higher Education. EUREDOCS has likewise played a key role in bringing together cutting edge research to focus on the various aspects of higher education policy in Europe and the European Union. CIPES was also a member of the EU PRIME Network of Excellence.

These international partnerships are essential in laying down a solid basis for our work. And for this we are grateful indeed to our colleagues and fellow research centres in Europe and beyond.

To some, higher education is not an autonomous discipline. It is rather a field of research to which many disciplines contribute. CIPES' work is fully within this perspective. It has both benefited from and profited by being a multidisciplinary community.

CIPES' researchers hail from very different disciplinary backgrounds: engineering, economics, management, sociology, philosophy, psychology, education sciences, history and geography. Each of its research projects draws strength from the diverse backgrounds of its members. Not only is the sum greater than the individual and disciplinary parts, the same feature protects and prevents the domain of higher education from that stultifying form of intellectual and institutional isolation that can only undermine its scientific, scholarly and public standing.

The volume Higher Education in Portugal 1974–2009: a Nation, a Generation is a good example, as well as being a synthesis, of what CIPES has been able to achieve over some 15 exciting and intensive years of exploring the Portuguese higher education system. The chapters in this book are the outcome of many years reflecting on the major changes the Portuguese system has been through over the past few decades. The impact they have had on the institutional fabric of higher education is carefully weighed up. The chapters also reflect the way this intellectual venture has been embedded in a multidisciplinary approach, which is clearly echoed across their conceptual, methodological and analytical foundations.

Another hallmark of CIPES' 'work style' is its collaborative nature. As the only research centre in Portugal specialised in higher education research, CIPES takes as part of its mission to engage in a sustained dialogue with other institutions concerned with the study of higher education–related topics. It is then not surprising in the least that this volume was drawn up together with Portuguese scholars unaffiliated to CIPES but well-known for their commitment to a long-term view on the political, economic, societal and cultural transformation Portugal has been through.

Another further characteristic of CIPES' 'style' also clearly reflected in this volume is its resolutely comparative approach. From the first, CIPES set out to engage in a dialogue with the international community of scholars working in higher education, both to integrate the Portuguese experience as well as to highlight marked differences in shaping the Portuguese higher education system. This volume firmly places the last three decades of Portugal's higher education development against broader international trends. In this way, CIPES has sought to ensure that its account of higher education in Portugal is complemented by a firm grasp of the wider international developments that shape higher education within the Nation as they do beyond it.

In the course of the past four decades, Portuguese higher education has undergone deep and complex changes. These changes entailed elements that drew the system closer to its European counterparts. At the same time they revealed certain peculiar features of the Portuguese system that demand a thorough grasp of the country's history and the way this latter shaped its political, economic, social and cultural fabric. Higher education in Portugal is a fertile ground for developing a research agenda that is both substantial and challenging. This volume, I would suggest, not only bears witness to how much has been achieved over a relatively short period, it also hints at the promise of further and no less exciting journeys around higher education in the future.

Pedro Teixeira
Director, CIPES

Contents

**1 Introduction. On Exceptionalism: The Nation,
a Generation and Higher Education, Portugal 1974–2009** 1
Guy Neave and Alberto Amaral

Part I Shaping the Nation

**2 National Identity and Higher Education:
From the Origins till 1974** 49
José Manuel Sobral

3 University, Society and Politics 67
Luis Reis Torgal

**4 Cultural and Educational Heritage,
Social Structure and Quality of Life** 89
José Madureira Pinto

**5 From an Agrarian Society to a Knowledge Economy?
The Rising Importance of Education to the Portuguese
Economy, 1950–2009** 109
Álvaro Santos Pereira and Pedro Lains

Part II Shaping Higher Learning

**6 From University to Diversity: The Making
of Portuguese Higher Education** 137
Ana Nunes de Almeida and Maria Manuel Vieira

**7 Changing Legal Regimes and the Fate
of Autonomy in Portuguese Universities** 161
Maria Eduarda Gonçalves

8	Science and Technology in Portugal: From Late Awakening to the Challenge of Knowledge-Integrated Communities.. Manuel Heitor and Hugo Horta	179
9	Governance, Public Management and Administration of Higher Education in Portugal.. António M. Magalhães and Rui Santiago	227
10	Quality, Evaluation and Accreditation: from Steering, Through Compliance, on to Enhancement and Innovation?.............. Maria J. Rosa and Cláudia S. Sarrico	249
11	The Impacts of Bologna and of the Lisbon Agenda............................ Amélia Veiga and Alberto Amaral	265

Part III Shaping the Institutional Fabric

12	Patterns of Institutional Management: Democratisation, Autonomy and the Managerialist Canon... Licínio C. Lima	287
13	The Changing Public–Private Mix in Higher Education: Analysing Portugal's Apparent Exceptionalism .... Pedro N. Teixeira	307
14	Shaping the 'New' Academic Profession .... Teresa Carvalho	329
15	The Rise of the Administrative Estate in Portuguese Higher Education... Maria de Lourdes Machado and Luisa Cerdeira	353
16	The Student Estate .... Madalena Fonseca	383

Index... 417

List of Contributors

Alberto Amaral A3ES, Praça de Avaladade 6-5 Frente, 1700-036 Lisbon, Portugal, alberto.amaral@a3es.pt

Teresa Carvalho Departamento de Ciências Sociais, Políticas e do Território, University of Aveiro, CIPES Rua Primeiro de Dezembro 399, 4450-228 Matosinhos, Portugal, teresa.carvalho@csjp.ua.pt

Luisa Cerdeira Rectorate, University of Lisbon, Alameda da Universidade, 1600 Lisbon, Portugal, lcerdeira@reitoria.ul.pt

Ana Nunes de Almeida Instituto de Ciências Sociais, University of Lisbon, Av Prof. Aníbal de Bettancourt 9, 1600-189 Lisbon, Portugal, ana.nunes.almeida@ics.ul.pt

Madalena Fonseca A3ES, Praça de Avaladade 6–5 Frente, 1700-36 Lisbon, Portugal, madalena.fonseca@a3es.pt

Maria Eduarda Gonçalves Departamento de Economia Política, ISTCE Lisbon, Av das Forças Armadas, 1649-026 Lisbon, Portugal, maria.eduarda.goncalves@iscte.pt

Manuel Heitor Centro de Estudos em Inovação, Tecnologia e Políticas de Desenvolvimento, IN+, Instituto Superior Técnico, Technical University of Lisbon, Portugal, mheitor@ist.utl.pt

Hugo Horta Centro de Estudos em Inovação, Tecnologia e Políticas de Desenvolvimento, IN+, Instituto Superior Técnico, Technical University of Lisbon, Portugal, hugo.horta@dem.ist.utl.pt

Pedro Lains Instituto de Ciências Sociais, University of Lisbon, Av Anibal de Bettancourt 9, 1600-189 Lisbon, Portugal, pedro.lains@ics.ul.pt

Licínio C. Lima Departamento de Ciências Sociais da Educação, University of Minho, Campus de Gualtar, 4710-057 Braga, Portugal, llima@ie.uminho.pt

Maria de Lourdes Machado CIPES, Rua Primeiro de Dezembro 399, 4450-227 Matosinhos, Portugal, lmachado@cipes.up.pt

António M. Magalhães CIPES, University of Porto, Rua Dr Manuel Pereira da Silva, 4200-392 Porto, Portugal, antonio@cipes.up.pt

Guy Neave CIPES, 31, square St Germain, 78100 St Germain en Laye, France, guy.r.neave@gmail.com

Álvaro Santos Pereira School for International Studies, Simon Fraser University, 515W Hastings Street, V6B 1M1 Vancouver, Canada, apereira@sfu.ca

José Madureira Pinto Instituto de Sociologia, Faculdade de Letras da Universidade do Porto, Via Panoramica s/n, 4150-584 Porto, Portugal

Faculdade de Economia do Porto, Rua Roberto Frias, 4200-464 Porto, jmp@fep.up.pt

Maria J. Rosa Departamento de Economia, Gestão e Engenharia Industrial, University of Aveiro, Campus Universitário de Santiago, 3810-193 Aveiro, Portugal, mjrosa@ua.pt

Rui Santiago Departamento de Ciências Sociais, Políticas e Jurídica, University of Aveiro, Campus Universitário de Santiago, 3810-193 Aveiro, Portugal, rui.santiago@ua.pt

Cláudia S. Sarrico ISEG, Universidade Tecnica de Lisboa, Rua Miguel Lupe 20, 1249-078 Lisbon, Portugal, cssarrico@iseg.utl.pt

José Manuel Sobral Instituto de Ciências Sociais, University of Lisbon, Av Prof Anibal de Bettencourt, 1600 Lisbon, Portugal, jose.sobral@ics.ul.pt

Pedro N. Teixeira CIPES, University of Porto, Rua Primeiro de Dezembro 399, 4450-227 Matosinhos, Portugal, Pedro@cipes.up.pt

Luis Reis Torgal Centro de Estudos Interdisciplinares do Século XX da, Universidade de Coimbra, Rua Filipe Simões, 33, 3000-186 Coimbra, Portugal, lrtorgal@netcabo.pt

Amélia Veiga A3ES, CIPES, Rua Primeiro de Dezembro 399, 4450-227 Matosinhos, Portugal, aveiga@cipes.up.pt

Maria Manuel Vieira Instituto de Ciências Sociais, University of Lisbon, Av Prof. Aníbal de Bettancourt 9, 1600-189 Lisbon, Portugal, mmfonseca@ics.ul.pt

About the Editors

Guy Neave is Scientific Director of CIPES (Portugal) and Professor Emeritus of the Centre for Higher Education Policy Studies, Twente University, The Netherlands. An historian by training, he has written extensively on higher education and comparative Higher Education Policy in Western Europe. He was the Professor of Comparative Education at the London University Institute of Education from 1985 to 1990 and served as Editor in Chief with Burton R Clark for the Encyclopedia of Higher Education (4 vols 1992) was Founder Editor of Higher Education Policy (Palgrave Macmillan) In 1998, he was elected Foreign Associate of the National Academy of Education of the USA. His principle interests lie in the area of government/university relationships, the post war history of universities in Europe and European Integration. He holds a doctorate from UC London in French political history and lives in the Far West of the Paris basin.

Alberto Amaral is professor at the University of Porto and president of the Portuguese Quality Agency. He has been the chairman of the Board of the Consortium of Higher Education Researchers, is a life member of International Association of University Presidents, and member of the OECD-based programme Institutional Management in Higher Education. He is editor and co-editor of several books, including Governing Higher Education: National Perspectives on Institutional Governance (2002), The Higher Education Managerial Revolution? (2003), Markets in Higher Education: Rhetoric or Reality? (2004), Reform and Change in Higher Education (2005), From Governance to Identity (2008) and Essays in Supportive Peer Review (2008).

About the Authors

Álvaro Santos Pereira is currently Minister of Economic Affairs in Portugal and was an associate professor at the School for International Studies, Simon Fraser University, Vancouver, Canada. He has published three books on the Portuguese economy, including Portugal's Moment of Truth: How to overcome the national crisis (2011), Lisbon; The Fear of Failure: History and Economic Policy in Portugal (2009), Lisbon: Esfera dos Livros; and The Myths of the Portuguese Economy (2007), Lisbon: Guerra e Paz Editores.

His most recent publications in English include papers in the Journal of Economic History, the Journal of International Development, the European Review of Economic History and Historical Social Research.

His current research centres are on the evolution of macroeconomic variables in Portugal, the economic legacy of the Portuguese empire in Africa and prices and wages in Portugal since 1500; he has also published on the economic impact of tuberculosis since the late nineteenth century.

Teresa Carvalho is Professor at the University of Aveiro and Senior Researcher at CIPES. Her main research interests are institutional governance and management, the academic profession and gender in higher education. Recent publications include articles in: Higher Education, Higher Education Quarterly, European Journal of Education, Higher Education Policy, Journal of Higher Education Policy and Management, Journal of Management Research, Tertiary Education and Management and Equal Opportunities International. She is also co-editor of The Changing Dynamics of Higher Education Middle Management (Springer, 2010).

Cláudia S. Sarrico is associate professor at the School of Economics and Management, Technical University of Lisbon and researcher at the Centre for Research in Higher Education Policies of Portugal. Her main research interests are in public management, in particular issues of performance management and governance in education and higher education. She has published in management, public management and higher education studies journals. She is Europe Regional Editor of the International Journal of Productivity and Performance Management. She is a member of the Consortium of Higher Education Researchers.

Ana Nunes de Almeida is a Sociologist and Research Professor in the Instituto de Ciências Sociais, University of Lisbon (Portugal). She was born in Lisbon in 1957. She holds a Licence en Sociologie (Faculté des Sciences Économiques et Sociales, Geneva, Switzerland), PhD in Sociology (ISCTE-IUL, Lisbon). She is a Pro-Rector at the University of Lisbon and coordinator of the Observatory of Students' Trajectories. Her research domains include: school and family, children and the Internet, youth and social inequalities. Her latest publications include: História da Vida Privada em Portugal (Ed.), Lisboa: Círculo dos Leitores, 2011; Para uma sociologia da infância, Lisboa: ICS, 2010.

Madalena Fonseca is a Geographer, Assistant Professor at the Universidade do Porto and researcher at the Centre for Research on Higher Education Policies (CIPES). At present, she is Secretary General of the Portuguese Agency for Accreditation and Assessment of Higher Education (A3ES) in Lisbon. She has been Consultant in planning, regional development and evaluation of European projects since 1994. She was a Guest Researcher at the University of Bayreuth, Guest Professor at the Chemnitz University of Technology, Germany and Visiting Professor at the Universities of Maputo (Mozambique), Complutense de Madrid (Spain), Frankfurt-Main and Regensburg (Germany).

As Member of the Regional Studies Association, she has published on industrial relocation and regional upgrading. Her recent publications (since 2008) include reports and research on the Portuguese higher education network.

Maria Eduarda Gonçalves, LL.M., Harvard Law School, Doctorat d'État en Droit (University of Nice), is Full Professor of Law at the Higher Institute of Business and Labour Sciences Lisbon University Institute (IUL) and at the Faculty of Law of the New University of Lisbon. A member of the Centre for the Study of Socio-economic Change and the Territory, her research interests include European law and policy, information technology law, risk regulation and the relationship between policy-making and scientific expertise. Participant in several multidisciplinary research projects sponsored by FCT/Portugal or the European Commission, she has published widely in both Portuguese and international journals in these fields. She is co-author of Taking European Knowledge Society Seriously? (2007), the report by the EC Expert Group on Science and Governance.

Manuel Heitor was until June 2011 the Secretary of State for Science, Technology and Higher Education. He was founding director of the Center for Innovation, Technology and Policy Research at the Instituto Superior Técnico (IST), the engineering school of the Technical University of Lisbon. After earning his PhD at Imperial College, London in 1985 and post-doctorate study the year following at the University of California San Diego, he took post as Professor at IST, becoming its Deputy-President from 1993 to 1998. Heitor is Research Fellow of the Innovation, Creativity and Capital (IC2) Institute at the University of Texas at Austin. Amongst his books are Combusting Flow Diagnostic and Unsteady Combustion. From 1996 to 2005, he chaired the Organizing Committee for the International Conferences on 'Technology Policy and Innovation'. He sits on the editorial boards of several journals, including

Technological Forecasting and Social Change and the International Journal of Technology, Policy and Management.

His research includes publications on technology management, the development of engineering and innovation policies and engineering design. He represented Portugal on the OECD project 'Steering and Funding of Public Research' and on the 'Futures Programme'. In 2003 he coordinated a national exhibition on 'Engineering in Portugal in the twentieth century', for which the Society for the History of Technology, SHOT conferred its Dibner Award. Cofounder in 2002 of 'Globelics – the global network for the economics of learning, innovation, and competence-building systems', Heitor is member of the Science and Technology Council of the 'International Risk Governance Council', IRGC.

Hugo Horta currently at the Centre for Innovation, Technology and Policy Research at the Instituto Superior Técnico (IST) at the Technical University of Lisbon. After completing his PhD in Management and Industrial Engineering at the Instituto Superior Técnico (IST), in 2007, he embarked on postdoc research into academic inbreeding in Portugal and Japan, an enquiry involving the Centro de Investigação e Estudos de Sociologia, ISCTE, Portugal and the Center for the Advancement of Higher Education (CAHE), Tohoku University, Japan. His publications focus on higher education diversity, scientific policies and funding, comparative scientific national structures, scientific productivity, internationalisation of higher education and academic mobility and have appeared in such international journals as Management Science, Technological Forecasting and Social Change, Science and Public Policy, Higher Education, Higher Education Policy, Studies in Social Science and Asia Pacific Education Review. He is on the editorial boards of the Mexican Journal of Research in Education and Asian Pacific Education Review. He is national delegate to the European Research Area Steering Committee on Human Resources and Mobility.

José Madureira Pinto is Professor (Retired) at the Social Sciences Department of the Faculty of Economics in the University of Porto (Portugal) and Researcher at the Institute of Sociology in the Faculty of Arts at the same university. His current interests include the sociology of education and cultural practices, the sociology of classes and social recomposition, the analysis of the social foundations of economy, as well as the methodology of the social sciences. He has published and edited several books and dozens of articles and book chapters on these topics, some of which were based on prolonged research in the field.

Pedro Lains is a research professor in Economic History at the Institute of Social Sciences, University of Lisbon and a visiting professor at the Faculty of Economics, Catholic University. His most recent publications in English are Paying for the Liberal State. The Rise of Public Finances in Nineteenth Century Europe, Cambridge: Cambridge University Press, 2010 (Co-edited with J. L. Cardoso); Agriculture and Economic Development in Europe since 1870, London: Routledge, 2009 (Co-edited with V. Pinilla); "The Portuguese economy in the Irish mirror, 1960–2002", Open Economies Review, 19 (5), 2008: 667–683; "The power of peripheral governments. Coping with the 1891 financial crisis in Portugal", Historical

Research, 81, 2008; "Growth in a protected environment: Portugal, 1850–1950" Research in Economic History, 24, 2007; and Classical Trade Protectionism, 1815–1914. London: Routledge, 2006 (jointly edited with J.-P. Dormois).

Licínio C. Lima was born in 1957 in Porto, Portugal. He is Full Professor of Sociology of Education and Educational Administration at the Department of Social Sciences of Education, Institute of Education of the University of Minho, Campus de Gualtar, Braga, Portugal. He has been the Director of the Research Centre for Education and Psychology (1994–1997), Head of the Unit for Adult Education (1984–2004), Head of Department (1998–2004), and Director of the PhD in Education at the University of Minho. Lima has been Guest Professor in various European and Brazilian universities. He is an author of many academic works published in 13 countries and 6 languages, including 30 books.

Luisa Cerdeira received her PhD in Educational Sciences, Specialty Policies and Organisation of the Educational System from the University of Lisbon and Master's Degree in Education, specialising in School Administration from the University of Évora and a Licenciatura in Economics from the Lisbon Technical University (Portugal). She is Pro-Rector at the University of Lisbon and Professor of the Institute of Education, University of Lisbon. Currently, she is external consultant to the World Bank in higher education financing. In recognition of her work, she was elected member of the HUMANE Executive Committee (Heads of University Management & Administration Network in Europe) and member of the Executive Secretariat of RAUI (Iberian-American Network of University Administrators).

Maria de Lourdes Machado holds a Licenciatura in Economics from the University of Porto, Post-Graduate Studies in Administration and a PhD, both from the University of Minho (Portugal). She was Head of Administration at the Polytechnic Institute in Bragança (Portugal). She is a Senior Research Associate at the Center for Research on Higher Education Policies (CIPES), Portugal. Her areas of research include management, strategic planning and gender studies. She is the author of books on higher education legislation, strategic management, gender studies, non-university sector and other publications in European and American journals such as European Journal of Education, Higher Education Policy, Planning for Higher Education and Tertiary Education and Management.

António M. Magalhães is associate professor at the Faculty of Psychology and Education Sciences at the University of Porto, Portugal, and a senior researcher at CIPES (Centre for Research in Higher Education Policies), Portugal. He researches in the areas of regulatory mechanisms in education and the relationship between state and higher education, higher education governance and its theories and methods of policy analysis. On these topics he has published widely in both national and international journals and publications.

Maria J. Rosa is assistant professor in the Department of Economics, Management and Industrial Engineering at the University of Aveiro and a researcher at CIPES. Her research topics are quality management and quality assessment in higher education. Publications include articles in journals such as Total Quality Management, Higher Education Quarterly, European Journal of Education, Quality Assurance in Education and Quality in Higher Education. She is co-editor of Cost-sharing and Accessibility in Higher Education: A Fairer Deal? (2006), Quality Assurance in Higher Education. Trends in Regulation, Translation and Transformation (2007) and Essays in Supportive Peer Review (2008). She is a member of Consortium of Higher Education Researchers and of the Executive Committee of European Association for Institutional Research.

Rui Santiago is a professor at the University of Aveiro and a senior researcher at CIPES. His main research interests are institutional governance and management and the academic profession. His recent publications include articles in Higher Education Quarterly, Higher Education, Higher Education Policy and European Journal of Higher Education. He is also co-editor of Non-University Higher Education in Europe (Springer, 2008) and of The Changing Dynamics of Higher Education Middle Management (Springer, 2010).

Jose Manuel Sobral, a historian and anthropologist, is Senior Research Fellow at the Instituto de Ciencias Sociais da Universidade de Lisboa, Portugal, where he also teaches on the Graduate Programme in Anthropology. He has researched and published on family and kinship, power and politics, social structure, epidemics, social memory, the history of anthropology and, more recently, on food and cuisine and nationalism, ethnicity and racism. Among his recent works are Trajectos: O Passado e O Presente na Vida de uma Freguesia Rural (Imprensa de Ciencias Sociais, 1999) and as editor and contributor, A Pandemia Esquecida: Olhares Comparados sobre a Pneumonica (1918–19) (with Maria Luisa Lima et al., Imprensa de Ciencias Sociais, 2009), Identidade Nacional, Inclusão e Exclusão Social (with Jorge Vala, Imprensa de Ciencias Sociais, 2010).

Pedro N. Teixeira is Associate Professor at the Department of Economics (University of Porto) and Director of CIPES (Centre of Research on Higher Education Policy). His research interests focus on the economics of higher education, notably on markets and privatisation, and the development of human capital as a research programme. He is the author of Jacob Mincer – A Founding Father of Modern Labour Economics (Oxford UP, 2007). He has co-edited two volumes: Markets in Higher Education – Reality or Rhetoric? (Kluwer, 2004) and Cost-Sharing and Accessibility in Higher Education – A Fairer Deal? (Springer, 2006).

Luis Reis Torgal is Professor Emeritus of Contemporary History, Faculty of Arts at Coimbra University and Director of Research at the Centre for the Interdisciplinary Study of the Twentieth Century at the same university. He has published extensively on Education and on the University in particular from both a historical and critical perspective. He is currently preparing a collection of studies entitled 'What University?'.

Amélia Veiga is researcher at the Agency for Assessment and Accreditation of Higher Education (A3ES) and has been researcher at Centre for Research in Higher

Education Policies (CIPES) since obtaining a master degree. She holds a PhD from the University of Porto, Portugal. Her main research interests lie in comparative studies in higher education, in particular European integration and governance and the institutionalisation of a European dimension in education viewed from the perspective of policy implementation.

Maria Manuel Vieira is a Sociologist and Research Fellow at the Social Sciences Institute, University of Lisbon (Portugal). She has a PhD in Sociology (1998, ISCTE, Lisbon) with a thesis on elite education ("Educar Herdeiros. Práticas educativas da classe dominante lisboeta nas últimas décadas", Lisboa: Fundação Calouste Gulbenkian, 2003). Her current research interests include education systems and modernity, schooling and individuation processes and schooling as an affiliation link between parents and children. She is Coordinator of the Permanent Observatory of Youth (ICS-UL). Her recent publications include: Vieira, M.M. and Resende, J. (Eds.). (2009). The Crisis of Schooling? Learning, Knowledge and Competencies in Modern Societies. Newcastle: Cambridge Scholars Publishing; and Vieira, M.M. (2011). Aprendizagens, escola e a pedagogização do quotidiano. In A.N. Almeida (ed). História da Vida Privada em Portugal. Os nossos dias., vol 4. Lisboa: Círculo de Leitores/Temas e Debates.

Chapter 1
Introduction. On Exceptionalism: The Nation, a Generation and Higher Education, Portugal 1974–2009

Guy Neave and Alberto Amaral

Introduction

The history of the University in Europe is long always; nuanced, inevitably so; most assuredly complex and occasionally inspiring (Ruegg and de Ridder Simoens 1994–2011). Yet, irrespective of whether the shaping of contemporary Europe is the child of a broader, planet-wide drive towards what is variously described as the 'Knowledge Economy', the 'Knowledge Society' (Sorlin and Vessuri 2007) or the 'Learning Economy' (Lundvall and Johnson 1994), the very fact that today we can look upon the university as a manifest form of 'Europe re-emerging' reflects the University's perceived and abiding centrality. Nor, for that matter, is the central and symbolic value of the University as a revived expression of a Europe quâ a regional 'learning area' to be ignored. Rather the contrary. A careful examination of the names appended to the various programmes, launched by the European Commission, Tempus, Erasmus, Socrates, Leonardo da Vinci, Marie Curie, to name but a few, are themselves redolent of the wish at one and the same time to present current policy as the natural heir to and continuation of, the centuries-long history of learning in Europe. The deliberate choice of these particular figures as symbols has another and most definitely explicit purpose. That purpose is to re-state a basic continuity with a very old image indeed of the University. To be sure, in the strict meaning of the term, the University no longer has, as it did until recently, the monopoly over the transmission of higher learning and still less the exclusivity over developing knowledge whether fundamental or applied. The permeation of these functions into

G. Neave (✉)
CIPES, 31, square St Germain, 78100 St Germain en Laye, France
e-mail: guy.r.neave@gmail.com

A. Amaral
A3ES, Praça de Avaladade 6-5 Frente, 1700-036 Lisbon, Portugal
e-mail: alberto.amaral@a3es.pt

other institutions – some of them forming a subset within 'tertiary education', others firmly ensconced in business, industry and commerce – is today an integral part of the dynamic that the Knowledge Society has created and which it needs for its survival, if not always its well-being. Seen from this perspective, the rise of the 'Learning Society' has driven the universality of higher learning beyond the groves of academe. Learning has, in short, taken on a new 'dimension' in its universality. The University is but one part in it, though no less vital for all that.

European Higher Education Policy as Eschatology

There is, however, a further element in the eschatology of higher education in present-day Europe. It has to do with two key issues, namely economic integration on the one hand and attempts to firm up a 'European Identity', on the other. In this, bureaucratic jargon is not always endowed with poetic and historical imagination. But the ties by association between what the analyst knows as the 'European Dimension' in higher education policy and the explicit harking back to a time when higher learning knew little if any physical frontiers, a blessed moment when the universities in Europe were coterminous with Europe itself, provides a vision that is powerful in its appeal if not always in its historical accuracy. Indeed, if we take this vision at face value, it could certainly be argued that the basic rationale of the European Union itself – the mobility of capital, ideas and labour – is simply a vastly enlarged application of one of the basic principles that was itself an integral feature of the medieval university, namely the *peregrinatio academica* – the ancient practice of students moving across kingdoms, dukedoms and counties, seeking out learning wherever it was to be found. Both the European Research Area and the European Higher Education Area stand as latter-day re-enactments of this principle, though on a scale both financial and in terms of the number of individuals involved far beyond that known – or even thinkable 600 years ago.

European Higher Education Policy as Ambition

In short, higher education policy in Europe is engaged in a venture so ambitious in its geographical extent and in the number of systems involved that one is hard pressed indeed to find an exact parallel, though the analogy itself is evident, (Neave 2001: 13–73) across the nine centuries since the legendary founding at Bologna (Italy) of what some regard – and others just as hotly dispute – as the first of Europe's universities in the Year of Grace 1088 (Ruegg 1992: 4–6). That venture is nothing less than the forging of a Continent-wide, multi-national system of higher education, rooted in the European Higher Education Area, sustained by the European Research Area and urged on by the Bologna 'Process' and by the Lisbon Agenda (Amaral and Neave 2009b: 281–300).

European Higher Education Policy as Historical Paradox

There is, even so, a certain paradox in such a bid to have higher education 'progress to the past'. For just as the rise of prototypical forms of the 'Nation State' in the course of the fifteenth century undermined and ultimately dissolved the medieval vision of 'the European University' as an institution under a single and supreme authority of the Pope (De Groof et al. 1998) so, more than half a millennium later the revival of a 'European' vision for the University in turn rested upon and built out from, equally unprecedented and sustained efforts within the Western Nation States of Europe to modernise their systems of higher education. This they did under pressure from social demand, from insistent calls to give further recognition to merit and worth – the two are very far from being the same, as Rothblatt has pointed out (Rothblatt 2007: 301–311). Individual Nation States in Europe mobilised higher learning to keep abreast of social and knowledge demands, equally pressing, that technological and economic change had thrown up. Each Nation adapted the construct and provision, structure and content that had shaped its individual and highly variegated system of higher education.

The break-up of what has been termed the 'elite' University and the birth of its 'mass' offspring were not, however, universal developments, though the earliest impulses can, depending on the particular system involved, be traced back as early as 1955 in the case of France (Ruegg 2011: 13–14). Eastern Europe and more particularly those systems shaped by the Soviet model of higher education and driven by a command economy remained aloof from the trends emerging in the West (Neave 2011: 46). Only after the Berlin Wall fell in ruins in 1989 did the satellites of the now defunct Soviet bloc begin to 'massify' their own universities, a step that took place under conditions often bordering on the chaotic. (File and Goedegebuure 2003). Nevertheless, 'massification' was wholly and utterly the work of the individual Nation State. Over the four and a half decades from 1950 onwards, national policies of higher education raised the number of universities in Europe from around 200 to 800 by 1995 (Ruegg 2011: 21). Crudely stated, the return of the University as a prime vector for European cooperation, integration, research and culture began to take on operational form in the mid-1980s initially in the shape of student mobility programmes. Even so, it cannot be denied that these first operational initiatives at European level rested on a trajectory, which had been determined, laid down and realised within the Nation State.

Beginning in the early nineteenth century and from then on, the Nation State had steadily assumed responsibility for, and been the exclusive architect of, both the modern research university and its successor in mass form (Nybom 2006: 3–16). What some scholars have qualified as 'the University *for* Europe' (Barblan 2011: 574) is, in effect, a recent graft on a very old root.

Whilst the European Dimension in higher education policy built on the achievements of the Nation State, it also brought in its wake a fundamental change in the basic paradigm on which European higher education policy rests today. This too is the product of Nation State initiative. The onset of neoliberalism – sometimes alluded to as 'Ultra Liberalism' – as the basic doctrine that today drives higher education policy in Europe emerged from the same source – first in the UK and the Netherlands during the early 1980s. By the following decade, it had taken root in the newly liberated States of Eastern Europe (File and Goedegebuure 2003) at the same time as they groped belatedly towards massification.

A Watershed

From this perspective, the 1980s were a watershed in the history of Europe's universities. That decade saw the unfurling of neoliberalism as the new *Weltanschauung*. In the course of the ensuing 15 years, neoliberalism ousted the long-established paradigm, which previously governed the relationship between the polity, society and higher education and had done so over the previous century and a half (Neave and van Vught 1991). The earlier paradigm is best described as 'political'. It was intimately taken up with the modernisation of government, with the professionalisation of public administration and the forging of national identity. In this, the University in Europe was taken over as a public service provided by the State, which also guaranteed varying degrees of self- determination, to ensure the renewal of Nation's future administrative, professional and intellectual elites (Neave 2007: 56–74). By contrast, neoliberalism focuses not on the political modernisation of society so much as the modernisation of the economy principally through its transformation from a manufacturing to a service – or non-material – economy. Neoliberalism is a marked breakaway from the political and historic paradigm that shaped the Universities of Western Europe up to the end of the 1970s; it is concerned less with the Nation State as an independent sovereign entity so much as the place the Nation State occupies as an interdependent unit in an economic order, variously defined as regional – or global. In effect, the neoliberal paradigm inverted the fundamental assumptions that governed both institutions and progress. For whilst the political paradigm regarded the purpose of institutions – and the University not least – as upholding social stability and coherence as prior conditions for progress, neoliberalism stood this relationship on its head. Economic efficiency, performance and output are today deemed to be the prior and necessary condition for social stability. In short, Adam Smith triumphed over Thomas Hobbes (Neave 2006: 382–403).

Higher Education's mission under the new paradigm is less to do with social behaviour, socialisation and enculturation so much as the provision of skills, which a service and technologically driven economy demands on a scale even greater and for a broad range of occupations which, whilst more diverse, are also less stable in their 'expectation of sustained relevance' than ever before. Some have argued that neoliberalism re-introduced a market that had never in effect been entirely absent (Ruegg 2011: 21). Whilst it is certainly true that from an economic perspective, higher education had never been entirely divorced from 'the market', the political paradigm served largely to feed the 'fixed price labour market' (Kerr 1986) of public sector employment. In effect, mass higher education and neoliberalism together served not merely to fragment the hitherto dominant market to which higher education responded. By the same token, it also multiplied the range of markets with which higher education has today to deal.

The triptych of market, competition and demonstrated institutional performance thus assumed the primary role in shaping higher education at the Nation State level (Dill et al. 2004). It brought to an end that paradigm which, for the best part of a century and a half, had driven higher education within the European Nation State as the highest level of political, legal and cultural aggregation (Huisman, Maassen and Neave 2001: 13–75).

New Vistas and Perspectives on Europe's Higher Education

Not surprisingly, this paradigm shift is interpreted in different ways: as the end of the neo-Keynesian consensus of deficit funding in public policy, as the destruction of the Ivory Tower university, its replacement by the Entrepreneurial University (Clark 1997; Ruegg 2011: 15) or, alternatively, as the triumph of the American model of university over its European fellows. Whatever the analytic perspective chosen, the consequences for the universities in Europe which the paradigm shift brought about in the course of the 1990s were profound: the privatisation of higher education, the introduction of fees – otherwise known under the feline phrase of 'cost sharing' – closer and more rigorous public oversight over academic quality, performance, productivity and output, a rejuvenation of the 'leadership principle' and the realignment of university management around supposedly best commercial practice. These measures appear even more radical when set against the broader collective cultural mission the Nation State university fulfilled when the dominant paradigm obeyed a political rationale as opposed to an economic purpose set in within a regional – if not a global – economy. As the earlier political paradigm acquired weight and substance during the nineteenth and twentieth centuries, the university served as guardian of the Nation's intellectual memory and thus its identity. Both were grounded in those scientific, literary, artistic and political achievements that made up the national self-image and forged an awareness of being part of that collective identity. The university also prepared, educated and socialised those who formed 'value allocating bodies' in society – the Law, the Church, the Medical Profession, as well as a national civil service firmly grounded on the principle of merit. Whilst these latter functions still pertain and very often characterise the older and more prestigious amongst a Nation's establishments of higher learning, they have become marginal by comparison with the central task the university is now required to fulfil – namely the provision of services directed primarily at the private sector, whilst generating revenue as well as capital, human and fiduciary, rather than re-distributing it.

Four Points in Justification

This summary excursion across the broad trends that shaped the universities of Europe has one simple purpose. It is to state a basic and evident truth, which in turn governs both the rationale of this study and the way we have gone about it. That evident truth is simply this: irrespective of the degree of complementarity, integration or collaboration which the European Dimension aims for and represents, higher education has not detached itself from its roots in the Nation State despite the argument, fashionable amongst some, that the past 20 years have seen a drastic weakening in the Nation State's viability. If the truth were out, complementarity – the capacity through exchange and collaboration for the strength of one system of higher education to remedy the shortcomings of its neighbours – points in two directions. It may just as well contribute to the strengthening of higher education within the Nation State as it develops a new awareness of the potential and significance that come from extending the 'outreach' of its universities to operate beyond it.

To this, one may add a further justification for focusing on one particular Nation – in this case, Portugal. For whilst none would waste their breath by denying the significance of the European Dimension as a further stage in the ongoing saga of higher education, how far its aims and its intent translate into concrete outcomes and practices are still determined within the individual Nation State if not always by it. Seen from this perspective, whatever 'success' there is to be had by 'European' as opposed to Nation State initiatives is dependent on whatever fate, reception and take up occur at the Nation State level. At a time when evaluation and public accountability are the watchwords of the hour, it is arguable more than ever that the Nation State system of higher education stands literally as the acid test by which the objectives, goals and principles enshrined in European level initiatives are themselves weighed in the balance rather than being taken on faith through the overblown rhetoric that often accompanies their launching (Neave and Amaral 2008: 40–62).

Time and Circumstance

Research – whatever the field involved – rarely fulfils a single purpose. From this axiom, this book does not stand aside. In drawing it up – and clearly given what has been discussed up to this point – this volume sets out to deal with a number of issues key to understanding the current situation of higher education in one country. And, no less important, how *over time*, such issues assumed their importance – an aspect that many studies of higher education leave aside the better to devote themselves to diagnosing the current condition – or 'solving the current problem' – rather than delving into how that problem came to be what it is today. Thus, this study sets itself the ambition to show how such issues as system growth, changes in institutional and managerial latitude, changes in the way government and academia conceive their responsibilities and the way the shifting *Weltanschauung* examined earlier have in

Portugal as elsewhere in Europe moved higher education away from its historic place as a subset of the political system to assume its contemporary status as a key instrument in advancing the economy of Nations or, as we have suggested at various points in this overview, the economy of a continent.

The Place of Context and the Context of Place

Second amongst the explicit issues this book addresses is the setting of higher education, its response to policy and its evolution within a broad context, that is to say, within the deep sociological, political, demographic, economic shifts and forces of collective psychology that have fundamentally reshaped Portuguese society as a whole over the past four decades. Setting the broader scene provides a necessary and inseparable preliminary to a more focused examination of how higher education in Portugal unfolded over these same years. This is important for other reasons as well.

Ours is not the intention deliberately to limit readership to students of higher education. Nor, for that matter, do we see this undertaking as an account presented for Portuguese readership alone. Clearly, it would be folly of the worst kind to presume that non-Portuguese readers have the same familiarity with, and sensitivity to, those features in Portuguese society and politics that are the daily lot of the Portuguese citizen, tax payer, academic or student!

Even within the study of higher education, there are very substantial differences in the weight scholars assign to what is all-too-often passed over lightly by summoning up the utterly meaningless phrase, 'The External Environment'. Cruel though it might be to say so, this is a facile and cavalier way of dealing with a highly complex issue, if it is not itself a devastating example of a wider and no less deleterious phenomenon of the 'Evacuation of Meaning' from which neither higher education nor the scholarship devoted to it is immune (Neave 2011). Simply to concentrate on higher education in isolation from the context – political, economic or sociological – in which it is set is a curious, though sometimes justifiable, perspective, for it leaves itself open to the unkind accusation of being 'Ivory Tower' erudition or, in the words of the English sociologist, Roger Dale, to be seen as a species of 'higher educationism' (Robertson and Dale 2009). That is to say, boiling the analysis of higher education down to a perspective bounded by the apparently neutral and uncontroversial ends couched in terms of processes, goals and objectives without the slightest attention being paid to the consequences in terms of their impact beyond the Groves of Academe and still less what may follow in the way of shifts in social values, ethics and behaviour for society at large.

Playing fast and loose with the broader social, economic or political context that surrounds higher education may, of course, be precisely the price some are prepared to pay for a finer and more discriminating portrayal of the internal displacement of power and authority, performance and responsibility, not to mention the level of efficiency each of these dimensions may demonstrate within academia itself. Yet, as the rise of neoliberalism in Europe generally and its somewhat belated arrival in the theatre of higher education policy in Portugal both show as clear as the day is long, radical change in higher education, as Clark Kerr pointed out more than half a century ago, comes rather from without the university though intellectual change from within remains its essential business (Kerr 1963).

Agendas: Inside and Outside

Third, this study is the work of 'insiders'. All those contributing to it are, in one way and other, active in higher education and in research on higher education, in defining, shaping, administering and analysing policy – or all four. They are, in short, students of higher education in Portugal or are part of the Portuguese Diaspora abroad. Here again, there are benefits and drawbacks to the 'insider' view just as there are to an outsider's perspective. The advantages are obvious: deep and personal experience of higher education and of its evolution that come from having been through it, allied with a sensitivity to the way higher education in Portugal shapes both itself and the perceptions of itself – a natural subtlety that is not always readily accessible to the outside observer. On the other hand, however, it may be argued that in no small degree, Exceptionalism or singularities that sometimes appear so striking to the outsider are often apt to be precisely what the insider takes for granted. And whilst this Introduction seeks deliberately to espouse a standpoint more akin to the outsider view by dint of one of us being precisely that, we take the view that readers will have their own perceptions of what appears to be exceptional in addition to those grosser dimensions which we will deal with later. Given this ambition, it is in all probability the lesser of two evils to place our trust in the accounts and perceptions of our colleagues 'deep inside the whale'.

Pedagogy

Finally, despite the tedium that 'pedagogy' often evokes, this book has a very definite 'pedagogical purpose'. This purpose relates back to the disciplines and perspectives that illuminate the institution of higher education.[1] Here, we find ourselves faced with a double task. First, to give real expression to the argument that higher education is a multidisciplinary domain. This requires a coverage of disciplines and perspectives that reflects the line-up and configuration as they are currently employed in the analysis of higher education as a national institution. Second, to do so in such a way that the different methods of analysis emerge clearly, though whether they are complementary to, or in conflict with, one another is a very different matter.

These two considerations have direct implications for both the structure of this volume as indeed they do for the way each discipline or perspective handles its account of higher education in Portugal over the past four decades. In effect, the synthesis is established primarily *within* the particular discipline or perspectives prominent in the study of higher education. Arguably, the task we set our colleagues and ourselves does not seek to set out a synthesis *across* fields. And for this too, there are good reasons. Since the aim of this study is to provide as clear a demonstration as possible of how different criteria and concepts, canons of scholarship and their interpretations are applied and brought to bear on analysing the place higher education occupies in different areas of the life of the Nation – in Politics, the Economy and in the Nation's cultures – clearly overlaps between the scope such different perspectives entail cannot be avoided. Nor have we sought to do so. To have eliminated overlap, different weight attached to, and interpretations placed on, the same events, situations and trends would, we feel, have taken the edge off our showing both the analytical techniques and methodology that set one discipline – or perspective – off from another. Had we sought to avoid duplication and overlap, we would have compromised the very purpose this study sets out to address – first, to give a dynamic account of higher education developing in one country across four decades and, second to provide clear examples of how different canons of scholarship are currently employed in laying bare the multiple dimensions and functions of Higher Education.

From this it follows that overlap of events, trends and topics is very far from being the result of editorial sloth. It is, rather, a deliberate device of this book. For this reason and to underline particular events or the interpretations of them that emerge from the different scholarly accounts, we have included a system of cross-referencing that points the reader towards similarities, issues or themes that find echo in other chapters.

Structure and Rationale

The structure of this study takes the form of a 'reverse pyramid', that is, a pyramid standing on its apex rather than on its base. We proceed from the general – the broad sweep across the major dimensions that shape the life of the Nation and its higher education – down to the very specific and particular at the institutional level. In this, it is only correct to have that Estate on whose behalf policy has been drawn up and for whose future, reform and all that follows therefrom are intended to advance and improve, should figure as the final account. Precisely because what is today fashionably alluded to as the 'higher education enterprise' is neither higher education, still less an enterprise when devoid of students, to reserve the Student Estate until last is to recognise its undisputable importance.

The book is organised into three distinct parts. These are:

1. Shaping the Nation
2. Shaping higher learning
3. Shaping the institutional fabric

All three parts address one central issue: How far is Portugal an exception in the way its higher education system has evolved over the past 40 years? What form does this 'Exceptionalism' take? How has Portuguese higher education policy sought to deal with this? What have been the consequences that resulted, both for the world of higher learning within the Nation as well as the place the Nation sees itself occupying today in the broader European panorama? How has higher education in Portugal sought to accommodate the initiatives, increasingly bold and certainly more complex, that tie it into the European Union?

These questions form the Leitmotif to this book. By their very nature, they demand a very particular analytic perspective, one which combines both internal and external viewpoints the better to marry together the interplay between the shaping of higher education and the policy which sets the bounds to that exercise as they play out on two levels – the Portuguese and, for lack of a better term, the European Dimension itself. Quite obviously, such an approach seeks to take full account of the interplay between two 'policy dynamics', the former being within Portugal, the latter the broader backdrop unfolding on the larger, European stage. This we seek to make explicit by this Introduction. To say the least, it is a challenge and a delicate one at that. It is delicate not simply because much can happen – and did – in the years following the Revolution of the Carnations in 1974. The task is made no less formidable because developments in the study of Higher Education itself over the same period are equally dynamic. For this reason, we need to be alert to changes in meaning, in different understandings and rise of new concepts that provide us with further insights into the workings and perceptions we have of the institution we study.

Accordingly, this Introduction, as indeed the book's title, makes use of an unusual unit of analysis to develop a long-term perspective – namely a generation. Such a category is, we believe, justifiable precisely because it imposes a perspective inseparable from the long term. It obliges us to set recent trends and current initiatives in a context more comprehensive and, we would argue, more sensitive to broader trends in Society than simply confining ourselves to the immediate present. The University is, after all, one of the most evident and enduring of Society's historical institutions (Kerr 1963). Against this backdrop, we then return to the central question: What does the evolution of higher education in Portugal tell us about its often singular features, about what some would see as its break-neck dash to growth? Is Portugal simply following broad trends visible elsewhere in Europe? Or is it a pioneer? If the latter, on what grounds may its system of higher education lay claim to such a title? Has the country's revolutionary inheritance in higher education vanished entirely or is it still a conditioning factor in the values that attach to higher education and which add spice to the debates that sometimes give the reform of higher education liveliness, venom and sparkle? Dissecting Portugal's revolutionary inheritance is not, however, an indulgence in nostalgia, still less a backhanded form of regret for what might have been. It is important because it illustrates some of the explicit assumptions made about the legitimate role of the State. In Portugal, such concepts are very far from being a perfect reflection of the basic belief that nourishes neoliberalism *à l'anglo-saxonne*.

Before turning our attention to the various analytic thrusts in each of the three parts around which the corpus of this study is arranged, it is as well to address the prior context, if only to give some immediate answers to the questions raised here.

This 'preliminary briefing' takes the form of five theme sections prior to making an overview of the detailed analyses that form this study. These five themes are:

1. Changes in European Higher Education.
2. The Study of Higher Education: a Brief History.
3. Portugal: Exception, Pioneer or Partner?
4. On the Road to neoliberalism.
5. A Rapid Flight over a Complex Terrain.

The fifth and final topic in this Introduction returns to the three parts round which this book is arranged. It provides a summary – a species of route map – that takes us through the main lines and perspectives developed by the 15 chapters that follow. It identifies topics and trends which cross different disciplinary perspectives and in so doing give rise to different interpretations, sometimes complementary to one another, sometimes as alternative explanations.

Changes in European Higher Education Policy

Though the tests of feasibility, relevance and appropriateness, as we have suggested, remain firmly in the hands of the Nation State, this does not mean that the vexed issue of the balance of power in higher education policy between Nation State and Europe is settled. On the contrary, how far the balance between these two spheres is shifting is an issue hotly disputed by students of higher education policy (Gornitzka 2007; Musselin 2010; Gornitzka and Maassen 2007: 81–98). Indeed, the injection into the policy arena by Bruxelles of the so-called Open Method of Coordination in the wake of the Lisbon Agenda first aired in the year 2000 added further impetus to the debate. Equally contentious is the effective impact such developments as the Bologna Process have had so far beyond the mere statement of aims and principles and very specifically their impact on the institutional fabric and day-to-day workings of higher education across different national systems of higher education (Veiga 2010).

Yet, since 1999 and the signing of the Bologna Declaration, the European Dimension has acquired and that rapidly a solid institutional framework in the shape of 2-year meetings of Ministers in charge of higher education within the framework of the Bologna Process together with the European Higher Education Area and the European Research Area. The establishment of 'institutions of public purpose' and agencies of cross-national oversight, for instance, The European Network of Quality Assurance Agencies (ENQA) and the European Quality Agency Register for Higher Education (ENQAR), lends further institutional substance to the European Dimension. In effect, institutional coalescence brings another and very different dynamic into the domain of cross-national comparison. And with it comes a new meaning to the term 'Exceptionalism' as a descriptive condition of higher education systems compared cross-nationally. Whilst students of higher education and political scientists in particular (Olsen 2007: 25–54) may quibble over how far or how rapidly initiative in shaping higher education policy is shifting away from the Nation State to other sites, networks, regions or to agencies operating across the historic frontiers of Europe's Nations – one of the more significant though less commented upon consequences that follow from reshuffling the pack of power, decision-making and influence in higher education is the emergence of new meanings and with them a new range of priorities attendant upon the notion of Exceptionalism itself.

Exceptionalism Shifting

Changes in meaning are never coincidental. Nor is it with the shift in meaning attached to Exceptionalism. This linguistic displacement – a phenomenon well known to the practitioners of discourse analysis – revolves around what in the lexicon of that field is termed a 'floating signifier'. A 'Floating Signifier' emerges in very particular circumstances and especially when different discourses struggle to invest their specific meaning into a well-established term. Thus, according to Philips and Jorgensen, "the term 'floating signifier' belongs to the ongoing struggle between different discourses to fix the meaning of important signs" (Phillips and Jorgensen 2002: 28).[2] And inasmuch as policy implemented is of necessity in a democracy, the result of debate, strife and contention of ideas, how those ideas are expressed, what terms are used to express them and how the meaning of an established term evolves represent an important, if preliminary, stage in the shaping of the policy that results from the earlier battle to attach new meaning to an established concept. For this reason, it is important to attend to the way the notion of Exceptionalism has mutated when taken into the sometimes-exotic terminology of European higher education policy.

Interlocking Developments

Two interlocking developments, inseparable from what some see as the 're-construction' of higher education in Europe, others as its 'modernisation' (EU 1991), redefined the notion of Exceptionalism.

The first involved strengthening the legal basis of what earlier was alluded to as the 'European Dimension' in education generally and more specifically in higher education. Providing a legal basis for EU activities in this area, beginning with the Gravier Judgement in 1985 (Court of Justice of the European Communities 1985: 593), was confirmed and added to by the Treaty of Maastricht, which, in 1992 for the first time included education and vocational training as one of six new areas coming under community oversight. Leaving aside the precise and detailed significance of other marker points in the saga of European Integration, the first steps towards the foundation of a multi-national system of higher education were taken in the Bologna Declaration of 1999. Putting in place a permanent institutional framework to implement the Bologna process may be seen as the second impulse in re-defining

Exceptionalism. Certainly, the institutionalisation of Bologna, and with it the substitution of 'European' for 'national' standards in respect of the duration of studies, was a central factor. The 3:5:8 model set out a Continent-wide template for study duration across the three cycles of Bachelor, Master and later, Doctorate. Nor did the prime influence in redefining Exceptionalism spring from a similar degree of cross-system homogeneity that aligned student performance and achievement on criteria grounded in the European Credit Transfer Scheme, key though those functions had been in the generic process of certifying the attainment of *national* standards. These two operational priorities and objectives provided datum points, a base line for comparing progress towards their fulfilment which the representatives of Europe's universities had voluntarily and curiously fixed at 10 years – that is, to be in place by the year 2010.

The Role of Convergence as a Policy Dynamic

Against this backdrop, the central notion that imparted a new meaning to Exceptionalism lies in the process of 'Convergence', a policy construct which first saw the light of day in the Maastricht Treaty of 1992 when it then applied to such matters as a common currency, social legislation and to laying down the rights of EU citizens. The Bologna Declaration of June 1999 in effect set in place both the criteria for evaluating higher education's 'convergence' and the schedule for its completion. Convergence is a code word for the progress made in implementing measures designed to secure objectives shared and jointly agreed upon. It is also a process of verification. How far have individual national systems of higher education gone in meeting or implementing 'European' objectives, norms and practices? 'Convergence' is not just a watchword. It is, on the contrary, tied in intimately with a very specific policy dynamic which bids fair to change the relationship between the three levels of decision-making – European, national and institutional. The assumption implicit in the policy of Convergence operates a profound change in the role and status of the national level in the overall process of policymaking in general and very particularly so when the matter in hand concerns the construction of a multi-national system of higher education. Higher education policy, from being an activity of *sovereignty* by the Nation State, instead sees the Nation State acting as *executor* of policy drawn up and agreed upon at European level. Though nowhere stated as such, what is implied by the very notion of Convergence as a policy dynamic is the unspoken assumption that progress – or, for that matter, lack of it – in attaining the goals set is the responsibility of the national level.

How effective the gambit of public praise for those successfully meeting 'European' norms has in fact been in establishing the three cycles of the Bologna degree structure, ECTS, the Diploma Supplement or quality assurance techniques and practices and how effective public chastisement is for those who appear to be lagging in their duty remains for the moment an open issue (Purser and Crosier 2007; Veiga 2010; Neave and Amaral 2008: 40–62). Yet the urging on of

'European norms' by carrot and stick, often alluded to as 'Naming and Shaming' (Gornitzka 2007), brings two major consequences in its train. First, in its new meaning as convergence around 'European' rather than 'national' norms, Exceptionalism discards the essentially historical portrayal of individual systems of higher education. Exceptionalism no longer singles out those particular and specific features, practices, perceptions and values that had accumulated around the practices, structures and customs to be found in the individual Nation State higher education system, features that sustained the claim of the Nation State to a particular standing and to a particular identity. Second, the 'European construct' of Exceptionalism is neither historical in perspective nor in the way it emerges operationally. On the contrary, it is rigorously rooted in the present and, moreover, comes as a fundamental reversal in the value of Exceptionalism itself.

Meaning Mutating

Since the basic dynamic in the early stages of constructing a multi-national system of higher education in Europe entailed a drive towards standardisation, the laying down of new norms and the putting in place of shared structures and provision for teaching, learning and research, clearly the end purpose underlines a homogeneity writ large, even if this latter is served up by officialdom with the sauce of a 'new architecture'. New the 'architecture' may well be. From an historian's perspective, the process beneath the happy descriptor may equally be seen as simply extending to the European level that basic characteristic of legal homogeneity which long served to shape higher education provision within the individual Nation States of Europe over the past century and a half (Neave and van Vught 1991; Neave 2007, 2009a). Even so, Exceptionalism in its new guise, operationalised around criteria deemed to be objective and measurable with precision, differs markedly from its earlier meaning in one outstanding feature: It is not regarded as either justifiable, desirable or as a legitimate expression of difference and diversity. On the contrary, the presence – let alone its persistence – of Exceptionalism is seen by those who plot the course of Convergence, as a sign of feet being dragged, as evidence of reluctance – or, worse, of the inability – to move wholeheartedly towards the cross-national norms that higher education voluntarily took upon itself at Bologna and onto which others are being grafted by the European Commission in the wake of the Lisbon Agenda (Maassen and Neave 2007).

Exceptionalism, rather than being as once it was, the outcome of higher education's adaptation over the long term within the Nation State – and legitimate on that account – has taken on a new meaning. In current European policy as it applies to higher education, Exceptionalism today carries a very different signal. It signals a clear and evident *failure* of a particular system to converge or, at a more charitable level, to do so with the same alacrity as others. From being a legitimate expression of national specificity, the concept of Exceptionalism in higher education policy-making at the European level has, in the course of the last decade or so, mutated into its very opposite. Today, it is viewed as an illegitimate brake upon the drive by Europe towards a multi-national system of higher education. In short, Exceptionalism is no longer taken to be the particular manifestation of national identity conveyed through and by higher education. On the contrary, the label now serves to point the finger at 'The Odd Man out', to single out on the European Parade Ground the notorious members in higher education's equivalent of the 'Awkward Squad'. That Exceptionalism has, in the terminology of the discourse analyst, taken on the trappings of a 'Floating Signifier' reflects a continuing and ongoing struggle over the balance of power and thus the part to be assigned, to the various levels of decision-making – European, national, regional and institutional – in the construction of a multi-national system of higher education as well as the pace at which the political domain reckons it ought to proceed.[3]

Plea for a Long-Term Perspective

If the notion of Exceptionalism is changing, in what way may Portugal be said to be exceptional? This is no idle question. Few – if any – studies of higher education in Portugal have over the past few decades set themselves the task to provide a 'grand narrative' or an overall synthetic account both of Portuguese higher education and of the policies that have shaped it across the years following the Revolution of 1974 on and up to the present day. In itself, such a task is not light. Redoubtable though it may be – and this is generally admitted by students of higher education and higher education policy[4] – this task is, we believe, more than necessary today.

Putting in place a multi-national higher education system in Europe, viewed within a very long-term perspective indeed, is strangely Jesuitical in the sense that Sobral, echoing Carvalho's history of education in Portugal, notes *en passant*, in the first chapter of this study.

> The school did not have a mother country. In the schools, Latin was spoken. Logic, Rhetoric, Arithmetic or any other subject was studied in Latin, followed the same rules, the same textbooks, and the same discipline. To study in the schools of the Company of Jesus at Évora, Salamanca, Paris, Rome or Bohemia, was exactly the same. (Sobral quoting de Carvalho 2008: 361)

Curious Analogues

Substitute University for school, English as *the lingua franca* for Latin and the defence of a belief grounded in the supremacy of Economics, Business and the cash nexus as an *Ersatz* for the Faith, trust and fear in the Hereafter, and the ultimate vision that looms over higher education from both Bologna and the Lisbon Agenda onwards appears not greatly distant from the 'cross-national' model of education put in place by the Company of Jesus four centuries earlier! This, together with what some sociologists see as the ambition of the European Commission to inject a goodly dose of homogeneity into the curriculum of higher education – all in the name of modernising the institution itself (Giddens 2006, quoted in Maassen and Musselin 2009: 9) – suggests that structure, duration and content of what is taught in higher education no longer serve as statements of national identity so much as criteria for assessing, and the ambition to move towards, cross-national similarity. If this is so – and in our view, the only issue is how far the thrust towards homogenisation will be permitted eventually to penetrate and in what areas of teaching, learning and research – the implications are obvious. If a modicum of intentional and deliberate diversity is to be upheld as legitimate and desirable in the future European construct of a multi-national system of higher education, other criteria will be needed to take full account of diversity within the individual system of higher education that forms part of the Continent-wide edifice.

By their nature, those criteria emerge *fully* and *only* when the evolution of a given system of higher education is weighed up over the long term. In effect, moving towards a multi-national system of higher education summons forth the need to redefine individual systems of higher education in terms of the *abiding, constant* and very particular characteristics intimately related to their advance over the long term. Such characteristics, because they are abiding, also enclose the short-term, often instantaneous 'snapshot' – league tables, system review, institutional performance and output – which are currently the major – if sometimes ephemeral – forms of intelligence currently available to policymakers, administrators, to parents as taxpayers and to the Student Estate as 'consumers'.

Such an approach does not decry the necessary part that disciplines other than history play in setting out an up-to-date and sustained account of the development in individual systems of higher education. What it does maintain, and this study we hope bears the view out, is that such disciplines contribute with even greater weight to re-stating national specificity when they are engaged in examining and testing for the presence and operation of factors inside a given country's system of higher education *over the long term*.

A Generational Perspective

Other considerations give further weight to higher education policy viewed *de longue durée*. Not least of them is a species of counter-trend that has become integral to contemporary policymaking in higher education. It is best presented as an acceleration – alternatively, as a foreshortening – of 'the expected time to implement' (ETI). In what many today regard as 'The Golden' 1960s, time for reform in higher education to work its way through and to embed itself into the institution as 'established practice' was reckoned to be in the order of some 30 years-in short a generation. By the 1980s, time to implementation was commonly held to be 15 years. And, as we have seen, the formal schedule its signatories set for implementing the Bologna Process serves as a further bellwether to the amazing reductions to the expected time to implement. Ten years – to lay down the foundations of a multi-national system of higher education – is not over generous, even if over-optimistic. And many will point out that at national level, ETI tends to be even shorter, often bringing it – or, more to the point, *seeking* to bring it – into the confines of a single legislature (Neave 2007), so success may be held up to an admiring citizenry.

In this collection of essays, we have resolutely set our faces against the short-term, preferring a chronologically broader sweep that allows us to integrate momentary oscillations in the performance and 'responsiveness' of higher education into what we see as a more powerful 'generational perspective'. True, such a stance leaves itself open to the accusation of being nostalgia in scholarly form. There are equally powerful arguments in its favour, however. Not least amongst them – and no less significant when leadership is being hawked around as a panacea to many of the ills higher education is currently held to display – is the fact that a 'generational account' is precisely that. It allows us some grasp over just what has been achieved by that generation which in the Portugal of its salad days were the fiery young sprigs who allied with the Armed Forces Movement in the heady days of 1974 and who, today, are amongst the nation's elders in politics, business and academia! What has changed, what has endured and what has 'gone the way of Nineveh and Tyre' during their rise to the stewardship of the Nation?

The Grand Narrative: An Unfashionable Genre

Clearly, such a purpose is not greatly different from what is often presented as The Grand Narrative. Grand narratives have their appeal – above all for historians. Still, it has to be admitted that this particular *genre* does not enjoy a whole-hearted endorsement from many of the other domains and disciplines that contribute to the study of higher education or which scrutinise the policies applied to it (Barnett 2007: 295–300; Neave 2010a: 175). There are many reasons for this querulousness. Not least the unprecedented growth over the past five and thirty years past in the size of the three Estates – the Student Estate, the Academic Estate and the Administrative Estate – that bore higher education forwards as much in Portugal as in Europe generally. The swelling of higher education's Constituent Orders in turn mirrored a corresponding growth in the range of fields, disciplines and perspectives that served to unveil the complexities, subtleties and nuances that came to occupy scholarship as higher education drove rapidly towards its present condition. Baldly stated, the contemporary study of higher education never rested on a single corpus of knowledge.

The Study of Higher Education: A Brief History

Some 40 years ago, when the first pioneering steps were taken by the late Burton R. Clark, then at Yale University, to make comparative *higher* education a self-standing area of systematic and sustained scholarly investigation, four disciplines were held to be key to the purpose: History, Politics, Sociology and Economics (Clark 2000: 2–34).

Clark's place in shaping the study of cross-national higher education as an academic domain is only with great difficulty underestimated. In the area of methodology, he introduced the basic framework of institutionally grounded broad-scale analysis of national systems, which he set down in his seminal work *The Higher Education System: academic organisation in cross-national perspective*, the fruit of some 30 years work in the USA and Italy (Clark 1983; Neave 2010c: 209–216). Equally significant, he introduced the concept of higher education as a 'system', thereby injecting a basic and fundamental construct that derived from Organisational Sociology into the analytical armoury of higher education studies. To see higher education in this light is not, it has to be admitted, particularly novel in Western Europe, where legal codification and a high degree of central government control over such key functions as academic appointment to post, over promotion, curriculum and the setting of admission standards made higher education a 'regulated area' (Moscati 2008: 134). Rather, the originality of Clark's scholarship lay in applying the notion of 'system' to higher education in the Anglo-Saxon world and getting it accepted.

The Concept of 'System': A Seminal Point

This was a major feat. The predominant vision that hitherto permeated Anglo-Saxon literature on higher education tended to portray it as a series of self-standing institutions – as a de facto federation of individual universities engaged, more by empirical and organic evolution in a broadly similar purpose and task than as the outcome of a legally and formally regulated 'system'. Nor, it should be noted, was Clark's notion of a system grounded in legal codification. The Clarkian notion of 'system' rested on dimensions of formal organisation, to which the legal stood, if it stood at all, as a subset. Nevertheless, for higher education to be considered as a 'system' was a perspective both powerful and, more to the point, one that opened a broad highway for comparison between countries just as it also hastened the transfer of experience between them, making it applicable to the other across both Anglo-Saxon and 'Continental European' fields of scholarship.

Shaping the cross-national study of higher education was then the product of a dual evolution – of the 'system approach' forged within academia and the 'economic perspective' which if no less present in academia, had powerful sponsorship from international organisations and agencies – the World Bank, the International Monetary Fund and the Organisation for Economic Cooperation and Development being the most prominent. It was also a highly dynamic in one dimension in particular – an aspect that the American historian, Walter Metzger has termed 'subject parturition'. Subject parturition is that unceasing activity of disciplines to coalesce, break up and re-align with other cognate and similar domains (Metzger 1987: 123–196).

'Subject Parturition': A Constant Feature

Subject parturition is a marked characteristic in the field of comparative higher education. It is nowhere better illustrated than in the work of the British scholar, Tony Becher, who, early in the 1990s, identified some 20 fields and perspectives that dissected, and intersected across, the study of higher education (Becher 1992: 1763–1766). They ranged alphabetically from Anthropology through to Women Studies. Nor, in the meantime, has the assimilation of new domains into the analysis of higher education in all its multiple facets ground to a halt. The years immediately following Becher's review saw the advent of Quality Studies, Evaluation and International Relations, the latter a somewhat confusing title assigned to research into cross-system student flows and exchanges together with cross frontier working together and formal linkages between universities and polytechnics across the face of Europe.

Some Basic Dilemmas the Student of Higher Education Faces

To draw up an overarching account that works across all these domains into a judicious and even-handed analysis is – and, if anything, it understates the difficulties involved – a Herculean task, not lightly to be undertaken and nigh on impossible for the individual scholar, however polymathic he – or she – might believe themselves to be! This does not mean, however, that the attempt should not be made even in face of the claim by many students of higher education that, since the Grand Narrative is a 'mission impossible', to attempt it at all is to risk dismal failure or, worse still, to succeed only at the price of telling a partial, if not an unintentionally biased, tale.

Whatever the criticism different disciplinary canons may level against the Grand Narrative, there is a further consideration. It is both weighty and to a large extent built into the study of higher education. If the Grand Narrative is not always viewed with great sympathy within the bounds of one country, modest as this ambition might appear, it is subject to even greater suspicion when applied to many.

Such a view, unadventurous, pessimistic though it is, is not without justification, particularly in the area of comparative or cross-national study of higher education. Indeed, the comparative dimension is more than usually delicate, forcing the unavoidable choice between the range and the number of systems to be examined and the depth, detail and *finesse* in the analysis required. As with that eternal dilemma between gastronomy and a slim waist line, so with comparative higher education. One can opt for one. Or go for the other. It is, however, rare indeed to be able happily to combine both! One may cover many systems but at the price of sacrificing depth, detail and nuance, or by concentrating on a limited range of topics or variables. Alternatively, one may plumb for depth and detail, but the number of systems one may cover – even with teams of colleagues – rarely exceeds single figures – more often than not, at the low end of the single figure scale.

Hubris

Still, like it or not, even the detractors of the 'Grand Narrative' have their very own version of hubris – that sin of overweening pride that the Greek gods of old never failed to punish, often with madness! It must remain a matter of personal choice whether the globalisation of higher education is not a latter-day form of this state of mind. Certainly, globalisation must be the grandest narrative of them all since by sheer definition, there can be none greater. When the origins of globalisation as an historical process, as opposed to the coining of the construct itself, began to emerge – and where – remain a sore trial to those who have embraced in this intoxicating perspective (Marginson 2004), though some attempt has been made by scholarship prior to the surfacing of globalisation as an analytical concept, principally by Immanuel Wallerstein's earlier perspective of World Systems Analysis (Wallerstein 2004).

Portugal: Exception, Pioneer or Partner?

As the chapters in this book show, Exceptionalism in its historic interpretation rather than as the contemporary handmaiden of Convergence has four dimensions. The first turns around the very specific circumstances, values and interpretations, which accompany the evolution of higher education and which may found only in one particular system. The second dimension of Exceptionalism relates to policies or outcomes, which whilst they may be shared across different systems are more intense or present to a higher degree in one than in the remainder. The third dimension, which this book develops within the Portuguese setting, is that Exceptionalism emerges in different forms depending on the level of analysis – national, regional or institutional. And finally, it emerges from the particular disciplinary perspective – or combination of disciplinary perspectives employed in the analysis.

Techniques of Comparison

Just as there are many ways to skin a cat, so there are many ways to analyse a system of higher education, which in this case, focuses on Portugal both as an exemplar and as a vehicle for illustrating the wide-ranging and very different perspectives that may be brought to bear. One of the most commonly used typologies for classifying higher education systems is their size. This is usually expressed in the sheer numbers of the Student Estate, the percentage of the relevant age group entering higher education or both. Drawn up more than 40 years ago by the American policy analyst Martin Trow, higher education systems are placed in one of three categories, depending on whether the numbers of the Student Estate are less than 15% of the relevant age group – an 'elite' system – range from 15% to 40% – a 'mass' system – or 40% and above of the relevant age group in which case Higher Education is construed as providing 'universal' access (Trow 1974).

Trow's classification has great virtue and convenience. It is dynamic. It shows the quantitative pace of change in one country. It is gratifyingly actual and like most indicators can be used comparatively to show where one country figures amongst many. Similarly, it may also illustrate the first two dimensions of Exceptionalism just mentioned. It may equally show whether Portugal's claim to Exceptionalism is born out in quantitative terms. As many of the accounts presented here make plain, Portugal very certainly *cannot* claim to be exceptional in the drive towards mass higher education and beyond. Rather, Portugal is a partner in the drive to massification. Others have been there before. France, for instance, crossed the border from elite to mass higher education the early 1970s, (West) Germany in the middle of the same decade and the United Kingdom somewhat later during the mid-1980s (Neave 1985: 347–361).

In short, along that specific dimension of Exceptionalism which seeks to identify the unique, Portugal is very clearly *not* exceptional at all. However, there *are* other grounds for claiming this condition. They are to be found in the second dimension of Exceptionalism, namely in the intensity or the speed at which Portugal accomplished this transformation and very especially the 15 years from 1985 to the year 1999/2000. These years saw higher education rush headlong beyond massification and on towards the threshold of universal status which it attained at the end of the 1990s and at a level of 50% of gross participation (Magalhães and Amaral 2007: 1–24).

… and Their Critique

Indispensable though such quantitative scales are in plotting the fortune or fate of higher education across countries and across time, they are open to criticism. They are, to use a Gallicism, simply a *constat* – statement of condition. Certainly, that condition may be used – and very certainly is – to spur further efforts on to consolidate national achievement or to avoid national ignominy. But this approach can also be seen as one example of what was alluded to earlier as 'Higher Educationism'[5] that is, as a deliberate evacuation of the broader political, economic and social context the better to concentrate on higher education as a de-contextualised entity. To put matters slightly differently and to draw upon a term sometimes used by historians, such a method also stands as a monument to the 'Historical Attention Span Deficit Disorder' – Alzheimer's disease in a bureaucratic form – which some historians professed to have detected in the late 1980s and early 1990s, a feature they hold to coincide inter alia with the application of New Public Management to some of the more sensitive areas of the British Civil Service (Andrew 2009: 848–849).

The various accounts presented here, however, depart precisely from the contrary perspective. But what light does this approach, which could, with similar inventiveness be seen as 'an historical memory compensatory strategy,' shed upon the historic dimension of exception in the higher education of Portugal? Does it change at all the ways in which its evolution is to be interpreted and understood?

Portugal as Pioneer: The Revolutionary Inheritance

Foremost amongst the features that set Portugal aside, though less as an exception so much as a pioneer, is the 1974 Revolution. Though the sceptical may argue that this watershed is in part an artefact by the nature of the period this study covers, the subsequent development of higher education is, as practically all the chapters show in varying degrees, inseparable from the events of 1974 to 1976. Agreed, most of the proposals, forged in the white heat of enthusiasm, did not long survive, as Torgal notes. The University of the Revolution was radical, generous – and short-lived. But the influence of the Left in drawing up the 1976 Constitution and the enunciation of certain principles enshrined in that Constitution – university autonomy, participant democracy, quality control and access to higher learning, for example – remained. Over the ensuing two decades, as the accounts presented in this study insist on time and again, these principles were taken into law and shaped higher education. If the 'political university' was stillborn, the inheritance of the Revolution lived on as a guiding force in the Nation's higher education policy.

Thus, Portugal, if chronologically the first amongst the present-day member states of the EU to see its higher education shaped, if not wholly by a post-war Revolution, then certainly by its immediate aftermath, is far from being unique. On the contrary, if we cast our net further afield, it brings in, though a decade and a half later, virtually all EU members in East and Central Europe (File and Goedegebuure 2003; Dima 2001; Duczmal 2006). And, no less interesting, the impact of upheaval in releasing pent-up 'social demand' for higher education in those lands followed a course every bit as comparable as it had been in the immediate aftermath of the Revolution 15 years previously in Portugal.

First of the New or Last of the Old?

Not surprisingly, differences are to be seen between Portugal as a system of higher education evolving out of Revolution and those on the Eastern Marches of the EU. The former was driven onwards by a social vision that owed much to the radical Left. The latter, by contrast, looked for salvation to the free market and the individual freedoms the free market was held to symbolise. In short, revolution in Central and Eastern Europe moved briskly and directly towards neoliberalism. It set about rapidly re-shaping its systems of higher education around the principles of privatisation (Levy and Slancheva 2007) and modernising the public sector by a rapid dash into management rationality as the operational expression of the new economic theology.

Leaving aside the diametrically opposed ideological thrust that accompanied the demise of the *Anciens Régimes* in Eastern Europe, it is self-evident that a group of higher education systems in the EU has one shared characteristic, namely their revolutionary origins. From this standpoint, Portugal may claim, as we have suggested, the title of pioneer. If, however, we differentiate these systems in terms of their *ideological* drivers, then a good case can certainly be made for seeing Portugal as indeed exceptional. The Revolution of the Carnations drove to the Left. The Velvet Revolution and its emulators, if they did not turn to the Right, most certainly fled from the Left as fast as their heels could carry them.

Such differences raise other issues as well. These issues have a certain bearing on how the Revolution of 1974 is interpreted. And, as we have already noted, such an ideological difference is crucial in determining whether being driven by revolution is in truth a Portuguese Exceptionalism or, less audacious but no less flattering, whether Portugal stands the first amongst many that may also assert this claim. Seen from outside Portugal and with hindsight – that most beneficial of human frailties – the nature of the Revolution, as many essays point out, can bear other interpretations. Indeed, in one respect, and seen from the standpoint of the Student Estate, the May days in the France of 1968 were not without their imitators in Portugal, a point Fonseca makes. Analysed from this perspective, Portugal's Revolution of 1974 was the last of Left-wing-inspired uprisings that Western Europe was to know. From this angle, the Revolution of 1974 stands as the last of the old rather than the first of the new, though no less exceptional on that account.

Thanks for the Memory

Yet, such dramatic events often shape the perceptions of those who have been through them or who see themselves as heirs to the values for which such events stood, or against which they strove. If Revolution does not always produce what the French call '*droits acquis*', though the Portuguese Welfare State is very certainly one, the memory it shapes nevertheless serves to keep hopes and even political agendas alive. Thus, revolution possesses a species of perceptual half-life, which becomes emblematic of what social institutions – and in this case, higher education – ought to be. It becomes part of a political 'value set' in the democratic life of the Nation. There is, in many of our colleagues writings, clear evidence of the continued power of this 'half-life' of the Revolution in shaping higher education, if only for the fact that key legislation in the latter part of the 1980s and early 1990s built firmly upon those principles which the Constitution had preserved.

It is precisely the very weight and legitimacy that attached to this perceptual 'half-life' which account for that other feature of higher education policy in Portugal, namely the reluctance to embrace the toils of neoliberalism and the consequences it brought in its train for higher education. For whilst the drive towards neoliberalism and the implementation of New Public Management both began to take root in Western Europe from the 1990s onwards, it was only a decade later that Portugal moved along the same path to salvation. Indeed, as late as 2001, as one of us has argued elsewhere, the place in Portugal of New Public Management and Managerialism, the two handmaidens of neoliberalism inside the world of academia, was more rhetorical than substantial (Amaral and Magalhães 2001: 7–20). Clues as to why this should be so are, we believe, to be found in 'the Revolutionary Heritage' on the one hand and in the values best represented by 'the Generation of Reform', on the other.

A Generation of Exception

In Portugal, just as in Western Europe generally, the generation that is about to take its final bow was both part of, and the instrument for, the most remarkable period of growth in higher education since that institution was founded (Neave 2009c). In Portugal, under its stewardship, a new sector – private higher education – was founded. And plans for a non-university, polytechnic-based system, were brought to final fruition, developments that echoed similar achievements in France (Doumenc and Gilly 1977), West Germany (Teichler et al. 1996: 219–249) and the United Kingdom (Pratt and Burgess 1974), *entre autres.*

The most significant contribution this generation has made in Portugal must surely lie in the area of national self-perception. Precisely because national self-doubt had been an abiding feature of Portuguese society and politics – it had surfaced time and again over the past 200 years – here was the opportunity finally to give that doubt the lie. Agreed, higher education was not the only area where such newfound confidence bubbled up. It was equally evident in the founding of the Welfare State in Portugal. And though the expansion of higher education – as elsewhere in Europe – was part and parcel of that overall monument to collective solidarity within the Nation, the latter is not our prime concern.

Irrespective of how the principle development which both accompanied and which, retrospectively is intimately associated with the stewardship of that generation, is described – whether as an 'Explosion in Higher Education', as the Rise of the Teaching Nation (Neave 1992b) or as the advent of the 'Learning Society' (Chap. 8: Graves 1994) – this was the generation that mobilised around higher education. It propelled the Nation along a trajectory, which in the space of a quarter century thrust it forwards to reach what in Trow's classification placed it in the 'universal' category of that scale. No less noteworthy, it was a trajectory, which for other Western European systems of higher education that had reached a similar condition, had taken them the best part of five and thirty years, an institutional saga that had begun in the mid 1960s and spread out over two phases, the first lasting until the mid-1970s, with a second that began in the mid-1980s. Portugal, by contrast, saw expansion compressed into one single phase whose take-off began in the late 1970s and persisted until the turn of the millennium.

Mobilising and the Mobilised

It is not misplaced then to see the generation whose record in higher education this book covers as a 'mobilising generation'. Yet, it is useful to distinguish two elements within it: those who brought mobilisation about and those who were mobilised. This is after all one of the pragmatic boundaries between the political and the social dimensions in higher education policy. That the former achieved this feat, owed much to a sustained political consensus around the strategic importance of higher education, a consensus that held together despite differences that separated Left from Right over such matters as private higher education. It extended university self-government in the form of the 1988 Act on University Autonomy. It entrusted university leadership with developing a performance-driven evaluation system. In short, such a consensus held and gave operational expression – a species of *droit acquis* – that consolidated the principles grounded in the 1976 Constitution.

For those who mobilised, the sheer speed – and strength – of their response, though at times directly and explicitly stimulated by considerations of a political order, above all in the mid-1980s as Fonseca reminds us, had other consequences as well. Amongst the most telling – and also the most subtle – lay in the symbolism of higher education itself. This symbolism was both a cause and a consequence of the sheer rapidity of growth in higher education which both unleashed and accentuated deep social change already building up in the latter days of the *Ancien Regime* as Portuguese society began finally to cut its ties with an agrarian past. That education was increasingly seen as an avenue for social mobility, rather than a threat to the income of the traditional rural family by luring individuals away to the city, that opportunities both in higher education and in the economy were obviously available – and more rewarding – as too the opportunity to realise them through higher education – were powerful agents indeed for social mobilisation. It was powerful precisely because of the 'lagged response' of Portuguese society to 'modernisation'. Indeed, many saw as the New State's authoritarianism as a means of holding modernisation at arm's length and not least in higher education. Faced with this situation, growth in higher education took on a dual symbolism of Emancipation: an emancipation *from* traditional society and, at the same time, an emancipation *from* a regime and its ideology that were inseparably associated with that past. In other words, what outside observers and national leadership may interpret as 'Portugal catching up with Modernity' may, by the same token and from the standpoint of the citizen and scholar, also be seen as the *distance* placed between themselves and what the British political and social historian, Peter Laslett, once termed 'the world we have lost' (Laslett 1965) – in many cases, thankfully!

In the space of one generation, higher education in Portugal ceased to be 'something for other peoples' children'. Instead, it became the reasonable affair of Everyman, or, as many of the analyses make abundantly clear, Everywoman. Still, disparities in participation between social class and income levels remain. No less relevant, this remarkable achievement had been set in train by a model of relationship between government and society which, if evolving from State control towards 'state supervision' (Neave and van Vught 1991) retained the long established convention of higher education as a subset of national politics whereas, elsewhere – in Britain, the Netherlands for instance – the relocation of higher education firmly within an economic discourse had advanced by leaps and bounds. On the contrary, Portugal remained steadfastly wedded to an agenda firmly rooted in the application and extension of 'Participant Democracy' to academia.

On the Road to Neoliberalism

The weight that an abiding consensus in higher education commanded, in its turn, raises the question 'How and why did neoliberalism and its operational expressions of New Public Management and Managerialism in Portugal pass onto the statute book?' There are excellent reasons for raising it. In the first place, neoliberalism may be seen as an economic construct with an explicit transnational application.[7] In the second place, it altered, and that profoundly, the setting in which the University was located. It redefined the University's purpose and ushered in unprecedented changes both in the relationship between University, Government and Society and, within the groves of Academe, re-set the historic balance of power between the three Constituent Orders. This doctrine swept across the EU, beginning in the Netherlands and the United Kingdom in the mid to late 1980s.[8] It spread rapidly into East and Central Europe with the fall of the Berlin Wall, and in so doing boosted the pace of change further still in Western Europe. In Portugal, as many of the accounts in this volume show, only in 2007 in the shape of the Higher Education Guideline Law were the tenets of neoliberalism officially and explicitly taken on board as a principle driver – a new Orthodoxy – for higher education policy.

Orthodoxy is a belief, theory, or body of knowledge that possesses 'authoritative status'. In its religious form, Orthodoxy enforced correct observance through a monopoly wielded over the interpretation of an 'authoritative text' – the Scriptures for Christians, the Koran for Mohammedans. The task of enforcing such correctness – Orthodoxy – amongst the community of believers fell to what in contemporary jargon is a single external body or agency of oversight: Rome, Mecca or in the case of neoliberalism, the World Bank in Washington DC or its branch office at the OECD in Paris (Amaral and Neave 2009a). In many of its features, not least in the ardour with which its supporters propagate it, neoliberalism may be viewed as a present-day equivalent of Orthodoxy – a secular expression of belief and faith in Economics as the central driver of human purpose. As belief, whether religious or secular, acquires authoritative status, it is both presented by its adepts and often seen by its potential converts as the sole and inevitable 'solution'. It is The Right Road towards The Right Thing. There is no alternative. Equally powerful, Orthodoxy rewrites History in the light of its own triumph. Retrospectively, the passage of a political statement from declaration or agenda to Orthodoxy endows those pioneering that policy with an additional power of persuasion and an enhanced legitimacy.

This it does by suggesting that the necessity as to the correctness of the doctrine its pioneers first devised for themselves possesses even greater correctness, appropriateness and validity by dint of others subsequently following in their footsteps. In Economics as in Religion, the power of Orthodoxy consists in the ability to compel the Heathen – whether Humanists or Marxists – to the Faith and in either case to make the Sceptical the Faithful. There are other reasons as well for paying close attention to the rise of neoliberalism. Prime amongst them, that precisely because of its contemporary pervasiveness, it constitutes both the ideological and operational basis on which Europe's bid to create a multi-national system of higher education proceeds.

In exploring this issue, we do not contend and even less challenge the interpretations colleagues have developed. They speak for themselves. Our concern is to place their accounts in a broader setting. In short, we provide a supplementary account that builds upon the various analyses through developing what may be seen as a third party perspective.

Portuguese Perspectives on Neoliberalism

In this book, the infiltration of neoliberalism into Portuguese higher education policy is treated within a number of different contexts – historical, legal, from the standpoint of Economics, Public Administration and Science Policy just as it is addressed within such themes as the rise of Managerialism, the development of private higher education, the impact neoliberalism holds out for Governance and for the distribution of power, authority and oversight both external and internal in Universities and Polytechnics. That it is a central and recurrent theme across so many domains is a gauge both of its strategic significance and of the radical nature of the changes it seeks to bring about. That its advent is looked upon askance by many – though not all – of those whose accounts figure in this volume – as an explicit and renewed attempt to create a 'political university' by Torgal, or, by Gonçalves as a desperate last recourse by a political party formally of the Left to force legislation through the National Assembly – hints at the presence in Portugal of very different forces and factors of reference than tends to be the case in other countries, where neoliberalism and its operational expressions of Managerialism and New Public Management were largely the work of the Right. The battle to set in place what the French term *La Pensée unique* appears in Portugal to involve what military historians would call 'A Battle on Reversed Fronts'. That is, the engagement sees the army with its back to its enemy's frontier – or in this case, a political party finding itself in the passably curious position of advocating measures that elsewhere were the work of its ideological adversaries!

Why this should be so in Portugal reflects the weight of certain political values which occupy a very different place both in recent policy and in the recent history of higher education, values which, if not entirely absent elsewhere amongst the forces that neoliberalism rallies, were far more influential in Portugal. These central values may be divided along two dimensions – the basic assumptions made in the relationship between State and Society on the one hand and the path of development in higher education on the other.

Anglo-Saxon Presumptions and Attitudes

The basic presumption the prototypical Anglo-Saxon form of Liberalism made about the status and role of the State had little place in Portugal. The belief, fundamental to both British and American political systems, of the necessity to keep the State at arm's length – above all in the domain of culture and education by extension – found little or no echo in Portugal. The tension that Anglo-American political theory held to exist between the individual and the collectivity took a very different form and drew upon very different social and political constructs in Portugal. These constructs drew upon Social Catholicism in the case of the Right and various shadings of Marxism and Socialism for the Left. Each in its own way sought to create a social model, primarily to address the issue of social change and thus political organisation to counter what each in its own manner saw as the unacceptable face of industrialisation. For Social Catholicism, this took the form of grouping society around associations, or 'corporations', hence the notion of the Corporative State found in Portugal. In the case of the Socialist or Marxist Left, taking command of taking of the means of production via nationalisation and collectivisation performed a similar task.

Neither doctrine placed the same weight upon *differences* of interest between collectivity and the individual. Nor for that matter, did either decry the notion of a strong State as the legitimate means of ensuring whatever differences emerged, were dealt with within the framework of formal equality of the law. The State's prime function was to ensure the equitable application of the decisions the representatives of the Nation reached. For this, a strong and centralised State was a *conditio sine qua non*. A strong State, however, does not mean an authoritarian State. Indeed, this distinction was both an integral and an essential part in the architecture of the post-Revolutionary consensus, shared by both Right and Left and, as has already been pointed out, the foundation stone on which higher education policy rested.

From this basic premise of legitimacy that attached to the strong State, it naturally followed that the notion, fundamental to neoliberalism that private initiative could, outside such areas as tariffs, taxes, defence and foreign policy, legitimately substitute for a strong State, held little sway. In short, the assumption that stood as a necessary prior condition for slimming Leviathan down the better to strike off the chains that held entrepreneurdom and individual initiative in thrall commanded very little credence in Portugal. On the contrary, the private sector generally, as it certainly did in higher education, looked to the State to create conditions favourable to its interests – a stance very different from the central tenet of neoliberalism, which conceives private interests as complementing those of the State. A final operational marker set Portugal well apart from the Anglo-Saxon values that neoliberalism enshrined. This difference is reflected in the latter's determination to maintain a clear line between the State, the local community and its culture by assigning responsibility for education to municipalities or to self-standing universities (Neave 2003: 141–164). In Portugal under the Constitution of 1976, Education and higher education by extension were part of the national collectivity and as such came under the direct responsibility of the State.

The Tensions of Progress

Taken together, these values suggest that amongst the motives underlying the rise of neoliberalism in Portuguese higher education policy, the legitimacy of the State was not one. On the contrary, with the State committed to participant democracy, coupled with an ongoing commitment to expanding higher education, suggested that both State and Nation were clearly in harmony. The issue lay elsewhere. It lay in the very speed at which higher education had grown, both in volume and complexity. Both outstripped the technical capacity of central national administration both to track and to keep pace with it (Amaral and Carvalho 2008). The cost of massive growth, as Machado and Cerdeira point out, had by the end of the 1980s, became a source of disquiet to *le pays politique*. Such tensions, however, did not bring into question the legitimacy of the State. Rather, they were pragmatic issues of husbandry. They could be accommodated in their initial phase, which lasted until the late 1990s, within the strategy that had been in place since the late 1970s – namely extending the principle of Participant Democracy. In effect, this latter could – and did – provide an acceptable and stable policy framework for offloading part of the task of detailed enactment to both Universities and Polytechnics, the former in the 1988 University Autonomy Act and its polytechnic counterpart in 1991. Similarly, the task of developing an appropriate system for quality assessment was offloaded to university leadership.

In these circumstances, with a high degree of consensus across both Left and Right that saw the expansion of higher education as a very real and successful example of collective effort carried out by the State, for neoliberalism to gain a purchase over Portugal's higher education policy was no small matter. It could not, as in the UK, for instance, argue that higher education had held itself aloof from Society. On the contrary, the evidence that higher education had proven itself remarkably and rapidly resilient to social demand could not in good faith be denied. Nor could it easily be argued either that the State had overstretched its limits since the strength of the State was the ark of covenant for both Right and Left.

Exquisite Dilemmas

Yet, the dilemma governments faced was not light. Reduced to its essentials, it involved reducing public expenditure on the one hand whilst, at the same time, enhancing the technical capacities of the State to steer policy, on the other. Budget cuts are always painful and not only to those who find their resources suddenly shrunk. And whilst we deny neither the difficulty nor the importance of the challenge both issues posed, arguably the prime issue as it always is when such decisions, fraught as they are, have to be taken is precisely how they may be made acceptable or how the bitter pill may be rendered less bitter in default of being sugared. There is, in effect, a distinction to be made between policy as content – leading up to a legal enactment – and policy as presentation – that is, the adjustments in rhetoric – often held up as 'spin doctoring' – to win support by appealing to groups and interests to support its content, though in real life the two tend to be inextricably entwined with each other.

Importing neoliberalism as a way to introduce new priorities and procedures into Portuguese higher education may be interpreted as the second of these two analytical phases – that is, policy as presentation. And, together with Gonçalves, we see neoliberalism as the deliberate and considered 'solution' to another, equally ticklish 'problem'. The problem neoliberalism was brought in to deal with lay precisely in the power of consensus that had urged on the expansion of higher education over the previous two decades. For those on whose shoulders the burden of 'cost compression' rested, that consensus was remarkably constraining. To begin with, the memory of what the Revolution had achieved – what we alluded to earlier as its 'perceptual half-life'[9] – was very much alive if only because many of those who had been young in the days of upheaval now occupied positions of responsibility in higher education. Furthermore, the key dimensions in that consensus involved sensitivity in the extreme and very especially to the possibility that a strong State which acted as guardian for the independence of higher learning (Amaral 2008) could overstep the boundaries of mere strength and revert towards a 'policy style' (Premfors 1981: 253–262), not easily distinguishable from authoritarianism. The memory of the corporatist doctrine of the *Estado Novo* had not entirely died the death. Last, but not least, was pedagogic autonomy, which the government rescinded, ostensibly to restore a parity of condition to polytechnics, which had not been granted it.

Conjuring up the shades of Adam Smith and Milton Friedman provided a doctrine to outflank the blocking power of higher education's political and constructive consensus since 1976. But outflanking the consensus also entailed shifting both the underlying paradigm and thus the criteria by which higher education was viewed and publicly judged.

Shift in Discourse as Handmaiden to Policy

The shift in discourse neoliberalism brings with it has been criticised on many grounds: as the rise of the immediate, the triumph of the short term, the primacy of the utilitarian, as the predominance of the economic over both the political and cultural, quite apart from re-engineering the paradigm of higher education as a cultural institution to become an instrument of production in the service economy. Its mission has been redefined from meeting social demand to supplying knowledge as a tradable and saleable commodity. Such a change in the way the purpose of higher education is construed is not, however, a philosophic or intellectual concern alone, although often it is easily dismissed as such. On the contrary, it has consequences both political and operational. By re-stating the mission of higher education exclusively in functional and operational terms, as opposed to realising such broad social objectives as equity and social demand, a new series of criteria could be introduced and the performance of Portuguese higher education reassessed in their light. Change in paradigm changed the way the achievements of consensus could be presented – and were – not as success so much as failure that retrospectively could be burnt on the altar of the very issues that were central in justifying and giving credence to the neoliberal agenda for higher education in Portugal. Thus, the concept of the strong State was no longer held to be a virtue so much as a manifest example of Portugal's persisting where others had moved on. Reductions in public expenditure could thus be presented as a non-negotiable and as an overdue correction to past error and profligacy. Within the same perspective, participant democracy – the touchstone on which the two previous decades of higher education policy had rested – could equally be held up as a telling example of the way academia sought to advance its own sectional interests rather than advancing the competitive demands of a modern economy.

Bonfire of the Vanities

Such efforts put in place an alternative interpretation and, as do most Orthodoxies, sought to rewrite History as well as justifying the measures Government envisaged. By the same token, the advent of neoliberalism in Portuguese policymaking also sought to gain general recognition of the practical difficulties funding and financing higher education faced. It also brought other consequences in its train. Amongst the most paradoxical was, as we have already remarked, the quest by Government for an alternative set of values from those that upheld the established consensus in higher education the better to argue later that there was no alternative to what Government proposed! Another was to light a bonfire around the vanities of the historic interpretation of Portuguese Exceptionalism. By so doing, that process, analysed earlier in this Introduction[10] in terms of the mutation in defining Exceptionalism, wrought an equally dramatic reassessment on Portuguese higher education policy. No longer the gauge of achievement and rapid adjustment to Society's demands on the home front, the policy that had driven the Nation forwards over three decades was now dismissed as a manifest example of failure, as the root cause of the gap between higher education policy in Portugal and emerging European norms.

As other contributors to this book have noted, three features stand out in the introduction of neoliberalism to justify pragmatic issues in policymaking. The first is the contrast between Portugal's drive towards *La Pensée Unique* and its counterpart in the UK. For whilst the UK grafted an ideological rationale *after* expenditure reduction took place (Dill et al. 2004), the Portuguese Government sought an ideological justification *before* introducing the operational consequences of neoliberalism – New Public Management – in the shape of the 2007 Higher Education Guideline Law. The second – and as we have pointed out at various points in this introductory overview – is the highly compressed time scale that accompanied the two phases of presentation and enactment. The third feature – perhaps the most revealing of the three – was the role played by external, international agencies, principally the OECD and ENQA in giving weight and legitimacy to what, from a long-term standpoint, amounted to nothing less than a 180° turn, an 'about face', in the central values that had shaped Portugal's policy towards higher education.

It remains a matter of the nicest judgment to determine whether so marked a departure from historically rooted values and their replacement by an undeniably partisan agenda is best seen as an Act of Oblivion or as a deliberate example of the Historical Attention Span Deficit Disorder wreaking its ravages Portuguese-style! Whether the Government of the day sought benediction from abroad in default of gaining it wholeheartedly at home is a point that a number of contributors raise and not simply in the immediate background to the legislation of 2007. If this is so, then the Bonfire of the Vanities, which Government lit around higher education's achievements of the years of consensus, appears to have found other potentially inflammable material, despite the efforts and prior recommendations amongst others of the OECD, brought in to act neoliberalism's equivalent of the Fire Brigade.

A Rapid Flight over a Complex Terrain

This Introduction has set out a broad background to the evolution of higher education in Portugal across four decades and has done do so against a wider backdrop of parallel developments taking place elsewhere in Europe. We have sought to draw up a species of overview, the better for our readers to grasp the finer and more detailed analyses our colleagues have made. At this point, to return to an earlier metaphor, attention turns from the 'route map' to a rapid flight over the terrain explored – or theme addressed. The disciplinary perspectives employed and the specific issues raised may then be seen at one and the same time as an abstract or as a 'curtain raiser' to the substantive points and arguments developed.

Shaping the Nation

The First Part of this book, Shaping the Nation, sets the general background to the rise of Portugal as a Nation and the place of education – and higher education as a subset – in forging the national identity. The four accounts presented place a particular weight on the historical approach though the basic perspectives range from Sociology, Political History, the History of Ideas and Ideologies, Cultural History through to Social Psychology.

Sobral's chapter sets out the long-term historical background to higher learning in Portugal. He takes us forward from the fifteenth century to the fall of the so-called New State in 1974. Sobral's account identifies some of the enduring themes and characteristics that emerge over the centuries. Two are of particular interest: first, the recurring conviction that education could serve as a prime lever for political and social change; second, the equally recurrent theme of comparing Portugal's condition to other European countries – a theme that, beginning in the eighteenth century, surfaced time and again in moments of crisis and very often national self-doubt.

From the standpoint of chronology, Torgal takes Portuguese higher education forwards from the Revolution of the Carnations in 1974 up to the present. As an historian, Torgal sets out to explain how the Revolution of 1974 failed in its ambition to create a 'political university'. He takes the narrative up where Sobral left off. Torgal provides a complementary introduction to the 1974 Revolution and its aftermath. Interestingly, his examination of the interplay between the University, Society and Politics ends by broaching the delicate issue of whether the Revolution's failure to establish a 'political university' did not, in effect, re-emerge later and in under very different ideological wraps with the advent of neoliberalism as the major impulse behind recent developments in Portuguese higher education.

Madureira Pinto provides a parallel analysis of the remarkably rapid changes in social structure, values and quality of life that, in the space of less than a half-century, urged Portugal on from being a largely traditional, agrarian land to take on many of the characteristics of a modern service society. Shifts in population, the flight from the countryside, which took place later though more rapidly in Portugal than in other European countries, massive emigration, changes in the quality of life – all set the stage for broad-ranging themes that are taken up later and more specifically in the impact in shaping Higher Education and, in particular, the constituent bodies within it – the Academic, Student and Administrative Estates. Amongst them, the spectacular rise in the participation of women and girls and the growing range of occupations opened to them beyond the limited activities once allotted by a deeply traditional society – a trend largely precipitated by the colonial wars of the 1960s and 1970s and as such yet another example of the way war hastens social change (Marwick 1974; Neave 1992a: 84–127, 2010a, b, c: 47–48). A second Leitmotif, which is taken further in the Second and Third Parts, is the mobilising effect of shifts in popular attitudes towards Education, no longer shunned as the object of distrust and suspicion – above all, by the more traditionally minded, rural population.

Pereira and Lains tackle the strictly economic dimension to Portugal's developmental trajectory. This, in the space of a half-century, saw the country move from an economy based on agriculture to its present status of standing on the threshold of a Knowledge Economy. From being a country of low growth and low openness, its economy drove forward to become an industrialised society based on high growth and high openness. Here too, Portugal along with Ireland, displayed a pace in economic growth that matched the highest in Europe, though this upwards spiral began to flag from the 1990s onwards. Though the authors do not rule out the transition towards a Knowledge Economy, this step presents more than usual difficulty, difficulties that have in the meantime, become greater with the deepening of the financial crisis.

Shaping Higher Learning

The Second Part of the book, Shaping Higher Learning, as its title suggests, hones in on the higher education system as its central focus rather than locating higher education within the broad lines of the Nation's political, cultural or economic saga. Six clearly delineated topics are brought together beginning with an overview by Nunes de Almeida and Vieira on the build-up of Portugal's higher education system over the past 30 years, the emergence of a multi-sector binary model, split between an historically grounded public sector and the rise in the course of the 1980s of a private sector.

The forces that bear down on higher education in Portugal are examined by addressing the various instrumentalities involved in its re-configuration. Prime amongst them, though it rarely figures in mainstream accounts of higher education development, is the legal perspective and trends in legislation – an analysis of the formal legislative enactments, decrees and circulars which, if indispensable to the ongoing venture of higher education in what Clark termed 'the Continental (European) model' (Clark 1983), tends to be less prominent or, to nuance matters somewhat, is less usual in collections of essays that deal with higher education. The central role of legislation, the twists and turns in the relationship between Government, Higher Education and Society, are examined by Gonçalves. Over and above her analysis of the legislative dynamic, Gonçalves sets it against the ebb and flow of party politics in Portugal. Particularly telling is her account of how legislation in the shape of the 2007 Higher Education Guideline Law extended the imperatives of neoliberalism into higher education.

The chapter on Science Policy provides another perspective, again rarely found in run-of-the-mill studies of higher education. The strategic centrality of Science Policy is traced in great detail by Heitor and Horta who take us back to the early beginnings of science research in the 1920s. The wealth of detail they bring to bear and the initiatives launched by the Ministry of Science and Technology to forge links and partnerships between university and industry as well as between the Universities of Portugal and world leading research universities underscores the importance of Science Policy as an instrument for mobilising the Nation's inventiveness and research capacity. In advanced societies, whether already engaged on, or seeking actively to make, the transition towards the 'Knowledge Economy' (Sorlin and Vessuri 2007), the Science perspective is a crucial and essential development in contemporary higher education. It is a shaping factor of supreme importance. Whilst Knowledge Economy and the parallel perspective of the 'Knowledge Society' are often treated within disciplines of the Social Sciences, the major focus in this domain is, not surprisingly, a direct extension of the Sciences – Natural, Exact, Biological or Medical.

Science Policy as treated from a Science perspective not only involves a different value set from either the Social Sciences or the Humanities. It is concerned with very different basic issues: the attainment of 'critical mass' amongst research units, the intensity and scale of operation and, above all, the crucial issues of output and creativity, measurable international standing, quality and originality (Lindqvist 2006: 77–90).

Science Policy stands at a different interface. It revolves around the generation and diffusion of highly specialised knowledge between the Nation's research system of which higher education is part and the application and – hopefully rapid – transfer of that knowledge to production in firms, enterprises and business. In short, whilst for the majority of chapters in this book, the *institution* of higher education is the independent variable, in Heitor and Horta's contribution, it is the *type* of knowledge and the conditions of its optimisation which provide the focus.

Heitor and Horta start from the basic premise that a Knowledge Economy is itself driven by a more fundamental concept that of a 'Learning Economy' which is both dynamic and best understood by examining its course historically. As with other chapters, the authors go back to the various attempts to provide Portugal with a vestigial research base during the Estado Novo. They then trace the gradual build-up of a national Science and Technology system in considerable and authoritative detail. The 'late awakening' of S&T in Portugal, they argue, took place during the decade 1985 to 1995, a decade during which systematic evaluation of research output linked to funding was introduced – a turning point in Portugal's shift towards market-driven change. It is very clear that Science Policy in Portugal was amongst – if it was not *the* earliest vehicle of external reference having the explicit purpose to bring the country up to internationally comparable levels of output and to this extent was – and remains – proactive in its basic purpose. Other areas of policy by a similar token tend to be reactive to what is viewed as a *fait accompli*.

Analysing the 'instrumentalities' of change shifts is focused in Chap. 9. They move us deeper into the interface between those forces that work *within* the system of higher education to urge on change and responsiveness and those that bear down on it from *without* and from *above* which is the salient feature of both legislation and Science Policy. As students of Public Administration and Sociology, Magalhães and Santiago examine the evolution of three dimensions in the 'coordinative instrumentality' of Portuguese higher education: Governance, Public Management and Administration. Their account is more than usually sensitive to the usefulness of weighing matters up over the long term. Indeed, they extend the chronological framework backwards to include the First Republic, which saw the light of day in 1910. By doing so, they branch out from the purely historical accounts presented in the First Part by Sobral and Torgal. This approach has its benefits. It reveals a certain measure of continuity despite the evident rupture represented by the disappearance of the New State in 1974, a degree of continuity that others also point to. Amongst the elements of continuity, one may count the first steps towards a non-university sector and the laying down of a national research infrastructure.

Magalhães and Santiago show very clearly that different disciplines or disciplinary perspectives often give rise to very different chronological frameworks, a point that weighs heavily against the Grand Narrative[11]. By the same token, however, it is no less a powerful device in giving additional credence and purchase to the notion of synthesis within disciplinary perspectives when applied across time. In their scheme of things, the unfolding of Governance, Public Management and Administration falls into five clear phrases: the Years before the 1974 Revolution, the Days of Revolution (1974–1976), the Period of Normalisation (1976 to 1986), the Decade of Massification (1986 to 1996) and finally, the Rise of Managerialism (1996 to the present day).

Rosa and Sarrico extend the examination of the 'instrumentalities of coordination' further. They deal with the issue of Quality, Evaluation and Accreditation. The origins of what is sometimes termed 'The Evaluative State' (Neave 2009c: 3–22) are often traced back to the creation in 1984 of the French *Comité National d'Evaluation*. In Portugal, the first expression of the intent to monitor and assess the output of higher education appears in the Constitution of 1976, though operational reality of the principle stated was taken only 18 years later.

As in other systems of higher education in Europe, quality and evaluation, though relatively recent procedures, are extremely powerful in ascertaining how the individual institution responds to national priorities. They are no less potent in weighing up the viability of the policy such priorities underpin, though this latter use is by no means routine. Such an instrumentality is even more powerful when allied, as has been the case in Portugal since 2008, with accreditation as part of the overall remit of a single national agency.

Rosa and Sarrico trace the various attempts – some happy, others less so – to set evaluation in place. Not surprisingly, their periodicity differs from that of Magalhães and Santiago. Rosa and Sarrico, for instance, divide their chapter into three sections: Quality Drift: a legislative account, which may be seen as building on from Gonçalves' analysis, with the substantive issue being addressed in two further sections playfully entitled From Learning to Walk to Dysfunctional Teenager 1994–2005 and Coming of Age: From 2006 to the Present. Continuing their metaphor of Evaluation as one of three stages in the life of man, they turn to the future. Will it lead on to Uneventful Middle Years – or a Ripe Old Age? Higher Education in Portugal, they conclude, will henceforth increasingly be driven by competition and by market forces. However, the authors are adamant in upholding the point that trust between universities, polytechnics and the public must be won back if evaluation is to realise its full potential and to avoid the taint of being seen by the first two as an adversary and as a source of conflict.

Chapter 11 may likewise be seen as analysing an instrumentality. Both the Bologna Process and the Lisbon Agenda involve restructuring those key functions which earlier we argued were the structural concomitants in shaping the specific identity of higher education within the Nation State: study duration, certification and assessment mechanisms of student performance. Quite apart from the significance of both the Bologna Declaration and the Lisbon Agenda as steps towards a Continent-wide higher education system, and leaving aside the fact that for the first time in their history, large numbers of States are currently engaged upon the same enterprise at the same time, Bologna and Lisbon also serve as a species of litmus paper to test the presence, strength as well as to tease out the 'dimensionality' of national singularities in higher education.

Viewed in this light, Veiga and Amaral's account of the impact of Bologna and of the Lisbon Agenda carries across two dimensions: its impact direct and its impact indirect. The former examines the different arguments and views of contending interests – authorities and government included. They assess the impact of both agendas and the methods used by those involved to estimate both the progress made by, and the consequences that follow for, the national system. The second dimension is more subtle. It examines the stance taken less by the reforming than by those having reform done to them, namely universities, polytechnics and their three Constituent Estates. Both perspectives are particularly revealing. They show the confused – and often contradictory – results that occur when the forces of Convergence attempt to bring moral suasion to bear on both national and institutional levels. They also shed a most valuable insight into the ways by which the historic and historically based definition of Exceptionalism is translated through a series of often hilariously contradictory signals into a normative goal.

Introducing the Bologna structures into Portugal took place later than elsewhere. And whilst, for Amaral and Veiga, the three cycles, together with European Credit Transfer Scheme and the Diploma Supplement, were certainly taken up by both Universities and Polytechnics, Bologna was an affair of haste and precipitation, one amongst other far-reaching domestic reforms if anything more radical still in their immediate consequences for higher education. Certainly, Bologna allowed national administration to hold back the licentious proliferation of degree programmes – an unexpected blessing, which shows clearly that in Portugal, as elsewhere, France for instance (Musselin 2010: 181–206), the European agenda also served as a Trojan horse for specific national issues to profit from the unwonted window of opportunity Bologna and the Lisbon Agenda unintentionally opened.

Shaping the Institutional Fabric

The Third Part, Shaping the Institutional Fabric, pushes the analytical focus down to the institutional level and builds out from the underlying logic and rationale that permeate this study. Whilst the Second Part concentrates on policies emerging at the interface between national and institutional levels, the five chapters in the Third Part move us further into issues of direct consequence for the individual university and polytechnic. Here, the question 'What has changed in the Universities and Polytechnics of Portugal?' is addressed. The various answers given both echo and at the same time move further forwards on themes already present in Part II. Overlap, as we pointed out earlier, should not, however, be seen as effort wastefully duplicated. On the contrary, it allows us to delineate a boundary, a marker point, between the different perspectives that the study of higher education employs. Ostensible overlap in some of the themes and topics already broached at the intermediary level – what we termed earlier the 'interface' between the national and the institutional levels – often make for a very different account indeed when pressed into an institutional framework. In effect, patterns of development in higher education are often dependent on the level at which the analysis takes place (Neave 1996: 27).

The Third Part shows an increasing disciplinary eclecticism – though in varying degrees. Amongst the techniques, methods and canons of scholarship woven into the five accounts are Management Studies, the Sociology of Organisations, Political

Science, Economics, Economic History and Economic Theory, the Sociology of Education, the Sociology of Status, Public Administration and Implementation Studies, Geography and Economic Geography.

According to the periodicity delineated in Part II by Magalhães and Santiago, the Leitmotif for the years 1996 to the present could be satisfied within the overall theme of 'the Rise of Managerialism'. Lima drives this theme further forwards. He concentrates on Patterns of Institutional Management examined along the dimensions of democratisation, autonomy and what he presents as 'the Managerialist Canon', culminating in the Higher Education Guideline Act of 2007. This Act injected new patterns of governance and management into the institutional fabric. As has been pointed out earlier, higher education in Portugal rests on a legally codified system. Since much of Lima's examination involves the impact of legislation in setting the legal framework for the three issues – democratisation, institutional autonomy and the management imperative – the analysis he undertakes is a complementary picture to those presented on the one hand by Gonçalves and on the other by Magalhães and Santiago.

The re-arrangements that followed the overhaul of institutional management – increasingly centralised decision-making, boosting the authority of the Rector as institutional leader – brought with them a hyper-bureaucratic pattern of vertical power structures, technical rationality and standardisation, traits that cannot fail to have a familiar ring for students of New Public Management elsewhere. In the Portuguese setting, as Lima remarks, this was unprecedented and no less so for the fact that 20 years previously a marked degree of formal institutional autonomy had been conferred upon the University though not the polytechnic sector. In short, seen from an Anglo-Saxon standpoint, if universities and polytechnics in Portugal had long held out against the wiles of Managerialism, nevertheless embrace that doctrine they did, though not without heart-searching, regret or second thoughts (Santiago et al. 2006: 215–250).

Teixeira traces the course of one particular development that recent scholarship holds to be a very clear example of Portuguese Exceptionalism – namely the mushrooming of a substantial private sector of higher education over the 20 years beginning in the mid-1980s (Amaral and Teixeira 2001: 245–266). Though the rise of private higher education is not in itself a Portuguese exclusivity, the speed of its growth – at the height of its fortunes, private higher education drew in more than one third of the Student Estate – and the speed of its subsequent decline in the latter part of the 1990s, most certainly were. In seeking to account for the strange fate of private higher education in Portugal, Teixeira ranges far beyond the canon of Economics and Economic History into such aspects as long-term demographic trends, changes in the political environment and, last but not least, lax regulation by decision-makers.

Thus, the spectacular rise of the private sector in Portuguese higher education gave way to an equally spectacular shrinkage. Agreed, the private sector played its part in 'demand absorption'. To that extent, it played a significant role in the country's thrust towards mass higher education. In a scrupulous and even-handed assessment, Teixeira concludes that despite its marked contribution in advancing equity by giving individuals the opportunity to move on to higher learning, the great expectations private higher education nurtured at the outset – greater external efficiency and greater responsiveness to market demand, more sensitive and more rapid – were, for that very reason, almost as spectacular in the deception that resulted from their non-fulfilment.

The three chapters that bring the Third Part to a close delve deeply into what was earlier presented as the Constituent Orders in higher education: The Academic, Administrative and Student Estates. However, this particular terminology is not always accepted in the working vocabulary of scholarship in higher education. In its early usage, the term 'Academic Estate' served to draw a distinction between Academia as a profession, which tends to be the way it is conceived in Anglo-American literature (Perkin 1969; Clark 1987: 21–42; Rhoades 1998), and Academia as a category of public service, which was, until very recently, the predominant and formal legal status of its members in Continental Europe, Portugal included (Neave and Edelstein 1987: 211–270; Neave 2009d: 15–17).[12]

In her chapter on the development of academia in Portugal, Carvalho reviews the major theories dealing with the definition and status of professionals in English, American and also French literature – Bourdieu and Foucault in the main. Carvalho recasts the location of the Academic Estate, arguing that simply to see it as a subset of National Administration tends to play down the degree of difference and the conflict of interests within that Estate itself. A more profitable perspective, she argues, is to be found in Gramsci's theory of the central role played by 'organic intellectuals' in society. The main function of 'organic intellectuals', Gramsci held, lay in transforming technical knowledge into political knowledge.

Seeing the Academic Estate as a subset in the ranks of 'organic intellectuals', a broader though less precise category, provides a powerful and alternative theoretical framework through which Carvalho pinpoints, assesses and explains changes in the status and condition of academics in Portugal. Key to her argument is the basic assumption that academia is not a uniform whole. Rather it consists of different groups, each of which has its own 'interpretive scheme' and normative identity, an assumption she shares with Becher in respect of differences in 'disciplinary culture' (Becher 1992; Becher and Trowler 2001).

Carvalho identifies three major developments in the Academic Estate, which fragment it further in addition to the tribal lines of disciplinary cultures and interests. These are its rapid feminisation, though less in the Hard Sciences; its further organisational and structural split resulting from different conditions of employment in the non-university and private sectors of higher education; and, finally, and perhaps the most significant, the rise of the Administrative Estate which, she argues, bids fair to put an end to academia's hegemonic status of 'organic intellectuals'. The counter hegemonism of the Administrative Estate rests, she asserts, on representing itself as 'the primary competitive group in the jurisdictional field'.

Machado and Cerdeira turn our attention to the Administrative Estate, a difficult topic to tackle if only for the fact that even at national level, statistics that would otherwise give purchase over that Estate's evolution across time, not to mention possible shifts in its structure and distribution across different ranks, are remarkably opaque and far from easy to access. Such opacity is not a perverse phenomenon limited to Portugal alone. It is equally evident for instance, in the United Kingdom (Whitchurch 2006) despite the fact that the 'empowerment' of the British Administrative Estate has been uninterrupted these three decades past.

In the saga of the Administrative Estate in Portugal, the two authors take up some themes already developed by others in a different context, notably by Magalhães and Santiago, Lima and, not surprisingly, by Carvalho. Indeed, the dominant issues they examine closely reflect timelines developed earlier. Machado and Cerdeira trace the Rise of the Administrative Estate across the Years of Revolution, the Period of Normalisation, the Drive to Massification and the Period of Consolidation. They ask how far national policies affected the fortunes of the Administrative Estate and, no less important, how far it was also shaped by 'Europeanisation'.

Numerically speaking, growth in Administrative Estate outstripped that of the national civil service as a whole over the years from 1987 onwards though it plateaued out in 2001, only to pick up again in 2008. Against a background set in parallel trends elsewhere in Europe that accompanied, where they were not instrumental in conferring, a new centrality upon the Administrative Estate, Machado and Cerdeira follow a line of argument very similar to earlier interpretations of the rise of Managerialism in Portugal, though their reasoning and vocabulary both differ. They point out that Portugal displayed a 'lagged response' to the benefits of neoliberalism. Nor do they depart from Carvalho's argument about the displacement of 'hegemony' from the Academic to the Administrative Estate. They differ however, in their estimation of the timing of the full impact the reform, thrust forward in the name of neoliberalism, is likely to have. The saga of re-shaping the Administrative Estate around the tenets of New Managerialism has certainly begun. But, Machado and Cerdeira depart from the usual view held. If the legislation of 2007 marks a new stage in this overall process, the final impact upon patterns of authority and thus the balance of influence between Academic and Administrative Estates, they conclude, has yet to make itself felt in full.

In the final essay in this study, Fonseca sets herself a most comprehensive remit, which places growth of the Student Estate firmly in a statistical, historical and cultural setting. As other studies, notably Almeida and Veiria, have made plain, Fonseca shows in considerable detail that the decade 1985 to 1995 saw a tripling in the size of the Student Estate from around 100,000 to over 300,000. The peak year – 2002 – saw some 400,000 enrolled, a figure which, after a fall-off between 2005 and 2007, appears subsequently to have stabilised. This is a development of more than passing concern though whether similar phenomena will emerge elsewhere as a result of the financial crisis eating its way deeper into the social fabric, or following on the frenetic efforts of Governments to save by cutting back the higher education budget, is an issue on which a jury has yet to reach a verdict. By the same token, the slowdown in student applications begs the question whether Portugal might not be amongst the first of EU states to have reached a natural threshold in demand. Not without significance is the fact that from the turn of the millennium onwards, Portuguese higher education found itself with more than enough places for all those applying. Whether this means that Portugal has attained the upper limit on the demand for higher education is a question well worth the posing.

Fonseca, however, goes beyond the Student Estate viewed as a self-standing, self-contained and, more recently, a predominantly female institution. She reinserts it into the obvious, but often less noted ties, between family, friends, hometown and the broad cultural shifts that unfolded across the past three and a half decades. In this respect, her essay takes up themes developed earlier, principally by Madureira Pinto. Particularly interesting is her account of the Student Estate on the eve of the Revolution, an approach that allows us to link back to the two historical accounts of Portuguese higher education by Sobral and Torgal – a complementary perspective seen from the Student Estate, which, from 1956 onwards, entered into a phase of opposition to the Ancien Régime. In doing so, Fonseca opens up a further dimension to issues first discussed by Magalhães and Santiago and later, by Lima in the general perspective of Governance, Public Administration and Managerialism considered as part of relations between University and Government as opposed to the relationship which Fonseca develops, between University and Students.

Equally fascinating is the subsequent 'demobilisation' of the Student Estate. It is clear that despite recent studies of this phenomenon, de-mobilisation has been gathering strength well before it attracted the attention of scholarly curiosity. As Fonseca points out, demobilisation is not confined to political activism. It takes other forms, not least a dissolving of student identity derived from the act of study and from the once-esteemed status associated with being part of the Student Estate. If anything, the once-militant Student Estate, which in the heady days of the Revolution and its aftermath saw itself as part of the vanguard of the Revolution, is today a vestigial and sartorial rump on a broader and more amorphous Youth Culture.

Envoi

This introductory overview set out to develop a broad-ranging and complementary perspective the better to highlight the close and detailed analyses our colleagues present in this book. To the focused accounts that only insiders and experienced scholars can bring about, ours is a parallel view that sets out to provide what best may be seen as a series of unifying themes that serve as a general backdrop. These themes were:

1. Changes in European Higher Education.
2. The Study of Higher Education as a field of scholarship.
3. Portugal: Exception, Pioneer or Partner?
4. On the Road to Neoliberalism.
5. A Rapid Flight over a Complex Terrain.

Another task, which is the natural lot of Editors, is to draw attention to the way different disciplinary perspectives throw up different interpretations to common events or situations; in short, to bring out explicitly the ways independent scholarship adds depth and nuance to its own material, whilst shedding a complementary light on that of others.

In setting ourselves this remit, we have been sensitive above all to the demand, more than ever necessary given the present juncture at which higher education in the European Union finds itself, to place the saga of one country against developments, sometimes similar, at others different, that unfolded elsewhere in Europe before, during or after those in our referent system – namely Portugal. As we have seen, though the pace of change in Portugal's system of higher education has, in many respects, been spectacular, it also displays what clearly amounts to a 'lagged response'. Yet, the very notion of 'a lagged response' requires attention be paid to those that first of all set the pace or ushered the key development in. A 'lagged response' is not necessarily either a handicap or, for that matter, a disadvantage. Indeed, one of its advantages may well be the opportunity to profit from the experience of others to avoid some of the pitfalls their enterprise and initiative occasionally led them into, *quitte enfin* to creating one's own!

From this viewpoint, if Portugal embarked late on the drive to massification – to cite but one instance – late starting did not prevent catching it from up rapidly.

Pierre Bayle, the seventeenth century Huguenot father of the theory of political Toleration, once pointed out in his Historical and Critical Dictionary, 'Gratitude is owed one's patrons.' Gratitude is also owed one's colleagues, above all in a collective enterprise such as this. The Editors have much to be thankful for: punctuality in delivery; forbearance and remarkable self-control when one sees one's text ill treated, if not mangled; and finally, a nigh-godlike patience as the 'final touches' surpass the understanding of man, woman and scholars all. We have had proof in assembling this volume that our colleagues possess these qualities in almost superhuman measure. From this two things follow: errors and infelicities that may remain are those of the Editors. Editorial gratitude must be in just the same measure as the qualities just mentioned were shown by each and every one of those whose chapters form the substance of this study.

Notes

1. See below pp. 9–10.
2. We are indebted to our CIPES colleague Sofia Branco de Sousa for calling our attention both to the concept and to the exact terminology involved.
3. If Exceptionalism is construed as negative, pejorative even, what can we call those instances of foreign practice that are held up as 'the way to go' and enviable on that account? Let us suggest the term 'Exemplarism' for this category. The essential difference between Exceptionalism and Exemplarism resides in the fact that the latter entails recognition of such practices is voluntary to the individual nation and undertaken in terms of its own self-defined convenience, rather than using external moral suasion to urge on convergence around a cross-national norm, which, as we have argued, is Exceptionalism in its contemporary meaning.
4. Why the Grand Narrative should be held in such scepticism is tackled in greater detail below. See *The Grand Narrative: an Unfashionable Genre* p. 16.
5. For this see above p. 7.

6. We would wish to thank Magali Neave, graduate student in the War Studies Department at King's College, London for drawing our attention to this point.
7. See above pp. 3–4.
8. See above, pp. 3–4.
9. See above pp. 21–22.
10. See above pp. 10–13.
11. See above p. 16.
12. There are, of course, other descriptors – Academic, Administrative and Student *Constituencies* – for instance. And indeed, there are good reasons for the use of this alternative term. For a discussion of the forces that moved the Estates over to becoming Constituencies, see Neave 2009d, especially footnote 1 pp. 32–33.

References

Amaral, A. (2008). *Reforma do Ensino Superior: Quatro Temas em Debate*. Lisboa: Conselho Nacional de Educação.
Amaral, A., & Carvalho, T. (2008). *Autonomy and change in Portuguese higher education*. Matosinhos: CIPES (Xerox).
Amaral, A., & Magalhães, A. (2001). On markets, autonomy and regulation: The Janus Head revisited. *Higher Education Policy, 14*(1), 7–20.
Amaral, A., & Neave, G. (2009a). The OECD and its influence in higher education: A critical revision. In R. M. Bassett & A. Maldonaldo-Maldonaldo (Eds.), *International organizations and higher education policy: Thinking globally, acting locally?* London: Routledge.
Amaral, A., & Neave, G. (2009b). On Bologna, weasels and creeping competence. In A. Amaral, G. Neave, C. Musselin, & P. Maassen (Eds.), *European integration and the governance of higher education and research* (pp. 281–300). Heidelberg/London/New York: Springer.
Amaral, A., & Teixeira, P. (2001). The rise and fall of the private sector in Portuguese higher education. *Higher Education Policy, 13*(3), 245–266.
Andrew, C. (2009). *The defence of the realm: The authorized history of MI5*. London: Allen Lane.
Barblan, A. (2011). From the university in Europe to the universities of Europe. In W. Ruegg (Ed.), *A history of the university in Europe, Vol. IV. Universities since 1945*. Cambridge: Cambridge University Press.
Barnett, R. (2007). Wit and wisdom in the study of higher education. In J. Enders & F. van Vught (Eds.), *Towards a cartography of higher education policy change*. Enschede: Centre for Higher Education Policy Studies, Twente University.
Becher, R. A. (1992). Disciplinary perspectives on higher education. In B. R. Clark & G. Neave (Eds.), *Encyclopedia of higher education. Vol. 3. Analytical perspectives, section V: Disciplinary perspectives on higher education*. Oxford: Pergamon Press.
Becher, R. A., & Trowler, P. (2001). *Academic tribes and territories: Intellectual enquiry and the cultures of discipline*. Milton Keynes: OU Press for SRHE.
Clark, B. R. (1983). *The higher education system: Academic organization in cross-national perspective*. Berkeley/Los Angeles/London: University of California Press.
Clark, B. R. (1987). *The Academic Life: Small worlds, different worlds*. Princeton: Carnegie Foundation.
Clark, B. R. (1997). Small worlds, different worlds: Uniqueness and troubles of American academic professions. *Daedalus, 126*(4), 21–42.
Clark, B. R. (2000). Developing a career in the study of higher education. In J. C. Smart (Ed.), *Higher education: Handbook of theory and research* (Vol. xv). New York: Agathon Press.
Court of Justice of the European Communities. (CJEC). Judgment of 13 February 1985, Françoise Gravier v City of Liège, Case 293/83, in *Reports of Cases before the Court*. 1985: 593 on http://www.ena.lu/judgment_court_justice_gravier_case_293_83_13_february_1985–020002987.html

de Carvalho, R. (2008). *História do Ensino em Portugal* (3rd ed.). Lisboa: Fundação Calouste Gulbenkian.
De Groof, J., Neave, G., & Svec, J. (Eds.). (1998). Governance and democracy in higher education, vol. 2, in the Council of Europe series. *Legislating for higher education in Europe*. Dordrecht: Kluwer.
Dill, D., Jongbloed, B., Amaral, A., & Teixeira, P. (Eds.). (2004). *Markets in higher education: Rhetoric or reality?* Dordrecht: Kluwer Academic Publishers.
Dima, A.-M. (2001). Roumanian higher education viewed from a neo institutionalist perspective. *Higher Education in Europe, 23*(1), 397–406.
Doumenc, M., & Gilly, J. C. (1977). *Les IUTs: ouverture et idéologie*. Paris: Editions du Seuil.
Duczmal, W. (2006). The rise of private higher education in Poland: Policies, markets and strategies (Ph.D. Thesis, Twente University, CHEPS, Enschede, the Netherlands).
European Commission. (1991). Memorandum on higher education in the European community. In *COM (91) 349 final*. Luxembourg: Office for Official Publications of the European Communities.
File, J., & Goedegebuure, L. (Eds.). (2003). *Real-time systems: Reflections on higher education in the Czech Republic, Hungary, Poland and Slovenia*. Brno: Vuilin Publishers.
Giddens, A. (2006). *Europe in the global age*. (Cambridge: Polity Press) quoted in Maassen and Musselin (2009) 9.
Gornitzka, A. (2007). The Lisbon process: A supra national policy perspective. In P. Maassen & J. P. Olsen (Eds.), *University dynamics and European integration* (pp. 55–178). Dordrecht: Springer.
Gornitzka, Å., & Maassen, P. (2007). An insstrument for national political agendas: The hierarchical vision. In P. Maassen, & J. P. Olsen (Eds.), *University dynamics and European integration*. Dordrecht: Springer.
Graves, W. H. (1994). The learning society. *Educom Review, 29*(1).
Huisman, J., Maassen, P.A.M., & Neave, G. (Eds.). (2001). *Higher education and the nation state*. Oxford: Elsevier-Pergamon for IAU Press.
Kerr, C. (1963). *The uses of the university*. Cambridge: Harvard University Press (Godkin Lectures).
Kerr, C. (1986). The employment of university graduates in the united states: The acropolis and the agora. In A. Bienaymé, L. Cerych, & G. Neave (Eds.), *La Professionnalisation de l'enseignement supérieur*. Paris/Amsterdam: Fondation Européenne de la Culture.
Laslett, P. (1965). *The World we have lost: England before the industrial age*. London: Methuen.
Levy, D., & Slancheva, S. (Eds.). (2007). *Private higher education in east and central Europe: The quest for legitimacy*. New York: Palgrave Academic Publishers.
Lindqvist, S. (2006). The R&D production model: A Brueg (h) elesque alternative. In K. Blueckert, G. Neave, & T. Nybom (Eds.), *The European research university: An historical parenthesis*. New York/London: Palgrave Macmillan.
Lundvall, B. & Johnson, B. (1994). The learning economy. *Journal of Industry Studies, 2*: 23–42.
Maassen, P., & Neave, G. (2007). The Bologna process: An intergovernmental perspective. In P. Maassen & J. P. Olsen (Eds.), *European integration and university dynamics* 35–154. Dordrecht: Kluwer.
Maassen, P.A.M., & Musselin, C. (2009). European integration and the Europeanisation of higher education. In A. Amaral, G. Neave, C. Musselin & P.A.M. Maassen (Eds.), *European integration and the governance of higher education and research* (pp. 3–14). Dordrecht: Springer Books.
Magalhães, A., & Amaral, A. (2007). Changing values and norms in Portuguese higher education. *Higher Education Policy, 20*(1), 315–338.
Marginson, S. (2004). *National and global competition in higher education: Towards a synthesis (theoretical reflections)*. Presentation to the 2004 Conference of the American Society for Higher Education, Kansas City, April 3–4, 59 pp.
Marwick, A. (1974). *War and social change in the twentieth century*. London: Macmillan.
Metzger, W. (1987). The academic profession in the USA. In B. R. Clark (Ed.), *The Academic Profession: National, disciplinary and institutional settings*. Berkeley/Los Angeles: University of California Press.

Moscati, R. (2008). Transforming a centralized system of higher education: Reform and academic resistance in Italy. In A. Amaral, I. Bleiklie, & C. Musselin (Eds.), *From Governance to identity: A festschrift for Mary Henkel*. Heidelberg/London/New York: Springer.

Musselin, C. (2010). The side effects of the Bologna process on national institutional settings: The case of France. In A. Amaral, G. Neave, C. Musselin, & P. Maassen (Eds.), *European integration and the governance of higher education and research*. Heidelberg/London/New York: Springer.

Neave, G. (1985). Elite and mass higher education: Britain, a regressive model. *Comparative Education Review, 29*(3), 347–361.

Neave, G. (1992a). War and educational reconstruction in Belgium, France and the Netherlands, 1940–1947. In R. Lowe (Ed.), *Education and the second world war* (pp. 84–127). London: Falmer Press.

Neave, G. (1992b). *The Teaching Nation: Prospects for teachers in the European community*. Oxford: Pergamon Press.

Neave, G. (1996). Homogenisation, integration and convergence: The Cheshire cats of higher education analysis. In V. L. Meek, L. Goedegebuure, O. Kivinen, & R. Rinne (Eds.), *The mockers and mocked: Comparative perspectives on differentiation, convergence and diversity in higher education*. Oxford: Pergamon.

Neave, G. (2001). The European dimension in higher education: An excursion into the modern use of historical analogues. In J. Huisman, P. Maassen, & G. Neave (Eds.), *Higher education and the nation state*. Oxford: Elsevier-Pergamon for IAU.

Neave, G. (2003). The Bologna Declaration: Some of the historic dilemmas posed by the reconstruction of the community in Europe's systems of higher education. *Educational Policy, 17*(1), 141–164.

Neave, G. (2006). On time and fragmentation: Sundry observations on Research, the University and Politics from a waveringly historical perspective. In K. Bluchert, G. Neave, & T. Nybom (Eds.), *The European Research University – a historical parenthesis?* (pp. 63–76) New York: Palgrave Academic.

Neave, G. (2007). A privatização da Educação Superior e a Dinâmica do Estado Avaliador. In *ANAIS Educação Superior: questão de Estado prioridade social* (pp. 109–192). São Paulo: FNESP.

Neave, G. (2009a). The evaluative state as policy in transition: An historical and an anatomical study. In R. Cowen & A. M. Kazamias (Eds.), *The international handbook of comparative education* (pp. 551–568). Heidelberg/London/New York: Springer.

Neave, G. (2009c). Institutional autonomy 2010–2020. The tale of Elan – Two steps back to take one very large leap forward. In B. Kehm, J. Huisman, & B. Stensaker (Eds.), *The European higher education area; perspectives on a moving target* (pp. 3–22). Rotterdam: Sense Publications.

Neave, G. (2009d). The Academic Estate revisited; reflections on academia's rapid progress from the Capitoline hill to the Tarpeian rock. In J. Enders & E. de Weert (Eds.), *The changing face of academic life: Analytical and comparative perspectives*. New York/London: Palgrave Macmillan.

Neave, G. (2010a). Introduction to federalism in American higher education. In M. Burrage (Ed.), *Martin Trow: Twentieth century higher education – Elite to mass to universal*. Baltimore: Johns Hopkins University Press.

Neave, G., de Groof, J., & Svec, J. (Eds.). (1998). Governance and democracy in higher education, vol. 2, in the Council of Europe series *Legislating for higher education in Europe*. (Dordrecht: Kluwer).

Neave, G. (2010b). Grundlagen. In W. Ruegg (Ed.), *Geschichte der Universitaet in Europa, Band IV vom Zweiten Weltkrieg bis zum End des Zwanzigsten Jahrhunderts*. Munchen: Beck Verlag.

Neave, G. (2010c). Burton R. Clark 1921–2009: The man, his saga and his times. *London Review of Education, 8*(3), 209–216.

Neave, G. (2011). El Estudio de la gobernanza en la educación superior: Vaciamento, re-construcción y re-ingeniería del significado. In Rocio Grediago Kuri y Romualdo López Zárate (Eds.), *Aportaciones a la agenda de investigación sobre educación superior 2010–2020* (pp. 261–298). Mexico: Universidad Autónomia Metropolitana, Unidad Azcapotzalco.

Neave, G., & Amaral, A. (2008). On process, progress, success and methodology or, the unfolding of the Bologna process as it appears to two reasonably benign observers. *Higher Education Quarterly, 62*(1–2), 40–62.

Neave, G., & Edelstein, R. (1987). The academic estate in western Europe. In B. R. Clark (Ed.), *The academic profession: National, disciplinary & institutional settings*. Berkeley/Los Angeles: University of California Press.

Neave, G., & van Vught, F. (Eds.). (1991). *Prometheus bound: The changing relationship between government and higher education in Western Europe*. Oxford: Pergamon Press.

Nybom, T. (2003). The Humboldtian legacy: Reflections on the past, present and future of the European University. *Higher Education Policy, 16*(2), 141–169.

Olsen, J. P. (2007). The institutional dynamics of the European university. In P. Maassen & J. P. Olsen (Eds.), *University dynamics and European integration*. Dordrecht: Springer.

Perkin, H. (1969). *Key profession: The history of the association of university teachers*. London: RKP.

Phillips, L. J., & Jorgensen, M. W. (2002). *Discourse analysis as theory and method*. London: Sage.

Pratt, J., & Burgess, T. (1974). *The polytechnics*. London: Pitmans.

Premfors, R. (1981). National policy style and higher education in France, Sweden and the United Kingdom. *European Journal of Education, 16*(2), 253–262.

Purser, L., & Crosier, D. (2007). Trends V: Key messages, *4th Convention of European Higher Education Institutions*, Lisbon, March (power point presentation).

Rhoades, G. (1998). *Managed professionals: Unionized faculty and restructuring academic labour*. Albany: State University of New York Press.

Robertson, S. L., & Dale, R. (2009). *The world bank, the IMF and the possibilities of critical education*. London: Routledge.

Rothblatt, S. (2007). *Higher Education's abiding moral dilemma: Merit and worth in the cross Atlantic democracies 1800–2006*. Oxford: Symposium Books.

Ruegg, W. (1992). Mythology and historiography of the beginnings. In W. Ruegg (Ed.), *History of the universities in Europe. Vol. 1. The middle ages*. Cambridge: Cambridge University Press.

Ruegg, W. (2011). Themes. In W. Ruegg (Ed.), *A history of the university in Europe, Vol. iv. Universities since 1945*. Cambridge: Cambridge University Press.

Ruegg, W., & de Ridder Simoens, H. (1994–2011) *A History of the University in Europe* (4 vols). Cambridge: Cambridge University Press.

Santiago, R., Carvalho, T., Amaral, A., & Meek, V. L. (2006). Changing patterns in the middle management of higher education institutions: The case of Portugal. *Higher Education, 52*(2), 215–250.

Sorlin, S., & Vessuri, H. (Eds.). (2007). *Knowledge society vs. Knowledge economy*. New York/London: Palgrave Macmillan.

Teichler, U., Daniel, H.-D., & Enders, J. (1996). Hochschulen und Gesellschaft als Gegenstand der Forschung – Bilanz und Perspektiven. In U. Teicher, H.-D. Daniel, & Enders Juergen (Eds.), *Brennpunkt Hochschule: neuere Analyse zu Hochschule, Beruf and Gesellschaft*. Frankfurt am Main/New York: Campus Verlag.

Trow, M. (1974). *Problems in the transition from elite to mass higher education*. In General report on the conference on future structures of post-secondary education. Paris: OECD.

Veiga, A. (2010). Bologna and the Institutionalization of the European Higher Education Área (2 vols). Porto: Faculdade de Psicologia e de Ciências da Educação, Tese de Doutoramento em Ciências da Educação.

Wallerstein, I. (2004). *World-systems analysis: An introduction*. Durham: Duke University Press.

Whitchurch, C. (2006). *Professional managers in UK higher education. Preparing for complex futures: Interim report*. London: Leadership Foundation for Higher Education.

Part I
Shaping the Nation

Chapter 2
National Identity and Higher Education: From the Origins till 1974

José Manuel Sobral

National Identity, Nation, Nationalism

What are the connections between the images – or representations – of Portuguese national identity and the evolution of higher education in Portugal? For reasons associated with both the national dimension and with higher education, this chapter will pay more attention to recent centuries whilst putting the topic it deals with against a broader historic panorama and backdrop.

First, let us clarify the meaning of the concepts this chapter deals with. Higher education embraces that level of education, which historically has always been considered the most advanced and the most sophisticated. Though changes have taken place across its centuries-long existence, changes that made it an institution with highly distinctive features, the university has always stood at the apex of learning. It is not the only institution to occupy this position, however. From the start of the nineteenth century, institutions such as advanced schools or academies – polytechnic or medical – made their way into what is currently understood today as 'higher education'.

Problems abound when it comes to defining 'national identity'. To simplify matters, to have a 'national identity' is to be conscious of belonging to a nation and acting like a member of one (Hutchinson 2001: 215). As for what a nation is, a broad definition holds it to be 'a group connected by a strong feeling of shared values, cultural characteristics such as language and religion and a history perceived as common' (Giddens 2009: 1126), or, alternatively, it has been presented as 'a social relationship of a collective awareness' (Grosby 2005: 10). The nation is not to be confused with

---

J.M. Sobral (✉)
Instituto de Ciências Sociais, University of Lisbon,
Av Prof Anibal de Bettencourt, 1600 Lisbon, Portugal
e-mail: jose.sobral@ics.ul.pt

the State, which is 'a political apparatus (government institutions and administration) that governs a particular territory and whose authority is based on the law and the ability to use force' (Giddens 2009: 1134). There are nations without a state – like Kurdistan nation, states in which the state is associated with the nation – like Portugal or Denmark and multinational states – like the United Kingdom and Spain.

Nations are the product of history. Today, there is a lively debate between those who defend the ancient and historical origins of nations (Hastings 1997), those who hold to its modern origin (Gellner 1983; Hobsbawm 1990) and a third school of thought, which whilst admitting that nations derive some of their features from modernity, see them as grounded in earlier cultural realities and ethnic differences (Smith 1991). To pursue this debate here is inappropriate. In our view, there is no single type of explanation, no single theory that can account for the sheer variety and variation that exist in the building of nations. Suffice it to ponder for a moment on what in historical terms separates ancient national profiles, be they European or Asian, from nations that were the outcome of colonial occupation, which had little time and even less respect for ethnocultural identity. Nations are the work of history, and in this, we subscribe to an argument that others too have endorsed (Llobera 1994) inasmuch as it applies to the Western European context of which Portugal is a part – namely that the nation and the identities to which it refers are the product of processes that work out over the long term (Sobral 2003). Furthermore, the profile of nations and of national identities ties in with nationalism. Yet, this term covers a number of distinct and different connotations. If nationalism is to be understood as:

(…) an ideological movement that is looking to obtain and keep autonomy, unity and identity for a population some members of which think of building a nation,

Then it is an essentially modern phenomenon that emerged in the course of the past two centuries (Smith 1991: 73). If, however, we conceive nationalism as a particularistic and ethnocentric notion, clearly the nationalism involved will be older by far (Hastings 1997: 4–8).

Since the national existence of Portugal as an entity is centuries old (Sobral 2003, 2006), it is useful to retain both meanings of nationalism. One takes its shape through the expression in collective experience and rejection of foreigners – through ethnocentrism and xenophobia. The other emerges in the form of explicit ideologies that exalt and extol the nation. Both are associated with forging national identity. They are intertwined. The former emerges little by little, incrementally, as an outcome of a common, that is to say, an increasingly shared history of the collectivity that in the fullness of time will define itself as a nation. This was what happened with the inhabitants of the Kingdom of Portugal. At the same time, confrontation with, and differentiation from others also moved forward. The latter of these two dynamics rallies around a set of principles and representations, the drivers of political action, which spread from political and intellectual centres out into the periphery. In the precise sense of the term, nationalism is a discourse or ideology, in which the Nation is a source of legitimacy for political power. It is also the supreme value that permeates and inspires not only political life, but also knowledge, particularly the Humanities, Arts and Sciences. It is, however, a later dynamic, one that only triumphed fully in the nineteenth century (Schulze 1996: 137–302). This particular strain of political and cultural nationalism raises and strengthens earlier feelings of national identity to new heights. It is precisely what took place in Portugal.

Both the State and its servants, together with educated elites, fulfil a crucial role in constructing and spreading this national identity. It is taken aboard and taken in as something natural and unquestionable, an outgrowth of everyday life inserted into social and political patterns and habits that are differentiated from other earlier ones.

This interpretation is close to Bourdieu's concept of national *habitus*, the unconscious perceptions and behaviour acquired by dint of living in a particular nation state, being subjected to its specific beliefs, *mores* and culture. As Bourdieu pointed out:

> (…) Culture is unifying. The state contributes to the unification of the cultural market by unifying all the codes, juridical, linguistic, metric, and by operating forms of homogenization, namely the bureaucratic (by means of, for example, forms, applications, etc.). Through the systems of classification (…) registered in law, through bureaucratic procedures, school structures, and social rituals (…) the state models mental structures and imposes common principals of vision and division, forms of thinking that relate to cultivated thought like the primitive forms of classification of Durkheim and Mauss related to savage thought, by this fact contributing to constructing what is commonly called *national identity* – or, what in an older expression was called the national character… (Bourdieu 1994: 114–115; Sobral 2006)

Under these categories, symbolic production may also be associated, for instance, with a distinct name for a collective territory, for its inhabitants, a name linked to an official language or to the coining or perpetuation of stereotypes about 'nationals' and 'foreigners'.

Clearly, the State plays the central role in constructing national identities. It is an important purveyor of ideology. Amongst the strategies the State uses to construct a single identity for its inhabitants (Guibernau 2007: 25) are disseminating a specific national *image* through drawing up a common history, shared culture, defining a particular territory, the devising and spreading symbols and rituals to instil a sense of community among the population; the definition of citizenship with specific rights and the separation between those who have right to it and those refused; the designation of common enemies, namely through war, as a potent unifying force; progressive build up of national systems of education and communication as keys to promoting images, symbols and national narratives, thus completing what has been called the 'nationalization of the masses' (Mosse 1975). National identity is then reproduced in everyday life by the mere fact of living on the territory where social life is filled with so-called 'banal nationalism' (Billig 1995) that constantly insists and persists, through diverse forms, in distinguishing between 'us' (nationals) and 'them' (foreigners).

Particular attention will be paid to the way the State and official nationalism were both used to refine national identity. This process intensified over the last three centuries, when nationalism, in various guises – liberal, authoritarian, democratic – emerged as a central element in State ideologies. Similarly, and at this self-same moment its presence in education and, through schools, the use of the latter to inject specific characteristics and dimensions into national identity, come to the fore.

The Kingdom of Portugal in the Middle Ages and the Role of the Studium Generale

In Portugal, evidence of nation building and, correlatively, the shaping of national identity date from the end of the medieval period, which is not overly odd in the European context (Huizinga 1984: 97–117). The Kingdom of Portugal took shape during the so-called Christian Reconquista and pushed southwards toward territories then under Islamic dominance. Features that later were to differentiate it from other kingdoms in the Peninsula emerged gradually. Frontiers, the beginnings of a native vernacular language, later transformed into the official language, Portuguese, the appearance of a telling symbol, the coat of arms of the Kingdom, the distinct ethnic name assigned to the territory thus defined, Portugal and the ethnic name of its inhabitants, the Portuguese, the striking of its own coinage, these were elements that defined and differentiated (Albuquerque 1974; Mattoso 1985a, b; Sobral 2003). The same applied to the war that broke out after the death of the King D. Fernando at the end of the fourteenth century. The dispute over inheritance brought by D. Fernando's legitimate daughter and her husband, the King of Castela, a dispute involving access to the Throne, gave free reign to xenophobia, of raising the Portuguese up and putting the foreigner down. Looked at from a slightly different angle, this particular episode saw the raising up of the collective Portuguese identity as a 'social relationship' set apart from Castelhano, a proto Spanish dialect, which was to endure across centuries before the latter finally gave place to Spanish (Sobral 2003).

Evidence for the awareness of national identity concerns only a highly limited minority. Little or nothing is known of the perceptions held by the majority of the population in the matter of national identity, because there are almost no written records of their feelings and behaviour. These appear only in late medieval chronicles. Even so, it should not be forgotten that these chronicles were the work of Fernão Lopes, himself a literate man and one dedicated to upholding the cause of independence of the Kingdom of Portugal against Castilian claims, whose own interpretation could be seen as adding to the 'nationalist' overtones. Still, a goodly number of historians agree that a distinct Portuguese identity was visible at the end of the Middle Ages (Mattoso 1985a, b; Godinho 2004; Disney 2009: 96–97). Documentary support for this identity – or its awareness – first appears in Court circles or in institutions linked to it. Only later did they extend to broader social milieux (Mattoso 1985b: 211–212).

For his part, Rómulo de Carvalho (Carvalho 2008: 61), the historian of Education on whose work this Chapter systematically draws, takes the existence of the Portuguese nation in the Medieval period as given. He connects the creation of the *Studium Generale* at the end of the thirteenth century to this period in the phase of national construction. To us, this does not seem warranted. He does not draw the distinction between the political entity – the Kingdom of Portugal – and the cultural collectivity – the nation – as determined by its borders. Thus, so it appears to us, he sees the making of the nation as a *fait accompli* long before it was possible to speak of its existence as a fact lived and experienced by a large part of the population.

Moreover, there is no basis in *national* terms for establishing the Studium Generale. Rather, the motives he mentioned refer to the usefulness of the Studium Generale for the State, for the prestige the Studium Generale might confer and its importance in the defence of religious orthodoxy. The letter, in which Portuguese prelates asked the Pope's permission to set the Guild up, reads:

> (...) As Kingly Might should be marked not only by weapons but also by laws, for the Republic to be ruled in times of war and of peace, because the world is illuminated by knowledge, and the life of the Saints better informed to obey God and His Ministers and Masters, the Faith is strengthened, the Church raised up and may defend itself against the perverse heresies... (Carvalho 2008: 47)

The university would teach knowledge of the world (science), qualify specialists in law and enhance teaching of the true religion against heresy, the extirpation of which was the constant preoccupation of the Medieval Church. The initial curriculum did not include Theology, Mathematics (Arithmetic) and other sciences, but rather Arts – Grammar, Logic and Music – and Physic that is, Medicine, but above all Laws and Decrees, i.e. Law, all figured as necessary for educating specialists in the new political entity, the Kingdom of Portugal (Carvalho 2008: 57–63). The Law, Civil and Canon, continued to hold primacy into the fifteenth century, which finally saw the inclusion of Theology (Carvalho 2008: 114).

University During the Golden Age of Empire

The launching of Portuguese imperial dominance with the conquest of Ceuta at the beginning of the fifteenth century, and a policy of promoting overseas voyages, both would have profound effects on Portugal. They do not seem to have had great impact on what today would pass for higher education. There was no link between the so-called discoveries and university education. Nor was one necessary. For many years, the circulation of nautical skills and techniques via manuals put together by specialists outside the university, had flourished. Portuguese navigation of that era was eminently practical and based on long accumulated experience (Carvalho 2008: 108–109, notes 32, 33).

In his examination of the Manuelin statutes of the Studium Generale, for example Carvalho found no hint that either sea travel, which he regarded as innovation, or the Renaissance had an impact on the curriculum (Carvalho 2008: 142).

This period, which also embraced the period of the Iberian monarchy from 1580 to 1640, witnessed the outpourings of a patriotic/nationalist sort (Figueiredo 1993; Boxer 1969; Albuquerque 1974; Marcu 1976) as it did in other parts of Europe, where historical studies were spurred on by the advent of Humanism (Schulze 1996: 114–131). The Age of Discovery and overseas expansion were, time and again and for many strains of Portuguese nationalism, alluded to as Portugal's Golden Age.

> (...) The transformation of Portugal into a commercial Empire is accompanied by the construction of a "distinct national image", which exalted the territory and its inhabitants. (Sobral 2003: 1109)

Both Historiography and epic poetry – particularly Camões's 'Os Lusíadas' – played a fundamental role in this respect (Albuquerque 1974). During the reign of D.João III 'an event related to education and of the greatest importance for the consolidation of national awareness' (Carvalho 2008: 265) took place. This was the publication in 1536 of the first grammar for the Portuguese language, which lauded its qualities, of course, and was followed immediately by a second. At that time, reading manuals and elementary schools proliferated (Carvalho 2008: 267–277). This increased number of schools was part the King's initiative, which on the one hand, met the need to educate individuals able to serve in State and Church – hence the importance paid to educating lawyers and the clergy – and, on the other, the wish to raise the Kingdom's prestige, in the footsteps of what was currently in hand abroad. No motivations of a national nature were mentioned in connection with the King's undertaking – this was at a time when nation-building was intense. Nor was the royal progamme an exaltation of Portugal and Portuguese in the meaning that Albuquerque (Albuquerque 1974) examined in detail. Yet, the practice of spreading the vernacular tongue, common to all, backed by the press – though its readers were limited in numbers – showed that 'a nationalization of minds' (Hermet 1996: 57–58) was underway.

Higher education was dominated by the Counter-Reformation and deeply hostile to innovative learning, philosophical and scientific. University reform, taken in hand by D. João III, plus the setting up of new institutes of schooling in various diocesan centres shows the continuity afforded to 'medieval thinking and pedagogy' (Carvalho 2008: 238–239). Thus, for instance, the University of Évora, founded in 1557, was a church university with the mission to train theologians (Carvalho 2008: 307–308).

Protected by the royal prerogative, the Jesuits settled in Portugal and flowed across the Portuguese Empire, dominating education, save in the University of Coimbra. Even so '(…) there was no distinction between Jesuits and university masters of Coimbra. They all served in the same army (…) united by the same objective, which was the active defense of the Catholic Church through education (…). National educational life was to remain peaceful for almost two centuries' (Carvalho 2008: 330).

Such an educational orientation tied in closely with the identification of Portugal as a Catholic monarchy, a feature that underlined the special connection between Portugal and divine providence. This 'very special relationship' was, according to legend, first to be seen in the intervention of the Godhead in favour of the first Portuguese king, Afonso Henriques, at the Battle of Ourique by granting him victory over the Moorish kings. The same eschatology emerged in the belief that the Portuguese were the people chosen by divine providence to evangelise the world, an idea inseparable from Portugal's expansion into an Empire (Albuquerque 1974: 337–373).

Rómulo de Carvalho has pointed out that '(…) D. Francisco Manuel de Melo, in the 17th century… glorified the "blessed Catholic Faith" that allowed the Portuguese Nation "with religious awe to be wary of any opinion, art or custom that was not in favour of Christian mercy" and praised the Portuguese for being "always suspicious of any dangerous speculation and for being content with knowing just that which was necessary to manage the actions of body and soul without any mixing of unnecessary areas of knowledge..."' (Carvalho 2008: 369–370).

In the sixteenth and seventeenth centuries, education – and particularly what today would pass for higher education – did not carry with it any connection with the notion of being 'national', despite the clergy's part in Portugal's struggle to free itself from the Iberian monarchy of the Habsburgs. As one educational historian, who was extremely attentive to the role education played in moulding and strengthening national awareness, has observed:

> Neither the objectives of education, nor the school curriculum, selected manuals, or methodology, had any intention of enhancing the national (...) National languages and history, which in the future were to become the educational foundations for the readiness of the masses to defend and maintain a society divided into nations, was not part of educational programmes in those days. Any Master or any student who moved from Portugal to another country or vice versa felt no hindrance at what he had done or in how he progressed. The school did not have a mother country. In the schools, Latin was spoken. Logic, Rhetoric, Arithmetic or any other subject was studied in Latin, followed the same rules, the same textbooks, and the same discipline. To study in the schools of the Company of Jesus at Évora, Salamanca, Paris, Rome or Bohemia, was exactly the same. (Carvalho 2008: 361)

In general, education in Portugal not only remained on the sidelines but also, with little exception, treated the philosophical and scientific movements of the seventeenth century with hostility. In 1746, for example, a statement by the Rector of the Coimbra Arts College roundly condemned those opposing Aristotle's teachings and considered the ideas of Descartes and Newton to be useless (Carvalho 2008: 389; Albuquerque n.d.: 228–233).

The Enlightenment: Concerns of the Portuguese Nation and Its Educational Inertia

The reign of D. João V saw signs of a broader receptivity in Portugal to changes in science, scholarship and learning elsewhere in Europe. The monarch subsidized the Astronomical Observatory at the Jesuit College of S. Antão and another at the Royal palace (Carvalho 2008: 393–394).

The thirst for knowledge and scientific discovery was widely shared at the court of D. João V. During this period, the Royal Academy of Portuguese History in Lisbon (1720) and in Porto, an Academy of Medicine, albeit short-lived, were founded. Enthusiasm for Natural Philosophy and Experimental Physics flourished. A work of Newton was translated. Bluteau's Portuguese Vocabulary – a seminal work – was published. D. João V looked kindly on the Oratorian religious Order, which in turn looked kindly on Cartesian thought. For the Order, the king acquired a Cabinet of Experimental Physics and a well-endowed library (Carvalho 2008: 400).

The reign of D. João V saw the appearance of a 'work of great value' on elementary education, 'The new school to learn how to read, write and count', written around 1722 by Manuel de Andrade de Figueiredo (Carvalho 2008: 398–402). It was the first of its kind in Portugal. A further feature deserves highlighting, however. The author of the new school explicitly saw it as a work of comparison between the Portuguese and other 'nations':

> (...) all other nations have printed books that teach how to write with rules very similar to Art. *Our Portuguese nation* [our italics], not being inferior, has failed in this part of having its masters publish their teachings. In other words, they avoided the job or did not wish to submit themselves to censure. (Carvalho 2008: 405)

Be that as it may, its appearance provides further proof that the idea of 'a nation' as a collective entity continued to make its way under monarchical absolutism.

Education in Portugal felt the impact of the Enlightenment. Verney, an ardent defender of teaching Portuguese in place of Latin and a supporter of the equality of women in education, was well known. In higher education, he paid special attention to medical education, stressing that it demanded knowledge of Physics, Chemistry, Botany and even Mathematics (Carvalho 2008: 415–419).

D. José's reign, with the government centralised around the person of the Marquis de Pombal, was marked by a range of educational initiatives, at different levels and largely without precedent. The expulsion of the Jesuits in 1759 put an end to the Order's predominance in Portuguese education. Following this step, several innovations were taken. Attention returned to basic studies. A plan for Minor Schools in continental Portugal and in the Empire, involving almost 900 masters and professors, was put in hand. A College for the Nobility was founded in 1761, a school for the sons of the aristocracy, where 'humanities' were taught along with an ambitious science provision, which lasted a decade. However, the study of science was abolished in 1772, thereafter only literary disciplines remained. The Royal College at Mafra was founded in 1759 for the quaintly termed 'Civil Aristocracy', described as those who 'live with decency' together with a Class for Trade to teach its practical side. Still, despite the secularisation of education in the Minor Schools and despite the expulsion of the Jesuits, the Church continued to 'be highly dominant in education' (Carvalho 2008: 446–467).

In the area of higher education, most important was the reform of the Portuguese university undertaken by the Marquis de Pombal (Chap. 9). Its most noticeable and radical element lay in the development of science education. Faculties of Medicine, Mathematics and Philosophy were established, the latter including Experimental Physics, Chemistry and Natural History. The structures and equipment were brought in for teaching such domains as involved observation and experimentation. For Medicine, it took the form of the Teaching Hospital, the Theatre of Anatomy and a Pharmaceutical Dispensary. In Mathematics – an Astronomical Observatory; in Philosophy – a Natural History Collection, a Botanic Garden, a Cabinet of Experimental Physics and a Chemistry Laboratory (Carvalho 2008: 465–466).

The Pombalian reforms unfolded against the backdrop of an Absolutist State and drew heavily on so-called 'Enlightened Despotism'. What this entailed was very clear. Those powers and authorities that promoted the advancement of science and literary culture in their own bailiwick did so without the slightest intention of cutting back their own sovereign power, still less that such power should be questioned and challenged.

Intervention by the Absolutist State was urged on by a concern with Portugal's condition in the field of education, and this, in turn, was represented as bonding together a desirable presence in the area of science and knowledge with Portugal's historic past – along with an explicit comparison of Portugal with 'other nations'. Here then is further proof, and yet a further example of the way representation of the country as a nation spread across Portuguese society. Equally interesting is what may be termed as the 'eschatological justification' for this initiative. A much envied innovation in science was compared to, and associated with, what was held to be the 'high point' in Portuguese history, namely, the 'Discoveries'. As evidence of this link, we have the introduction to a scientific monograph of 1753, which urged the King (D. José) to promote the sciences:

> If God moves our King's will (…) if God moves this Sovereign will to establish in this Kingdom an Academy and a Science Observatory where the first form is Natural Philosophy, the world will admire in Portugal its men as great as in Rome and Florence's Galileos, Torricellis (…). Foreigners will see that Portugal too succeeds in scientific discoveries as (it has) in world discoveries. That just as it had Magalhães (Magellan) who made the first circumnavigation of the globe, so it would have many others who would give their best to any Faculty. Just as there was a da Gama who discovered and became the Master of the East, so there would be many who would discover and become Masters of Science. Just as the Portuguese were the first Argonauts who cast their anchors where Saint Augustine with all his wisdom, had not ventured, so they would reach out through their understanding where other nations had not yet travelled. (Carvalho 2008: 857).

The theme of Portugal in decline when compared to other nations – and, not without significance – to its own past, more glorious by far than the present – a theme that would become prominent in representations of national identity during the centuries following, is already visible. A document signed by D. José in 1770, creating the *Junta de Previdência Literaria* alluded to the 'decadence and downfall' (sic) the Jesuits brought to minor and major studies, made clear mention of this Leitmotif:

> And because as King … and as Protector of this university it is up to Us to examine the causes of its decadence and its present state of decay… (Carvalho 2008: 873).

It was a decay, which the action of the State would self-evidently bring to a halt.

The theme of the relationship between university and Nation was in its turn developed by the Rector of the University of Coimbra, D. Francisco de Lemos, who also saw the university's purpose to carry out the training of State elites, in these terms:

> The University (…) is a great corporation, formed by Kings and magnificently endowed by them, with the purpose of becoming a **General Seminary of the Nation** [our italics], where the Youth, noble and non noble from all walks of life is taught the Sciences and the Arts. (Carvalho 2008: 480–481).

With the death of D. José and the subsequent withdrawal from power of the Marquis de Pombal, higher education (in Coimbra) did not develop along the lines foreseen. The Academy of Sciences in Lisbon, created in 1779 as an institution for the literary elite, had amongst its purposes 'the advancement of *National Instruction*' [our italics]', 'perfecting the mechanical Arts and Sciences' 'and the increase of industry amongst the people' (Carvalho 2008: 513–515).

Other institutions for the dissemination of specialised knowledge appeared. Today, they would be placed in the different 'sectors' of 'higher education'. Amongst those associated with the development of the State or the economy were two Naval Academies; the Engineering School for Naval Constructors in the naval Arsenal; the Royal Academy of Fortification, Artillery and Design for training army officers; the Royal Academy for the Merchant Marine and Trade in Porto; and the Military Academy. In Lisbon, the Casa Pia, an establishment for the care of poor and abandoned children who were taught from primary school through to university degree, was also set up (Carvalho 2008: 513–524).

By the end of the eighteenth century, the existence of a formal *'National Training Plan'* [our italics] provided further proof of the representative spread of Portugal as a nation, though it has to be admitted that virtually nothing in it touched on higher education (Carvalho 2008: 507–511).

Higher Education in the Era of Nationalism

Whilst for some, to speak of nations and nationalism as a way of distinguishing reality, social, political and ideological prior to the end of the eighteenth century is a matter of the highest controversy, the existence and importance both acquired over the two centuries that followed (Schulze 1994; Hermet 1996) commands wide consensus. Even so, it would be clearer to speak about nationalisms in the plural. Nationalism in its singular form tends to be contradictory inasmuch as its substance may be liberal and democratic, as was the case in the first half of the nineteenth century. It may, however, take on a totalitarian and even racist character, which it increasingly assumed towards the end of the same century (Mosse 1988: 65–84). Either way, the celebration of the nation and its people as a collective representation, whether as an ideology of social and political groupings and movements or as an ideology of State, permeated into most of the varied and differing spheres of culture and human action. The Nation, represented as a supreme value, became itself a source of sovereignty and in the first document of Portuguese liberalism – the Constitution of 1822 – was defined as 'a union of all Portuguese from both hemispheres' (Soares n.d.: 159–163).

This was a watershed. Never again would the Portuguese State be endowed with a legitimacy other than the national. The substance devoted to defining, bolstering and re-stating national identity – the dominant representation of the nation – became profoundly marked by cultural production, by nationalist activism, and most particularly by specifying the State's responsibilities in the course of the nineteenth and twentieth centuries (Matos 1998; Ramos 1994; Torgal et al. 1998a, b). From this standpoint, the relationship between nationalism and education, and higher education in particular, took on a new centrality. Here, our focus shifts. It concentrates on how the preoccupations of nationalism and its different forms and expressions – liberal and republican, authoritarian and fascist as well as democratic – shaped the politics of higher education.

One theme persists across all these discourses and, as a recurrent Leitmotif, moulded literary representations of national identity amongst both liberals and republicans. But, as has already been pointed out, it was an idea that had been circulating well before. The recurrent theme of Portugal's decadence when set against other societies, was taken up time and again by 'successive regenerative' movements which promised its eradication from the nation (Serrão n.d.: 508–517; Serrão n.d.: 270–275). As the influential romantic historian, Alexandre Herculano, declaimed:

> Who are we today? (…) A nation that tries to regenerate itself (…) because it is irritated with its own decadence… (Serrão n.d.: 272).

The first Portuguese liberal government of 1820–1823, short-lived and riddled by crises though it was, gave way to a period of great unrest and civil war between the adepts of Absolute Monarchy and the Liberals, which carried on till 1834. It was not a period conducive to reforming education. Still, the idea was not entirely dead. It surfaced in the proposal made by Luis da Silva Mouzinho de Albuquerque (Albuquerque n.d.: 389–391) and dedicated to the 'Portuguese nation'. The proposal called for the creation of Academies in Lisbon, Porto and Coimbra, each having five faculties (Carvalho 2008: 538–539). Interesting though it was, the project went no further, however.

The second decade of the nineteenth century witnessed the founding of Royal Schools of Surgery at Lisbon (at S. José Hospital) and Porto (S. António Hospital) structured around 5-year programmes. A Veterinary School affiliated to the military saw the light of day during the reign of D. Miguel (Carvalho 2008: 540–544), despite the repressive and regressive nature of his policies towards both education and academics.

With Liberalism definitely established in 1834, various measures in the area of education were introduced. Already in 1835 Rodrigo da Fonseca Magalhães sketched out provision for public primary education, made it obligatory, which placed Portugal on a similar footing with other nations in Europe:

> Mistakes and prejudice of different sorts have precluded this branch of public Education [primary education] from being accepted among us just as they held back the move that, in the majority of European nations, has raised it (primary education) to the level of perfection and development expected. (Carvalho 2008: 888).

The legislative agenda of da Fonseca Magalhães covered the whole of education from primary school to higher learning, which involved setting up an Institute of Physical and Mathematical Sciences, a project that remained stillborn. (Carvalho 2008: 554).

By far the largest number of proposals for reform, which concentrated on secondary (liceal) education in Portugal, were put forward by the Septembrist leader Passos Manuel. His programme did not greatly change the Pombalian University. In the wider field of higher education, concern for the advance of technical scientific education bore fruit. Two new schools were founded in 1837 with objectives similar to those of the Faculty of Philosophy at Coimbra which had reached out to include Agriculture, Rural Economy, Veterinary Medicine and Technology in the new fifth year. Previously the course was taught in 4 years. The reform was introduced by decree in December 1836. The two institutions were the Polytechnic School of Lisbon – which placed weight on scientific education and was, like its French counterpart, linked with military Technology and specialisation – together with the Polytechnic Academy of Porto, equally strong in sciences, but intended to train engineers, pilots, merchants, farmers, factory managers, etc. Passos also overhauled the Medico-Surgical Schools at Lisbon and Porto (Carvalho 2008: 560–571).

These proposals for reform contained as well both discourses and representation of the Portuguese nation and did so persistently along the lines mentioned above in connection with the plans of Rodrigo da Fonseca Magalhães. Discourses and representation dwelt long on the backwardness of the Portuguese nation, when compared to those which acted as referents in the task of diagnosis and of defining identity. European nations where change brought about by revolutions, economic and political, were held up literally as 'noteworthy'. Without going into a more exhaustive and detailed pursuit of this constant theme, we will presume such discourses also pervaded the reforming impulse in higher education, which proceeded throughout the nineteenth century. Suffice it to note the reforms put in hand by Fontes Pereira de Melo: the founding of the Industrial Institute of Lisbon and the Industrial School of Porto, along with agriculture education which, at the third level – higher education – was to be seen in the Agriculture Institute, founded in Lisbon in 1853 (Carvalho 2008: 588–590). Another initiative concerned the establishment of the Higher Programme in the Humanities under the patronage of Pedro V (Carvalho 2008: 592–593). Given the importance assigned to education, a new government agency emerged in 1870 – the Ministry of Public Instruction though its life was short (Carvalho 2008: 599–600).

To review *in extenso* all the proposals for reforming higher education during the nineteenth century would be intolerably tedious. Rather, attention will concentrate on the images they projected of the Nation and its identity. The representation of Portugal as a nation decadent endured and was present at the end of that century. Indeed, it fed the rise of Republican Nationalism as a force for social and political revival. Some echo of those times may be gathered from a book, published by Adolfo Coelho in 1890 that carried the tile, significant in itself, *A draft program for an anthropological, pathological and demographic study of the Portuguese people*. Here we read

> The principal and determinant cause' [of the country's decadence] "seems to us to be in the lack of an education able to instil in all vital institutions, society's living expression of its organic wholeness, the practices that ensure their normal balanced functioning. (Carvalho 2008: 658).

When Coelho penned his study, discussion, both influential and weighty, of Portuguese decadence was widespread. For instance, in the writings of both Antero de Quental and Oliveira Martins, amongst other far less famous authors. Antero, in his influential essay, *The Causes of Decadence of Peninsular People,* claimed that one of the principal factors in such decadence lay in the absence of modern science in Portugal (Chap. 3) (Serrão no date: 273). Science that higher education advanced elsewhere in countries seen as the 'Significant Other' (Triandafyllidou 1998) against which images of Portuguese national identity were constructed.

Educational Reform, Higher Education and the Republic

Nationalism was fundamental to the Republican movement that triumphed in 1910. It came to power to resurrect a homeland held to be decadent, threatened in its colonial engagement – and undervalued, a Mother country of illiterates, predominantly rural and in marked contrast with industrialised, urban societies, the epitome of modernity in science and technology. Republicanism set great store by education as a lever for social transformation. Already in 1911, primary schooling was overhauled, a measure which would move Portugal in terms of education, up to a level of more advanced countries – should it be implemented even minimally (Carvalho 2008: 665).

Legislation built upon two dimensions – nationalism and democracy – as basic blocs in constructing the nation around a community of citizens. This imperative was set out explicitly in the introduction to the Decree of March, 29th 1911 (Chap. 9) which justified reorganising primary education. The purpose of reform was plain: '(…) Portugal needs to make citizens, the first resource of all homelands'. Primary school was to play a crucial role in socialisation in its broadest sense. On completing compulsory schooling, the young Portuguese was expected to love '(…) with conscious and reasoned love the region where he was born, the homeland where he lives, and humankind to which he belongs.' (Carvalho 2008: 894–895.)

Antonio Sérgio, a short-term Minister of Public Education – restored to office in 1913 – wrote a work in 1918 with the significant title *Education as a Factor in National Recovery*. In it, he argued:

> 'The role of a school is' (…) 'to inoculate, perform, and develop the ideal of the Portuguese, the ideal of the Nation, but never that of a sect or a party'. 'At the moment, we do not have a plan of a collective life.' (Carvalho 2008: 707).

A Decree dating from 1918 at the time of Sidónio Pais, a more conservative Republican, proclaimed:

> The value of people, a safe avenue down the path of progress, an intense vibration of patriotism, the unity of intentions able to lead on to a nation's historic purpose, has only one origin, a single and unique source, (that remains) immutable across all ages, constant in all civilisations: education. (Carvalho 2008: 696).

Higher education too underwent major changes under the Republic. As has already been pointed out, Republican lawmakers set their sights principally on the two extreme points in the hierarchy of education – primary school and higher education. They did not, however, pay much attention to secondary schooling. As early as 1911, two universities – Lisbon and Porto – (Carvalho 2008: 688) were founded, which extended the number of places available in higher education and smashed the monopoly hold of Coimbra University over university study at the same time. The Industrial and Commercial Institute of Lisbon was elevated to form two autonomous schools (1911) – the Technical University Institute and the Commercial University Institute (Carvalho 2008: 695) (Chap. 3).

The Decree founding the two new universities reflected the twin driving forces of democratisation and nationalism. Their mission was, on the one hand:

> (…) to promote a methodical study of national problems and disseminate high culture among national masses by the methods of university extension. (Carvalho 2008: 689)

On the other hand, in a Decree of 42 articles length, 41 were given over to laying out the conditions for scholarships, the purpose being to make higher education accessible:

> to many students with merit and aptitude but without funds. (Carvalho 2008: 688)

Although paying attention to changes in attendance level and to content taught do not fit easily within the scope of this essay, nevertheless the Republic saw the numbers of students and schools increase just as it did changes in student distribution across courses and Faculties. Student moves into Sciences and Medicine, which overtook Law (Carvalho 2008: 714–716) may be seen as another instance of the culture of science that went hand in glove with Republicanism (for a parallel discussion on this phenomenon see Chap. 3). Clearly, such developments did not proceed without conflict quite apart from the feeling that in no way brought about the revival many hoped for (Carvalho 2008: 708–709).

Higher Education, Authoritarian Nationalism and the New State

Under the Corporatist New State, established in 1933, which succeeded the military Dictatorship ensconced since 1926, higher education suffered. School growth, ushered in by republican nationalism, stopped. The impact of the New State's ideology was redoubtable. Higher education also suffered the consequences of cuts in budget to reduce the deficit in Portugal's public expenditure – which in some cases led to schools closing, albeit temporarily – as part of the measures to deal with economic crisis and recession that marked the run up to World War II. Those in power sought to have the university mirror the regime, as a university of 'national corporatism' (Torgal 2009: 22–23). Attempts were made to have higher education defend the corporatist 'world vision' that embraced authoritarian and imperial nationalism in which Catholic religiosity returned to occupy the prominent place it had lost to Republican secularism. Ideological control of Universities led to abandoning those disciplines where teaching and research were accused of being to all intents and purposes polemical – Sociology and Psychology, for example (Torgal 2009: 18). Formal oversight of contents and of academic staff at different times brought about the removal of the more dissident amongst its members. The strand of nationalism the New State purveyed, harked back to an old theme, though this time played to a new variation. It too symbolised resurgence in the face of decay. The variation, however, lay in equating decay and 'disorder' engendered by the Republic the New State replaced and which its military predecessor had overthrown (Catroga 1998: 264).

Yet, educational policy under the New State was not monolithic. The days of Fascism which inspired it, were followed by the post-war period, which saw Fascism vanish into the oubliettes of History. Against a backdrop of a predominantly rural and illiterate land, seen as backward compared to more developed countries, the theme of national identity broke surface once more. In the words of the Engineer Leite Pinto who in the 1960s was Minister of Education, this 'deplorable backwardness' contributed strongly to the lack of specialists in Science and Technology (Carvalho 2008: 794). The ideology of development, that would become so influential, began to take shape. As Sedas Nunes (1969) argued in an influential report of the time, specialists after whom the advocates of modernisation hankered were just not there. Still, some modernisation of education took place during the 1960s. The School Leaving Age was raised. In higher education, General University Studies were put in place in the then colonies of Angola and Mozambique. There, the Portuguese State was engaged in armed conflict with movements of national liberation, a conflict that in 1974 was to bring down the curtain on the New State itself as it did on the imperial nationalism, which had given birth to it.

The most radical transformation of Portugal's higher education system during this period was introduced under the direction of Veiga Simão as Minister of Education. Veiga Simão took office following the replacement of Salazar as President of the Council of Ministers and thus the major driving force in the Estado Novo, by Marcello Caetano. With the priority of 'democratising education', (Carvalho 2008: 808) Veiga Simão drew up a major agenda for reform from preschool through to higher education, which was implemented under Decree–Law no. 402/73 of August 11th (Chap. 3). In it, a line was drawn between universities and university institutes. New universities were founded and one university institute. Particular importance was laid on technical and scientific courses with polytechnic education to strengthen technical–vocational training, and Colleges of Education to train teachers in preschool and basic education. In effect, the groundwork for what was to become higher education in the aftermath of the Revolution of the Carnations of April 25th 1974 was laid down (Stoer 1983: 819).

Yet, Veiga's programme was the subject of considerable misgivings on the part of conservatives who clung to a particular definition of nationalism – one that enshrined an official national identity, part of which revolved around the Catholic religion and corporatism. The teaching of Political and Administrative Organisation of the Nation, a course which defined, justified and defended the corporatist ideology of the New State, Veiga had made optional. It is, however, only fair to add that this discipline enjoyed but a secondary significance in the curriculum (Carvalho 2008: 811). Even so, values for which it stood continued to inform official and national identity up to the last. Galvão Teles, minister during the 1960s, launched some measures of modernisation – he was, for instance, responsible for introducing a preparatory cycle (*ciclo preparatório*). The *ciclo preparatório* replaced the first 2 years of secondary schooling and raised compulsory education from 4 to 6 years. He also founded the Teleschool, which used television broadcasting to disseminate the new preparatory cycle in those places where school provision was not available. Galvão Teles was, in short, a figure of consequence. He argued that education should uphold loyalty to the 'great constants of Christianity and Lusitaneity' (Carvalho 2008: 798).

In the minds of the New State's ideologues, the quintessential character of the nation lay in its definition in terms of religion and ethnic myth with Lusitanians as the forebears of the Portuguese. As António Reis, an Opposition member, pointed out, Veiga's reform, on the one hand, represented an important break in the regime's nationalist ideology by seeing in the democratisation of education a principle agent of progress for the country's future in contrast to the exaltation of the past, to dreams of greatness and cultural elitism (Stoer 1983: 795). On the other hand, this strain of nationalism remained no less evident in the text of the 1973 Reform itself, which alluded to Portuguese identity as Christian and as defender of homeland and family (Stoer 1983: 805). Furthermore, Portugal's identity encompassed the 'overseas provinces,' for the Minister also alluded to Portuguese living in the 'arid savannah.' (Stoer 1983: 799.)

The uproar which Veiga Simão's reform provoked in Universities – for being technocratic and capitalist (Chap. 3) – cannot be separated from questioning what precisely the official national image was of an exceptional Portugal. This exception – a Portugal without colonies and refusing the notion of racial hierarchy or racial supremacy – as too the colonial wars fought to sustain it – were both hotly contested by the student movement of the day. This, together with April 25th gave birth to a new image, both official and national. Here indeed was a new identity, which in the immediate aftermath of the Revolution sought to affirm itself as democratic and socialist and appeared to link in with change in higher education (Chaps. 3, 9 and 7). As a result, between 1974 and 1977, expansion in higher education was inseparable from the rise of a new representational image in – and of – the Nation (Oliveira 2000: 104).

References

Billig, M. (1995). *Banal nationalism*. London: Sage.
Bourdieu, P. (1994). *Raisons Pratiques: Sur la Théorie de l'Action*. Paris: Editions du Seuil.
Boxer, C. R. (1969). *The Portuguese seaborne empire, 1415–1825*. London: Hutchinson.
Catroga, F. (1998). As Ritualizações da história. In L. R. Torgal, J. A. Mendes, & F. Catroga (Eds.), *História da História em Portugal (séculos XIX-XX): da Historiografia à Memória Histórica* (pp. 221–361). Lisboa: Temas e Debates.
de Albuquerque, M. (1974). *A Consciência Nacional Portuguesa*. Lisboa: M. de Albuquerque.
de Albuquerque, L. (n.d.). Ensino Liceal. In J. Serrão (Ed.), *Dicionário de História de Portugal* (Vol. III, pp. 389–391). Porto: Livraria Figueirinhas.
de Albuquerque, L. (n.d.). Universidade. In J. Serrão (Ed.), *Dicionário de História de Portugal* (Vol. VI, pp. 228–233). Porto: Livraria Figueirinhas.
de Carvalho, R. (2008). *História do Ensino em Portugal* (3rd ed.). Lisboa: Fundação Calouste Gulbenkian.
de Figueiredo, F. (1993). *A Épica Portuguesa no Século XVI* (2nd ed.). Lisboa: Imprensa Nacional.
Disney, A. R. (2009). *A history of Portugal and the Portuguese empire* (Portugal, Vol. I). Cambridge: Cambridge University Press.
Gellner, E. (1983). *Nations and nationalism*. Oxford: Blackwell.
Giddens, A. (2009). *Sociology*. Cambridge: Polity Press.
Godinho, V. M. (2004). *Portugal: a Emergência de uma Nação (das raízes a 1480)*. Lisboa: Edições Colibri.

Grosby, S. (2005). *Nationalism: A very short introduction*. Oxford: Oxford University Press.
Guibernau, M. (2007). *The identity of nations*. Cambridge: Polity Press.
Hastings, A. (1997). *The construction of nationhood: Ethnicity, religion and nationhood*. Cambridge: Cambridge University Press.
Hermet, G. (1996). *Histoire des Nations et du Nationalisme en Europe*. Paris: Éditions du Seuil.
Hobsbawm, E. (1990). *Nations and nationalism since 1780*. Cambridge: Cambridge University Press.
Huizinga, J. (1984). *Men and ideas: History, the middle ages, the Renaissance* (3rd ed.). Princeton: Princeton University Press.
Hutchinson, J. (2001). National identity. In A. A. Leoussi (Ed.), *Encyclopaedia of nationalism* (pp. 215–217). New Brunswick/London: Transaction Publishers.
Llobera, J. (1994). *The God of modernity: The development of nationalism in Western Europe*. Oxford: Berg.
Marcu, E. D. (1976). *Sixteenth century nationalism*. New York: Abaris Books.
Matos, S. C. (1998). *Historiografia e Memória Nacional no Portugal do Século XIX (1846–1898)*. Lisboa: Edições Colibri.
Mattoso, J. (1985a). *Identificação de um País: Ensaio sobre as Origens de Portugal 1096–1325* (Oposição, Vol. I). Lisboa: Editorial Estampa.
Mattoso, J. (1985b). *Identificação de um País: Ensaio sobre as Origens de Portugal 1096–1325* (Composição, Vol. II). Lisboa: Editorial Estampa.
Mosse, G. L. (1975). *The Nationalization of the masses: Political symbolism and mass movements in Germany from the Napoleonic wars through the Third Reich*. Ithaca/London: Cornell University Press.
Mosse, G. L. (1988). *The Culture of Western Europe. The nineteenth and twentieth centuries*. Boulder/London: Westview Press.
Nunes, A. S. (1969). *A Universidade na vida portuguesa*. Lisboa: GIS.
Oliveira, L. (2000). Desafios à Universidade: Comercialização da ciência e recomposição dos saberes académicos. *Sociologia, Problemas e Práticas, 34*, 93–116.
Ramos, R. (1994). *A Segunda Fundação (1890–1926)*. Lisboa: Círculo de Leitores.
Schulze, H. (1996). *States, nations and nationalism: From the middle ages to the present*. Oxford: Blackwell.
Serrão, J. (n.d.). Liberalismo. In Serrão, J. (Ed.), *Dicionário de História de Portugal* (Vol. III, pp. 508–517). Porto: Livraria Figueirinhas.
Serrão, J. (n.d.). Decadência. In Serrão, J. (Ed.), *Dicionário de História de Portugal* (Vol. II, pp. 270–274). Porto: Livraria Figueirinhas.
Smith, A. D. (1991). *National identity*. London: Penguin.
Soares, M. (n.d.). A Constituição de 1822. In Serrão, J. (Ed.), *Dicionário de História de Portugal* (Vol. II, pp. 159–163). Porto: Livraria Figueirinhas.
Sobral, J. M. (2003). A formação das nações e o nacionalismo: Os paradigmas explicativos e o caso português. *Análise Social, 38*(165), 1093–1126.
Sobral, J. M. (2006). Memória e identidade nacional: Considerações de carácter geral e o caso português. In N. C. Silva (Ed.), *Nação e estado. Entre o local e o global* (pp. 27–49). Porto: Afrontamento.
Stoer, S. R. (1983). A reforma de Veiga Simão no ensino: projecto de desenvolvimento social ou 'disfarce humanista'? *Análise Social, 19*(77–78–79), 793–822.
Torgal, L. R. (2009). Estudo Introdutório. In A. Vilela (Ed.), *Lobo Vilela e a Polémica sobre a Universidade e o Ensino nos Inícios do Estado Novo* (pp. 11–78). Lisboa: Fundação Calouste Gulbenkian.
Torgal, L. R., Mendes, J. A., & Catroga, F. (1998a). *História da História em Portugal (Séculos XIX-XX): a História através da História*. Lisboa: Temas & Debates.
Torgal, L. R., Mendes, J. A., & Catroga, F. (1998b). *História da História em Portugal (Séculos XIX-XX): da Historiografia à Memoria Histórica*. Lisboa: Temas & Debates.
Triandafyllidou, A. (1998). National identity and the 'Other'. *Ethnic and Racial Studies, 21*(4), 593–612.

Chapter 3
University, Society and Politics

Luis Reis Torgal

The Revolution of 1974: How the Attempt to Create a 'Political University' Failed

The idea of the 'Political University', both in theory and in practice, is a concept that appears to us today as indelibly associated with totalitarianism. The university, conceived thus, can do no other than fall in with the political ukases laid down by the State that, within the boundaries defined by a single ideology and by a single party, identifies itself with the nation. Such a model of university was clearly present in Nazi Germany. It also had its repercussions in Portugal both in articles written by German professors and published in Portugal and in Portuguese writings 'from the radical right' at the outset of the New State and the 'National Dictatorship'.

Such was the case, for example, of an article by Adolf Rein, Rector of the University of Hamburg, which in 1937 was published in the *Boletim do Instituto Alemão*, (Bulletin of the German Institute) (volumes VI–VII) in the Faculty of Arts at the University of Coimbra. The article was entitled 'The Idea of the Political University' and appeared together with two others that developed the same line of argument. The latter were summaries (the complete document must have figured in the 'Publications of the German Institute') of articles on 'National Socialism and Science' by the Reich Minister for Science, Education and National Culture, Bernard Rust, with a second – 'The Problem of the Objectivity of Science' – written by the Rector of the University of Heidelberg, Ernst Krieck. Both speeches had been delivered to mark the jubilee of Heidelberg University in 1936. The accompanying leaflet 'The University Problem in Portugal', published in 1934 by Vanguard press, was

L.R. Torgal (✉)
Centro de Estudos Interdisciplinares do Século XX da, Universidade de Coimbra,
Rua Filipe Simões, 33, 3000-186 Coimbra, Portugal
e-mail: lrtorgal@netcabo.pt

the work of a Portuguese, though his name did not appear in the booklet. There, the anonymous author wrote: 'Inside the New State there are no – and cannot be – two opinions: in the State of totalitarian tendencies, the university problem has to be subordinated in its solution to ideological directives that inspire the New State' (pp. 11–12).

The Soviet State was likewise totalitarian and dominated at that time by Stalin. Even after his death in 1953, 'de-stalinisation' of the State was never fully undertaken and never entirely complete. Thus, as Adolf Rein suggested in his presentation, the Soviet university was also a species of 'Political University' in which science and technology were wholly at the service of the Marxist system of ideology. Rein also took the view that the 'Popular University', which enshrined 'bourgeois individualism', was in effect the forerunner of that type of university.

In Portugal, however, the New State officially rejected the logic of totalitarianism – even though totalitarianism was present in the argumentation of some theorists of Salazarism (Torgal 2009c: I, 249–288) just as it was evident in practice or in certain practices. Yet, the university did not necessarily become a 'Political University'. Under the influence of corporatist doctrine, the New State sought to preserve the idea of the university as a 'corporation of masters and students' together with their 'liberties' which were upheld so long as both groups did not question the fundamental ideas of 'national unity'. Non-observance of this structure entailed the dismissal of academic staff, which indeed happened, for example, in two significant purges in 1935 and 1937, and continued sporadically until 1974. Students faced suppression in various guises – sometimes individually, sometimes institutionally. The latter instance involved closing student associations down or placing them directly under State oversight by means of State-nominated administrative commissions. Even the *Mocidade Portuguesa* (Portuguese Youth Movement), contrary to what happened in Falangist Spain with the *Sindicato Español Universitario* (Spanish University Union), never exercised a significant role save in organising university student residences and dormitories.

Similarly after 25 April 1974 – which represented a 'revolutionary' movement against the New State, in contrast to the 'transition' that took place in neighbouring Spain[1] – the push to set up a State of socialist Marxist persuasion took shape, especially during the years 1974–1976, then heralded as the PREC, that is, 'the Revolutionary Process Unfolding'. Thus, there was certainly a move to set up a 'Political University', which had its roots in the universities themselves and with the backing of some interim governments. But the truth remains that the 'cleansing' by faculty assemblies of academic staff identified with the political 'right', and for that reason, deemed unsuitable in the university of this type – despite opposition from a few professors and students and despite the very real personal damage it caused, especially to 'university assistants' who did not enjoy public servant status – had little legal consequence. On the other hand, *curricula* – especially in social sciences – were organised along Marxist lines, less as the pure doctrine of Karl Marx so much as what emerged from manuals like those of Marta Harnecker, especially her 1973 Brazilian publication *Elementary Concepts of Historical Materialism*. This effervescence, which bubbled on for some 2 years, was eventually discarded, as was the bid to build 'the system' into a socialist State. After the months of 'troubles' and following the first elections, which saw the socialist party of Mário Soares victorious, the 1976 Constitution was approved by the Constituent Assembly on 2 April of the same year. It reorganised and gave formal institutional shape to the bodies of faculty administration, which had been created spontaneously in the turmoil of the Revolution (Decree-Law 781 A/76 of 28 October) and laid down new curricula for programmes of study (Chaps. 7 and 9).

In 1998, existing public universities were, until 25 April, the Universities of Coimbra,[2] Lisbon and Porto,[3] the Technical University of Lisbon[4] and an autonomous establishment, the Higher Institute of Work and Enterprise Sciences (ISCTE) created in 1972. The Universities of Aveiro, Nova de Lisboa, Évora and Minho created in 1973; the universities of Beira Interior and Trás-os-Montes were first founded as Polytechnic Institutes in 1973, transformed into University Institutes in 1978 and finally into Universities in 1986. The University of Azores was established in 1976, Algarve in 1979 and Madeira and the Open University in 1988. Their legal basis rested on the University Autonomy Act, known as 'Magna Charta of the Portuguese Universities' (Law 108/88 of 24 September), and was ratified by the government, the first being of the University of Aveiro in June 1989.

Constitution of 1976 and Its Contradictions in Education

The Constitution of 1976 possessed a democratic logic, or better still, a logic of liberal democracy, although in certain cases, not without contradiction, it was couched in Marxist terminology which was watered down by subsequent legal revisions.

Among the 'rights, freedoms and guarantees', the freedoms to learn and to teach were re-affirmed in paragraph 1 of Article 43: 'The freedom to learn and to teach is guaranteed'. The separation of education from religious beliefs – Article, no. 3 – and exclusion of the State from imposing a 'system' were also upheld: 'The State cannot attribute to itself the right to programme education and culture according to any philosophical, aesthetic, ideological or religious guidelines' – Article no. 2.

Thus, the Constitution, although maintaining the fundamental character of public education, in Article 75, which dealt with 'public and private education', opened the way for creating private schools – and not just universities – which it defined, however, as 'supplementary' and therefore always subject to inspection:

1. The State shall create a network of official educational establishments to cover the needs of the whole population.
2. The State shall recognise and inspect private education, as laid down by law.

The process that led to establishing private universities goes back to the beginning of the 1980s and owed much to a dynamic rooted in business and commerce. It derived in no small part, from the fact that public universities failed to respond to the drive of more students into higher education (Chap. 13). Private universities, by contrast to primary and secondary schools, shone by their absence in the New State until the Marcelist period. In the case of the Catholic University, certain militant groups urged its foundation especially during the 1950s, arguing on the experiences of other countries and even citing the passably obscure Article XX of the 1940 Concordat with the Holy See. From 1967, Salazar merely tolerated the Catholic University, largely because of pressure from both the Pope and the Patriarch of Lisbon, Manuel Gonçalves Cerejeira. Effectively, the Catholic University gained a *droit de cité* only during the Marcelist period, thanks to the Decree-Law of 15 July 1971. Drawing on Article XX of the Concordat, the State recognised the Catholic University. In 1972, the first non-ecclesiastic course – Business Sciences – started up in the Faculty of Humanities. After 1974, and in the years following, a number of private universities sprang forth and came together around an organisation called APESP – The Portuguese Association of Private Higher Education. In addition, the 'public' standing of the Catholic University was strengthened further when its rector – in contrast to other private universities – was accepted into the Council of Rectors of the Portuguese Universities (CRUP) by Decree-Law 107/79 of 2 May, subsequently modified.

Added to this, Article 76 of the April Constitution had already embarked on a *numerus clausus* logic. It set the number of yearly admissions for each course – a provision that remains in place to this day but which, then, was couched in a 'labourite' language in the following terms: (Chap. 13)

> Access to university should take into account of the country's need for a qualified work force and stimulate the entry of workers and children of working class origin.

In the same spirit, paragraph (d) of Article 74 guaranteed all citizens, according to their ability, 'access to higher degrees of education, scientific research and artistic creation', whilst paragraph (e) required the State to 'Establish progressively at all levels education free of charge'.

Successive revisions in 1982, 1989, 1992, 1997, 2001, 2004 and 2005 changed the terms and the meaning of the Constitution (Chap. 7). In respect of education, all 'ouvriériste' allusions were weeded out whilst emphasising, albeit in a general way, those aspects that placed the relationship between university, education and competition around the explicit hallmarks of today's society driven by forces of neo-liberalism and globalisation. Thus, for example, the current version added a fourth paragraph to Article 73 after the revision of 1997 so that it now reads:

> The State shall stimulate and support scientific research and creation and technological innovation, in such a way as to ensure their freedom and autonomy, reinforce competitivity and ensure cooperation between scientific institutions and businesses.

Furthermore, also following 1997, an attempt was made to define the nature of the evaluation to which universities should be subjected, whilst strengthening their autonomy, (Chap. 10) a combination that bade fair to change the university fundamentally. Paragraph 2 of Article 76 took on the following wording:

> As laid down by law and without prejudice to an adequate assessment of the quality of education, universities shall autonomously draw up their own bye-laws and shall enjoy scientific, pedagogical, administrative and financial autonomy.

By end of the twentieth century, a new shift in paradigm stood in the offing. In the intervening period, surprisingly and paradoxically, paragraph (e) of Article 74, which dealt with the gradual establishment of non-fee paying education at all levels, was retained, despite all that had changed both in the financing of the university and higher education and their social objectives. Indeed, so great was the change that the Article can now be considered as little more than a dead letter.

Higher Education at the End of the Twentieth Century: The Change in Paradigm

The binary nature of Portuguese higher education – Universities and Polytechnics – posed great difficulty when it came to defining the two types. The upshot was to create a species of identity best presented in the notion that institutes were close to universities – from bachelor level study, polytechnics began to move from granting short cycle diplomas toward granting *licenciaturas* and masters degrees, whilst Universities in certain instances began to take on features of polytechnics in the presentation of their courses, especially in the quest for new students. Universities became 'polytechnicised'. From the 1980s onward, private education exploded (Chap. 13). Today, private higher education brings together several dozen universities, university institutes and their respective satellite branches. Drawing on academic staff from public sector higher education to pad out their own numbers and, moreover, by holding out the prospect of an extra salary for individuals already teaching in public sector higher education, the private sector introduced into Portugal a phenomenon well known elsewhere, principally in France and Italy, in the person of the 'turbo prof' – 'high-speed academics' who shuttled hastily between public and private higher education. Such a practice was damaging to public education. It also prevented many private universities from both training and controlling the quality of their own academic staff, a burden some of them were more than reluctant to assume.

Far more than these perverse effects, however, what shaped the university, especially after the 1990s, stemmed in large part from the pragmatism of the European Union that had started out as the European Economic Community. Equally influential was the strong attraction exerted by North American models of higher education. Taken together, these two 'shaping forces' brought about a complete change of paradigm. Stated slightly differently, the European University forgot its guild, communitarian and social origins, and sought to be seen primarily as an instrument at the service of wealth, first of all, by posing a lesser burden on the public's funding of higher education and then by mutating into a necessarily profitable business.

By analysing what is happening both in and to the university and by scrutinising the policy of government towards higher education, both the direction and the dynamic may be clearly perceived. To do this, a broad backdrop is needed. First, we ought not to forget that Portugal joined the European Community in 1986, a community transformed into the European Union by the Maastricht treaty of 7 February 1992. In short, the transition from an economic to a political community brings other type of relationships in its train, especially – and contrary to the formal nature of that very change from economic to political union – those of an economic nature, despite the assertion that educational or cultural issues now formed the central part of the union's agenda. Yet, any attempt to organise independent and self-standing bodies of citizens, especially intellectuals and university professors who early on foresaw the direction 'Europe' would follow, as a way to consolidate and deepen cultural relations beyond the terms laid down by the EEC/EC/EU, was doomed to failure. European bureaucracy and technocracy, riddled by their economistic world view, triumphed indeed, though their self-proclaimed success owed more than a little to programmes such as ERASMUS, which in large part were both educational and cultural.

Furthermore, it is worth remembering that the government of Mário Soares, despite the practical aspects of its political agenda, also carried with it a history of ideological struggle. With the exception of António Guterres, prime minister from 1995 to 2002 and an engineer by profession, successive governments in Portugal were formed by 'political professionals' or technocrats, such as the economist and university professor Cavaco Silva,[5] lawyers like Durão Barroso[6] and Santana Lopes[7] or the engineer José Sócrates.[8] A similar check on the governments of some of the most significant countries in the EU suggests the situation is not greatly different. Durão Barroso became president of the European Commission in 2004. The same period in the United States saw the presidency of George H.W. Bush (1989–1992/1992), of Bill Clinton (1993–2000/2001) and of George W. Bush (2001–2008/2009). It also witnessed the Iraq invasion (2003), organisation and intervention in Afghanistan of NATO forces, backed by the UN Security Council (end of 2001), and a major rise in petrol prices, largely the result of further deterioration in the long-running Arab-Israeli crisis.

Leaving aside whatever political and ideological values one may have – and this is not the place to dissect them – we have to consider what change would take place in the university, at a time when paradigms were shifting and attempts were being made to put others in their place. Faced with this task, the historian must, by the nature of his craft, bear such events in mind and not least amongst them the international financial crisis of 2008/2009, comparable in its gravity – despite some notorious differences – to the Krach of 1929. Even if the immense scientific and technological advances of this period in the fields of health, telecommunications and informatics are not subject to question, today's world is characterised by the logic of consumerism, monopoly capitalism, internet banking, instantaneous financial traffic and neo-liberalism. In this world, the State interferes only when it is in its interest to do so or to attain certain specific objectives. Thus, as Bill Readings pointed out, in a book published by Harvard University, in the shade of competition and summoning up 'beautiful concepts', such as 'Excellence', the Entrepreneurial University was called into being. In these terms, Readings, a specialist in comparative literature at the University of Montreal, dealt with the *University in Ruins* (Readings 1996/2003) – the ruination of one paradigm as a step *towards* another or, as the French philosopher Jacques Derrida argued in 1998 at a conference held at Stanford University, a step *away* from his notion of the university as an unfettered ideal, which he developed in *L'Université sans condition* (Derrida 2001/2003).

Reverting to the Portuguese case, the Basic Law for the Financing of Higher Education (Law 113/97 of 16 September) set certain restrictions on public universities, in particular a much-debated staff to student ratio, that is, the number of students per member of academic staff. The background to this initiative lay in the increasing bureaucratisation of public finances and major difficulties in managing administration, science and education (Chaps. 7, 10 and 11). In addition, the law put a stop to what could be called 'free higher education' and, for the first time since 1941, raised tuition fees from the symbolic 1,200 Escudos – *grosso modo*, 6 € – to around 1,000 € per annum for a *licenciatura*, thereby rendering paragraph (e) of Article 74 of the Constitution to all intents and purposes null and void. The Law 37/2003 of 22 August subsequently confirmed this directive by requiring each university to have a budget determined by a set of rules grounded in an evaluative logic, which increasingly became the basic credo in the new university liturgy. Thus, the 'base budget of educational and instructional activities of institutions, including their basic units and specific structures', set out under Article 4 of that law and operationalised in paragraph 2, was even more detailed:

> Funding ... is indexed on the reference budget, with appropriations calculated according to a formula based on objective criteria of quality and excellence, default values and performance indicators being equitably defined for all institutions and taking into consideration evaluation reports for each course and institution.

After evaluation was applied to public universities in 1999, and following the successive revocation of other legal norms, the Law 38/2007 of 16 August was adopted. In the same year, a 'foundation governed by private law', the Higher Education Evaluation and Accreditation Agency, (A3ES) was set up by Decree-Law 369/2007 of 5 November. Its Board of Trustees was nominated at the Council of Ministers on 23 May 2008 (Chap. 10).

In the same year, the XVII Constitutional Government, directed by José Socrates and with the minister responsible for higher education Mariano Gago, sought to consolidate higher education legislation into one single document in an effort to clarify some aspects and to innovate in others. The outcome was Law 62/2007 of 10 September 2007 legally known as the 'Juridical Regime of Higher Education Institutions' (RJIES) (Chap. 7).

As has already been noted, an attempt was made to define a binary system by setting out the differences between universities and polytechnics:

Article 6

Higher Education Institutions

1. Universities, university institutes and other institutions of university education are institutions of higher level oriented for creation, transmission and dissemination of culture, knowledge and science and technology, through the connection of study, teaching, research and experimental development.
2. Universities and university institutes grant *licenciatura*, masters and doctor degrees, according to the law.
   [...]

Article 7

Polytechnic Education Institutions

1. Polytechnic institutes and other institutions of polytechnic education are institutions of higher level oriented towards creation, transmission and dissemination of culture and knowledge of professional nature, through the connection of study, teaching, targeted research and experimental development.
2. Institutions of polytechnic education grant *licenciatura* and masters degrees, according to the law.

Apart from a certain ambiguity in the discourse that tried to distinguish between the two types of education, the practice set up over the past few years, motivated partly by legislation in place, may well have caused irreversible confusion, at least for some universities, certain polytechnics and their course offerings (Chap. 6).

Title IV sought to clarify structural and functional rules for private higher education establishments. In effect, the available mode of supervision, which was either non-existent or was downplayed in the intervening period, regulated the private sector. Despite some honourable exceptions, it faced multiple crises (Chap. 13). The greater attraction that public higher education had for students, not to mention cases of outright fraud in the certificates awarded, was evident in some and predictable for the rest.

Above all, the novelty of the RJIES lay in the institutional management of higher education. It cast aside the much-lauded *Magna Charta* of autonomy which had a record of great dignity in following the logic of the community University and which in any case, was in keeping with a long tradition in European universities, as has been noted previously. Without going into detailed analysis of the law, more specifically title III, baldy stated, entailed a change in paradigm. Confining ourselves solely to university management, provision was made for a limited 'General Council' of 15–35 members, from which representatives of non-academic staff may be excluded. Academic staff, researchers and students alone make up membership, along with 'external members of recognised merit, not belonging to the institution but with knowledge and experience relevant to it' (Article 81). The latter accounts for '30% of the total members of the General Council' (Article 81, no. 5, b). Among its other functions, this curtailed council has the responsibility for the election of the rector who can be from the same university or from another, including universities abroad (Article 86, no. 3). The 'Executive Board' chaired by the rector consists of no more than 5 members (Article 94, no.1).

Seen from the perspective of 'management/governance' (Chaps. 9 and 12), the university community had sought to involve a large part of university members in its running, but above all, those having the knowledge to debate its main problems. Here, a clear shift was visible. Management/governance was presented as more 'business-like', though the presence of outside members appears – at least to our way of looking at matters – more like a formal attempt to project a 'business image' than, as arguably it ought to be, acting as an element of broad social engagement. Furthermore, the new legislation was redolent with allusions to a model that owed more to business autonomy than to its academic counterpart.

The option for universities to become a foundation university, less dependent on the State, but functioning rather as 'autonomous foundations' (IV, Articles 129 ff) drew its model from university organisation of American provenance, which has a long history, some being centuries old. It is then quite appropriate that some of them had figured in certain discussions at the beginning of the twentieth century, often held up – to paraphrase Ortega y Gasset's (Ortega y Gasset 1930/1946/2003) ironic description – as 'universities of exemplary countries'. The truth is, however, that only experience will tell if the achievements of 'foundation universities', at the time of writing only three universities opted for this format, the University of Porto, ISCTE Lisbon and the University of Aveiro, have the slightest significance – or not – for the Portuguese context.

That said, our interpretation – when linked in with such processes as reorganising scientific research, (Chap. 8) with Bologna, with overhauling Ministries (Chap. 15) and even with the new terminology much *en vogue* – suggests we are faced with a new university paradigm. If, to be sure, it is not an 'Entrepreneurial University', it is at least the 'paradigm of the university with entrepreneurial features', adapted to a neo-liberal society, now in crisis.

Two in the Place of One

It goes without saying that the *Fundação para a Ciência e a Tecnologia* (Foundation for Science and Technology FCT) was not Portugal's first body for promoting and coordinating scientific research. Rather, it replaced the *Junta Nacional de Investigação Científica e Tecnológica* (the National Board of Scientific and Technological Research JNICT) whose first president had been an ex-Minister of National Education, Francisco de Paula Leite Pinto. The National Board had been set up in 1967 (Decree-Law 47 791 of 11 July) during the Salazar government – a time of renovation in the final phase of the New State. Surprisingly, the JNICT was not subordinated to the Ministry of National Education, but it was directly answerable to the Presidency of the Council of Ministers. In terms of science policy, it was a consultative body, submitting proposals for the development of research (Chap. 8).

In the aftermath of 25 April, another organisation was established to foster science. The National Institute of Scientific Research (INIC), founded on 9 July 1976 (Decree 538/79), replaced the Institute of Higher Culture, created in 1936, which in turn, had emerged from the basic law of National Education (Law 1941 of 11 April). In this complicated administrative genealogy, the Institute of Higher Culture had been heir to the National Education Board (JEN) whilst the National Education Board had seen the light of day during the Military Dictatorship, more precisely one year before the Technical University of Lisbon was founded, in 1929 (Decree 16 381 of 16 January).

With the closing down of JNICT in 1995 – INIC had vanished 3 years before (Decree-Law 188/92 of 27 August) – the Foundation for Science and Technology

(FCT) took over the full range of coordinating scholarly endeavour across the fields of the Exact, Natural and Applied Sciences, Technology and the Social Sciences, Humanities and Arts. Under the government of Antonio Guterres (1995–1999), for the first time, a Ministry of Science and Technology was inaugurated, headed by a professor of Engineering from the *Universidade Técnica de Lisboa* (Technological University of Lisbon), Mariano Gago. The new ministry began the reorganisation of research and the evaluation of its affiliated research units in 1997.

With priority laid upon research and on higher education – statistics pointed up many shortcomings in those two areas – came the decision to establish a Ministry of Higher Education, with a second ministry in charge of the remaining levels of education. Thus, from 6 April 2002, during Durão Barroso's premiership and for the first time in Portugal, the Ministry of Science and Higher Education was hived off from the Ministry of Education. The first Minister of Higher Education, Pedro Lynce, had graduated in Agronomic Engineering from the Technical University of Lisbon, and his successor, Maria da Graça Carvalho, hailed from the Technical Institute of the same university. During the premiership of José Socrates, the ministry changed in 2005 to become the Ministry of Science, Technology and Higher Education, headed by Mariano Gago, after a brief interim when it had carried the title of Ministry of Science, Innovation and Higher Education during the short term in office of the Santana Lopes government between 2004 and 2005, when Graça Carvalho was minister. Thus, universities and polytechnics obtained their own ministry. They were no longer subordinate, as had been the case hitherto, to the Ministry of Education, which once exercised oversight across higher education, pre-school, primary and secondary education. Thus, authority in education was divided into two. The presence of Ministers of Science, whether combined or not with higher education, who had been trained at the Technical University and, above all, from the Technical University Institute, was a constant feature that also applied to the presidents of FCT: Luis Magalhães, Fernando Ramôa Ribeiro and João Sentieiro. A comparable profile may be seen in respect of Ministers of Education since at least 1981. Many were educated at the Technical University of Lisbon or had trained in fields connected with Exact, Natural Sciences, Technology or Business Studies.

The division of educational policy across two ministries, quite apart from echoing what was happening elsewhere in Europe, has a long history, though clearly unrelated to the way the ministry remit was defined. Indeed, nobody we know defended this arrangement in this way. Rather, they argued in favour of the relative separation between research and teaching. Such an argument took weight from the moment when some of the best researchers began to appreciate how difficult it was to divide their work between teaching and research. More than a decade earlier, Joaquim de Carvalho, professor and researcher in the History of Philosophy and Culture, had already broached this theme in one of the most interesting articles about the university (Carvalho 1933).

Thus, in parallel with a teaching career in university and polytechnic, legislation outlined a career path in research (Decree-Law 415/80 of 27 November and Decree-Law 365/86 of 31 October). It did not have great impact, in part because of its lukewarm reception by the university, which remained wedded to the notion that only teaching combined with research could be justified, because of the way the law was applied and, last but not the least, because of the use made of legislation to boost the status of university laboratory technicians. Successively updated (Decree-Law 219/92 of 15 October and Decree-Law 124/99 of 31 March), the law now stands as lynch pin in contemporary science policy by bringing new full-time researchers into research centres, especially in associated laboratories (Chap. 8). It gave them a genuine role in the field of research, even though newly engaged researchers are always subject to a temporary status.

The significance of the work undertaken in Portugal in recent years on behalf of science and technology is clear and evident. Research units were reorganised into State laboratories, associated laboratories and other research and development units; their financing was raised, their creation speeded up and the number of posts for PhD researchers, even temporary appointments, expanded. It is not without reason that Mariano Gago, the minister in charge of this area, has not only been the longest in office. Sobrinho Simões, one of the leading specialists in oncology research and director of the well-known Institute of Pathology and Immunology at the University of Porto (IPATIMUP), considered Mariano Gago to be 'the best Minister of Science that we have had.' (*Público*, 24.10.2009: 4). Leaving aside whether such esteem is more applicable to science than to higher education, which in our opinion it is, there appears to be an equally unquestioning view that considers R&D units as the true place where science is practiced, where 'scientific elites' have their being. By the same token, the same view considers education, even university education and especially polytechnic education, as a sector of practical training. For the rest, already in March 1997, the coordinator of evaluation, Luis Magalhães, in the Overall Evaluation Report of 1996, called attention to an excessive number of teaching hours in higher education, proposed a maximum of six teaching hours per week and outlined the possibility for university teachers to move over to devote themselves exclusively to research for 3 years, though in practice institutional constraints meant this seldom happened. Thus, the criticism, already voiced by Joaquim de Carvalho in an article dating back to 1933, was repeated. The problem of 'over teaching' rather than being resolved was made worse by the 'Bologna process', which seems to prove that it served as a mere device for the university, which transformed itself into a place of training rather than a place of scientific and cultural learning.

Under the Sign of Bologna

The Bologna declaration, signed on 19 June 1999 by 29 European ministers – in the Portuguese case, by the Minister of Education, Eduardo Marçal Grilo, another alumnus of the Technical University Institute – had set out to make both curricula and degrees converge in the European Higher Education Area (Chap. 11). However, it transmuted into a political process leading on towards uniformity, a process that in Portugal was put in train through Decree-Law 74/2006 of 24 March. Pedro Lourtie – likewise from the Technical University Institute, who had been the Director

General of Higher Education (1996–2000) and, later, Secretary of State of Higher Education (2001–2002) during the government of Antonio Guterres – was nominated in November 2005 by Mariano Gago, already minister under the government of Jose Socrates, to be president and representative of the Bologna Follow-Group to oversee the Bologna process.[9] Its current president, Professor Feyo de Azevedo, is an engineer from the University of Porto.

The Bologna process has been a decade under way and, according to newspaper reports, 'Ten years on: Portugal passes the Bologna test well' (*Público*, 21.09.2009). From the Internet, it is to be gathered that Pedro Lourtie, together with Paulo Fontes from the Catholic University, who delivered a keynote address to a closed colloquium at the Calouste Gulbenkian Foundation in September 2009, have recently completed a report, 'The future of Bologna, 10 years later'. It looks at what happened in Portuguese universities. Naturally, it views the relationships forged by this European initiative in its bid to set up a European Higher Education Area positively. Yet, the question remains: Is this process a benefit or has it set artificial boundaries around learning and scholarship, both of which remain fundamental? Does it uphold an education of culture that is capable of sustaining a vision of the world in which we live?

In universities, the criticism of academics and students seems frequent. Certain prominent figures in the university world who opted for teaching, research and their organisation, as a calling as distant from bureaucracy as possible, protested against the massification and proliferation of the *licenciaturas*, which will soon extend upwards into masters degrees and even into PhDs. 'Massification' does not necessarily mean that *some* masters and *some* PhDs do not uphold the gold coin of excellence. Massification is not necessarily synonymous with 'democratisation.' It does not always challenge the place and function of social and economic elites. That said, practices *à la Bolognaise*, far from being a cause, are more of a consequence that flows from the logic of neo-liberalism, the guiding concept of which remains the profitability of the university, of scholarship as producers of wealth, and which seems to be the principle purpose of this venture.

Many scholars have set out to address this problem, amongst them are a French philosopher, Jacques Derrida, a Canadian professor of comparative literature, Bill Readings – both of whom were mentioned earlier – a professor in the Philosophy of Education at Hamburg University, Andrea Liesner (Liesner 2006), an Oxford sociologist, Hermínio Martins (Martins 2004, 2007) and, dare I say it?, myself. All have written and lectured extensively on this topic (Torgal 2008a, b, 2009a, b). And if more names are needed of those who tackled the issue in the broader perspective of 'the education system', one might add the French mathematician Laurent Laforgue, dismissed from the *Conseil Supérieur d'Éducation* for taking the view that the French education system was in the process of active 'self destructing' by setting value not on knowledge so much as on pragmatic goals of organising society around market mechanisms. This was *'L'Affaire Laforgue'*, to which the Portuguese mathematician Jorge Buescu drew attention. Then, there are passionate writings of the mathematician Nuno Crato (Crato 2006), who set about critically deconstructing the use and abuse of pedagogical or pseudo-pedagogical methods currently in vogue.

The issue of 'modernity' and its contradictions merit closer scrutiny. To do this, we will concentrate on one work that may be considered particularly revealing. The introduction to the proceedings of a conference on *Les ravages de la 'modernisation' universitaire en Europe* (Charle and Soulié 2007) allows us to explore this topic in greater detail. The title alone casts modernity at best in terms of 'loss' or, at worst, the wreckage that 'modernisation' has wrought on universities in Europe.

The author, Christophe Charle, a leading historian at the University of Paris I, set out by analysing the various declarations uttered by the European Union, culminating in the Bologna statement of June 1999. From then on, he argued, and following the strategy adopted at Lisbon in 2000, a new discourse emerged around such catch-phrases as the 'qualification of the work force', pointing economic changes in the direction of the knowledge economy, preparing ongoing research for economic needs, international cooperation between European graduates who benefited from studying abroad and who were adjusting to the practices of their national and cultural neighbours as companies became international. As a round up to his overview, Charle concluded:

> Loin de donner un supplément d'âme culturel et civique à l'Europe, c'est plutôt l'enseignement supérieur qui se trouve soumis aux principes généraux économiques, voire économicistes de l'Europe des Six initiale: marché ouvert, concurrence, compétitivité, efficacité. Loin de préserver la diversité culturelle et échange entre les traditions intellectuelles, ces nouveaux objectifs aboutissent à une normalisation qui ne tient compte ni des spécificités disciplinaires, ni des particularités régionales ou nationales, ni même de la diversité des rapports des individus à la demande d'enseignement supérieur et des diverses fonctions possibles de l'enseignement supérieur. (Charle and Soulié 2007: 11–12)

In his appreciation of contemporary 'economistic' mentality, Charle stressed the emergence of certain fields that converged around that same species of logic, in other words, the applied disciplines at the expense of the theoretical, the fundamental sciences or the humanities. Management, Informatics, some Engineering sciences, Communications, Education, all figure prominently in this line up. In their practicality lies the attraction of professional masters programmes and the Master of Business Administration in particular, which see the economic elite mesmerised by the American economic model. The more backward the country, the more easily are such reforms accepted, if only for the simple reason that there are no favourable conditions for significant resistance to take root in the face of a propaganda that seeks to persuade that indeed 'there is no alternative'. Thus, a myth of 'Anglo-Saxon' universities, especially the American, flourishes. What is forgotten is that these universities are 'exceptions functioning'. They are grounded in a history that cannot be compared to the reality of European countries, whose university history is very different indeed. Thus, Charle argued, the Anglo-Saxon system benefits only a small elite, not the majority of higher education institutions, nor the majority of students who constitute a mass increasingly amorphous and largely uncultivated:

> Un tel système ne peut donc fonctionner que pour quelques établissements d'élite. Il n'est pas généralisable pour l'ensemble d'un système pour des raisons d'équilibre sociale. Les universités d'élite américaines et anglaises peuvent s'en sortir parce qu'elles cumulent en fait des ressources multiples, absentes des autres pays: des systèmes de paiement inégalitaire,

le mécénat des riches anciens élèves, les contrats de recherches avec l'argent public et privé, et surtout la rente de situation de l'exploitation du capital symbolique de la langue anglaise comme instrument de mondialisation et le mythe, savamment entretenu pour tous ceux qui y ont intérêt, de la supériorité des établissements anglo-saxons. Cette croyance se traduit en fluxe d'étudiants étrangers aisés vers ces établissements et donc en manne financière. Par une alchimie qui rappelle le griffe des grands couturiers, ce capital symbolique se transforme alors en capital tout court grâce aux droits d'inscription des étudiants nantis des pays moins avancés venus acheter des diplômes haut de gamme comme ces touristes japonais qui font l'emplette de sacs, de parfums ou de montres de luxe quand ils viennent faire un tour à Paris pour démontrer qu'ils ont bon goût. (Charle and Soulié 2007: 29)

These are bitter words. They convey not only the sense of loss that bites deeply into contemporary France but also a loss all the more poignant given that France's language, culture and that some of its universities once provided – though today less so – a symbolic capital of considerable attractiveness. Charle also makes plain that the neo-liberal system of globalisation works to the benefit of some, by creating regions where national (or international) scientific and technological prestige is tied in with interests that extend beyond borders, that benefit international capital and that will not profit the third world or less developed countries to the slightest degree. For these countries, production – fundamental as much for their independence as it is for their development – is ousted by 'consumption cities' and consumerism even by those without the money to consume. Such a condition is consistent with neo-liberal theories of the American Milton Friedman, who died in 2006, and which the recent crisis has put to the question, though explanations finally emerged, though reluctantly by dint of parliamentary questions (Gonçalez 2009).

Contrary to what is stated, teaching, compressed into 3 years of the *licenciatura* – the so-called first cycle, practically useless as a self-standing degree, followed by 2 years' masters courses that do not necessarily look for originality in research, still less critical interpretation, that make up the second cycle and PhDs, lasting 4 years constitute the third cycle – far from advancing scientific training and the induction of students to scholarship served only to ramp up the number of graduates, poorly trained by an education increasingly less demanding.

New Vocabulary, New Values, New Realities

Today's new paradigms, because we refuse to confer the descriptor of 'novelty' on these notions which are probably better qualified as 'old-new' paradigms, above all, place value on an economic mental set, even in a society beset by the turmoil of a very real crisis in its development. These paradigms encompass, condition and even shape Science, Culture, Teaching and Education. In their turn, they engender a different vocabulary or alternatively impart different meaning to an already existent and established vocabulary, giving it an overlay of 'modernity'. This new terminology, however, should not be confused with the vocabulary born from the rationale of enlightenment-liberalism, from the rationale of liberal democracy and even less from their social democratic or socialist counterparts which already anticipated society's path towards the current species of capitalism and its disarray in the shape of the ongoing financial crisis.

Current formulas and fashionable phraseology, spurred on by the revamped concepts of 'progress' and 'development', push more for 'excellence' than for 'intelligence'. 'Evaluation' and 'certification' ease aside 'the pedagogical and scientific quality of institutions'. The press for 'competence', which springs from the same etymological root as 'competition', replaces 'knowledge' and 'culture'. 'Critical mass'– a notion imported from chemistry and nuclear physics – is held more desirable than 'critical awareness'. 'Profitability' replaces 'theoretical and practical learning'. 'Competitiveness' takes the place of 'solidarity'. 'Economic sustainability' and 'wealth creation' have priority over the 'social interest', whilst 'internationalisation' and 'globalisation' edge out 'cosmopolitanism' and 'ecumenism'. Ultimately, an 'entrepreneurial university' and 'schools of productivity' are deemed more 'successful' by far than a 'guild' or the university as an element at the service of 'democracy' or, for that matter, the 'school as a key element of culture and community', whilst 'privatisation', intended to make everything 'profitable', ousts 'public education'.

This curious lexicon that has grown up around the reorganisation of education and society is concerned less with content, with *nómenos*. It is, on the contrary, given over more to form and *phenómenos*. Etymologically, this latter noun comes from the Greek verb *pfáinô*, 'what appears'. In short, the new vocabulary emphasises 'appearances', in a world of 'events' or, alternatively 'what happens' in the world projected as a show or a spectacle, replete with communication and information and dedicated to performance and profitability. Such a representation trails dehumanisation in its wake, just as it displays disinterest in Linguistics, History, Literature, Mathematics, Physics, Chemistry, Biology, Geology and Ecology. In short, the 'new' terminology dismisses Culture as the vehicle for critically understanding the world, save under the wrappings this self-same perception imposes on it. It is a 'culture to be consumed'. What it is not is Culture as a form of reflection. It is far removed from the values of democratic liberalism.

We ought to ask ourselves whether we live in a free world or whether 'freedom' has simply become a service element in the development of capitalism. Does the absence of State intervention in key areas – even in States governed by 'socialists' – not consolidate this capitalism, a capitalism in crisis but constantly trying to renew itself? Is 'globalisation' merely a justification for importing and exporting models, templates and practices as a substitute for a genuine and real advancement of critical knowledge? For indeed, as we used to say, there is no knowledge without critical knowledge, constant questioning, thought and pondering, which has humanity as its purpose. Knowledge, as Sílvio Lima pointed out in an article old but always germane, is always an 'essay', an attempt, a quest – but never a certainty (Lima 1944).

Rankings, 'Faculty Strife' and the 'Cultural University'

The University in Portugal, and in the world generally, is at base governed by market rules, which the new paradigm imposes and where rankings and international reports appear as the 'Great Spectacle'. OECD (Organisation for Economic Cooperation and Development) reports, essentially 'managerial' and 'economistic' in nature, crowd in on one another, generating criticism and counter-criticism in Portuguese society. This happened, for example, with the review of Portuguese tertiary education of 7 March 2008, signed by Abrar Hasan, then Head of the Educational and Training Policy Division in OECD's Directorate of Education, and by four experts, an Irishman, an Australian, a Finn and one other from the UK. There were no specialists from Latin countries.

More recently, ranking by the weekly Times Higher Education placed Coimbra – according to newspaper reports (*Diário de Coimbra*, 10.10.2009: 2) – 366th, an opinion that brought forth few signs of natural rejoicing. Earlier, the Rector of Coimbra, Fernando Seabra Santos, then president of CRUP – the Council of Rectors of the Portuguese Universities – made the point that, having looked at investment in science and scholarship, it was as well to examine the funding of universities, (*Público*, 6.10.2009: 14–15) as well as their political role, all-too-often overlooked. Candidates for rectoral appointment made much play in their electoral manifestos of putting in hand a policy to ensure that, during their eventual term of office, the university would figure prominently in international ratings, despite the fact that such rankings are merely indicative – a general pointer rather than an exact statement. Even so, newspapers also reported a citation study of researchers publishing in international journals, which showed that of all Portuguese institutions of higher education, the Technical Institute had the highest citation rate – occupying the 314th place (*Público*, 20.10.2009: 5).

The overhaul of university statutes and the establishment of new rules of management have had a significant impact on the disciplinary background of rectors. The trend amongst the recently elected confirms the weight attached nowadays to the Exact and Natural Sciences – Medicine included – as well as to the Applied and Technological Sciences. In contrast with earlier days, rectors in the main hail from these disciplinary areas. Of the 14 rectors of public universities, three alone were from the Humanities: History, Language and Literature, or Educational Sciences. And in a university where one might expect such a pattern to emerge, the Technical University of Lisbon the rector, significantly, comes from the Technical Institute of Lisbon. Furthermore, though it did not involve exhaustive search, some presidents of university General Councils were drawn from business and banking, a gesture towards pragmatism and productivism held to be so lacking in higher education. To this, one might add that the Board of Trustees of the Agency for the Evaluation and Accreditation of Higher Education (A3ES) is composed in the main of professors of Medicine, Applied Mathematics and Engineering. There is one exception, however: a lawyer, who apart from being active in scholarship, teaching and legal practice, also had a political profile.

Be that as it may, if the significance of the data presented here is to be grasped to their full extent, they need to be firmly set in historical perspective.

The 'quarrel of the faculties' is a feature present in higher education from the eighteenth century onwards. This we have explored in some articles (e.g. Torgal 1989), which revert to the same title as Immanuel Kant gave to his famous essay of 1798, *Der Streit der Fakultäten*. This essay also traced the influence of the model developed in Pierre Bourdieu's analysis of the sociological characteristics of *homo academicus* (Bourdieu 1984). In Portugal, beginning with the Enlightenment *en passant par* the first Liberal Revolution of 1820, the most ardent defenders of a new educational policy, which formed an inseparable part of the ideals of early liberalism, were to be found in the Exact and Natural Sciences. They held out against the arguments of conservative lawyers, initially, those versed in Canon Law and theologians (see also Torgal and Vargues 1984). A perusal of the nineteenth and the early twentieth centuries reveals something similar. One has only to recall the impact of the famous speeches *de Sapientia* by the Coimbra professors: Sidónio Pais, (Mathematics), Bernardino Machado, (Physical Anthropology then in the Faculty of Philosophy, that is Natural Philosophy) or Sobral Cid (Medicine). Nor should we forget the importance of the educational policy of the First Republic, carried out by António José de Almeida, a medical doctor by profession, as too was the deputy, and subsequently Minister of Public Education in 1923 and 1925, José João da Conceição Camoesas, who, in his turn, presented one of the most interesting proposals in the reform of education. Presented to parliament in 1923 as an attempt to modernise education in Portugal in the light of what might be learnt from the First World War, it envisaged setting up an education *system*, from primary school to higher education. It remained stillborn. Significant too were the reforms of Leonardo Coimbra, especially the creation of the Faculty of Arts at Porto in 1919, which introduced the concept of a multi-faceted culture, based on ideas that drew on the Exact and Natural Sciences, on the Social Sciences and on the Humanities. Equally important were educational ideas of the intellectuals in the *Seara Nova* movement, António Faria de Vasconcelos, Jaime Cortesão and António Sérgio. The first held a degree in law but had studied the work of Belgian reformers of the 'new school'. The other two had fundamentally a 'scientific' culture in the Exact, Natural and Applied Sciences; the former in the field of medicine, which he did not practice, and the latter in Nautical Science.

Even those members of academia, who were dismissed by Salazar in 1935 and 1947 fought for a democratic school and for the expansion of scientific research and were, in the main, from Medicine, Life Sciences, Physics, Engineering etc., with others from the Humanities, Philosophy and Psychology, Linguistics and Literature. The same applied to the intellectuals in the 'Democratic Renewal' movement, who took up cudgels against the Law Faculty, then considered the most conservative, and against the dominance of 'legalism' in Portuguese society, though their educational background was very different (Vilela et al. 2009). They subscribed, however, to the concept of the 'Cultural University', based on the ideas of Ortega y Gasset, which he set out in the famous *Misión de la Universidad*. For the Spanish philosopher, the university had a triple obligation – to educate professionals, to advance original research and to hand on culture. Of these three, the last was the most important. Without culture, the whole of life risked fragmentation. Under such conditions, to understand, critically and with awareness the significance of the direction it took, would be impossible:

> Life is chaos, a wild jungle, confusion. Man is lost in it. But his mind reacts to this feeling of sinking and wastage: it works to find in the jungle "tracks" and "roads", that is: clear and firm ideas about the universe, positive beliefs about what things and the world are. Their combination, their system is the culture in the true sense of the word, quite the contrary to the ornament. Culture is what saves him from the sinking in life, (it is) what allows Man to live without his life being a senseless tragedy or radical degradation. We cannot live as humans without ideas.... (Ortega y Gasset 1930: 57–59)

Antonio Lobo Vilela, a mathematician and a geographical engineer, one of the most influential personalities in the 'Democratic Renewal' movement and a proponent of the concept of the 'Cultural University', believed deeply that science itself was not enough. Looking particularly at the case of Nazi Germany, he wrote:

> One of the most evident causes of the social and political crises of our time is the lack of *general culture*, the narrowness of the horizon of a *scientific technician* who tends to extrapolate his specialised experience and supposes it is valid in any other area, or isolates himself in his cave world, oblivious to most of the issues in which he should give a fair opinion or intervene with his clear mind. The revival of fanaticism and despotism are closely related to the discredit of the values associated with intellectual culture.
>
> In Germany, where the social and political crises took the most disgusting forms with Nazism, Arnold Berliner[10] felt the need to start a magazine aimed at *correcting the inefficiency of specialised research*, by offering researchers – the most highly qualified specialists – an overview of *problems*, *methods* and *results*, obtained in the various branches of knowledge. Referring to this magazine, Einstein wrote: 'He who wants to do serious research, painfully feels this involuntary limitation to an increasingly narrowing circle of understanding which threatens to deprive the wise man of great perspectives and demean him to artifice'. In a letter addressed to Sigmund Freud, he proposes the creation of an *International Society of Men of Science* who would be distinguished by their work and stay in permanent contact to intervene effectively in the resolution of political problems, which would distinguish it from the *Commission on Intellectual Cooperation* created by the former League of Nations (Vilela 1995; Vilela et al. 2009: 383–385).

When we look at the Portuguese case in particular, we wish simply to point out this: There are cultural concepts in scientists and scholars of all backgrounds. Science and scholarship can live in the laboratory as well as in the library or in the archives. It is an insult – as indeed we have recently argued (Torgal 2009b) – to speak of science and scholarship as mere appendages of 'useful science' that 'begets wealth'. Such a narrow and pejorative restriction in meaning is rampant in today's world. In point of fact, the cultural concept of science and scholarship first saw the light of day – and then not without difficulty – in a rationale that pushed for openness and, sometimes, stood in 'quasi-opposition' to a conservative world during the latter days of the New State. In its happier form, it served to organise science under the dictatorship as, for instance, with the creation of JNICT or, earlier, of the

National Laboratory of Civil Engineering – LNEC – founded in 1946 (Chap. 8). Other initiatives were evident in the Ministry of Education during the term in office of Veiga Simão, professor at the Faculty of Sciences at the University of Coimbra, or, in the National Assembly, the proposals of Miller Guerra, (Guerra 1970) professor at the Faculty of Medicine of Lisbon. Another example of this mobilisation was the organisation of SEDES – the Society for Economic and Social Development – on 25 February 1970 by individuals on the most liberal wing of the regime, who had graduated in fields ranging from Law to Economics and Technology.

Even though 'technocrats' existed already at that time, the truth is that a certain degree of idealism was present in this bid to drive towards development and modernisation and, in certain instances, to move towards democracy. To be sure, this idealism can still be found, but so embedded in a neo-liberal system that it is hard to find a clearly defined cultural boundary. It is this lacuna that, in Portugal has triggered as it has in other countries, a sense of outrage among scientists and academics who find the 'conditioned' university highly unappealing.

A New Vision of the Political University?

At the outset of this chapter, the 'Political University' was considered a characteristic of totalitarian countries. But might it not be that a 'new Political University' is emerging in democratic countries, one that is eased into the credos of neo-liberal capitalism?

This is our parting question as well as our Parthian shot. The new vision of the university has generated the idea of a dependent university, at the service of capitalism and, after the current crisis, at the service of capitalism rehabilitated, though so far capitalism has been unable to understand life from a cultural perspective, just as it has proven impotent to conceive society as having a sense of solidarity, or to interpret science and scholarship beyond the closed circuit of self-interest and 'wealth creation production'. And yet, there cannot be a university, at least as Europe conceived it, that is devoid of cultural and scholarly idealism.

Etymologically speaking, university means 'corporation' (*universitas*) or, in the language of mediaeval times, a 'guild'. In this meaning, or in the sense of a community, it is at the service of science, culture and society that the university ought to be understood. In contemporary terms, it ought to be a community at the service of social democracy. In its dependency on enterprises, businesses and firms as a generator of wealth, it is anything but a university.

The course of the Portuguese University or higher education in its binary form from 1974 onwards cannot be sundered from the broader process of evolution in Portuguese – and international – society. As historians, we cannot see it otherwise. We have presented this account as not only an objective but also an interpretative vision, if only because history has of necessity to interpret reality critically, that is with equity and judgement, subtlety and nuance.

Notes

1. *La Transición* in the political language of the day.
2. Founded in Lisbon in 1288–1290 and permanently transferred in 1537 to Coimbra.
3. Founded by the Provisional Government of the First Republic in 1911.
4. Created in 1930 during the 'National Dictatorship'.
5. Prime minister from 1985 to 1995.
6. Prime minister from 2002 to 2004.
7. Prime minister from 2004 to 2005.
8. Prime minister from 2005 to 2009 and current incumbent.
9. Not to be confused with his son, also Pedro Lourtie, one-time *Chef de Cabinet* to Prime Minister José Sócrates and presently Secretary of State for European Affairs. He studied Economics at the Higher Institute of Economics and Management in the Technical University of Lisbon. He has a diplomatic career.
10. Arnold Berliner (1862–1942), a German physicist, founded the scholarly review *Die Naturwissenschaften*, of which he was a director from 1913 till 1935.

References

Bourdieu, P. (1984). *Homo Academicus*. Paris: Editions de Minuit.
Charle, C., & Soulié, C. (Eds.). (2007). *Les ravages de la "modernisation" universitaire en Europe*. Paris: Éditions Syllepse.
Crato, N. (2006). *O "eduquês" em discurso directo: uma crítica da pedagogia romântica e construtivista*. Lisboa: Gradiva.
de Carvalho, J. (1933, Novembro 8). Reflexão outonal sobre a Universidade de todo o ano, *Diário Liberal*, Lisboa.
Derrida, J. (2003). *L'Université sans condition*, Paris, Éditions Galilée. Translation in Portuguese: *A Universidade sem condição*. Coimbra: Angelus Novus.
Gonçalez, R. (2009). *Que crise é essa?* Curitiba: Editorial Juruá.
Guerra, M. (1970). *As Universidades tradicionais e a sociedade moderna. Aviso prévio efectuado na Assembleia Nacional em 14 de Abril de 1970 seguido do respectivo debate*. Lisboa: Moraes Editores.
Liesner, A. (2006). Education or service? Remarks on teaching and learning in the entrepreneurial university. *Educational Philosophy and Theory, 38*(4), 483–495.
Lima, S. (1944). *Ensaio sobre a essência do ensaio*. Coimbra: Arménio Amado Editor.
Martins, H. (2004). http://www.adelinotorres.com/sociologia.
Martins, H. (2007). The marketisation of universities and some contradictions of academic knowledge-capitalism. In *Metacrítica. Revista de Filosofia*, no 4, 2004.
Ortega y Gasset. (1930). Edições portuguesas: (1946) *Missão da Universidade*. Versão portuguesa de Sant'Anna Dionísio, Lisboa, Seara Nova; e (2003) *Missão da Universidade e outros textos*, Coimbra, Angelus Novus, com uma Introdução de Iñaki Gbaráin. (1930) *Misión de la Universidad*, Madrid: Revista de Occidente.
Readings, B. (2003). *The University in ruins*, Harvard University Press, 1996. Edição portuguesa: *A Universidade em Ruínas*, Coimbra, Angelus Novus.
Torgal, L. R. (1989). Universidade, ciência e "conflito de faculdades" no Iluminismo e nos primórdios do liberalismo português. In *Claustros y estudiantes* (Vol. II, pp. 291–299). Valencia: Facultad de Derecho.
Torgal, L. R. (2000). *Caminhos e contradições da(s) Universidade(s) Portuguesa(s). Centralismo e autonomia. Neoliberalismo e corporativismo*. "Cadernos do CEIS20". Coimbra, Centro de Estudos Interdisciplinares do Século XX da Universidade de Coimbra.

Torgal, L. R. (2008a). *A Universidade e as "condições" da Imaginação.* "Cadernos do CEIS20". Coimbra: Centro de Estudos Interdisciplinares do Século XX da Universidade de Coimbra.

Torgal, L. R. (2008b). A Universidade entre a Tradição e a Modernidade. In *Revista Intellectus*, ano 07, vol. I – Rio de Janeiro, UERJ, 2008[2], 40 pp. http://www.intellectus.uerj.br.

Torgal, L. R. (2009a). Ciência e Cultura, Ensino e Educação. Entre a "imaginação" e as "fronteiras". In *XIII Encontro de Educação em Ciência*. Castelo Branco, 24–26 Setembro 2009[1]. Pode ser solicitado a Encontro Nacional do Ensino das Ciências: enec2009@ese.ipcb.pt.

Torgal, L. R. (2009b). Educação, liberdade e relações internacionais. Ideais, ideologias e práticas políticas do fim do século XVIII aos inícios do século XXI. *Opening lecture of the VIIth Hispanc Colloquium of the History of Education (Parades, 18–19 September 2009) on the theme "Exílios e viagens. Ideários de liberdade e discursos educativos. Portugal-Espanha séc. XVIII-XX"*.

Torgal, L. R. (2009c). *Estados Novos, Estado Novo.* 2 vols. Coimbra: Impensa da Universidade, 2.ª edição, Setembro de 2009[3].

Torgal, L. R., & Vargues, I. N. (1984). *A Revolução de 1820 e a Instrução Pública.* Porto: Paisagem.

Vilela, A. C. L. (Selecção, fixação de textos e notas), Torgal, Luís Reis (Introdução) e Grilo, Eduardo Marçal (Prefácio) (2009). *Lobo Vilela e a polémica sobre a Universidade e o Ensino nos inícios do Estado Novo*, Lisboa: Fundação Calouste Gulbenkian – Serviço de Educação e Bolsas.

Vilela, A. E. L. (1955, December 12). Especialização e cultura. *Diário de Lisboa*.

Chapter 4
Cultural and Educational Heritage, Social Structure and Quality of Life

José Madureira Pinto

Introduction

Portuguese society is frequently regarded, both by analysts and by lay observers, as somewhat unexplainable and surprisingly unpredictable. Sometimes, it displays a rather 'European appearance'. At others, it seems to be a sort of entry port to the 'third world'. Sociologists have characterised Portugal as a 'semi-peripheral' society, as a society of 'unachieved modernity' or as an example of 'intermediate development'. They have a common and real concern with this contradictory condition, which is held to be a combination of sudden change, historical specificity and social inertia, or, alternatively, as the accumulation of persistent dualisms, if not a unique and paradoxical juxtaposition of backwardness and progress.

One of the aims of this chapter is to propose a plausible explanation for the 'unexpectedness' those observations of Portuguese society pose, particularly those aspects that whether *directly or indirectly* concern the advancement of the nation's learning and higher education.

However, before presenting a systematic analysis of the main features and trends which, from the standpoint of the social sciences, must be tackled, two mathematical notions (or ways of reasoning) will serve to express the contradictory – and in certain aspects, singular – nature of social reality in Portugal.

J.M. Pinto (✉)
Instituto de Sociologia, Faculdade de Letras da Universidade do Porto,
Via Panoramica s/n, 4150-584 Porto, Portugal

Faculdade de Economia do Porto, Rua Roberto Frias, 4200-464 Porto
e-mail: jmp@fep.up.pt

Two Mathematical Concepts

The first mathematical concept is based on the distinction between the value of the function and the value of the *derivative* of that function. Whereas the former allows the intensity of a phenomenon, expressed by the function, to be measured at a given point or moment, the latter sets out to evaluate the behaviour of the phenomenon around or, more simply put, before and after that point or moment. The value of the derivative of the function is sensitive both to the path of evolution *and* to the initial condition of that same phenomenon. To bear this distinction in mind is central whenever we seek a plausible explanation for several characteristics in Portuguese society. Often, their 'strangeness' derives from the fact that, although the rhythm of change shown by the feature under scrutiny is remarkably intense, its value appears to be still *too high* or *too low* when set against comparable developments in other European nations. The present condition of the phenomenon under analysis, being genuinely 'anomalous' in the light of relevant indicators, is in large part the deferred effect of the no less 'anomalous' starting condition of that same phenomenon.

A second form of mathematically related reasoning is equally useful in helping us to grasp the specificity – and unpredictability – in the evolution of Portuguese society. It rests on the distinction between, and the joint application of, measures of central tendency *and* measures of dispersion. When studying structural features or significant social change, the question is now how to take adequate account of the significant, and sometimes profound, *inequalities* that persist in Portuguese society. To obtain a realistic portrait of the country, all the *average* figures we must collect to characterise it – from the purchasing power *per capita*, the schooling levels or the rates of participation in adult training to access to justice and to healthcare or even to the competencies that allow full integration in the information society – need to be set against, and balanced out by, the corresponding measures of dispersion, that is, the range of *variance* displayed. All the optimism that accompanies the undeniable, and sometimes very impressive, improvement in the average values of many social indicators that followed the reintegration of Portuguese society with democracy ought not to be dissociated from paying systematic attention to the level of dispersion entailed once attention turns to specific contexts – for instance, across different regions, social class, gender, age and so forth.

Economic Structure, Employment and Migration Movements

In studying the evolution of cultural and educational background, social structure and quality of life in Portuguese society over the past three decades, we start by scrutinising some key changes that took place in the *economic and employment systems* during those years.

The first of these witnessed a sharp and sudden *decline in the economic relevance and the place of agriculture as a sector of employment.*

By the mid-twentieth century, primary activities still accounted for half of the total active population. In the more developed economies of Europe, it varied from between 15% and 30% (Lopes 2004: 41). In 1970, according to the National Census, almost one-third of the Portuguese labour force still worked in the primary sector. Twenty years later, that figure had dropped to 10.8%. By 2001, it amounted to no more than 5%. Clearly, a true revolution had taken place in the Portuguese countryside over the past three decades (Instituto Nacional de Estatística 1970–2001). Yet, this very impressive and marked change does not alter the fact – and it stands as an eloquent example of the 'awkwardness' of Portuguese development – that comparatively speaking, many Portuguese people still work in agriculture. Indeed, other official sources suggest that the proportion of those working fully or partially in agriculture is significantly more than 5%.[1] No less important – and here we return to the inequalities and uneven development already mentioned – in some Portuguese regions, often covering vast areas especially in the interior, but also in some not greatly distant from the metropolitan regions along the coast, the percentage of the labour force employed in agriculture and their family members living on farms is significantly higher than the national average.

Leaving aside some well-defined regions where agriculture was modernised and competitive, those where the primary sector still predominated faced great difficulties in retaining the young generation on the land. An intense rural exodus to foreign or national destinations, persistent demographic decline, a rapid ageing of the population remaining, together with a marked dependency of family budgets on largely inadequate welfare assistance, were the downside to this trend.

Even where rural regions had diversified their productive methods and techniques, they were frequently associated with activities of low value added and with a low- or semi-skilled labour force. With such an employment structure and with limited job prospects, studying beyond the 9 years of compulsory schooling, on into secondary and higher education, was an opportunity rarely taken up by most families. The traditional peasant resistance to, and suspicion of, schooling, due largely to disbelief in the opportunities for social mobility the school held out, was replicated even as the country entered the 'knowledge century'. Once again, early school leaving and precarious access to the labour market emerged – a very important point to be born in mind above all given the overall purpose of this study.

Naturally, the evolution of Portuguese society during the last few decades cannot leave aside *industrialisation and the rise of the service sector* in the economy of the Nation (Chap. 5).

Briefly put, after a period of intense growth of employment in the secondary sector during the 1960s and 1970s, a decade of stagnation followed. The industrial labour force began to drop steadily and regularly up to the present, whilst tertiary activities increased their part in both national production and overall employment. This was not just a normal consequence of modernising the systems of production. It also followed on as an outcome of building up a welfare state that, prior to 1974, was to all intents and purposes non-existent. Education, health and social security created large numbers of jobs in the intervening period (Almeida et al. 2007: 48–49).

By 2001, according to National Census data, almost 60% of the Portuguese labour force was employed in the tertiary sector of the economy, as against no more than 35% in the secondary activities.

The transition from an agrarian to a service society occurred in an amazingly short period – some three decades (Chap. 5). It is then self-evident that Portugal's social structure has changed radically and recently. Even so, when the same phenomenon is looked at from the consequences it had on intergenerational mobility and institutional restructuring, there is much to suggest that the contemporary history of Portugal generates many hypotheses and very certainly challenging ones to the analysis of social change.[2]

This became even more evident once one recalls that this same transition was accompanied by two further significant changes in the Portuguese employment system: first, the dramatic *increase of female participation in the labour market*, and second, the overall *recomposition of migration patterns*.

In 1970, compared to other European countries, the female employment ratio in Portugal was very low: only 29% of women aged between 16 and 64 were then on the labour market. Three decades on, the employment of women had become significantly higher than most southern European countries and near to the northern model, although with a far lower proportion of part-time jobs. To be precise, by 2001, almost 65% of women in the age range mentioned above were in employment. Furthermore, almost 80% of women with children under 12 years were working in full-time jobs (Aboim 2009). This striking structural shift is currently interpreted as an outcome of other specificities in Portuguese society, such as: (1) the progressive acquisition of autonomy by women in managing family affairs, a trend stimulated in the 1960s more by necessity – in particular, by the absence of adult males engaged in fighting colonial wars and by intense migration flows out of the country – than by ideology; (2) the impetus given by the democratic revolution to the general climate of women's emancipation; and (3) the persistence of low salaries and low family income amidst growing consumption and equally growing aspiration to social mobility (Chaps. 6 and 16).

That said, however, from the perspective this chapter sets out to develop, it is interesting to pay some attention to certain concomitants which the employment of women had, albeit indirectly, for the learning opportunities and career development of the younger generation.

Despite a very real impact of egalitarian views on issues of gender (Aboim 2007), social research has shown that increasing participation by Portuguese women at all qualification levels of the labour market, in practice, went hand in hand with a significant (although diminishing) withdrawal by men in sharing many aspects of the domestic burden. On the other hand, support by the Portuguese welfare state to families remains both weak and incomplete. Many women face considerable pressures in their daily life. This situation gives rise to very real difficulties for the Portuguese family above all in its relationship with the school, and with regular parental follow-up and support for their children's learning activities. If, for many, this involves offloading educational responsibility onto a 'distant' school, for others it merely heightens stress and anxiety.

The very pronounced fall in fertility rates – from an *'anomalous'* peak in 1970 (3.0) to an equally *'anomalous'* low in 2001 (1.3), plus the fall in the average number of family members from 3.7 in 1970 to 2.8 in 2001, has necessarily to be set against the backdrop of drastic change in female employment rates. But they are also part of an important drift towards a 'European' pattern of values and social aspirations. They determine how the middle-aged and younger generations experience love and affections and how they plan their families. Without putting in cause the importance subjectively attributed to family ties as a source of effective support in social contexts which are becoming intrinsically precarious and uncertain, these facts in connection with many others (rising divorce rates, non-religious marriages, decrease in nuptiality rates) show the rise in Portuguese society of the processes of individualisation and de-formalisation of family relations – a very outstanding change in a country which was considered, not so very long ago, to be a traditional Catholic bastion.[3]

Both Portuguese society, as a whole, and its employment system, in particular, have been marked by important changes in migration patterns.

At the start of the 1970s, Portugal served as one of the main labour-exporting countries in Europe. In the second half of the decade, however, the sudden return of more than half a million of Portuguese citizens from African ex-colonies took place, an event that coincided with a significant drop in labour demand by most developed countries and, as a result, a slowdown in Portuguese emigration.

Almost without realising it – both official and contemporary speeches on migration movements continued to direct their attention to the so-called Portuguese Diaspora – Portugal itself became, in the last quarter of twentieth century, the haven for many migrants especially since the 1980s those from the ex-colonies and, during the second half of the 1990s, from South America and Eastern Europe.

Though, in the past, both people and politicians had been absorbed by the problems of social integration for successive waves of emigrants into their host societies abroad and with re-knitting economic and symbolic ties between large Portuguese expatriate communities and the motherland, more recently they found themselves obliged to focus attention and public policies on the conditions to integrate incomers in Portugal. Amongst them, poor African communities highly concentrated within the Lisbon Metropolitan Area. That, in a short space of time, the proportion of immigrants resident in Portugal rose, from quasi negligible levels to around 5% of resident population and 9% of total employment, is a clear illustration of the degree of demographic shift entailed.

From becoming the end-destination of migration flows from countries with weak or highly de-structured economies, Portugal still remains a labour-exporting country, though present emigration flows are less intense than in the mid-1970s. In keeping with the drive by productive and employment systems towards flexibility – a salient feature in the recent phase of economic globalisation which also gave rise to a kind of *just-in-time* model of mass migration – Portuguese emigration flows have changed. Today, they are temporary – sometimes seasonal – in the main. They involve nontraditional host countries – Switzerland, Spain, and the United Kingdom.

Paradoxically (or maybe not), in these new host societies, the majority of Portuguese emigrants fill the very kind of non-qualified jobs, which at home are vacant and therefore open to immigrants.[4] Recently, increased outflows of qualified young people have also to be taken into account. They too are an indirect pointer to some of the central features in the Portuguese employment system.

Urbanisation

If change in the Portuguese social structure in recent decades is to be fully grasped, one has also to bear in mind that both intense and contrasting urbanisation took place at the same moment.

The most marked feature of that process was the creation of a notorious *coastal strip*. By 2001, 65% of residents lived on this coastal area, strongly concentrated around the two great traditional urban centres – Lisboa and Porto (*bipolarisation*). Although these two cities are clearly subject to demographic decline since the 1980s, the surrounding metropolitan areas have grown with considerable intensity. By the beginning of the twenty-first century, no less than 38% of the overall resident population was concentrated in the metropolitan areas of Lisboa and Porto.

Two other dimensions of occupied space characterise Portuguese urbanisation.

The first is the low population density or *diffuse urbanisation*, predominantly in the northern and central regions of the country. Here, agricultural activities have significantly dropped away though, thanks to part-time work in small family farms, they still survive. Industry is based on small and micro firms. This extensive and diffuse logic of spatial organisation contributes to sustaining rural lifestyles in large parts of the country. It is, however, not without significant disparities in terms of citizens' access to physical infrastructure and social service networks. In effect, urbanisation seldom coincides with urbanity (in the sense of providing the alleged 'specific' or 'genuine' amenities of city life).

A second tendency in spatial occupation emerged over the last few decades of middle-sized urban centres that form a kind of 'archipelago' in the country's interior. The build-up of these *new midlevel towns*, which springs in part from the attractiveness and social dynamism generated by higher education and other public services, offset in recent times some of the large-scale regional imbalance. Even so, the new attractiveness could not cancel out intense demographic decline, nor economic rundown in the countryside surrounding those urban 'islands'.[5]

Taken together, these tendencies that characterise Portuguese urbanisation confirm the deep asymmetry in the developing patterns of Portuguese society. Yet, they also help us anticipate the intensity and diversity of social changes – at the objective (economic, demographic, educational…) or the subjective (ethical, ideological…) levels – that may have taken place in broad sectors of Portuguese society in recent times.

Illiteracy and Schooling

The stimulus given to the social demand for schooling is one of the most important dimensions, as well as a very powerful catalyst in the overall process of social transformations which ran in parallel to urbanisation.

Despite the fact that Portugal was a pioneer in legislating the compulsory attendance of basic schooling, the generalisation of elementary instruction amongst Portuguese children occurred only at the onset of the 1960s. Thus, with the return to democracy in 1974, one Portuguese citizen in four was illiterate. Entry to higher education was an opportunity reserved to very few.

The past three decades witnessed a very substantial and positive shift in the nation's educational panorama. Briefly stated: (1) compulsory schooling level (9 years) is taken up almost without exception by today's younger generations; (2) the number of students attending the third level of basic studies and tripartite secondary schooling tripled – a phenomenon which, given the fall in the fertility rate mentioned earlier, is explainable only by the very low rates of school attendance at the beginning of the period; and (3) the number of those attending higher education multiplied ten times (Almeida and Vieira 2006: 31–39).

Over and above these tendencies, two further factors must be considered in order to get a more realistic purchase over the educational condition in Portugal. They are, first, regional disparities, which characterise Portuguese schooling, and second, the growing presence of girls in the Portuguese student population – to the point that now they make up the majority in all post-compulsory education, in contrast to trends that lasted until the 1970s.

Tables 4.1–4.4 present a more precise statement of the real impact and accumulated consequences of these developments. They compare several educational indicators across different phases in recent Portuguese history. In addition, they set

Table 4.1 People with extreme cultural deprivation (1960–2001)

	People with extreme cultural deprivation (%)								
	1960			1981			2001		
	M	W	MW	M	W	MW	M	W	MW
Portugal (Mainland)	48.1	61.9	55.4	14.3	24.3	19.5	6.1	11.5	8.9
Porto Metropolitan Area	38.0	56.9	48.3	7.1	16.9	12.3	3.0	7.4	5.3
Vale do Sousa Urban Comm.	48.5	65.4	57.3	13.0	22.4	17.8	5.5	10.0	7.8

Sources: Instituto Nacional de Estatística – Portugal, *Recenseamentos Gerais da População*, 1960, 1981 and 2001
Notes:
Extreme cultural deprivation: literal illiteracy + semi-illiteracy (can read and write, without any formal school certificate)
1960: illiteracy in 7-year olds and over; 1981 and 2001: illiteracy in 10-year olds and over
In 2001, the population census stopped recording semi-illiteracy (in the sense used until then). So, the rate of extreme cultural deprivation corresponds to the (literal) rate of illiteracy, since this is the most reliable indicator of extreme lack of educational qualification

Table 4.2 Nine-year schooling success rate (1981–2001)

	Nine-year schooling success rate (%)								
	1981			1991			2001		
	M	W	MW	M	W	MW	M	W	MW
Portugal (Mainland)	15.5	12.8	14.1	23.9	22.1	22.9	39.2	37.5	38.3
Porto metropolitan area	19.7	15.7	17.5	28.6	25.6	27.0	45.2	42.0	43.5
Vale do Sousa urban comm.	5.2	4.8	5.0	8.9	9.1	9.0	20.6	21.3	20.9

Sources: Instituto Nacional de Estatística – Portugal, *Recenseamentos Gerais da População*, 1981, 1991 and 2001

Note: Numbers correspond to proportions relating to the population above 15 years old

Table 4.3 Twelve-year schooling success rate (1981–2001)

	Twelve-year schooling success rate (%)								
	1981			1991			2001		
	M	W	MW	M	W	MW	M	W	MW
Portugal (Mainland)	8.2	6.8	7.5	13.9	13.2	13.5	22.4	23.8	23.1
Porto metropolitan area	11.0	9.0	9.9	17.9	16.4	17.1	27.3	27.6	27.4
Vale do Sousa urban comm.	2.4	2.7	2.6	4.3	5.1	4.7	9.0	11.3	10.2

Sources: Instituto Nacional de Estatística – Portugal, *Recenseamentos Gerais da População*, 1981, 1991 and 2001

Note: Numbers correspond to proportions relating to the population above 18 years old

Table 4.4 Higher-education attendance rate (1981–2001)

	Higher-education attendance rate (%)								
	1981			1991			2001		
	M	W	MW	M	W	MW	M	W	MW
Portugal (Mainland)	3.6	3.7	3.6	8.7	8.5	8.6	13.7	15.4	14.6
Porto metropolitan area	4.8	4.9	4.9	11.9	11.1	11.5	17.2	18.4	17.9
Vale do Sousa urban comm.	1.0	1.8	1.4	2.4	3.4	2.9	4.6	6.8	5.8

Sources: Instituto Nacional de Estatística – Portugal, *Recenseamentos Gerais da População*, 1981, 1991 and 2001

Note: Numbers correspond to proportions relating to the population above 18 years old

out the situation for *three different regions*: Mainland; the Porto Metropolitan Region, the second largest urban pole in the country; and Vale do Sousa Urban Community, an area that abuts on the administrative limits of the Porto Metropolitan Region.

The tables provide a *general* overview of what may be seen as the 'cultural heritage' in the setting of Portuguese society. Including the Vale do Sousa Community in our portrayal of the Portuguese educational panorama may appear a trifle strange. In fact, its inclusion may be justified on the grounds that it makes explicit, and is thus in keeping with the main lines of analysis laid down at very beginning of this chapter, that in a region which covers six municipalities characterised by its relatively young population, its traditional, but nonetheless dynamic, industrial sector, *plus its favourable location*, not far from the coast and from major urban centres, it is nevertheless possible for educational indicators to assume very low values. Not only is this a clear contrast with national average standards. It also contrasts with the levels displayed by its metropolitan neighbour area.[6]

Table 4.1 shows very clearly how severe the consequences of educational deprivation in Portuguese society were until very recently and particularly so when outside the metropolitan urban areas.

Progress in access to basic education achieved over the past three decades is obvious and no less gratifying. Even so, data conveyed by Tables 4.2–4.4 indicate that the country has still to face up to important cultural disparities and deficits.

Effectively, in the year 2001, those completing secondary education were less than a quarter of Portuguese population aged 18 years and above. Roughly 15% of the same age range attended higher education. Equally salient because present in all tables, regional variation in educational standards remains sharp and persistent, even when comparisons are made between two adjoining coastal areas of Portuguese territory alleged to be more 'developed'.

The significance of these statistics – especially those referring to the Vale do Sousa Community, on the edge of the Porto Metropolitan Area – stands revealed once these general trends, already developed in relation to social demand, family investment in schooling and the demand by employers for qualifications, are intertwined and reciprocally interact with one another to reproduce educational deficits in some Portuguese regions.

The economic structure of Vale do Sousa – which is far from exceptional – rests on small- and medium-sized firms, mostly family owned, with incipient levels of technological and organisational innovation. For the most part, labour is recruited informally, through family and social networks. Atypical kinds of employment and poor working conditions are common. For most industrial employers in the region – and this is a crucial point – level of education is not a factor in wage differentiation. Often, the wages of employees with the equivalent of 4 years' schooling do not vary significantly from the wages paid to employees with today's compulsory schooling (9 years).

Where (1) there is no sign of any fundamental change to the profile of educational qualifications in industry employment and when (2) the slight decline in the weight of industrial jobs is offset by the rise of branches of activity equally undemanding in terms of qualifications – for example, building construction for men, and restaurants, domestic service and social care for women – a real shift in the patterns of educational demand and in the recognition of educational ability by the regional system of production seems improbable. Studies pursued at secondary level and *a fortiori* in higher education are opportunities rarely if ever taken up by most families in the region. Even when they include in their aspirations vague aims of social mobility based on the education of their younger members, many families tend to avoid the costs and risks they associate to long-term investment with education.

In a region with low family purchasing power, early entry to the labour market meets the need to raise the family budget through youngsters gaining early access to the benefits that come with adult status. Consumer aspirations and personal independence are both fulfilled. Individual emancipation and the prospect of mobility seem to many of the locals to depend less on school certificates, which demand long-term investment, have high opportunity costs and a dubious pay-off, than on becoming a wage-earner as soon as possible. This is an easy solution and offers instant benefits to whoever achieves this condition.

International surveys on literacy skills, the *IALS* reports, show that Portugal ranks amongst the least-favoured positions. Moreover, they also suggest that the literacy profiles amongst Portuguese are worse than what would normally result from converting schooling certificates into literacy skills. This gap, at least in part, may be explained by the high incidence, in the daily life of many Portuguese citizens, of practical contexts (namely, at family and work) in which contact with the written document and other forms of cultural capital is rare or virtually absent. The value of academic qualifications tends to wear away in such an environment (Ávila 2006: 243–263, 2009: 31–34). A more realistic picture of the economic opportunities some Portuguese regions command at the dawn of the 'knowledge century' requires careful reflection on all that applies to the context of family and work in Vale do Sousa. There are good reasons for thinking that, as in this specific instance, literacy deficits are not simply a cause but also a *consequence* of the particular patterns of a region's development.

Tables 4.1–4.4 open the way to further comments on the participation of women and girls in Portuguese schooling.

Once again, we are confronted with a surprising evolutionary trajectory.

Having passed from being a minority to becoming a majority amongst those aged 18 years and above who completed *12-year schooling* and attended or completed *higher education* (see Tables 4.3 and 4.4), Portuguese women seem to have definitely overcome that massive handicap they still faced in the 1960s, when almost 62% – compared to 48% of their male counterparts – faced extreme levels of cultural deprivation (Table 4.1). The growing and, nowadays, clearly hegemonic participation of girls in *higher education* – in 2001, 56.4% of students attending higher education were women – confirms the intensity of the shift in gender balance (Almeida and Vieira 2006: 35–36; Ribeiro 2007).

Although today's hegemonic participation of girls in the educational dynamics of Portugal remains stable across both national and regional levels of analysis, it is nevertheless worthwhile attending to those differences between the immediate values that characterise each level. Surprisingly, in 2001 the proportion of women and girls attending higher education in the Vale do Sousa Community was *less than half* of the corresponding statistic at national level. Once more, the imprint of regional handicap, already observed at the start of the period in question, endures, despite important changes in the meantime. There are, it would seem, specific objective limits to the increase in the overall propensity of Portuguese girls to engage in educational investment.

Class Structure and Social Recomposition

Given all that has been said about economic, demographic and educational change in Portuguese society, a synthesis of their combined effects can be made by examining the evolution in the *class structure*. The class divisions set out here (see Table 4.5)

Table 4.5 Individual social class fractions in the population with economic activity in 1970 and 2001 (%)

Class fractions	1970 Mainland	2001 Mainland	Vale do Sousa
Entrepreneurial and executive bourgeoisie	3	9	8
Managerial bourgeoisie		3	2
Intellectual and scientific (professional) Petty bourgeoisie		7	2
Traditional petty bourgeoisie	7.3	5	5
Managerial and technical petty bourgeoisie	4.9	8	4
Routine petty bourgeoisie	19.4	32	19
Peasants	15.2	2	1
Agriculture working class	16.2	2	1
Industrial working class	34.0	30	56

Sources: Instituto Nacional de Estatística – Portugal, *Recenseamentos Gerais da População*, 1970 and 2001
Distribution by class calculated by Almeida et al. (2007) for 1970 and Silva and Pereira (2008) for 2001

follow those which have been applied and broadly tested in Portuguese sociological literature. Here we will identify – as the specific purpose of class analysis – those positions in the social field which, by acting as different sets of structural constraints and opportunities based on access to economic and educational resources, determine – although in a non-deterministic way – practices and power of their agents. So as to give further depth to the issue of regional asymmetries in Portuguese society, information on the class structure as it was in 2001 in the Vale do Sousa Community is set out in Table 4.5.

Table 4.5 shows clearly – and given what we know already, this will not be surprising in the least – that the proportion of individuals economically active in agriculture – whether as wage-earners ('agricultural working class') or as independent workers in family exploitations ('peasants') – has sharply decreased over the decades. In 2001, these categories accounted for no more than 4% of the total – and even less in the Vale do Sousa.

The waning of the industrial working class in Portuguese social structure – from 34% in 1970 to 30% in 2001 – is another remarkable, but not altogether surprising, trend. It is the corollary of some social processes already touched upon: for instance, the rise of tertiary sector economy and urbanisation. In some sense, it is the counterpart of the rise to statistical and social relevance of those mentioned in Table 4.5 as 'routine petty bourgeoisie' (workers occupying less-qualified non-industrial salaried jobs in the employment system): 19% in 1970 and 32% in 2001. This contrasts sharply with the social profile of the Vale do Sousa. Thirty years ago, the peasant economy remained prominent in the region. Today, the industrial working class, which accounts for 56% of the population, stands clearly as the modal social grouping.

The rise of 'intellectual and scientific professionals' and of workers in 'intermediate managerial and technical' positions within the productive processes – both of which are in relative terms socially privileged – is another aspect that merits consideration. Very obviously, it echoes those changes, already mentioned, in educational demand and school certification by younger generations together with the modernisation of certain sectors of the economy. Yet, when set against the equivalent statistic in Europe, in Portugal these proportions still appear relatively low and as such point towards some of the more worrying weaknesses the country continues to suffer from within the global economy.

Another facet associated with the class realignment in Portugal relates to the loss of statistical and social weight by small owners and, conversely, the growing presence of the salary-earner pole in the social structure. This phenomenon was particularly pronounced in agriculture. Peasantry has declined dramatically from around 15%, in 1970, to 2%, in 2001 – surely, a phenomenon fraught with consequence for value systems, ideologies and life styles in Portugal.[7]

Economic Inequalities and Poverty

Yet, the vast universe of wage-earners can also be differentiated by indicators other than social class. It may equally be subjected to other criteria, by position in the wage hierarchy or by job security, for example.

Between 1995 and 2005, the average wage rose almost 20% before taxation, despite a levelling out in wage increases since 2002. Meanwhile, the proportion of low wage workers remained significant. In 2005, 13% of Portuguese workers earned less than 432€, that is, two thirds of the median wage of that year (Comissão do Livro Branco das Relações Laborais 2007: 37–43).

The political intention to increase the national minimum wage in a sustainable way may be expected to diminish in the near future the numbers of very low wage-earners on the Portuguese labour market. Still, there are reasons enough to think that this will not significantly reduce large disparities in income and wage distribution in Portugal. According to Eurostat, the ratio between the percentage of income earned by the richest sector of the Portuguese population and the corresponding figure for the poorest (S80/S20) in 2005 was in the order of 6.9 – well above the average for Europe of the 15 of 4.8 and the 4.9 for Europe of the 25. Income differences in Portugal were amongst the highest in the enlarged European Community. Detailed studies (Rodrigues 2008) demonstrated that, after a small lowering in income inequalities during the second half of the 1990s, between 2000 and 2005 the gap once more began to widen. Whilst these years coincided with a slight improvement in income distribution for the 20% worst off, such a trend reflected not simply a fall in income for the intermediate quintiles. It reflected above all, an improvement in the income of the richest 20%. The analysis of wage distribution data confirms this recent strengthening of high income differentials. It also suggests that poverty is beginning to hit the employed as well.

One study, covering the years from 1995 to 2000, which focused on vulnerability and social exclusion, concluded that more than half of the families that had fallen at least once into the poverty trap during these years derive their main income source from employment (Costa 2008). Another national inquiry into family income and expenditure in 2005/2006 confirms that whilst the risk of poverty falls with participation on the labour market, a significant proportion of those employed live in poverty. Around 70% of poor families in the 34–54 age group were regularly employed (Alves 2009). This suggests that, in Portugal, *primary* wealth distribution patterns lie at the very base of some of the fundamental factors of social vulnerability. In short, poverty is structurally tied in with the weakness in, and in certain cases the inequities of, the economy. Nor is poverty due simply to feeble policies of social redistribution, though the relatively low level of minimum and social pensions, which in 2001 affected more than 7% of the resident population, acts as an important poverty factor in Portugal (Capucha 2009: 173).

Sharp segmentation in the labour market, plus an increasing recourse by employment through 'atypical' forms such as fixed-term contracts and pseudo-independent work, above all, hit young people. It acts then as an additional factor that cannot be dismissed if we seek a realistic tableau of Portuguese society.

In the future, the chances of an effective professional and social integration of young people will depend to a significant degree on the ability of Portuguese society to deal with precisely those weaknesses in the labour market that have been outlined. These weaknesses are particularly harmful to the less educated amongst the younger generation. Nor for that matter will those same fragilities, which, as we have seen, are more pronounced in certain regions, leave the better educated entirely unscathed. Agreed, on the whole, educational qualifications are a shield against unemployment. They still guarantee relatively high returns on the labour market, not to mention other social and symbolic benefits. But empirical evidence indicates that, even for the educated, the probability of obtaining a stable, well-paid job, at least in the early years of a professional career, is falling, especially in a situation of persistent economic crisis. For the holders of certain high school diplomas, the withdrawal from state intervention, together with the corresponding cutbacks in public employment, will serve to compound those difficulties further (Alves 2008: 282–306).

Development, Welfare and Quality of Life

The tableau of Portuguese society we have sketched out has underlined a series of structural traits which, in addition, hint at important developmental disadvantages Portuguese society faces. Such a canvas may perhaps feed the impression that social change of the last few decades in effect failed to realise many of the progressive programmes drawn up by the supporters of the 1974 democratic revolution.

Yet, the impression itself must be significantly corrected in the light of some of the indicators conventionally used for international comparisons in development. One of these – the Human Development Index (HDI/PNUD) – is a composite indicator, combining 'GDP *per capita*', 'educational level' and 'life expectancy'.

The scores HDI assigned to Portugal have clearly improved over three decades. To be precise, they rose from 0.793 in 1975 to 0.897 in 2005. They show some convergence towards the EU15 average, which was respectively 0.847 and 0.943 (United Nations Development Programme 2007: 234). With a very unfavourable position at the starting block, Portugal's path of convergence could not have been met without a relatively positive meshing of social policies with institutional reform, which the process of democratisation made possible.

The stimulus given to the basic schooling of the young generation stands as one of the most solid pillars in that positive effort. The creation of the public health service, where a number of coordinated measures were followed through, brought other important improvements in its train. Not the least amongst them is the 'near-miracle' which drastically reduced infant mortality from a tragically high rate of 55.5 per thousand in 1970 to an exceptionally low 3.5 per thousand in 2005. As a basis for comparison, the average infant mortality rate in 2004 for Europe of the 15 was 4.1 per thousand (Barros and Simões 2007: 6).

Against this backdrop, it is as well to take account of some specific features of Portugal's welfare system.

The first steps in establishing welfare provision date back to the mid-1970s, when its counterparts in Northern and Central European countries were already mature systems, though under financial constraint as a result of the economic crisis during the 1970s.

Constructing the institutional framework of the Portuguese welfare state started with the approval of the 1976 Constitution. From the very first, the welfare state had to contend with highly polarised issues both political and social. The decade following 1974 was marked by such events as the nationalisation of, and state intervention in, large companies, agrarian reform as well as two programmes to adjust the balance of payments, headed by the IMF. After 1985 and to meet the requirements for EC membership, a series of important reforms were undertaken. They revised institutions, adapted regulations in the economy in a liberal direction – cutting back in state intervention, giving free reign to the financial sector – injected a new 'flexibility' into labour laws and aligned the country around the conditions set out in the Maastricht Treaty. More recently, additional efforts have been made to fall in with the budget demands of the European Monetary Union. These adjustments imposed severe financial constraint on the infant Portuguese welfare state.

Today, it is clear nevertheless that Portuguese citizens benefit from a system of social protection more sophisticated by far than the embryonic form that characterised it 30 years ago. Despite gaps and certain inconsistencies, not to mention financial difficulties, it is inconceivable that the Portuguese welfare state should stand as anything other than a very positive legacy both of the democratic revolution and of the country's membership of the European Union.

In short, dealing with important structural disadvantage and pressed by financial and political difficulties in part arising from the enlargement of the EU, the Portuguese welfare system, and thus the quality of life of the citizenry, continues to be a net beneficiary of improvement in that same process. Still, given the nature of the inequalities and regional disparities in the structure of Portuguese society, decentralisation and subsequent integration of different public services and social security around the regional level would appear to hold out much promise in reforming the still fragile Portuguese system of welfare.

Value Systems and Cultural Dynamics

In Portuguese society, the economic, demographic, educational and political changes this chapter has explored intertwined with important shifts in the symbolic and cultural field. Values, as organised and relatively stable sets of preferences that provide a framework for the individual's perceptions, beliefs and practices, represent an important dimension in that general movement.

The rise of *individualism* is one of the shifts in the value system that deserves further attention. The decay in the propensity of individuals to fall in with community or family norms, to delay personal satisfaction, pleasure and consumption and to ensure family or group survival runs in parallel with the assertion of attitudes and practices grounded in personal goals, personal achievement and ambitions centred around the self. These latter attitudes, which are highly influential in shaping educational and career trajectories, also drive towards a more intense and immediate experiencing of the here and now. Such an ideological shift towards *individualism* does not necessarily loosen the ties of family affection and still less involves an universal casting off of other traditional points of reference. In Portugal, the incidence of these phenomena cannot be fully understood without mentioning several features already dissected in this chapter. It is the case of the de-structuring of peasant society. In fact, it led to the weakening of localism and other ideological reference points centred in the traditional community, thus stimulating the emergence of individualistic traits in large sectors of Portuguese society. The growing participation of women in work progressively brought about the objective and subjective liberation of the 'second sex'. And even consolidating the policies of the welfare state, which endowed the population with an unprecedented range of social rights, drove in the same direction.

One major salient feature in the changing value system is the *secularisation* of life, that is, the rising prevalence of the profane over the sacred in frameworks of individual and collective judgement and practice. Secularisation is not necessarily an irreversible movement. Nor does it oust every dimension of religiosity in society. Self-identification with Catholicism remains high in Portugal – around 84% of the population in 2001. In certain regions, it is very high – for instance, in the municipalities of the Vale do Sousa, where, in the same year, more than 90% of the inhabitants declared themselves to be Catholic. For all that, regular weekly Church attendance by the faithful has steadily deteriorated nationwide from 28% in 1977 to 26% in 1991. The corresponding statistic for the Vale do Sousa Community shows higher absolute values, but a similar trend, falling from 57% in 1977 to 35% in 2001.[8]

After 1974, the overthrow of ideological control exercised by the dictatorship for nigh on a half a century unleashed a lively confrontation in public debate between conservative, reformist and revolutionary programmes. In a second phase, it gave birth to a *pluralistic coexistence of values and ideological systems* similar to those in 'stable' and 'mature' democracies. Whilst several indicators show the level of political commitment, participation and the trust of Portuguese citizens to be significantly lower than in many other European countries (Almeida et al. 2006; Viegas and Faria 2009), there is no reason to believe that Portuguese society is moving towards the 'end of ideology'. In Portugal, as with many other 'modernist' national settings, ideological pluralism and political cleavage tend to live cheek by jowl with an opening up to otherness and to a kind of personal *bricolage* of ideas, value orientations and cultural choice. Thus, traditional ideological affiliations yield before the logic of utilitarianism and individualism, and, in the sphere of politics, are replaced by self-reflexive and autonomous opinions and decisions. A similar tendency colours the relationship of individuals with the sacred. The individualisation of religious experience and the privatisation of faith are commonly held to be two evident traits in the religious dynamic of Portuguese society.

Media exposure and the degree of passively oriented cultural practices are important components in the symbolic-ideological processes discussed here. International comparisons show Portugal belongs to that group of countries where television viewing largely outstrips the reading of newspapers. Such close bonding with audio-visual culture is particularly intense amongst the older and less educated – those who, at the same time, have low levels of access to Internet services (Torres and Brites 2006: 330–337).

A dissection of 'high culture' audiences unearths significant degrees of class selectivity. To be more precise, it reveals that belonging to socially and culturally privileged strata seems to be a condition necessary, but not sufficient – *loin s'en faut* – to avail oneself of high culture's institutions and *oeuvres*. Recently, efforts have been made by both national and local authorities to enlarge both readership and the 'cultivated' public. Amongst these initiatives are the construction and networking of libraries, museums and other cultural facilities; the launching of reading incentives by involving basic and secondary schools; and integrated cultural policies of adult education at local and regional level. Hopefully, these efforts to extend access to high culture will, over the long term, raise not only the level and quality of democratic life but also spur on the objective conditions for artistic and cultural creation. But this is a topic too complex to be dealt with here.

Conclusion

The idea that Portuguese society changed very significantly in the last three decades commands a wide consensus. This chapter developed that same idea, but tried not to confine it, as frequently is done, solely to the political dimensions of the process of democratisation begun in 1974.

The chapter began with an analysis of the most influential changes in economic structure, employment system and migration movements. A drastic shrinkage in the importance of agriculture and the peasantry in the economy, the emergence of immigration as an important vector in the dynamics of demography and the very significant increase of female participation in the labour market were some of the main features considered (Chap. 6). They were followed by a broad inventory of the specific trends of the urbanisation process during the last decades. Here the emphasis was put on the persistent concentration of population in the metropolitan areas of Lisboa and Porto, a phenomenon which ran parallel with the consolidation of other important asymmetries in the Mainland territory.

Given the overall purpose of this study, it will not be surprising that the trends of schooling and literacy in the democratic era were also analysed in some detail. Impressive improvements in the access of the younger generations to instruction were registered. But our text also demonstrates that the latter phenomenon cannot be regarded as a homogeneous movement towards higher levels of instruction. On the contrary, its incidence differs very significantly across regions, gender and social status. With the combined effects of economic, demographic and educational changes in mind, we could then point up the broad tendencies, and regional variants, of class recomposition and social mobility – a very useful key to grasp at a glance the overall transformation of Portuguese society in the last decades.

Having announced, since the very beginning of the chapter, that Portuguese society is marked by very significant social asymmetries, we could not but cautiously discuss the most important issues concerning poverty and economic inequalities, as well as quality of life and welfare support. Value systems and cultural dynamics were the last features to be put under scrutiny. The results obtained led to the conclusion that the twin impulses of democratisation and modernisation that followed the fall in 1974 of the old authoritarian regime touched not only the 'material infrastructure', but also, in a very impressive way, the 'symbolical superstructure' of social life.

Notes

1. According to the Instituto Nacional de Estatística (1999), the number of family agricultural population (people living on farms) as a percentage of the total resident population still corresponded, in 1999, to 11.4%.
2. For a brief and overall analysis of social change and the reproduction of 'institutional inconsistency' in Portuguese society along the last decades, see Pinto and Pereira (2006).
3. For a general assessment of the main demographic trends and family changes in twentieth-century Portuguese society, see Rosa and Vieira (2003), Almeida (2003) e Leandro (2001: 92–106). More specific analysis on conjugality and domestic structures in Portugal will be found in Wall et al. (2001), Wall (2003), Torres (2002) and Aboim (2006).
4. See, for a comprehensive panorama of Portuguese migration patterns, Ferrão 1996; and Malheiros 2005.
5. For an analysis of the urbanisation process in Portugal during the last decades, see, amongst others, Gaspar (1987), Rosa and Vieira (2003), Portas et al. (2003), Ferreira and Castro (2007) and Carmo (2008).

6. The main arguments and empirical evidence presented in the following numbers (4.2. and 4.3.) are fully developed in Queirós and Pinto (2008).
7. For a detailed analysis of the empirical data considered in this section, see Almeida et al. (2006, 2007), Costa et al. (2000) and Silva and Pereira (2008).
8. For an analysis of religion and religious practices in Portugal, see Fernandes (2004) and Vilaça (2006).

References

Aboim, S. (2006). *Conjugalidades em mudança*. Lisboa: Imprensa de Ciências Sociais.
Aboim, S. (2007). Clivagens e continuidades de género face aos valores da vida familiar em Portugal. In K. Wall & L. Amâncio (Eds.), *Família e género em Portugal e na Europa* (pp. 35–91). Lisboa: Imprensa de Ciências Sociais.
Aboim, S. (2009). Igualdade Gualdade e diferença: género e cidadania em Portugal. In *Le Monde Diplomatique* (Vol. 36/II). Lisboa: Outro Modo.
Almeida, A. N. (2003). Famílias. In Instituto Nacional de Estatística (Ed.), *Portugal Social (1991–2001)* (pp. 51–68). Lisboa: INE.
Almeida, A. N., & Vieira, M. M. (2006). *A escola em Portugal*. Lisboa: Imprensa de Ciências Sociais.
Almeida, J. F., Machado, F. L., & Costa, A. C. (2006). Classes sociais e valores em contexto europeu. In J. Vala & A. Torres (Eds.), *Contextos e atitudes sociais na Europa* (pp. 69–96). Lisboa: Imprensa de Ciências Sociais.
Almeida, J. F., Capucha, L., Costa, A. F., Machado, F. L., & Torres, A. (2007). A sociedade. In A. Reis (Ed.), *Retrato de Portugal. Factos e acontecimentos* (pp. 43–79). Lisboa: Círculo de Leitores.
Alves, N. (2008). *Juventudes e inserção social*. Lisboa: Educa/Unidade de I&D de Ciências da Educação.
Alves, N. (2009). Novos factos sobre a pobreza em Portugal. In *Boletim Económico do Banco de Portugal* (pp. 125–146), Primavera. Lisboa: Banco de Portugal.
Ávila, P. (2006). A literacia dos adultos: competências-chave na sociedade do conhecimento (PhD dissertation, ISCTE).
Ávila, P. (2009). Literacy and social inequalities in the knowledge society. In A. F. Costa, F. L. Machado, & P. Ávila (Eds.), *Knowledge and society* (pp. 21–44). Lisboa: CIES, ISCTE-IUL/Celta.
Barros, P. P., & Simões, J. A. (2007). Portugal: Health system review. *Health Systems in Transition, 9*(5), 1–142.
Capucha, L. (2009). Poverty and social exclusion. In M. D. Guerreiro, A. Torres, & L. Capucha (Eds.), *Welfare and everyday life* (pp. 169–186). Lisboa: CIES, ISCTE-IUL/Celta.
Carmo, R. M. (2008). Portugal, sociedade dualista em questão: dinâmicas territoriais e desigualdades sociais. In M. V. Cabral, K. Wall, S. Aboim, & F. C. Silva (Eds.), *Itinerários. A investigação nos 25 anos do ICS*. Lisboa: Imprensa de Ciências Sociais.
Comissão do Livro Branco das Relações Laborais. (2007). *Livro Branco das Relações Laborais*. Lisboa: MTSS.
Costa, A. B. (Ed.). (2008). *Um olhar sobre a pobreza. Vulnerabilidade e exclusão social no Portugal Contemporâneo*. Lisboa: Gradiva.
Costa, A. F., Mauritti, R., Martins, S. C., Machado, F. L., & Almeida, J. F. (2000). Classes sociais na Europa. Sociologia. *Problemas e Práticas, 34*, 9–46.
Fernandes, A. T. (2004). *Prática dominical. Sua redefinição em novos universos simbólicos*. Porto: Voz Portucalense.
Ferrão, J. (1996). *A Demografia Portuguesa*. Lisboa: Cadernos do Público.
Ferreira, V. M., & Castro, A. (2007). O território. In A. Reis (Ed.), *Retrato de Portugal. Factos e acontecimentos* (pp. 43–64). Lisboa: Círculo de Leitores.

Gaspar, J. (1987). *Ocupação e organização do espaço. Retrospectiva e tendências.* Lisboa: Fundação Calouste Gulbenkian.
Instituto Nacional de Estatística. (1970–2001). *XI, XII, XIII e XIV Recenseamentos Gerais da População.* Lisboa: INE.
Instituto Nacional de Estatística. (1999). *Recenseamento Geral da Agricultura.* Lisboa: INE.
Leandro, E. (2001). *Sociologia da família nas sociedades contemporâneas.* Lisboa: Universidade Aberta.
Lopes, J. S. (2004). *A economia portuguesa no século XX.* Lisboa: Imprensa de Ciências Sociais.
Malheiros, J. M. (2005). Jogos de relações internacionais: repensar a posição de Portugal no arquipélago migratório global. In A. Barreto (Ed.), *Globalização e migrações* (pp. 251–272). Lisboa: Imprensa de Ciências Sociais.
Pinto, J. M., & Pereira, J. V. (2006). Trinta anos de democracia: mudanças sociais e inconsistência institucional. In M. Loff & M. C. M. Pereira (Eds.), *Portugal: 30 anos de democracia (1974–2004)* (pp. 133–151). Porto: Editora UP.
Portas, N., Domingues, A., & Cabral, J. (2003). *Políticas Urbanas. Tendências, estratégias e oportunidades.* Lisboa: Centro de Estudos da Faculdade de Arquitectura da Universidade do Porto/Fundação Calouste Gulbenkian.
Queirós, J., & Pinto, J. M. (2008). Estruturas produtivas, escolarização e desenvolvimento no Vale do Sousa. Análise da reprodução da condição social periférica numa região metropolitana portuguesa. *Cadernos de Ciências Sociais, 25*(26), 309–356.
Ribeiro, A. A. (2007). A vantagem escolar das raparigas no secundário: resultados escolares e identidades juvenis numa perspectiva de género. In M. M. Vieira (Ed.), *Escola, jovens e media* (pp. 109–136). Lisboa: Imprensa de Ciências Sociais.
Rodrigues, C. F. (2008). Desigualdade económica em Portugal. In *Le Monde diplomatique* (Vol. 23/II). Lisboa: Outro Modo.
Rosa, M. J. V., & Vieira, C. (2003). *A população portuguesa no século XX.* Lisboa: Imprensa de Ciências Sociais.
Silva, E. G., & Pereira, V. (2008). Actividade Económica e formação de classes na região do Vale do Sousa (1950–2001): considerações preliminares para a respectiva conceptualização. *Cadernos de Ciências Sociais, 25*(26), 357–390.
Torres, A. (2002). *Casamento em Portugal. Uma análise sociológica.* Oeiras: Celta.
Torres, A., & Brites, R. (2006). Atitudes e valores dos europeus: a perspectiva do género numa análise transversal. In J. Vala & A. Torres (Eds.), *Contextos e atitudes sociais na Europa* (pp. 325–378). Lisboa: Imprensa de Ciências Sociais.
United Nations Development Programme. (2007). *Human Development Report 2007/2008.* Nova Iorque: Palgrave MacMillan.
Viegas, J. M., & Faria, S. (2009). Political participation: the Portuguese case from a European comparative perspective. In J. M. Viegas, H. Carreiras, & A. Malamud (Eds.), *Institutions and politics* (pp. 53–70). Lisboa: CIES, ISCTE – IUL/Celta.
Vilaça, H. (2006). *Da Torre de Babel às Terras Prometidas. Pluralismo religioso em Portugal.* Porto: Edições Afrontamento.
Wall, K., (Ed.). (2003). Dossiê: Famílias no Censo 2001. In *Sociologia. Problemas e práticas* (Vol. 43). Lisboa: CIES/ISCTE.
Wall, K., Aboim, S., Cunha, V., & Vasconcelos, P. (2001). Family and informal support networks in Portugal: The reproduction of inequality. *Journal of European Social Policy, 11*(3), 213–249.

Chapter 5
From an Agrarian Society to a Knowledge Economy? The Rising Importance of Education to the Portuguese Economy, 1950–2009

Álvaro Santos Pereira and Pedro Lains

From Growth to Stagnation

In the twentieth century, the poorer economies on the European periphery experienced rapid economic growth and fast convergence of per capita income levels vis-à-vis the most advanced economies in the world. In Europe, for the first time since the onset of industrialisation, the gaps between average country incomes, as well as a subsequent decline in cross-country income inequalities, were considerably reduced (Bourguignon and Morrison 2002). The Portuguese economy was one of the great success stories in the process of economic convergence. Since the 1950s, it had made a remarkable transformation. In a relatively short period, Portugal moved from a low-growth, low-openness and an agrarian-based economy to a largely high-growth, high-openness and industrial economy. From the late 1950s until the mid-1970s, the country not only industrialised but also achieved some of the highest rates of economic growth in Western Europe (Crafts and Toniolo 1996). It also, and perhaps not coincidently, managed to open itself to the rest of Europe by entering the European Free Trade Area (EFTA) in 1960 and by substantially expanding its export base. After 1973, the rate of economic growth fell. Still, the Portuguese economy was able to absorb relatively well a sharp shift in economic and fiscal policy after the implementation of democracy in 1974, the loss of colonial markets that gave rise to a sudden diversion of trade, the nationalisation of major companies

---

A.S. Pereira (✉)
School for International Studies, Simon Fraser University, 515W Hastings Street,
V6B 1M1 Vancouver, Canada
e-mail: apereira@sfu.ca

P. Lains
Instituto de Ciências Sociais, University of Lisbon, Av Anibal de Bettancourt 9,
1600-189 Lisbon, Portugal
e-mail: pedro.lains@ics.ul.pt

during the revolutionary period of 1974 and 1975, as well as two significant financial crises in the late 1970s and early 1980s.

Economic growth picked up after macroeconomic stabilisation was achieved in the mid-1980s and following the country's joining the European Economic Community in 1986, which further increased the country's openness. Economic liberalisation and a privatisation programme also contributed to rapid growth. By the early 1990s, Portugal was being solicited for its economic success (Mateus 1998; Neves 1994) and for its speed of convergence (Barros and Garoupa 1996). Since the late 1990s, however, the Portuguese economy began to display several structural problems, especially with regard to productivity as well as substantial fiscal and external imbalances. In the decade following, and even though Portugal joined the European Monetary Union, the Portuguese economy stagnated. Unemployment rose to historical levels. There was a significant resumption of emigration (Pereira 2010, 2011).

Given its trajectory within Europe, Portugal provides an interesting example of how countries on the European periphery adapted to broader changes in the European economy and how poorer countries sought to close the structural gaps in human and physical capital with the most advanced economies. The recent Portuguese experience also provides valuable lessons on how countries adapted to the euro since the late 1990s.

Accordingly, this chapter sets out the main features of the Portuguese economy since 1950. It tries to understand the reasons behind the extraordinary turn events took over the past few decades. It does this by surveying the main causes behind the recent stagnation in the economy. One of the main reasons behind the second slowdown in the Portuguese economy was the steady but inexorable decline in the trends in productivity growth since at least the end of the 1990s. Based on an historical account for the sources of economic growth, human capital arguably will also have an instrumental role in the resumption of productivity, and consequently, of economic growth in Portugal.

The chapter proceeds as follows: The next section discusses the main trends in the Portuguese economy since 1950, focusing particularly on the period after the fall of the Dictatorship, in 1974. The section "Explaining the Decline in Economic Growth: the Nineties and Their Aftermath" examines the main factors behind Portugal's disappointing economic performance since the late 1990s, whilst the section "From Agriculture to a Knowledge Economy?" analyses the contribution of human capital to economic growth and assesses Portugal's transition from an agrarian society to, possibly, a knowledge-based economy. The conclusion is set out in the last section.

The Portuguese Economy Since 1950

Portugal entered the twentieth century as one of the poorest countries in the Western world and with one of the highest emigration rates (Baganha 1994). In contrast to other Western European countries, Portugal then was predominantly an agrarian society, with most of the population still living in rural areas (Chaps. 4 and 6).

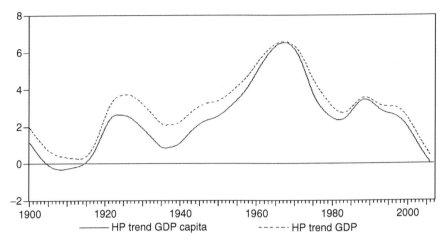

Fig. 5.1 Trend growth in GDP and GDP capita, 1900–2008 (Source: Calculated from Maddison (2003), The Conference Board *Total Economy Database*)

Portugal also displayed one of the lowest levels of human capital in the West, both in terms of literacy and enrolment rates, and thus a marked educational gap vis-à-vis other European countries (Amaral 2002; Reis 2004). Over the decades that followed, the country's economic backwardness persisted, and the living standards of the average Portuguese remained low. During the first part of the twentieth century, the structure of the Portuguese economy changed little. By 1950, more than half of those employed still worked in the agricultural sector. The big breakthrough for the Portuguese economy occurred when industrialisation gathered speed as hundreds of thousands of people left their occupations in the countryside and flocked to the cities in search of urban and industrial jobs, or emigrated.[1]

In order to grasp the development of Portugal's economy over the long term, Fig. 5.1 shows the evolution of Portuguese GDP and GDP per capita since 1900.[2] Portugal's GDP increased throughout most of the twentieth century and accelerated significantly in the post-war period, especially after the mid-1950s, at which point and at long last, the country finally began to industrialise. From 1960 until 1973, the Portuguese economy reached some of the highest rates of growth in the world and, as will be shown, set it on a path of rapid convergence of Portugal's level of income per capita in relation to that of the wealthiest European countries (Maddison 2003).

The trend in economic growth peaked in the early 1970s, declining subsequently in the decades following. Economic growth slowed down afterwards due, in part, to lower foreign demand caused by the first 'oil shock' and subsequent recession, and also due to the political and economic instability that followed the return to democracy in 1974. In spite of this downturn, the trend in economic growth remained, by historical standards, high.

In 1986, the economic growth trend accelerated after Portugal's accession to the European Economic Community, which saw a wave of institutional reform, an

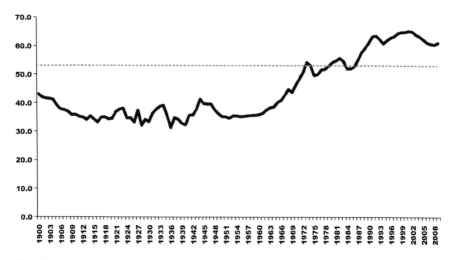

Fig. 5.2 Portugal's convergence to the European core (=100), GDP per capita, 1900–2009 (Source: Calculated from Maddison (2003), The Conference Board *Total Economy Database*)

Table 5.1 Growth of real income per capita on the European periphery, 1913–2009

	Portugal	Spain	Greece	Ireland	European core
1913–1929	1.35	1.65	2.45	0.33	1.39
1929–1938	1.28	−3.53	1.50	0.87	1.16
1938–1950	1.56	1.48	−2.72	0.94	1.00
1950–1973	5.47	5.63	5.99	2.98	3.55
1973–1986	1.52	1.31	1.75	2.47	2.01
1986–1998	3.45	2.65	1.39	5.42	1.88
1998–2009	1.00	2.8	3.3	3.5	1.31
1913–1998	2.79	2.20	2.29	2.19	2.06

Source: Lains (2003b), The Conference Board *Total Economy Database*

ambitious agenda of economic liberalisation and the privatisation of several of Portugal's major companies. However, acceleration in economic growth was short-lived. By the end of the 1990s, the trend started to fall off – gradually but inexorably. Economic stagnation ensued.[3]

Effective convergence with the European core countries followed a similar path to that of economic growth. This is set out in Fig. 5.2, which represents the distance between the Portuguese economy and the European core from 1900 until 2009. The dotted line shows the level of Portuguese GDP per capita in 1974, when democracy was restored. Table 5.1 compares the growth of real income per capita in Portugal and other countries in the European periphery with the European core from 1913. During the first half of the twentieth century, Portugal's real income per capita relative to that in the European core remained, to all intents and purposes, constant. In other words, the Portuguese economy converged towards Europe's most advanced countries only slightly.

During the interwar years, income per capita in Portugal and in the European core grew at similar rates, with the relative gap between them remaining fairly stable. Despite substantial political instability and macroeconomic volatility in the years after World War I, the Portuguese economy still expanded at a rate higher than the early years of the twentieth century (Lains 2007; Neves 1994). Expansion occurred in the teeth of problems associated with the country's balance of payments, brought about by a substantial fall in the money sent back from Brazil by emigrants as well as by a sharp fall in revenue from colonial re-exports. Thus, at the onset of the Great Depression, the Portuguese economy managed to grow, whilst most of the other national economies did not, which gave rise to a short period of convergence with the European core. However, shortly after, under Salazar's stabilisation plan of the 1930s, the economy stagnated, and with the winds of recession blowing from Europe, convergence regressed.

During World War II, the Portuguese economy picked up once again, growing faster than the European core. Neutrality allowed Portugal not only to avoid the destruction of human and physical capital but also to see a substantial increase in exports of wolfram – a key strategic material – textiles and wine to the belligerents (Mateus 1998). Exports surged with the increase in foreign demand and an improvement in Portugal's terms of trade. During the war years, the economy converged rapidly towards the European core, not least because the latter were badly affected by the war itself. However, once again, convergence was brief. The escudo rose in value and caused a fall in both exports and economic growth at the end of the 1940s. Happily, from the decade following, convergence with the European core resumed and did so strongly. During the 'European Golden Age', which lasted from 1950 to 1973, Western Europe's most advanced countries grew at historically high rates, driven on by rapid growth in productivity, capital accumulation and technological progress (Crafts and van Ark 1996; Maddison 2003)

During these years, despite rapid growth at the European core, the Portuguese economy showed unprecedented rates of convergence in income per capita, closing the gap vis-à-vis European core countries at an average of 1.85% per annum (Table 5.2). On the European periphery, Portugal grew at a rate similar to, albeit slightly lower than, that of Greece and Spain.

In the aftermath of the 1974 Revolution, Portugal's relative performance was not so impressive. With the nationalisation of major industries during the revolutionary period, with the financial and political instability that ensued, economic growth fell in the latter half of the 1970s. As a result, between 1973 and 1986, real convergence regressed. Portuguese real income per capita moved apart from the European core at a rate that oscillated around 0.5% per annum. Convergence returned with the mid-1980s. The country joined the European Economic Community, and a sweeping programme of economic liberalitation started. Between 1986 and 1998, Portugal's economy moved towards the European core by some 1.54% per year, markedly higher than the rate of convergence of Spain – average rate 0.76% per annum – though less than the sparkling performance of the Irish economy, which clipped along at annual rate of 3.48%.

Table 5.2 Convergence of real incomes per capita in the European periphery, 1913–1998

	Portugal	Spain	Greece	Ireland
1913–1929	−0.04	0.26	1.04	−1.04
1929–1938	0.12	−4.64	0.33	−0.29
1938–1950	0.55	0.47	−3.69	−0.06
1950–1973	1.85	2.01	2.36	−0.55
1973–1986	−0.49	−0.69	−0.26	0.45
1986–1998	1.54	0.76	−0.48	3.48
1913–1998	0.72	0.14	0.23	0.13

Source: 1913–1990: Lains (2007), 1998–2009: calculated from The Conference Board *Total Economy Database*

Notes: Convergence is defined according to:

$$\phi = \left[\left(y_i / y_9 \right)_{(t+1)} / \left(y_i / y_9 \right)_{(t)} \right]^{[1/(t+1-t)]}$$

where y_i denotes income per capita for country i and y_9 is an income index for the nine European core countries

Table 5.3 Sources of Portuguese economic growth, 1910–2009

	Annual growth rates					As per cent of output growth			
	Labour	Human capital	Capital	TFP	GDP	Labour	Human capital	Capital	TFP
1910–1934	0.33	0.70	0.42	0.72	2.17	15.4	32.1	19.2	33.3
1934–1947	0.44	0.38	1.30	−0.02	2.09	20.8	18.2	62.0	−0.10
1947–1973	0.23	0.82	2.58	1.53	5.17	4.5	15.9	49.9	29.7
1973–1990	0.02	1.61	1.74	0.56	3.93	0.5	41.0	44.3	14.2
1990–2000	0.73	1.27	0.8	1.5	3.17	20.9	36.3	42.8	
2000–2009	−0.03	0.80	−2.46	−0.1	0.89				
1990–2009	0.38	1.09	1.41	0.7	2.14				

Source: Lains (2003b), Barro and Lee (2010), AMECO, Freitas (2005)

If the whole period from 1913 to 1998 is taken into account, the Portuguese economy grew faster than its European counterparts, including the other economies on the European periphery, which brought about a swift convergence in both incomes and living standards. More specifically, and as Table 5.3 shows, between 1913 and 1998, the rate of convergence of the Portuguese economy with the European core – 0.72% per year – was significantly higher than that of Spain at 0.14%, that of Greece at 0.23% and that of Ireland with 0.13%. Even so, since the late 1990s, the tide of convergence is again on the ebb. Not only that, divergence with the core economies has been the longest and most sustained since the end of World War II. From the last decade of the twentieth century, the Portuguese economy, when compared to other economies in Europe and other countries on the periphery – Ireland and Spain, for example – has clearly been underperforming.

Nevertheless, in the course of the last century, Portugal mutated from being an agrarian economy to become a middle-income, industrialised country. The country became an exporter of traditional products, such as textiles, shoes and clothing, as well as certain intermediate products, namely, electronic components and industrial moulds.

Although the drivers of industrialisation may be traced back to the late 1950s, economic convergence with the European core and relatively fast economic growth carried on during the first decades of a democratic Portugal – a trend especially noticeable between 1986 and 1998, the years of European integration and the introduction of liberalisation, economic and institutional. Yet the past decade has seen the economy stagnate and unemployment soar. The factors that lay beneath the recently underperforming Portuguese economy are now analysed.

Explaining the Decline in Economic Growth: The Nineties and Their Aftermath

Several possible explanations are to hand to account for the literal reversal of Portugal's fortunes. First and probably foremost, the past decade saw a substantial slowdown in productivity, which contributed to the fall in economic growth. Although the drop in the growth rate of productivity has not yet been fully analysed at an empirical level, the most likely villains include structural change (Lains 2008), relatively low rates of accumulating human capital (Pina and St. Aubyn 2005), plus an increase in unemployment (Jalles and Pereira 2010). Second, economic growth was also hindered by a difficult adjustment to the euro, which slowed down job creation and lowered export competitiveness (Blanchard 2007; Eichengreen 2007). Third, although the rapid and unprecedented rise in investment rates over the last few decades has contributed to rapid economic growth, increasing evidence suggests that capital accumulation may have reached a threshold of diminishing returns. Fourth, economic policy aggravated the situation by exacerbating the internal imbalances and the structural weaknesses of the Portuguese economy, namely, in the realm of public finances, as well as the fact that the economy is still too dependent on a low-skilled labour force. These explanations will now be pursued in greater detail.

The Drop in Productivity

One of the most striking developments in the Portuguese economy has been a significant decline in productivity. This has worsened over the last few years. This trend stands out in Fig. 5.3, which plots growth in labour productivity, measured as total output per hour, between 1957 and 2009.[4] As expected, growth in labour productivity followed a path similar to economic growth, increasing during the early industrialisation phase, falling in the 1970s and early 1980s. However, contrary to growth of GDP per capita, trend in the growth of labour productivity did not rise in the late 1980s.

Still, it is worth noting, during this period, that the drop in the trend of productivity growth, which had taken place since the 1970s, was halted temporarily. In fact, the mid-1990s saw a small rise in the trend of labour productivity, although soon

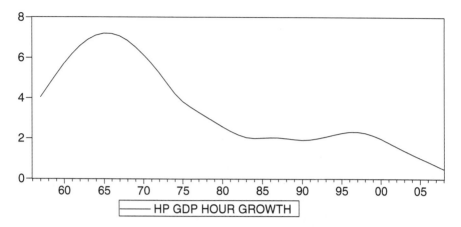

Fig. 5.3 Productivity GDP per hour growth, 1957–2009 (HP filter) (Calculated from Maddison (2003), The Conference Board *Total Economy Database*)

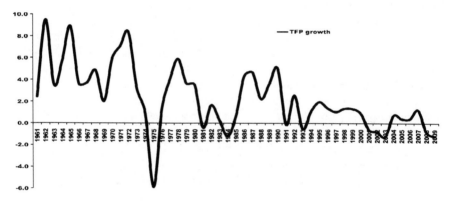

Fig. 5.4 Total factor productivity growth, 1960–2009 (Source: Lains (2003b) and AMECO)

after – in 1998 – it resumed its downward course. By 2005, the trend in GDP per hour grew at a rate close to zero per cent per annum, a performance that did not alter in the years following.

This steady decline in productivity is also clearly visible when total factor productivity (TFP) growth, which measures changes in the productivity of both labour and capital, is examined. Figure 5.4 shows that TFP growth was relatively high during the period of industrialisation in the 1960s, dropped during the period of political upheaval that followed the 1974 revolution but picked up again – though briefly – later in the same decade.

In the 1980s, TFP growth fell during the years of financial uncertainty and the subsequent austerity measures that followed, but rose again with the country's adhesion to the EEC and with the move towards policies of privatisation and economic liberalisation that marked the end of the decade. However, once again, the gains were ephemeral, and the 1990s unfolded against the backdrop of a steady decline in growth of TFP, which fell even further during the first years of the new millennium to become negative with the recession at its outset and in 2008–2009.

The importance of TFP growth for the performance of the Portuguese economy since 1973 is underlined further by Table 5.3. It sets out the sources of Portuguese economic growth over the 100 years from 1910 to 2009.[5] Thus, in the interwar years, capital accumulation accounted for almost two thirds of the economic growth, whilst human capital and labour made more modest contributions – around 20%. TFP was, for all intents and purposes, residual, with an average growth of −0.2% per annum.

In the afterwar years and on until 1973, capital accumulation continued to be the most important source of growth for the Portuguese economy, causing it to expand at an average rate of 2.58% per year, sufficient to account for almost half of all growth. Human capital also expanded more rapidly after 1947, to the tune of 0.82% per annum, whereas labour, undermined by high emigration rates, rose by only 0.23% per year. In turn, and as Fig. 5.4 already made clear, TFP accelerated substantially, as did its contribution to economic growth, which accounted for around one third of total growth. After 1973, growth decreased. It became less capital intensive. By contrast, urged on by the unprecedented investment in education undertaken by democratic governments, the contribution of human capital as a proportion of total economic growth reached around 41%.

All in all, the main source of Portuguese economic growth in the twentieth century was capital accumulation. The contribution of labour to economic growth over those years was small – not greatly surprising, given the high emigration rates that persisted across the century. Yet, human capital was a crucial source of growth during these ten decades. Though this will be developed in greater detail later, despite the fact that indicators of Portugal's educational dynamic showed it to be weak by European standards, nevertheless, they rose significantly throughout the century, with a positive impact on economic growth. With a certain similarity to the development processes of the Asian Tigers – South Korea, Taiwan, Singapore and Japan (Young 1995) – the growth in TFP was less substantial in Portugal than it was in other Western economies. Nevertheless, as Table 5.3 shows, the decrease in economic growth since 1973 can be attributed in greater part to the fall in TFP growth. In other words, the Portuguese economy was employing more people and using more capital but using them in a less efficient way, in contrast to what happened before 1973.

Other studies bear these findings out. Afonso (1999), for example, provides additional evidence of the contribution that total factor productivity makes to Portugal's economic performance. He pointed out that the rapid rise in economic growth in the years 1960–1973 can be attributed to total factor productivity and the growth in capital stock, which account to 93.4% of growth in GDP. Lains (Lains 2003a) used the variables on Levine and Renelt (1992) and showed that whilst their model replicates Portuguese growth performance from 1910 until 1973 relatively

Table 5.4 Output and productivity growth by economic sector, 1950–1990

	1950–1973	1973–1990	1990–1999	2000–2009
Agriculture				
Output	1.3	1.2	1.5	−0.4
Employment	−2.2	−2.8	−3.7	−0.6
Productivity	3.5	4.0	5.2	0.2
Industry				
Output	7.6	2.5	−3.3	−0.2
Employment	1.8	1.8	−8.0	−2.0
Productivity	5.8	0.7	4.7	2.2
Services				
Output	6.0	3.7	3.9	1.8
Employment	1.6	3.8	2.9	1.3
Productivity	4.4	−0.1	1.0	0.5
Total GDP				
Output	5.7	2.9	3.4	0.9
Employment	0.2	1.7	0.8	0.2
Productivity	5.5	1.2	2.6	0.7

Source: Lains (2003b), AMECO

well, it does not account for the post-1973 growth slowdown. After all, Portugal's investment and school enrolment ratios remained high over the ensuing period. Lains claimed that the decline in TFP growth is crucial in any explanation for the drop in growth after 1973. Mateus (Mateus 2005) reached similar conclusions about the main sources of Portuguese economic growth. He estimated that capital accumulation contributed between 31% and 46% to economic growth in 90 years from 1910 to 2000 but was particularly significant during the years of the Golden Age from 1950 to 1973. Mateus's findings also confirmed the increasing importance of human capital as a driver of growth, accounting for 31% of total growth over the two and a half decades from 1975 to 2000. According to these figures, investment in education was of paramount relevance for the growth of the Portuguese economy in that period.

What explains the decline of TFP growth in the 1990s and in the following decade? One possible explanation for the disappointing level of productivity may lie in the substantial structural change that took place over the past few decades (Table 5.4). Rapid industrialisation after the 1960s triggered off an unprecedented increase in industrial employment. The services sector grew as well. The transfer of labour and other resources from a low-productivity sector, such as agriculture, over to a high-productivity industrial sector was an important generator of productivity and economic growth in the 1960s and early 1970s (Lains 2003a). Precisely the reverse mechanism operated in recent decades. As the agricultural labour force declined, labour productivity increased from 3.5% per year (from 1950 to 1973) to 4% (from 1973 to 1990). In parallel, industrial labour productivity fell from 5.8% between 1950 and 1973 to only 0.7% between 1973 and 1990. Labour productivity fell dramatically in the services sector – from 4% a year between

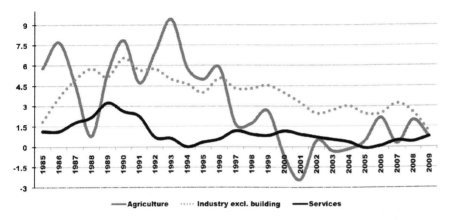

Fig. 5.5 Growth in value added by sector (5-year averages), 1985–2009 (Source: Calculated from AMECO)

1950 and 1973 to −0.1% over the period 1973–1990. During the decades that followed, the services sector continued to attract an increasingly large share of total employment, though productivity growth remained low. In effect, the transition of the Portuguese economy from an industrial to a more service-based economy brought about both a lower rate of productivity growth and a drop in economic growth.

These trends stand forth in Fig. 5.5. It shows the growth of value added since 1985 by sector. Over the past quarter-century, of all sectors, the agricultural sector underwent the greatest volatility in terms of growth in value added, which grew rapidly in the years following the country's entry to the EEC. Thereafter, it fell drastically, even showing rates of negative growth early in the new millennium. Value added in agriculture recovered in some measure after 2005, but its average rate hovers around 1% per year. Another sector with a disappointing performance in terms of value added is construction and building, with negative growth rates since the early 1990s. Its level of value added fell significantly over the past 20 years.

Growth in the value added by industry also declined since 1990, though at a rate somewhat slower than in other sectors. Thus, from 1990 until 2000, industrial value added grew at a healthy average of 4.9% per annum and fell back to an average of 2.6% between 2000 and 2009. If growth in value added of the services sector was steadier, it was also much smaller. From the early 1990s, value added by services never grew faster than an average of 1% per year, dropping back to 0.5% between 2001 and 2009.

Structural change apart, what other factors explain the decrease in TFP growth? Several studies have shown that TFP growth is also strongly correlated with labour productivity. Thus, its drop is likely to be related with a decline in labour efficiency. This is indeed so, as Fig. 5.6 illustrates. It shows strong correlation between TFP growth (on the horizontal axis) and labour productivity (on the vertical axis) over the years 1960 and 2009.

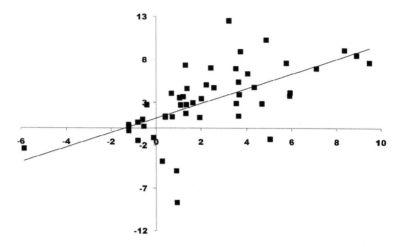

Fig. 5.6 TFP growth and labour productivity growth, 1960–2009

Mateus (2005) argued that the behaviour of TFP growth in Portugal is probably related to the degree of openness of the economy, to macroeconomic stability, as well as to institutional factors. Jalles and Pereira (2010) found that it had been influenced by unemployment rates and by the level of human capital. More empirical research is certainly needed, and we are certain that the decline in productivity will be actively researched in the near future.

Adjusting with Difficulty to the Euro

Blanchard (2007) and Eichengreen (2007) pointed out that a difficult adjustment to the euro was one of the main reasons behind Portugal's profile of low growth and high unemployment over the past decade. They claimed that wages and unit labour costs increased faster in Portugal than they did for traditional competitors of Portuguese exports in international markets. Thus, the Portuguese economy lost competitiveness and stagnated. Bento (Bento 2009) argued that unit labour costs rose more in Portugal than in Germany due to low wage restraint and a rapid rise in wages in the non-tradable sectors, such as the construction and the electric power industries. Rising unit labour costs are clear in Fig. 5.7, which shows the evolution of nominal unit labour costs in selected European economies, in Germany and in the eurozone.

Portuguese unit labour costs rose faster than those in the eurozone, in countries such as Germany, which, in the decade past, stood by a policy of wage restraint. Rises in unit labour costs similar to those of Portugal were seen in other Southern European countries, which had the effect of cutting back their competitiveness and accumulated considerable deficits in their current account. Thus, it is tempting to

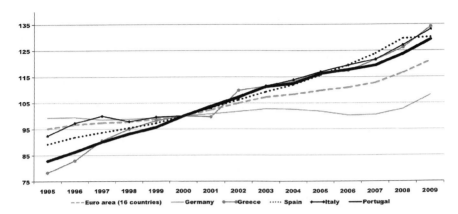

Fig. 5.7 Nominal unit labour costs in selected European countries, 1995–2009 (2000 = 100) (Source: AMECO)

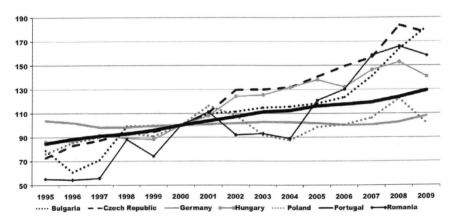

Fig. 5.8 Nominal unit labour costs in Portugal and Eastern Europe, 1995–2009 (Source: AMECO)

conclude that loss of competitiveness and low economic growth were, in large part, caused by rises in unit labour costs. However, once the evolution of nominal unit labour costs in Portugal and some Eastern European countries – traditionally regarded as competitors of Portuguese exports – is examined, Portugal's loss of competitiveness is less clear. Figure 5.8, which plots unit labour costs for Portugal and several Eastern European countries, shows that practically all large Eastern European countries saw unit labour costs rise and far more than Portugal. Poland is the exception in managing to place a fairly effective control over the growth in unit labour costs during the past decade.

Indeed, evolution in *real* unit labour costs was even more modest[6]. Between 2000 and 2009, *real* unit labour costs in Portugal increased by mere 1.3% points, nothing that would undermine export competitiveness, much less explain the extent of the recent economic slowdown. More revealing still, the main increase in real unit labour costs took place between 2008 and 2009, rising by 3.2% points and not from the start of the decade when the Portuguese economy felt the onset of slow growth and low job creation. Though a relative loss of competitiveness certainly seems to have occurred in all likelihood, it was not sufficiently marked to account fully for the depth in the slowdown over the past 10 years.

Yet, other studies highlighted the loss of competitiveness. Alexandre et al. (2009) showed that the Portuguese exchange rate in the 1990s and the first decade of the millennium appreciated in real terms by some 7%, which brought about a drop in the competitiveness of some of the country's main exports. Such a loss of competitiveness occurred mainly in export sectors with lower value added and productivity growth. Cabral (2004) and Amador and Cabral (2008) confirmed that Portuguese exports suffered significant losses in the international market between 1997 and 2006. More specifically, the main losses in market share hit some of Portugal's traditional exports – textiles, clothing and footwear. Between 2002 and 2006, loss of market share extended to the export of motor vehicles, wood and paper. This loss of market shares, the writers argued, can be explained in part by the rising costs of Portuguese exports and also by the appearance on the main international markets of new competitors – China and Eastern Europe – as contenders with Portugal's traditional exports.

In a nutshell, difficulty in adjusting to the single European currency was in part to blame for Portugal's economic woes, not only an appreciating real exchange rate but also loss of competitiveness brought on by a rise in unit labour costs at a rate faster than that in many countries in the euro area. Yet evidence of the importance of unit labour costs remains, in our view, inconclusive. Part of the recent loss of international market share may well be attributed to the arrival of important competitors on the long-established markets for Portuguese exports. To our best belief, no study on the loss of competitiveness has yet been able to distinguish between these two factors. Nor does the loss in competitiveness on its own seem able to account for the marked slowdown of the last decade.

Decreasing Returns to the Accumulation of Capital?

Since capital deepening, or the increase in the amount of capital available per worker, has been an essential explanatory variable in the performance of the Portuguese economy over the past half-century – more important than for most OECD economies – growth in, and the effectiveness of, capital accumulation might explain the recent slowdown in growth. Several studies have stressed its importance to the growth of the Portuguese economy. Pereira and Andraz (2005) suggested that, from the 1960s onwards, public works and public infrastructures had a positive impact in the economy not only because of their positive rates of return but also because of their positive effect on private investment (the so-called crowding-in

5 From an Agrarian Society to a Knowledge Economy? The Rising Importance...

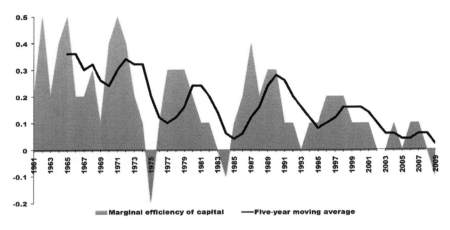

Fig. 5.9 Marginal efficiency of capital, 1960–2009 (Source: AMECO and authors' calculations)

effect). Moreover, it provided positive externalities on private investment. They also found that capital accumulation in infrastructures had significant dynamic effects on the economy. Pina and St. Aubyn (2005) noted that between 1960 and 2005, public investment yielded greater profitability in terms of economic growth than either private or human capital investment. Afonso and St. Aubyn (2009) reached similar conclusions, whilst Freitas (2005) confirmed that capital accumulation was crucial to Portugal's economic growth.

Nevertheless, researchers are not at one in praising the importance of public investment for the performance of the Portuguese economy. Afonso and Sousa (2011), using quarterly data from 1977 until 2008, found contradictory evidence about the role of public investment and public expenditure. They showed that it had a negative impact on private investment and consumption.

Evidence on the role of capital accumulation is not, at first sight, clear-cut. It may hold true only for the recent past but not for earlier decades. Data on the marginal efficiency of capital seem to support the notion that the law of diminishing returns, in some form, applies to the accumulation of capital and might operate in Portugal. As Fig. 5.9 reveals, the marginal efficiency of capital has been steadily declining over the years and, in the last decade or so, has been very near to zero.

That returns on the accumulation of capital may have fallen in recent decades has been suggested in other studies. Freitas (2005) presented new time series data on the evolution in capital stock. Freitas (2005) showed that the average productivity of capital decreased substantially since the 1960s. Furthermore, Jalles and Pereira (2010) reported that whilst the marginal efficiency of capital certainly contributed to economic growth since the 1960s, there was evidence aplenty to support the hypothesis of decreasing returns to capital accumulation in more recent times.

Still, this interpretation does not command consensus. Pereira and Andraz (2005) took the view that substantial dynamic and long-run effects on investment, especially of the public variety, were still present. Despite evidence that purports to support the thesis of declining returns to capital accumulation, Freitas (2005) argued that capital accumulation in Portugal had not been 'excessive' since, by the year 2000, the economy still showed a capital-to-labour ratio that was only 0.64 of its American version and as such, far less than the difference seen in other European economies – for instance, Ireland at 0.94, Spain at 0.91 and even Greece with 1.2.

All in all, whilst research literature seems to support the view that since the 1950s, capital accumulation had an important role in economic growth for Portugal, whether capital accumulation has reached the point of diminishing returns – or not – remains unresolved. Studies showed that diminishing returns to capital accumulation might have had some effect on the slowdown of the past decade, but the data are not wholly conclusive. Further clarification will need more empirical evidence.

Turning to the question of human capital, research demonstrated that it became increasingly important as a source of economic growth in Portugal. As far as we are aware, no study has yet suggested that decreasing returns to the accumulation of human capital in Portugal might be significant. In fact, as the section "From Agriculture to a Knowledge Economy?" will show, Portugal, compared to other OECD countries, still lags considerably on most indicators relating to human capital. Yet, as Table 5.3 indicated, human capital seems to be replacing physical capital as the principal source of growth in the economy. The section "From Agriculture to a Knowledge Economy?" addresses this question in greater detail.

Summing Up

Several factors lie behind the pronounced slowdown in the Portuguese economy since 1974 and apply, more specifically, to the economic stagnation of the past decade. Sagging productivity, a difficult adjustment to the euro and lower returns to the accumulation of capital all seem to have had their part in the stagnation that has set in since 2000. Over the past few years, economic policy may well have exacerbated the structural problems in the Portuguese economy by being overly procyclical and too expansionary (Lopes 2004) and by being unable to tackle the main brakes on the economic slowdown (Pereira 2009, 2010). In truth, economic policy has been singularly ineffective in combating the fall in productivity, for, as we have seen, the latter seems to have been the major factor in the steady fall-off in economic growth since the mid-1990s at the very latest.

Human capital has gradually increased its importance for output growth in Portugal. Capital deepening and total factor productivity were crucial during the phase of industrialisation. Since 1974, however, human capital has become an important source of growth. There still remains a substantial gap between Portugal and most of its European partners in terms of the quality and quantity of human capital. The option for Portugal to invest more in the knowledge-based and knowledge-intensive sector as a means of boosting its productivity is well worth pursuing further. This issue will be examined in the following section.

From Agriculture to a Knowledge Economy?

The disappointing performance of Portugal's economy over the past decade suggests that a return to productivity growth is a necessary prior condition for achieving higher rates of economic growth and thus a rise in the standard of living. Since a strong link exists between productivity and both quality and quantity of human capital, investing in a knowledge-based economy might be an appropriate strategy to bring Portugal's stagnation to an end and improve the country's rate of economic growth. Here, attention focuses on the question whether the Nation's economy is moving from a post-agrarian society onwards and towards a knowledge economy. This is a crucial matter. Potentially, important productivity gains can be obtained from a knowledge-based economy, as other OECD countries seem to show. As was argued earlier, between the 1950s and the end of the twentieth century, Portugal evolved successfully from an agrarian economy to an economy dominated by the industrial and the services sector, a transition that was one of the principal reasons for rapid productivity growth during the period. Can Portugal replicate this experience in its drive towards a knowledge economy? Can a knowledge economy help raise the country's export competitiveness? These questions are addressed in this section by looking at the technological content of Portuguese exports and by analysing the main human capital indicators in a cross-country perspective.

The Technological Content of Exports

In the twentieth century, the make-up and content of Portuguese exports changed considerably as structural changes in the economy moved ahead. Early in the twentieth century, Portuguese exports were chiefly primary products and re-exports of colonial products. Changing from an agrarian society to an industrial- and service-based economy involved significant change in the composition of exports. As Fig. 5.10 shows, industrialisation and the opening up of the economy following Portugal's entry to EFTA spurred on an extraordinary rise in the exports of textiles, clothing and shoes, as well as investment goods, such as machines. The specialisation of exports progressed even further in the years immediately before and following Portugal's joining the European Economic Community; at the same time, the relative importance of goods with lower technological content, as well as primary products in total exports, fell.

Increased specialisation was stimulated further by a significant rise in the market share these products won on international markets. Amador and Cabral (2008) estimated that between 1977 and 1986, the market share of Portuguese exports increased by 5.6% and by a further 3.8% between 1987 and 1991, with an additional 2.5% for the years 1992–1995. From the mid-1990s onward, textiles, clothing and shoes saw their relative importance in the country's total exports' fall. In part, this rollback stemmed from the loss in market share of Portuguese exports, reckoned between 1997 and 2006 to be about 2.4% (Amador and Cabral 2008).

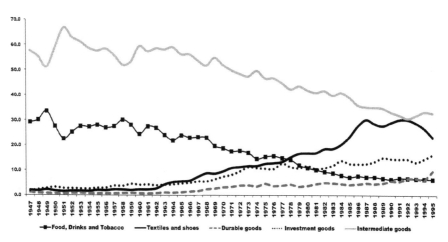

Fig. 5.10 Main exports by type of product as % of total exports, 1947–1995 (Source: Alves et al. (Eds.) (2009))

If the composition of Portuguese exports is examined over the past two decades, some interesting changes occurred in their technological content. From the mid-1990s, they became less 'traditional'. They were no longer goods with low value added that drew on the intense use of unskilled labour. Rather, they began incorporating more medium and medium-high technologies, such as rubber and plastic products, machinery and electrical equipment, motor vehicles and chemical products, particularly in the case of industrial exports, as can be seen in Table 5.5, which sets out the sector's share of all industrial exports. The technological element in exports rose. Exports based on high- and medium-high technology currently account for about 40% of all manufactured products (Cabral 2008). Conversely over the same period, the share of exports with low-technology input fell. Even so, this positive development does not necessarily imply that Portugal's crossover to a knowledge economy has taken place or that it is successful. Two considerations impel caution. First, statistics about the technological content in exports cover manufactured products only. They omit such important exports as services. Whilst the service sector includes companies commanding a high degree of entrepreneurship and innovation, especially in information and communications technologies, the part of this sector in the economy has not, over the past decade, grown markedly. The share of information and communications technologies in gross fixed capital formation remained fairly constant over the last 15 years (Pereira 2010). Second, Table 5.5 shows that the technological content of Portuguese exports appears to have moved from low-tech to medium-tech products, but not necessarily on to high-tech goods. Between 2001 and 2008, the share of medium and medium-low technology in total exports rose from 13.5% to 23.7% of all manufactured exports. On the same base, the share of low-tech exports declined from 45% to 34% of all manufactured exports (Pereira 2009). Though the level of technological input

Table 5.5 Sector share in total industrial exports

	1990	2000	2006
High tech	5.56	9.19	14.6
Pharmaceutical products	0.63	1.15	2.28
Clerical equipment and computers	0.64	0.36	3.76
Radio, TV and communication equipment	3.68	6.77	7.87
Medical, optical and precision instruments	0.61	0.81	0.7
Medium-high tech	21.5	32.12	30.73
Machinery and electrical equipment	4.07	7.17	3.47
Motor vehicles, tows and semi-trailers	7.44	14.43	15.05
Chemical products, except pharmaceuticals	5.61	4.58	6.29
Railroad equipment and transport equipment	0.20	0.38	0.52
Machinery and equipment (non-electrical)	4.18	5.56	5.4
Medium-low tech	10.1	12.84	20.41
Construction and naval repair	0.55	0.26	0.24
Rubber and plastic products	1.39	2.79	4.23
Oil refining, petrochemical and nuclear fuels	0.08	0.8	2.58
Non-metallic mineral products	4.48	3.66	5.11
Metallurgy	1.26	2.53	4.42
Production of metallic products (machinery and equipment)	2.35	2.8	3.83
Low tech	62.44	44.82	34.26
Other manufactures and recycling	2.16	2.15	2.97
Paper pulp, paper, paperboard and printing industry	6.4	5.6	2.51
Foodstuffs, beverages and tobacco	6.61	6.23	8.21
Textiles, apparel, leather and footwear	40.61	25.94	16.37
Wood and cork and wood products	6.67	4.91	4.2

Cabral (2008)

apparently increased since the 1990s, Portugal does not seem as yet to have crossed over to a high-productivity, high-value-added knowledge economy.

Though the pointers towards the improving technological content of Portuguese exports are encouraging, data also show that the step up the quality ladder has been rather towards medium and medium-low technologies, and not the high-tech sectors, usually associated with a knowledge economy.

That said, successful technological adoption goes hand in hand with improvements in human capital (Easterlin 1996; Lipsey et al. 2005; Stoneman 1995). Both export competitiveness and the technological content of its exports could be improved if Portugal is able to improve considerably its human capital. Key to this is the evolution over recent decades in certain indicators of human capital. This, and the role of human capital in constructing a knowledge economy in Portugal, is pursued below.

The Role of Education for a Knowledge Society

Despite considerable investment in both the quantity and quality dimensions of human capital that democratic governments have made since 1974, Portugal is still subject to significant shortcomings in its education when set against other OECD countries. In part, the persistence of low levels of educational provision in Portugal can be seen in the legacy of the past. Portugal has lagged on most education indicators, literacy and enrolment rates, since the nineteenth century at least (Chaps. 2–4). In 1870, for instance, primary school enrolments in Portugal were around 13.4% of the relevant age cohort, lower by far than the average for other Southern European countries (30.4%), below Eastern Europe (16.9%) and considerably behind the European core (61.8%) (Benavot and Riddle, 1988) (Chap. 2); Portugal continued to trail behind other European countries. By 1940, the Nation's primary school enrolment had risen to 28.6%, still substantially below the European core (73%), Eastern Europe (50.9%) and even Southern Europe (54%) (Benavot and Riddle 1988). Literacy rates were much lower in Portugal than in most other European countries (Reis 2004).

Though indicators of the state of Portuguese education improved, particularly enrolment and literacy rates, the gap between Portugal and the other Western European countries moved apart during most of the period from 1926 until 1974, when Portugal was under the grip of Dictatorship. The regime did not attribute much value to education as an important source of growth (Amaral 2005). In 1950, around 46% of the Portuguese population aged 15 years and over were unschooled. Only 20% completed primary education (see Table 5.6). Some progress was made. By the late 1960s, universal primary schooling was finally attained (Amaral 2005) some decades after the European core. Even so, by the end of the *Estado Novo*, one third of all the Portuguese were illiterate, one third of those aged 15 or older had full primary education, 3% had completed secondary education and a residual 0.6% had undergone university education (Amaral 2005).

In sharp and deliberate contrast, democratic governments devoted substantial public resources, both in absolute terms and in percentage of GDP, to education in an attempt to catch up with Europe. Between 1974 and 2000, public expenditure on education rose from 1.8% of GDP to about 3.7% in 1980 and to 6.9% GDP in 1999 (Lopes 2005). This unprecedented effort to improve the country's human capital was reflected both in literacy rates and in the average years of schooling. In Table 5.6, illiteracy rates – that is, the percentage of population with no schooling – fell from around 30% of the population in 1975 to 8% in 2010.

The average years spent in school steadily rose, almost doubling from 4.7 years in 1974 to 8.26 years in 2010. The numbers of those reaching upper secondary and tertiary education grew substantially since the return of democracy and tripled since 1975.

Such an improvement in human capital was an important factor in explaining Portugal's growth performance from the mid-1970s onwards. However, substantial evidence suggests that improvement in the absolute levels of education did not necessarily translate into a marked closing of the educational gap with other European and OECD countries (Alves et al. (Eds.) 2009). First, as the OECD's PISA inquiries show, the quality of Portuguese education was low (OECD 2010). Portuguese students had amongst the lowest PISA scores of all countries in math, science and reading (OECD 2004, 2007, 2010). Second, Portuguese education is not overly efficient.

Table 5.6 Average years of schooling in Portugal, 1950–2010

Year	No schooling	Primary Total	Primary Completed	Secondary Total	Secondary Completed	Tertiary Total	Tertiary Completed	Average years of schooling	Population (1,000s)
		(% of population aged 15 and over)							
1950	46.1	49.5	20.3	3.4	1.9	0.9	0.4	2.656	5,927
1955	42.3	52.5	22.6	4.2	2.2	1	0.5	2.911	6,142
1960	38.1	55.9	25.5	4.9	2.4	1.1	0.5	3.207	6,276
1965	39	53.3	30.4	6.3	2.9	1.4	0.6	3.471	6,387
1970	37.8	53.3	35.7	7.4	3.2	1.4	0.6	3.778	6,184
1975	29.7	55.7	40.1	11.9	4.9	2.7	1	4.709	6,554
1980	21.9	58.7	44.8	15.9	6.3	3.5	1.3	5.53	7,231
1985	16.9	58.8	46.3	18.4	7.4	6	2.2	6.212	7,657
1990	13	57.7	47	21.3	8.5	7.9	2.9	6.784	7,948
1995	11.8	54.2	45.6	25.5	10.4	8.4	2.9	7.16	8,253
2000	10.4	49.7	43	29.8	12.5	10.1	3.4	7.647	8,567
2005	12.8	46.2	41	31	13.4	10.1	3.3	7.583	8,826
2010	8	43.9	39.9	37.3	16.7	10.8	3.3	8.26	9,043

Source: Barro and Lee (2010)

Table 5.7 Average years of schooling, all levels, 2010

	All levels	Secondary	Tertiary
Bulgaria	9.838	2.132	0.528
Czech Rep.	12.137	3.377	0.318
Estonia	11.805	4.982	0.850
Finland	9.987	3.513	0.700
France	10.533	5.234	0.593
Germany	11.825	7.439	0.573
Greece	10.677	3.903	0.924
Holland	11.023	4.512	0.738
Hungary	11.651	3.424	0.578
Ireland	11.646	3.757	0.984
Italy	9.875	4.839	0.336
Poland	9.872	2.084	0.488
Portugal	8.259	2.578	0.282
Romania	10.527	3.426	0.388
Slovakia	11.161	3.028	0.373
Slovenia	8.912	2.452	0.476
Spain	10.382	4.293	0.778
Sweden	11.571	4.959	0.756
United Kingdom	9.752	3.183	0.766

Source: Barro and Lee (2010)

As a percentage of its GDP, the country spends more than the OECD average and gets a lower return from it (OECD 2006; Pereira 2009). Third, the school dropout rate remains very high, greater than that of other OECD countries, with the exception of Mexico and Turkey.

The latest figures from the Barro–Lee international dataset on average years of schooling bear out the presence of several shortcomings in the formation of human capital in Portugal. Table 5.7 shows that, on average, Portugal has the lowest number of years spent in school at all levels and in the whole European Union. Similarly, Portugal has one of the lowest rates in the average of years spent in secondary schooling – better than only Bulgaria, Poland and Slovenia – and the lowest average of years spent in university education in the whole European Union.

In effect, the relative gap between Portugal and the most advanced countries in Europe stayed at the same level over recent decades. In assessing the gap in average schooling, Fig. 5.11 compares Portugal with five advanced economies (France, Germany, Italy, the Netherlands and the UK), which constitute the European core. It plots the relative distance between the average years spent in schooling for the European core countries with its counterpart in Portugal for all levels of education, for secondary and tertiary. Since the return of democracy, the differences in average years of school narrowed significantly. However, despite resources invested in the education sector, the relative gap between Portugal and the European core over the last two to three decades remained virtually constant.

Thus, considerable expansion and major investment in education were not enough to *reduce* the relative gap between Portugal and the European core, at least to average of years schooling spent in school.

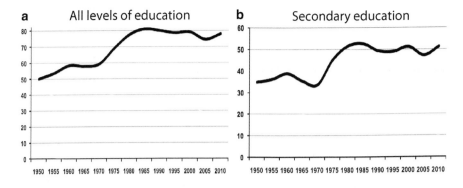
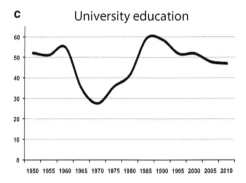

Fig. 5.11 Average schooling years in Portugal relative to European core (European core = 100) (**a**) All levels of education (**b**) Secondary education (**c**) University education (Source: Calculated from Barro and Lee 2010)

In face of improvement in the absolute levels of education, Portugal still lags a considerable education lag vis-à-vis most OECD economies. For these reasons, and given the technological content of Portuguese exports, we take the view that at this stage, given the evidence on which we have relied upon, Portugal has not made the shift over to a knowledge economy – yet.

Conclusion

Though the Portuguese economy has been successful in moving on from an agrarian society to an industrial-based economy, it has been less successful in changing over to a knowledge-based economy. Despite substantial improvement since the return to democracy, improvements that showed up in several educational indicators, the relative gap in educational progress between Portugal and the European core countries is large and, over the last few years, has remained relatively unchanged.

This is disconcerting and has several implications for policy. First, since human capital has been the most important source of growth in the Portuguese economy after 1974, that Portugal has not been able to close the human capital gap vis-à-vis the European countries we used here as a benchmark could hold future growth back. Second, Portugal needs to improve the effectiveness of its education provision and the quality of education and to explore more assiduously the markets for education (Amaral et al. 2004) (Chap. 10). Third, improvement to its human capital and a faster transition to the knowledge economy may turn out to be important factors for recovering growth in productivity, and, following this, for economic growth to begin again. Portuguese data show a strong correlation between growth not only in labour productivity and but also in total factor productivity. The slowing down in growth seems to be strongly associated with a drop in the latter component. Since there are significant interactions between human capital and gains in productivity, a more rapid thrust towards the knowledge economy will, in all likelihood, be instrumental for improving the performance of Portugal's economy in the near future.

Notes

1. 1960s was also a period of high emigration (Baganha 1994).
2. Economic growth is smoothed by the Hodrick–Prescott (HP) filter, which removes short-run fluctuations and extracts the long-term trend in growth.
3. These broad tendencies of Portuguese economy are also corroborated by a recent study (Jalles and Pereira 2010), in which the trend in the growth of the Portuguese economy was estimated by using the Basic Structural model and a corresponding Kalman filter.
4. As before, the data are smoothed by the Hodrick–Prescott filter.
5. Data on labour were obtained from National Institute of Statistics labour force statistics, data on capital accumulation were from Lains (2003a) and Freitas (2005), whilst human capital growth is measured as the average years of schooling of the active population.
6. Nominal cost includes inflation. Real costs do not include inflation; they are, in short, deflated.

References

Afonso, O. (1999). *Contributo do Comércio Externo para o Crescimento Económico Português, 1960–1993*. Lisbon: Conselho Económico e Social.

Afonso, A., & St. Aubyn, M. (2009). Macroeconomic rates of return of public and private investment: Crowding-in and crowding-out effects. *The Manchester School, 77*(Supplement 2009), 21–39.

Afonso, A., & Sousa, R. M. (2011). The macroeconomic effects of fiscal policy in Portugal: A Bayesian SVAR analysis http://ideas.repec.org/a/spr/portec/v10y2011i1p61-82.html, *Portuguese Economic Journal* http://ideas.repec.org/s/spr/portec.html, *10*(1), 61–82.

Alexandre, F., Bação, P., Cerejeira, J., & Portela, M. (2009). Aggregate and sector-specific exchange rate indexes for the Portuguese economy. Estudos do Grupo de Estudos Monetários e Financeiros, No. 5.

Alves, N., Centeno, M. e Leal, A. C. (Eds.). (2009). *A economia portuguesa no Contexto da Integração Económica, Financeira e Monetária*. Lisbon: Banco de Portugal.

5 From an Agrarian Society to a Knowledge Economy? The Rising Importance...

Amador, J., & Cabral, S. (2008). The Portuguese export performance in perspective: A constant market share analysis. *Banco de Portugal Economic Bulletin*, Autumn pp. 201–221.

Amaral, L. (2002). *How a country catches up. Explaining economic growth in Portugal in the postwar period*. Unpublished PhD dissertation, European University Institute, Florence.

Amaral, L. (2005). O trabalho. In P. Lains & A. Álvaro Ferreira da Silva (Eds.), *História Económica de Portugal, 1700–2000* (Vol. III). Lisbon: Instituto de Ciências Sociais.

Amaral, A., Rosa, M. J., & Teixeira, P. (2004). Is there a market in Portuguese higher education. In A. Amaral, D. Dill, B. Jongbloed, & P. Teixeira (Eds.), *Markets in higher education*. Dordrecht: Kluwer.

Baganha, M. I. (1994). As correntes migratórias portuguesas no século XX e o seu impacto na economia nacional. *Análise Social, 29*(4), 959–980.

Barro, RJ., & Lee, JW. (2010). A new data set of educational attainment in the world, 1950–2010 (NBER Working Paper 15902) (data are available at www.barrolee.com).

Barros, P. P., & Garoupa, N. (1996). Portugal-European Union convergence: Some evidence. *European Journal of Political Economy, 12*, 545–553.

Benavot, A., & Riddle, P. (1988). The expansion of primary education, 1870–1940: Trends and issues. *Sociology of Education, 61*(3), 191–210.

Bento, V. (2009). *Perceber a Crise para Encontrar o Caminho*. Lisbon: Bnomics.

Blanchard, O. (2007). The difficult case of *Portugal*. *Portuguese Economic Journal, 6*(1 April), 1–21.

Bourguignon, F., & Christian Morrisson, C. (2002). Inequality among World Citizens: 1820–1992. *The American Economic Review, 92*(4), 727–744.

Cabral, S. (2004). Recent evolution of Portuguese export market shares in the European Union. *Banco de Portugal Economic Bulletin*, December: 79–91.

Cabral, M. (2008). *Export diversification and technological improvement: Recent trends in the Portuguese economy* (GEE Papers no 6). Gabinete de Estratégia e Estudos, Ministério da Economia.

Crafts, N., & Toniolo, G. (1996). Post-war growth: An overview. In N. Crafts & G. Toniolo (Eds.), *Economic growth in Europe since 1945*. Cambridge: Cambridge University Press.

Crafts, N., & van Ark, B. (Eds.). (1996). *Quantitative aspects of post-war European economic growth*. Cambridge: Cambridge University Press.

de Freitas, M. L. (2005). O capital. In A. Álvaro Ferreira da Silva (Ed.), *História Económica de Portugal, 1700–2000* (Vol. III). Lisbon: Instituto de Ciências Sociais.

Easterlin, R. (1996). *Growth triumphant*. Ann Arbor: University of Michigan Press.

Eichengreen, B. (2007). The breakup of the Euro area (NBER Working Paper No. 13393).

Jalles, J. T., & Alvaro Santos Pereira, A. (2010). *The great Portuguese decline: Assessing Portugal's extraordinary reversal of fortunes, 1900–2010*, mimeo.

Lains, P. (2003a). *Os Progressos do Atraso*. Lisbon: Instituto de Ciências Sociais.

Lains, P. (2003b). Catching up to the European core: Portuguese economic growth, 1910–1990. *Explorations in Economic History, 40*, 369–386.

Lains, P. (2007). Growth in a protected environment: Portugal, 1850–1950. *Research in Economic History, 24*, 121–163.

Lains, P. (2008). The http://www.ics.ul.pt/corpocientifico/plains/pdf/2006-01/growth_in_a_protected_environment.pdf. Portuguese economy in the Irish mirror, 1960–2002. *Open Economies Review, 19*(5), 667–683.

Levine, R., & e Renelt, D. (1992). A sensitivity analysis of cross-country growth regressions. *American Economic Review, 82*, 942–963.

Lipsey, R., Carlaw, K., & Bekar, C. (2005). *Economic transformations: General purpose technologies and long-term economic growth*. Oxford: Oxford University Press.

Lopes, J. S. (2004). *A economia portuguesa no século XX*. Lisboa: Imprensa de Ciências Sociais.

Maddison, A. (2003). *The world economy: Historical statistics*. Paris: OECD.

Mateus, A. (1998). *Economia Portuguesa. Crescimento no Contexto Internacional (1910–1998)*. Lisbon: Verbo.

Mateus, A. (2005). A tecnologia. In P. Lains & A. F. da Silva (Eds.), *História Económica de Portugal, 1700–2000* (Vol. III) O Século. Lisbon: Imprensa de Ciências Sociais.

Neves, J. César das (1994). *The Portuguese economy: A picture in figures. XIX and XX centuries.* Lisbon: Universidade Católica Editora.

OECD. (2004). *Learning for tomorrow's world. First results from PISA 2003.* Paris: OECD.

OECD. (2007). *PISA 2006 science competencies for tomorrow's world.* Paris: OECD.

OECD. (2010). *PISA 2009 results: Executive summary.* Paris: OECD.

Pereira, A. S. (2009). *O Medo do Insucesso Nacional.* Lisboa: Esfera dos Livros.

Pereira, A. S. (2010). *The return of Portuguese emigration: Net migratory flows and the balance of payments, 1850–2009*, mimeo.

Pereira, A. S. (2011). *Portugal na Hora da Verdade. O que Fazer para Vencer a Crise Nacional.* Lisboa: Gradiva.

Pereira, A. M., & Andraz, J. M. (2005). Public investment in transportation infrastructure and economic performance in Portugal http://ideas.repec.org/a/bla/rdevec/v9y2005i2p177-196.html, *Review of Development Economics* http://ideas.repec.org/s/bla/rdevec.html, 9(2), 177–196.

Pina, Á., & St. Aubyn, M. (2005). Comparing macroeconomic returns on human and public capital: An empirical analysis of the Portuguese case (1960–2001). *Journal of Policy Modelling, 27*(5), 585–598.

Reis, J. (2004). Human capital and industrialization: The case of a late comer, Portugal, 1890. In J. Lungbjerg (Eds.), *Technology and human capital in historical perspective* (pp. 22–48). Basingstoke: Palgrave Macmillan.

Stoneman, P. (Ed.). (1995). *Handbook of the economics of innovation and technological change.* Oxford: Wiley-Blackwell.

Young, A. (1995). The tyranny of numbers. Confronting the statistical realities of the East Asian growth experience. *Quarterly Journal of Economics, 110*, 641–80.

Part II
Shaping Higher Learning

Chapter 6
From University to Diversity: The Making of Portuguese Higher Education

Ana Nunes de Almeida and Maria Manuel Vieira

Introduction

Today, Portuguese higher education differs radically from those features that distinguished it a mere four decades back. It has acquired new dimensions and a new public. It has been regionalised. The barriers of exclusivity that surrounded the 'classical' university have been overturned and a wide range of students admitted. It has also become more diversified, adding a new polytechnic sector alongside the existing university. For the public, private higher education is now available in certain academic fields (Chap. 13). The student body was quickly feminised, thereby standing its traditional masculine predominance on its head and revealing academic excellence amongst female students as well as their over-representation at undergraduate level. In its recruitment, higher education became more diverse admitting students of all ages, social backgrounds, even working professionals. Such trends went hand in hand with growing internationalisation, which encouraged mobility in both scientific and academic fields. If the sum of such a dynamic is not in itself new – the same is happening in the rest of Europe – the fact remains that it constitutes an eloquent change in the Portuguese setting, which earlier had been marked by considerable modesty in its educational achievements[1] (Chaps. 4, 12 and 13).

In this chapter, the origin and the development of the dual system in Portuguese higher education are explored. The outlines of its different subsystems are set out, and the main evolutionary tendencies of the last few decades analysed. To do this, a dual perspective was used. On the one hand, an internal and descriptive look at its institutional structure was combined, on the other, with an outside perspective of the higher education system, looking into the background and the contexts into which it

---

A.N. de Almeida (✉) • M.M. Vieira
Instituto de Ciências Sociais, University of Lisbon, Av Prof. Aníbal
de Bettencourt 9, 1600-189 Lisbon, Portugal
e-mail: ana.nunes.almeida@ics.ul.pt; mmfonseca@ics.ul.pt

was sited. The chapter starts by identifying the main themes and the outcomes achieved during the period of democratic consolidation in Portugal. Subsequently, it goes on to single out and characterise the dimensions that against a European backdrop pinpoint the specificities of Portuguese higher education. The final reflections enclose this discourse, sustained by the available empirical evidence of the themes discussed.

From Simple to Complex: Diversification in Portuguese Higher Education

The origins of the binary system in Portugal's higher education go back to the 1970s when an ambitious reform – the so-called 'Veiga Simão Reform' – was outlined. It was part of a broad ranging plan to accelerate modernisation and to open up the education system from basic school through to higher education (Vieira 2001). Higher Education, at that time, was highly restricted (Nunes 1969) (Chap. 7, 9 and 13). Mainly public and largely non-fee-paying, only 3% of young people aged between 20 and 24 years attended school in the 1960s (Almeida and Vieira 2006). Of all students enrolled, only 4% came from working class families (Machete 1969) (Graph 6.1).

In response to this situation, a significant re-dimensioning of the education system was set in hand in the public sector. It gave rise to a binary system, which focused on drawing in and advancing the educational profile of a broader student body with very different educational and social backgrounds. The new system included, on one hand, short-cycle higher education with a predominantly vocational character, which focused on the transition of students to the employment market, an emphasis held to be more attractive for students from less well-off backgrounds, whilst on the other hand, maintaining a *university* perspective that is, training with a strong theoretical bias, grounded on a long cycle, a format traditionally preferred by better-off students. Decentralising the supply of higher education, previously concentrated in three centres – Lisbon, Porto and Coimbra – completed this new model, the purpose of which was to make higher education both available to students in their region and to speed up the dynamics of regional development. Thus, the availability of higher education was determined by the pressing needs of the local economy. The political change of 1974 brought this reform to a halt, though the binary concept of higher education that underpinned the abortive reform was to endure up to the present.

The transition to democracy in April 1974, and the promise it held out, raised social aspirations. Hopes for social equality and for education were particularly high, and received solid expression in the large numbers of students registering in higher education establishments in that year. Pressure of demand forced the authorities to seek solutions to relieve it, not least because the majority of student demand – 96% in 1976 – lay in the public sector. At the height of the Democratic Revolution, a 'civic service for students' was put in place for students in their last year of high school. Lasting 1 year, it sought to put students in direct contact with members of the

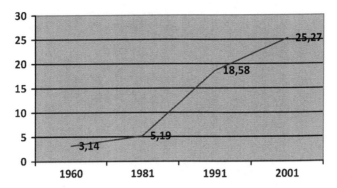

Graph 6.1 Participation rates of young people aged between 20 and 24 years in higher education (%) (Source: Adapted from Alves 2008: 251. Reprinted by permission of the publisher)

working class, and very especially in respect of those professional and vocational fields the individual student would take up at the university (Oliveira 2004). Such an arrangement was seen as a means either to confirm – or alternatively, orient students away from – the university before embarking on their first year studies at the university. Its failure, after no more than 2 years, spurred on the quest for other solutions to the problem of admission to higher education. The creation of a *numerus clausus*, that is a system restricting the number of places available in each faculty, was introduced as an experiment in 1976–1977 and applied to all degrees the year following. In effect, access to higher education was determined by the grade the individual applicant achieved and by the number of places available in each institution. Here was a solution, which put a damper on the high hopes that rested on education. Classified according to the grades awarded by a national competitive examination at secondary school meant that access to places in higher education was, effectively, rationed and with it the very real possibility that applicants were either excluded from higher education or faced being placed in a degree programme or a higher education institution they had not chosen (MCTES 2007).

Even though the education system had become massified, grade competition took firm root and was particularly intense in secondary education. Success, however, was not unrelated to a well-grounded preparation in the early years of an individual's school career. On the other hand – and especially so in the metropolitan area of Lisbon and, at a certain extent, Porto as well – a competitive market at school level was present within the region. Several institutions of higher education competed with one another to attract students, especially the best (Chap. 4).

The imbalance between supply and demand since then has been a permanent feature in access to higher education. Despite progressive decentralisation (between the years 1974 and 1983, eight new public regional universities were founded, as well as a network of polytechnic institutes and a limited number of private and cooperative institutions – both university and polytechnic) the truth remained that the oldest universities and the more prestigeful ones enjoyed the preference of

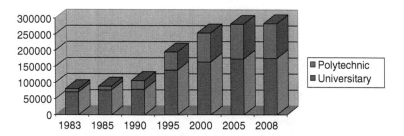

Graph 6.2 Students registered in public higher education: universities and polytechnics (Source: INE (National Institute of Statistics), 'Statistics of Education', Lisbon MCTES, 'Registered in higher education by educational subsystems', Lisbon)

students coming from the urban coastal strip and from privileged homes (Chaps. 4 and 12). On the other hand, within the public sector of higher education, consolidating the polytechnic subsystem took far longer than it did for the university subsystem.

During the 1980s, despite the growing number of places available in higher education, the number of applicants largely outstripped them. By the end of the decade, the number of students seeking access to higher education was two and a half times more than the places on offer (Vieira 1995). For those successful, the majority found that the place assigned to them did not correspond to their first choice, a situation of which the least that can be said is that it raised frustration, if it did not actively compromise success in earning a degree.

These points are interesting since they also form the basis of the argument used by the adepts of private initiative in higher education, once the political and ideological obstacles that largely invalidated it in the 1970s lost their strength (Chap. 13). Over the decade from 1980 to 1990, the number of students enrolled in the private sector of higher education grew from 9% to 28% of total student enrolments and reached a peak of 36% in 1996 (Graph 6.2).[2] The modest social standing of this subsystem, in part because of its recency, in part because of its ambiguous academic and pedagogical credibility, made it a species of fallback for students failing to get a place in the public sector rather than being their first choice. Even at the apogee of its popularity, for the majority of its students, private higher education was not their first choice which would otherwise have been a public establishment, even though many were in fact following the course they wanted (Balsa 2001). Evidence from the two main metropolitan urban areas, where the majority of students are recruited, suggests that private universities restrict themselves to degrees broadly similar to those in public universities, mainly in fields less demanding in equipment and in infrastructure, such as Social Sciences, Management, Economics and Law (Chap. 13) (Graph 6.3).

Rather than offering an innovating alternative to the public sector, the private sector set itself up as a replica of its public counterpart, and for this reason is

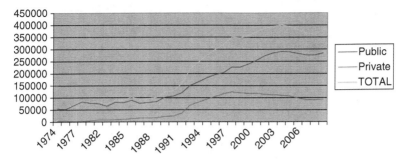

Graph 6.3 Students enrolled in public and private higher education, 1974–2008 (Source: INE (National Institute of Statistics), 'Statistics of Education', Lisbon (1974 to 1997); MCTES 'Enrolled in Higher Education by subsystems' (1998–2008))

vulnerable to shifts in demand. In effect, from the late 1990s, the plateauing out in the numbers of applicants to higher education, plus the increasing vacancies in the public sector, brought about a fall of the number of students enrolled in private universities and even the closing of certain amongst them – a fate the polytechnic subsystem escaped.

Fragmentation, Diversification and Opacity

Today, higher education offers more degrees and boasts more institutions than ever before, rising from 34 educational institutions in 1964 to 291 in 2007. New institutions were brought together in self-standing units, distributed across the length and breadth of the whole country, thereby ensuring easier access to higher education for locally based students. The upshot of this development has been the fragmentation in the private and cooperative subsector of the self-standing – so-called 'organic' – units – mainly within polytechnic establishments – a situation that stands in marked contrast with the high degree of regional concentration evident in the public subsector (Fig. 6.1).

Clearly more dynamic from the perspective both of research and of academic excellence, academic staff in the public university subsystem stands at the peak in the hierarchy of qualifications held. In 2007, 64% of academic staff in public universities held a PhD degree as against 15% of their counterparts in public polytechnics (MCTES 2009b). Such a 'qualifications gap' between academic staff in universities and polytechnics has an important bearing on the decisions of the most ambitious students as to which establishment they shall apply (Balsa 2001; Fernandes 2001).

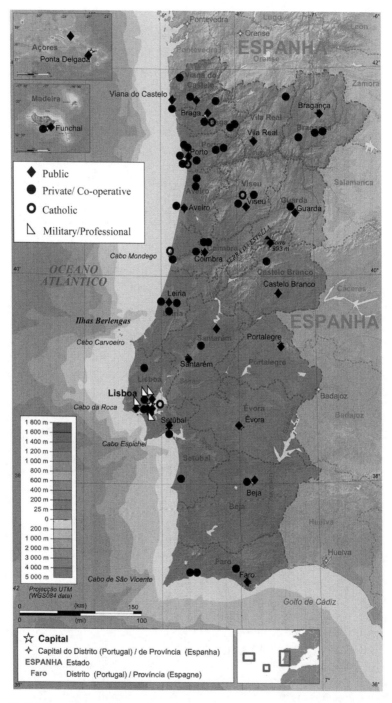

Fig. 6.1 Higher education in Portugal in 2007 Universities and polytechnics (public and private) Public Private/ Co-operative Catholic Military/Professional (Source: Adapted from Costa and Lopes 2008: 110. Reprinted by permission of the publisher)

This is not to say that the supply of public sector higher education is restricted. Despite being strongly concentrated in the coastal regions, public higher education covers the whole country and, in 2008, enrolled 75% of the student population. Even if supply is strongly grouped around the two main metropolitan areas of Lisbon and Porto, the hegemony of the coastal strip is offset and balanced out by the spatial location of polytechnic education, which from North to South, from Braga to Lisbon (Costa and Lopes 2008), fulfils its regional engagement (Leão 2007).

Overall, higher education today caters for ten times more students than it did 30 years ago – around 373,000 compared to 39,000 in 1970 – in truth, an 'educational explosion'. Today, one in every four young people aged between 20 and 24 attends higher education (see Graph 6.1). This speedy 'catching up' with traditionally 'more educated' countries unveils a very rapid drive onwards towards higher training, which took place within the space of one generation (Grácio 2000).

From the year 2000, however, the numbers of new students entering directly from secondary schools have dropped, as have birth rates. This situation, at least at the first stage of its onset, is compensated by the significant growth in the numbers of post-graduate students – one of the consequences of the Bologna Treaty – that rose from 25,000 in 1997 to 50,000 in 2007. It was also boosted by the move towards higher education of adults already in working life and aged 23 years or more. These 'new students', in the year 2007–2008, represented 14% of all entering higher education institutions, though they tended to be concentrated mainly in private institutions, and rather less in public polytechnics.

Abiding Cleavages

Yet, this dual process, on the one hand of 'opening up' and on the other of massification, took place against a social landscape marked by persistent fault lines and cleavages (Chap. 12). Despite the generalisation of access to higher education, the fact remains that the possibility for different social groups to place their children in higher education is still far from being equal. If the year 2004 is taken to illustrate these social disparities, highly qualified professionals have eight times more probability of their offspring attending higher education than do industrial workers (Mauritti and Martins 2007).

Furthermore, the process of massification itself took place against a backdrop marked by cleavages that, within this dual-faceted system of higher education, worked within a setting itself highly favourable to replicating and perpetuating social reproduction. To be sure, generalisation of access to higher education alters long-established hierarchies of prestige associated with higher studies. Yet, social and educational differentiation based solely on the length of study time has not entirely disappeared. Rather, it tends to take on new patterns of hierarchisation based on the type of degree and on the particular institution.

Leaving aside for the moment such internal differences between disciplinary domains or educational fields, the most prestigious university degrees are still taken up by students from families of privileged socioeconomic status – 61% of students in public education come from the middle and upper middle class ('businessmen, leaders and the liberal professions', 'technical professionals and vocational professionals') compared with only 29% of students from working class or lower middle class ('clerical support workers' and 'service and sales workers'); 41% are from families with a first degree.

When the social background to recruiting for polytechnic degrees is examined, clearly it is broader, with an over-representation of students from socially disadvantaged milieux: 41% are children of 'industrial workers' and of 'manual workers'; 63% of the families of origin have not gone beyond basic education (Martins et al. 2005; Mauritti and Martins 2007). The academic trajectory of polytechnic students tends to involve a lower performance level than university students. Such a profile allows us to grasp how economic factors – regional proximity and reduced expenses that such proximity may imply – as well as academic considerations – lower entrance grades, for instance – influence candidates to apply to polytechnics (Balsa 2001).

Against such a differentiated social landscape, private provision represents yet another opportunity for access to higher education – especially for students of privileged social backgrounds, thereby extending the imbalances mentioned above. In fact, despite a profile very similar to students in public universities – 43% of students in private higher education have parents holding a first degree – private higher education students are weaker in academic performance, which translates into a higher failure rate in high school and in lower average grades when entering higher education (Cruz et al. 1992; Balsa 2001).

These distinct social profiles are amplified by the increasingly internationalised nature of academia. Recognised as a valuable educational experience, internationalisation of careers in academia, of contacts and learning takes on a stronger relevance still when placed against the globalisation of education and research systems. It opens up further options for those who embark on such paths. Furthermore, the direct building up of international partnerships between higher education institutions became a key strategy in stating one's claim to standing and excellence in the world of international competition in academia (Chap. 8). Diversity and quality, which such partnerships engender, are amongst the main criteria in the academic hierarchisation and differentiation between higher education institutions. Those establishments with few international ties are relegated to lower positions in the rankings of prestige and standing.

Earlier, it was pointed out that other forms of social reproduction were emerging, which worked in favour of perpetuating, though often by different means, those social and cultural cleavages long in place in Portuguese society. The drive to internationalisation may well work to the same effect. The student population – both public and private – is highly cosmopolitan. Three times more university students have had experience of education abroad and in all forms – a study period at a foreign university or college, an internship, language course or similar – compared to polytechnic students (Martins et al. 2005). In the polytechnic sector, the very inequalities that characterise the panorama of Portuguese society are equally visible (Costa et al. 2007), giving rise to differences in the opportunity to have access to mobility programmes. In Europe, and taking the Erasmus Programme as indicator,

Portugal ranks amongst such countries as Bulgaria, Greece, Romania, Slovenia, Spain and Turkey, where the economic factor is crucial in whether to apply for a place on the programme (Otero and McCoshan 2006).

Portuguese higher education is then socially diversified and built around academic hierarchy.

Backstage: The Social Construction of Educational Inequalities

As has already been suggested, the explosion in higher education is inseparable from the massification of access to education at basic and secondary levels. In turn, this was also the outcome of strong and effective investment via the public sector in democratising the school system since 1974. It was also a result of a new and intense demand for education by families in their daily quest to improve their children's educational lot. The vertiginous drop in the Portuguese birth rate since the second half of the 1970s is a pointer to this watershed, which went hand in glove with a new notion of childhood and infancy, and their relationship to schooling (Graph 6.4).

The idea of the child as a small adult, working for the family from an early age because physically able, and thus, quite literally, just passing through school, contradictory though it is, has not entirely vanished. Yet, Portuguese families rapidly moved on to an ideal of childhood, more modern in concept.

The practice of multiple offspring yielded before the notion of a planned and chosen child within a partnership or as an individual's choice. The environment of socialisation was no longer the workplace but rather the school, where the child was one amongst others of the same age range, where, together, all learn, in a pedagogical relationship with teachers, acquire technical knowledge and moral judgments that will accompany them as adults, wholly integrated into a society where school is increasingly a necessary requirement to enter the job market as well as a vehicle of social mobility. It is therefore the child's, and then the youngster's responsibility, to develop the 'job of studying'. As an individual, achieving autonomy, relative to the adult, whilst simultaneously being in major part dependent on parents for both affection and support *sensu lato,* stands as the obverse of massification's medal. It is also one of the more powerful incentives in limiting the birth rate that makes such benefits possible.

That school became mandatory and universal did not mean that all children and young people who went through it do so in the same way. Whether the starting point is more – or less – favourable is heavily influenced by the level of parental educational capital, which in turn is a powerful force in shaping unequal educational trajectories – some longer or shorter, some more successful than others, and which lead on to institutions of greater or lesser standing, all of which build up those profiles that are reflected in differential access to higher education. From a very early age and within an increasingly diversified and hierarchical school system,

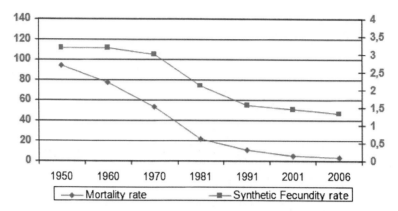

Graph 6.4 Infant mortality rate (per 1000) and synthetic fertility index (num.), Portugal, 1950, 2006–2007 (Source: INE, demographic indicators; adapted from Barreto 2000. Reprinted by permission of the publisher)

privileged families plan out strategies of success for their children: the careful choice of school or even the particular grade subdivision class; participation in extracurricular activities or leisure activities with an educational value; support for the child's performance at school – alternatively, at home or through a tutor (Almeida 2005). These are examples of parental mobilisation. In the bigger picture, the destinies of these children continuously diverge from those hailing from less favoured families.

Today, the impact of social background emerges less in access to higher education, which in effect is open to every potential candidate, so much as in the type of entry into higher education and at what level. Families that can draw on precise and wide-ranging information create a solid basis of support for the young person's decisions: choice between subsystems, institutions – their standing, reputation and ranking in the academic, social and employment stakes – or between degrees more or less prestigious. Choice becomes more precise and focused than those based on less informed, tentative options without family backing – a situation typical for youngsters from families traditionally excluded from higher education. Families with substantial educational capital are clearly over-represented amongst students with better grades in higher education institutions and who consequently enter the most selective degree courses – Medicine and Health and some of the Fine Arts degrees. Individual merit, attested through national entry examinations to higher education, is strongly tied in with family and social structures.

Since 2003, the University of Lisbon gathered systematic information on its students' profiles, which may serve to illustrate these processes (Almeida 2009a, b, c, d; Curado and Machado 2006). Its different organic units, which cover different degrees, bring together students with very different social and family origins and trajectories (Graph 6.5):

6 From University to Diversity: The Making of Portuguese Higher Education

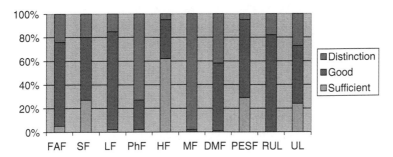

Graph 6.5 Entry grades by faculty, 2008–2009 (%). *FAF* Fine Arts Faculty; *SF* Science Faculty; *LF* Law Faculty; *PhF* Pharmacy Faculty; *HF* Humanities Faculty; *MF* Medical Faculty; *DMF* Dental Medicine Faculty; *PESF* Psychology and Educational Sciences Faculty; *RUL* Rectoate of the University of Lisbon (Health Sciences Degree) (Source: ALMEIDA, Ana Nunes de (2009). OPEST – Observatory of Students' Paths/RUL – Rectorate of the University of Lisbon. Reprinted by permission of the publisher)

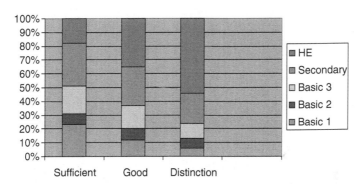

Graph 6.6 Mother's education level by student's entrance grade 2008–2009 (%) (Source: ALMEIDA, Ana Nunes de (2009: 120). OPEST – Observatory of Students' Paths/RUL – Rectorate of the University of Lisbon. Reprinted by permission of the publisher)

In 2008–2009 – but also part of a regular pattern in recent years – entry grades of first year students in the first cycle were distributed in a pattern statistically significant across the different faculties. The grade of 'Sufficient' (≤135/200) was over-represented in the Humanities and in a lesser degree in Sciences, Psychology and Educational Sciences. 'Good' grades (136–165/200) were clearly represented in the Law faculty and in the Fine Arts faculty, in the course of Health Science and, again, in Psychology and Educational Sciences. 'Distinction' grade (≥166/200), the pathway leading to a real academic elite, formed the strong majority of students in Medicine, was significant in the Pharmacy faculty and, in some degree, in the Faculty of Dental Medicine. Which social strata lie behind these particular results?

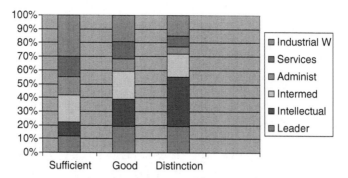

Graph 6.7 Father's occupation (past or present) by student's entrance grade 2008–2009 (%). *Leader* Leader positions and higher ranks; *Intellectual* Intellectual professionals; *Intermed* Technicians and Intermediate positions; *Admnist* Administrative workers; *Services* Services and Salesmen; *Industrial W* Farmers, fishermen, industrial workers and non-qualified workers (Source: ALMEIDA, Ana Nunes de (2009: 121). OPEST – Observatory of Students' Paths/RUL – Rectorate of the University of Lisbon. Reprinted by permission of the publisher)

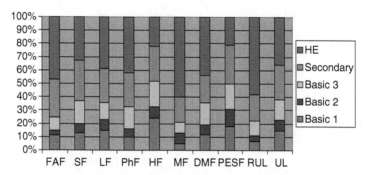

Graph 6.8 Mother's education level by faculty of entry: first year students, 2008–2009 (%). *FAF* Fine Arts Faculty; *SF* Science Faculty; *LF* Law Faculty; *PhF* Pharmacy Faculty; *HF* Humanities Faculty; *MF* Medical Faculty; *DMF* Dental Medicine Faculty; *PESF* Psychology and Educational Sciences Faculty; *RUL* Rectorate of the University of Lisbon (Health Sciences Degree) (Source: ALMEIDA, Ana Nunes de (2009: 97). OPEST – Observatory of Students' Paths/RUL – Rectorate of the University of Lisbon. Reprinted by permission of the publisher)

Graphs 6.6–6.9 set out results that were statistically significant after controlling for such variables as: mother's education level, father's occupation and student's entry grade in the national examination for admission to higher education. The percentage of mothers with higher education dropped drastically between students with Distinction (53.8%) and those with Sufficient (18.4%). At the same time, the proportion of mothers with basic education grew with respect to those two grades – from 23.6% to 51%. Likewise, fathers in 'leader positions and higher ranks' and especially 'intellectual professionals', two of the highest occupational categories, were over-represented in the case of students with Distinction (54.4%). Students

6 From University to Diversity: The Making of Portuguese Higher Education

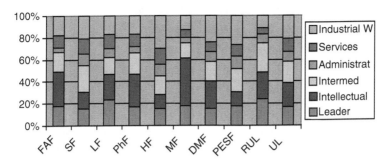

Graph 6.9 Father's occupation by faculty of first year students, 2008–2009 (%). *Leader* Leader positions and higher ranks; *Intellectual* Intellectual professionals; *Intermed* Technicians and Intermediate positions; *Admnist* Administrative workers; *Services* Services and Sales men; *Industrial W* Farmers, fishermen, industrial workers and non-qualified workers (Source: ALMEIDA, Ana Nunes de (2009: 99). OPEST – Observatory of Students' Paths/RUL – Rectorate of the University of Lisbon. Reprinted by permission of the publisher)

graded as 'Sufficient' were predominant amongst the less qualified occupational categories: 'administrative workers', 'services and salesmen' and 'farmers, fishermen, industrial workers and non-qualified workers' (57.6%). Clearly, the socioeconomic background of students' families played a decisive role in shaping their academic pathways, and through that the creation of internal diversity within higher education.

Turning to the final data set on diversity, the graphs below show the relationship between mother's level of education and father's occupation for the first year student population at the University of Lisbon to be statistically significant. The different degrees cater for highly diverse social strata. Highly competitive degrees, which demand a high entrance grade (Medicine, Health Sciences or Fine Art), are attended in the main by the 'heirs' of families traditionally having higher education degrees – as well as the presence of parents with high professional standing ('leader positions and higher ranks', 'intellectual and scientific professionals'). On the contrary and at the other end of the continuum are faculties such as the Humanities, Psychology and Educational Sciences, which are distinguished by low levels of the mother's education – more than 50% did not attend high school – and the non-qualified occupations of the fathers – 'administrative workers, services, salesman, industrial workers'. This generation was the first to enter higher education, which earlier had no part in their family history.

The structure of higher education in Portugal, as in the remainder of the countries in Europe, is a product of the formal and internal dynamics in the education system, shaped through political decisions or institutional logic. It is also a result of investment and external appropriation made by social strata and families for whom school is an instrument for the distinction and preservation of privileged positions, or serves as a point of access to new positions in the social structure and as a channel of mobility to them.

Singularity in Plurality – Portuguese Higher Education in the European Landscape

By comparison with Northern and Central European countries, Portugal caught up late with modern demography – and with educational modernity (Europeia 2000). Modernisation came through different groups in different regions and at different times (Chap. 4). Since then, change proceeded at a very brisk pace giving rise to the hybrid and complex features found in its present condition. Stories and accounts cross at different times, some distant, others less so but all layered atop one another within the universes of practice and representation.

In fact, indicators and statistical averages that relate to the contemporary population in Portugal hide contrasting generations from the standpoint of their education level (Chap. 12). In the course of 30 years, Portugal rushed through developmental stages far faster than other countries (Grácio 2000). Evidence for this claim is plain. Portugal, with 18% of enrolments in tertiary education – graduate and post-graduate degrees alike – as a percentage of all students, tops the average in Europe of the 27, which stands at 16.4% (Eurostat 2007).

This singular characteristic of Portuguese education has several consequences, which are reflected in the upper levels of the education system. First, there is the issue of the characteristics of the students enrolled and the buildup of a particularly wide gap between the education level reached by different generations (Mauritti 2002; Estanque and Bebiano 2007). We will begin with the first level, that is basic education.

The educational *explosion* that reflected the opening up of access to higher education from 1974 raised to this level of the education system swathes of a population by tradition non-educated. There is, in short, a 'double pattern of student recruitment' (Machado et al. 2003) of which the University of Lisbon is, as was shown above, a remarkable example. The 'double pattern' is to be seen in a socially selected group – effectively, the majority – for which an undergraduate degree ensured and reproduced a privileged position, joined by a new wave of newcomers to higher education caught in a process of rising mobility. The diversity in origins and trajectories in the school population is clearly accentuated.

Data between 2005 and 2008 from *Eurostudent* pointed out the marked underrepresentation of students from disadvantaged socio-economic backgrounds in the higher education systems of Europe. The Portuguese case was particularly clear: 'children from blue collar backgrounds are extremely under represented at institutions of higher education in Germany, Austria, France and Portugal'. In fact, when the weight of the 'working class' parents of Portuguese students in higher education is compared to the weight of the same status in the male population of the corresponding age group, the percentage grows from 19% to 40% (Eurostudent Report 2005: 60). And likewise with mothers: 'the findings confirm the unbalanced chances for children from different social origins to the disadvantage of blue collar families' (Eurostudent Report 2005: 63).

Social barriers, it seems, may be easily overcome in countries like Ireland, Finland and Spain. The situation is identical with reference to educational background.

In Portuguese higher education, the proportion of students' fathers with an undergraduate degree stands at 29% (against 5% of the whole male population in the same age group). When the analysis turns to the mothers of students, the percentages are 28% and 6%, respectively. These values place Portugal as the lead country in terms of social selectivity, insofar as it is coterminous with this indicator.

Other characteristics distinguish Portuguese students from their European colleagues. Portuguese students are younger – an average of 22 years old, 22.4 for men and 21.7 for woman – due to the fact that they are full-time and exclusively students who proceeded directly from secondary school to higher education. Alternative pathways in parallel to full- or part-time jobs or leading to late entry into higher education – for example, after time spent on the job market or following a gap between leaving school and entering higher education – remain relatively rare in Portugal.

Eurostudent data from 2005 bears this situation out. Work experience prior to entering higher education involved 19% of Portuguese students – amongst the lower figures for the countries under scrutiny – by contrast to 64% in Germany, 45% in Latvia and 42% in Finland, for example. Furthermore, student employment during term time was minimal in Portugal – 20% against 91% for the Netherlands, 68% for Ireland, 67% for Austria, 66% for Germany and 65% for Finland. Even neighbouring Spain with 49% of students working in term time outdistanced Portugal on this indicator. Despite exceptions for some degree courses – Art, Humanities and Educational degrees, for example – and the considerable level of work experience before entry to polytechnics – 24% compared to 14% for the university – there is a clear dissociation between school and work in Portugal.

Also related to the age profile of Portuguese students is the low percentage of those married – 4.7% – or with children – 4.5%. In what seems to be a characteristic of southern Europe, the vast majority (55%) lives with its parents in what Machado Pais (2001) termed a 'welfare family' regime, which he saw as a positive benefit.

Several factors may explain such a pattern. Besides the argument that highlights the importance of family values in Portuguese culture, one should mention: tight family budgets, reduced offer for the student population in the house rental market, few possibilities for part-time employment, inexistent state support for the independence of young people. This latter point merits further development empirically, since it serves to underline the very considerable variation in patterns of student support across different countries. Independence is not simply a matter of individual will or family culture. It is also a condition that public policy may – or may not – make available to young people. The table below sets out on one hand the level of state aid and on the other the average monthly support allowance in a selected number of European countries. There is a clear alignment with the situation set out in Table 6.1: the higher the state aid, the more frequent the student's independence. In Portugal, the family is the major source of financial support for the living expenses of students in higher education to the tune of three times the level of support from the state, work or other sources (Cerdeira 2009; Mauritti et al. 2005) (Table 6.2).

Table 6.1 Students living with parents/relatives (%)

Italy	76
Spain	69
Portugal	55
France	42
Latvia	38
The Netherlands	37
Ireland	35
Austria	24
Germany	23
United Kingdom	22
Finland	5

Source: Martins et al. 2005; Eurostudent 2005 – National profiles: 70. Reprinted by permission of the publisher

Table 6.2 State aid for all students

Country	State assistance rate (%)	Average monthly allowance for recipients, in euros
UK	85	694
Finland	71	427
The Netherlands	62	342
Ireland	31	317
Austria	27	343
Portugal	24	49
Germany	23	352
Spain	23	134
Italy	9	159

Source: Martins et al. 2005; Eurostudent 2005 – National profiles, p. 70. Reprinted by permission of the publisher

Thus, the belated democratisation of Portuguese higher education tends to have maintained a certain traditional student profile: young, single, living with the family, entirely given over to study and who does it full time. For the vast majority, study and work, study and having a family are mutually exclusive.

The 'Inheritors', those for whom there is a tradition of higher education study in the family, re-knit the experience of their parents. They enjoy an element of continuity, whereas others face an element of dissociation between the generations. As for the first generation of newcomers to the educational system, educational mobilisation by their families imparts a new centrality to schooling just as it casts other sideline work activities aside, as threatening the success of its commitment to their children's education.

For many parents, this unwavering focus on their children's education as a way to shape social mobility demands considerable financial effort, given the lack of state support. Yet, it was precisely this heavy investment in their children's education that in the space of a generation altered the Portuguese educational landscape

Table 6.3 Cultural background of HE students and mother's education level (%)

	Elementary (%)	Upper secondary (%)	Higher education (%)	Total
Level of education of the HE students' mothers	52.6	15.6	31.8	100.0
Level of education of the Portuguese populationn (40–60 years)	81.3	8.9	9.8	100.0

Source: CIES-ISCTE, Eurostudent 2005, in Martins et al. (2005: 38). Reprinted by permission of the publisher

out of all recognition. Even if, from a cultural standpoint, students in higher education form a select part of the population, the distance travelled between the two generations is remarkable. Today, no less than 68% students in higher education have gone beyond the level of education reached by their mothers (Table 6.3).

This accelerated change, which stands in contrast to the low education level of the Portuguese adult population, drives a very wide gap indeed between the generations, a situation liable to provoke misunderstanding between parents and children over such matters as values and life chances, or even to cause the inter-generational transmission of culture to break up. Yet, such differences can also serve to urge parents to go back to school and thus bring about an unusual mobilisation of the less-educated adult population towards the opportunities schooling holds out. Most recent data on the popularity of adult education seem to confirm this trend.

Early Feminisation of Higher Education

Another specificity of Portuguese higher education is its early feminisation. Even though the presence of the first female students in Portuguese universities goes back to the end of the nineteenth century (Soares 1985a, b), it was sporadic and largely an exception to the male majority. Quitting school – frequently associated with marriage – appears to be a structural characteristic amongst the female university population at that time. It also took place at the same time as the prolongation in study duration amongst their male counterparts.

It was in the course of the 1960s that the drive of women into higher education became unstoppable. In 10 years, female participation grew from 29.5% in 1960 to reach 44.4% by the end of the decade. Growth followed on a considerable opening up, at the level of social representation, of education for women – a movement driven forwards through the growth of women and girls in secondary education. With male conscription reaching new heights with the colonial wars in Africa,[3] new job openings developed in the job market for women undergraduates. However, only a few could effectively link higher education with their future. For all that, the 1960s *boom* served merely to extend the pattern of socially restrictive recruitment to higher education to the female population. For female students, their social origins, as research pointed out at the time, were exactly the same as their male fellows.

During the 1980s, the 'tipping point' when the number of women students surpassed the number of male students in Portugal was reached. Against a broader European backdrop, Portugal, together with France, was the first country to achieve this point (CE 2000). Iceland, Sweden and Norway reached their 'tipping point' in 1985. With a few years delay, countries such as Denmark, Spain, Italy, Finland and, more recently, Ireland, Luxemburg and the UK attained this condition.

Today, this shift is a characteristic shared by most western countries – the dominance of the numbers of women in higher education has become a permanent feature.

After decades of camouflaged and limited access to the higher level of education, female students have moved massively into higher education, largely on account of their success in high school in the form of better grades than their male peers (Grácio 1997; Ribeiro 2007). Compared to male students, females are more likely to complete their studies – a characteristic that holds good irrespective of the particular sector or subsystem in higher education in which they enrol (MCTES 2009a, b, c, d; OCES 2007).

Specificity of Portuguese higher education relies not only on having girls in the majority of the student population. Female students not only arrived earlier in higher education. They also moved earlier into certain disciplinary fields, usually considered as 'masculine' preserves. Not only was the first degree course coordinated in 1894 by a woman to be in Mathematics. During the twentieth century, female undergraduates in Sciences, Pharmacy and Medicine were common, these disciplines being exceeded only by the Humanities in the subject choice made by the limited numbers of female graduates admitted by Portuguese universities (Soares 1985a, b).

During the 1960s, some questions were posed about the motives underlying the subject choice of women, especially those opting for courses in the Science faculties, second in popularity only to the Humanities. The reason was clear, however. Science degrees led to careers in teacher training at secondary school level (Nunes 1968), a career path deemed better suited to female than to male ambitions. Over the past half century, this trend has continued to grow. In doing so, not only did it confirm Portugal's status as 'early developer'. It raised female participation in all fields to an even higher level in such disciplines as Education, Humanities and Arts, Social Sciences, Business and Law, Science, Mathematics and Computer Science, Engineering (industrial and construction), Agriculture and Veterinary Science, Health and Welfare services, than the European average. It was a trend particularly evident in fields such as Science, Mathematics and Computers, where, in 2004, Portuguese female students were well above the average gender balance for Europe of the 27, which stood at 37.5%, as against 49.2% for Portugal (Eurostat 2007).

Undergraduate Degrees: Relative Phenomenon, Promised Benefits

Portugal's delay in opening up access to higher education brought additional features in its wake. The rarity of these degrees – and here it must be born in mind that in the European Union of the 15, Portugal had the lowest rate of undergraduate students in higher education (Mauritti and Martins 2007) – endowed their holders with symbolic advantage as well as the promise of economic reward. In the 1990s, and across Europe, debate about the job market for first-degree holders waxed hot (Alves 2007). It was as much a subject for social concern – as was the role of measuring the quality of higher education (Chap. 10). To this debate, Portugal remained aloof. The relatively low numbers of undergraduates in the Portuguese population, combined with a period of economic prosperity and growth in the service sector, kept such concerns at a distance and upheld the optimistic expectations that were associated with obtaining a degree. Indeed, data gathered during that decade proved the reasons for optimism to be well founded (Chap. 13). Between the years 1982 and 1993, salary differentials between first-degree holders and non-undergraduate certificate holders rose significantly (Gracio 1997). For many attending higher education, the conferment of an undergraduate degree represented not only a better level of job on the labour market by dint of being better qualified. It opened the door to better-off and more privileged social circles. It also led on to rewarding posts.

Only recently has the problem of employment for undergraduate degree holders arisen in Portugal. From 2001 onwards saw a steady rise in unemployment amongst degree holders (Gonçalves 2005). Cutbacks in the public sector, traditionally responsible for taking on significant numbers of the newly graduated, plus a striking degree of economic instability in the private sector over the last few years saw the employment of such professionals shrink or, at the very least, a new feeling of vulnerability amongst them. Even if unemployment is on the upturn, it remains more frequent still amongst those with lower levels of education. And as for the precariousness of work contracts, it is far from being exclusively a problem for undergraduate degree holders. It affects all categories in the labour force (Alves 2007).

Nevertheless, the value of a university degree has depreciated. At the onset of the 1990s, a recent graduate earned three times as much as a person without a degree who entered the job market at the same moment. By 2002, this advantage dropped to 1.7 times as much (Escaria, quoted in Alves 2008). Yet, higher education is still a profitable economic investment. Portugal, in what appears to be a genuine exception in the European context, continues to pay higher salaries to employees with an undergraduate degree (Alves 2000, 2005, 2008) – something that may perhaps be explained by the rareness in the number of cases involved.

Against this backdrop which in general remains positive, there are certainly differences in the rewards undergraduates from different subsectors and subsystems in Portuguese higher education enjoy. Though very little research has been done on this area, still it has singled out some very interesting tendencies. First, studying in the public sector carried more guarantees of employment than studying in the private sector. This was the conclusion reached by research on the insertion of recent undergraduates from both higher education sectors into the job market. It covered the 5 years following their concluding their studies. It showed clearly higher rates of unemployment amongst students with an undergraduate degree from a private higher education institution (ODES, quoted in Alves 2007). As in the case of other European countries with a binary system of higher education – for instance, France, Germany and, until 18 years ago, UK – so in Portugal: transition to working life is more difficult for undergraduates from polytechnics than for their colleagues in university (Alves 2007).

Conclusion

Over the last few decades, Portuguese higher education has expanded – an expansion that yielded remarkable growth, both in the number of new institutions and in the numbers of students. Growth took shape in a strong tendency towards specialisation in the internal structure of higher education, both in supply and provision, split between universities, polytechnics, private and public institutions, and demand, expressed through the different types of school population that applied. Growth was to hand as well in the geographical distribution of higher education. The coastal regions have not lost their weight. They are rather being balanced by the presence of polytechnics in the inland regions of the country. The higher education system is now larger and more complex, following on what seems to be a dynamic adjustment to the construction, in different dimensions and at different rhythms, of a late but fast modernising society.

A deep understanding of the movements and forces in society is, therefore, indispensable to understand the forms assumed by the structure of the higher education system. In this change, a new representation of children and youngsters was ushered in and played out. Such a new depiction was definitely and exclusively linked to the educational condition of children and young people, just as it was to their role as students. Through the younger generation, families create and, from an early age, put strategies in hand to gain access to the highest levels of the education system. In particular, such strategies are made easier and more successful in families possessing a higher level of education, with better knowledge to understand an increasingly complex field, families who may bring their own educational experience and their complicity with it to build up strategies for access. Today, despite increasing openness in the Portuguese higher education system and in its more prestigious and selective sectors especially so, these latter draw in the 'heirs' and 'inheritors', the sons – and daughters – of well-educated and high-status parents, with school trajectories of excellence. On the contrary, students with less-favoured social background concentrate mainly in the polytechnic sector and in less demanding degrees. Whilst internal diversity of the higher education system is one of its main characteristics, this internal diversity, as has been argued throughout this chapter, is not randomly organised.

Compared to other European countries, the Portuguese higher education system presents distinctive characteristics. First, it operates a very steep social selectivity in its access and most of all in the modality of access. The probability of entering the most demanding degrees and institutions for students from less-favoured social origins is notoriously inferior to that of youngsters from a privileged socioeconomic background. Second, Portuguese students follow a relatively traditional profile. Most are dependent residentially and financially on their parents and are committed full-time to their studies. Access to higher education is determined in the setting of secondary school and is rarely combined with other experience, be it work, marriage or parenthood. Third, the massive advance of women into higher education and polytechnics, their distinctive presence in degrees that demand excellence in school or in traditionally masculine degrees – such as the Natural Sciences – count amongst the other specific characteristics of the Portuguese higher education system.

Finally, and despite disparities amongst subsystems, degrees awarded by Portuguese higher education institutions serve as a strong instrument for employability and as a facilitating factor along the path to better rewards and salaries. The gap between undergraduates and non-undergraduates remains noteworthy.

These recent tendencies in Portuguese higher education pose important challenges for the future. First of all, the steep fall in fecundity, confirmed over the last decade, will affect the dynamics of the quest by young people for education – for now, and provisionally postponed by the recent raising of the school leaving age until secondary education, may, for some, provide an extension to their studies. Linked to this is the push to open higher education in universities and polytechnics to older age groups, who seek to improve their education to strengthen their employability, to acquire new skills through re-conversion and/or to meet demands for mobility to ensure future employment.

Demographic pressure will force the strengthening of the education network – both in terms of the regional distribution of supply and, in organisational terms, through promoting institutional partnerships or even mergers between academic institutions. Such adjustments might also come about as a result of raising scientific standards, itself a possible outcome of disseminating international models of quality evaluation and of inserting Portuguese higher education into the globalised ethic of competitiveness.

Given that scientific, scholarly and educational internationalisation is the goal of education policies at the European level, strengthening state-based financial support for students in higher education – especially the less favoured – may be hoped for together with support necessary for the international mobility of students. Without such support, the risk remains of exacerbating the social inequalities, present today in Portugal's system of higher education.

Notes

1. In 2001, the Portuguese Census showed only 12% of the Portuguese population aged between 25 and 64 had an undergraduate diploma (Mauritti et al. 2005). The EU (15) average was, at that time, 22%.
2. See Graph 6.2.
3. The war in the former Portuguese colonies in Africa (mainly Guinea-Bissau, Angola and Mozambique) lasted throughout the 1960s until 1974, with the independence of the colonies following the return of democracy to Portugal.

References

Almeida, A. N. de (2005). O que as famílias fazem à escola… pistas para um debate. *Análise Social, 176*, 579–593.
Almeida, A. N. de (2009a). *O sucesso escolar na Universidade de Lisboa, 2007–2008. Quadros-Resumo (Relatório)*. Lisboa: OPEST/Reitoria da Universidade de Lisboa.

Almeida, A. N. de (2009b). *Os estudantes à entrada, Universidade de Lisboa, 2008–2009. (Relatório).* Lisboa: OPEST/Reitoria da Universidade de Lisboa.

Almeida, A. N. de (2009c). *À entrada: os estudantes da Universidade de Lisboa, 2003–2008. Números e figuras. (Relatório).* Lisboa: OPEST/Reitoria da Universidade de Lisboa.

Almeida, A. N. de (2009d). *Estudantes da Universidade de Lisboa. Imagens do quotidiano escolar a partir dos "Inquéritos à satisfação" (Relatório).* Lisboa: OPEST/Reitoria da Universidade de Lisboa.

Almeida, A. N., & Vieira, M. M. de (2006). *À entrada: um retrato sociográfico dos estudantes inscritos no 1º ano.* Lisboa: Reitoria da Universidade de Lisboa.

Alves, N. (2000). *Trajectórias académicas e de inserção profissional dos licenciados 1994–1998.* Lisboa: Universidade de Lisboa.

Alves, M. G. (2007). *A inserção profissional de diplomados de ensino superior numa perspectiva educativa: o caso da Faculdade de Ciências e Tecnologia.* Lisboa: Fundação Calouste Gulbenkian.

Alves, N. (2005). *Trajectórias académicas e de inserção profissional dos licenciados pela Universidade de Lisboa: 1999–2003.* Lisboa: Universidade de Lisboa.

Alves, N. (2008). *Juventudes e inserção profissional.* Lisboa: Educa.

Balsa, C. (2001). *Perfil dos estudantes do ensino superior.* Lisboa: CEOS.

Barretto, A. (2000). *A situação social em Portugal. 1960–1999* (Vol. II). Lisboa: Imprensa de Ciências Sociais.

Cerdeira, L. (2009). *O Financiamento do Ensino Superior Português. A partilha de custos* (dissertação de doutoramento em Ciências da Educação, Faculdade de Psicologia e Ciências da Educação, Lisboa).

Costa, A. F., Machado, F. L., & Almeida, J. F. (2007). Classes sociais e recursos educativos: uma análise transnacional. In A. F. Costa, F. L. Machado, & P. Avila (Eds.), *Portugal no Contexto Europeu* (Sociedade e conhecimento, Vol. II). Lisboa: CIES-ISCTE, Celta.

Costa, A. F., & Lopes, I. T. (Eds.). (2008). *Os Estudantes e os seus trajectos no ensino superior: sucesso e insucesso, factores e processos, promoção de boas práticas.* Lisboa: CIES.

Cruz, M. B., Cruzeiro, M. E., Leandro, M. E., & Mathias, N. (1992). *A PGA e os estudantes ingressados no ensino superior.* Lisboa: ICS.

Curado, A. P., & Machado, J. (2005). *Factores de sucesso e insucesso escolar na Universidade de Lisboa.* Lisboa: Reitoria da Universidade de Lisboa.

Curado, A. P., & Machado, J. (2006). *Estudo sobre o abandono.* Lisboa: Reitoria da Universidade de Lisboa.

Estanque, E., & Bebiano, R. (2007). *Do activismo à indiferença. Movimentos estudantis em Coimbra.* Lisboa: Imprensa de Ciências Sociais.

Fernandes, A. T. (Ed.) (2001). *Estudantes do ensino superior no Porto – representações e práticas culturais.* Porto: Afrontamento.

Gonçalves, C. (2005). Evoluções recentes do desemprego em Portugal. *Sociologia, 15*, 125–163.

Gracio, S. (1997). *Dinâmicas da escolarização e das oportunidades individuais.* Lisboa: Educa.

Gracio, S. (2000). Educação e Emprego: reflexões suscitadas pela Semana da Educação. In *Educação, formação e trabalho. Debates Presidência da República* (pp. 129–137). Lisboa: Imprensa Nacional Casa da Moeda.

Leao, M. T. (2007). *O ensino superior politécnico em Portugal. Um paradigma de formação alternativo.* Porto: Edições Afrontamento.

Machado, F. L., Costa, A. F., Mauritti, R., Martins, S. C., Casanova, J. L., & Almeida, J. F. (2003). Classes sociais e estudantes universitários: origens, oportunidades e orientações. *Revista Crítica de Ciências Sociais, 66*, 45–80.

Machete, R. (1969). A origem social dos estudantes portugueses. In A. S. Nunes (Ed.), *A Universidade na vida portuguesa* (Vol. I, pp. 213–224). Lisboa: Gabinete de Investigações Sociais.

Martins, S., Mauritti, R., & Costa, A. F. (2005). *Condições socioeconómicas dos estudantes do ensino superior em Portugal.* Lisboa: Direcção-Geral do Ensino Superior, Ministério da Ciência, Tecnologia e Ensino Superior.

Mauritti, R. (2002). Padrões de vida dos estudantes universitários nos processos de transição para a vida adulta. *Sociologia – problemas e práticas, 39*, 85–116.
Mauritti, R., & Martins, S. (2007). Estudantes do ensino superior: contextos e origens sociais. In A. F. Costa, F. L. Machado, & P. Avila (Eds.), *Portugal no Contexto Europeu, Vol. II, Sociedade e Conhecimento*. Lisboa: CIES-ISCTE Celta Editora.
Nunes, A. S. (1968). A população universitária portuguesa: uma análise preliminar. *Análise Social, I*(22–23–24), 295–385.
Nunes, A. S. (Ed.). (1969). *A Universidade na vida portuguesa* (Vol. 1). Lisboa: GIS.
Oliveira, L. T. (2004). *Estudantes e povo na Revolução. O serviço cívico estudantil (1974–1977)*. Oeiras: Celta.
Otero, M.S., & McCoshan, A. (2006). *Survey of the socio-economic background of Erasmus students. DG EAC 01/05. Final report*. Birmingham: Ecotec.
Pais, J. M. (2001). *Ganchos, tachos e biscates Jovens, trabalho e futuro*. Porto: Âmbar.
Ribeiro, A. M. (2007). A vantagem escolar das raparigas no secundário: resultados escolares e identidades juvenis numa perspectiva de género. In M. M. Vieira (Ed.), *Escola, jovens e media*. Lisboa: Imprensa de Ciências Sociais.
Soares, A. J. (1985a). *Saudades de Coimbra. 1901–1916*. Coimbra: Almedina.
Soares, A. J. (1985b). *Saudades de Coimbra. 1917–1933*. Coimbra: Almedina.
Vieira, M. M. (1995). Transformação recente do campo do ensino superior. *Análise Social, 131*(132), 315–373.
Vieira, M. M. (2001). Ensino superior e modernidade. *Forum Sociológico, 5/6*, 169–184.
Vieira, M. M. (2007). Recém-chegados à universidade: entre constrangimentos sociais e projectos individuais. In M. M. Vieira (Ed.), *Escola, jovens e media*. Lisboa: Imprensa de Ciências Sociais.

Primary Sources

Europeia, C. (2000). *Os números chave da educação na Europa*. Luxemburgo: Serviço das Publicações Oficiais das Comunidades Europeias.
Eurostat. (2007). *Key data on higher education in Europe 2007 edition*. Luxembourg: Office for Official Publications of the European Communities.
Eurostudent. (2005). *Social and economic conditions of student life in Europe*. Hannover: HIS Hochschul-Informations-System. http://www.his.de/Eurostudent/report2005.pdf.
INE. *Educational statistics*. Lisboa: Instituto Nacional de Estatística.
MCTES. (2007). *Acesso ao ensino superior*. www.acessoensinosuperior.pt.
MCTES. (2009a). *Inscritos em cursos do Ensino Superior por estabelecimento, no ano lectivo de 2008/09*. Lisboa: Gabinete de Planeamento, Estratégia, Avaliação e Relações Internacionais.
MCTES. (2009b). *Docentes do ensino superior (2001 a 2007)*. Lisboa: Gabinete de Planeamento, Estratégia, Avaliação e Relações Internacionais.
MCTES. (2009c). *Diplomados do ensino superior (2000–2001 a 2007–2008)*. Lisboa: Gabinete de Planeamento, Estratégia, Avaliação e Relações Internacionais.
MCTES. (2009d). *Inscritos no ensino superior com provas para maiores de 23 anos*. Lisboa: Gabinete de Planeamento, Estratégia, Avaliação e Relações Internacionais.
OCES. (2007). *Sucesso escolar no ensino superior. Diplomados em 2004–2005*. Lisboa: OCES.

Chapter 7
Changing Legal Regimes and the Fate of Autonomy in Portuguese Universities

Maria Eduarda Gonçalves

> *Mudam-se os tempos, mudam-se as vontades, ... E, afora este mudar-se cada dia, Outra mudança faz de mor espanto: Que não se muda já como soía.*[1]
>
> (Luís de Camões, 1524–1580)

Introduction

In recent years, Portuguese universities have undergone major legal and institutional change. Following up the Bologna process,[2] a new framework law was passed by Parliament in 2007.[3] It replaced the University Autonomy Act in force since 1988.[4] New legislation introduced a noteworthy revision to the system of internal governing for public universities. It converted what might be viewed essentially as a cultural institution, based on democratic management, to a passably functional establishment concerned predominantly with raising its performance in teaching, research and in its ties with society.

This legislative saga unfolded against a background of the two outstanding political events in Portugal's contemporary history: first, the Revolution of 25 April 1974 with its democratic and socialist ethos; and second, the accession in 1986 of Portugal to the European Communities and with it the opening up to, and growing penetration of, domestic policies by external, mainly European, influences. With this backdrop in mind, it is not unreasonable to ask how far the principles and rules, the policy options for higher education enshrined in the legislation of 1988 and 2007, were shaped by the broader political setting.

M.E. Gonçalves (✉)
Departamento de Economia Política, ISTCE Lisbon, Av das Forças Armadas,
1649-026 Lisbon, Portugal
e-mail: maria.eduarda.goncalves@iscte.pt

Whilst law is often considered from the standpoint of its normative and mandatory features, a view that corresponds to the prevailing positivism, a growing current in legal scholarship underlines the importance of understanding the law for its instrumental function as well. In other words, its use as a means to pursue political and policy goals. Viewed thus, law may well be compared to a mirror for the evolving visions and choices in any specific domain of social life – higher education, for instance – in addition to its setting down the basic framework for its structuring, organisation and operational ruling.

Against considerations such as these, the central purpose in this chapter is to review and compare the legal basis that the legislation of 1988 and 2007 provided the Portuguese university. By this means, the chapter will identify and explore the leading ideas legislation set out in respect of the missions of the university, the institutional conditions laid down for the accomplishment of these missions contained in them. In doing so, this chapter draws extensively on the proceedings of the debates in the Assembly of the Republic, Portugal's Parliament. In this way both the shifting and sometimes conflicting perceptions of the university, and hopefully the dynamics contained in the internal and external influences that brought about change in the university's legal basis may emerge with greater clarity.

In that connection, a key notion surfaces almost by instinct. That is the principle of university autonomy. Throughout the past 30 years, autonomy has remained a central focus in the debate about the public university in Portugal. Around it, the university's place in society, its relationship with the State and the university's byelaws, its internal regulations and governing modes revolved and were discussed. Not surprisingly, with the passing of time, the ways autonomy was regarded, its purpose and its scope were subject to variation as the vision of the institution itself evolved (Chaps. 9 and 12).

Has the scope of university autonomy been regarded primarily in terms of self-government or as acknowledging academic freedom? How has its scope been delineated? Which components were included? How does autonomy relate to the founding and organising of a university's governing bodies? These questions will guide us through the analysis that follows of the 1988 and 2007 Acts of the Portuguese Parliament.

Two Legal Acts in Historical Perspective

Twenty years separate the publication of the two main university framework laws Portugal adopted since the 1974 Revolution. The University Autonomy Act of 1988 may well have been a belated end result of the Revolution. The '25th of April' terminated the system of autocratic management with extreme prejudice, thereby putting an end to the 'long-lasting and humiliating dependence on political power' (Cardoso 1989: 132) that characterised the Portuguese university under the totalitarian grip of the 'Estado Novo' ('the New State') (1926/1974). In the wake of some experiments and incidents involving attempts to install direct democracy in the affairs of the university (Chaps. 2, 3 and 12) during the heady days of Revolution, the general principles and rules for university government were progressively laid down. Such a 'normalisation' process (Grácio 1981: 117) drew heavily from socialist ideology, subsequently set into the Constitution of the Portuguese Republic that was promulgated in 1976.

The Constitution defined education, including higher education, as a public responsibility of the State (Article 74).[5] Thus, the State's duty to set up the legal framework for the organisation and functioning of the university in compliance with constitutional guarantee was thereby recognised. The Constitution also underlined close ties between education and democracy, and both with social renewal. It affirmed the freedom of research and teaching, as it did the democratic management and participation of all the corps in the university to be its fundamental principles (Copetto 2002: 104–105).[6] The principle of autonomy of the university was eventually taken into the Constitution through the revision undertaken in 1982.[7] Yet only in 1987 was a legislative initiative, designed to clarify the meaning of those principles, launched.

The University Autonomy Act, Law 108/88, which resulted from this initiative, was the outcome of a wide-ranging and intense political negotiation within the Assembly of the Republic (AR). All political parties represented there, as well as the government – then the centre-right Social Democratic Party – came forward with their own proposals.[8] Despite their diversity, the debate in Parliament was carried out in an atmosphere of dialogue and mutual understanding. Each and every political interest made clear its determination to contribute to a legal framework, based upon broad consensus. Eventually the law was approved unanimously, an achievement heralded later as exemplary.

In fact, consensus that gathered around Law 108/88 rested on the recognition of autonomy as an essential condition for the institution to accomplish its central mission. It was rooted, however, in a struggle, which had its origins in resistance to the New State regime (Cardoso 1989: 125 ff; Copetto 2002: 133).[9] As a Member of Parliament pointed out, autonomy had been:

…claimed strenuously during the dictatorship by successive generations of professors and students, the universities' autonomy and the schools' democratic governance were made possible by the liberating revolution of the 25th of April.[10]

The parliamentary commission for Education, Science and Culture confirmed the convergence of all legislative proposals around two fundamental principles:

1. The understanding that university autonomy was an assumption of responsibilities, as well as the democratic participation of the academic community, namely through the setting up and voting of representative bodies; and
2. The necessity of ensuring an exchange between university and society designed to promote national and regional development.[11]

Thus, the well-established claim for self-government and independence vis-à-vis the State came together with the belief that only a free and democratic regime with the university itself could guarantee the fulfilment of its mission, that is to say, the production of scientific knowledge and its handing down through learning. On the one hand, the history of the subordination of Portuguese higher education to political power under the repressive authoritarian regime of the 'Estado Novo' underlined the need for self-rule alongside the guarantee of the freedoms to research and teach and, more generally, of freedom of thought (Chap. 3). On the other hand, internal democracy and the active participation of all its members were deemed a necessary requirement for any university within a democratic society (Cardoso 1989: 136). In 1988, the university's organisational paradigm was thus deeply embedded in the democratic and participative culture and was thus at one with the spirit and the letter of the 1976 Constitution, which itself stood as an ideological backdrop to the long-established ideal of academic freedom. As Russell reminds us, autonomy to govern their own affairs is an essential condition for academics to exercise their basic rights of freedom of speech and of thought (Russell 1993: 3).

The legal grounding for higher education institutions, published in 2007 (Law no. 62/2007 of 10 September) sprang from a very different political context. In contrast to the University Autonomy Act, which, as has been noted, rested on a broad consensus amongst parliamentary groups, the new enactment was but the result of a government-sponsored bill.[12] Moreover, time for discussion was short,[13] which was strongly disapproved in Parliament:

> In a submission to the chairman, members of parliament Luís Fazenda (Bloco de Esquerda (BE), João Oliveira (PCP), Diogo Feio (CDS-PP) and Pedro Duarte (PSD) stressed the lack of political conditions for the pursuance of the discussion of (the) proposal of law....[14]

Parliamentarians were backed in this criticism by one of the major official consultative bodies, the National Council for Education (CNE). The Council complained about the limited time allotted to express its recommendations. It also called for a wider agreement as a prior condition to make the Bill's contents acceptable to interested parties.[15] Impervious to such requests, the Minister for Science, Technology and Higher Education, supported by representatives of the governing Socialist Party, gave answer by stressing the urgency of the matter: 'The reform of Portuguese higher education is urgent, indispensable and cannot be delayed', stated the Minister.[16] Willy nilly, the government pushed on down the path towards what became Law 62/2007, which eventually was passed by the Assembly of the Republic with the votes of the Socialist Party alone supporting it.

The new law was the child of an 'original sin', that is to say, the absence of conditions necessary for a thorough-going discussion of its rationale and the likely repercussions it would have both in Parliament and beyond in the academic community. To quote Kant's 'Transcendental Principle of Publicity' (Kant 2003), the procedure lacked desirable legitimacy.[17] What was striking in 2007, as it was in 1988, both governments could count on absolute majorities in Parliament, the latter drawn from the Conservative PSD and the former from the Socialist Party, respectively. What explains the difference in stance both governments took over the issues of negotiation and consensus building?

Difference in circumstances may provide a partial explanation. In 1988, the notion of the university's autonomous governance drew upon a belief, widely shared in both academic and political circles, that of the university's quintessential function as a space for free thinking and collegial self-government. Two decades later, the push to reform lacked support from both university and polity. As a result, the government may have placed a premium on the need to present a stance of firmness and resolution, itself rooted in weighty and credible external sources, the better to avoid a debate which it anticipated would be difficult to handle.[18]

Tensions Between External and Internal Drivers of Institutional Change

> Going back now some 20 years, our universities were amongst the most free in the world. The successive governments decided they needed reform. This was based on no evaluation of what they were doing but was part of the general move to weaken the power of free professions and make them subject of the power of the market and of an increasingly dominant state. (...) I greatly hope that Portuguese universities will not be made to follow the British example. We had a good system that needed improvement, not distortion (Kogan 2005: 96–97).

This powerful statement was delivered to a Portuguese audience at a conference held in Lisbon in 2003. It provides a fine starting point for assessing how policies rooted in foreign countries may have shaped recent university reform in Portugal.

It is a matter of record that the Portuguese government chose to ask the Organisation for Economic Co-operation and Development (OECD) to evaluate higher education in Portugal and that the government built up its proposal primarily on the basis of the OECD experts' recommendations, which were delivered in 2006. During parliamentary debates, international and foreign examples were indeed intensely pored over to justify reform. In this respect, the law of 2007 differed significantly from its predecessor, which was hammered out mainly by inside forces and dynamics.

As has already been pointed out, the model of governance embedded in the University Autonomy Act of 1988 built out from a set of principles rooted in the 1974 Revolution and incorporated into the 1976 Constitution. Article 2 of Law 108/88, entitled 'Democracy and participation', categorically affirmed these principles:

> Universities shall guarantee scientific and technological freedom, ensure the plurality and free expression of positions and opinions, promote the participation of all the corps of the university in the common academic life and ensure methods of democratic management.

The autonomy of the institution in its various dimensions – scientific, pedagogical, disciplinary, administrative and financial – was explicitly protected, whilst the State's responsibility to provide the means necessary was clearly stated (Articles 6–9; Article 8, paragraph 2). The main governing bodies of the university were the Assembly, the Rector and the Senate. The Assembly was designed to prevent the concentration of powers in the Rector and the Senate (Cardoso 1989: 141). All three governing bodies were to be elected by a broad body of voters. Though universities were allowed to define the make-up of both Assembly and Senate, the law required parity between representatives of academic staff and students (Articles 17 and 24). In addition, the statutes allowed each university to establish other bodies to share some of the functions of the Senate, in particular, Scientific or Pedagogical Councils, which in effect they did.

This model was in full accordance with the recognition – as valid 20 years ago as it remains today – that the essential mission of the university is incompatible with forms of close control and is carried out more efficiently through responsible, democratic and transparent self-government (Pedrosa and Queiró 2005: 61). Indeed, the notion that the same democratic principle underlies both a progressive society and the university is entrenched in an enduring and diffused tradition which regards the university institution as the main setting for the individual to acquire higher learning 'together with the liberal and pluralistic values which are believed to go with it' (De Groof et al. 1998: 5). This conviction lies beneath the adoption, from the 1970s through to the 1990s, of tripartite parity in the representation of teaching staff, students and administrative staff across a number of European countries, including Portugal.

From this standpoint, Law 62/2007 brought radical change to the preceding state of things. The main governing bodies became the Rector and the novel General Council. The Rector's competences and powers were strengthened greatly. General Council replaced the Senate as the main decision-making body on strategic and management matters, though with a profoundly altered membership. Whereas in the Senate all the corps of the university were represented in a relatively balanced manner, in the General Council, the composition of which may range from 15 to 35, academics acquired more than 50% of total membership (Chap. 12 composition by statutes, Chap. 9). The presence of students was significantly reduced and staff excluded unless the total number of members on Council exceeded 33. Likewise, the Scientific Council, which encompassed the whole universe of academic staff holding the PhD under the terms of Law 108/88, was converted into a representative body with a maximum of 25 members including representatives of academic departments and research centres in the university.

Concentration and centralisation of power emerged, therefore, as distinguishing features in the new mode of governance for the public university. Democratic management, a principle protected in the Constitution, was removed from the law's lexicon. So too was the principle of freedom of research. Freedom is mentioned marginally in Article 73, which refers, symmetrically, to the 'intellectual freedom of both professors and students in the processes of teaching and learning'. It crops up again in Articles 152 and 157 in connection with situations of crises and with responsibility arising from damage caused to third parties.[19]

Yet, the most groundbreaking feature of Law 62/2007 may well be the inclusion of external personalities on the General Council. They command as much as 30% of total membership, the chairman being of their number. These personalities are co-opted through a majority vote by the elected members of the General Council, in effect, primarily the professors, given the very reduced presence of students.

All things considered, rather than being a mere improvement on the previous statute, the 2007 reform marked a profound change not only for the systems of governance but also for the traditionally basic principles of the university, or so one may argue. In effect, this reform went a good deal further than what it would otherwise have been expected to address, which could reasonably have included some of the problems identified by earlier assessments, either domestic or international, and including the 2006 OECD report itself. This report stated that tertiary education in Portugal needed more 'modern and efficient' systems of governance, which in turn raised the issue of examining the institutions' legal status and regulatory framework. For their part, the outside experts were prudent indeed. The only changes that should be undertaken, they suggested, should be 'in a way to foster their own independence in guiding the frontiers of science and knowledge' (MCTES 2006: 4). Recommendations of such delicacy pose foursquare why the letter of the Law of 2007 went so far in disregarding well-established principles of democracy and freedom in the conduction of university affairs.

Some clues are to hand when one turns to the speeches delivered in the National Assembly by the Prime Minister and by the Minister for Higher Education. In late 2006, in a speech to the Assembly of the Republic, the Prime Minister laid out the principal grounds for the reform then contemplated. His plea rested on two heads: the invocation of foreign advice plus the imperative need to modernise higher education.

> The government believes, 'the Prime Minister stated', that reform is necessary ... (to) overcome the insufficiencies of the system. (...) The assessment undertaken, at the request of the government, by qualified international organisations has mapped out the difficulties and the critical points. (...) First of all, on the institutions' governance. Here, problems are well known: uniformism, closeness to the outside world, weak capacity to generate strong and mobilising leadership. (...) Mechanisms will be introduced to stimulate and enhance the acquisition of funds by the institutions (...) this is the *modern way* to sustain the development of higher education.[20]

Later, and in a similar vein, the Portuguese Minister for Science, Technology and Higher Education affirmed, eloquently and ardently, to Parliament:

> The future of employment, the economy, and culture and science in Portugal depends nowadays on the courage *to modernise our higher education* (...). This reform ... may perhaps disturb vested interests, conservative, immobilising and backward, but we do not resign ourselves to mediocrity. (...).[21]

Playing up the need for greater efficiency, the Minister rallied members of the parliamentary majority:

> With organs congested by their very size and clearly undermining elected bodies, universities will become as a result of this proposal ... trouble-free and more efficient organisational structures....[22]

Thus in the rhetoric of the political theatre was modernity welded onto leadership, onto its presumed benefits for the institution's efficiency and onto the university's openness to society and the economy. At the same time, the university was lampooned as an entity, well advanced in decay.[23] Strikingly, as if to add strength to his position, the Minister resuscitated judgments on the Portuguese university made more than four decades earlier:

> Time has shown the wisdom of Miller Guerra who as early as the 1960s stated that 'university institutions are not capable of self-reform'.

In its appeal to modernity and its reliance upon external advice, the government's posture brings to mind a trend presented in the 1980s and early 1990s as an indicator of the peripheral or semi-peripheral character of Portuguese society (Santos 1994: 87). That trend took the form of mimetic behaviour towards foreign models and examples, of recourse to international expertise as a means to give legitimacy to a particular agenda, which, in all likelihood faced hearty, vigorous – and expected – opposition (Gonçalves 1996: 294 ff.). Yet, more than 30 years had elapsed since the 1974 Revolution. In the meantime, accounts of higher education and science in Portugal were fairly positive. More to the point, the dour picture of the Portuguese university sketched out by government was in flagrant contradiction with the overall appraisal of the OECD report, the very source the government used to justify the reform proposed. This report explicitly acknowledged the positive results achieved by Portuguese higher education in the recent past:

> Over the last decades, Portugal has been able to increase its higher education system at a growth rate that has no parallel in other European countries and today participation (18–22 years) corresponds to a gross enrolment rate over 50%, with the number of enrolment students increasing almost 800% relative to the student population in 1974 (…). Research activities also increased substantially over the last decade: the number of PhDs in Portuguese research units increased over 130% from 1996 to 2003, the yearly number of new PhDs more than trebled from 1990 to 2004, while the number of Portuguese scientific publications increased fourfold between 1991 and 2001 (MCTES 2006: 173).

The European Commission also cast Portugal as one of the countries with a low technology intensity that showed a more developed dynamic in closing the gap between itself and the more advanced European economies (European Commission 2008). In view of these achievements, the sketch drawn by the government may perhaps be understood better when stacked alongside the pessimistic philosophy, which accompanied similar reforms in such European countries as Britain or, more recently, France.

Like the Portuguese Higher Education Guideline Act of 2007, the French '*Loi des libertés et responsabilités des universités*' (August, 2007)[24] was couched in a deeply gloomy language when describing the current state of the French university. In turn, commentators saw the French government's rhetoric as an exercise in 'storytelling', that is, a deliberate mystification to justify the political decision (Brisset 2009; Destemberg 2009: 120). The reform '*ne pouvait relever que du parti pris idéologique*', was one harsh conclusion (Brisset 2009: 34). Pessimism towards and distrust of the university, it has been argued, may make setting in place new forms of regulation or constraints easier whilst at the same time denigrating previous optimism about the capacity of universities to discharge their missions (De Groof, Neave and Svec 1998: 131).

In fact, leaving aside the posturing of political rhetoric, the substance itself of the institutional reform set out in Law 62/2007 was largely influenced by foreign example. However, the Portuguese reform appears to have been inspired far more by the doctrines of New Public Management than by the general recommendations of the OECD and by the rhetoric of politicians. Initially launched in Britain and the Netherlands during the 1980s and 1990s, the doctrine of New Public Management set about strengthening administrative functions, with increasing emphasis on cost control and visible returns in public universities (Leisyte 2006).[25]

At the end of the day, the British example tells us that the primary reason for the appropriation of market values by the university has been the decline of public funding, and with it the need to diversify funding sources that lent weight to centralised managerial practices to the detriment of collegial ones (Russell 1993: 6–7; Beer 2007: 16).[26] It is not then surprising that the will to open up higher education to the outside world should be interpreted in Portugal – as elsewhere – as intended principally for the business sector as a potential source of future revenue. From this it may be inferred that a key – though hidden – goal of the 2007 regime for the Portuguese university may have well been the sharing of costs with the private sector. This follows the general line of argument Fuller developed, namely that 'universities are losing their autonomy because a weakened State exposes them more directly to the market' (Fuller 2006: 369).

A further look at some of the most prominent features of Law 62/2007 may provide a clearer picture of both the law's rationale and its likely implications for the autonomy of Portuguese public universities.

New Management, External Involvement and University Foundations: The Changing Meanings of University Autonomy

Three provisions in the 2007 Law are likely to have special bearing upon the autonomy of Portuguese universities. These are: changes in democratic rule, direct involvement of external personalities in the decisions of university's management and the introduction, as an option, of a new kind of organisational arrangement, the university foundation run by private law. All three raised considerable controversy in Parliament.

Democratic management lay at the heart of Law 108/88, in accordance with the 1976 Constitution, as we have seen. It can cause surprise to none that substantial reduction in student participation and the virtual exclusion of staff from the governing bodies under the terms of Law 62/2007 raised grave doubts as to their constitutional validity. As one Member of the Opposition observed:

> ...in view of the exclusion of staff from the institutions' management, the enormous reduction in students' participation in that management, concentration of powers in the General Council and in uninominal organs ... I would like to know if government perceives all these proposals as compatible with the democratic and participative construct of higher education as foreseen by the Constitution....[27]

Legal opinions were distant indeed from the parliamentary consensus of 1988 around the involvement of students then regarded as 'formidable agents of reform'.[28] Some Members of Parliament now regretted the weakening of participation on grounds of its being detrimental to the workings of the university:

> 'What has been a fruitful tradition of student participation in the management and government of the institutions is over', one of them complained.[29]

Likewise, centralisation of power about the Rector together with reductions in the composition of the electoral college were seen as reversing the earlier confidence in decentralisation and pluralism as prior condition for ensuring the accountability of all partner interests.[30] In a formal statement, the National Council for Education considered that: '...the Rector should be elected by an enlarged electoral college expressing the feeling of the academic community, as it is the case at present' (CNE 2007: 28405).

Though limiting eligibility for the post of Rector to academics, the new legislation gave a decisive place to outsiders who made up one third of members on the General Council, the main governing body. Opening the university to outside interests was acceptable to members of the Socialist Party in Parliament on the understanding that the prevailing situation limited the university's responsiveness to market needs:

> ...opening universities and polytechnics to the most dynamic actors of civil society, ending a detrimental separation between them: isn't the country fed up with hearing enterprises saying that higher education training does not meet their needs? Isn't it a shame that a qualified workforce and young graduates are found to be unemployed because of the inadequacy of their education?[31]

This particular situation is not devoid of ambiguity, however. It may be interpreted as useful and necessary for the university's lobbying and fund-raising capacities. Equally, it may be looked upon as putting the institution's independence from economic and political interests in jeopardy. Whatever the motives, perceptions or the expectations, it is a move that will most assuredly entail some degree of corporate or political influence upon the strategic and management options of universities.

Furthermore, the issue of the autonomy of universities became more crucial when set against that other major legal innovation of the 2007 regime, to wit, the public university foundation. Here again the Portuguese Minister for Science, Technology and Higher Education summoned the international example to his side:

> We must follow the best available international practices. (...) I must tell you that the regime of foundations for all public higher education institutions in Portugal – the OECD, for example, recommended it in the long-term – is very similar to the regime in force in many European countries (...).[32]

Though in principle open to any university, the special statute of 'foundation university' was boosted by the government as an 'opportunity' merited only by those institutions 'that demonstrate (themselves) to be in a position to benefit from a higher degree of autonomy',[33] a sibylline phrase taken to be a function of their ability to raise funds from non-governmental sources. Accepting private law for the public university is indeed hard to grasp except as a step towards a more general privatisation particularly with respect to funding.[34] In this light, the government's decision, in 2009, to allow additional financial openings to universities that requested such status[35] looks paradoxical since it was not based on any kind of competitive call for tender and even less an evaluation of their respective capabilities to successfully meet the conditions required.

An additional source of controversy lay in the possible impact foundation status might have on the university's autonomous decision making. In the words of the Minister, the foundations' Board of Trustees, designated by government according to Law 62/2007, were simply to take over the powers exercised by the Minister vis-à-vis universities run under administrative law. 'What happens is a transfer of powers from the competent ministry to the board of trustees', the Minister informed Parliament.[36] This explanation does not stand up against a comparative reading of the competences and powers assigned to trustees and to the Minister for Higher Education.[37] For whilst the Minister's role is limited to the 'homologation or registration of the statutes of higher education institutions and their modifications' and to the 'definition of the maximum number of new admissions and enrollments',[38] the Board of Trustees is granted an incomparable array of powers that include approval of all major deliberations of the General Council on strategic and action plans, budgetary and accounting proposals, and general guidelines in the areas of scholarship and teaching.[39]

Hence, the university foundation may be said to carry with it an intrinsic contradiction between a rhetoric, which praises the merits of private management for the autonomy of the institution, and the strengthening of oversight by trustees and government itself. The latter received the power to approve 'the outline' of the university foundation and its development plans. In Parliament, this contradiction did not go unnoticed: 'Linking the foundations to the autonomy of the institutions and then realising that government intends to designate the whole board of trustees is untenable', one Member remarked.[40] '...What is this but universities becoming more dependent on government?', noted another.[41]

It is of course too soon to evaluate the full extent of the practical effects of the 2007 legislation. Nonetheless, some thoughts may by now be entertained on the general impact the Law holds out for the concept of university autonomy itself.

Dimensions of Autonomy

Etymologically, *autonomia* is the power to rule oneself. Applied to the university, it includes first of all, the freedom to make up one's mind, and subsequently independence vis-à-vis external powers, economic, political or ideological (Prado 2009: 11–12). The whole history of the university assumes this principle. Guaranteed by Article 76 of the Portuguese Constitution, the principle was interpreted in legal terms as including two main dimensions: the personal and the institutional. Personal autonomy is the individual right of each member of the academic community to freedom to teach and to carry out research, whereas institutional autonomy refers to 'a fundamental right of the university itself' (Canotilho and Moreira 1993: 373).

As a very old aspiration indeed of the Portuguese academic community, autonomy of the university was deemed a requisite not only for its separation from State control and interference, but above all for the quality and effectiveness in accomplishing the university's scientific and cultural mission. As a Member of Parliament stated during the debate on the 1988 law:

> The autonomy of the university has a rare and unique status in our constitutional law.... Universities are granted a special treatment that is not comparable to any other public institute, enterprise, foundation, and administration or directorate-general.[42]

Autonomy was viewed then as a fundamental, all-encompassing principle, the distinctive hallmark of an institution dedicated to the creation and transmission of knowledge, and therefore requiring the authentic condition of intellectual freedom and free initiative:

> There is a relatively broad consensus about the constituent parts of the universities' autonomy: administrative, financial, pedagogical, scientific, patrimonial and disciplinary autonomy, as well as the elaboration of its own statutes and the election of its organs and governing and management positions represent a unique reality in our community.[43]

Thus a clear link was established between autonomy and the mode of governance in the university: 'Autonomy by the means of democratic and participatory practices ... prevents the maintenance of short-sighted corporatism and archaic bureaucracies', it was stressed.[44]

This principle resurfaced as a key topic in the parliamentary debate of 2007. Yet, its meaning had clearly changed. In particular, emphasis was laid primarily on the implications of university autonomy for financial and administrative management as conditions for raising efficiency in management, rather than of scientific and pedagogical autonomy per se. In the opinion of the Minister:

> Higher education institutions receive by the means of this proposal of law the greater autonomy ever. Autonomy for financial management and human resources with more responsibility and decision and managerial capacity....[45]

The intrinsic connection between autonomy and the academic community's participation in decision-making as envisaged in the 1980s gave place to limited and indirect representation. Indeed, not a single reference to democratic management can be found in Law 62/2007, despite the constitutional status of the principle. Quite on the contrary, growing involvement of outsiders came about as one major way to ensure transparency and watchfulness on the institution's administration. Emphasis on the university foundation as an opportunity to deepen the autonomy of the institutions also underlined the interpretation of autonomy above all as administrative and financial. The connotations associated with the concept thus changed significantly as emphasis shifted from autonomy understood primarily as a requirement for the free determination of research and teaching to autonomy perceived as administrative or financial self-management. Hence, in the heart of Portuguese policy for higher education, means appear to change place with ends in a number of dimensions. Focusing on means risks undermining the university's essential goals. Baldly stated, the central question is whether and how far the *'autonomie des modernisateurs*' (Montlibert 2009: 66–69) endangers scientific and teaching autonomy. Where autonomy was once regarded as a condition for fulfilling the university's prime missions, it implied that the State's responsibility lay in providing the necessary resources. Remodelling this responsibility as primarily administrative and financial is likely to pressure the university to rely less and less on public funding. True, in the eyes of some, this may not necessarily be a bad thing. Even so, it remains a matter of opinion whether the road to the future this provision has opened up will not bring about a fundamental mutation in what were once taken to be the abiding values of the university.

Conclusion

In a recent book, '*Le Principe d'Université*', Prado analysed the essence of the values and ends of the university. He regretted today's tendency to extend the law of investment returns to the '*travail de l'esprit*': 'For the university time is no more that of savants and philosophers, but rather of administrative staff and their managerial approach', he wrote (Prado 2009: 27).

Behind the shifts in the legal framework we have examined here lay two drastically divergent concepts. One is that of a university as a public service and the responsibility of the State, a university guided by the values of academic freedom. It looks forward to a university based on horizontal-like participatory democracy, seeking the collective construction of consensus amongst all the institution's agents. This vision was contained in Law 108/88. There is a second vision – that of a university shaped by market-based incentives and criteria, one predominantly given over to institutional performance and to return on its 'products' and 'services'. It is the shape of a university relying on quasi-private, vertically structured modes of governance. Here was the vision embedded in Law 62/2007.

Both models set out to achieve excellence though through different ways, the 'voices of modernisation' may argue. In the end, however, the peril is far from absent of a profound, albeit subtle and slow transformation of the practice and the spirit within the university, ousting its long-established liberal ethos and putting in its place a form of behaviour better adapted for self-adjustment to the presumed preferences of the State, university administrators, Boards of Trustees or corporate sponsors. Paring participation back is likely to be antithetical to a milieu committed to creativity even when such reductions do not work against a sense of partnership and shared, collective responsibility.

Can the Portuguese university retain its authentic institutional autonomy through such change? In my view, higher performance by Portuguese universities will hardly be achieved simply through organisational reform alone and certainly not when one considers the route map recently laid out. Even less can enhanced performance and output be guaranteed merely by concentrating power and authority and by curtailing the academic community's active participation. Most of all, what is required is, I believe, the sustained expansion of higher education in keeping with the commitment to equal opportunity begun 30 years ago. Such an engagement should be consolidated by strengthening scientific research as the indispensable basis for good teaching (Chap. 8).[46] Such goals require further public investment by the State, not disinvestment. They require the preservation of a culture of freedom and participation. In recent years, the prospect of market-driven reforms for the university as an autonomous institution has been openly taken up by technologically advanced countries. Such threat is likely to be more serious for a country like Portugal where fragility of the research base in industry is only too evident (Chaps. 5 and 8).

Still, as the French sociologist Michel Crozier observed more than three decades ago, '*On ne change pas la société par décret…*'.[47] The outcome of the new institutional arrangements will be carried out not through new laws and regulations alone. They will also advance and perhaps more significantly so through further exploration and discussion of the university's purpose, role and mission. In today's world, universities face having to reconcile further constraints created by external and domestic policies with their basic freedom to create, and to meet the expectations society has raised. Recent calls to hold out against these new pressures the better to safeguard the university's essential values (Derrida 2003; Prado 2009) are, given the changes the university is being asked to take on board, not entirely unexpected.

Notes

1. *Times change, Desires change…. And, besides this change every day, Another change is even more amazing: That is that change is no more than it used to be* (ad hoc translation).
2. The Bologna process purports to create a European Higher Education Area through progressive convergence of the conditions for access and student mobility amongst universities in Europe. See the official Bologna process website at http://www.ond.vlaanderen.be/hogeronderwijs/Bologna/.
3. Lei no. 62/2007, de 10 de Setembro – Regime Jurídico das Instituições de Ensino Superior (RGIES) (New Regime for Higher Education Institutions), *Diário da República, I Série, no. 174*, 10–9–2007: 6385.
4. Lei no. 108/88, de 24 de Setembro – Lei da Autonomia Universitária, *Diário da República, I Série, no. 222*, 24–9–1988: 3914.
5. Article 74 (Education), paragraph 2: 'In carrying out its education policy, the State has the duty to: (d) Guarantee to all citizens, according to their capacities, access to the higher levels of education, scientific research and artistic creation, and (e) To establish progressively the gratuity of all levels of education'.
6. Article 77 (Democratic participation in education), paragraph 1: 'Professors and students have the right to participate in the democratic management of schools, in accordance with the law'.
7. A new paragraph 2 was then introduced in Article 76 (University and access to higher education) stating that: 'Universities enjoy, in accordance with the law, statutory, scientific, pedagogical, administrative and financial autonomy, without prejudice to adequate evaluation of the quality of teaching'.
8. Projects of law no. 230/V (Autonomy of universities), presented by the Partido Socialista (Socialist Party) – PS; 243/V (Framework law for the universities), presented by the Partido Comunista Português (Portuguese Communist Party) – PCP; 252/V (Autonomy of universities), presented by the Partido Renovador Democrático (Renovating Democratic Party) – PRD and 256/V (Law on the autonomy of public universities), presented by the Centro Democrático

Social (Democratic Social Centre) – CDS, and the government's proposal of law no. 62/V (autonomy of universities).
9. That the adoption of this law occurred 2 years after Portugal's accession to the European Communities in 1986, which demanded almost 10 years of negotiations, seems irrelevant in view of the absence of true guidelines for higher education at European level at the time.
10. Statement by Jorge Lemos (PCP), *Diário da Assembleia da República*, I Série, V Legislatura, 1ª Sessão Legislativa, no. 97, 8 June 1988: 3937. Translations to English of excerpts from these proceedings, as well as of the relevant constitutional and legal provisions, will be the author's responsibility.
11. *Relatório e Parecer da Comissão de Educação, Ciência e Cultura*, 7 June 1988 (Rapporteur: Jorge Lemos).
12. The Social Democratic Party, the main party of the opposition, submitted a project of its own (Project no. 271/X – Law on the autonomy and management of higher education institutions) 6 months in advance of the governmental bill, but this project was not put onto the parliamentary agenda until later and was not discussed jointly with the governmental proposal.
13. Introduced in May 2007, the proposal was eventually approved on the 29th of June 2007.
14. *Diário da Assembleia da República*, I Série, X Legislatura, 2ª Sessão Legislativa, no. 100, 29 June 2007: 2.
15. See CNE, 2007: 28406. One of its members questioned the process by which the proposal of law was brought to the parliament 'letting one believe that neither the government nor the AR were interested in knowing the advice of the CNE or of other entities concerned'.
16. *Diário da Assembleia da República*, I Série, X Legislatura, 2ª Sessão Legislativa, no. 100, 29 June 2007: 28.
17. Kant (2003): Appendix 2.
18. The hostile atmosphere involving the parliamentary debate was somewhat aggravated by the backdrop of a tension between the Minister and university rectors around the diminishing financial investment for higher education.
19. Article 152 – Crisis situation: '1 – In case of serious institutional crisis of public institutions which cannot be overcome within its autonomy, the government ... may intervene in the institution and take the appropriate measures including the suspension of statutory organs...'. '2 – This intervention cannot affect the cultural, scientific and pedagogical autonomy of the institution, nor put into question the academic freedom or the freedom to teach and learn within the institution'. Article 157 – Responsibility of higher education institutions: '1 – Higher education institutions are accountable for the harm caused to third parties by the heads of their organs, staff or agents in accordance with the law, without prejudice of academic and scientific freedom'.
20. *Diário da Assembleia da República*, I Série, X Legislatura, 2ª Sessão Legislativa, no. 31, 22 December 2006: 7 ff.
21. *Diário da Assembleia da República*, I Série, X Legislatura, 2ª Sessão Legislativa, no. 100, 26 June 2007: 26.
22. *Diário da Assembleia da República*, I Série, X Legislatura, 2ª Sessão Legislativa, no. 100, 26 June 2007: 37.
23. *Diário da Assembleia da República*, I Série, X Legislatura, 2ª Sessão Legislativa, no. 100, 26 June 2007: 38.
24. Loi no. 2007–1199 du 10 août 2007 relative aux libertés et responsabilités des universités in http://www.nouvelleuniversite.gouv.fr/IMG/pdf/loi100807universites.pdf.
25. Under these doctrines, some fairly new features were introduced to universities, namely: priority setting by government and within institutions, assessment of targets and outputs, the use of performance indicators brought in from commercial practice rather than from disciplinary cultures traditionally based mainly on peer review methods of evaluation (Taylor and Miroiu 2002; De Groof et al. 1998: 131). New managerialism also favoured the reinforcement of executive leadership in detriment of collective professional roles in decision-making (Leisyte 2006: 3).
26. Deterioration of the student/professor ratio, growing pressure on professors whose number tended to decrease and increasing fees were some of the effects of the application of the new methods in Britain (Lorenz 2007: 33–52, 47–48).

27. Statement by João Oliveira (PCP), *Diário da Assembleia da República*, I Série, X Legislatura, 2ª Sessão Legislativa, no. 100, 29 June 2007: 26–27.
28. Statement by António Barreto (PS), *Diário da Assembleia da República*, I Série, V Legislatura, 1ª Sessão Legislativa, 8 June 1988: 3934.
29. Statement of Ana Drago (BE), *Diário da Assembleia da República*, I Série, X Legislatura, 2ª Sessão Legislativa, no. 108, 20 July 2007: 58.
30. Statement of Isabel Espada (PRD), *Diário da Assembleia da República*, I Série, V Legislatura, 1ª Sessão Legislativa, no. 97: 3941.
31. Statement by Manuel Mota (PS), *Diário da Assembleia da República*, I Série, X Legislatura, 2ª Sessão Legislativa, no. 100, 29 June 2007: 38.
32. *Diário da Assembleia da República*, I Série, X Legislatura, 2ª Sessão Legislativa, no. 100, 26 June 2007: 38.
33. Declaration by the Minister, José Mariano Gago, in http://jpn.icicom.up.pt/2008/01/16.
34. From a legal standpoint, the assignment of private law regimes to such foundations was even deemed unconstitutional in view, in particular, of the ensuing exemption of public universities from administrative law (Antunes 2007: 268).
35. The Universities of Oporto, Aveiro, and ISCTE (The Higher Institute for Labour and Management Sciences), just renamed ISCTE – Lisbon University Institute.
36. *Diário da Assembleia da República*, I Série, X Legislatura, 2ª Sessão Legislativa, no. 100, 26 June 2007: 38.
37. See Decretos-Lei nos. 95/2009 (ISCTE), 96/2009 (University of Oporto) and 97/2009 (Universidade de Aveiro), *Diário da República*, Iª Série, no. 81, 27 April 2009.
38. Article 27, paragraph 2, of Law 62/2007.
39. See Articles 129–135 of Law 62/2007 and Article 9 of the Statutes of the Foundations in the annexes to Decretos-Lei nos. 95/2009, 96/2009 and 97/2009.
40. Statement by José Paulo Carvalho (CDS-PP), *Diário da Assembleia da República*, I Série, X Legislatura, 2ª Sessão Legislativa, no. 108, 20 July 2007: 60.
41. Statement by Diogo Feio (CDS-PP), *Diário da Assembleia da República*, I Série, X Legislatura, 2ª Sessão Legislativa, no. 100, 26 June 2007: 30.
42. Statement by António Barreto (PS), *Diário da Assembleia da República*, I Série, V Legislatura, 1ª Sessão Legislativa, no. 97, 8 June 1988: 3932.
43. Ibidem.
44. Statement by Jorge Lemos (PCP), *Diário da Assembleia da República*, I Série, V Legislatura, 1ª Sessão Legislativa, no. 97, 8 June 1988, p. 3934. In the same vein, statement by Isabel Espada (PRD), ibidem: 3941.
45. *Diário da Assembleia da República*, I Série, X Legislatura, 2ª Sessão Legislativa, no. 100, 26 June 2007: 26.
46. At the start of this decade, only 9% of the Portuguese population between 25 and 64 years old had completed higher education against 24% in OECD countries; the number of researchers for each 1000 workers was 3.3 when the average number in the European Union was 5.4 (MCTES 2006: 26).
47. See Crozier (1979).

References

Antunes, L. F. C. (2007). Da Belle Époque à Mauvaise Époque. A propósito das neofundações legislativas. *Revista da Faculdade de Direito do Porto, IV*, 265–277.

Beer, C. (2007). La Grande-Bretagne à la croisée des chemins. In C. Charle & C. Soulié (Eds.), *Les Ravages de la "Modernisation" Universitaire en Europe*. Paris: Éditions Syllepse.

Brisset, C.-A. (2009). La 'guerre de l'intelligence' m'a tuer. In C.-A. Brisset (Ed.), *L'Université et la Recherche en Colère. Un Mouvement Social Inédit* (pp. 5–38). Broissieux: Éditions du Croquant.

Canotilho, J. K., & Moreira, V. (1993). *Constituição da República Anotada*. Coimbra: Coimbra Editora.
Cardoso, A. H. (1989). A universidade portuguesa e o poder autonómico. *Revista Crítica de Ciências Sociais, 27/28*, 125–145.
Conselho Nacional de Educação. (2007). Parecer N° 6/2007 – Regime jurídico das instituições de ensino superior, *Diário da República*, 2ª Série, N° 188, 28 September 2007.
Copetto, M. (2002). *Autonomia Universitária. Enquadramento histórico, político e legislativo*. Lisboa: Universidade Autónoma de Lisboa.
Crozier, M. (1979). *On ne change pas la société par décret*. Paris: Fayard.
De Groof, J., Neave, G., & Svec, J. (1998). *Democracy and governance in higher education*. The Hague/London/Boston: Kluwer Law International.
De Montlibert, C. (2009). Oui chef, bien chef. In *L'Université et la Recherche en Colère. Un mouvement social inédit* (pp. 63–84). Broissieux: Éditions du Croquant.
Derrida, J. (2003). *A Universidade Sem Condição*. Lisboa: Angelus Novus.
European Commission (2008) *Key figures*. Bruxelles: DG Research.
Fuller, S. (2006). Universities and the future of knowledge governance from the standpoint of social epistemology. In G. Neave (Ed.), *Knowledge, power and dissent: Critical perspectives on higher education and research in knowledge society* (pp. 345–370). Paris: UNESCO Publishing.
Gonçalves, M. (1996). The politics of science policy in the periphery of Europe: The case of Portugal. *Science, Technology & Society, 1*(2), 291–310.
Grácio, R. (1981). *Educação e Processo Democrático em Portugal*. Lisboa: Livros Horizonte.
Kant, I. (2003). *Perpetual peace: A philosophical sketch 1795*. Indianapolis: Hackett Publishing Company, Inc.
Kogan, M. (2005). The mission of the university. In J. Pedrosa & J. F. Queiró (Eds.), *Governar a Universidade Portuguesa* (pp. 85–97). Lisboa: Fundação Calouste Gulbenkian.
Leisyte, L. (2006). *The effects of new public management on research practices in English and Dutch universities*. Paper presented at the UNESCO forum on higher education, research and knowledge. Colloquium on research and higher education policy. Universities as centers of research and knowledge creation: An endangered species? Paris: Unesco.
Lorenz, C. (2007). 'L'économie de la connaissance', le nouveau management public et les politiques de l'enseignement supérieur dans l'Union Européenne. In C. Charle & C. Soulié (Eds.), *Les Ravages de la "modernisation" universitaire en Europe*. Paris: Éditions Syllepse.
MCTES – Ministry of Science, Technology and Higher Education. (2006, April). *Tertiary education in Portugal. Background report prepared to support the international assessment of the Portuguese system of tertiary education*. A working document: Version 1.1.
Pedrosa, J., & Queiró, J. F. (2005). *Governar a Universidade Portuguesa. Missão, Organização, Funcionamento e Autonomia*. Lisboa: Fundação Calouste Gulbenkian.
Prado, P. (2009). *Le Principe d'Université*. Clamecy: Lignes.
Russell, C. (1993). *Academic freedom*. London/New York: Routledge.
Santos, B. de S. (1994). *Pela Mão de Alice. O Social e o Político na Pós-Modernidade*. Porto: Afrontamento.
Taylor, J., & Miroiu, A. (2002). *Policy-making, strategic planning and management of higher education*. Papers on higher education, on http://unesdoc.unesco.org/images/0012/001295/129524eo.pdf

Chapter 8
Science and Technology in Portugal: From Late Awakening to the Challenge of Knowledge-Integrated Communities

Manuel Heitor and Hugo Horta

Introduction

The evolution of science and technology (S&T) in Portugal and its impact on the modernisation of higher education is analysed and discussed through the unfolding relationship between knowledge and the development of Portuguese society within both the European Union and also in a world increasingly globalised. This Chapter draws on the work of Conceição and Heitor (2005) whilst the analysis builds on the seminal work of Lundvall and Johnson (1994). Lundvall and Johnson challenged established views by introducing the simple, but powerful, idea of *learning*. They speak of a 'learning economy', not a 'knowledge economy'. This is a dynamic construct and therein lies its fundamental difference. Some knowledge does indeed assume great importance, but some does not. Both knowledge creation and knowledge destruction are part of this dynamic. By forcing us to look at learning rather than at the mere accumulation of knowledge, Lundvall and Johnson added a dimension that renders discussion more complex, more uncertain, but also more interesting and intellectually more rewarding.

At the centre of learning societies are *people* and *institutions*. As time progresses, both learn. Both acquire experience. Hence, to understand a science system, it is absolutely necessary to view it within an historical context in which each social,

---

M. Heitor (✉) • H. Horta
Centro de Estudos em Inovação, Tecnologia e Políticas de Desenvolvimento,
IN+, Instituto Superior Técnico, Technical University of Lisbon, Portugal
e-mail: mheitor@ist.utl.pt; hugo.horta@dem.ist.utl.pt

political and historical moment both influences, and helps explain, how decisions were taken and how the events that flowed there from came about.

We start with a statement that has become common in Portugal: *scientific backwardness followed Portuguese society through the last centuries*. Originally, this statement was attributed to Anastácio da Cunha, an artillery Lieutenant who later became full professor at the University of Coimbra during the eighteenth century. In his book *Literary News of Portugal* of 1780, which was edited by Joel Serrão in (1966), he wrote:

> We had some painters whom we should not overlook, but no great painter. We do not have a single statesman, a single architect who can be compared with mediocre ones in France or Italy. In short, the sole person who deserves to be considered a great man is still, and forever, our great poet [Camões].

Less than a century later, in 1895, Oliveira Martins wrote in his work *Contemporary Portugal*:

> Besides lacking coal, a vital industrial resource, we also lack key resources (that are) far more important: temperance, knowledge, education, tradition, steady governance and intelligence when investing. All of these flaws, and the gain achieved by other European peoples, give us no choice but to farm the land or emigrate to Brazil.

More than 100 years on, in his *Manifesto for Science in Portugal* of 1990, José Mariano Gago described Portugal as a

> ...poor and unequal country, where the low levels in the quality of life are articulated – in terms of the scientific and technological system – with obsolete, rigid, isolated, highly dependent, and non-innovative institutions of production.

Conditions began to change, slowly at first, in April 1974 with the Revolution of the Carnations. It brought in a democratic Government and with it, a more sustained and accelerating momentum as Portugal integrated with the European Union. Still, only in 1996 did scientific establishments start to be independently evaluated by international peers, a marker event in the evolution of the Portuguese science system (see Heitor and Conceição (2005); also Chap. 10).

Since Portugal's integration with the European Union in 1986, the S&T system displayed a largely uncoordinated pattern of development, which although progressive and sustained, to a large extent centred on the state. Development of the Portuguese S&T system was, until the 1970s, characterised by its small size and loose articulation mainly as a consequence of the totalitarianism of the *Estado Novo*, which inflicted a weak science culture and a restricted technological base on Portuguese society (Gago 1990).

As it expanded so the S&T system linked up with higher education, a development which stands as a Leitmotif in this chapter and one particularly evident over the last 20 years, though it has to be said that the S&T system evolved independently of higher education and, very often, in marked contrast to the latter's institutional conservatism (Heitor and Horta 2004). Such a dynamic gave rise to a set of 'new' institutions. True, they faced a number of structural difficulties (Horta 2008). Nevertheless, they are considered the most innovative and forward-looking elements

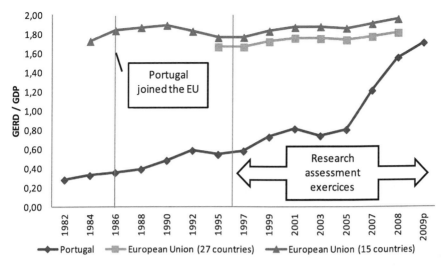

Fig. 8.1 Gross expenditure on research and development as a percentage of the gross domestic product, for Portugal and the European Union average, 1981–2009 (Source: OECD, OLIS dataset – MSTI)

in Portuguese society, as well as harnessing the driving forces for modernising higher education. Strongly urged forward since 1996 by public policies based on systematic and internationally based research assessment exercises, university research centres and independent research institutes promptly took up best international practice and became the drivers of change for modernising the university in the early twenty-first century.

Against this backdrop, the first decade of the twenty-first century saw science investment increase significantly (Fig. 8.1). Public policy upheld international research assessment exercises as a regular practice, assessing the output of scientific establishments, and concentrating on increasing what is termed 'critical mass'.[1] Sustained importance was laid on creating job openings in science to bring new blood into the science domain to enhance critical mass. Much emphasis was placed on setting up international partnerships to foster scientific networks and industry-university partnerships, and on strengthening the bonds between graduate education and research. The last few years saw the emergence of two distinct, but inter-related trends: first, a remarkable increase in business expenditure on research and development (BERD) and in industry's capacity to undertake research in collaboration with academic research centres. Business expenditure on research and development (R&D) rose from 425 million Euros in 2005 to over 1,300 million Euros in 2009. The second trend involved a marked increase in academia's research capacity, which, taken together with the legal reform of higher education, saw the number of PhD fellowships and postdoctoral research contracts rise more than twofold.

Path Development of Science Policy and Science and Technology in Portugal

According to the chronological framework set out in the work of Beatriz Ruivo (1995) and Heitor and Horta (2004), the unfolding of the Portuguese S&T system (Table 8.1) in its relationship with higher education and, in general, with Portuguese society, divides into five main periods. Suffice it to say that the effective establishment of the S&T system took place only when independent and international research assessments were activated in the mid-1990s. In this respect, the first decade of the twenty-first century consolidated and strengthened earlier policies begun during the previous phase of development when vigorous public investment in R&D leveraged business sector expenditure on research activities at the same time as the Portuguese knowledge base accelerated a strong drive towards internationalisation.

Up to 1967: A Residual Scientific Base

At the start of the twentieth century, Portuguese science and technology may be summarised in terms of sporadic and limited initiatives by the Academy of Sciences, created in 1779 (Caraça and Pernes 2002). In addition, the *Associação dos Engenheiros Civis Portugueses* (Association of Portuguese Civil Engineers) debated, disseminated and published within a narrow range of engineering subjects (Rodrigues 1999). The Republican Revolution of 1910 sought to change this by founding the universities of Lisbon and Porto as 'modern universities'. Their statutes included research to underpin teaching quality and to open up the university to society. These features aimed at developing a model that differed from the classic education of the University of Coimbra, primarily by the importance laid upon a research university model where 'the professor should not live for the student nor the student for the professor, but both to science, collaborating incessantly in the discovery and conquest of the new scientific truths' (Coelho 1962).

Whilst the first phase points to the early glimmerings of a science base, the two that followed are associated with a late and deficient launch of a national scientific base.

These ideals received further endorsement with the founding in 1911 of the *Instituto Superior Técnico* (IST). The central features of IST drew heavily on the Humboldtian model of experiment-based university education, grounded in the basic principles of autonomy, academic freedom, teaching through academic knowledge and the unity of research and teaching. Alfredo Bensaúde, IST's first President, put these ideas into practice, working closely with a group of professors who had also trained abroad, whom he managed to attract to IST. They included Charles LePierre, Ernest Fleury, Adam Droz, Giovanni Costanzo and Léon Fesch

Table 8.1 Main phases in the evolution of the S&T system in Portugal and its relation with higher education and, in general, the Portuguese society

Periods	Identification	R&D expenditure GERD, gross expenditure in R&D (% GDP) Portugal	BERD, business expenditure in R&D (% GDP) Portugal	GERD, gross expenditure in R&D (% GDP) European Union	Human resources in R&D Researchers (per 1,000 labour force) Portugal	Researchers (per 1,000 labour force) European Union
Until 1967	Residuals of a scientific base	<0.2	<0.09	<1.65	<0.9	<3.5
1967–1985	The beginning of scientific planning	0.28 (1)	0.09	1.65 (x)	0.9	3.5 (5)
1985–1995	The late awakening of the scientific base	0.49 (2)	0.13	1.88 (x)	1.6	4.4 (6)
1995–2005	Striving towards the European average	0.76 (3)	0.21	1.74	3.2	4.5
2006–...	Reinforcing critical masses to foster knowledge-integrated communities	1.71 (4)	0.80	1.81	8.2	6.3

Sources: For Portugal, EU and US: OECD, OLIS; For the US also: NSF (2002) *Science and Engineering Indicators*, For Portugal also: Ruivo (1995); Caraça and Pernes (2002)

Notes: (1) data refers to 1982; (2) data refers to 1990; (3) data refers to 2000; (4) data refers to 2009, preliminary; (5) data refers to 1983; (6) data refers to 1995; (x) data refers to EU-15

(Bensaúde 1922). Despite his efforts, scientific activity in Portugal did not greatly change. As Vítor Crespo has pointed out, neither the science nor the social system at the time possessed the

> necessary conditions to absorb, transmit and advance scientific and technical progresses in the same way it was happening in other industrialised countries. The research activities were particularly poor in the exact and natural sciences (Crespo 1993: 11).

The lack of scientific equipment, he observed, permitted neither advanced research nor incentives to stimulate research, which were bedevilled by bureaucratic heaviness and by conditions that could scarcely be met.

With apathy towards, and negligence of, both science and education, the Portuguese population of 1930 when compared to every other European country displayed the lowest levels of schooling at all levels of education. This situation did not, however, alarm the Government which held that 'ignorance was a synonym of happiness' (Crespo 1993). The *Estado Novo* was not interested in raising either schooling or the educational level of the population, still less in fostering general access to higher education (Amaral and Magalhães 2005; see also, Chaps. 2, 3 and 9). Rather, it preferred to graduate a limited number of individuals to become part of the élite. Small numbers were more easily controlled (Torgal 1999). A feeble human capital and a flaccid political will to change the situation account for the country's slow educational and scientific development. Still today, this is reflected in Portugal's backwardness compared with other European countries in the formal qualifications held by its population (see Chap. 5). Nor should it be forgotten that during the *Estado Novo* many university professors were expelled, dismissed or forcibly retired, a clear demonstration of the brutality that accompanied the negation of free thinking and free speech, so essential to research and teaching (Marques 1986).

The *Junta Nacional de Educação*, created in 1929, transformed into the *Instituto para a Alta Cultura* (IAC) in 1936, had the mandate formally to support research. Science research establishments outside academia could undertake fundamental research and award research scholarships abroad. Thus, IAC supported internships at large national Laboratories in Europe, laid down the first contacts with international science organisations, particularly in the fields of mathematics, physics and chemistry. In 1952, the *Instituto para a Alta Cultura* became the *Instituto de Alta Cultura*, with the principle objective to bolster the self-standing nature of Portuguese science by financing research centres outside the control of universities, thereby outflanking the centralising tendencies in the Portuguese university. In addition, the IAC was charged with 'increasing scientific research and to coordinate cultural relations with foreign countries' (Decree-Law 38680, of 17 March 1952). It mutated yet again to become the *Instituto Nacional de Investigação Científica* (INIC) in 1976.

Yet, the Government continued to distance itself from science in general, and from scientific culture, in particular (Nunes and Gonçalves 2001). Government policies were generally 'short term', associated with negligible investment in science and technology (S&T). Combined with the flight of scholars and intellectuals abroad, this situation brought about a partial closing down of both S&T and higher education systems. The few exceptions involved supporting applied research that tied in with the main policy concerns of the moment (Ruivo 1995). In focusing on applied research, the *Laboratórios do Estado*, i.e. state laboratories, were singled out as favoured research institutions. They included the *Estação Agronómica Nacional*, created in 1936, the *Junta de Investigação do Ultramar*, founded in 1945 and, most important, the *Laboratório Nacional de Engenharia Civil* (National Laboratory of Civil Engineering*)*, set up in 1946. Some 10 years later, driven by the challenges of the 1950s to modernise, the *Committee of Nuclear Energy* was established in 1954, and the *Instituto Nacional de Investigação Industrial* (National Institute of Industrial Research) in 1957. The year 1961 saw the founding of the *Laboratório de Física e Engenharia Nuclear* (Physics and Nuclear Engineering Laboratory), equipped with an American reactor through the Programme 'Atoms for Peace'.

During those times, a few research scholarships abroad were awarded, primarily to earn doctorates in physics, chemistry and engineering sciences. The *Marshall Plan for European Reconstruction* opened the way for knowledge transfer programmes and advanced training of Portuguese engineers in the United States of America (Rollo 1994). The 1960s saw the creation of the *Gulbenkian Institute of Science* in 1961 – of particular importance given its research emphasis in such fields as biology and automatic calculation methods. One indicator of importance is, of course, the overall level of gross expenditure on research and development (GERD) measured in terms of the gross domestic product (GDP). In 1964, for Portugal, this stood at some 0.28%. In 1945, for the United States alone, the corresponding statistic already stood at 0.5% of GDP.

Significantly, research – relatively isolated – undertaken by state laboratories was relevant only to an industry with extremely low levels of technological development, as Ezequiel de Campos (1943) has shown. De Campos analysed the industrial sector as a preliminary to discussing how economic development, based on the build-up of 'modern industry', could be advanced, given the country's structural backwardness. Against the then current state of development in the science system, launching the *I Plano do Fomento* (First Development Plan) in 1953 was a marker event. Its importance lay in the favourable conditions that followed the end of the Second World War (Rosas 1995; see also Chap. 5) and in the electrification programme, drawn up by Ferreira Dias (1998), an engineer and Minister of the Economy at that time. In Ferreira Dias' view, the first development plan stood as, 'the reinforcement of the technological and industrial capability of the country, both representing the great strengths of nations'. He added 'it is more useful to give the right conditions to an engineer to open a new venture than placing dozens of manual workers in routine work' (Dias 1961). Taking this priority up, the *Associação Industrial Portuguesa* (Portuguese Industrial Association) sponsored inter-university field visits for senior students on technical courses to develop contacts amongst them and to exchange knowledge. This, however, was a limited initiative. Field visits did not exceed 100 students a year. Furthermore, contemporary industrial development in Portugal then entailed considerable technological dependency. Portuguese firms manufactured or assembled components designed and developed abroad, in the company's country of origin. The latter retained the technological know-how, the basic conception and the management of the overall project. Portuguese firms assembled the components. There was no technological transfer (Ribeiro et al. 1987).

Basically, industrial research in Portugal was non-existent (Heitor and Horta 2004), except for a research centre associated with the *Companhia União Fabril* (CUF) in the field of chemical processes. This research centre eventually closed some years later. Meanwhile, the onset of the colonial wars and the subsequent withdrawal of state participation from private projects of large Portuguese financial and industrial groups weakened the economy. The banking sector was concentrated and re-organised and had increasing recourse to foreign capital (Macedo 1970). Certain protectionist policies were abandoned and several attempts made to stimulate a technologically more advanced and more productive industrial sector (Ribeiro et al. 1987).

On the university front, the founding in 1962 of the *Estudos Gerais Universitários* (University General Studies) was particularly important. It extended Portuguese university law to Angola and Mozambique and placed them under the control of both the *Ministério da Educação Nacional* (Ministry of National Education) and the *Ministério do Ultramar* (Ministry for the Colonies). This measure led to the creation of the University of Luanda in Angola and the University of Lourenço Marques in Mozambique, designed to meet regional and local needs. These universities had a reasonable impact on their regions. They funded scholarships and awarded merit prizes for the best students. To the same end, training programmes to qualify academic staff through scholarships to *licenciados* (graduates from 5-year programmes) from Portuguese universities to continue studying up to PhD level were particularly important. More than a decade later, many academic staff from those universities returned to Portugal, which eased the creation of new universities, put in hand in 1973 by Veiga Simão (see, for example, Chaps. 2 and 9). These latter universities – amongst which the New University of Lisbon, the University of Aveiro and the University of Minho – were to play an important part in generating a much-needed 'critical mass' that was to be key to the development of Portugal's science system.

To summarise, in the first phase seen in terms of 'a residual science base', Portuguese development plans (especially the second development plan, 1959–1964) included few incentives for R&D activities in a non-integrated system. It was a system structurally averse to scientific knowledge where state laboratories were the main centres of scientific activities. The successful case of the *Laboratório Nacional de Engenharia Civil* (LNEC) was the exception, not the rule, in a system where the universities were blocked off from science development by the Estado Novo.

1967–1985: The Onset of Scientific Planning: Anticipating Linear Technological Change

The *Junta Nacional de Investigação Científica e Tecnológica* (National Committee of Scientific and Technological Research – JNICT), established in 1967, marked the beginning of science planning in Portugal. It was the outcome of several NATO studies during the early 1960s. It was driven forward by the OECD Project 'Pilot-Teams in Sciences and Technology' for Portugal, a project commissioned by Minister Francisco Leite Pinto as follow-up to the 'Regional Mediterranean Project', which had focused on the condition of education in Portugal (see Conceição et al. 2004). JNICT took over responsibility for the coordination, planning and advance of science and technology, as a means to advance economic and social development. JNICT become fully operational in 1969. It reported directly to the Presidency of the Council of Ministers until 1975, when it came successively under the ambit of several different ministries until 1986, when it was incorporated into the Ministry of Planning, later the Ministry of Territorial Planning and Administration.

Ruivo (1995) divided this period in science policy (1995) into three phases:

1. From 1969 to 1971: Corresponding to the third development plan, which applied a model of technological change that was remarkably linear. It emphasised fundamental research (i.e. *Science Push*).
2. From 1972 to 1974: Still within the framework of the third development plan, emphasis in this phase centred on supporting applied research. It retained the previous commitment to a linear perspective of innovation.
3. From 1978 to 1985: The main objective was to reduce Portuguese technological dependence on foreign countries. Whilst it obeyed a linear perspective of technological change, emphasis now lay on market mechanisms (i.e. *Market Pull*).

The third development plan, launched in 1968, set out to nudge Portuguese industry towards international markets by implementing massive industrial initiatives. It broke from earlier industrial planning which had focused on internal and colonial markets (Rollo 1996). The major financial groups began expanding beyond their core business and did so in conjunction with international industrial and financial groups of world dimension which controlled raw materials, and investment in large-scale infrastructures, in industrial conglomerates. They also had access to technology and marketing networks (Santos 1996). The plan had limited impact. Throughout the 1970s and 1980s, Portuguese industrial structure retained its base in sectors of low technological intensity, in part because industrial strategy set much store by low wages and reduced value added. The search for new knowledge by the business sector was negligible.

In the absence of incentives to promote the social and economic dimensions in the search for knowledge, Minister Veiga Simão launched the education reform of 1973 and through it laid down the foundation for growth in Portugal's science base. Grounded in an expanded higher education system, including new universities, this reform, in particular, was to be shaped by a legal enactment to recognise the equivalence of doctoral degrees obtained abroad and to restructure the career path of academic staff (see, for example, Chap. 10). These legislative acts were passed more than 10 years after Manuel Rocha's statement to the first congress of engineering education that

> the fundamental aim of the university is to teach and disseminate culture, and this function cannot be performed without research activities (Rocha 1962: 19).

These ideals were only to be carried into effect in 1979 when the *Estatuto da Carreira Docente Universitária* (Statute on the careers of academic staff in universities) took effect. It gave final and formal expression to the obligation on academic staff at university wholly and exclusively to undertake teaching and research. We hold this step to be decisive in establishing the science base in Portugal. It stipulated the necessary and basic conditions for R&D effectively to be set up in universities.

Against this background which laid out the groundwork of the Portuguese science system, JNICT unveiled the *Plano Integrado de Desenvolvimento* – PIDCT (Integrated Development Plan). The Plan turned around clearly defined measures for science policy, with implications for technological policy during the early 1980s. The PIDCT promoted university-industry projects. It encouraged state laboratories to undertake research together with firms. It proposed an innovation agency. As a pointer to the nascent dynamism thus unleashed, between 1967 and 1986 overall expenditure in R&D rose from 0.25% to 0.36% of GDP. In 1982, across all subject areas, the country mustered 5,736 research staff and by 1986 9,258. During this phase immediately prior to Portugal's accession to the EU, the Ministry of Industry, working through the National Laboratory for Industrial Research (LNETI), brought out the National Technological Plan. The Plan built on specific experiences in Asia developed by the Massachusetts Institute of Technology (MIT). It received little immediate echo. It did, however, trigger off an institutional conflict with JNICT's policy, a conflict that dragged on until the end of the century, damaging attempts to integrate coherent science and technology policy with industrial strategy.

To recapitulate: During the second phase that may be characterised as 'the beginning of scientific planning', establishing the JNICT was the first attempt to lay out a science and technology system. It was based on centralised coordination, on a policy of distributing research scholarships and on the expectation that technological change would be a linear process.

1986–1995: Late Awakening of the Scientific Base: Structural Delay and the Creation of New Institutions

Accession to Europe came as a very real opportunity for Portuguese science and technology development. The phase from 1986 to 1989 saw science policies guided by a more complex model of technological change and by a growing intensification in international cooperation. Becoming a member of such international organisations as the *Centre Européen de Rercherche Nucléaire* and the European Space Agency was particularly important. It furthered the international engagement and presence of Portuguese research staff (Horta 2010). Above all, the period is indelibly marked by the setting up of countless 'interface' institutions, usually non-profit making and associated with university bodies. These were seen as the counter to bureaucratic rigidity in public administration, and more particularly in the university's access to public funds.

In the 1987 *Jornadas Nacionais de Investigação Científica e Tecnológica*, JNICT drew up the *Programa Mobilizador de Ciência e Tecnologia* (Mobilising Programme for Science and Technology) to define and implement at national level a set of S&T projects in specific areas (e.g. Caraça 1993). In the 1990s, a number of new programmes were implemented, supported from European structural funds. The CIÊNCIA Programme, between 1990 and 1993, promoted advanced training and the build-up of physical infrastructure. Under this programme, 3204 fellowships – roughly half at PhD level – were granted and brought about a considerable increase in the numbers of Portuguese research staff. Several of these fellowships supported doctoral degrees abroad (54% of the total PhD fellowships awarded). Through them, access to international research networks was acquired (Horta 2010). Universities throughout this period played a preponderant role in attracting structural funds from CIÊNCIA and other programmes.

In the matter of public expenditure on R&D, most outstanding feature during the period 1986–1995 was the decrease of expenditure in the state sector and the growth of expenditure in higher education and private non-profit institutions. The part assigned to universities increased substantially, from 21% in 1982 to 43% in 1992. In terms of R&D expenditure, universities formed the predominant sector. However, in relative terms, equally noticeable was the decreasing participation of firms whose part in 1995 was 20%. Here was a trend counter to that observed in more advanced economies and in face of the European average. Thus, in 1995, compared to other European countries, Portugal still presented a relatively low R&D effort. Spain, which in the 1960s displayed a R&D effort lower still, had in the meantime overtaken Portugal. Portugal's outlay on R&D in 1995 remained below 1% of GDP, the second lowest figure amongst OECD countries. It is worthwhile recalling that, even in the more pessimistic scenario outlined by Murteira and Branquinho (1968), Portugal should have reached that important threshold by 1980.

To summarise, during the third period, 'the late awakening of the science base', the integration of Portugal in the EU facilitated the internationalisation of the economy and launched the bases for a organised R&D system, with increasing international links (including entry to CERN). New programmes and R&D activities developed and funding forged ahead. The institutional rigidity of universities led to the emergence of new 'interface' institutions to draw on European Union funds, to encourage the flexible transfer of technology and, above all, for hiring research staff.

1995–2005: Struggling Towards the European Average: Promoting Human Resources, Strengthening Scientific Institutions

In 1995, the incoming Government created the *Ministério da Ciência e Tecnologia* (Ministry of the Science and Technology; see also Chap. 3), a move that involved profound changes to public institutions associated with science and technology.

Functions previously allocated to JNICT were reassigned between the *Fundação para a Ciência e Tecnologia* (Science and Technology Foundation – FCT) which had both evaluation and funding responsibilities, the *Instituto de Cooperação Científica e Tecnológica Internacional* (Institute for International Cooperation in S&T – ICCTI) and the *Observatório da Ciência e Tecnologia* (Observatory of Sciences and Technologies – OCT) with responsibility for monitoring, inquiry and analyses.

The Portuguese S&T system was stimulated further by fundamental reform in the assessment of R&D institutions. The new assessment exercise of R&D units guaranteed the independence and effectiveness of evaluation, the publication of the methodologies employed and the results obtained, together with the right of appeal. This exercise included state laboratories and research units funded through the FCT. It encompassed the implementation of new programmes for advanced training at PhD level. It addressed the issues of renewal and the mobility of human resources. The evaluation of state laboratories in 2000 revealed considerable variety and variation. Links to society in general and to firms in particular needed to be strengthened further as did aligning such activities on national priorities, and the need for further institutional reforms to introduce more flexible organisation.

For university-based public-funded R&D units, the funding programme, begun in December 1993, was also subject to national evaluation. Evaluation panels, organised by scientific field, drew on Portuguese research and academic staff. Amongst the evaluation criteria included was size of the research team, its scientific objectives for the coming 5 years, the team's scientific achievements over the previous half decade, its financial situation, as well as joint funding foreseen for the 5 years ahead. Three hundred and thirty-four R&D units applied for recognised status. Two hundred and seventy were deemed eligible for public funding. A new funding model was drawn up in 1996. It rested on parameters intended to secure organisational stability, international evaluation and responsibility. The evaluation of R&D units was undertaken by panels of international research staff – in all some 100 foreign scientists from 14 countries. The panels were chaired by a Portuguese researcher, whose function was not to evaluate, but to facilitate exchange between members of the R&D units and evaluators. Base funding was indexed on the number of research staff having a doctoral degree and to the rating the unit obtained. Base funding was complemented by special programmatic funding to meet the specific needs of some R&D units.

R&D units were classified on a five-point scale, from excellent, very good, good, fair to poor. Those classified poor – 6% of all units evaluated – saw their funding terminated and their recognition withdrawn. The remainder were funded according to the classification they obtained. By the end of the 1996 evaluation exercise, 257 R&D units had been funded. Sixty-seven new R&D units were approved in 1998. By 2000, the programme oversaw 337 R&D units, with some 5,000 research staff having a doctorate. R&D units classified at different points on the scale were 19%, 38%, 27%, 12% and 4%, respectively. This compared with 16%, 28%, 31%, 19% and 6% for the 270 R&D units evaluated in 1996, and 15%, 30%, 36%, 13% and 6% for the 84 R&D units evaluated in 1997–1998 (for a detailed account see Heitor 2001).

The results show clearly that the most frequent classification of R&D units changed from good in 1996 to very good in 1999. Indeed, whilst 44% of the 270 R&D units had been classified excellent and very good in 1996, by 2000, 57% reached this level. Furthermore, the proportion of doctorate degree holders in R&D units attaining this rating rose from 56% in 1996 to 65% in 1999. Of those evaluated in 2000, only 10 obtained a poor rating. Their size ranged from 5 to 17 doctorate holders, and accounted for 2% of research staff with this qualification.

Funding increased significantly. For publicly funded university-based research units, funding rose from 7.5 million Euros in 1995 to 25.5 million Euros in 1999. In 1999, overall expenditure on R&D accounted for 0.76% of GDP. The European average was 1.74%. Accelerated growth in annual scientific output stood at 16% whilst the corresponding statistic for the European Union between 1995 and 1998 averaged only 3%.

The evaluation exercise of 1999–2000 confirmed that successive evaluations of S&T institutions since 1996 had injected a dynamic of change into the Portuguese research community, a change that had brought about a rapid increase in the numbers of young doctorates, PhD students and international connections (Heitor 2001). The steady increase in the number of doctorates, seen against European and international statistics, was seen by the majority of evaluation panels as decisive in upholding critical mass in scientific development (Heitor 2001). Even so, in the year 2000, the number of research staff plotted against the active population still remained about half the European average – respectively 2.9 and 4.9, for every 1,000 inhabitants. Clearly, further initiatives were warranted. Evaluation panels recommended *entre autres* reinforcing the infrastructure, boosting technical and administrative support, opening complementary lines of public R&D funding around thematic programmes, multidisciplinary in nature, making the integration of research staff in science-based networks more easy, internationalising the science base whilst backing mobility, implementing a coherent policy on Intellectual Property Rights and developing skills in technology management.

Structural deficiencies in the organisation and composition of the majority of R&D units led evaluation teams to propose such measures as improving the articulation between education and research, especially workloads for teachers and students, renewing research and academic staff by extending employment in science, improving existing support structures, adopting development strategies and flexible approaches to teaching, learning and research. Evaluation panels pointed out that direct funding from industry, reduced as it was, had no significant impact on the quality of research and had, almost exclusively, been used for short-term projects (Heitor 2001). That said, the business share of gross expenditure on R&D (BERD) grew by 71% between 1995 and 2005, a figure unmatched in Europe. From 2005 onwards, business expenditure on R&D exceeded that of higher education institutions, with overall figures surpassing one billion Euros from 2007 onwards.

A summary of the fourth phase, around the theme 'Striving Towards the European Average', turns around the creation of the Ministry of science and technology. It marks the effective establishment of a national system of S&T. In this, the setting up of independent and fully international research assessment exercises for R&D units was critical. The training of highly qualified human resources moved ahead. Growth in funding and in doctoral output per year was considerable. The progress of research institutions now rested on international criteria and terms of reference.

From 2005 Onwards: Reinforcing Critical Mass, Fostering Knowledge-Integrated Communities, Promoting Internationalisation

At the end of the first decade of the new millennium, science investment in Portugal took on a new lease of life. It broke with the earlier pattern of relatively sluggish or fluctuating investments. It reached unprecedented levels of development. Above all, the impact of the build-up across two decades of public funding for the advanced training of human resources and laying down new scientific institutions started to bear fruit. Particularly clear was the impact on qualifications and on modernising both higher education and business based R&D, which increased considerably during these years. In 2006, the historical tipping point of 1% of GDP invested in R&D was finally reached. Three years later in 2009, it was to attain 1.71%. Thus, Portugal overtook countries that historically had always invested more in R&D, amongst which Italy (1.19%), Ireland (1.43%) and Spain (1.35%). At the same time, the share of business expenditure in the gross expenditure on R&D increased from some 20% to 50%, representing in absolute terms a threefold increase in business expenditure on R&D, which rose from about 400 million Euros in 2005 to 1,300 million Euros in 2009.

The recent speeding up in the development of the Portuguese S&T system went hand in hand with its capacity to attract and train human resources. It clearly bolstered the critical mass factor in academic institutions. It launched 'new' provision which concentrated researchers across disciplines and built-up *knowledge integrated communities* with an increasingly marked international outreach. Thus, in Portugal research staff expressed as the number of researchers per 1,000 employees in the labour force, reached the OECD average. In 2009, this stood at 8.2 per 1,000, a level similar – even higher in some cases – to Spain, Ireland, Italy, Germany, the Netherlands and the United Kingdom.

In terms of total full time equivalents (FTE) of research staff per 1,000 workforce, Portugal in percentage growth rates was second highest with some 34%, well above the European average, which between 2003 and 2006 grew only by 5.4%. In effect, Portugal outstripped Spain (13%) and Ireland (7%). In the business sector, R&D personnel between 2005 and 2007 rose by 111% and 164% between 2005 and 2008, from 4,014 to 10,589 FTE. Moreover, Portugal displays a remarkably high ratio of female research staff, particularly in academia research (see, for example, Chap. 4). As a proportion of all research staff, in 1997 women accounted for some

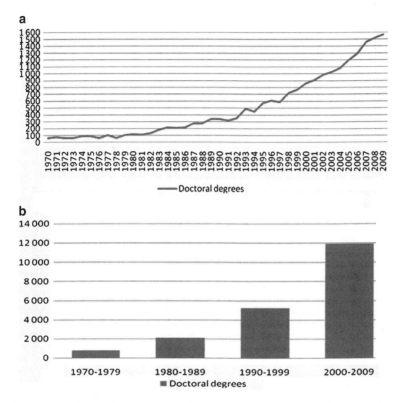

Fig. 8.2 Doctoral degrees done at or recognised by Portuguese universities, by year and decade since the 1970s to 2009 (**a**) Doctoral degrees done at or recognised by Portuguese universities, per year, (**b**) Doctoral degrees performed or recognised by Portuguese universities, by decade (Source: GPEARI 2009b)

41% and 44% in 2009. Yet, R&D personnel as a percentage of all employees is still rather low in Portugal – less than 10% in 2005 – when compared with countries like Finland or Sweden with 32% and 28%, respectively.

Even so, increases in the ranks of research staff and especially the 12,000 FTE doctoral level research staff, who in 2009 were active in university R&D centres, are a clear pointer to the consolidation of both Portugal's knowledge base and the status of science in its universities. Equally encouraging were the growing numbers of new PhDs awarded between 2000 and 2009 – in all 11,932. Over the past 9 years, Portuguese universities awarded or recognised more new PhDs than during the three previous decades when between 1970 and 1979, 8,047 new PhDs were awarded – 769 between 1970 and 1979, 2,065 from 1980 to 1989 and 5,213 from 1990 to 1999.

By 2008, Portugal had already fulfilled the target set for 2010 – more than 1,500 new PhDs a year, doubling the number of awards made throughout the 1970s (see Fig. 8.2). Significantly, this same year saw new PhDs awarded to women passing the 50% mark, the highest ever. In science and engineering, new PhDs currently account for almost half the total (46%) of all new PhDs – a figure that held constant since the early 1990s. Corresponding statistics for 1990 amounted to 47%. In absolute terms, however, numbers rose from 161 in 1990 to 717 19 years on. When expressed per 1,000 of population aged 25–34, the ratio of new PhDs in science and engineering reached 0.42 in 2007 compared with 0.3 in 2001. It is in details like these that the rise in capacity of Portuguese universities to offer PhD programmes and also to work across frontiers is reflected (Horta 2010). By the same token, it also posed the question of guaranteeing quality of PhD programmes, of extending further their international outreach and setting up international networks for doctoral study and research, where PhD students serve as essential links.

The drive to internationalise the science system has long been part of Portugal's agenda for science policy. In this, most recent amongst government initiatives has been to draw up strategically oriented international partnerships with leading American universities. It echoes previous policies that combined internationalising individuals and institutions with qualifying human resources and building up institutional maturity in science organisations. International partnerships launched in 2006 went further, however. They focused on stimulating the integration of national institutions with emerging international science and technology networks involving both business and industry, with mobility of students and academic staff, the better to strengthen scientific and academic exchange and collaboration within those networks. With this broad mandate in mind, the strategic programme of international partnerships in science, technology and higher education was introduced in 2006. By September 2007, the first doctoral and advanced studies programmes were officially launched. They brought several Portuguese universities together with leading world universities, MIT, Carnegie Mellon University and the University of Texas at Austin. Unprecedented in Portugal, these programmes opened the way in 2007 for effective market-demand theme networks, which drew in a large number of Portuguese institutions. These networks boosted internationalisation at institutional level and, through advanced studies and ongoing projects, generated new knowledge, developed new ideas by working with firms and with internationally renowned universities (Heitor and Bravo 2010). The end purpose of these networks is to enhance the technical capacity of Portuguese firms by working closely with universities and the research community and thus to improve their penetration in emerging markets worldwide.

Together with growing investment in science, much emphasis was placed on the qualifications of academic research staff as well as creating science-based job opportunities. The latter was tackled by a programme, launched in 2007, to support contractual arrangements for research staff. By the summer of 2009, some 1,200 new PhD researchers were given contracts – 41% of whom were non-Portuguese nationals. Hopefully, this initiative will mobilise the academic community and inject new blood into teaching and research in Portuguese universities. Moreover, national and international mobility amongst new PhD holders tends to lie mainly within the Europe. Given this situation, extending the international engagement of research units is particularly important in view the current stage of development in Portugal's S&T system.

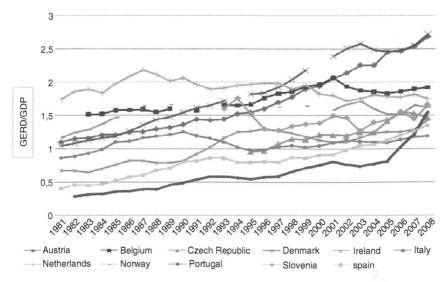

Fig. 8.3 Evolution of GERD as a percentage of GDP in selected European countries, 1981–2008 (Source: OECD, OLIS, MSTI)

Impressive though the increased investment in science in Portugal has been in recent years – the GERD reached the same investment levels as it had in other European countries – still, this does not guarantee scientific maturity. Rather, given the development trajectory of Portugal's science system, it is more appropriate to regard investment as further step in the recovery from a late awakening and a slow – often intermittent – move along the path to maturity. The recent positive trend in science investment is best understood by comparing it with other European countries, not only over the same period, but over a longer time frame as well. From this longitudinal perspective (see Fig. 8.3), two main results emerge: First, that despite reaching the same levels of investment as Spain, Italy or Ireland, the level of Portugal's *accumulated* science investment over the past few decades was not even close to the level in those countries. Building up the nation's scientific development to a position similar to the countries just mentioned requires both a far larger and sustained investment in science, at a rate faster than those countries and over a long period. Second, despite heavy investment in S&T, Portugal is still far from the investment levels of other small- and medium-sized countries in the European Union, Belgium, Austria, Denmark or Finland, for instance. One indirect consequence of these two features is the persistent 'infantile status' in industry-science relationships and the present 'immaturity' in both industry and academia to plan joint ventures over the long term. This is certainly affected by the structure of business enterprises, by the lack of large companies in sectors traditionally involved in advancing these ties in other industrialised countries, not least in the aeronautical and automobile industries.

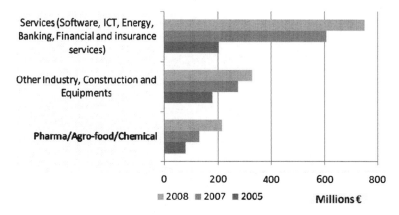

Fig. 8.4 Main sectors of business R&D expenditure in Portugal, 2005–2008 (Source: GPEARI/MCTES)

Still, the growth in public investment in science in recent years remains a crucial factor. Scholarly literature has shown that nurturing and maintaining excellence in the knowledge infrastructure is the most effective way public funding may provide resources – including qualified human skills – for firms. This, in turn, stimulates their own investment in S&T and strengthens the entrepreneurial environment for innovation (see, for a rather detailed discussion, Conceição and Heitor 2005). In effect, the recent rise of Portugal's public investment in R&D is matched by a steep rise in firms investing in R&D. Business share in the gross expenditure on R&D (GERD) grew by 71% between 1995 and 2005, a figure unmatched in Europe. Only from 2005 onwards did business expenditure on R&D overtake that made by higher education. In 2005, these changes coincided with a review of the tax system for corporate R&D, to encourage business to spend both on R&D and on employing research personnel in firms. By 2008, R&D expenditure by business enterprises as a percentage of GDP surpassed the whole of higher education, the not-for-profit private sector and the government sector combined, to reach 0.8% of GDP.

The analysis of recent growth in R&D expenditure by business (BERD) in Portugal is of particular interest, and no less so when placed against more than a century of development when business scarcely took any part at all (Fig. 8.4). This reflects the structure of business enterprises, which lacked large companies in sectors traditionally associated with industry-science relationships in industrialised countries, including aeronautics and automobile. In recent years, knowledge-intensive services – software industry, computing services, communications, financial services and insurance – showed the highest levels of investment in R&D. Between 2005 and 2008, theirs was the highest growth rate, together with the energy sector – the fastest growing during these years – together with the automotive industry. Since 2005, R&D investment in knowledge-intensive sectors quadrupled. Financial services and insurance accounted for the highest increase – a ninefold rise. Communications registered an eightfold increase, followed by computing activities, which rose six times. In the energy sector, business R&D expenditure multiplied 80-fold, whilst the automotive sector increased seven times over. Similarly, the food industry sector increased 3.5 times and the pharmaceutical industry a mere 1.5 times. On the other hand, the years 2005–2007 saw R&D expenditure decrease in the electrical appliance and construction sectors, though overall the absolute level remained relatively low. In part, this is the reflex of methodological issues – for instance, classifying firms according to sector and also market-related adjustments in two sectors, both deeply affected by demand, to wit, construction and particularly public works and infrastructure.

Analysing the structure of Portuguese BERD in terms of the concentration in R&D funding is also revealing. It tracks the relative spread across the number of firms investing in R&D. This grew considerably. But the five most R&D intensive firms account for only 30% of BERD, the top 20 for 59%, and the top 100, for some 80%. These figures suggest that Portuguese business R&D is not dependent on a few large companies. This comes as a 'green light' in the overall goal of raising and sustaining the business sector's participation in the national drive to increase technological intensity in the nation. Yet, analysis also suggests that large companies certainly need to increase their R&D investment significantly, if science-based job openings are to increase in the business sector and if further specialisation in the skills required by these emerging areas is equally necessary if both are to advance.

In all probability, recent trends in the Portuguese BERD have helped the penetration of Portuguese firms into competitive and emergent markets (see, for example, Chap. 5). In 2007, for the first time, Portugal's technology based balance of payments[2] became positive. This trend was the result of a rise in income from a broad range of markets, including the US, UK and France. In 2009, the credit analysis of this same item revealed a diversified market portfolio. The UK accounted for 15% – the largest market share in terms of credit, followed by Germany (12%), Spain (11%) and the US (9%). Portugal acquires most of its technology-based services (19%) from Spain, followed by the UK (16%) and Germany (15%). Equally significant, the emerging market of Angola registered the most positive balance, though in 2009, Angola represented only 8% of total credit and 2% of total debit. A longitudinal analysis of the state of Portugal's technology balance of payments, this time focusing on markets, highlighted the enhanced competitiveness of Portuguese firms in highly competitive markets. Over the past 2–3 years, the technology balance of payments with the Netherlands became positive since 2008, with France since 2007, UK since 2009 and US since 2007. With Germany from 1999 to 2009, however, it remained in the red. Spain – except for 2007 – and Switzerland – save for the years 2003 and 2004 maintained a positive income flow.

Even so, the average funding per researcher in Portugal – currently US$ 44,000 per head – is less than half the OECD average, which stands at US$ 101,000 per capita. On this criterion, Portugal is similar to Hungary, Poland, the Russian Federation or Romania. On the other hand, Portuguese research staff can count on only 66% of the funding their Spanish or Czech colleagues receive. This applies to funding per researcher across different output sectors, even those where researcher numbers increased most (Table 8.2).

Table 8.2 Expenditure in R&D by researcher in 2008 or latest year available

	R&D expenditure per researcher 1,000 US dollars PPP/researcher (headcount)			
	Total	Private sector (firms)	Higher education	Government institutions
Austria	126	194	62	130
Belgium	120	210	46	187
Czech Republic	71	126	28	69
Denmark	102	126	72	73
Finland	113	164	52	88
France	130	170	65	196
Germany	134	209	49	165
Hungary	48	90	19	66
Iceland	71	98	57	48
Ireland	105	162	54	266
Italy	131	237	76	125
Japan	138	179	47	292
Korea	128	147	52	268
Luxembourg	201	253	51	122
Netherlands	162	165	161	149
New Zealand	41	74	18	129
Norway	83	109	56	96
Poland	35	87	16	80
Portugal	44	81	25	46
Slovak Republic	23	90	8	45
Slovenia	80	150	26	72
Spain	67	136	31	89
Sweden	147	227	65	182
Switzerland	174	523	58	57
Turkey	58	144	36	109
United Kingdom	86	230	31	304
Argentina	38	132	18	49
Romania	39	55	20	75
Russian Federation	45	51	34	39
Singapore	158	209	85	167
South Africa	91	252	25	211
Chinese Taipei	117	158	41	159
OECD average	101	169	49	133
Portugal/OECD average	44%	48%	52%	35%

Source: OECD, OLIS, data extracted on September 29
Notes: (1) last available year: Austria, United Kingdom: 1998; Belgium, Denmark, Greece, US: 1999; France, Ireland, Italy, Netherlands, EU15, EU25; Turkey, Switzerland: 2000; (2) the values refer to current US dollars (PPP); (3) values referring to 2000: Switzerland and Turkey, values referring to 2001: Greece, Ireland, Belgium, Netherlands, Italy and Sweden

That said, any analysis of the dynamic in the Portuguese science system remains incomplete if it does not take developments in the higher education system into account and, in particular, the growing levels of qualification in the Portuguese labour force, most especially the younger age groups. Over the past 3 years, total enrolment by 20-year-olds in tertiary education rose by more than 10% to reach some 36% of the age group compared to 30% in 2005. At least one in three 20-year-olds in Portugal attends tertiary education – a statistic, whilst near the European average, is still below most industrialised regions. Expansion reflected the increase of places available in polytechnics, which grew far faster than universities. Amongst the adult population, the qualifications level has also risen. Total enrolment in tertiary education by adults aged 30–34 over the 3 years 2005–2008 rose by 20% to reach 4.1% of the corresponding age group compared to 3.5% in 2005. The annual graduate output between 2005 and 2007 for its part rose by about 19%, whilst S&T graduates numbered approximately 18 per 1,000 of the population aged between 20 and 29 years – well above the EU average.

Rapid massification of higher education and rising qualification levels in the general population are critical if the science system is to develop further. Opening up access as a means to raise participation rates in tertiary education is no less essential if equality of access for students from all social classes is to be improved. Equally important is a human resources pool to meet the rising need for qualified resources in both the work force and the science system (Heitor 2008). No less vital in this regard is to bring the population more closely into contact with science as well as policies intended specifically to enhance the culture of science within the general population. Initiatives for the dissemination and vulgarisation of science and technology were put in hand in the closing decade of the twentieth century. As part of national science policy, they were well received. Schools and other institutions – particularly science centres and science museums – had, and still have – an important role in rousing curiosity and interest in scientific knowledge. The European report 'Benchmarking the Promotion of RTD Culture and Public Understanding of Science' (Miller et al. 2002) paid tribute to the leading role of such national programmes as *Ciência Viva*, under way in Portugal since 1996.

Support for promoting the cultures of science and technology accounts for 5% of public S&T funding. The national network of some 21 *Ciência Viva* centres covers the country, though plans are to increase this number. Projects to boost the experimental teaching of science in primary and secondary schools, to enhance science and technology culture involve close cooperation with schools and research centres. In 2007–2008, the programme was backed to the tune of some 14 million Euros from public funds. In addition, the *Ciência Viva* vacation programme places secondary school students in research and higher education institutions. Since 1997, more than 5,800 secondary school students took part in the vacation programme. The active involvement in summer classes by children and their families in astronomy, biology, geology and engineering is now an established feature of *Ciência Viva* centres. In 2008, for the first time, *Ciência Viva* included an exchange programme between Portugal and Spain.

To summarise the most recent phrase, 'reinforcing critical mass to move beyond the European average': it focuses on international partnerships, on fostering graduate education, university-industry links, the qualification of human resources in R&D

and drawing in knowledge and people. Above all, it is tied in with strong public investment in science as a way to foster investment in R&D by the business sector.

Tracking the Portuguese science system during the first decade of the twenty-first century shows that whilst development was rapid particularly in recent years, it has yet to reach a state of maturity evident in other European countries. If this maturity is to be attained, investment set aside for science ought to continue. The science system still faces several challenges. Some – expanding and maintaining critical mass, reinforcing the institutional strength of science establishments, for instance – stem from the system's own internal dynamic. These issues will now be addressed in depth. Other challenges entail the priority to be given in times of financial stress, to keeping up investment in research and development, to continued support for integrating international networks and to strengthen links between graduate education and research. They will be discussed later.

Discussion: People, Institutions and Ideas

The developmental path of science and technology in Portugal and with it science policy's ongoing challenge, namely, to sustain the momentum in higher education and research, have been explored. Clearly, the system has been successful in meeting some unanticipated goals. Challenges still persist, however. Here, we consider four in particular: the scaling up of the system, increasing its intensity, whilst at the same time raising academic quality and intensifying interaction and exchange between establishments of science and education and, finally, better and deeper integration with society at large and with industry in particular. Such goals demand a thorough grasp of how the S&T system is evolving. This is analysed in the following paragraphs along three lines of approach: people (i.e. human resources), institutions and ideas, generated through science-based activities.

People: Training Human Resources and the New Challenges of Scientific Employment in the Push for Critical Mass

In Portugal over the past half century, training human resources in science and technology encompassed programmes funded by a variety of institutions, amongst which the *Instituto para a Alta Cultura* (IAC), NATO, the *Fundação Calouste Gulbenkian*, the *Fundação Luso-Americana para o Desenvolvimento* (FLAD), the *Junta Nacional de Investigação Científica e Tecnológica* (JNICT) and the *Fundação para a Ciência e Tecnologia* (FCT). Human resources training focused almost exclusively on academia. Hitherto, those obtaining a PhD flowed into higher education, mostly to public universities.

Until 1960, the system was funded mainly through the *Instituto para a Alta Cultura* (IAC). Two rationales predominated: (1) better-prepared academic staff meant better teaching quality; (2) fundamental research advances when academic staff are better prepared (Crespo 1993). Scholarships granted by IAC supported internships with large European laboratories, where networks came together, especially in the exact sciences – physics, chemistry and mathematics, all key elements in launching the national science base (Horta 2010). Later, the Portuguese S&T system benefited from the scholarship programme sponsored by NATO's Scientific Committee. Between 1959 and 1967, the Committee handed out 123 scholarships to be taken up in Portugal and a further 189 abroad. These scholarships played a significant part in establishing international ties. In turn, such ties had an important impact on JNICT's initial planning. In 1956, the *Fundação Calouste Gulbenkian* awarded its first postgraduate scholarship. Thenceforth, the Foundation held annual competitions, which from 1968 extended to all science domains, with priority on scholarships at doctoral and postdoctoral levels.

Between 1985 and 2002, support from Foundations for the advanced training of human resources saw the FLAD granting about 3,928 awards for 'individual support'. The FLAD programme, including scholarships at doctoral and master's degree level, supports for internships in US technology-based firms, laboratories and hospitals, also covered support for the attendance of Portuguese research staff in international congresses. Conversely, it also funded US faculty to attend congresses in Portugal and supported lecturing programmes for visiting professors in Portuguese universities. Ninety percent of all awards for 'individual support' were granted in the broad areas of the hard, pure and applied sciences.

Only after 1986, following Portugal's accession to the European Union, were European structural funds used for advanced training. From the 1990s onwards, this task was assigned to such programmes as CIÊNCIA, which ran until December 31st 1993 – and between 1994 and 1999 to PRAXIS XXI. Until 1997 both were coordinated by JNICT. This arrangement not only permitted previous initiatives be multiplied by several orders of magnitude. At long last, it contributed in an effective manner towards raising the production of human resources in science and technology.

From 1997 onwards, this funding source was managed by the FCT. Priority was placed on doctoral and postdoctoral fellowships, based on competitive evaluation, which gradually became more demanding. Between 2003 and 2008, these fellowships represented more than 90% of all ongoing fellowships funded by FCT. Thus, over the 11 years from 1997 to 2008 (Table 8.3), more than 13,000 doctoral and 4,500 postdoctoral fellowships across all scientific areas were awarded. Of the doctoral fellowships granted during these years, 21% were awarded in engineering and in the social sciences, 17% in the natural sciences, with between 11% and 13% falling to the humanities, to the exact sciences and health sciences. Together, exact sciences, natural sciences and engineering accounted for 2/3 of all fellowships.

The fellowships made a substantial contribution both to the mobility of human resources and to their internationalisation. More than 1,000 were awarded to foreign scholars, as were 34% of all postdoctoral awards. Of the doctoral fellowships granted between 1997 and 2008, 41% involved foreign study or covered a stay of several months abroad. 'National' doctoral fellowships also allowed their holder to

Table 8.3 Fellowships awarded and ongoing by *Fundação para a Ciência e Tecnologia*, by year and scientific area, from 1997 to 2008

	1997	1998	1999	2000	2001	2002	2003	2004	2005	2006	2007	2008
Exact science	96	135	90	118	120	118	93	148	138	200	182	179
Natural sciences	97	127	135	171	169	192	137	218	181	281	289	261
Engineering and technology sciences	135	175	155	139	152	149	133	285	245	403	439	448
Health and medical sciences	73	46	78	80	85	86	108	151	159	200	246	216
Agrarian sciences	22	31	26	35	20	34	30	53	43	72	78	83
Social sciences	114	161	149	162	128	172	104	245	264	360	479	419
Humanities	62	84	81	92	93	97	82	133	165	223	316	329
Total	599	759	714	797	767	848	687	1233	1195	1739	2029	1935

Source: FCT

spend up to 3 months abroad. Of the postdoctoral fellowships handed out over the same period, fellowships for study abroad amounted one in four. This is not unexpected. The great majority of postdoctoral fellowships were more often than not taken up at Portuguese universities. From 1997, the FCT also gave out advanced training fellowships within the general framework of R&D projects. Distributing this latter type of award lay in the discretion of the project's principal researchers, and of the universities where the project was based.

The number of fellowships awarded generated a substantial increase in the number of doctoral degree holders[3] and had major impact on the number of research staff holding a PhD. In 2008, the latter were 11,500, roughly 29% of all full time equivalent research staff. The qualifications held by Portuguese academics also improved.

Three surveys of former FCT scholarship holders, carried out between 1999 and 2001, showed that the vast majority were employed in Portugal, mainly in higher education. Given that both training capacity and the power to draw in new PhD holders determine the maturity of the science system, creating science-based employment is especially important, above all when inserted into scientific networks which generate and sustain solid links between university-based R&D units, state laboratories and firms. Science-based employment in such networks operating at the science base reduces the perverse effects associated with undersized R&D units. It creates and diffuses knowledge. It instils in science development a dynamic of continuous change. It extends internationalisation into Portugal's science base.

A new programme, recently launched, has also boosted science-based employment through the renewal of academic staff in Portuguese universities. This initiative, unveiled in 2007 and based on open competition, provides postdoctoral researchers with a 5-year contract-based employment. Over 1,200 new contracts with Portuguese universities and research units were signed by the end of 2009. Forty-three percent of those hired were concentrated in the exact and natural sciences, with a further 24% in engineering and technology. Social sciences and humanities accounted for some 20% with 10% from health and medical sciences. Significantly, 41% of those engaged were foreign. Of this 41%, 18% were from other EU countries, 4% came from Lusophone countries, for example Brazil. The remaining 19% hailed from countries such as China, India, Russia or the United States. These figures underline both the growing attractiveness of the Portuguese S&T system as well as its international outreach.

These and other initiatives to increase the size and raise the qualifications of the human resource pool in science and technology saw a steady growth in the number of researchers in Portugal. By 2008, more than 75,000 were engaged in research in Portugal compared to less than 30,000 in 2000. Their numbers grew in all fields of science (Table 8.4). In the natural sciences and engineering, their total strength – more than 51,000 in 2007 – was more than double the corresponding statistic for 2000. In the social sciences and humanities, numerical growth was even more pronounced. With more than 23,000 in 2008, it had tripled over the same period. From a purely numerical perspective, the knowledge base in Portugal today is stronger in the exact and natural sciences and engineering, each field drawing on nearly 20,000

Table 8.4 Researchers (headcount) by scientific area in Portugal, 2000–2008

		2000	2001	2002	2003	2004	2005	2006	2007	2008
Natural sciences and engineering	Exact and natural sciences	7,377	7,812	8,249.5	8,687	8,782.5	8,878	10,780	12,682	18,764
	Engineering	7,228	7,434	8,090	8,745	9,214	9,682	13,647	17,611	19,982
	Medical sciences	4,223	4,268	4,528	4,788	5,093	5,398	5,609	5,821	10,665
	Agricultural sciences	2,192	2,151	2,277	2,403	2,263	2,122	2,132	2,142	2,478
Sub-total 1: Natural sciences and engineering		21,019	21,665	23,144	24,623	25,352	26,080	32,168	38,256	51,889
Social sciences and humanities	Social sciences	5,325	5,549	6,294	6,241	6,146	6,051	7,245	8,439	15,466
	Humanities	2,253	2,272	2,538	3,602	3,632	3,661	4,205	4,748	7,717
Sub-total 2: Social sciences and humanities		7,578	7,821	8,832	9,843	9,778	9,712	11,450	13,187	23,184
Sub-total 3: Not elsewhere classified		1,164	1,660	1,525	1,389	1,683	1,977	989	0	0
Total: All fields of science		29,761	31,146	33,501	35,855	36,812	37,769	44,606	51,443	75,073

Source: OECD, OLIS, Research and Development Statistics; data for 2008: GPEARI/MCTES

research staff. Admittedly, in 2000, these same areas also had the most research staff. The highest *growth* rates in researcher strength lay in the social sciences and humanities, although both fields departed from a relatively restricted number of researchers. Agricultural sciences, unlike other fields, however, showed relatively small growth during the early years of the new century.

The recent and rapid rise in human resources engaged in research and development activities during the last phase of Portugal's developing science system acquires even greater significance once the dynamic in human resources active in research and development is itself placed against a longer-term historical perspective (Table 8.5). Compared with current researcher strength, their ranks over the 10 years from 1995 to 2005 represented in absolute figures 40% of today's research body. A similar calculation for the decade 1985 to 1995 shows the nation's research strength then to be 17% of what it is today. And, using the same calculation, the onset of planning science policy saw the strength of the nation's research arm at some 8% of its present-day level. Clearly, such statistics are an eloquent testimony to the solidity that, as time went by, accompanied the engagement in science and technology. By the same token, however, these same statistics also reflect the protracted nature of the dynamic involved. Between 10 and 12 years are necessary for researchers to double in number. As we have seen, however, the last phase is clearly one of speeding up. In 8 years, the number of researchers grew one and a half times, with a telling impact on the build-up and attainment of critical mass in academia's research capacity.

When the low numbers on which the S&T system had first to build are born in mind, this is no small feat. When the planning of S&T was put in hand, the ratio of the number of researchers per 1,000 in Portugal's labour force stood at 21% of the average for the European Union. This is an achievement very far indeed from being negligible. Yet, other indicators point to the need to invest further in the consolidation and growth in the nation's human resource base in science. First, the number of researchers holding a PhD only represents 31% of all researchers (in spite of almost doubling from the previous period to the current one), thus suggesting the need for a further emphasis on the advanced training and qualifications of human resources engaged in research and development activities. Second, the percentage of researchers in the business sector in Portugal in 2008 is only 24% of the total number of researchers, a situation that is dissimilar to the one of countries with more mature scientific human resource base (e.g. in the Netherlands it is 52%, in Finland is 51% and in Belgium is 40%).[4]

The recent and rapid expansion in the number of researchers increased the size of R&D units. By 2007, the average number of PhDs per unit had almost doubled since 1996, from 14 to 27. As expected, the critical mass in Associated Laboratories was larger than other R&D units, the former averaging 58 PhDs per unit, the latter only 23 (Sunkel 2009). The development of research activities in larger R&D units stimulates collaborative research amongst Portuguese researchers both at national and international levels (Horta and Lacy 2011 forthcoming). The same study also found that researchers in larger research units tend to publish more in international outlets, a finding that reflects increasing collaboration with foreign-based scientists as measured by patterns of joint authorship in scientific publications.

Table 8.5 Evolution of human resources in R&D for the evolutionary phases of the S&T system in Portugal

Periods	Total personnel in R&D Headcount	Total personnel in R&D FTE	Total researchers Headcount	Total researchers FTE	Researchers holding a PhD (headcount)	Academic staff (PhD holders headcount)	Researchers in the business sector (headcount)
1967–1985 The beginning of scientific planning (1)	N/A	8,552	5,736	3,962.5	N/A	N/A	878
1985–1995 The late awakening of the scientific base (2)	18,953	12,042.6	12,675	7,736.3	N/A	N/A	1,417
1995–2005 Striving towards the European average (3)	38,018	21,887.7	29,761	16,738.3	12,152	9,465	3,977
2006–... Reinforcing critical masses to move beyond the European average (4)	87,572	47,881.7	75,073	40,408	23,125	14,205	18,206

Sources: For Portugal, OECD, OLIS, GPEARI/MCTES
Notes: No data available for the period 'until 1967'; N/A: no data is available; Notes: (1) data refers to 1982; (2) data refers to 1990; (3) data refers to 2000; (4) data refers to 2008

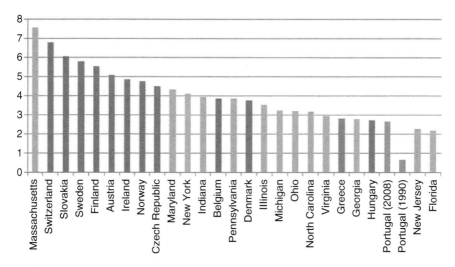

Fig. 8.5 Number of new PhD per 10,000 labour force in selected US states and European countries, 2008 (Note: US labour force refers to the civilian labour force; the countries and US states have a small-medium-sized labour force comprised between 2 and 9.5 million individuals. Data refers to headcounts) (Source: NSF/NIH/USED/USDA/NEH/NASA, 2008 Survey of Earned Doctorates; Eurostat; GPEARI/MCTES)

Rapid growth in the number of researchers had significant repercussions in particular on the qualification level of academic staff across all sectors of higher education, public and private universities and polytechnics. From 2001 to 2009, the proportion of faculty holding a PhD rose in public universities from 48% to 68%, from 21% to 39% in private universities, from 7% to 19% in public polytechnics and from 8% to 19% in their private counterparts. By 2009, of 15,000 faculty members in public universities, more than 10,000 were doctorate holders – a growth of some 47% over the course of the preceding 9 years GPEARI (2010b).

To complete our analysis of Portugal's drive towards attaining critical mass demands an assessment both external and, very particularly, comparative in perspective. Both are necessary because, despite accelerated growth in human resources for science and technology, their growth rate in Portugal remains relatively low compared with other European countries and US states (Fig. 8.5). This emerges clearly when the numbers of new PhDs produced each year are plotted against the country's labour force. On this indicator, in 2008, Portugal created 2.7 new PhDs per 10,000 labour force. By contrast, the Commonwealth of Massachusetts, Switzerland, Slovakia, Sweden and Finland produced more than twice that number. Particularly revealing in this regard is the number of new PhDs awarded per 10,000 labour force in the Commonwealth of Massachusetts. It stands at 7.6 and for Switzerland at 6.8 – a growth rate almost triple that of Portugal. Even so, Portugal can count on more doctoral awards per year than such US states as Florida or New Jersey, having reached that position from a very weak starting line. Twenty years ago in 1990, Portugal turned out a mere 0.68 new PhDs per 10,000 labour force.

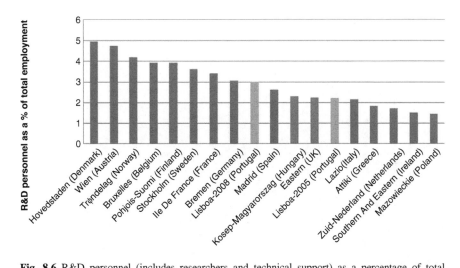

Fig. 8.6 R&D personnel (includes researchers and technical support) as a percentage of total employment in the regions with the greatest critical mass for selected European Union countries, 2007 or latest available year (Note: Data for 2007: Denmark, Austria, Norway, Belgium, Finland, Sweden, Spain, Hungary, UK and Portugal; Data for 2005: Germany, Italy, Greece, the Netherlands; Data for 2001: France. Data refers to headcounts) (Source: OECD, OLIS Regional Statistics dataset)

Both current and past disparities in the numbers of new PhDs impact on the available pool of qualified human resources engaged in research. Such impact is evident at the national level, where only recently has Portugal begun to reach the average levels found in the European Union. However, such disparities also have a regional dimension. It is at regional level that concentrating critical mass is vital for developing poles of excellence to generate additional employment, create wealth and develop the economy (Saxanian 1994; see also, Chaps. 4, 5 and 13).

It has become commonplace to argue that the concentration of critical mass is key to sustaining the quality of research, to forging stronger links between the different sectors engaged in research and to spurring on creativity and innovation regionally and nationally (Baptista and Mendonça 2010; Saxanian 1994). Bearing this in mind, the Lisbon region with most people employed in R&D in Portugal represents only 61% of its counterpart in Hovedstaden (Denmark), the European region that enjoys the most R&D personnel (Fig. 8.6). Compared to Lisbon, the regions of Wien (Austria) and Trøndelag (Norway), for instance, have more than 40% R&D personnel. Despite the rapid rise over the last few years in the number of R&D personnel as a proportion of all employment in the Lisbon area, this region, which concentrates the country's largest critical mass, is still relatively low when compared with others abroad. In the UK, for example, levels of R&D personnel are spread relatively evenly amongst its regions, which hints at a critical mass relatively strong in terms of R&D personnel across all regions – and at national level. By contrast, in Portugal disparities in R&D personnel across regions are substantial (Table 8.6; OECD 2009). In 2008, 45% of all R&D personnel concentrated in the

Table 8.6 Total R&D personnel and researchers by regions in Portugal, 2008

Portuguese Region	Total personnel in R&D (headcount)	%	Total personnel in R&D (FTE)	%	Total researchers (headcount)	%	Total researchers (FTE)	%
Norte	24,051	27	12,408.8	26	20,432	27	10,515.3	26
Centro	17,040	19	8,852.8	18	14,367	19	7,453.9	18
Lisboa	39,245	45	22,778.8	48	34,121	45	19,342.8	48
Alentejo	3,771	4	1,913.6	4	3,242	4	1,541.3	4
Algarve	1,930	2	992.5	2	1,790	2	895.1	2
Azores	787	1	491.6	1	586	1	364.2	1
Madeira	748	1	443.5	1	540	1	295.4	1
Total	87,572	100	47,881.7	100	75,078	100	40,408	100

Source: GPEARI

Lisbon area. This share has decreased slightly over the last decade. In 2001, Lisbon accounted 53% (GPEARI 2010a). Such statistics strongly suggest that raising the number of highly qualified human resources should be a priority for Portuguese science policy over the coming decades if both Portugal and its regions are to attain sufficient critical mass.

For Portugal, quantitative change in human resources for science and technology cannot be divorced from measures to raise the public's understanding of science. Expanding both the number of centres and *Ciência Viva*'s activity is evident from the agency's increasing centrality in nurturing science. Since 1997, for instance, some 7,600 youngsters have held internships in R&D units and laboratories. Between 1997 and 2006, the experimental programme for science teaching in schools engaged more than 4,000 projects, beginning with 216 projects in 1997 and reaching 932 in 2006. Activities of *Ciência Viva* centres often take the form of partnerships with regional or local authorities, with higher education institutions, schools and other bodies. They are in close touch with the science community. Researchers often design the exhibitions, act as project managers, advisors and coordinators, all of which helps establish linked and lateral learning processes between participants. Raising both awareness and interest in science, the advancement of learning in a broad sense, sharpening a critical mind-set amongst individuals and groups, are all seen as prior conditions for fostering research and improving its organisation, as well as defining the role of individuals and groups in what may be called 'global citizenship' (Costa et al. 2002). Indeed, the paradigm involved in vulgarisation and disseminating science to the population and to young people is itself changing, from the public understanding *of* science to the public engagement *with* science and technology (see Delicado 2010; Miller 2001; Bodmer 1985).

A recent study suggested that the *Ciência Viva* programme mobilised widespread support in advancing the culture of science. A wide range of initiatives, exchange programmes and partnerships, by bringing together innovative projects across several institutions, focusing its projects on different sections of the public, all contribute to its growing visibility (Costa et al. 2005). Of major importance is the assumed positive impact *Ciência Viva* activities have on young people's career decisions, their subject choice at secondary school which gradually inclines towards the fields of science and nature.

Institutions: From State Laboratories to Reinforcing R&D Laboratories and Forward-Looking Universities

For most of the twentieth century in Europe, strengthening S&T establishments involved developing state laboratories. State laboratories first appeared in Portugal in the late nineteenth century. They focused on such areas as health and the agricultural sciences (Ruivo 1995). During the first Republic (1910–1926) other areas developed – maritime biology and animal and veterinary sciences (see Chaps. 2 and 3). Developing the institutional base of state laboratories received particular attention during the *Estado Novo* (1933–1974) mainly between the 1930s and 1960s when development addressed several goals:

1. To open up research beyond the rigidities of the university system. The founding of the *Laboratório Nacional de Engenharia Civil* – LNEC – provided a clear evidence of this.
2. To meet the interests of new scientists and engineers in keeping with the interests of the *Estado Novo*.
3. To meet the emerging requirements of industry. The LNEC, created in 1946, provides a referential case study, given the quality and the international standing it achieved in the field of civil engineering. Other state laboratories also represent steps to institutionalise scientific research in the public interest and to support government strategies, which naturally came under the control and supervision of the *Estado Novo*.

As with other OECD countries, even those with a more developed science system, state laboratories followed the pattern of bureaucratic organisation that characterised most public bodies under state control. Faced with the need to enhance science and to meet the requirements scientific enquiry posed, the use of continuous evaluation procedures remained unconsidered or ill considered. Their apparent irrelevance to the S&T system of the day reflected a growing deficit in material resources per researcher, ageing staff and infrastructures, an advanced training of increasing obsolescence and the extreme paucity of researchers holding a doctoral degree. According to a survey recently conducted by JNICT, during the 1980s, only 5% of research staff in state laboratories were PhD holders. After 28 years, it stands at 25% (GPEARI 2010a). To correct this situation, international evaluation procedures were put in hand in 1996, which drew upon both international and national experts. As a direct consequence, 2 years later, FCT introduced a programme to reform Sate laboratories. The programme set out guidelines for specific projects in the public interest, introduced management by objectives, renewed human resources for R&D, organised project teams lead by a principal researcher, extended both autonomy and flexibility in managing these teams and placed them under the responsibility of a principal researcher appointed to this task (FCT 2002).

Even so, continuous absence of autonomy for state laboratories, difficulties in making the state accountable especially for institution-based activities of a public nature, worked in such a way that the remit and mandate of state laboratories was fulfilled simply by dint of their providing services. Not only did this situation reduce their contribution to the nation's scientific and technological development. It meant in the main that S&T development was led by university-based R&D units, which covered a variety of science domains and fields of specialisation. In the late 1980s, however, the institutional environment in Portuguese universities plus the administrative workload led several researchers to set up non-profit institutions, focusing on knowledge creation and on disseminating academically generated knowledge to society at large, and to the business sector, in particular. In effect, they became 'interface' institutions between higher education and society (Table 8.7). Since their staff often included faculty from different universities

Table 8.7 Main institutional breakthroughs experienced in the last 40 years, as fostered through increasing academic and research capacity

Period	Main institutional breakthrough	Rationale for breakthrough	National research assessment exercise	National university assessments
1967–1985 (late part of this period)	Non for profit institutions, fostered through academic research (a leading example is INESC, as created in 1980)	Knowledge creation and dissemination in institutions outside the reach of the university bureaucracy	–	–
1985–1995				
1995–2005	Associate Laboratories, to foster research excellence through networks of academic research centres (as created since 1999, with a few initial developments in biomedical and physical science, but reaching 25 Laboratories by 2007)	Fostering critical masses, aggregating several R&D groups and attracting new talents, under the direct support of FCT	1996/19997 exercise 1999/2000 exercise 2002/2003 exercise	–
2006–....	University Foundations (includes three leading examples in 2008, including University of Porto, University of Aveiro and ISCTE business school)	Enabling flexible management and organisational mechanisms; institutional autonomy and responsibility of higher education institutions; having more responsive institutions	2007 exercise	The Agency for Assessment and Accreditation of Higher Education (A3ES) through the assessment and accreditation of study cycles in higher education institutions is impacting their education (About 1,200 courses are to be discontinued)
	International partnerships, as thematic research and advanced training networks (includes partnerships with MIT, CMU, Harvard and UT Austin in emerging themes, including ICTs, energy, bioengineering, design, clinical research)	Networks of research centres across leading Portuguese universities, brought together to cooperate with world leading institutions, involving business industry		

(for example, *INESC Lisboa – Instituto de Engenharia de Sistemas e Computadores*, drew its staff members from universities based in and around Lisbon), knowledge transfer took place through articles, consultancy, research projects and the employment of students in firms. Significantly, contact between faculty and the business sector created 'spin-offs' that still play an important role in the latter's research performance (Marques et al. 2006).

In support of academic research and to strengthen R&D units, Decree-law 125/99, known as the *Regime Jurídico das Instituições de Investigação* (Legal Framework for Research Establishments), was passed in 1999. It granted the status of *Laboratório Associado* (Associated Laboratory) on those research establishments demonstrating scientific excellence as recognised by external evaluation. The first Associated Laboratories were set up in November of 2000. By 2001, 15 laboratories, bringing together 31 research institutions and staffed by more than 2,200 researchers, of whom 880 were PhD holders, were active in R&D. By 2009, the network of scientific institutions encompassed 510 research centres – 257 as a result of the evaluation in 1996 and 25 Associate Laboratories, the first three of which had been set up in 2001. Overall, institutional funding amounted to some 80 million Euros compared with five million Euros a decade earlier.

One of the main objectives assigned to Associated Laboratories called for an increase in science-based jobs by recruiting both doctoral level research staff and additional technicians. As a result, the average number of PhDs in Associated Laboratories is twice that of general R&D units. A second objective set out to develop critical mass in each and every scientific discipline by bringing together comparatively large research consortia engaged in thematic networks across a number of institutions, selected by international assessment. The launching of Associated Laboratories was part of the transition towards a non-material economy, based on producing intangibles, a development seen elsewhere in Europe. Being both stable and drawing on a strengthened research staff basis, they were indispensable if science development in Portugal was to tackle the systemic problems of scale and intensity. Associated Laboratories opened the way for a new science culture, grounded in institutional autonomy, upheld by incentives and urged on by regular and ongoing recourse to independent scientific evaluation, a culture that had been developed and implemented in both the OECD countries and in most established and mature science systems, such as the UK (Roberts 2003).

In 2007, the reforming impulse in Portuguese higher education received a further boost with new Legal Framework for higher education institutions[5] (i.e. the 'RJIES'). The new framework (Chaps. 7, 10 and 12) laid down organisational principles for the higher education system, defined institutional autonomy and accountability. It established Governing Boards with external participation. It recognised research units as part of the university management structure. Not only did the Framework Act anticipate greater openness of universities to society in general. It also made provision for a more direct and clearer involvement of research staff in university decision-making. In effect, it addressed one of the oft-mentioned and abiding obstacles to the build-up of knowledge bases in Portuguese universities (see Horta 2008).

The Legal Framework ushered in greater institutional diversity. It changed the legal status of public higher education establishments. Henceforth, they may opt for independent legal status as public foundations governed by private law (Hasan 2007). Granting independent legal status to public universities and polytechnics is one way to give them greater autonomy. University foundations have a number of advantages. First, institutional leadership has the widest latitude to pursue its goals with little external constraint. Second, leadership can plan over the long term without being subjected to shifts in government budgetary policies. Third, new opportunities for generating additional resources were opened up. Finally, accountability was vested in those on whom responsibility rested. Yet, legislation also contained potential shortcomings. Managing a foundation requires different and sometimes new skills. These, institutional leadership may find difficult to acquire. Staff may also see the move away from the status of public servant to university employee as fraught with risk and uncertainty.

Concern about the viability of the foundation model was not absent – for example, insufficient scale to permit economies to be made; expertise inappropriate for running a foundation. Still, the expectation remained that universities, which opted for the status of public foundations, would become more flexible, more adaptable to society's demands and more alert to the structural problems that might affect both their research proficiency and productivity. By the end of 2009, three universities volunteered for this status, the University of Porto, the largest Portuguese public university with some 30,000 students, the University of Aveiro, a medium-sized university with some 13,000 and ISCTE-IUL, a small university institute with approximately 6,000 students (MCTES 2010).

Strategically oriented, international partnerships are a key element in bringing higher education reform into close alignment with the goal of raising national research capacity. Their prime focus lies in modifying the approach to institutional development. Conceived as top-down initiatives, partnerships are thematically oriented with the express aim of nurturing national networks, lead by world-recognised institutions (see further details below). To galvanise scientific activity in networks engaged in inter-institutional projects, particular weight is placed on cooperation at national and international level.

The strategic programme of international science, technology and higher education partnerships was unveiled in 2006. By September 2007, the first doctoral and advanced studies programme was running. It brought together several Portuguese universities with other world-ranking universities, including MIT, Carnegie Mellon University, Harvard Medical School and the University of Texas at Austin. These initiatives, unprecedented in Portugal, opened the way in 2007 for setting up a number of thematic networks. Networking brought together a large number of Portuguese institutions, extended their international outreach through advanced studies projects. Ongoing ventures to generate new knowledge and exploit new ideas together with firms and institutions enjoying high international repute and standing were an integral part of the strategy.

Recently, two innovative institutions with an international focus and intimately bonded with quality-driven science took their place in the Portuguese S&T

firmament: the International Iberian Nanotechnology Laboratory (INL) and the Champalimaud Foundation. The first, a joint Portuguese and Spanish partnership, aims at building up a strong base for close collaboration at the cutting edge of science. The INL is currently under construction at Braga, in the north of Portugal. Its first director, the Spanish professor José Rivas, has been appointed. The INL will bring together some 200 research staff, recruited worldwide. It will be jointly funded by both Spanish and Portuguese Governments. The laboratory is backed by a long-term financial commitment. Each Government will underwrite, in equal parts, public funding to the tune of 30 million Euros. Such conditions, together with the openness and visibility, flexibility and stability in decision-making, plus the status of an international research organisation, are expected to make this laboratory an international reference point, which in future other countries may join.

The second establishment, the Champalimaud Foundation, was created by the bequest of the Portuguese industrialist and entrepreneur, the late António Champalimaud. It focuses on biomedical science. The Champalimaud Foundation seeks to extent research in the fields of oncology, neuroscience and to advance the field of ophthalmology.

Knowledge and Ideas: Processes of Technical Change: The Challenge of International Science and Technology Networks

Growth in the numbers of research staff, the rise in their qualifications and the maturity of scientific establishments, all had marked impact on Portuguese scientific output, particularly that which is internationally refereed. The number of internationally cited, scientific publications doubled since 2002 and almost tripled over the period from 2000.

Figure 8.7 measures the scientific competitiveness of several European countries. It shows Portugal, with some 703 scientific publications per million inhabitants in 2009 to be the country where output grew most since 2000 (Table 8.8). Portugal's science base is now internationally competitive. However, when set against other European countries – Sweden with 1,831 publications over the same period or Denmark with 1,777 – clearly such growth needs to be sustained by raising the critical mass that the concentration of knowledge-integrated communities requires.

Overall publication output grew 1.65 times since 2000. Output is greater still when compared to the days when science planning was in its infancy or when the science base began belatedly to awake. In terms of sheer volume of internationally refereed publications, the earlier period saw output rise more than nine times and by a factor 25 when plotted against the latter. The citations received by publications authored by researchers based in Portugal also point to the growing visibility and impact which research based in Portugal is having internationally. Both suggest that Portugal's contribution to the world 'knowledge pool' is greater than ever.

What may be learnt from this analysis? It is this: the increasing intensity of collaboration with international partners deserves close attention. 'Internationalising'

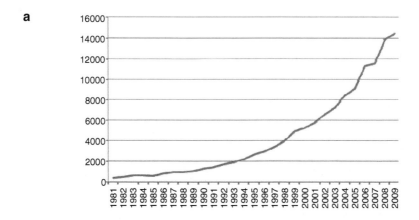

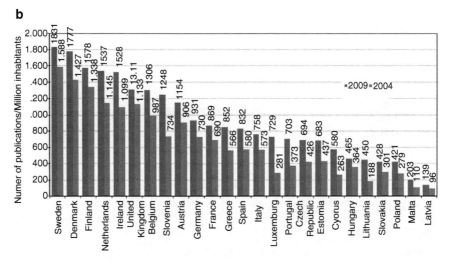

Fig. 8.7 Evolution of the Portuguese scientific production measured by number of international publications (referred by ISI), 1981–2009 (**a**) Portuguese scientific production measured by number of international publications (referred by ISI), 1981–2009, (**b**) Number of publications by million population, 2004–2009 (Note: Data for 2009 is provisional) (Source: GPEARI 2009a)

Portugal's science base is strongly associated with public policies, which simultaneously drove its development forwards as they urged on the dynamic of internationalisation (Horta 2010). High levels of collaboration between Portuguese researchers and their foreign-based colleagues are in keeping with trends observed in other small- and medium-sized countries. Not surprisingly, the rationale that justifies intensifying international collaboration stems from small critical masses, from the need for access to more advanced equipment and facilities, and, last but not least, from international collaboration as a facilitating factor in integrating global scientific communities (Hakala 1998).

Analysing Portugal's collaborative projects also provides an insight into the patterns building up during the different phases of development through which the national

Table 8.8 Main identified periods of the evolution of the S&T system in Portugal

Periods		Total publications	Citations	Percentage of publications done in collaboration	Top five countries (collaborations)
1967–1985	The beginning of scientific planning	388	1,652 (1981–1985)	N/A	N/A
1985–1995	The late awakening of the scientific base	970	5,748 (1990–1994)	39%	UK, US, France, Germany, Netherlands
1995–2005	Striving towards the European average:	3,792	14,457 (1997–2001)	46%	UK, US, France, Spain, Germany
2006–...	Reinforcing critical masses to move beyond the European average	10,081	34,971 (2005–2009)	48%	Spain, UK, US, France, Germany

Sources: for Portugal, EU and US: OECD, OLIS; for Portugal, GPEARI/MCTES

Notes: No data available for the period 'until 1967'; (1) data refers to 1982; (2) data refers to 1990; (3) data refers to 2000; (4) data refers to 2009; the information regarding citations is presented in 5 year periods following the traditional scientometrics approach

S&T system passed. Joint research with Spain in particular has burgeoned in recent years (Castro-Cruz and Menéndez 2005). Such a dynamic seems to follow the phenomenon detected by Smeby and Trondal (2005) in other European states. For Smeby and Trondal, it was a dynamic propelled by both 'Europeanisation and globalisation movements'. That these two factors are also present in Portugal suggests that the Nation's science effort has become fully integrated with the European Research Area.

When we place the process of knowledge diffusion against a broader historical perspective and most especially if we set industry-science links and the impact they have on technical change, clearly this is not a short-term policy. On the contrary, planned initiatives to speed knowledge diffusion, disseminate 'new ideas' and create networks to tie research together between university and industry *stricto lato* was a strategy in place since the early 1980s. The initiative was first launched by the *Ministério da Indústria e Energia* (Ministry of Industry and Energy). It was grounded in Industrial Development Contracts, which in turn were part of the *Plano de Desenvolvimento Tecnológico da Indústria Transformadora* (Technological Development Plan for the Manufacturing Industry). In all, some 60 contracts were signed. Each required its beneficiaries to take up R&D services for an amount that, at minimum, represented 5% of the total funding the contract brought with it. These contracts played a decisive role in integrating young researchers, returning from doctoral studies abroad, into R&D teams. They were key also in setting up R&D teams, which from 1986 onwards, competed for European Community funds. With additional backing from projects financed by JNICT's *Programa Mobilizador de Ciência e Tecnologia* (Programme for Mobilising Science and Technology) between 1988 and 1990, this objective was attained.

With the onset of the 1990s, scientific and technological development took on further momentum thanks to programmes like CIÊNCIA and PRAXIS XXI, which drew on the European Union's structural funds. In turn, such programmes received further support for advanced training through human resources programmes,[6] and the PRODEP and PEDIP programmes in particular. The latter funded the build-up of physical infrastructure. Between 1996 and 2002, some 70 million Euros were invested through PREDIP II in 19 projects[7] that boosted technological and industrial development in different sectors of the economy.

In particular, the build-up of Portugal's scientific output in technology areas benefited from the European Commission's Framework Programmes, which started up in 1984. University-based teams, often working with private sector non-profit institutions, took part in these programmes, as did private sector firms, though on a limited scale until the Fifth Framework Programme. The first Framework Programme gave priority to information technologies, which accounted for 33% of all groups taking part. Of the Portuguese tenders retained, 72% were concentrated around the Lisbon region. Evidence of the maturity the nation's scientific community now enjoyed stood out in the Fifth Framework Programme, which ran from 1998 to 2002. In more than 180 projects focused on competitive and sustainable growth, in 170 projects dealing with information technologies and 140 projects that addressed the issue of the quality of life, Portuguese R&D teams actively participated. Thirty-two percent of the country's total participation in Fifth Framework Programme was firm-based. The EUREKA programme raised this further. In all, and over the 15 years from 1985 to the year 2000, projects awarded to Portugal numbered 165, with 60 being coordinated by Portuguese institutions.

The influence exerted by incentive-based funding programmes in promoting R&D was both self-evident and decisive. Even so, different forms of incentive need complementary action to raise both intensity and scale of R&D. Contract research was particularly important. If research is to assume a new dynamic, other incentives have to be brought to bear. And private sector firms, in particular, require other forms of encouragement – for instance, tax breaks for those actively engaging in research and innovation.[8] In short, priority in developing the science system rests on a variety of incentives.[9]

In this, Portugal's trajectory in science and technology owed much to two recent incentive-driven programmes for promoting R&D. The first, in 2005, overhauled the tax system for corporate R&D. Initially introduced in the late 1990s, it was designed to encourage business spending on both R&D and research personnel in the private sector. Firms applying for this tax break, less than 300 in 2003, rose to more than a 1,000 in 2009. The opportunities the SIFIDE tax system provides are considered amongst the most attractive in Europe. Tax liability may be reduced by some 32.5% of the total expense on R&D. To this can be added a further deduction of 50% on the increase in expenditure on R&D over the previous 2 years, up to a maximum of 1.5 million Euros. In all, deductions can reach 82.5% of the total invested in R&D. In addition, a recent adjustment to the tax system for corporate R&D, which took effect in 2010, allows the cost of employing PhD researchers to be totally deducted during the first year. The overall tax credit set aside in the state budget for 2010 is about 50 million Euros, as against 27 million Euros in 2008.

The second incentive programme concentrated on laying out structures and procedures to enhance consortia-based research. To this end, international partnerships, as we have already noted, were introduced. They introduced a new slant on institutional development, very specifically intended to offset the disadvantages of scale, which limited size imposes on some research units. Multiplying science-based networks stimulates the generation and diffusion of new knowledge. It drives scientific development forwards at a time of constant change when the internationalisation of the science base is itself a phenomenon in constant flux. Strengthening the international dimensions in higher education and in S&T is a well-established way to integrate national institutions in science networks as they emerge at the international level. From this, it follows that internationalisation should be a central component in most, if not all, science and education oriented projects. Internationalisation spurs on the mobility of academics, research staff and students. The benefits are considerable. Mobility early in a research career is highly important in determining the work that will be carried out in the future just as it is in forging international ties as part of academia's Invisible College (Horta 2009). With such considerations in mind, each programme is tied in with an international partner, strategically and carefully selected in the light of those specific and equally strategic objectives that identify and differentiate each programme from others (Table 8.9).

Table 8.9 Main strategically oriented international partnerships fostered since 2006 to foster excellence in academic research and knowledge integrated communities with international relevance

Strategic partnership	Launched	Brief description and evolution
MIT-Portugal	October 2006	Focused on the field of 'engineering systems', with special emphasis to the complex processes associated with industrial production, sustainable energy, bioengineering and transport systems, in which Portuguese and MIT faculty and researchers identified three main thematic areas for research and development in close cooperation with an industrial affiliation programme. They include sustainable energy and transportation systems, stem cell engineering for novel therapies in regenerative medicine, and materials and design-inspired products with specific applications in electric mobility and new medical devices. Overall, the programme involved over 340 master and doctorate students at the beginning of its third year in September 2009
		Recently strengthened and opened to additional partners through three thematic research networks, namely on: (1) The Sustainable Cities Forum and Research Network; (2) Sustainable Energy Systems and Electric Mobility Research Platform and Network, or the 'E2 Research Net'; and (3) Stem Cell Engineering and Clinical Research net, or 'StemCellnet'
		Through the joint programme with MIT, co-operation with the Sloan School of Management was strengthened through an international MBA programme, 'Lisbon MBA'. This involves co-funding from seven major Portuguese companies and banks in a way that will stimulate new research and the quality of education in management sciences in Portugal
Carnegie Mellon-Portugal	October 2006	Focused on information and communication technologies, in particular the so called Future Internet technologies and services, and involving dual professional masters and PhD programmes by Portuguese institutions and Carnegie Mellon University. The areas covered include new generation networks, software engineering, cyber-physical systems for ambient intelligence, human-centric computing (including language technology), public policy and entrepreneurship research, and applied mathematics. Overall, the programme involved about 170 master and doctorate students at the start of its third year in September 2009
		Three new innovation networks were launched at a later stage, whose goal is to consolidate and expand the successful cooperation amongst all partner institutions and industrial affiliates: (1) Security and Critical Infrastructure Protection (NET-SCIP); (2) Future Internet Services and Technologies (NET-FIT); and (3) Services and Technologies for Interactive Media (NET-STIM)

UTAustin-Portugal	March 2007	The programme 'International Collaboratory for Emerging Technologies, CoLab' focuses on collaborative research in advanced interactive digital media and integrating advanced computing and applied mathematics. Overall, the programme involved about 70 doctorate students at the start of its third year in September 2009 Under the joint collaboration with the University of Texas in Austin, a 'University Technology Enterprise Network, UTEN' was established in 2007 and oriented towards international technology commercialisation and the professionalisation of university technology managers
Fraunhofer Portugal Research Association	May 2008	Establishment in Portugal of the first Fraunhofer Institute in Europe outside Germany. This project focuses on emerging information and communication technologies, such as 'Ambient Assisted Living', to be complemented by the establishment of R&D consortia and co-operative projects involving several Portuguese institutions and Fraunhofer institutes in Germany
Harvard Medical School-Portugal	May 2009	Focus on translational research and information fostering translational and clinical research programmes and the development of a new infrastructure for delivering medical information produced by medical schools to medical students across the academic institutions, to health practitioners and to the general public, thus contributing to strengthen the relationships of medical schools and health science institutions with their main constituencies
International Iberian Nanotechnology Laboratory	July 2009	It is the first research laboratory set up under international law in the Iberian Peninsula, and it is the first such institution worldwide explicitly focused in nanotechnology. It is expected to achieve a reputation as an international institution of excellence in application areas of food and water quality, environmental monitoring and nanomedicine, conceived for about 200 researchers from all over the world, a total of 400 people, and an annual investment and operational budget of around 30 million Euros that is being funded equally by both countries. It is expected that this laboratory will develop strong links with industry and will attract the membership of more European countries and countries of other continents

In addition to the strategic international partnerships just mentioned, other projects, directed towards Portuguese industry, were started recently. Thus, the synergy generated by cross national partnerships within academia extends onwards to industrially linked programmes – to stem cell engineering for regenerative medicine, automotive engineering, low-energy systems through the MIT-Portugal joint venture, telecommunications and information systems with the Carnegie Mellon-Portugal partnership, the Fraunhofer-Portugal association and the UT Austin-Portugal Programme. A network of technology transfer offices supporting the development and internationalisation of technology-based entrepreneurial ventures is moving ahead within the University Technology Enterprise Network (UTEN).

Summary

This analysis of the development over time of Portugal's science and technology system and the impact it has had on modernising higher education underlines three crucial aspects:

(a) *Scale* of the system, placed against the need for continued public support for the *advanced training of human resources* through R&D, and particularly, to increase further the current number of research staff and personnel engaged in S&T activities.
(b) *Diversification*, tied with the need to differentiate the role of public and private funding for science whilst preserving the integrity of institutions and the freedom of thought.
(c) *Time*, reflecting a basic truth namely, that evolution in the S&T system is a continuous process. It requires both stability and the ongoing engagement of *people* and *institutions*.

At the onset of the twenty-first century and against this background of change, debate about the future of the Portugal's science system continues. Certainly, investment in science at last has reached – and gone beyond – the long-awaited moment when the amount set aside for research and development topped 1% of GDP. In 2009, general expenditure on R&D attained 1.71%. Yet, the nation's R&D system needs to maintain its investment in science if it is to acquire further sustainability and maturity. Both are vital if stability is to be ensured, if the modernisation of higher education is to continue and if further goals are to be met. At this juncture, our argument is clear. Developing the science system further and the policies necessary to this purpose need to be brought together more closely and interlocked with the development of the higher education system itself and with those policies that address these tasks.

Why this is so, is clear. Qualifying human resources, raising the critical mass further both remain as pressing and as vital today and in the immediate future as they were yesterday. Despite the speeding up, which we have analysed and noted in the growth of human resources for S&T, together with the accompanying rise in qualifications and skills, nevertheless Portugal produces fewer highly qualified human resources than other states in Europe and in the US. Even the nation's most R&D intensive region is still far from enjoying the levels of R&D personnel its counterparts command in most European countries. Our analysis suggests that the basic dynamic that has driven Portugal forward, also opens up a new potential for that nexus, of increasing importance, between science policy and higher education policy, just as it reveals the growing significance of the role S&T plays in modernising higher education.

In terms of human resources, it is equally clear that sustainability of the S&T system depends on the continuous flow of graduates from tertiary education. In its turn, that depends on a no-less vital condition namely, the ability of tertiary education to attract the talented and well qualified. Only by opening tertiary education to a wider constituency, drawn from all social classes and economic conditions may the levels of qualification in the labour force be raised, and, by so doing, guarantee the necessary pool of the well-qualified to feed the research system (Chaps. 7 and 10). It goes without saying that such a goal requires a broad range of policies to raise participation rates further. Innovative and creative funding schemes to improve equality of access are not the least amongst them. In this, Portugal has recently seen further initiatives in a policy specifically designed to have three principal points of impact – on the systems of higher education, on the science system and on the economy (Heitor 2008; Heitor and Bravo 2010). This triple focus, we believe, not only reflects current views on emerging learning societies. It is a configuration emerging in a world that is globalising. This triple alignment drives the referential exemplars and institutional arrangements that have worldwide significance. In short, the *rapprochement* of higher education policy and science policy is, to echo Victor Hugo, an idea whose time has come.

Yet, dimensions remain in Portugal's S&T system that still show frailness and vulnerability. Correctives to them must be found and developed. So too must appropriate incentives to allow both institutions and projects to flourish in more stable environments where practice and process may be strengthened. In this, quality assurance remains essential. Scientific quality must remain the prime driver of system evolution in the future, both by assigning funding and in evaluating research establishments. For their part, both research establishments and higher education must advance and do so autonomously. With these priorities in mind, that the state continues to recognise and reward the initiatives shown by research establishments through its diversifying of resources and funding is vital. That research establishments, universities and polytechnics are themselves active in advancing their own autonomy, is no less so.

Today, more than ever before institutions of research and of higher education are held accountable to society. In this, they are similar to the state itself. They are answerable to a growing and perhaps not always predictable range of interests – to the public, to 'stakeholders', to 'external interests', for instance – which impose on them the onus, not just of demonstrating but being *seen* to demonstrate a measurable and increasing capacity to generate and disseminate knowledge. They are being asked to do so in ways that are perceived as relevant, if not always immediately applicable by those who require accounts to be rendered. This, universities, polytechnics and research establishments are being asked to do in a world where human and material resources are scarce. They must do so in a world of great financial uncertainty where resources and cash both demand wise and nicely calculated use. Against such backdrop of financial difficulty and with limited public budgets, it is no less vital for the state to continue to underwrite the autonomy of both S&T and higher education, by increasing the numbers of research staff, material resources and by shaping public policies appropriate to Portugal's development.

Notes

1. The term 'critical mass' refers to the minimum required resources (often referring to the size of personnel engaged in R&D) needed to assure a dynamic and continuous performance of research and development activities with minimum levels of quality and success.
2. The technology balance of payments records commercial transactions related to international technology and know-how transfers. It consists of capital paid or received for the use of patents, licences, know-how, trademarks, patterns, designs, technical services (including technical assistance) and for industrial research and development (R&D) carried out abroad.
3. See section People: Training Human Resources and the New challenges of Scientific Employment in the Push for Critical Mass; Fig. 8.5.
4. Data for the last available year: Finland: 2008; Netherlands and Belgium: 2007; Source: OECD, OLIS
5. RJIES; Law 62/2007, of 10 September 2007.
6. See above check pp.
7. Data provided by the *Gabinete de Coordenação da Inovação Tecnológica, Ministério da Economia*
8. Tax breaks to firms engaging in R&D activities were in place during the last years of the twentieth century.
9. For a detailed discussion see Conceição et al. 2004.

References

Amaral, A., & Magalhães, A. (2005). Implementation of higher education policies: A Portuguese example. In A. Gornitzka, M. Kogan, & A. Amaral (Eds.), *Reform and change in higher education – Analysing policy implementation*. Dordrecht: Springer.
Baptista, R., & Mendonça, J. (2010). Proximity to knowledge sources and the location of knowledge-based start-ups. *The Annals of Regional Science, 45*, 5–29.
Bensaúde, A. (1922). *Notas Histórico-Pedagógicas sobre o Instituto Superior Técnico*. Lisboa: Imprensa Nacional.
Bodmer, W. (1985). *The public understanding of science*. London: Royal Society.
Campos, E. de. (1943). *O Enquadramento Geoeconómico da População Portuguesa Através dos Séculos* (2nd ed.). Lisboa: Revista Ocidente.
Caraça, J. (1993). *Do Saber ao Fazer: Porquê Organizar a Ciência*. Lisboa: Gradiva.
Caraça, J., & Pernes, F. (2002). *"Ciência e Investigação em Portugal no século XX" in Panorama da Cultura Portuguesa no Século XX*. Porto: Edições Afrontamento.

Castro-Cruz, L., & Menéndez, L. S. (2005). Bringing science and technology human resources back in: The Spanish Ramón y Cajal programme. *Science & Public Policy, 32*(1), 39–53.
Coelho, E. (1962). *Da problemática da Universidade, o seu sentido ecuménico e nacional.* Lisboa: Imp. portuguesa.
Conceição, P., & Heitor, M. V. (2005). *Innovation for All? Learning from the Portuguese Path to Technical Change and the Dynamics of Innovation.* Praeger: Westport.
Conceição, P., Heitor, M. V., Sirilli, G., & Wilson, R. (2004). The 'swing of the pendulum' from public to market support for science and technology: Is the US leading the way? *Technological Forecasting and Social Change, 71*, 553–578.
Costa, A. F., Ávila, P., & Mateus, S. (2002). *Públicos de Ciência em Portugal.* Lisboa: Gradiva.
Costa, A. F., Conceição, C. P., Pereira, I., Abrantes, P., & Gomes, M. C. (2005). *Cultura Científica e Movimento Social.* Oeiras: Celta Editora.
Crespo, V. (1993). *Uma Universidade para os Anos 2000 – O Ensino Superior numa perspectiva de futuro.* Mem Martins: Editorial Inquérito.
Delicado, A. (2010). Exhibiting science in Portugal: Practices and representations in museums. *Portuguese Journal of Social Science, 9*(1), 19–32.
Dias, J. F. (1961). *A posição Actual da Indústria Metalomecânica.* Lisboa: Associação Industrial Portuguesa.
Dias, J. N. F., Jr. (1998). Linha de Rumo I e II e Outros Escritos Económicos, 1926–1962. In J. M. Brandão de Brito (Ed.), *Colecção de Obras Clássicas do Pensamento Económico Português,* (20, 3 vols.). Lisboa: Banco de Portugal.
Fundação para a Ciência e Tecnologia (FCT). (2002). *Relatório: Cinco anos de Actividades 1997 a 2001.* Lisboa: FCT.
Gago, J. M. (1990). *Manifesto para a Ciência em Portugal – ensaio.* Viseu: Gradiva.
GPEARI. (2009a). *Produção Científica Portuguesa, 1990–2008: séries estatísticas.* Lisboa: GPEARI.
GPEARI. (2009b). *Doutoramentos realizados ou reconhecidos por universidades Portuguesas: 1970 a 2008.* Lisboa: GPEARI.
GPEARI. (2010a). *Inquérito ao Potencial Científico e Tecnológico Nacional.* Lisboa: GPEARI.
GPEARI. (2010b). *Docentes do Ensino Superior 2001–2009.* Lisboa: GPEARI.
Hakala, J. (1998). Internationalisation of science. Views of the scientific elite in Finland. *Science Studies, 11*(1), 52–74.
Hasan, A. (2007). *Independent legal status and universities as foundations.* Paper prepared for the Portuguese Ministry of Science, Technology and Higher Education.
Heitor, M. (2001). *Relatório da Avaliação de Unidades de Investigação financiadas pelo programmea plurianual – 1999/2000.* Lisboa: MCT.
Heitor, M. (2008). A system approach to tertiary education institutions: Towards knowledge networks and enhanced societal trust. *Science & Public Policy, 35*(8), 607–617.
Heitor, M., & Bravo, M. (2010). Portugal at the crossroads of change, facing the shock of the new: People, knowledge and ideas fostering the social fabric to facilitate the concentration of knowledge integrated communities. *Technological Forecasting and Social Change, 77*(2), 218–247.
Heitor, M., & Horta, H. (2004). Engenharia e desenvolvimento científico. In J. M. B. Brito, M. Heitor, & M. F. Rollo (Eds.), *Engenharia em Portugal no Século XX.* Lisboa: D. Quixote.
Horta, H. (2008). On improving the university research base: The technical university of Lisbon case in perspective. *Higher Education Policy, 21*, 123–146.
Horta, H. (2009). Holding a post-doctoral position before becoming faculty member: Does it brings benefits for the scholarly enterprise? *Higher Education, 58*(5), 689–721.
Horta, H. (2010). The role of the state in the internationalization of universities in catching-up countries: An analysis of the Portuguese higher education system. *Higher Education Policy, 23*, 63–81.
Horta, H., & Lacy, T. A. (2011). How does size matter for science? Exploring the effects of research unit size on academics' scientific productivity and information exchange behaviors. *Science and Public Policy, 38*(6), 449–460.

Lundvall, B., & Johnson, B. (1994). The learning economy. *Journal of Industry Studies, 1*(2), 23–42.
Macedo, J. B. (1970). A dívida externa portuguesa. In *Cadernos de Ciência e Técnica Fiscal*. Lisboa: Centro de Estudos Fiscais da DGCI, Ministério das Finanças.
Marques, A. H. O. (1986). *História de Portugal* (Vol. II). Lisboa: Pala Editores.
Marques, J. P. C., Caraça, J. M. G., & Diz, H. (2006). How can university–industry–government interactions change the innovation scenario in Portugal? —The case of the university of Coimbra. *Technovation, 26*(4), 534–542.
Miller, S. (2001). Public understanding of science at the crossroads. *Public Understanding of Science, 10*, 115–120.
Miller, S., Caro, P., Koulaidis, V., Semir, V., Staveloz, W., & Vargas, R. (2002). *Report from the Expert Group Benchmarking the promotion of RTD culture and Public Understanding of Science*. ftp://ftp.cordis.europa.eu/pub/era/docs/bench_pus_0702.pdf
Ministério da Ciência, Tecnologia e Ensino Superior (MCTES). (2010). *A new landscape for science, technology and tertiary education in Portugal*. Lisboa: MCTES.
Murteira, M., & Branquinho, I. (1968). Desenvolvimento de Recursos Humanos e Ensino Superior: Problemática Portuguesa numa perspectiva comparativa. *Análise Social, 6*(20–21), 81–95.
Nunes, J. A., & Gonçalves, M. E. (2001). Introdução. In J. A. Nunes & M. E. Gonçalves (Eds.), *Enteados de Galileu? A semi-periferia no sistema mundial de ciência* (pp. 13–31). Afrontamento: Porto.
OECD. (2009). *OECD regions at a glance*. Paris: OECD.
Oliveira Martins, J. P. (1895). *Portugal contemporâneo – 1845–1894*. Lisboa: Livr. de Antonio Maria Pereira.
Ribeiro, J. F., Fernandes, L. G., & Ramos, M. M. C. (1987). Grande Indústria, banca e grupos financeiros – 1953–73. *Análise Social, XXIII*(99), 945–1018.
Roberts, G. (2003). Review of Research Assessment preparado por solicitação, em Junho de 2002, dos quatro *Higher Education Funding Councils*. London: HEFC
Rocha, M. (1962). *A Reforma do Ensino da engenharia – A Educação Permanente – A Investigação em Portugal*. Lisboa: LNEC.
Rodrigues, M. L. (1999). *Os Engenheiros em Portugal*. Oeiras: Celta.
Rollo, M. F. (1994). Portugal e o Plano Marshall: história de uma adesão a contragosto (1947–1952). *Análise Social, 29*(4), 841–869.
Rollo, M. F. (1996). Indústria/Industrialização'. In F. Rosas & J. M. B. Brito (Eds.), *Dicionário de História do Estado Novo*. Lisboa: Círculo de Leitores.
Rosas, F. (1995). *Portugal entre a Paz e a Guerra*. Lisboa: Editorial Estampa.
Ruivo, B. (1995). *As políticas de ciência e tecnologia e o sistema de investigação*. Lisboa: INCM.
Santos, A. R. (1996). Grupos económicos/Conglomerados. In F. Rosas & J. M. B. Brito (Eds.), *Dicionário de História do Estado Novo* (Vol. I). Lisboa: Círculo de Leitores.
Saxanian, A. (1994). *Regional advantage: Culture and compatititon in silicon valley and route 128*. Cambridge: Harvard University Press.
Serrão, J. (1966). *Notícias Literárias de Portugal*. Lisboa: Seara Nova.
Smeby, J.-C., & Trondal, J. (2005). Globalisation or Europeanisation? International contact among university staff. *Higher Education, 49*, 449–466.
Sunkel, C. (2009). *Research units evaluation – 2007 global report*. Lisbon: FCT.
Torgal, L. R. (1999). *A Universidade e o Estado Novo*. Coimbra: Minerva.

Chapter 9
Governance, Public Management and Administration of Higher Education in Portugal

António M. Magalhães and Rui Santiago

Introduction

This chapter examines higher education governance models in Portugal over the past three decades. The different forms of steering and governance will be linked, on the one hand, to public management and administration perspectives in which they evolved and, on the other hand, to the general development of the Portuguese higher education system and its institutions as a whole.

Concepts such as administration and governing, governance and management are often used as if their nuances were self-evident or taken for granted. However, this is not so. To clarify our understanding of such concepts, the chapter begins by providing the reader with our views on the matter. Despite their different meanings, governance and management are used frequently and indiscriminately. Gallagher noted that 'governance' is the structure of relationships that provides organisational coherence, authorised policies, plans and decisions. 'Management' corresponds, however, to the accomplishment of desirable goals through allocating resources, assigning responsibility and the monitoring of both their efficiency and effectiveness (Gallagher 2001: 2). Whilst 'governing' is associated with setting social, economic and political goals and objectives, the meaning of 'governance' is associated with political instrumentality, its elaboration and assessment in the field of higher education. Yet, governance and management cross-cut with the notion of institutional autonomy. Whether applied to activities of scholarship, the freedom to teach,

---

A.M. Magalhães (✉)
CIPES, University of Porto, Rua Dr Manuel Pereira da Silva, 4200-392 Porto, Portugal
e-mail: antonio@cipes.up.pt

R. Santiago
Departamento de Ciências Sociais, Políticas e Jurídica, University of Aveiro,
Campus Universitário de Santiago, 3810-193 Aveiro, Portugal
e-mail: rui.santiago@ua.pt

or to govern its own affairs, the autonomy of the university, nevertheless, entails States, in varying degrees, steering and administering the individual university and the system of which it is a part. Hence, the executive branches of government, often referred to as 'Administration', were – and for that matter, still are – more than marginally involved in the autonomy of universities and polytechnics.

The chapter falls into the following time frame: the years before the 1974 Democratic Revolution; the Days of Revolution (1974–1976); the Period of Normalisation (1976–1986); the Decade of Massification (1986–1996) and the Rise of Managerialism (1996 to present). The basic assumption is that higher education governance cannot be isolated from the political context – i.e. the structures and instances engaged in national and international power and decision-making as well as the actors and agents involved. In short, it is taken as given that management models are linked to the frameworks of public management within which they are both sited and have evolved.

The Years Before the 1974 Democratic Revolution

Since medieval times, the State has intervened in the university's internal life. If, in the thirteenth and fourteenth centuries, Studium, Sacrum and Imperium were ideologically and effectively integrated,[1] the following centuries saw the strengthening of European monarchies and a corresponding decrease in the autonomous and institutional privileges universities once had (Cardoso 1989: 127). The Statutes of 1503 (*Estatutos Manuelinos*) stated that the university tutor – that is, the monarch himself – was entitled to lay down the university's statutes and to confirm the rector's election. On the other hand, the university was entitled to possess property and manage its own finances. It also retained the right to apply the law to its members in independence from public administration and from the law as it applied ordinarily to society outside the university. In the eighteenth century, the Statutes promulgated by the Marquis de Pombal (*Estatutos Pombalinos*) in 1772 increased state interference in the university's inner life. The Enlightenment reforms impinged not only on administrative aspects but also – and significantly so – upon scholarship and teaching (Carvalho 1986) (Chaps. 2 and 3).

By 1911, 1 year after the foundation of the Portuguese Republic, the University of Coimbra was the sole Portuguese university. Though founded in the thirteenth century, not until the twentieth century was this institution to see its place and status in higher education[2] contested. Two new universities were established by the decree of 22 March 1911. These were the universities of Porto and Lisbon. The framework of the modern Portuguese higher education system was thus set out in keeping with the winds of modernisation that then were blowing across Europe, or so contemporary rhetoric argued. Universities saw their institutional autonomy reinforced. The University Constitution of 1911 (*Constitutição Universitária*) endowed universities with economic and scholarly self-government (Chap. 2). At the same time, the Constitution laid upon the Directorate General for Secondary and Higher Education

(*Direcção Geral da Instrução Secundária e Superior*) responsibility for exercising economic, administrative and pedagogical oversight (Article 16). It also defined both the organisation and mandate of university government. The University's governing bodies were to be the Senate, the Rector, the General Assembly of the University and the Councils of Faculty and Schools. The Senate was designated as the 'supreme university authority' (Article 20). It was composed of professors, students and – an interesting provision rarely found at a similar level or having official status in other systems of higher education at the time – one alumni representative. Local authorities in the persons of municipal and civil governors also made up the Senate. The Rector was appointed by the government after the General Assembly of the University had submitted a list of three candidates from which the government chose one. The law granted institutions financial autonomy, that is, the right to draw up their own budget, to manage their subsidies and income derived from fees. Universities were also tax exempt.

From 1926 to April 1974, Portugal lived through a dictatorial regime. The Dictatorship deeply influenced – and in many respects still 35 years later continues to mark – Portuguese society, institutions and individuals. It shaped the role and place of the State and its structures. To do so, it drew on a pervasive political and ideological control that embraced the army, justice, security and the social as well as educational sectors. Public Administration in the New State ('Estado Novo') rested upon a highly centralised system. It was, however, a mixed regime: a pre-Weberian pattern based on 'informal' and ideological political networks; and Weberian with respect to the functional aspects, that is to say, the structural component of hierarchy and the allocation of power.[3] With no clear separation between political and administrative spheres, which was unusual in modern administrative systems, autonomy in public administration shone by its absence (Chap. 3).

Against this setting and background, higher education developed over half a century. Thus, the state control model intertwined with authoritarian and anti-democratic elements, which rendered the governance of higher education largely dependent on the structure and processes of the 'Estado Novo' as they operated within the realm of administration.

Five months after the Dictatorship established itself, on the 2 October 1926, a new legal framework (*Estatuto da Instrução Universitária*) for higher education was promulgated in the shape of Decree 12 426. It introduced a long and violent phase in the relationship between State and Universities. In fact, all those whether by thought or deed who opposed the regime – whether students, professors or non-academic staff – were actively hounded, ostracised and expelled from the institutions, or arrested.

The new regulations pruned back the role of the General Assembly of the University. Power to take decisions was concentrated in the Senate and in the person of the Rector. Following the Decree-Law 16 623 of 18 March 1929, the Rector was appointed by the Ministry. There were, however, substantial changes to the 'constituency' from which rectoral appointment could be made. It was extended beyond the professoriate to include judges from the Supreme Court of Justice, to individuals prominent in the field of the Sciences and Arts (Article 8). State control was enforced not only by the heavy homogeneity of law, norms and rules. It was extended by means of an all-embracing ideological and police surveillance of university activities. The nature of the oversight exercised seriously undermined Portuguese academia both as a social and political body and as the locus of knowledge production and diffusion. Under the Dictatorship, the political police undertook – and indeed they had a formal and mandatory obligation to do so – to seek information on researchers, professors and on public servants generally as well as those employed in State Laboratories (*Laboratórios de Estado*) and universities. A simple list of those academics the Dictatorship expelled from Portuguese universities is an eloquent comment on the unacceptable nature of the regime. By far, the greater majority of those dismissed stayed in Portugal. Interior exile was the price of survival (Marques 1981: 499).

Public administration and the steering of higher education policy together with institutional management were firmly placed under the authoritarian and ideological control of the State. These three dimensions of governance tended, by and large, to converge around the will and the ways of the New State (*Estado Novo*). Such a profile may be interpreted as an extreme version of the legal homogeneity model (Neave and van Vught 1991, 1994; Neave 1998). That said, up to 1952 the universities of Coimbra, Porto and Lisbon enjoyed a considerable degree of internal administrative decentralisation. At university level, their Senates, faculties and non-integrated schools had a margin of discretion: they could take administrative decisions. However, Rectors saw their mandate reduced to a role not dissimilar to that of a mere representative of government. They were directly answerable to the Director General in charge of the appropriate sector of national administration (Cardoso 1989: 133). Within the institution, rectoral power was shared with full professors (*professores catedráticos*) in line with a collegial/hierarchic/corporative model (Lima 1998) from which the participation of other academic ranks, students and administrative staff was utterly absent.

The Decree-Law 38/692, 21 March 1952, confined university management to mere administrative duties. It stipulated that neither University Senate nor School Councils could undertake the administration of the establishment. By its nature and function, university management was to be executed by a small board, consisting of the Rector, the Secretary of the university and the Finance Officer (an accountant).[4] The hold of Authoritarianism over the universities grew in direct proportion to the State's curtailing their institutional autonomy, as it did indirectly by imposing the same legal framework on them that also applied to public administration in general.

The linkage between the State's control and higher education autonomy was changed only at the start of the 1970s when the Minister Veiga Simão embarked on a comprehensive reform of the education sector. By then, the regime had reached its limits and, subjected to both internal and external pressures, sought to 'modernise' from within (Stoer 1986; Magalhães 2004) (Chap. 2). New universities were founded and granted both administrative and financial autonomy (Decree-Law 402/73, 11 August 1973). As set out in the Guideline Law for Higher Education (*Projecto de Diploma Orientador do Ensino* Superior) 'universities are legal entities that own their own patrimony and are provided with pedagogic, scientific and cultural, administrative, financial, and disciplinary autonomy, without any restriction beyond those imposed by law' (Article 13). The Veiga Simão reform was cut short by the outbreak of 1974 Revolution a few days after the final document had been approved.

The Days of Revolution (1974–1976): Nudging Higher Education Towards Socialism

The revolutionary period flourished in a socialist and egalitarian climate that permeated both higher education governance and management. The State was paralysed by the unfolding of the Revolution, whilst actors such as students' unions and teachers' associations strengthened their influence (Chap. 3). They became main players in the democratic reshaping of universities. In the aftermath of the Revolution, all Rectors and Vice-Rectors of Portugal's universities, all Directors and Sub-Directors of faculties and schools were dismissed. The provisional government appointed Rectors and administrators ad interim. Events within the universities echoed those taking place beyond the Gates of Academe. Teachers' Associations and Students' Representative Associations, which had been important actors in resisting the 'Estado Novo', abounded and gave higher education institutions a very unusual joie de vivre, which ranged from 'de-fascising' the curricula to 'substituting' those members of academic staff deeply compromised with the Old Regime.

The collegial/hierarchic/corporative model of university was rapidly rejected by both teachers' associations and students' unions. Both pressed for representative and participative democracy at the university central level and in the governance and management of faculty/schools. Election of Rectors, Deans and Heads of school should be based on the participation of all university bodies – academic staff, students and administrative staff. This requirement emerged as one of the major items in the collective drive towards democratising the inner life of Portugal's universities. In addition, political pressures for embedding a model of representative democracy redrew the university's power structure. Power was to be redistributed both vertically – proceeding from Rector, down to faculty/school and departments – and horizontally – across the fields of scholarship and teaching. Such reconstruction was no isolated phenomenon. It replicated the spirit of the moment – revolutionary and socialist. It also expressed the firm intent to democratise the Portuguese State. Public administration was simultaneously perceived as an instrument for maintaining the functions of ideological control and, more important, as a potential lever in the reform of the old 'civil society' and paving the way for a socialist economy.

The involvement of higher education in the socialist agenda, promoting equality of opportunity, seeking new answers to national, social, cultural and economic issues by placing higher education's scientific and technical resources at the service of the Nation, itself anticipated radical change in public administration. It also had its counterpart in the issue of university governance. Such narrative elements formed the reservoir from which actors in university politics drew their legitimacy to demand a new model of governance in keeping with democracy newly installed in the university. Teachers' associations and students' unions were fully recognised by Portuguese political parties as important social agents for reconstructing Portuguese universities. To a certain degree, students, and particularly student unions, acted as 'go betweens' for Portuguese political parties to reshape governance and management in the Nation's universities. At system and institutional levels, Portuguese higher education was governed during these days by an arrangement that is perhaps best characterised as a more 'radical' version of the 'garbage can' model (Cohen et al. 1972) intermixed with a political-participative model (Lima 1998) (Chap. 12).

With the passing of Decree-Law 781-A/76, which settled the issue of higher education governance and administration, the way was opened for the Period of Normalisation. The Decree-Law referred back to the previous law of 1974 (Decree-Law 806/74). But it also made plain that its present purpose was to provide legal grounding for the demands of the Revolution. Its intention not to let anarchy triumph, however, was quite explicit (Stoer 1986). Legal support, it argued, was required, to offset:

> (…) activists, minorities, demagogy and supremacy, which, by manipulation and coercion, secured a real dominium over the majority of higher education institutions, to the detriment of an efficient administration and financial management, of ideological pluralism quintessential to democratic, of teaching quality, of the urgent pedagogical renovation and a correct insertion of higher education in the cultural and socio-economic context of the country (Decree-Law 781-A/76)

Here was a step to neutralise the revolutionary impetus, to establish representative democracy in higher education and to 'normalise' university governance and management.[5]

The Period of Normalisation (1976–1986)

Decree-Law 781-A/76 set out and developed a model of democratic governance in higher education. It was a moderate edition of the political-participative model that evolved during the revolutionary period. In truth, it was more political than participative.

Embedding representative democracy was most evident at the university's mid level of governance, that is, at the level of faculties and schools. It gave rise to a form of bureaucratic-collegial model, based on election procedures as the main source of legitimation. Governance and management bodies at this level included a General Assembly, Assembly of Representatives, Board of Administration and Pedagogical Council. All were elected, and in their make-up, teachers and students were equally represented. These committees also included representatives of administrative staff. The Scientific Board alone was totally controlled by professors. However, the decisions they took were subject to the Rector's oversight. Interestingly, the Rector was appointed by the Minister of Education under the terms of a law passed at the height of the Dictatorship (Decree-Law 26 611, 1936). In an effort to 'normalise' both 'bottom-up dynamics' (Clark 1983) and to instil a rationale that was professional and academic, both procedure and decision-making in higher education were accordingly restructured.

Higher education governance was part of the wider normalisation of the Portuguese State and public administration. Major organisational forms emerged in other public systems. Amongst them was the drive to consolidate welfare provision, notably in the health sector, the creation of the National Health System (Law 56/79) and the consolidation and vertical integration of public administration. To use Weberian terms, such integration, by normalising hierarchic management in public systems, introduced more rationality in restructuring Portuguese society. At institutional level, rationalisation advanced largely through a combination of bureaucratic rationalism and the professional rationale, that is, between bureaucracy and professionalism. Similar to health sector reforms, the same forces were no less visible in higher education (Carvalho and Santiago 2007) (Chap. 14).

By the end of 1970s, the Portuguese polytechnic sector and the private sector began to develop – though with different governance structures. The Years of Normalisation saw the first lines sketched out that were to figure in the present blueprint for Portuguese higher education with the creation of the binary system and the first private institutions.

The decade saw a rapid increase in the number of private institutions. In 1977, the Catholic University, founded in 1971, was the only non-state higher education institution. In 1977, the Free University was created in Lisbon and in Porto. Two years on, the government granted it 'conditional permission' to provide higher education and, in 1983, to offer study programmes in both cities. In its models of political steering and governance, both the higher education system and institutions reflected characteristics of the Portuguese State as well as some features of Portuguese public administration. The Free University was defined as a 'collective person of public interest'; the purpose of which was to provide post-secondary education, along with other Portuguese universities.

'Conditional permission' is an interesting example of what has been termed 'the parallel State' in Portugal (Santos 1993),[6] which is also reflected in the process of public administration and management. Having recourse to this specific form of legal authorisation is in part due to de facto situations that governments could neither avoid nor solve easily. As V. Crespo, one-time Minister of Education, ruefully remarked: 'After hundreds or even thousands of students being enrolled, the Ministry became hostage to the legitimate interests and expectations of the students and their families' (Crespo 1993: 149). Founding private universities was mostly the result of this form of strategy by which the State 'turned a blind eye' and in which both governments and institutions acted as each other's accomplices.

The polytechnic sector made an important contribution to expansion and differentiation/diversification of Portuguese Higher Education (Decree-Law 427-B/77; Decree-Law 513-I/79). The binary system was designed to support economic development and to respond to the demands of the labour market. Human capital theories were highly influential, particularly those based on central planning, which was seen as the main instrument in reforming the public sector and Portuguese society. So too was the advice of the OECD and the World Bank. Setting up the binary system to enhance industrialisation and to accelerate development in the service sector of the economy at both national and local levels was a political priority. The importance government attached to the polytechnics in this task may well explain the closer control government maintained over their management, internal governance and the more circumscribed degree of autonomy granted to them in the Law of 1990.

In effect, polytechnic presidents and the other members of the Board of Direction were legally held to represent the government in founding and managing the new higher education institutions. They were granted extensive power over the appointments of schools' boards and over the recruitment and promotion of academic staff. Such responsibilities not only drew on hierarchic support, grounded in the 'rational-legal' legitimacy, expressed by the exceptional character of the legal framework that set up these new public institutions. They also operated horizontally through the influence that could bring to bear on the main collegial body in the academic sphere – the Scientific Council.

The Decade of Massification (1986–1996)

In 1986, the very year Portugal joined the European Economic Community, a Comprehensive Law of the Education System (CLES) (Law 48/86) (*Lei de Bases do Sistema Educativo*) was approved. It re-established the divide between universities and polytechnics by defining the social, economic and academic mandate of both.

Two years later, the 1988 University Autonomy Act (UAA) granted public universities the right to establish their own statutes. It also conferred scientific, pedagogical, administrative and financial autonomy. Only in 1990 (Law 54/90) were polytechnics granted autonomy, though less extensive than universities. From then on, public sector universities were exempt from the obligation to seek official and formal authorisation from the Audit Court (*Tribunal de Contas*) when appointing new staff, though the stipulation still applied to staff seconded from the civil service. In matters of finance, institutions became autonomous in the disposal of their assets, able to freely decide how to manage the funds allocated to them each year by formula funding and to shift money across different heads and budget accounts.

This revision was in keeping with the trend to decentralise public administration that had already taken place in the health sector during the first half of the 1980s. As was the case in many European countries at this time, quality, efficiency and competition became important reference points in political discourse on higher education. The entrepreneurial model of governance and management was introduced to the organisation and functioning of hospitals. Furthermore, the desirability of assigning a more active role to the private sector health system was recognised in both the act revising the Constitution of the Republic revision act (Article 64/1982) and in the new Health Act (Law 48/90) (Carvalho 2009).

Governing bodies of public universities were defined by law as the University Assembly, the Rector, the University Senate and the Administrative Council. The University Autonomy Act (UAA) entitled the University Assembly to discuss and approve university statutes, to elect – and dismiss – the rector without having to refer to central government. Responsibilities of the collegiate bodies were also set down in law and their composition defined by the institutions' statutes and bye-laws. Limits were set on the numerical composition of professors, other members of academic staff, students, management and administrative staff. Parity between the numbers of elected academic staff and students was retained, as was the principle of a balanced representation in the base units regardless of their size. Depending on the conditions set out in their statutes, University Senates could include external personalities up to 15% of their total membership. Mid-level governance of universities – faculties, schools, institutes or departments – included the Assembly of Representatives, the Administrative Board, the Pedagogic Council and the Scientific Council, alternatively a Pedagogical-Scientific Council.

Institutional autonomy was strengthened further by Law 252/97. It provided institutions with a larger degree of administrative and financial freedom, mainly for staff recruitment, though in the case of public higher education institutions, recruiting academic, management and administrative staff was subject to legal procedure. Public universities had been accorded the right to draw up their statutes and bye-laws, provided internal regulation complied with the appropriate legislation. Statutes defined the organic structure, the conditions of internal organisation for scientific, pedagogic, financial and administrative procedures and the degree of autonomy in its units. The main instruments that remained to government for regulating the public university system were rules and conditions of funding or by controlling student places by defining the *numeri clausi*.

For public sector polytechnics, the legal framework regulating their autonomy is contained in the Law of Organisation and Management of Polytechnic Institutes (Law 54/90). Polytechnics were defined as public collective entities with statutory, administrative, financial and patrimonial autonomy. However, in contrast to public universities, they were not authorised to create, suspend and cancel study programmes. Such changes required Ministry approval. Amongst the polytechnics' main governing bodies was an Electoral Assembly, 20% of whose members represented local authorities and different economic interests. The Assembly elected the President, who could be chosen from amongst the establishment's qualified academic staff, another higher education institution or from recognised personalities with appropriate professional experience. At the schools' level, governing bodies included the Director or the Directive Council, the Scientific Council and the Pedagogic Council, alternatively, the Pedagogical-Scientific Council, the Advisory Council and the Administrative Council.

For private higher education, governance structures were largely in the hands of the founding body, that is, the collective private bodies or foundations set up specifically for this purpose. The founder drew up the statutes of the institution and submitted them for Ministry approval. Private institutions enjoyed pedagogic, scientific and cultural autonomy, as set down in their statutes. Theirs was also the responsibility for administrative, economic and financial organisation together with the organisation of their management. Thus, the governing bodies of private sector higher education were similar to their public counterparts: Rector for university level institutions, President for polytechnics together with a Director or a Directive Council, a Scientific Council and a Pedagogic Council for the basic units.

These structures and processes of governance developed against a background of marked changes in the paradigm of 'system steering'. Elsewhere in Western Europe the historic state control model gave way before a state supervisory model (Neave and Van Vught 1991). During what we term 'The Period of Massification', Portugal appeared to embrace a pattern of political steering close to the state supervisory model by enhancing institutional autonomy. But, contrary to the pattern of development in most systems in the North and West of Europe, the University Autonomy Act built upon an initiative launched in 1982 by the Council of Rectors of the Portuguese Universities (CRUP *Conselho de Reitores das Universidades Portuguesas*) (Amaral et al. 2000). CRUP had been one of the main partners in dialogue in the paradigm shift. In short, the academy was the main architect of this important step towards a self-regulatory model of governance. In distinction from other European countries, in Portugal, the initiative to promote institutional autonomy as a form of relationship between State and higher education institutions was taken by the institutions themselves, i.e. by the CRUP, which acted as their direct representative.

Institutional autonomy, however, did not command a consensus. Some in Portuguese academia regarded such legal provision and the corresponding rationale of self-regulation as an 'imposition'. Autonomy and self-regulation were seen both as an intrusion from the world outside, and as the pusillanimity of a State bent on reneging on its obligations. For example, Queiró, himself an academic, argued:

> In fact, the autonomy that academics truly need – the pedagogic and scientific autonomy – can hardly, due to the very nature of things, be taken from them [...]. What other kind of autonomy can, or ought, to be needed by universities in such a small country as Portugal, given that their funding is made up in large part by the General Budget of the State? (Queiró 1995: 34–35)

Both Left and Right in academia shared a hearty mistrust of the benefits to be had from autonomy and from the political backing for self-regulation. In some quarters, liberation from detailed state control was seen more as a burden than as liberation. Indeed, the move from the state control model to its state supervisory equivalent was perceived by some actors as a loss of freedom for both the basic units level and for the individual. The reason for this stance may, in part, derive from the fact that the supervisory State brings an evaluative component in its wake (Neave 1988a, b). The formal setting up under law of a national system for quality assessment appeared to compensate increased institutional autonomy. Ultimately, it was the CRUP that assumed both the initiative for institutional autonomy and the responsibility for its political consequences. At that time, thanks both to its cohesion and to its political influence as a buffer institution, CRUP's authority was not questioned.

The reaction of universities and polytechnics to the Laws of Autonomy and their implementation was twofold, as autonomy not only brought about more self-regulation but also introduced other and more subtle forms of regulation in the shape of evaluation through quality assessment. From the perspective of political decision-makers, the UAA 'd[id] not provide for, in an appropriate form, the protection of national interests, as far as university policy is concerned' (Crespo 1993: 164).

Since institutional autonomy largely depended on financial resources, clearly the system of funding was a crucial factor. Article 11 in the University Autonomy Act stipulated that the State distributed the necessary funding between different higher education institutions annually. Yet, the growing complexity of tasks assumed by establishments of higher education was not compatible with a yearly financial cycle. Pluriannual financing and programme contracts seemed better suited to the situation and to the demands of governance and proactive management. Following this logic, institutions were allowed to organise their requirements in the framework of development plans.

However, self-regulation was inseparable from the logic of government steering. Such plans depended on the Minister's approval. Approving each higher education establishment's development plan preceded the drawing up of contracts, which presumed the existence of guidelines for education policy. So untidy a hybrid arrangement between the formality of law and the relationship between government and institutions posed a dilemma of the cruellest kind: whether to back the logic of self-regulation or to espouse central planning (Amaral and Magalhães 2001).

The same quandary was no less evident when it came to creating new faculties, schools, departments or research institutes in institutions already in place. In the case of public universities, the UAA stated, on the one hand, that the duty to approve the creation or closing, integration or modification, of any university structure was a matter for the Senate (Article 25). Yet, Article 28 stated that it was the Ministry's responsibility to authorise the creation or closing, integration or modification, of any university structure.[7]

That autonomy and the aims of political regulation by government were combined was clearly set out in the UAA: 'in accordance with their pedagogic autonomy and *in harmony with national policies of education*, science and culture, universities *shall have the right to create*, suspend and cancel courses' (Article 7) [our emphasis]. Hybridism also infested the relationship between State and private higher education. In Portugal, private higher education institutions were – and still are – less autonomous than public establishments – save in financial matters. They too depend on the Ministry for authorisation to start new courses and degrees, for the recognition of their diplomas and for the definition of their numerus clausus – or selective entry – programmes.

Public universities, however, enjoyed almost complete freedom to start, suspend or cancel courses – and they used this latitude extensively. This state of affairs created the view that institutions had 'too much' pedagogic autonomy and that it was virtually impossible to co-ordinate the sector as a result (Amaral et al. 1996: 32). The State possessed the capacity to steer neither the transition towards the new governing model nor the model itself, which forced the governments to revert to a more traditional mode of operation (Amaral and Carvalho 2003). Lack of expertise and lack of technical capacity to move political decisions along were a problem. Since the legislation on autonomy required polytechnics and private institutions to submit their new programmes to Ministry approval, the upshot was a spectacular overburden on central services. Weak regulation served to compound the hybridism previously mentioned. Thus, for instance, a lackadaisical attitude towards the private sector left governments encouraging the mushrooming of private institutions without much attention paid to either the academic and financial conditions of individual private sector establishments.

The need to set up a quality evaluation system in Portugal resulted directly from implementing the UAA and from problems of quality that the sudden creation and proliferation of a large number of private institutions had unleashed. The origins of the drive towards quality evaluation go back to 1992 when, as a result of an initiative by the CRUP, a nationwide trial evaluation of five disciplines took place. It focused on Physics, Computer Sciences, Electrical Engineering, Economics and French. The Council of Rectors negotiated a proposal for a law on quality assessment with the Ministry of Education. It was submitted to Parliament and approved in 1994.

The letter and spirit of Law 38/94 (21 November 1994) explicitly set about improving quality in the Nation's higher education. Its basic tenet was for results of the evaluation to be used mainly to improve quality. The law did not directly link results to funding. Because evaluation was seen as ameliorative, self-evaluation reports were the centrepiece in the evaluation and assessment system and assigned the key role in that process to the individual institution. The final reports of the evaluation were to be made public and were also to include comments from the evaluated institutions.

Interestingly, some former Ministers of Education agreed that evaluation should have financial consequences. At the same time they endorsed a more managerial vision for university governance. Amongst their ranks, Marçal Grilo pointed out that 'the worst that can happen to the Portuguese university in the funding area is to insist on an equal treatment of the institutions, as they are so different from each other'. Following up this line of argument, he held that the 'future must reward those who better manage and, above all, those who are capable of tracing objectives and taking on responsibilities, always within the logic that those who are different must be treated differently' (Grilo *Público*, 23 December 2000).

Grosso modo, academia saw quality assessment as a threat. The launching of evaluation drummed up considerable professional and subjective resistance. Yet, it was almost universally recognised by those involved that quality issues demanded urgent measures for higher education's own sake. The reasons for this ambiguity are many. The evaluation changes traditional institutional culture insofar as it was not immediately compatible with the prevalent Humboldtian ethos in the university – though mainly in the more traditional. To this may be added fear of the possible consequences of quality assessment: damage to the reputation of institution or programme or cuts in budget. Autonomy is not a stable state when it comes to setting policy objectives and the availability of money. Considerable uncertainty is inflicted at the basic unit and at the individual level. Even if the law stated there was no direct and immediate link between the outcome of quality assessment and the level of funding, this, however, did not exclude negative consequences for the institutions in the medium term, as Article 5 in Law 38/94 made plain.[8]

To sum up, the Portuguese version of the supervisory State model of regulating higher education seems to move towards the 'remote control' pattern (Neave and van Vught 1991: 253) found in other countries where the model developed earlier. Such change to State co-ordination of the system appears to align with the political mandate entrusted to higher education. This mandate is explicitly economy driven. And, as a result, the elements for an 'entrepreneurial narrative' and for a managerial approach to higher education governance appeared on the agenda.

Consolidating institutional autonomy cannot be seen then simply as a steering device planned solely by the State. Rather, it is set within a wider framework of the political context, which offered higher education institutions the opportunity to take on new strategies. The hybrid nature both of policies and their perception by actors has been examined. This characteristic seems to be also to apply to the strengthening of autonomy. On the one hand, it served as an instrument of co-ordination. On the other it became a tool used for their own purposes by the actors involved. As the entrepreneurial narrative of higher education permeates political discourse and decision-making processes, it is also possible to point to the behaviour of higher education institutions in the light of their official autonomous status. It is a perspective that presents an interesting margin both to manoeuvre and to take initiatives.

As Licínio Lima has noted, the institutional models that presided over and carried forward the development of the Portuguese university – the corporate, the political-participative and the managerialist model – can coexist simultaneously:

> At the exact moment when the new institutional political-participative model emerges searching for new organisational forms and new rules and new social practices, in tension with the centralist and corporate institutional model, deeply embedded in the normative instruments and in the habits of the actors who were socialised in it, there occurs a second tension with the rise of a third institutional model, the managerialist model. (Lima 1998: 68). (Chap. 12)

The Rise of Managerialism: 1996 to the Present

Whilst quality, quality assessment and the rationalisation of higher education took on increasing importance (Chap. 10), the issue of higher education governance during these years became pivotal.

By the end of the 1990s, discourses and practices of New Public Management (NPM) assumed a central role in public policies (Chap. 7). They reshaped the public sector. Political discourses seeking to inject a new 'common sense' about welfare, its provision, its structures and its actors pushed forward with the purpose of modernising the public sector. Policies to instil an entrepreneurial ethos and competition-driven behaviour amongst public institutions and actors pressed ahead. Incentives to develop competitive horizontal relations amongst autonomous institutions together with restrictions on professional power were the main political instruments employed. A whole array of new organisations emerged at system level – for example, intermediate regulatory agencies and foundations. The sphere of governance saw recourse to macro and micro technologies, which were brought to bear on evaluation and accountability systems. The development at the institutional level of individual contracts together with the strategic management of human resources and the alignment of productivity to management objectives were presented as the new way to regulate both institutions and their professionals in the public sector. The legitimation for these 'priorities' rested on two principles: economic rationalism and citizen–consumer sovereignty.

This approach to governance extended to higher education (Amaral and Carvalho 2003; Santiago et al. 2005; Santiago and Carvalho 2008; Carvalho and Santiago 2007, 2009). Indeed, the rise and recent broadcasting of the term 'governance' into the jargon of higher education is itself both a manifestation of, and a pointer to, the significance of the change it seeks to bring about.

From the end of the 1990s, Portuguese higher education was the object of important revisions in governance, in the form of changes to financing and fund allocation, in increasing weight placed on inter-institutional competition for research funds. It also made its way into the legal formalisation of evaluation and quality assurance practices and culture and from there mobilised change in science and technology policies by extending the relationship between knowledge production and the Portuguese entrepreneurial fabric (Chap. 8). Several political devices (Resolution 54/2001; Decree-Law 197/2001; Decree-Laws 125/99 and 91/2005; Regulation for the Financing of Research Units 1/98 of 1998) were introduced to stimulate scientific research and technological development through private–public partnerships with tax benefits for enterprises engaging in R&D projects. Basically, these instruments were supposed to improve competitiveness in the national economy, to address the challenges raised by economic globalisation and by economic networking on a worldwide scale and, finally, to attract foreign investments, both direct and in the area of technology.

In parallel with an emphasis on institutional autonomy, a seemingly more interventionary relationship between State and higher education institutions stood in the offing (Magalhães and Amaral 2009; Neave 2007). In public universities, pedagogic autonomy was 'the first casualty' (Amaral and Carvalho 2003). Bombarded by complaints from polytechnics and private higher education over the different degrees of autonomy they had been granted, which, they asserted, compared unfavourably with that conferred upon public universities, the government passed a law in 2000 (Law 26/2000) that granted the same degree of autonomy on all.

The takeover of 'quality' as a device in the political armoury bolstered the move towards a more nuanced view of institutional autonomy. Decree-Law 205/1998 established general rules for assessing higher education. The national quality assessment system was further reinforced by Law 1/2003. It laid out an academic accreditation system for both study programmes and institutions. It made abundantly clear the consequences that would follow from the refusal to seek accreditation. It extended the possibilities for state interference in higher education's internal life by setting out new conditions for validating new teaching programmes. Later, a new Decree-Law stipulated that[9] for new programmes to be accepted, they are required to have a minimum number of students – 35 in 2003, subsequently cut back to 20 by the government, returned in 2005. Furthermore, the state budget formula for funding to public higher education progressively incorporated performance and quality indicators.

In moving down this path, the government, which returned to office in 2005, commissioned ENQA (the European Association for Quality Assurance in Higher Education) to review the Portuguese quality assurance system and to advise on setting up an accreditation agency[11] according to the appropriate European standards. It also commissioned the OECD (OECD 2006) to examine Portuguese higher education.

The political driver of 'quality' linked it to the issues of governing and governance. In a 2005 research study, Santiago et al. (2005) analysed the discourses of key actors in Portuguese higher education – ex-ministers, rectors, polytechnic presidents and administrators. More particularly, they focused on criticism of state bureaucratic control and the perceptions of their interviewees of the way regulatory mechanisms had been implemented. They found that deregulation was correlated with institutional autonomy and was closely aligned assigning responsibility for decision making to professional managers to the detriment of academics and academic managers.

Earlier, CIPES (Amaral 2003) reported a survey on levels of participation by all involved in Portuguese higher education. The survey focused on how actors judged the need to modify and/or strengthen laws on the governance of higher education institutions. Students' unions were the main supporters of collegial governance in higher education institutions. For their part, the majority of professors and the major actors in higher education were critical, both of the collegial model and of the type of State relationship envisaged.

However, Carvalho and Santiago's study, undertaken in 2006 (2009) into the influence of NPM on higher education policies and institutions, showed the overall picture was more nuanced. They concluded that the interpretation and responses of higher education institutions to external pressures were strongly dependent on internal processes and on the initiatives and behaviour of academic actors. Amongst the latter, deans played a key role in both the power and sphere of action, which was central to coping with increasing managerial pressures the State brought to bear. Deans, when placed in an institutional setting, singled out the very pressures the government exerted (Carvalho and Santiago 2009). But when placed in an organisational environment, the majority adhered to the 'archetypical' collegial style of governance at the expense of a corporate-style governance 'archetype'.

The new Higher Education Guideline Law, 62/2007, of 10 September 2007, introduced important elements in the reconfiguration of governance in Portuguese higher education, both at system and organisational levels. The law laid out an institutional and organisational framework that departed from those based on academic collegial power. It also offered institutions the opportunity to opt either for a public institute regime or become a public foundation regulated by private law.

This new law drawn up explicitly under the influence of New Public Management (Moreira 2008) replicated the latter's political and managerial assumptions about governance faithfully: executive decision-making as opposed to collegiality; reinforcement of the presence of stakeholders on decision-making bodies; the concept of HEIs as 'total organisations' (Chap. 12).

Since it was promulgated in September 2007, it is too early to judge how it will develop or what the consequences for the inner life of Portuguese higher education – that is, teaching, research and service to the community – will be. Its main assumptions can, however, be identified.

In Articles 77, 78 and 79, the governance of universities and polytechnics is exercised by a General Council – the Rector in the case of universities or the President in the case of polytechnics – and an Executive Board. In both sectors across the binary divide, the law makes provision for other consultative bodies. For universities, 'the statutes may allow the creation of an academic senate constituted by representatives of the institutional units as a body that must be obligatorily consulted by the rector in issues defined by the statutes' (Article 77). The General Council must be made up of more than 50% of professors and researchers, by students –15% of the General Council – and by 'external prominent personalities with relevant knowledge and experience', who account for 30%. Though representation of non-academic staff is possible, it is not compulsory (Art 81). Whilst Rector – or President in the polytechnics – heads the governance body (Art 85), election is by the General Council (Article 86). The General Council's remit effectively covers any areas of executive responsibility (Article 82) that range from approving internal statutes, approving the institution's strategic plans and the assessment of the Rector/President's performance.

The assumption was that a General Council acted as a board of trustees. As such, it was an instrument dedicated to securing better institutional performance than would an arrangement based on collegial governance. Thus, at one and the same time, the General Council is both a diagnosis of higher education 'failing' in the domains of both management and performance and a remedy to those self-same failures.

The pattern that stands out in the provision the Law of 2007 made for governance is in line with the work by Bleiklie and Kogan (2007) which highlighted a tendency in the organisation and governance of European universities to create powerful managerial infrastructures that run in parallel and even replace academic committees and bodies, built around traditional academic leaders. They remarked that decision-making by academics has become integrated into the administrative line structure in universities. Academics appeared less and less academics and increasingly part of the institutional decision-making process (Bleiklei and Kogan 2007: 479).

The move from collegial and institutional governance to another that emphasises organisational rationales as opposed to the occupational or professional codes that bolstered organisational rationalism as opposed to occupational rationalism as the regulator of higher education institution's inner life was clear. The push for more professional management ultimately aims at ousting professionals/academic control over the internal life of higher education to be replaced by the power of managerialism.

Conclusion

This chapter analysed how governance in Portuguese higher education evolved from an Authoritarian State control model to a more institutional-driven system of steering. In fine, system governing shifted towards institutional governance. Yet, the road from state bureaucracy to a more autonomous form of institutional management is a long one. And whilst its end may be envisaged, it has yet to be completed. Until the 1980s, Portuguese universities enjoyed only a limited degree of autonomy. They and their governance structures were part of a national administrative chain of command. Internally, they were professional bureaucracies. In reality, higher education institutions drew on bureaucracy and very little at all on management.

From the 1980s onwards, massification, the modernisation of public administration and the development of public management in Northern and Western European countries have shaped policy steering and governance in Portuguese higher education. By and large, these developments were politically driven through various assumptions made about 'self-governance' such as horizontal competition amongst the 'self-governed' or autonomous institutions, by entrepreneurship, private management models and by concerns arising from the demands of 'citizen–consumers' in a bid to reflect social and economic efficiency and effectiveness more closely.

With the rise and consolidation of the 'evaluative State' (Neave 1988a, 1998, 2010) and haunted by the *Geist* of New Public Management, higher education institutions were expected to shift from being administratively subordinated institutions to becoming stronger and more autonomous organisations. This shift was accompanied by a second, which took higher education on from the rule of administrators and professionals to governance by managers, with an organisation rationale replacing its occupational forerunner in the shaping of institutional activity and behaviour.

However, these shifts are ambiguous. Similar to a pendulum, they are in constant movement between institutional autonomy and external coercive and inductive norms, which hang over the structures of governance and management. Self-government and management were assigned to the institutions of higher education at the same moment as their traditional regulatory boundaries, defined mainly by the funding system, were cast aside and new ones put in their stead. The systematisation of quality assurance, the drawing up of contractual duties, external audits and pressure to establish a 'new grid of visibilities' (Rose 1996: 55) today set the frame to the responsibility for university and polytechnic vis-à-vis the State and other external stakeholders. Such displacement is reflected inside institutions, in the modes of regulating professionals, and the injection into professional autonomy of a more stringent managerial control over academic work.

In the opinion of Bleikie and Kogan (2007), across the face of Europe, governance in higher education is moving on from the 'Republic of Scholars' to becoming 'a stakeholder organisation'.

Following in the footsteps of Ferlie et al. (2009), we take the view that it is important to bring in 'more generic concepts from political science and public management more fully into the study of HEIs' (Ferlie et al. 2009: 1). To look at higher education as a 'stand alone' impoverishes the analysis of its governing and governance systems. Arguably, it is crucial today to re-emphasise the continual repositioning of higher education within the public sector if we are to have a deeper understanding of the alterations and changes in its governing and governance models. Over the past few decades, these transformations have become more visible, in part through criticism levelled against 'welfarism', its administrative and managerial features, the impact of globalisation and the redrawing of formative action within the framework of the so-called new governance paradigm[10] (Salamon 2002).

Criticisms against 'traditional' welfare governance models and against policies developed under neo-liberal auspices have both played their part in public policy in remoulding the relationship between governing and governance. This process of reordering was already widely acknowledged in the field of policy studies. Salamon, for instance, argued that

> At the heart of new governance approach is a shift in the 'unit of analysis' in policy analysis and public administration from the public agency or the individual program to the distinctive tools or instruments through which public purposes are pursued (Salamon 2002: 9).

Because the State depends upon knowledge and expertise (Rose and Miller 1992) to address social, educational and economic problems, these displacements become more visible, above all in those areas where the State has not built up sufficient technical and political knowledge to 'conduct the conduct and actions' (Rose and Miller 1992) of public systems as actors. Amongst those areas where the knowledge that the State possesses is incomplete are higher education, health and local administration in contrast to other domains where it has much, for example, the army, justice, internal security and foreign affairs (Chap. 8).

Since the consolidation of massification during the Nineties, the influence of New Public Management, the accepted views of higher education's mission and the type of regulation over its processes and structures, the regulatory aspect of State policies all changed significantly.

Quality, efficiency and accountability became major topics of public discussion and political discourse. In parallel to changes in the political steering of the system, the distribution of power inside institutions also evolved: from bureaucratic-collegial-professional power to integrated organisational-managerial sets (Chap. 10). Power moved out from specialised knowledge enclosures based on the authority of experts – whether individuals or groups – to a more open 'site' of knowledge production driven by the interests of institution, and by stakeholders, through their choices and their understanding of what was 'relevant' or 'appropriate'.

Gradually, overhaul of higher education governance at the system and institutional levels was implemented. Promulgation of the Juridical Regime of Higher Education Institutions (Law 62/2007 – RJIES) stands, at least formally, as the political fulfilment of this programme. At system level, new governance technologies, the result of reciprocal adjustments deriving from horizontal interactions between higher education institutions and their external stakeholders, came into place (Chap. 7). At institutional level, each institution is increasingly viewed as an individual organisational actor, better positioned to create strategies for building up local knowledge and better suited to new social and economic conditions and challenges. However, this is only one part of the complex and multidimensional process of reconfiguring the Portuguese State and public administration.

Notes

1. In the theocratic societies of the Middle Ages, the universities – the Church – and the political power were closely intertwined, mutually supporting their missions both sacred and profane.
2. There were, at the time, other institutions of higher education with university characteristics such as the Polytechnic School of Lisbon (*Escola Politécnica de Lisboa*), the Polytechnic Academy of Porto (*Academia Politécnica do Porto*), the Schools of Medicine and Surgery at Porto and Lisbon (*Escolas Médico-Cirúrgicas do Porto e de Lisboa*) and Higher Course of Letters (*Curso Superior de Letras*). Nevertheless, the University of Coimbra, as Oliveira Marques has pointed out, continued throughout the nineteenth century to be 'the alleged owner of university studies, in spite of the fact that the majority of its professors did not manage to follow the pace of the amazing progress that was happening all over the world in all fields of knowledge' (Marques 1981: 130–131).
3. For the consequences this arrangement had for the Academic Profession see Carvalho pp.
4. Salazar did not believe that academics should govern their own institutions. They were scientists, philosophers, historians and not managers: 'It is not wise to ask men who by the force of their minds' prevailing concerns should not be bothered by administrative affairs, to commit themselves to such affairs for which they have neither training nor inclination, thus sacrificing their prime function' (Decree-Law, no. 38692 of 23 March 1952).
5. Nevertheless, this very same 1976 Decree-Law considered this governance model, when compared to other countries', to be '(…) the most daring and progressive, combining democracy and responsibility as it should in a society ruled by social democratic principles and where all elected bodies must be accountable for their actions' (Decree-Law 781-A/76).
6. 'With such a Constitution [1976 Constitution], the distance between the institutional framework and social and political practices would have to be enormous. In fact, the Constitution did not have a State that was willing, and with suitable conditions, to implement its program. […] In this fact resides the first characteristic, of a constitutional type, of what I call the *Parallel State*: a constitutional State concerned with the building of a modern capitalist democracy while its constitution foresaw a socialist society without classes' (Santos 1993: 30). The gap between the legal regulatory forms and actual institutional practices derived not only from the historical features of the Portuguese State but also from the fragilities brought about by the normalisation process itself. The normalisation process intended precisely to stabilise the legal architecture and the actions of the newly created democratic State.
7. However, it also stated that dividing a faculty or a school into smaller units (departments) or creating new ones inside an already existing faculty or school is a decision internal to the university.
8. 'If the results of the continuous evaluation of the higher education institutions are negative, the following measures may be applied: (a) reduction or suspension of public financing whenever the institutions do not follow the recommendations made to correct (the situation); (b) suspension of recognition of the courses in the public higher education system; (c) revocation of the authorisation for the functioning of courses in the public higher education polytechnic system; (d) revocation of the authorisation for the functioning of courses or the recognition of degrees in the private higher education system. Art 5.'
9. The Higher Education Accreditation and Assessment Agency (A3ES) was created by the 2007 Decree-Law 369/2007 5th November. For a more elaborate account see below the Chap. 10.

10. According to Salamon, the new model, which he terms *third-party government,* has two main features: 'The *first* of these signified by use of the term 'governance' instead of 'government' is an emphasis on what is perhaps the central reality of public problem solving for the foreseeable future – namely, its *collaborative nature,* its reliance on a wide array of third parties in addition to Government to address public problems and pursue public purposes. Such an approach is necessary, we would argue, because problems have become too complex for Government to handle on its own, because disagreements exist about the proper ends of public action, and because Government increasingly lacks the authority to enforce its will on other crucial actors without giving them a meaningful seat at the table. The *second* feature, signified by the use of the term 'new' is a recognition that these collaborative approaches, while hardly novel, must now be approached in a new, more coherent way, one that more explicitly acknowledges the significant challenges that they pose as well as the important opportunities they create' (Salamon 2002: 8).

References

Amaral, A. (Ed.) (2003). *Avaliação, Revisão e consolidação da Legislação do Ensino Superior.* Matosinhos: CIPES.
Amaral, A., & Carvalho, T. (2003). Autonomy and change in Portuguese higher education. In Observatory for Fundamental University Values and Rights (Ed.), *Case studies: Academic freedom and university institutional responsibility in Portugal.* Bologna: Bononia University Press.
Amaral, A., Correia, F., Magalhães, A., Rosa, M., Santiago, R., & Teixeira, P. (2000). *O ensino superior pela mão da economia.* Matosinhos: CIPES.
Amaral, A., & Magalhães, A. (2001). On markets, autonomy and regulation: The Janus-Head revisited. *Higher Education Policy, 14,* 7–20.
Amaral, A., Magalhães, A., & Teixeira, P. (1996). *Management structure in the European Union and South African higher education systems.* Porto: University of Porto.
Amaral, A., Magalhães, A., & Santiago, R. (2003). The rise of academic managerialism in Portugal. In A. V. Amaral, V. L. Meek, & I. M. Larsen (Eds.), *The higher education managerial revolution?* (pp. 131–153). Dordrecht: Kluwer Academic Publishers.
Bleiklei, I., & Kogan, M. (2007). Organisation and governance of universities. *Higher Education Policy, 20*(4), 477–494.
Cardoso, A. H. (1989). A Universidade e o Poder Autonómico. *Revista Crítica de Ciências Sociais, 27*(28), 125–145.
Carvalho, R. (1986). *História do Ensino em Portugal.* Lisboa: Fundação Calouste Gulbenkian.
Carvalho, T. (2009). *Nova Gestão Pública e Reformas da Saúde: o profissionalismo numa encruzilhada.* Lisbon: Edições Sílabo.
Carvalho, T., & Santiago, R. (2007). *Still academics after all.* Paper presented at the SRHE annual conference, Brighton, 11–13 December 2007.
Carvalho, T., & Santiago, R. (2009). NPM and 'middle management': How deans influence institutional policies. In V. L. Meek, L. Goedegbuure, R. Santiago, & T. Carvalho (Eds.), *Changing deans:Higher education middle management in an international perspective.* Dordrecht: Springer.
Clark, B. R. (1983). *The higher education system: Academic organisation in cross-national perspective.* Berkeley: University of California Press.
Cohen, M. D., March, J. G., & Olsen, J. P. (1972). A garbage can model of organisational choice. *Administrative Science Quarterly, 17*(1), 1–25.
Crespo, V. (1993). *Uma Universidade para os Anos 2000: O Ensino Superior numa Perspectiva de Futuro.* Lisbon: Editorial Inquérito.
Ferlie, E., Musselin, C., & Andresani, G. (2009). The governance of higher education systems: A public management perspective. In C. Paradise, E. Reale, I. Bleiklie, & E. Ferlie (Eds.),

University governance: Western European comparative perspectives (pp. 1–20). Dordrecht: Springer.
Gallagher, M. (2001). *Modern University Governance – A national perspective.* Paper presented at the conference on the idea of a University: Enterprise or Academy? The Australia Institute and Manning Clark House, Canberra, 21st July.
Lima, L. (1998). Universidade Portuguesa: Notas Sobre a Crise Institucional. In M. C. Morosini (Ed.), *Mercosul/Mercosur: Políticas e Ações Universitárias.* Porto Alegre: Editora da Universidade.
Magalhães, A. M. (2004). *A Identidade do Ensino Superior: Política Conhecimento e Educação numa Era de Transição.* Lisboa: Fundação Calouste Gulbenkian/FCT.
Magalhães, A. M., & Amaral, A. (2009). Mapping out discourses on higher education governance. In J. Huisman (Ed.), *International perspectives on the governance of higher education: alternative frameworks for coordination* (pp. 182–197). London: Routledge/Taylor & Francis.
Marques, A. (1981). *História de Portugal* (Vol. III). Lisbon: Palas Editores.
Moreira, V. (2008). O Estatuto Legal das Instituições de Ensino Superior. In A. Amaral (Ed.), *Políticas de Ensino Superior: quatro temas em debate.* Lisbon: Conselho Nacional de Educação.
Neave, G. (1988a). Recent trends in European higher education. *European Journal of Education, 23*(1–2).
Neave, G. (1988b). On the cultivation of quality. Efficiency and enterprise: An overview of recent trends in higher education in Western Europe. *European Journal of Education, 23*(1–2), 7–23.
Neave, G. (1998). The evaluative state reconsidered. *European Journal of Education, 33*(3), 265–284.
Neave, G. (2007). *From Guardian to Overseer: Trends in Institutional Autonomy, Governance and Leadership.* Paper presented at the conference organised by the Conselho Nacional de Educação on the Legal Status of Higher Education Institutions – Autonomy, Responsibility and Governance, Lisbon, February 2007.
Neave, G., & van Vught, F. (Eds.). (1991). *Prometheus bound: The changing relationship between government and higher education in Western Europe.* Oxford: Pergamon Press.
Neave, G., & van Vught, F. (Eds.). (1994). *Government and higher and higher education relationships across three continents: The winds of change.* Oxford: Pergamon Press.
OECD–Organization for Economic Co-operation and Development. (2006). *Reviews of national policies for education: Tertiary education in Portugal.* Paris: OECD.
Queiró, J. F. (1995). *A Universidade Portuguesa: Uma Reflexão.* Lisbon: Gradiva.
Rose, N. (1996). Governing 'advanced' liberal democracies. In A. Barry, T. Osborne, & N. Rose (Eds.), *Foucault and political reason: Liberalism, neo-liberals and rationalities of government* (pp. 37–64). Chicago: The University of Chicago Press.
Rose, N., & Miller, P. (1992). Political power beyond the state: Problematics of government. *British Journal of Sociology, 43*, 173–205.
Salamon, L. (2002). *The tools of government: A guide to the new governance.* Oxford: Oxford University Press.
Santiago, R., & Carvalho, T. (2008). Academics in a new work environment: The impact of new public management on work conditions. *Higher Education Quarterly, 62*(3), 204–223.
Santiago, R., Magalhães, A., & Carvalho, T. (2005). *O Surgimento do Managerialismo no Sistema de Ensino Superior Português.* Matosinhos: CIPES.
Santos, B. (Ed.). (1993). *Portugal: Um Retrato Singular.* Porto: Edições Afrontamento.
Stoer, S. R. (1986). *Educação e Mudança Social em Portugal: 1970–1980, uma década de transição.* Porto: Edições Afrontamento.

Chapter 10
Quality, Evaluation and Accreditation: from Steering, Through Compliance, on to Enhancement and Innovation?

Maria J. Rosa and Cláudia S. Sarrico

Introduction

This chapter describes and analyses the development and evolution of quality mechanisms in Portuguese higher education. In the first section, 'Quality Drift: A Legislative Account,' it provides an overview of the legislative intent behind setting up a 'quality' agenda in higher education. The narrative starts in the *Constitution of the Portuguese Republic* of 1976, passed by the Constituent Assembly, in the aftermath of the Revolution of April 25th 1974. It proceeds on through the first evaluation law of 1994 and ends with the spate of reforms undertaken by the XVII Constitutional Government between the years 2005 and 2009.

The second section develops around the metaphor 'From Learning to Walk to Dysfunctional Teenager: 1994 to 2005'. It analyses the first and second cycle of the first bid to evaluate higher education in Portugal at first-degree level. This exercise was undertaken according to the terms set out in the 1994 *Higher Education Evaluation Law*. The section closes with the abrupt termination of that evaluative initiative.

The third section, 'The Coming of Age: From 2006 to the Present' delves into more recent developments in quality evaluation in Portuguese higher education. This third phase in the dynamic of Quality Evaluation has its point of departure in the decision of the XVII Constitutional Government to commission two studies: a review of the higher education system by the Paris-based Organisation for Economic

---

M.J. Rosa (✉)
Departamento de Economia, Gestão e Engenharia Industrial, University of Aveiro,
Campus Universitário de Santiago, 3810-193 Aveiro, Portugal
e-mail: mjrosa@ua.pt

C.S. Sarrico
ISEG, Universidade Tecnica de Lisboa, Rua Miguel Lupe 20,
1249-078 Lisbon, Portugal
e-mail: cssarrico@iseg.utl.pt

Co-operation and Development (OECD) (OECD 2007) together with an examination of the quality assurance system by the European Network of Quality Agencies (ENQA) (ENQA 2006). The publication of these two reports coincided with the end of the evaluation system set up earlier by the Minister. It also marked a major change in the interests represented. The previous system of evaluation lay in the hands of groups representing institutions of higher education. Re-launching the system of quality evaluation, to which accreditation was added, marked a substantial change in the relationship between evaluation and the evaluated. The task of evaluation was confided to an independent agency, with representatives from both government and higher education.

The fourth section entitled 'What Will the Future Bring Forth: Uneventful Middle Age or Ripe Old Age?' muses on the possible outcomes the new evaluative regime may bring about. Will its influence turn out to be more hopeful, more positive? Or will it, on the contrary, be more pessimistic and inquisitorial? The chapter closes with some concluding remarks on the general theme it has developed.

Quality Drift: A Legislative Account

The Portuguese preoccupation with quality in higher education is evident at the highest level and from the very start of the country's return to democracy. Article 76 of the *Constitution of the Portuguese Republic* of 1976 (VII Constitutional Review of 2005) provided for an 'adequate assessment of the quality of education' to offset the degree of autonomy granted to universities (Chaps. 7, 9, and 12). This provision was strengthened further in the *Comprehensive Law on the Education System* of 1986. Specifically, it made mention of quality assurance in higher education (Article 12), as an addition to the general evaluation of the education system (Article 49), and the gathering of educational statistics as part of the instrumentality employed in system steering (Article 51). The need to evaluate the universities was brought up once again in the *Law on Universities Autonomy* of 1988, though the word 'quality' itself was never raised (for alternative interpretations of this law, see Chaps. 7 and 12). Two years later, the *Polytechnics Statute and Autonomy Law* of 1990 also mentioned the need to extend evaluation to the polytechnics. However, only in 1994 with the passing of *Higher Education Evaluation Law*, was the intent of previous Acts finally operationalised. Thus, evaluation and monitoring of quality in all universities and polytechnics, public and private, were broached, and the notion of incentives and penalties depending on performance made public. In turn, the Law of 2003 on the *Legal Basis for Development and Quality in Higher Education* reinforced the evaluative element of the earlier *Higher Education Evaluation Law*. By modifying Article 5, it introduced the option of closing down institutions directly in those cases where evaluated performance was found to be deeply wanting. In addition, a rating system, based on the results reported, together with accreditation procedures were added to the instrumentality of quality assurance. That same year also saw institutional performance linked for the first time to institutional funding through

Article 4 of the Law, setting out the *Basis for Financing Higher Education 2003*. Equally significant, the term 'educational indicators' figured for the first time in legislation applied to higher education. Funding the Nation's system of higher education was no longer simply a matter of 'educational statistics'.

Four years on, in 2007, saw further developments in laying down the conditions, structures and organisation of a more rigorous system of evaluation for higher education. The Law setting out the *Legal Basis for the Evaluation of Higher Education* opened the way for founding an Agency to carry out both evaluation and accreditation. Significantly, it was to be independent of both higher education and government. The Agency's mandate was laid out in the Law for the *Creation of the Agency for Assessment and Accreditation of Higher Education 2007*. Having defined the Agency's mandate, the attention of the legislator turned to more broad ranging matters of general reform in higher education. Amongst the torrent of legislation that poured forth from government was the Law setting out the *Juridical Regime of Higher Education Institutions* of 2007. It clarified the roles to be played by the State and by higher education institutions in the sphere of quality. At system level, the State was responsible for quality evaluation (Article 26). Furthermore, only accredited degrees could be taught (Article 61). At institutional level, however, responsibility for quality assurance lay with the Rector in the case of universities, or the President in other higher education institutions (Article 92). The arrangement assigned the task of 'quality improvement' to universities and polytechnics, acting within their sphere of autonomy. The 'accountability' dimension to quality evaluation remained in the purlieu of the State, which delegated its responsibility to an independent Agency, entrusted with the technical administration, design, definition and setting up the procedures for gathering the appropriate information, and the processing involved in the evaluation and accreditation of degrees.

From Learning to Walk to Dysfunctional Teenager: 1994 to 2005

The consensus that came together to create a quality assessment system in Portugal drew on several factors: the drive to extend the degree of autonomy, the questionable quality of a fast-developing private sector, and the gathering momentum in the development of a European level in higher education policy (Rosa et al. 2006).

In 1991, during the Dutch Presidency of the then European Economic Community (Council 1991), the Council and the Ministers of Education agreed that the Commission should strengthen evaluation in higher education at the European level. Amongst the preliminary initiatives to lay the groundwork for this strategy was a comparative study of evaluation methods employed by Member States. A small number of cooperative pilot projects were commissioned, as was a study of the mechanisms and procedures for strengthening European cooperation. It was, ostensibly, a pragmatic initiative, more akin to a review of experience built up with its accompanying practices already in place.

At that particular juncture in the development of higher education policy in Europe, this was a delicate undertaking. Despite the Gravier Judgement, and despite the interpretation handed down by the European Court of Justice in 1986 that higher education could be construed as essentially vocational and, therefore, had its place in the Communities' Founding Treaties, the notion of a single European model was deeply offensive to individual Member States (Neave 2003). Aware of such sensitivity, the Dutch Vice-President made very clear in a circular to Member State authorities the eventual problems that might arise from establishing a single, uniform system for quality evaluation across the face of the Community. In Portugal, the Vice-President of the Confederation of European Rector's Conferences hinted to the Portuguese Council of Universities Rectors (CRUP) that to set up a national system for quality evaluation system would be one way to side-track the launching of a European one.

At that moment, the 1988 Law on University Autonomy, though promulgated, had not been fully implemented (Chap. 7). The government had yet to approve the complementary legislation required to implement some of the provisions the law had made. Amongst them figured a Bill, yet to be laid before Parliament, for evaluating and monitoring university performance. The same situation held good for the Law on the status and autonomy of Polytechnics of 1990, which likewise contained provisions for a quality evaluation system to be applied to that sector.

The Rectors' Conference was well aware that it was in the interest of public sector universities to have a credible quality evaluation system. Evaluation would provide a clear statement and a guarantee of their quality and particularly so, given the spectacular rise in the numbers of private sector universities (Chap. 13). With such considerations in mind, CRUP launched the debate on quality evaluation for Portuguese higher education. In 1992, a seminar was organised at the University of Porto with experts from the Netherlands, France and the United Kingdom who compared their respective national systems of quality assurance. The outcome of this meeting saw the CRUP opting to follow the Dutch system, mainly because of the weight the Dutch placed on quality *improvement*, on their acknowledgement that HEIs themselves should be the main party responsible for quality, and, finally, because of the compatibility of the Dutch model with the 1988 Law on the Autonomy of Universities (Amaral and Rosa 2004).

An experimental phase was introduced with the technical assistance of the Dutch *Vereeniging van de Samenwerkende Nederlands Universiteiten* (VSNU) – the Dutch Universities' Association – and the University of Twente. The quality of degree programmes in public universities in Physics, Computer Sciences Electrical Engineering, Economics and French were externally evaluated. The scheme, beginning in 1993, set out to assess quality through a four-phase model: a self-assessment report by the degree evaluated, an external assessment by a committee of independent experts, a site visit and a final report by the assessors lodged with the institution thus evaluated. Those evaluated had the opportunity, if they so wished, to express their views of the assessment reached by the outside evaluators. Finally, the end report was published, if need be, together with views of those responsible for the programme under scrutiny. Both were made publicly available on the Internet.

The following year, after negotiation between the CRUP and the Portuguese Government, in which the Ministry of Education took account of CRUP's initiatives, the *Higher Education Evaluation Law* of 1994 was passed. It laid down the bases for a Portuguese system of quality evaluation that covered all higher education degrees, including both universities and polytechnics, public and private.

One aspect, of particular relevance and innovative character in the *Higher Education Evaluation Law* lay in Article 14, which provided for further elaboration in the law to be made by decree or by protocol. In effect, and as the Law made plain:

> the rules for the operation of the evaluation system, as well as the general principles for the recognition of the representative entities responsible for the coordination of the external reviews, can be established by the government in the usual top-down approach by decree-law or can be mutually agreed in a contractual way (Santos et al. 2006: 31–32).

Under the terms of this stipulation, the Ministry of Education in 1995 signed a protocol with the Presidents of CRUP and FUP (the Portuguese Universities' Foundation), which recognised the Portuguese Universities Foundation, created in 1993, to be the representative body of public universities and the Catholic University. The protocol also defined the general guidelines the evaluation system was to follow. An Evaluation Council was established as the Foundation's agent responsible for coordinating the evaluation of public universities. The council was granted scientific and pedagogic autonomy, together with the resources necessary for it to operate.

Thus, by 1996, the system of quality evaluation for Portuguese universities was in place, and the first cycle in the process of evaluating quality was concluded in 1999. It was a significant step in laying down a system to evaluate the quality of higher education, despite the fact that the Decree-Law creating Conselho Nacional de Avaliação do Ensino Superior (CNAVES) – National Council for the Evaluation of Higher Education – in 1998 and organising it was approved only when the process itself was well under way.

Only public universities together with the Catholic University took part in the first evaluation cycle. Two years after the passage of the *Higher Education Evaluation Law*, the system of external evaluation extended neither to the polytechnics sub-system nor to both sectors of private higher education, although some sporadic efforts had been made in this direction by both sectors to set up their own evaluation. For their part, public polytechnics, acting through the Coordinating Council of Public Polytechnics (CCISP), undertook the self-evaluation of some study programmes. Between the years 1996 and 1999, 83 self-evaluation reports had been made. But, it was not possible to move further with external reviews, largely because of delay by the Ministry of Education in recognising the body representing the polytechnic interest. A fact compounded by the Ministry's reticence to finance the process of evaluation (Santos et al. 2006).

Delay in setting up an external quality assessment system for both public polytechnics and private higher education forced the government in July 1996 to establish a working group to reflect on and monitor the process of evaluation itself. (*Setting up the Group for Reflection and Monitoring of the Process of Evaluation of Higher Education Institutions 1996*).

The group, of 11 prominent individuals, chosen by the government from the worlds of science, academia and the professions, represented interests in both public and private sectors of higher education. Its remit was to draw up a methodology for evaluating both the polytechnic sub-sector and private higher education. It was also called upon to make recommendations on the type of body to carry out the evaluation of the two sectors. Following up on the group's work, the Ministry of Education presented a set of general principles for defining the legal instruments to extend the scope of the *Higher Education Evaluation Law* (CRUP 1997). In the document of 1997 entitled the *Normative Development in the Domain of the Evaluation of Higher Education: launching of self-evaluation* of 1997, these principles were:

> The cohesion, harmony and credibility of the evaluation system will be guaranteed through a coordination system integrating:
>
> a) The first level of coordination for each one of the sub-systems constituted by
>
>   a1) an evaluation council for the University higher education;
>   a2) an evaluation council for the Polytechnic higher education;
>
> b) The second level of coordination, of a global nature, constituted by a National Council for the Evaluation of Higher Education Institutions.

These terms received concrete expression with the setting up of *CNAVES* in 1998. CNAVES organised the quality evaluation system in Portugal, established the National Council for the Evaluation of Higher Education, together with four evaluation councils, one for each of the sectors in higher education – public university, public polytechnic, private university and private polytechnic. They conducted all external review processes in their sector. In so doing, they appeared to infringe the tenets laid out in the document *Normative Development* that predated the document *The Creation of CNAVES*. Such infringement led to accusations that the introduction of quality evaluation reflected at one and the same time, both corporative interests and a conflict of interests. The motives behind this onslaught are far from clear. One explanation lies in the degree of distrust between the public and private sectors of higher education, distrust reflected in the presence of four independent evaluation councils. A situation, delicate in the extreme arose which saw each council bent on showing the particular sector for which it had charge in the best possible light. Such supposed partiality made the composition of external evaluation teams even more fraught, above all, when evaluating degrees in the same disciplinary field across both sectors, private and public. From the start, securing agreement on who should be invited on to the external review teams was subject to objection and strife between the evaluation councils representing the public and the private sectors.

Still, time is a great healer. Mutual suspicion between public and private higher education fell away, and the issue of who should figure on external evaluation teams became more a matter of consent than dissent. This change in attitude is also explained by the work of conciliation by CNAVES.

The CNAVES was established as the overall coordinating body in Portugal's system of quality evaluation. Uniformity and cohesion were maintained by that other area of responsibility CNAVES discharged, namely meta-evaluation. CNAVES was not directly involved in external evaluation. It laid down general directions, made recommendations and, finally, exercised oversight in approving the external evaluation teams, though these remained subject to the Minister's final approval. With the creation of CNAVES, agreements were signed with the Association of the Portuguese Public Polytechnics (ADISPOR) in December 1998 and the Portuguese Association of Private Higher Education (APESP) in March 1999, recognising both Associations as representing public polytechnics and private institutions, respectively. It was too late for them to join the first cycle of quality evaluation carried out by FUP. They took part only in the second cycle of evaluation, which ran from 2000 to 2005.

The first evaluation cycle, over the years between 1995 and 1999, may be considered 'an experimental phase, as part of a process to build up a sense of belonging and ownership in regard to a quality assurance system widely shared by all the relevant partners' (Santos et al. 2006: 33). Quality improvement, the basic purpose for which evaluation was set up, was more pronounced during the first cycle. Embedding a culture of self-evaluation at the institutional level was the main watchword of the hour, rather than creating rating and ranking systems, or comparing either degrees or establishments. Although each programme's strong and weak points were to be noted, the main purpose was to ensure the programmes' continuous improvement.

Experience gained in the first cycle allowed several changes to be made in the second, when other sectors in higher education joined the evaluation system. Common procedures and guidelines were laid out. Elements of accountability were introduced progressively, although driven onward by legislation (publication of the *Legal Framework for the Development and Quality in Higher Education* in 2003) (Santos et al. 2006).

A major effort was made to increase participation of international experts on evaluation teams, although financial difficulties and the use of Portuguese as the working language placed severe constraints on further internationalising the system of quality evaluation.

Formally, the second evaluation cycle included more items of accountability. The truth is they never worked as planned. Reports were somewhat inconsistent. Most were written in a way that did not permit easy comparison between study programmes, let alone to identify those clearly in default of quality. As Amaral and Rosa (2008: 75) remarked:

> the external reports were in general carefully drafted so that the public in general and the media in particular could not easily draw up league tables and very seldom offered a basis for ministerial decisions leading to the cancellation of study programmes.

In 2002, an incoming Minister complained publicly that the conclusions of external reports were obscure. He decided the quality system required changing. The *Legal Framework for the Development and Quality in Higher Education* of 2003, accepted by Parliament, set new conditions to the outcomes of assessment and the rating of programmes evaluated. The same Law introduced academic accreditation, which henceforth figured in the remit of those bodies responsible for quality evaluation. The Minister, by imposing an accreditation-type conclusion – a yes or no answer – sought a more expeditious basis for action. The Minister did not remain long in office. The law was never applied and accreditation was quickly forgotten (Amaral and Rosa 2008).

The system of quality evaluation that lasted from 1995 to 2005 was not greatly effective. Some claim that training and preparation of external evaluators were insufficient, which was reflected in very varied external evaluation reports, which lacked balance. Time spent laying out uniform criteria, procedures and processes was not as effective as it should have been. Another problem was excessive cost, especially the amounts paid to external evaluators.

Nevertheless, up to that point, the most telling shortfall of evaluation was its lack of outcome, impact and of visible results. To be credible, evaluation must have consequences visible to society. It must produce results. In the case of the Portuguese system of quality evaluation, the results were scarcely visible at all, though the Law on *Higher Education Evaluation* clearly set out the consequences study programmes repeatedly evaluated as 'wanting' would find themselves facing. Here, two points deserve raising. First, it was not up to CNAVES to decide on the measures to be applied to a study programme negatively assessed. The final decision lay with the Ministry. The truth remains, however, that no Minister ever possessed either the political will or was ready to decide precisely what measures should be meted out to the non-performing. Second, even if Ministers had girded up their loins to bring the full weight of the measures the law defined in such cases, it would have been arduous – though perhaps not impossible – to seek out peccant programmes by reading the reports of external evaluators. Whilst from 2003 onwards, review panels were asked to rate 14 'fields of appraisal' on a five-point scale from A (excellent) to E (negative), reports remained inconclusive. They seldom made unequivocal recommendations to the Minister (Amaral and Rosa 2008).

Finally, it is worth pointing out that even the improvements in quality that took place in higher education institutions as a direct consequence of the evaluation system (Rosa et al. 2006) have been less than fully visible because the CNAVES never pushed forward with real follow-up to the external evaluation. Nor, was CNAVES explicitly given that task.

At long last, in 2005, the incoming XVII Constitutional Government opened a new phase for quality assurance in Portuguese higher education.

In 1994, the system was engaged in learning the first steps in quality assurance. Good will abounded and perhaps some naivety as well about the political tensions such a process would throw up. Over the years that ensued, the evaluation system came to resemble a dysfunctional teenager, trying – unsuccessfully – to find its self. Should quality evaluation be a formative exercise, with emphasis on quality improvement or should it be a summative exercise, with emphasis on accountability? All in all, the salient feature of the first phase in the drive to quality assurance in Portugal was the emergence of trust amongst its principle actors and the wish to join together with the purpose of bringing a valid solution to 'quality problems' (Sarrico and Rosa 2008). The second phase, however, saw the erosion of that trust, as the next section makes abundantly clear.

Coming of Age: From 2006 to the Present

The year 2006 ushered in a new phase in the unfolding saga of quality assurance in Portugal. This second phase may briefly be characterised as the development of a new evaluation scheme that reflected the 'fashion mode of accreditation', chosen not on the evidence that it will work better in terms of improving the quality of universities and polytechnics but simply because it looked more attractive from a political perspective (Sarrico and Rosa 2008).

In 2005, ENQA was commissioned to do a review of the national accreditation and quality assurance practices and of CNAVES. The report was to make recommendations to both CNAVES and to the Ministry on academic and management structures for implementing appropriate practical measures for quality assurance and accreditation. ENQA was also asked to provide recommendations for the establishment of a national accreditation system within the framework of European Standards and Guidelines (ESG) for quality assurance, adopted at the 2005 Bergen Conference of European Ministers responsible for Higher Education (ENQA 2005). CNAVES was asked by the Minister to make the final report public and to organise public debate around it (Amaral and Rosa 2008). At the same time, the government encouraged and financially underwrote the participation of Portuguese universities and polytechnics – both public and private – in the Institutional Evaluation Programme of the European Universities Association (EUA/IEP).

As ENQA's review moved forward, the government announced that the current quality assurance system would be dismantled. It would be replaced by a new accreditation system in early 2007. Although this represented a significant change to the initial review exercise confided to ENQA, the ENQA review panel did not consider it 'to imply any changes to the already agreed terms of reference for the review' (ENQA 2006: 14). This provoked CNAVES into making a very tart comment indeed on ENQA's stance:

> … a change in the terms of reference was accepted by the panel in the middle of the process, as a consequence of the formal decision of the government to extinguish the quality assurance system under assessment without waiting for the results of the review. The nature of the exercise became unavoidably much different (CNAVES 2006: 3).

Despite strong objection from CNAVES, ENQA's final report, when viewed from a distance, is broadly fair and adequate. Leaving aside successive blunders in the process (Amaral and Rosa 2008), which culminated in the inadmissible final – and intolerable – episode of failing to circulate the report to the institution assessed and only to do after its unveiling to the press, the possibility remained that negative reactions could be played down and a more dispassionate reception made possible thereby. The ENQA panel recognised that the Portuguese model fitted the purpose for which it was first established. It graciously acknowledged that the Portuguese model had 'accumulated a number of positive experiences that should be considered and carried over into a new quality assurance system' (ENQA 2006: 6). The major strengths of the Portuguese model, ENQA opined, lay in its contribution to establishing a culture of self-evaluation, in its methodological model, which, in many aspects, complied with the ESG, and, finally, its comprehensiveness: it included all universities and all polytechnics. Amongst its major weaknesses were an apparently limited independence, which reflected the strong role exerted by institutions of higher education through their representative bodies, insufficient operational efficiency and consistency, primarily limited by staff resources, inefficient training of reviewer teams, inconsistencies in reporting, etc. To which was added a low level of international engagement, but, above all, a grave lack of measures having both consequence and impact (ENQA 2006).

The ENQA panel also noted that CNAVES already planned a third evaluation cycle where major shortcomings were to be corrected. In fact, CNAVES planned to launch a third evaluation cycle by the closing months of 2005. It would be based not on assessing degree programmes but take the form of a departmental evaluation – that is, a functional evaluation that would take each department's teaching staff, degree programmes, graduates, research and resources into account. The guidelines for this third evaluatory exercise had already been made public.

Dismantling the quality evaluation system in place until 2005 was due in part to the general view that it had not been greatly effective or indeed overly consequent. Other pressures came to bear, this time from European developments. As the agency responsible for running the evaluation system in Portugal, CNAVES did not meet the conditions required to be accepted on the European Register of Quality Agencies that had been conjured up in the meantime. The presence of bodies representative of the four higher education sub-systems was taken to signify, according to criteria for recognition as a Quality Agency, that the Portuguese evaluation of degree programmes was not a genuine external evaluation at all, since it was not undertaken in full independence from those evaluated.

The break-up of the evaluation system, erected around CNAVES, brought in a new phase in the development of quality assurance in Portugal. This phase was influenced largely by the developments in the European arena and by the Bologna Declaration in particular. It is a phase more influenced by far by the government than by polytechnics and universities. Trust, which was the lynchpin to the previous 'contractual model', yielded ground before a more politicised higher education system. The government, elected in 2005, took the view that the quality assurance scheme, then being drawn up, should be recognised internationally. In other words, it had to comply with principles internationally accepted in this area. In short, the new system should follow the recommendations in the ENQA report (ENQA 2006), as well as ENQA's Standards and Guidelines for Quality Assurance in the European Higher Education Area (ESG). With these conditions in mind, the *Legal Framework for the Evaluation of Higher Education* was passed in 2007. And, in the same year, the XVIIth Constitutional Government approved legislation for the *Creation of the Agency for Assessment and Accreditation of Higher Education* (Chap. 7). The enactment conferred on the new Agency responsibility for establishing procedures of quality assurance in higher education, including assessment and accreditation, to include Portugal in the European system of quality assurance in higher education and to ensure the overall internationalisation of its universities and polytechnic institutes.

The Agency for Assessment and Accreditation of Higher Education – A3ES (A3ES 2009a) is a foundation under private law, established for an unspecified period, possesses legal status and is recognised as being of public utility. A3ES is independent in its decisions, without prejudice of the guidelines fixed by the State. Its mission is to contribute to the improvement of the quality of Portuguese higher education, through assessment and accreditation of higher education institutions and their study cycles. The assessment and accreditation regime to be developed by the Agency was set out by the Law for the *Legal Framework for the Evaluation of Higher Education*.

A3ES became operational towards the end of 2008, a year after its creation. Its activity plan (A3ES 2009b) showed A3ES to be closely circumscribed by law. Legislation passed in 2008 – *Modification to the Juridical Regime of Higher Education Degrees and Diplomas*, stipulated under Article 83, that study programmes already in place when A3ES became operational were required to present themselves for accreditation. Their accreditation is to be complete by the end of academic year 2010/11. The same Decree-Law, under Article 54, announced that any new programme leading to a degree of *licenciado* (1st cycle), *mestre* (2nd cycle) or *doutor* (3rd cycle) must be pre-accredited. With some 5,000 programmes existing, the sheer size of the problem made it impossible for A3ES to use the habitual modes of assessment and accreditation and still meet these legal deadlines. A3ES introduced procedures for preliminary accreditation, with a more regular procedure to be launched later. Thus, in 2009/10 A3ES's major energies concentrated on pre-accrediting new study cycles and on granting preliminary accreditation to study cycles already in place. In a second phase, A3ES will move on to audits as a means of validating internal procedures of quality assurance developed by universities and polytechnics themselves. The implications are plain. Initially, in essence, A3ES's approach will focus on strengthening accountability, with the purpose of moving beyond this initial commitment to increasing the weight placed on processes for quality improvement, based primarily on embedding internal systems of quality assurance into university and polytechnic (A3ES 2009b).

The creation of A3ES together with its work programme for the ensuing two years appeared to tackle some of the weaknesses hinted at in its predecessor, amongst them the assertion of its independent status, making Portugal's higher education more aware of internationalisation and falling in with the exigencies of the European Standard Guidelines with which ENQA had endowed itself. Legally, A3ES is independent both from government and from higher education establishments. It moved swiftly onto the other two topics:

1. It set up a Scientific Council whose members are internationally recognised experts;
2. It has been accepted as an associate member of ENQA for 2009;
3. With the internationalisation of external evaluation teams, all reports are to be written in Portuguese and English.

Assessment and accreditation procedures together with guidelines for self-evaluation and external evaluation have been drawn up in line with the European Standard Guidelines. Provision has been made for the formal training for those individuals dealing with evaluation and accreditation processes inside universities and polytechnics. Training for external evaluation teams was also taken in hand.

In June 2009, A3ES consulted the members of its Advisory Council for their views and expectations of A3ES' role and the main aspects that should figure on its work agenda (Rosa et al. 2009). Despite some apprehensions, those polled were positive in their expectations for the new system and for its coordinating Agency. This points up a solid basis for implementation and operation. In particular, advisers looked forward to marked improvements in quality. They anticipated that A3ES would focus on assessment and accreditation at both institutional and programme levels. With accreditation singled out as a priority, grounded on a model for raising the level of institutional performance, clearly a more 'robust' system of evaluation stands in the offing. This prospect may well be explained in the light of what was seen as the 'inefficiency' of the system A3ES replaced, quite apart from its predecessor's marked lack of impact (Rosa et al. 2009).

Be that as it may, it is still too early to judge whether the new quality assurance system *will* be of consequence, just as it is to judge whether it has yet achieved visible results on Society's behalf and has thus overcome one of the earlier system's major weaknesses. In principle, with the disappearance of non-accredited degrees, it will prove easier to demonstrate impact. But it is no less important that the energies devoted to assessing and accrediting degree programmes lead on to improvement in their quality and thus raise the quality of the Portuguese higher education system as a whole. For the moment, the hope which springs eternal is that the second phase of quality assurance in Portugal will remedy that feature in the first phase which the ENQA review touched upon, namely its inability to bring about:

> (…) 'quality enhancement', i.e., encouraging the identification, communication and implementation of best practices in curricula design, teaching, student learning and institutional academic quality assurance (ENQA 2006: 35).

Hopes are high that the dysfunctional teenager, which by 2005 quality evaluation had become, will see a coming of age, during which the roles of each are more clear: the State underwrites accountability to society in general, whilst universities and polytechnics institutions take on what is theirs, that is to say an internal culture of quality assurance.

What the Future May Bring Forth: Uneventful Middle Age or Ripe Old Age?

At the end of the second evaluatory cycle, then carried out in April 2005 under the terms set out in the *Higher Education Evaluation Law*, CNAVES unveiled new guidelines for a third evaluatory cycle. The idea behind the 3rd cycle was no longer to accredit degrees, but rather to accredit 'functional units' in universities and polytechnics. It called for a significant amount of data from establishments of higher education, to serve in the construction of performance indicators, and at the same time, place each establishment's performance in context. The demise of CNAVES saw the demise of the proposed third evaluatory cycle as well. A 4-year interval ensued before A3ES was up and running. Such gap may well have impaired the general determination both to uphold and to advance the process and procedures of internal quality assurance in higher education institutions, further. It will, then, be especially interesting to see how A3ES' lighter touch, its plan for post initial accreditation (or not) of all degrees in place, by certifying internal quality assurance mechanisms, will fare.

The rise of market mechanisms in tandem with State mechanisms of quality control likewise merits further attention (Chaps. 3 and 9). In theory, market mechanisms may be strengthened by two main factors: demographics, on the one hand, and the increasing availability of information, on the other. In terms of demographics, the number of 'traditional' students moving on to higher education directly after secondary school is falling, a function of declining fertility rates (Chap. 14). This downward spiral might somehow be alleviated by the recent extension of compulsory education to the end of secondary education (12th grade), although the increase in numbers in secondary education is meant to be in vocational courses leading directly to the labour market, rather than in academic courses leading to higher education. In effect, higher education in Portugal shifted from being a supply-side to a demand-driven market. Currently, more places are available in higher education than applicants, who can, thus, despite the numerus clausus afford to be choosier. Yet places freed up by the shortage of 'traditional' students plus the massification of second cycle degrees (masters level) brought more 'mature' students to the system. They tend to be 'older and wiser', make greater sacrifice to study in terms of time and money and more demanding from higher education. The second argument that strengthens market mechanisms follows, paradoxically, from strengthening State mechanisms of quality evaluation and accreditation. In this, the State extends the dissemination of information. All external evaluation reports are public, so too under the new system, put in place by the 'reforms' of 2007, are self-evaluation reports. Over and above judgements expressed by internal or external evaluators, these documents provide data, and, significantly, indicators on the performance of universities and polytechnics. Given the massification in Portuguese higher education, what is relevant in the graduate labour market is less the *possession* of a degree, than the *perceived quality* of that degree. From this, it follows that higher education will, to an increasing extent, be 'sandwiched' between the State and the market (Sarrico and Dyson 2000). In all likelihood, further tensions, anxiety and lamentation from academia, increasingly worn out by unceasing 'reform', will arise. An alternative scenario would call for the enhancement of academia and with it a determination to develop and lay down internal quality assurance mechanisms in institutions, on their own terms, to reflect their autonomy. Will there be energy left to do so, after so many 'reforms', and after a four-year gap in the evaluation trajectory that took off in 1994?

The answer to that question will, surely, determine to some extent the success or absence of the latest quality initiatives. Is Portuguese higher education moving down the path towards compliance, ticking boxes in an increasing list of requests, hawked about by the State via A3ES, via the market with its higher education league tables in newspapers? Is it feeding a bulimia for performance indicators and artificial opinions, in ever increasing bureaucratic exercises, each with their own specialists and overseers? Or will universities and polytechnics take back the reigns of control, devise their own internal mechanisms of quality assurance and bring about improvement, innovation and, most important, student support, staff development and the motivation of both?

To these uncomfortable questions, there are two scenarios in guise of an answer. The first will inevitably end, like the Hans Christian Anderson fairy tale, with the loud and horrified cries 'the king is as bare as the day he was born' and, with it the passing of yet another system of quality assurance, dead of ripe old age. The second might, little by little, win back trust in Portugal's universities and polytechnics, open the way for a stable system that insures at institutional level both improvement and quality, and for Society general accountability and transparency, as evaluation moves on towards an uneventful middle age.

Envoi

In Portugal, the preoccupation of Public Administration with quality in higher education has never been absent (Chap. 9). And as a result, the insertion of quality assurance mechanisms and procedures progressed rapidly. Installing a system of quality evaluation in Portugal began in 1994 – or in 1993, if the pilot exercise undertaken by CRUP is brought into the reckoning. With the experience of a decade to draw on, clear responsibilities for improving accountability and quality were mingled together. They were not assigned unambiguously either to the State or to the universities and polytechnics themselves. Disillusion infected the government of the day which, in 2005, secured the termination with extreme prejudice of the pioneering system of evaluation and closed CNAVES down. Two years later, in 2007, a new independent agency was born – a new system of quality evaluation and accreditation with more teeth.

The proliferation of institutions and degrees, with no clear control over quality, demanded a further 'cleaning up' of the system, however. This took shape with a programme of cursory accreditation during the first 2 years of the new Agency's work plan. Only after this initial phase will the Agency be able to move on to a 'cruise control' mode. Yet, the idea has become current that trust in Portugal's higher education must be regained, before a less adversarial system of auditing internal quality assurance procedures may take root. The success of this mode of operation will be accomplished only when the responsibility of quality assurance is devolved to the institutional level. A further thrust in this latter direction will surely entail strengthening market mechanisms. In a shrinking pool of students, with better information to hand in the form of performance indicators and public judgments made by committees of external evaluation, university applicants will, like it or not, increasingly vote with their feet. At the same time, universities will be scrutinised by the State and by the market. They will be subject to increasing competition for the best students, the best staff, for State funding of teaching and research, and for earned income to make up the shortfall in State subsidies, a situation that massification precipitates. These pressures may perhaps lead on to some sterile jousting. They will, most assuredly, also provide an incentive (whether carrot or stick must remain for the moment hidden in creative obscurity) for further measures of internal quality assurance as a way to be better prepared to face them. The role of foundation universities, operating under private law, is also of more than passing interest in the impact they may have on the ability of institutions to improve their quality management.

Acknowledgment We would like to thank the following for having discussed with us their experience and knowledge on quality in higher education in Portugal: Alberto Amaral, António de Almeida Costa, Jacinto Jorge Carvalhal, José Veiga Simão, Sérgio Machado dos Santos and Virgílio Meira Soares.

References

1. Legislation

Constitution of the Portuguese Republic 1976 (2nd April, Constituent Assembly, VII Constitutional Amendment, 2005).
Comprehensive Law on the Education System 1986 (Law 46/86, 14th October, X Constitutional Government).
University Autonomy Law (Law 108/88, 24th September, XI Constitutional Government).
Polytechnic Statutes and Autonomy Law (Law 54/90, 5th September, XI Constitutional Government).
Higher Education Evaluation Law (Law 38/94, 21st November, XII Constitutional Government).
Constitution of the Group for Reflection and Monitoring of the Process of Evaluation of Higher Education Institutions (Ministerial Dispatch 147-A/ME/96, 29th July, XIII Constitutional Government).
Normative development in the domain of the evaluation of higher education: Launching of self-evaluation (Dispatch 72/97, 5th May, XIII Constitutional Government).
Development of the Law on Evaluation (Decree-Law 205/98, 11th July, XIII Constitutional Government).
Juridical Regime for the Development and Quality in Higher Education Law (Law 1/2003, 6th January, XV Constitutional Government).
Basis for the Financing of Higher Education Law (Law 37/2003, 22nd August, XV Constitutional Government).
Legal Framework for the Evaluation of Higher Education Law (Law 38/2007, 16th January, XVII Constitutional Government).
Creation of the Agency for Assessment and Accreditation of Higher Education (Decree-Law 369/2007, 5th November, XVII Constitutional Government).
Modification to the Juridical Regime of Higher Education Degrees and Diplomas (Decree-Law 107/2008, 25th June, XVII Constitutional Government).
Legal Framework of Higher Education Institutions (Law 62/2007, 10th September, XVII Constitutional Government).

2. Scholarly Literature

A3ES – Agency for Assessment and Accreditation of Higher Education. (2009a). On http://www.a3es.pt/en.

A3ES – Agency for Assessment and Accreditation of Higher Education. (2009b). Activity plan. http://www.a3es.pt/en/activity-plan.

Amaral, A., & Rosa, M. J. (2008). International review of national quality assurance agencies. The case of Portugal. In *Implementing and using quality assurance: Strategy and practice* (pp. 74–79). Brussels: EUA – European University Association.

Amaral, A., & Rosa, M. J. (2004). Portugal: Professional and academic accreditation. The impossible marriage? In S. Schwarz & D. F. Westerheijden (Eds.), *Accreditation and evaluation in the European higher education area* (pp. 395–420). Dordrecht: Springer.

CNAVES. (2006). Refutation to the report by the ENQA review panel – Quality assurance of higher education in Portugal. http://www.cnaves.pt/avaliacao_int/Final_refutation.pdf.

Council of the European Union. (1991). Conclusions of the Council and Ministers of Education meeting with the council of 25 November 1991. In (91/34/EC), OJ 91/C 321/02.

CRUP – Portuguese Council of Universities Rectors. (1997). A Avaliação Das Universidades Em Portugal. Da Génese Do Modelo De Avaliação À Integração Na Dimensão Europeia.

ENQA – European Association for Quality Assurance in Higher Education. (2006). Quality assurance of higher education in Portugal. In *ENQA occasional paper 10*. Helsinki: ENQA.

ENQA. (2005). *Standards and guidelines for quality assurance in the European higher education area*. Helsinki: ENQA.

Neave, G. (2003). The Bologna declaration: Some of the historic dilemmas Posed by the reconstruction of the community in Europe's systems of higher education. *Educational Policy, 17*(1), 141–164.

OECD – Organisation for Economic Co-operation and Development. (2007). *Reviews of national policies for education: Tertiary education in Portugal*. Paris: OECD.

Rosa, M. J., Santos, C. S., Cardoso, S., & Amaral, A. (2009). *The Portuguese system of quality assurance – New developments and expectations*. In 4th European quality assurance forum, creativity and diversity: Challenges for quality assurance beyond 2010. Copenhagen, Denmark.

Rosa, M. J., Tavares, D. A., & Amaral, A. (2006). Institutional consequences of quality assessment. *Quality in Higher Education, 12*(2), 145–159.

Santos, S. M., Gonçalves, L. C., Silva, J. D., Fonseca, L. A., Filipe, A. F., Vieira, C., Lima, M. J., & Oliveira, M. F. (2006). *Review of the quality assurance and accreditation policies and practices in the Portuguese higher education: Self-evaluation report*. Lisboa: CNAVES.

Sarrico, C. S., & Dyson, R. G. (2000). Using Dea for planning in UK universities – An Institutional Perspective. *Journal of the Operational Research Society, 51*(7), 789–800.

Sarrico, C. S., & Rosa, M. J. (2008). Qualidade E Acreditação No Ensino Superior. In A. Amaral (Ed.), *Políticas Do Ensino Superior: Quatro Temas Em Debate* (pp. 377–402). Lisboa: Conselho Nacional de Educação.

Chapter 11
The Impacts of Bologna and of the Lisbon Agenda

Amélia Veiga and Alberto Amaral

Introduction

Implementing the Bologna process in Portugal was a lengthy affair, for in effect, it began only in 2006. While the process dragged on, some heated public debates took place. One such debate addressed the compatibility of the binary system with the new two-tier degree system. Another turned around which higher education institutions should be allowed to confer postgraduate degrees. However, when legislation was finally passed, it became clear that the Government had opted to preserve, or even reinforce, the binary system.

Implementing the Bologna process and the Lisbon strategy both have recourse to the use of what in Commission jargon is termed 'soft law' as opposed to the established tactic of European-wide legislation. Soft law leaves the initiative of implementing to the member states in an effort to respect the principle of subsidiarity. For politicians, 'soft law' has a certain appeal. It allows Governments to shift the blame for unpopular domestic agendas onto the Open Method of Coordination (OMC) itself or onto the European Union (Zeitlin 2005; Mosher 2000; Schäfer 2002).

Soft-law procedures differ from formal legislation to the extent that they lack the power to enforce. Enforcement, however, defines 'hard' law. Some have questioned how far soft-law procedures may produce results when compared to other more or less formalised systems of coordination in complex, multilevel and functionally interdependent systems of governance (Borrás and Jacobsson 2004). However, although soft-law mechanisms are not efficient for close coordination, they appear

A. Veiga (✉)
A3ES, CIPES, Rua Primeiro de Dezembro 399, 4450-227 Matosinhos, Portugal
e-mail: aveiga@cipes.up.pt

A. Amaral
A3ES, Praça de Avalade 6 – 5 Frente, 1700-036 Lisbon, Portugal
e-mail: alberto.amaral@a3es.pt

able to bring change about. 'Most coordination processes are aimed at initiating or facilitating reforms to be conducted at the national level' (Dehousse 2002: 10). Convergence appears more as a by-product rather than as an end in itself. It is not a matter of institutions and concrete solutions so much as objectives, performances and outcomes. It is not surprising then that in monitoring Bologna's progress in 2007, the Trends V report (Crosier et al. 2007) identified a number of problems in implementing it, quite apart from various anomalies emerging at the institutional level. Thus, it remains to be seen whether soft-law mechanisms can cope with the present wave of transformation flooding European higher education and whether they are able, in the long run, to create a coherent policy framework.

In seeking to provide answers to these questions and to give greater purchase over the context of practice for the Bologna process as it unfolded in Portugal, this chapter draws upon a survey of all schools (university faculties, institutes and polytechnic schools) which presented their initial proposals for the new Bologna-type degree programmes or their proposed adaptation of existing programmes to the new structure Bologna called for. These submissions were laid before the Ministry of Higher Education, Research and Technology in March 2006.

The first part of this analysis focuses on the policy contexts (Bowe et al. 1992) that accompanied both the Bologna process and the Lisbon strategy in Portugal. The second part sets out the most salient aspects of the survey data to show how the policy context that accompanied Bologna was perceived by leadership in higher education institutions. The hypothesis being tested was that both the speed of implementation and its positive take-up are linked to a specific logic of action which set greater weight on form than on substance.

The Policy Cycle Approach

In the importance it lays on policy contexts, the policy cycle approach (Bowe et al. 1992) highlights different levels of empowerment in the institutions involved in policymaking at European, national and institutional levels. However, it ignores the State control model based on top-down implementation. Implementation processes are neither causal nor linear. In other words, policymakers do not control the meaning of their texts (Bowe et al. 1992). Policies change while moving across policy cycles – for instance, across the context of influence, on to the context of text production via the context of practice. The reason for different perceptions present in the *pays politique* and the *pays réel*, to use Neave's terminology (Neave 2005), is not an implementation gap in the sense that social actors or institutional arrangements are engaged on limiting implementation. Rather, it is the outcome of the presence of different beliefs, expectations and perceptions of goals and aims in the Bologna process. This juxtaposition depends on both the level of analysis and on the 'inter-organisational relationships, that is, between organisations and different stakeholders in the organisational environment' (Gornitzka et al. 2005: 49).

The analysis of multilevel policy processes such as the Bologna process and the Lisbon strategy using the lens of the policy cycle approach puts weight on those policy processes that are premeditated and are a political resource to feed national debates and stimulate policy change by stimulating interpretation and application to specific contexts within higher education institutions. The policy cycle approach expands the view that policy processes develop differently at European level, at national level, which comprises different national contexts, and within higher education institutions, which encompass a wide range of institutional fields. This chapter focuses on these policy processes at national level by using the lens of the policy cycle to analyse the Bologna process and the Lisbon agenda in Portugal.

The policy cycle approach brings five contexts together (Ball 2004). This chapter, however, will attend only to three. There is good reason for this. To analyse the context of outcomes and the context of political strategy would take us beyond the scope of this chapter by focusing on feedback loops that follow from the context of practice. These *prises de position* would generate other policy cycles, and consequently, their analysis would lead us in a different direction.

The context of influence covers that sphere where policy discourses are constructed, key policy concepts established and representatives of institutions included or excluded within the process that ascribes meaning. The context of text production involves the appearance of texts that represent policy. Formally and informally, such texts generate comments. They are the outcome of struggle and compromise. Thus, policy texts represent policy and take the form of official legal texts. Finally, the context of practice attends to the fact that while policies develop, those involved in practice may have different interpretations according to their own specific milieu, circumstances and condition.

The Context of Influence

The context of influence and, above all, the context of text production in the Bologna process and in the Lisbon strategy at European level had decisive influence at national level. Two factors contributed to this situation: firstly, the reinforcement of creeping competence by the European Community; secondly, the hefty use of 'weasel words' in bringing it about (Amaral and Neave 2009). The Commission's creeping power flowed from both its organisation and its financial capacity which gave its role increasing importance in setting the Bologna process. The use of 'weasel words' opened up room aplenty for different interpretations to flourish and to accommodate a wide range of interests. The European commission strategy included supporting policy developments in the member states while allowing them flexibility to choose the local responses that best addressed the challenges to local reform. In short, it eased acceptability to the member states.

The Bologna process stemmed from a political declaration signed by Ministers of Education of European States. The Lisbon strategy, by contrast, was archetypal of supranational decision made by the European Council. Transposition to national legislation was voluntary in the case of the Bologna declaration but compulsory for the Lisbon declaration.

The Lisbon strategy took the Open Method of Coordination (OMC) as a policy tool to promote developments, which in turn sought to make the EU the world's most dynamic and competitive economy. Improving skills and raising investment in research were elements the Lisbon agenda shared with the Bologna process (Chap. 8). In Portugal, the effects of OMC may be detected within the context of influence of both these processes. To some extent, national reforms are part of a new cycle of governance that emerges from the difficulty of achieving consensus among the member states. In such circumstances, the expression of policy is fraught with the possibility of misinterpretation when examined within the context of practice.

In 2000, 2001 and 2002, the objectives of the Bologna declaration as an intergovernmental process were extended, following decisions taken by the European Council. During these 3 years, the Council pushed strongly for convergence between the Bologna process and educational policymaking at the EU level (Bologna Follow-up Group 2003: 7). Policy discourse focused on widening access, increasing system diversity, stimulating the regional relevance of higher education and promoting social equity, elements, which, effectively, formed the context of influence around the Bologna process in Portugal.

Amongst the major preoccupations associated in Portugal with the implementation of Bologna was the fear of a drop in the per capita funding of higher education, a fall in the number of applicants, the rise in tuition fees and the possible merger of the binary system (Chap. 13). Increased tuition fees had met with strong opposition from students. Limitations on the State budget deficit to within 3% of GDP – or less – imposed by the EU, plus economic difficulties on the home front, created a situation of financial stringency. A fall-off in the number of applicants to higher education, itself a reflection of declining birth rates, forced universities and polytechnics, both public and private, to compete for students (Chaps. 10 and 13). To tackle this situation, some academics argued in favour of using the Bologna reforms as an opportunity to open up access to new categories of student and to lifelong education, with the idea of raising qualifications amongst both students and the labour force (Amaral 2003). These goals also fell in with the target of the Lisbon strategy. Thus, they gave the impression that in Portugal, the Bologna process was a means to fulfil the goals of the Lisbon agenda.

Discussions and information in two reports, commissioned by the Portuguese Ministry for Science and Higher Education, provided evidence on the context of influence both processes had in Portugal. Both articulated different interests within higher education institutions.

The first, a survey conducted by CIPES for the Ministry of Science and Higher Education, revealed a high level of awareness for implementing the Bologna process, but an awareness that went hand in glove with strong disagreement over the details of implementation. Among academics, consensus lacked over the duration to be assigned to elements in the two-tier structure. And agreement over the criteria to decide which kind of degrees each type of institution should be entitled to confer was even less. The Government's proposal provided for a first cycle leading to a degree of *licenciatura* in both universities and polytechnics. It employed the same descriptor for the more vocational degree awarded by polytechnics as it did for the degree of *licenciatura* already awarded by universities. In the long run, this situation had the potential to merge the binary system into a unitary system. In the context of text production, however, the threat was avoided, as we will see later.

The second report presented the findings of specialised commissions appointed by the Ministry of Science and Higher Education for each discipline or disciplinary area, and asked to make proposals for implementing Bologna across all disciplines. The report revealed a considerable divergence between proposals put forward by different disciplinary commissions, a level of discordance that suggested imposing a single structure across the whole system was not wise. In Portugal, the context of influence surrounding the Bologna process gave weight to the argument that the objectives of Bologna and of creating the European Higher Education Area would be best satisfied if discussions in different disciplines came up with conclusions shared across fields of specialisation.

The two reports made clear that the final structure to be implemented by universities and polytechnics would be strongly influenced by the public financing system, by competition for students and by the acceptability of the new degrees to the labour market. This observation raised another question that cropped up in many of the reports produced for the Ministry, namely, the need to distinguish between employability and professionalisation. The Bologna process sought to encourage employability, but did not mention professionalisation. Professional associations and academics, however, insisted on the distinction being drawn. The report on the Exact Sciences (Gomes 2004) stated that employability referred to generic competencies acquired after a 3-year degree and which had value on the labour market. Professionalisation, by contrast, referred to specific qualifications that demanded special education and training. The arguments put forward by professional associations that withheld professional accreditation to new degree courses shorter than the traditional length of studies served only to delay compromise. Thus, for example, the Engineers' Professional Association clung to the argument that only with 5 years study, corresponding to 300 credits, was it possible to master the knowledge and responsibility indispensable for the status of chartered Engineer (Conselho Directivo Nacional 2004).

The argument could, to some extent, be anticipated. If governments funded higher education to meet the demands of employability, as opposed to those required by the professional licence to practise, the outcome could only be to extend study duration further. Prolonging study time in turn bade fair to confound the clarity of the distinction between employability and professionalisation. The rise of integrated masters degrees, examined within the sphere of the context of practice, illustrates this latter tendency.

The Context of Text Production

Analysing the context of text production follows the assumption that texts represent policies. The established practice in Portuguese legislation is grounded in highly detailed and prescriptive laws (Chap. 7). In 1986, Parliament passed the Comprehensive Law of the Education System (Law 46/86 of 14 October). It laid out in considerable detail and strictly defined both the type and the duration of higher education degrees. It also stated which institutions were entitled to award them. To implement Bologna required the modification of this Act for the simple reason that, as it then existed, the structure of degrees was incompatible with the terms set out in the Bologna framework. This was no small matter. For several years, no government could count on a parliamentary majority. Thus, to the discomfort of many ministers and the desperation of HEIs, the process dragged on for a good long time against a backdrop of heated public debate.

In 2004, the Government enacted legislation, which regulated certain elements in the Bologna package, more precisely those which did not conflict with the Comprehensive Law of 1986. Amongst them was the introduction of a curricular credit system in keeping with the European Credit Transfer Scheme (ECTS) together with certain of its accompanying procedures – the learning contract, transcription of records, student and course information and the mandatory take-up of the Diploma Supplement.

A year later, a new Government came into office, this time commanding a parliamentary majority. On 30 August 2005, Parliament finally voted the Law 49/2005, which adapted the earlier Comprehensive Law of 1986. This opened the way for the Government to pass a new Decree-Law (74/2006 of 24 March 2006), which set out new terms for academic degrees and diplomas and brought the degree structure in Portugal into line with the Bologna framework. Setting aside the fear that a common designation of first cycle studies for universities and polytechnics would erode the binary divide, the policy these legal documents enshrined upheld the binary line where it did not reinforce it. This it did by a clear distinction between the mission of universities and polytechnics and differentiating between the degrees each may confer, their length and their vocational bias.

For Polytechnics (Chap. 6), the normal first cycle degree structure was based on 180 credits – that is, 3 years study time. Only in exceptional cases – when national or European legislation required more protracted studies in keeping with established practices in certain professions – was alternative provision envisaged. Such provision was both conditioned by and dependent on a well-established practice in 'referenced' establishments of higher education in Europe. Under these specific terms alone could Polytechnics offer extended first cycle awards of up to 240 credits over 4 years. Universities were free to put on a first cycle of 180 or 240 credits. They also exercised the exclusive right to dispense integrated master's courses between 300 and 360 credits which lasted between 5 and 6 years in those instances where European Law recognised a longer study duration or, once again, when in keeping with practices well established in Europe.

In 2006, the Ministry of Science, Technology and Higher Education commissioned an evaluation of the Portuguese higher education system by the Organisation for Economic Cooperation and Development (OECD) together with a report on the national quality assessment system from the European Network of Quality Agencies (ENQA) (Chaps. 7 and 9). In addition, it jointly funded the voluntary participation of higher education institutions in quality audits undertaken by the European Universities Association's Institutional Evaluation Programme. These initiatives laid out the conceptual grounding for a second wave of policies, this time linked to the legal status of higher education institutions and the accreditation of degree programmes. It was entrusted to the Agency for Assessment and Accreditation (A3ES), established in 2007. In 2008, a decree-law was passed to monitor progress made in shifting the paradigm from teaching to learning. Each university and polytechnic was required to produce a report. The effects these reports may have had, however, on advancing the Bologna process remain as yet to be seen.

The Lisbon agenda also had its impact on policies to improve skills and qualifications. For students not having standard entry qualifications, the special access route was broadened by lowering the age of potential applicants from 25 to 23 years, by replacing national examinations with entrance examinations conducted by the establishment and, finally, by recognising students' prior professional and work experience as qualifying elements for application to higher education. Programmes leading to professional qualifications were enlarged in scope with the development of postsecondary education. In the form of technological specialisation courses – CET – they were essentially non-degree-awarding programmes which did not confer academic diplomas. It was a measure designed to strengthen links between secondary and higher education as well as to reinforce the vocational dimension in polytechnics, which were responsible for its development.

The Context of Practice

Whilst the interpretation of policy texts takes place in specific settings across different levels – European, national and institutional – the context of practice, in turn, builds out from the way policy is interpreted in institutions. The context of practice is then a process of making sense of policy texts in the light of established practice. Here, we tackle this issue at the three levels mentioned – that is, at European, national and institutional.

Examining the European level draws on the various so-called 'stocktaking reports' lodged by the Bologna Follow-Up Group, which monitors progress on implementing Bologna (Bologna Follow-up Group 2005, 2007, 2009). For the Lisbon agenda, the 'Lisbon Scorecard Reports' (Tilford and Whyte 2009) provide the principal source of data. Since 2000, the 'Scorecard Reports' are regularly updated by the Centre for European Reform[1] despite the frivolous use of such quaint labels as 'heroes' and 'villains' to classify the feats of European member states. There is some advantage to be derived from both sources; for they, in their turn, draw on national reports which contain certain information that are useful for understanding the unfolding of both the Bologna process and the Lisbon strategy.

By contrast, analysis of national level draws on empirical data generated by setting new study programmes in place. The institutional level for its part relies on the conclusions of a survey undertaken in 2007, which concentrated on the views of institutional leadership in those schools that had made proposals to the first round of submission for the new study programmes.

The Bologna Score Cards

The Bologna stocktaking reports check the progress participating countries have made in implementing the Bologna process. In 2005 and 2007, these exercises drew up indicators and applied them to specific action lines. Amongst them are the degree system, quality assurance, recognition of degrees, study abroad, lifelong learning and joint degrees (see Tables 11.1–11.5). Each item was scored from 1 to 5 and tinted: 1 (red) – little progress; 2 (orange) – some progress; 3 (yellow) – good; 4 (light green) – very good and 5 (green) – excellent. This scale has an obvious optimistic bias as no colours are foreseen for 'no progress at all'. Some worry about whether a tinge can possibly be compatible with objective accuracy (Veiga et al. 2008; Veiga and Amaral 2009), a disquiet admitted by the 2009 stocktaking exercise, which purported to use more rigorous criteria. It resulted in scores lower than in previous years (Bologna Follow-up Group 2009) just as it also recognised that earlier country reports on progress toward reform were overly optimistic. In truth, the graphic presentation of the Bologna scorecard has 'become a lighter shade of green' than earlier. In the case of Portugal, the shades conferred as a result of the progress made in implementing the qualifications framework and for the level of international participation achieved in the quality system have taken on a slightly less nacreous tint, as will be seen later. Yet, change in shades also brought about a dilution in a hitherto unalloyed optimism. For the very first time, the Bologna Follow-up Group admitted that not all the goals of the Bologna Process will be achieved by 2010 (Bologna Follow-up Group 2009: 12).

Table 11.1 shows that in Portugal, all the items in degree system implementation have improved with the exception of the national qualifications framework. The score assigned to implementing the two-cycle system appears, however, to have taken formal adoption as the sole indicator. No barriers to transition between cycles were

Table 11.1 Degree system: comparing stocktaking results for Portugal

Degree system	2005	2007	2009
Implementation of the two-cycle degree system	2	3	5
Level of student enrolment in the two-cycle system	2	–	–
Access from the first to the second cycle	2	5	5
Implementation of the National Qualifications Framework	–	5	4

Green (5); light green (4); yellow (3); orange (2); red (1)

Table 11.2 Quality assurance: comparing stocktaking results for Portugal

Quality assurance	2005	2007	2009
Stage of development of quality assurance system	4	–	4
National implementation of standards and guidelines for QA	–	4	–
Key elements of the evaluation system	4	4	–
Level of student participation	3	4	4
Level of international participation	4	5	4

Green (5); light green (4); yellow (3); orange (2); red (1)

Table 11.3 Recognition of periods of study: comparing stocktaking results for Portugal

Recognition of periods of study	2005	2007	2009
Diploma supplement	3	5	5
Ratification of Lisbon convention and implementation of its principles	5	5	5
ECTS	3	3	5
Recognition of prior learning	–	–	5

Green (5); light green (4); yellow (3); orange (2); red (1)

Table 11.4 Stocktaking results for Portugal

Lifelong learning	2007
Recognition of prior learning	5

Green (5); light green (4); yellow (3); orange (2); red (1)

Table 11.5 Stocktaking results for Portugal

Joint degrees	2007
Establishment and recognition of joint degrees	5

Green (5); light green (4); yellow (3); orange (2); red (1)

unearthed, probably because 'studying a Master programme in another discipline than the Bachelor degree is quite rare and often connected to further obstacles' (ESIB 2007: 40). It is premature, however, to assess such problems, for the simple reason that in July 2006, the only students enrolled in second cycle were those who transferred from the old structure to the new.

No less astounding is the performance in implementing the National Qualifications Framework (NQF) despite its new – and adjusted – lower marks. The experience of NQF in countries such as Australia, New Zealand, South Africa, England, Scotland and Ireland shows clearly that implementation does not bring forth quick fulfilment of goals, largely, because of the complexity of the exercise. In 2007, the national report assumed naively that NQF was already operational, being inspired by the Dublin descriptors, a status that was very far indeed from reality. It was awarded a score of 5. By 2009, though in the meantime the Portuguese government had presented 'The Framework for Higher Education Qualifications in Portugal', the Nations performance merited but a four, doubtless because indicators had assumed a new rigour in the meantime. The accuracy of scorecards based solely on reporting from national authorities opens the way to more than a little quibbling.

Portugal's performance in quality assurance is no less surprising. Between 2005 and 2007, apparently, it improved whilst remaining consistently green. Yet, in that self-same year, no quality assurance system was in operation. Its predecessor had been suspended, and its replacement had not been made! The lower score given in 2009 to the level of international participation which the authors of the report explained as being the result of more demanding indicators surprises only by retaining the green colour, although slightly faded. No less amazing was the score of four assigned to the level of student participation in a quality system that had not even seen the light of day. Still, the Trends V report (Crosier et al. 2007) pointed out that only one-third – or less – of Portuguese higher education institutions mentioned the positive involvement of students in the process of policy reform. On this, European Students International Bureau commented

> From [...] Portugal there are indications that recommendations from the OECD have lead to, or might lead to, less student participation. This is a worrying development and Governments should take care that HEIs continue to be governed in a democratic spirit (ESIB 2007: 30).

Certainly, this statement did not directly *measure* the level of student involvement in quality assurance. But, it did most assuredly make hints about the state of student participation.

Implementing the Diploma Supplement and ECTS is impressive. For all that, the passing of national laws adopting the Diploma Supplement (DS) does not mean HEIs in fact issue it. As Trends V report agreed '20% or less are able to make this claim [to issue the DS to all graduating students] in (...) Portugal (...)' (Crosier et al. 2007: 43), a situation the three writers of the report explained by the costs of issuing the Supplement.

Portugal obtained the highest score for implementing the principles of the Lisbon Convention. The Trends V report (Crosier et al. 2007) announced that more than 60% of HEIs stated that no returning students had problems with credit recognition. Nevertheless, a research project into institutional responses to internationalisation and Europeanisation, dating from 2005, found that

> The interviewed students from all organisations reported problems at the level of credit recognition and transfer and there are cases where the grades obtained in a different organisation do not count for the overall classification (Veiga et al. 2005: 112).

Clearly, not only are the national governments painting a colourful picture. The same may be said of university leadership, which appears to have an attitude – and a judgment – more positive than tends to dominate in academia's lower orders.

Performance on implementing the curricular credit system (ECTS) seems good. But what evidence in the reform is there that points to awareness of student workload, not to mention the assessment of learning outcomes? Here, Trends V refers delicately and generally to the apparent fact that in many cases, the use of ECTS remains superficial and incorrect.

The instruments of recognition are not closely coordinated. It is perfectly possible to issue a Diploma Supplement without implementing the credit system, just as it is possible to ratify the Lisbon Convention without implementing its principles.

Not all instruments, even if fully implemented, work in the same way for academic recognition. Nor is it clear whether higher education institutions tackle the issue of academic recognition differently. Does the use of the Diploma Supplement ensure that academic recognition is more transparent, less difficult and more flexible? Or will those mobile obtain full recognition, based on the credit system, for the periods they stay abroad?

The system of credit accumulation underpins the recognition of prior learning – including non-formal and informal learning. In Portugal, lifelong learning is a policy area in the Lisbon agenda. It includes the new opportunities initiative established in 2005. However, since recognition of prior learning did not exist prior to this date, it is mayhap a trifle early to have assigned a maximum score to performance in this area.

Activating the *ERASMUS Mundus* programme allowed joint degrees to be established at national level. The score obtained points to a significant number of HEIs having already set up joint programmes and were awarding nationally recognised degrees. This assessment seems too optimistic. A survey on cooperation in establishing double, multiple or joint degrees in 2006 was registered only 7% for Portuguese universities (Maiworm 2006).

The Lisbon Score Cards

Turning our attention to the Lisbon strategy, its counterpart to the Bologna process trend reports is a scorecard exercise which pins one of two labels to European member states: 'Hero' for countries that achieved many or most[2] of the Lisbon targets and 'Villain' for laggards and those dragging their feet (Tilford and Whyte 2009).

Portugal was cast as 'villain' in respect of levels of employment and social inclusion, which focused on transition into the workforce, mainly because Portugal suffered 'from under-performing education systems, with poor records at both secondary and tertiary levels' (Tilford and Whyte 2009: 74). The same held good for upgrading skills. Portugal is amongst the least performing in the Programme for International Student Assessment (PISA) exercise despite spending a higher share of GDP on primary and secondary education than the EU average (Chap. 4). In higher education, less than 20% of young people aged between 25 and 34 years graduate (Tilford and Whyte 2009).

Following the European Commission's assessment of progress made, the Council set specific recommendations for each country. For Portugal, those linked to Bologna included the development of a vocational training system by the full implementation of the National Qualifications Framework through involving appropriate stakeholders (European Commission 2009: 46). This is a curious contrast, indeed, when placed against the results of the Bologna stocktaking exercise in this field, where Portugal was judged 'very good'. One explanation might possibly relate to different interpretations made in implementing the National Action Programmes for Growth.

Truth to tell, interpretations from the Lisbon Score Card and the assessment of the European Commission are at odds with the claim of national authorities in reports about the National Action Programme for Growth and Jobs. The national report of 2006 stressed 'very significant results obtained' (PNACE 2006: 27). The 2007 report alluded to 'their decisive evolution in 2007 are already known' (PNACE 2007: 38).

Interestingly, the content of the reports presented by national authorities to the Bologna process and to the Lisbon agenda produced contradictory results. In the Bologna process, Portugal received a very positive evaluation. In the Lisbon agenda, however, the nation was cast as a 'villain' in items related to education.

On questions of access for new students and new social groups to higher education, the Bologna stocktaking exercise reported a significant rise in the number of students after the introduction of a more flexible scheme of access (Bologna Follow-up Group 2009: 137) – a topic that also figured on the Lisbon agenda. However, greater though adult enrolments in higher education were, the reports showed neither where nor how they enrolled.

Equally puzzling was the Lisbon agenda's nomination of Portugal as one of the five countries – together with Denmark, Sweden, Ireland and Scotland – to receive positive evaluation on the Bologna 2009 stocktaking exercise. This too stood in contrast with the Lisbon assessment in which Portugal received a not so much as a single commendation as 'Hero'!

Implementing Study Programmes Under the Bologna Framework

The data submitted for the approval of new programmes or for the adaptation of those already in place open up further insights into the context of practice of the Bologna process in Portugal from the viewpoint of the national authorities, universities and polytechnics.

In March 2006, Decree-Law 74/2006 was passed. It set up the new Bologna-type degree structure and called for submissions to be presented within 2 weeks. The Ministry expected that only in exceptional instances would proposals be made. This was not to be. Rather, some 1,464 proposals were lodged, 33% being new study programmes and 67% being adaptations of old programmes to the Bologna-type structure. Twenty-eight percent came from public universities, 27% from public polytechnics and 45% from the private sector. One reason for this avalanche may be that higher education had been waiting for a long time for this new initiative. Another was the notion that the new requirements would not be difficult to achieve. However, the Ministry stipulated that the adaptation of existing undergraduate programmes could only originate a single first cycle, which explains the fact that the final number of single first cycle programmes in the public university was small compared with second cycle programmes.

11 The Impacts of Bologna and of the Lisbon Agenda

Table 11.6 Bologna-type degrees approved by the Ministry

Type of institution	Type of degree	Presented Adequacy	Presented New	Accepted Adequacy	Accepted New	Total
Public universities	1st cycle	427	111	410	100	510
	Integrated master	113	10	82	9	91
	2nd cycle	547	814	511	758	1,269
	3rd cycle	245	329	188	310	498
Public polytechnics	1st cycle	450	285	425	141	566
	2nd cycle	2	615	0	316	316
Private institutions	1st cycle	515	495	460	233	693
	Integrated master	35	22	25	0	25
	2nd cycle	130	961	122	355	474
	3rd cycle	17	121	17	16	33
Army and police	1st cycle	22	0	22	0	22
	Integrated master	21	0	21	0	21
Total						4,518

Source: DGES, December 2009

As Table 11.6 shows, by the end of 2009, the degree programmes approved amounted to 4,870.[3] At public universities, master's programmes – in all, some 1,269 – far outstripped first cycle degree programmes, which numbered 510. In all likelihood, a reflection of the legal restriction on the number of adapted first cycles, a restriction that did not apply to second and third cycles. However, the distribution between second cycle and first cycle degree programmes was inverted for public polytechnics (316/566) and the private sector (474/693). For public polytechnics, the low number of second cycles was probably an outcome of new legislation, which strengthened the link between polytechnics and labour market and raised the qualifications level required of their teaching staff. In private higher education too, first cycle programmes predominated – though that situation might also spring from their staff being less well qualified.

A comparison of proposals submitted, with submissions accepted by the Ministry, shows that public universities presented 538 first cycle proposals – 427 adjustments and 111 new programmes 5 were accepted. Public polytechnics presented 735 proposals (450 adjustments and 285 new programmes), of which 566 were accepted; whereas the private sector presented 1010 proposals – 515 adjustments and 495 new programmes. Only 693 were accepted.

Turning to second cycle degree programmes, public universities presented 1,361 proposals – 547 adjustments and 814 new programmes – of which 1,269 were accepted. Similarly, public polytechnics presented 617 proposals – 2 adjustments and 615 new programmes. Three hundred and sixteen were validated, and in the private sector, 1,091 proposals – 130 adjustments and 961 new programmes – of which 474 alone were validated. The large number of second cycle proposals suggests that higher education institutions were trying to recruit students more for the second cycle than first cycle degrees.

One hundred and twenty-three integrated masters[4] were submitted by public universities – 113 adjustments and 10 new programmes. Ninety-one were accepted, while for private universities, 77 proposals – 55 adjustments and 22 new programmes – brought forth only 25 validations. The Ministry only validated integrated masters once it could be shown that the practice was firmly established across Europe. Integrated masters in 'Engineering' and 'Psychology' met this requirement since the Ministry approved them. In fields of specialisation protected by European directives, accepting integrated masters programmes was easier since professional qualifications required a minimum number of years of study – six for 'Medicine' (European Parliament and European Council 2005: article 25), five for 'Dental Medicine' (European Parliament and European Council 2005: article 35) and Veterinary Surgeons (European Parliament and European Council 2005: article 38), at least five for Pharmacists (European Parliament and European Council 2005: article 44) and between 4 and 6 years for Architects (European Parliament and European Council 2005: article 46). In the other cases, we would argue that professional associations were proficient in protecting the scientific areas they represented.

Third cycle degree programmes replaced the earlier structure of doctoral studies and were based on a research project leading to the public defence of a thesis. Public universities presented 574 proposals – 245 adequacies and 329 new programmes – 498 were taken up while private universities presented 138 proposals – 17 adjustments and 121 new proposals – only 33 were recognised.

National data show that amongst their academic staff, private universities had a lower level of qualification (GPEARI 2010) while their research engagement is still embryonic (FCT 2010).

Survey Findings

Describing the context of practice as universities and polytechnics see, it draws finally upon a survey into the way the process of submission was conducted – its organisation, consultations with students and academic staff, methods of credit allocation and finally the strong – or weaker – points as they were perceived during the first round of submission in 2006.

The results seem to bear out the idea that Bologna was progressing as the Ministry hoped. Indeed, it was difficult to find reports that recognised problems with the Bologna reforms (Veiga and Amaral 2006, 2009). Yet, for the first time in that series, Trends V (Crosier et al. 2007) pinpointed some issues that could affect the setting up of the European Higher Education Area. Among them, some issues cropped up in the Portuguese context – problems in the articulation between cycles and the flow of students between polytechnics and universities. Other problems related to a certain lack of coherence between different types of masters programmes under development and particular problems with integrated masters' courses.

Problems with employability were also noted by the Trends V report, due in the main, to the failure to open up a broad debate on the matter between institutions, authorities, employers and the general public. The risk, so Trends V reckoned, was that absence of dialogue would blunt the impact of reform and lead to a general misunderstanding of the qualifications it put in place. In Portugal, the absence of dialogue gave rise to an apparent paradox between a reform that should have been marked by the responsiveness of higher education to societal demands on the one hand and to the demands of the labour market needs on the other, faced with the apparent difficulty (or unwillingness) of universities to put on first cycles seen as directly relevant to the labour market.

For institutional leadership, the main goal involved shifting from a teaching to a learning paradigm. Mobility and employability, taken for granted as Bologna's goals at national level by the Government and at European level by Ministers, were not the main priority for Portuguese Higher Education Institutions. Trends V professed to see a causal correlation between student learning, interpreted as a paradigm shift, and the objectives of Bologna:

> it (student learning) will enable students to become the engaged subjects of their own learning process, and also contribute to improving the many issues of progressing between cycles, institutions, sectors and countries. (Crosier et al. 2007: 2).

In Portugal, pedagogic and curricular reform, presented in Trends V as an add-on outcome to Bologna, were seen by HEIs as the main vehicle for bringing change about. Fulfilling the Bologna goals – mobility and employability, for instance – were, in the view of Portuguese higher education, themselves adds-on. In short, different perceptions gave rise to different goals and priorities. For many European institutions, however, mobility and employability were the prime goals of Bologna. A shift in paradigm, on the contrary, was something to be achieved as the Bologna process unfolded. Thus, Portuguese HEIs saw Bologna as a window of opportunity to introduce pedagogic and curricular reforms without harnessing reform to mobility and employability that is, to Bologna's official and formal goals.

Given the high expectations of leadership in the schools surveyed, one might have expected that student-centred learning, heralded by the writers of Trends V as 'the most significant legacy of the process will be a change of educational paradigm across the continent' (Crosier et al. 2007: 2), would urge on the Bologna reforms in Portugal, even if no evidence was to hand that this change was under way. From the standpoint of school leadership, shifting the paradigm of teaching/learning depended on changes in teaching methods. In the public sector, both universities (26 out of 30 answers received) and polytechnic schools (44 out of 46 answers) acknowledged change in this item. For the private sector, 38 university schools out of 49 and 15 polytechnic schools out of 26 pointed in the same direction. Changes in curriculum design did not, however, connect with other processes supporting the paradigm shift. For instance, positive assessment of defining the skills and abilities created by each study programme and course unit, plus the allocation of credits, were seen as more important than assessment of changes in the organisation of curricula. Polytechnic schools, both public and private, rated the processes of competency definition and credit allocation more positively than university schools (public and private). Interestingly, university schools were more confident about effective change in curricular organisation than were polytechnic schools. Expectations that these changes could reduce dropout rates were high. Less encouraging was the low expectation School leadership entertained about student mobility.

Differences in the way some of the Bologna instruments were employed, which Trends V had lit upon, were also visible in Portugal, principally the incorrect and token usage of the European Credit Transfer System (ECTS), the confused use of the Diploma Supplement and the lack of engagement of higher education institutions in developing the National Qualifications Framework. Despite the optimism of Trends V, which anticipated an increase in activities related to mobility, the data of the survey bore out neither an enlarged horizontal mobility nor an increase in vertical mobility.

Integration at the first cycle level will, some scholars believe, have substantial consequences for universities and polytechnics, one possibility being the establishment of a degree hierarchy, based on standards the individual university may set (Bleiklie 2005). In Portugal, Decree-Law 74/2006, which launched the Bologna process, created just such a hierarchy, based on study duration, on the qualification level of academic staff and on the type of degrees universities and polytechnics award. Polytechnics in particular resented deeply that tailoring the rules for awarding second cycle degrees should echo the characteristics of universities, a situation which confirmed Bleiklie's remark:

> a number of practically-oriented institutions may thus feel threatened by being integrated in a system where they are going to find their place in a hierarchically organised setting according to criteria that are alien to them (Bleiklie 2005: 43).

Implementing the Bologna process took place against a number of political contexts that were both dynamic and permanent. They not only applied to the economic, social or political contexts but also embraced appropriate features in the context of action. In fine, policy mutated according to different policy contexts. Thus, when one compares the intentions of national institutions vis à vis the Bologna reforms as against the perceptions of leadership in the schools in the survey, clearly, they do not match (see Table 11.7).

In the eyes of school leadership, issues associated with advancing the mobility of students and academics were seemingly connected exclusively to funding policies still to be developed at national level. HEIs took the view that funding policies for higher education and their distribution would be clarified and especially so in the matter of second cycle studies. These expectations found no response at national level since the Bologna reform's focus of intention at that level did not deal directly with issues arising from funding. Given the large numbers of second cycle degree programmes, here was an issue sensitive indeed.

Thus, amongst the obstacles that in the minds of school leadership, stood foursquare across Portugal's road to Bologna, was the absence of debate and a lack of flexibility in norms and regulations. Even so, some HEIs claimed to be reasonably successful in mobilising their constituencies and had put in place new internal regulations to meet the conditions in the legal framework. Lack of preparation in academic services, plus a degree of incoherence in institutional policies added further to the difficulties. Some HEIs also reported low levels of student participation in

Table 11.7 Intended focus of Bologna reforms in the context of practice

Intended focus of Bologna reforms as perceived by national institutions	Intended focus of Bologna reforms as perceived by HEIs
Administration	Administration
Degree system	Approval of new internal regulations
Diploma Supplement	
Pedagogic	Pedagogic
Credit system	Pedagogical training initiatives
Qualifications framework	Contracts targeting teaching methodologies
	Status of part-time students
Governance	Governance
Status of HEIs	Accreditation agency
Accreditation agency	Changes on the status of academic profession
	Allocation of further resources to HEIs
	Access to HE
Internationalisation	Internationalisation
	Funding

such decision as the assigning of credits to courses as well as a lack of coordination between study cycles.

Conclusion

The extremely short time for submitting the first round of Bologna-type programmes, plus the fact some legislation remained outstanding, may have meant that implementation was largely a matter of form rather than substance.

The Decree-Law 107/2008 of 25 June required higher education institutions to publish annual reports on implementing the Bologna process. An analysis of the information contained in those reports leads to the following conclusions:

(a) Universities and polytechnics were able to implement the Bologna structure inasmuch as it involved full implementation of the three-cycle structure and the use of certain instruments – the curricular credit system (ECTS) and the Diploma Supplement, for example.
(b) Constraints imposed on adapting previous degree programmes to the Bologna first cycle were successful in preventing an excessive proliferation of degrees.
(c) New requirements for the qualification of academic staff teaching at second and third cycle degree programmes have concentrated academic Master and PhD programmes into public institutions, where most research takes place.
(d) That most higher education institutions consider the move from a teaching to a learning paradigm as the most important issue to be addressed over the next few years is a positive development.

(e) That universities and polytechnics recognised academic staff require substantial training in new teaching methods if the learning paradigm is to be advanced successfully and must also be seen in a positive light.
(f) Universities and polytechnics are actively developing a number of initiatives in areas such as quality assurance, requests from students about new teaching methodologies, internationalisation, etc. This will inject a new dynamic into higher education policy.

Reports from the European level show Portugal to be performing well within the Bologna setting. They also cast Portugal as a 'villain' when it came to Bologna-related matters within the Lisbon agenda. Representations such as these are perhaps a trifle simplistic. Nevertheless, they illustrate very well that differing – not to mention contradictory – interpretations of broadly similar achievements are not just possible, but are part of official opinion. The question that arises from such versatility of views must surely be: 'What, given the conjoined nature of the Bologna process with the Lisbon agenda, may explain so apparent a paradox?'.

At the national level, it became evident that Bologna now fed into the Lisbon agenda, thereby aligning the European strategy of seeing Bologna as one instrument within the Lisbon agenda (Froment 2007). This re-alignment suggests that progress made within the Bologna process served to advance the Lisbon agenda with respect to the upgrading of skills. From the standpoint of pure logic if it is agreed that Portugal's performance within the Lisbon strategy was not satisfactory, how is it possible to evaluate the country's performance in the Bologna process as successful?

Neave explored the potentially conflicting nature between what he termed 'political time' and 'academic time' (Neave 2005). In his view, 'political time' flowed from the technological imperatives of the knowledge society and its 'productivist' ethic. It pervaded the Bologna process. 'Academic time', he argued, by contrast derived from the 'time required to assimilate a corpus of knowledge' and was usually decided by universities (Neave 2005: 18). That the political timing of the Bologna and Lisbon strategy ventures no longer coincides would serve seemingly to reinforce tensions between academic time and political time and, by so doing, bring immense pressure to bear on the window of opportunity available to both reforms. Making sense of practice, viewed at European and at national levels was thus shot through with contradiction. The consequences for subsequent policy cycles ought not to be passed over lightly, however. For not the least amongst the risks that may flow from such contradictions is the failure to connect national policies with initiatives taken at the institutional level.

To drive home the definite conclusions about implementing Bologna in Portugal would be precipitate and premature. This chapter may usefully end with a quotation from the University of Minho. It casts an interesting light on the process of implementation (Universidade do Minho 2008: 23).

> ... it is always difficult to change people and institutions. These changes, to be deep and meaningful, require human and financial resources and time to be embedded in institutional culture and practice... the 2010 deadline as the end point for the implementation of this process [Bologna] must be contextualised against to the vastness of its objectives. That deadline represents a time horizon too short for implementing and bringing the changes to maturity, especially when they focus on centuries old practices and attitudes...

Notes

1. The Centre for European Reform is a British-based think-thank given over to improving the level of debate about the European Union.
2. The cynical will doubtless recall the joke about primitive counting methods: one, two, many and all. Simple but decidedly neither precise, nor rigorous and very certainly neither scientific nor scholarly.
3. Data do not include the Catholic University, as this institution until quite recently did not need to submit its proposals to the prior scrutiny of the Ministry.
4. The integrated masters refer to both those specialisation fields where the directive 2005/36/EC (European Parliament and European Council 2005) establishes the number of years of study required for professional practice (general care, dental practitioner, veterinary surgeon, midwife, architect, pharmacist and medical doctor) and to those fields (e.g. 'engineering' and 'psychology') that apparently fit the notion of regulated profession (European Parliament and European Council 2005: article 3). The regulated professions often voice their arguments favouring longer studies based on the assumption that professional qualifications required by competent authorities demand additional years of study.

References

Amaral, A. (Ed.). (2003). *Avaliação, Revisão e Consolidação da Legislação do Ensino Superior* (Vol. 4). Matosinhos: CIPES.
Amaral, A., & Neave, G. (2009). On Bologna, weasels and creeping Competence. In A. Amaral, G. Neave, C. Musselin, & P. Maassen (Eds.), *European integration and the governance of higher education and research*. Dordrecht: Springer.
Ball, S. (2004). *Education reform: A critical and post-structural approach*. Buckingham: Open University Press.
Bleiklie, I. (2005). Organising higher education in a knowledge society. *Higher Education, 49*, 31–59.
Bologna Follow-up Group. (2003). *Work programme 2003–2005: from Berlin to Bergen – Responsibilities of the Board – Tasks of the Secretariat.* Italian Presidency of the Bologna Follow-up.
Bologna Follow-up Group. (2005). Bologna process stocktaking report. In *Ministerial meeting in Bergen*. Bergen.
Bologna Follow-up Group. (2007). Bologna process stocktaking report. In *Ministerial meeting in London*. London.
Bologna Follow-up Group. (2009). Bologna process stocktaking report. In *Ministerial meeting in Leuven/Louvain-la-Neuve*. Leuven/Louvain-la-Neuve.
Borrás, S., & Jacobsson, K. (2004). The open method of co-ordination and new governance patterns in the EU. *Journal of European Public Policy, 11*(2), 185–208.
Bowe, R., Ball, S., & Gold, A. (1992). *Reforming education and changing schools: Case studies in policy sociology*. London: Routledge.
Conselho Directivo Nacional. (2004). *Posição da Ordem dos Engenheiros relativamente ao processo de Bolonha*. Lisbon: CDN.
Crosier, D., Purser, L., & Smidt, H. (2007). *Trends V: Universities shaping the European higher education area*. Bruxelles: European Universities Association.
Dehousse, R. (2002). The open method of coordination: A new policy paradigm? In *First Pan-European conference on Europeia union politics*. Bordeaux.
ESIB. (2007). *Bologna with students' eyes*. London.
European Commission. (2009). *Implementation of the Lisbon strategy structural reforms in the context of the European economic recovery plan – Annual country assessments: Recommendation*

for a council recommendation on the 2009 up-date of the broad guidelines for the economic policies of the member states and the community and on the implementation of Member States' employment policies. Brussels: European Commission.
European Parliament and European Council. (2005). *Directive on the recognition of professional qualifications*.
FCT. (2010). *Unidades de I&D – Apresentação dos resultados da Avaliação de Unidades de I&D, 2007–08*. Lisbon: Fundação para a Ciência e Tecnologia (http://alfa.fct.mctes.pt/apoios/unidades/avaliacoes/2007/).
Froment, E. (2007). Quality assurance and the Bologna and Lisbon objectives. In L. Bollaert, S. Brus, B. Curvale, L. Harvey, E. Helle, H. T. Jensen, J. Komlejnovic, A. Orphanides, & A. Sursock (Eds.), *Embedding quality culture in higher education*. Brussels: EUA.
Gomes, J. F. (2004). *Implementação do processo de Bolonha a nível nacional: grupos por área do conhecimento – ciências exactas*. Lisboa: Ministério da Ciência e do Ensino Superior.
Gornitzka, A., Kyvik, S., & Stensaker, B. (2005). Implementation analysis in higher education. In A. Gornitzka, M. Kogan, & A. Amaral (Eds.), *Reform and change in higher education*. Dordrecht: Springer.
GPEARI. (2010). *Docentes do Ensino Superior (2001 a 2008)*. Lisbon: Gabinete de Planeamento, Estratégia, Avaliação e Relações Internacionais, Ministério da Ciência, Tecnologia e Ensino Superior.
Lisbon Strategy Portugal Anew – National Action Programme for Growth and Jobs (PNACE 2005–2008). (2006). In *Report on 1st year of implementation*. Lisbon: Cabinet of the National Coordinator of the Lisbon Strategy and the Technological Plan.
Lisbon Strategy Portugal Anew – National Action Programme for Growth and Jobs (PNACE 2005–2008). (2007). In *Report on 2nd year of implementation*. Lisbon: Cabinet of the National Coordinator of the Lisbon Strategy and the Technological Plan.
Maiworm, F. (2006). Results of the survey on study programmes awarding double, multiple or joint degrees. In *Study commissioned by the German Academic Exchange Service (DAAD) and the German Rectors' conference*. Kassel.
Mosher, J. (2000). *Open method of coordination: Functional and Political Origins*. ECSA review *13*(3), 6–7. Retrieved from http://eurecenter.wisc.edu/OMC/open12.html.
Neave, G. (2005). *On snowballs, slopes and the process of Bologna: Some testy reflections on the advance of higher education in Europe*. Oslo: University of Oslo. ARENA – Centre for European Studies.
Schäfer, A. (2002). *Vier Perspektiven zur Entstehung und Entwicklung der "Europäischen Beschäftigungspolitik"* MPIfG. Discussion Paper 02/09. Retrieved from http://www.mpi-fg-koeln.mpg.de.
Tilford, S., & Whyte, P. (2009). *The Lisbon scorecard IX – How to emerge from the wreckage*. London: Centre for European Reform.
Universidade do Minho. (2008). *Relatório de Concretização do Processo de Bolonha na Universidade do Minho*. Braga: Universidade do Minho.
Veiga, A., & Amaral, A. (2006). The open method of co-ordination and the implementation of Bologna process. *Tertiary Education Management, 12*(4), 283–295.
Veiga, A., & Amaral, A. (2009). Policy implementation tools and European governance. In A. Amaral, G. Neave, C. Musselin, & P. Maassen (Eds.), *European integration and the governance of higher education and research*. Dordrecht: Springer.
Veiga, A., Rosa, M., & Amaral, A. (2005). Institutional internationalisation strategies in a context of state inefficiency. In J. Huisman & M. Van der Wende (Eds.), *On cooperation and competition II: Institutional responses to internationalisation, Europeanisation and globalisation*. Bonn: Lemmens Verlag.
Veiga, A., Amaral, A., & Mendes, A. (2008). Implementing Bologna in Southern European countries: Comparative analysis of some research findings. *Education for Chemical Engineers*. doi:10.1016/j.ece.2008.01.004.
Zeitlin, J. (2005). Social Europe and experimental governance: Towards a new constitutional compromise? *La Follette School Working Paper* no. 2005–001. Retrieved from http://www.lafollette.wisc.edu/publications/workingpapers.

Part III
Shaping the Institutional Fabric

Chapter 12
Patterns of Institutional Management: Democratisation, Autonomy and the Managerialist Canon

Licínio C. Lima

Introduction

Society's buildup of the University unfolded across the centuries – Portugal's first university was founded in 1290. Even so, over the past few decades, the institution of higher education in Portugal has undergone considerable change. Organisation and management are engaged, so a recent study claimed (Amaral et al. 2003) in the throes of a 'managerial revolution'.

At first sight, the Portuguese case is no exception. Yet, given the institutional inertia that accompanied the years of Dictatorship from 1926 to 1974, the pace of change that followed on Portugal's Democratic Revolution surpassed its counterparts in most Western countries and most markedly so in the fields of governance and management. The reforming impulse in Europe had already begun to beat in the aftermath of the Second World War (Neave 1992: 84–127). By the 1960s, this first wave of change in Europe was called into question, thus sparking off new reforms (Ruegg 2011: 3–30). Reforms in Portugal's higher education, by contrast, were launched much later and as a direct result of political change born aloft on the wings of Revolution.

In just 35 years between 1974 and 2009, the 'corporative university' of the Salazar-Caetano regime underwent radical overhaul, propelled by the tensions and contradictions that ebbed and flowed across the early days of the return to democracy (Chaps. 2 and 3). Radical, the reforms proposed most certainly were, largely, it has to be said, because of the nature of political change and because of the extreme tardiness in opening up higher education in Portugal to the process of democratisation. Such factors combined to usher in profound and wide-ranging overhaul within what, from

L.C. Lima (✉)
Departamento de Ciências Sociais da Educação, University of Minho,
Campus de Gualtar, 4710-057 Braga, Portugal
e-mail: llima@ie.uminho.pt

a historical perspective, was an extremely short space of time. Higher education moved from *autocracy* in governance and state-dependent institutions (Miranda 2008: 108) on to revolutionary change, first in the practice of direct democracy and self-management (1974–1976), and subsequently with the constitutional normalisation of the political regime with the introduction of representative democracy and democratic management in the governance of educational institutions during the years 1976–1988. Massification of Portugal's higher education system followed and with it the onset of Europeanisation, a dynamic that involved establishing institutional autonomy together with new forms of control and accountability. Such developments took up the years 1988–2007. With the enactment of the Juridical Regime of Higher Education Institutions in 2007, new patterns of governance and management emerged, together with the paradigm of public foundations under private law assuming particular prominence (Chaps. 7 and 9). Stress was laid on competitiveness, effective institutional leadership and quality assurance, the latter following the recommendations made in 2006 at the request of the Portuguese government by the Organisation for Economic Cooperation and Development (OECD) and by the European Network of Quality Assurance Agencies (ENQA).

This timeline encompasses different phases in the construction of the young Portuguese democracy in the shape of the *Third Republic*, which began in the last quarter of the twentieth century. By the same token, it also reaches out to include different concepts of educational organisation: the rise of educational objectives and educational technologies, organisational morphologies, power and structures of authority, patterns of governance and institutional management.

This chapter follows a sociological approach to educational organisations. The analyses it embarks upon are based on the hypothesis that in each of the chronological phases mentioned earlier, the institutions of higher education are better interpreted by referring to different metaphors and 'images of organisation', (Morgan 1980, 1986) to 'faces' (Ellström 1983) or to 'models of educational management' (Bush 1995). This approach, which is marked by theoretical pluralism, opens the way for using various models of analysis to combine different organisational images and metaphors. Most appropriate amongst them is the *rational-bureaucratic model* (Weber 1964) together with the organisational images of *mechanicist* and *tight coupling*. Account must also be taken of the increasing relevance of the concept of *hyper-bureaucracy* and of the *political model* (Baldridge 1971) in analysing educational organisations. Attention will likewise be paid to the metaphor of the *political arena* (Mintzberg 1985), to *post-Weberian models* (Tyler 1988) or *ambiguity models* (Bush 1995). Particular emphasis will be laid on the image of *organised anarchy* (Cohen and March 1974) as too the concept of a *loosely coupled system* (Weick 1976).

None of the periods under scrutiny may be examined in isolation nor, for that matter, can they be treated in a completely homogeneous manner, still less do they display a strictly defined timeframe. Likewise, each organisational image, used for the purposes of interpretation, should not be understood as a sole and exclusive tool of analysis. On the contrary, the complexity and the tensions typical of each historical period and of the development of the higher education institutions may well require the employment of different theories, complementary organisation images and different analytical metaphors so as to be able to engage more fruitfully in organisational hermeneutics (Lima 2006). In summary, this chapter attempts to build multifaceted or varying combinations of *lenses* the better to sustain a multifocal interpretation of complex organisational phenomena.

With this end in mind, the chapter examines the most salient changes and reforms introduced in universities and later in polytechnics ('binary system') in Portugal between 1974 and 2009 (Chap. 6). In particular, it attends to those which had impact upon, and consequence for, governance and authority structures as well as on the patterns of institutional management. Attention will be paid to the institutional responses to these reforms, for such responses entail the *re-contextualisation* of public policies by the various educational organisations involved, not to mention the possible resistance shown by the actors.

For the period 2007–2009, the most important national and international policy documents, which shaped the reforms in Portugal, are examined as are the Programme of the XVII Constitutional Government and the new Juridical Regime of Higher Education Institutions passed by the Parliament in 2007. In addition, the statutes of each of the 15 existing public universities as well as those of one-third of Portugal's public sector polytechnics were comprehensively scrutinised. The latter were expressly selected to reflect both regional diversity and size.

From Self-management to Democratic Management: The Political Arena and Rational Bureaucracy

The process of democratising university governance and management began immediately after the 25th April 1974, following the collapse of the authoritarian regime that had held sway in Portugal for almost half a century. The dictatorship had forged an autocratic system of governance for higher education institutions, based on a centralised and *tightly coupled* administration and on a system of appointments of Rectors and faculty heads by ministerial order (Decree-Law 26 611 of 1936). Democratisation was a typically revolutionary process, conducted by academics and students through the practices of self-management and direct democracy. Deliberative assemblies were set up in each institution. Rectors, faculty heads and some professors were ousted. A range of new bodies was voted in. Changes in both teaching and assessment were introduced. These events brought about a 'shift in power' from Ministry of Education to universities, from the political centre to the periphery, a shift initiated by the universities. Such a process of decentralising power was never formally conducted by the State. Rather, it was the outcome of a social dynamic which managed to spearhead the revolutionary impetus in education as opposed to simply following in its wake, albeit briefly (Stoer 1986: 63). This moment of self-management, combining the revolutionary practices of radical democracy with direct participation, transformed the universities into *political arenas*, ideological battlefields or places of conflict. In organisational terms, the university may, at that instant, be interpreted as a *political system* rather than as a bureaucratic or as a collegial-type organisation.

Bureaucratic centralisation, the structure of authority and formal hierarchy, features typical of a technical-rational and instrumental concept (*organum*) and typical too of the idea of a *community* of academics, who shared values and cooperated harmoniously (*collegium*) provided images of academic organisation that possessed little value in interpretative terms. In both cases, the images focus on *shared* institutional goals, not on the *diversity* of goals, just as they focused on the struggle between their supporters (Ball 1987: 11). Governance and management of higher education institutions thus bore more similarity to political conflict and permanent struggle (*political arena*) than they did to a bureaucratic mechanism or to a communitarian-type system of coordination and cooperation. In effect, the political model of organisational analysis 'assumes that complex organisations can be studied as miniature political systems, with interest group dynamics and conflicts similar to those in city, state, and other political situations' (Baldridge et al. 1978: 34).

The first Provisional Government, however, quickly set about legalising – though retrospectively – measures that grassroots democracy in the shape of academic staff and students had already taken. A month after 25th April 1974, the Council of Ministers approved a short bill (Decree-Law 221/74) recognising the democratically elected collegial bodies, termed 'Management Committees'. Management committees were provisional. They remained in place until the Government could approve the new system of institutional governance. Made up of representatives from academic staff, students and non-academic staff, their selection procedure abided by no electoral rules nor did they respect any others that governed the composition of public bodies set by the Government. The powers and mandate of the democratic committees did not follow any regulation. The only restriction placed on them required that they should not exceed the responsibilities that legislation had attached to the bodies they replaced, which, in some cases, dated from the 1930s. At so revolutionary a moment, however, the social actors did not let their collective decisions be limited by formal rules. They introduced measures best qualified as a 'normative unfaithfulness' (Lima 1992) and, rejoicing in their autonomy, exercised powers of decision that went far beyond the legal limits, but in keeping with their ideologies and their political interests.

Given the 'heightened revolutionary pace' which coalesced earlier in education than in other social spheres, the Government, in December 1974, set about cutting back the influence of a number of vanguard movements which represented the *logics of action* (Bacharach and Mundell 1993) and which, in some quarters, were heralded as bringing 'power to the people'. As it contemplated the unfolding of the politics of revolution, the State sought to reassert its function of control over universities and faculties. This it did by passing Decree-Law 806/74 – a precipitate step, to say the least. The purpose of this move was to ensure the 'seriousness of the [representative] democratic process' through clear electoral rules, as well as the effectiveness of the schools, now seen as places of work, the better to rein in the agitation of 'spontaneous movements'.

The law focused on faculty management, provided for a school Assembly comprised of elected representatives of academic staff, students and non-academic staff, which could delegate powers to an Assembly of Representatives. An Executive Board, headed by an elected academic, was set up to manage and execute both governmental policies as well as the decisions reached by the Assembly. In addition, a Scientific Council and a Pedagogic Council were created in each faculty, despite the fact that institutional autonomy, not to mention scientific and pedagogic autonomy, had not been legally granted. It was a situation paradoxical in the extreme. For it meant that the formal system of university governance continued to be based on legislation passed during the authoritarian regime. The appointment of Rectors by order of the Minister of Education remained in place. In practice, however, academic activism in the faculties removed the formal obstacles that stood in the way of democratisation. Even so, legislation passed in late 1974 proved to be more relevant in terms of creating new organisational morphologies than it was in bringing about an effective and democratic normalisation, grounded in the rules of representative democracy. If the truth were out, legislation proved itself unable to return the long-established mode of institutional control to the Provisional Government, nor was it able to return it to the central departments of the national administration of higher education.

Only with the approval of the 1976 Constitution and the election of the first Constitutional Government, headed by Mário Soares, did the slow and oft-resisted process of political normalisation begin and formal procedures of representative democracy start to be introduced. An attempt was made to terminate self-management practices, which the Government now associated with 'chaos' and with a 'building in ruins', by legally introducing so-called democratic management in clear terms and with a universal application. Thus, democratic management became associated with order and with 'non-negotiable discipline' in contrast to the 'supremacy of activist minorities'. Thus, the task of democratic management was to 'separate demagogy from democracy', a mandate clearly set down in the preamble to Decree-Law 781-A/76 of 28th October 1976.

From that moment on, the rules of representative democracy and the responsibilities of each body were laid down in law and in great detail. An organisational structure, more complex than before, extending to all the faculties and clearly bureaucratic in nature was laid out. The enactment was so punctilious and detailed that it even set the timetables for meetings of different governing and management bodies, occasionally going so far as to specify the months as well, of course, as their general remit. Although both faculty governing bodies and their heads continued to be elected, with parity ensured between representatives of academic staff and students (with the exception of the Scientific Council), the fact remained that Rectors continued to be appointed by the Minister of Education.

Contradictions

Democratic management, introduced in 1976, underwrote the collegial character of both the faculties' system of governance at faculty level, specified their management structures, and the democratic election of heads and other members. On these criteria, it represented a very real step forwards in democratisation. Even so, it was for all that not devoid of contradiction. Democratic management within the faculties was both a hybrid and insular. It made no profound change in the overall pattern of university governance. On the contrary, it ensured the return of centralised bureaucratic control over academic institutions. Decentralisation of education administration and institutional autonomy were goals and words remarkably absent from the policy discourse of the day. The central power of the Ministry and its departments was rebuilt with the result that henceforth, each university was better viewed as a rational-bureaucratic organisation. To be sure, management structures were democratically elected. But they had no effective democratic system of governance that was underpinned by institutional autonomy.

Very rapidly, the legacies of the revolution – direct democracy and self-management – were replaced by a democratically legitimate centralised and bureaucratic pattern of management set in place during the period of *constitutional normalisation*. Highly valued, though it is in terms of political symbolism, paradoxically democratic collegiality revealed itself to be compatible both with the bureaucratisation of higher education institutions and with the re-centralisation of decision making. Thus, the *political arena* gave way to a *mechanistic* concept of organisation with supposedly consensual aims and with reliable management technologies, for the world a technical-rational tool to carry out policies, defined centrally, outside and above each institution. In short, here was an *atopic* system of governance, cut off from, or outside, its rightful place. As a result, institutional management of universities was construed as the organisational execution by elected bodies in each institution, of policies centrally defined by the State. Thus, the practice of democratic self-government and institutional autonomy was ruled out. Once again, *bureaucracy* and *policy* came together as 'soul mates' (Silva 2006), but only this time in a setting of political democracy.

Institutional Autonomy and Modernisation: The Political System and Organised Anarchy

In the decade following the approval of the 1976 legislation, higher education institutions still remained without statutes and byelaws. Their rectors were still appointed by the Minister of Education. Their collegial structures and democratic management practices had been taken aboard by faculties and schools. Their internal power structure centred on the Rector. Externally, they continued to be enormously dependent on government, even in day-to-day management issues, above all those of a financial nature.

By the early 1980s, for reasons of management effectiveness, but also because of the onset of massification in terms of university access in Portugal, a slow and fragmented process involving the transfer of competences from government to the universities set in. It involved recruiting non-PhD academic staff, granting equivalency to academic degrees obtained abroad, appointing professors to examining boards and allowing certain expenses up to an amount predetermined by the Ministry (Santos 1999).

In 1982, for the first time, an elected Rector was appointed by the Ministry. The procedure involved was closely akin to that then present in Belgium and the Federal Republic of Germany. Following a ballot, three names were submitted to the Government. The individual obtaining the most votes was appointed. In the same year, the Parliament launched the first review of the Portuguese Constitution, which established the principle of university autonomy (Article 76). Four years later, the Parliament approved the Comprehensive Law on the Education System (Law 46/86). It recognised the principles of democracy, representation and participation in educational management and assigned scientific, pedagogic and administrative autonomy to all higher education institutions. Financial autonomy, however, was limited to universities alone (Article 45). Only in 1988, 6 years after the constitutional revision, did Parliament unanimously approve the University Autonomy Act (Law 108/88). This law was the high point in a campaign which saw the Council of Rectors of Portuguese Universities (CRUP), created in 1979 to promote deconcentration and decentralisation in the national administration of universities, playing a part that was both active and influential.

The 1988 Law introduced a new and decentralised system of democratic and participatory university governance. It made specific reference to 'democratic management methods' (Article 2). Institutions were granted the power of self-government and endowed with statutory, scientific, pedagogic, administrative, financial, patrimonial and disciplinary autonomy. A new era of decentralisation modified the relationship between the Government and universities. Within the universities themselves, a more decentralised internal structure was also applied to both institutional governance bodies and governance and management bodies at the faculty and school level, although the latter, in structural terms, were still regulated by legislation dating from 1976.

Universities drew up their internal statutes and regulations through assemblies of representatives and, in accordance with the compulsory provisions in the University Autonomy Act, put in place a number of key bodies for internal self-governance. Amongst them was the University Assembly, with responsibility for approving internal statutes and byelaws and for electing the Rector. The Senate was elevated to become the most important collegial body for those decisions involving internal issues touching on academic matters and management. The Rector wielded powers of governance, institutional representation and management. Faculties or schools retained their governance and management bodies (Assembly of Representatives, Executive Board, Scientific Council, Pedagogic Council) but were given the option of exercising administrative and financial autonomy. Some of the older and/or larger universities took this option up, particularly financial autonomy. The freedom to set up other bodies in some universities generated a large number of coordination and advisory boards. Some of which included a few external members.

Despite widespread support for the 1988 Act, a certain ambiguity remained, principally over the universities' formal legal status. Certainly, universities were now more distant from the traditional and direct administration of the State.

Nonetheless, the situation, half way between indirect administration and autonomous administration, was anomalous. The absence of an overall policy for higher education, the lack of a law on public funding for institutions and the absence of an evaluation system did not go unnoticed. It was, as Santos (Santos 1999: 17–18) remarked later, tantamount to 'autonomy without foundations', which served merely to underline 'the reluctance of central administration to let go of power that it had held for a long time'.

Organisational Images

Generally speaking, higher education institutions – first universities, later polytechnics, although the latter possessed a more limited margin of autonomy – assumed a pattern of democratic governance together with dimensions of institutional autonomy unprecedented in the Portugal of the twentieth century. The legitimacy of this pattern of governance rested on democratic forms of organisation and management, on participation by academics, students, non-academic staff plus some external representatives. In effect, each institution may from an organisational point of view, be seen in terms of a *political system*, or *city* (*Polis*), grouping diverse but legitimate projects and interests, susceptible to conflict but conflict to be settled by democratic methods. The collegial pattern of governance and management was a central feature. So too was parity in the representation of academic staff and students on various governance and pedagogic management bodies. A more extensive internal decentralisation set in as patterns of democratic and collegial management extended to faculties, schools and other units and on to subunits, departments, sections or research centres. Trends towards a greater relative autonomy of each unit and subunit and towards greater diversity in terms of structures and management were clear. In some instances, this may have introduced a degree of internal fragmentation in the structures of governance and management. Moves to adopt more decentralised and participatory forms of coordination, which because more vague and indistinct, lend themselves less to traditional forms of bureaucratic and centralised coordination. The organisational image was one of a *loosely coupled system*, along the lines Weick (1976) developed. An alternative would be to see the institutional model in terms of a 'loose confederation' of faculties, schools and departments, an arrangement intellectually more productive than its polar opposite of a 'tight realm' or *bureaucratic organisation*, on which Baldridge's (1971) model rested.

From the mid-1970s onwards, higher education institutions could be construed as *organised anarchies* (Cohen and March 1974). Such a descriptor projects the image of an organisation characterised by vague and ill-defined aims, with unclear technologies and a fluid participation of its members. Rather than being a pejorative judgement on universities, the more typical metaphors contained in *ambiguity models* may be regarded as a complementary theoretical approach to the bureaucratic, mechanistic or formal analytical images. They present a powerful critique of rationalist theoretical representations. Within such a varied range of interpretation, rational choice theory also figures, though it has been radically challenged both by the concept of *sensible foolishness* and by the *garbage can model of organisational choice*, both of which minimise the role of rational appraisal, planning and the quest for the *optimum* in education organisation (Cohen et al. 1972).

With the passing of the University Autonomy Act and especially up to the mid-1990s, patterns of institutional management in the public universities of Portugal were heavily influenced by political and collegial dimensions, on the one hand, and by aspects of ambiguous and organised anarchy, on the other, in keeping with the theoretical categories developed by Cohen and March (Cohen and March 1974: 37–40). Rectors, for example, tended to assume institutional leadership roles that oscillated between the *political candidate* and the *catalyst*. In the former, they were aware of the need to fulfil their election promises. They also required negotiating skills to deal with the Government and mediation skills when dealing with the university on whose support they depended (*democratic political model*). In the latter, rectors sought to understand the *loosely coupled system* in its all complexity and diversity and come up with plausible solutions, which were not necessarily unified or centralised but rather *adaptable to localised situations* (*anarchic model*). Some of the main analytical dimensions in the *ambiguity models* of education organisation were recognised early on by Victor Baldridge and his colleagues (Baldridge 1971; Baldridge et al. 1978) as being compatible with the political model of organisational analysis. That was also the case with neo-institutional approaches (Meyer and Rowan 1977).

From the mid-1990s onwards, the aims of modernisation, rationalisation, effectiveness and efficiency, which had been set out years previously, took on a heightened centrality together with increasing attention in higher education, directed towards *Europeanisation*. The *Bologna Process* and the proposed construction of a *European Higher Education Area* loomed large in this new 'dimension' (Chap. 11). New forms of state regulation emerged; external evaluation as an imperative counterpoint to institutional autonomy was introduced; new rules for funding and accountability were voted. Managerialist-inspired political discourse gained visibility. 'Democratic management' began 'softly and silently to vanish away'. It became associated with irrational and ineffective management.

Collegial participative management came under increasing criticism, especially over the issue of equal representation for academics and students on some committees. The most influential actors, both within and outside higher education, became increasingly critical of the way the 1988 Act had been met by a corporatist attitude on the part of academia, a response which had distorted it (Amaral et al. 2003). Various authors (amongst others, Lima 1997; Amaral and Magalhães 2001; Seixas 2003; Magalhães 2004; Santiago et al. 2005) examined the tensions arising from confrontation between collegial governance and governance through management. *Excess of democracy* was criticised, as were academic leaders' management patterns that were subordinated to academic culture. Professional management and Boards of Trustees were looked upon as the main vehicles for hope and salvation, together with the power of the technostructure. Institutional autonomy was progressively hobbled by new forms of regulation, new public funding practices, not least. As the pendulum swung towards management, micro-regulatory interference by the Ministry of Science, Technology and Higher Education followed the same path.

Institutional autonomy was hampered further by the injection of inter-institutional competitiveness, reinforced by external evaluation, by the need to recruit more students and to compete internationally for research funds. That the Council of Rectors of Portuguese Universities and, to a lesser extent, the Coordinating Council for Polytechnic Institutes, went through a crisis in terms of representation and negotiating power with the Government also had a negative impact on institutional autonomy. The autonomy of higher education institutions (laid down in Law 54/90, for the Polytechnics) underwent a process of *loose articulation* with democratic governance. Rather, it was associated and linked up with a political agenda constructed around the catchwords of modernisation, rationalisation and international competitiveness. The new agenda focused on the effectiveness and efficiency of the structures and the pattern of institutions' management, swinging sometimes towards an instrumental, at others, towards an operational, concept of autonomy. Despite policies of privatisation, which flourished with governmental support between the mid-1980s and the mid-1990s, higher education policy in Portugal entered into a new phase. Unlike parallel measures in both the Netherlands and the United Kingdom, it was accompanied in Portugal by none of the intense commitment to *quasi-market* policies. Rather, the new phase in Portugal was marked by the intervention of major international agencies and also, though in diluted form, by the influence of some features of a 'managerial state' (Clarke and Newman 1997).

Against such a backdrop, riddled with contradiction and paradox, the managerialist canon debouched onto higher education in Portugal. Agreed, it was still a far cry from the strength wielded in other countries since the 1980s. But, in all likelihood, it had already gone beyond a merely rhetorical status that research associated with it a few years ago (Amaral et al. 2003: 150).

Competitiveness and the Effective Leader: Tight Coupling and Hyper-bureaucracy?

Originating in the 1970s, new theoretical approaches began to focus on the specificity of educational organisations. Indeed, educational organisations were now regarded as so unlike other organisations that applying a general theory of management, on the lines fleshed out by F. Taylor and H. Fayol in the early twentieth century, had little purchase. On the contrary, general opinion held that attention at any attempt to apply modern management techniques, current in the world of business, to universities demanded the utmost care and circumspection (Baldridge et al. 1978: 9).

Even so, educational reforms in Great Britain and the United States during the 1980s introduced the managerialist canon, then predominant amongst the prescriptive theories of educational management. It rested, however, on precisely the opposite premise. Economic and business organisations were now held up as the acme of *good management* – effective, efficient and innovative – whilst the management of public organisations, in particular schools and higher education institutions, was associated with bureaucracy, bumbling, inefficient, irrational, lacking in leadership and insufficient in customer focus.

The Litany of the Managerialist Canon

Difficult though it is to define in exact terms and without taking into account the social and political contexts in which it is embedded, it is my belief that the managerialist canon may be represented as a constellation of theoretical dimensions with varying degrees of empirical expression, as is also the case with the concept of bureaucracy, which is seen as an *ideal type* in Max Weber's work (Weber 1964). Without claiming to produce a comprehensive list, the following dimensions may, nonetheless, be highlighted: corporate culture; competitive performance and the creation of internal markets; individual leadership; effectiveness and efficiency, defined in strictly economic terms; rational and individual choice (within the larger context of *public choice theory*); clarity in the organisational mission and objective together with a strict definition of the aims to be achieved.

The managerialist canon was critical in the extreme of the welfare state model of social policies, above all of the State's role in provision and intervention. It was particularly incensed by bureaucracy and professionalism, which it deemed to be two institutional patterns of power and resistance to the reforms managerialism advocates. It is management – which, in a general framework, is sometimes still inaccurately called *New Public Management* – rather than policy, which is presented as a transformational force to cut back the traditional power of politicians and bureaucrats (Newman and Clarke 1994: 23) (Chap. 9). Organisational reform takes the shape of standardisation in addition to mechanistic and neo-Taylorist processes, which in some respects are similar to industrial optimisation and efficiency (Brunsson and Olsen 1993).

Amongst the dimensions of managerialism that surface most often in educational reform, the following stand out: centralisation in both policy formulation and decision-making processes; decentralisation or devolution of certain competences, mostly technical or instrumental in nature; less relevance placed on the processes of democratic control assigned to the bodies of collegial decision making; reinforcement of the power of managers and of the technostructure within the organisations or their units; the loss of influence by teachers, academics and knowledge elites; governance based on evidence and the evaluation of results; the introduction of market-type regulations; the reinforcement of vertical management structures (Smyth 1993; Fergusson 1994; Whitty et al. 1998; Maassen 2002).

When discussing higher education in Portugal in the mid-1990s (Lima 1997), I referred to the emergence of a managerialist pattern, which already had its adepts and which already incorporated some of the dimensions of the canon mentioned above. The most emblematic and radical legislative measures aimed at introducing an educational market have yet to be taken, which in itself is another of the specificities in the Portuguese case. This, however, may be explained by the fact that both the market and civil society have historically been weak. Nevertheless, the following dimensions were singled out: the modernisation of the higher education system in order to adapt to the imperatives of economic competitiveness; rationalisation measures with the purpose of obtaining internal efficiency gains; pressure to increase productivity; added importance of the institutions' private budgets and fund-raising activities; criticism of collegial governance and democratic management whilst adopting an operational concept of institutional autonomy and a concept of participation as a management technique; employment of business management methods; advocacy of total quality management and the transferral of management control from academics to new purpose-built technostructures (Lima 1997: 48–49). With these managerialist manifestations in mind, it was suggested, at least metaphorically, that universities were moving from their historical 'Ivory Tower' to a new status of being a 'modern service station'.

New Images of the University

In a setting where various managerialist dimensions emerge, higher education institutions are, in terms of organisational analysis, rather more rarely represented as organised anarchies, loosely coupled systems or even as political systems. Their theoretical portrayal is based rather on rational and technical-instrumental dimensions. As for the images of bureaucratic-rational organisation, emphasis lies on *tight articulation* between governance and management, aims and results, leadership and the success of the organisation, as well as on the synergy between institutional mission, strategic planning and organisational structures. Despite heavy ideological criticism, bureaucracy made a triumphant return together with its most important Weberian features, now frequently exaggerated and cried up: individual leadership; professional knowledge and power of the technostructure; technical rationality, accuracy, discipline and hierarchy; effectiveness and efficiency and an obsession with making optimal choices; competitive performance, neo-positivist institutional evaluation; division of labour between academics and managers; standardisation and centralisation.

Many of these phenomena, currently prevalent in higher education institutions, lurch towards an image of radicalised bureaucracy or *hyper-bureaucracy*. They are social phenomena, reproduced at a global level through the influence of powerful international agencies and bolstered by information and communication technologies. This is not something new. It is, in fact, a situation which was considered theoretically a few decades ago when attention was drawn to a number of issues: enlarged control by external agencies, the centralisation of academic management, the power of managers and technocrats, the change from governance shared by academics to a manager-led business-style management (Baldridge et al. 1978: 220–231). Indeed, the metaphor of university governance as a *competitive market*, developed by Cohen and March (Cohen and March 1974: 30–39), was also considered at that time, with the leadership role of *entrepreneur* being recommended for Rectors or Presidents rapidly to embrace.

The managerialist canon can be better interpreted, however, in the light of *hyper-bureaucracy* and in the image of a *tightly coupled* organisation. Issues such as the concentration of power, hierarchy, centralisation, the role of managers and technostructures and the transition from elected leadership to appointed leadership and from collegial bodies to individual leaders (De Boer 2003) all take on another meaning. Comparative studies and the examination of cases of *institutional isomorphism* between institutions of higher education and their units, identified by the neo-institutionalist approaches, also acquire added relevance.

It is still extremely important to seek out and examine possible national or regional specificities, on the one hand, and the distinct responses to the managerialist canon and its *re-contextualisations*, on the other. As De Boer (De Boer 2003: 92) observed, 'Why should, for instance, English, German and French universities respond to managerialism in the same way?' In the Portuguese case, this question is particularly pertinent when the most recent higher education reform launched by the XVII Constitutional Government (2005–2009) is subject to scrutiny. It is, as yet, premature to draw conclusions about the changes introduced to the management profile by the passing of Law 62/2007 (Juridical Regime of Higher Education Institutions) (Chaps. 7 and 9). Most of the statutes approved by the institutions have only very recently come into effect. It does, however, seem relevant to acknowledge that, in the current transition period, there is a certain degree of hybridism and some tension deriving from the clash between the collegial-participative model of governance (political system and organised anarchy) and the managerialist pattern (tight coupling and hyper-bureaucracy).

Competitiveness and the internationalisation of higher education figured as priorities in the Socialist Party's 2005 Election Manifesto (Partido Socialista 2005) together with institutional evaluation and accountability, flexibility of organisation and management practices and the strengthening of the power of executive bodies. Accordingly, the Government, with the support of the Socialist Party, commissioned studies, evaluations and recommendations from the OECD (2006) and the ENQA (2006) before passing the legislation.

Role of the OECD

The OECD review (OECD 2006) of higher education in Portugal did have a bearing on the reform put forward by the Government and approved by the Parliament, though some important recommendations of the OECD were not adopted or were only partially followed since they were not mandatory upon institutions; amongst them were widespread adoption of public foundation status under private law, the appointment of Rectors or Presidents, the appointment of faculty and department heads, an increase in external members on institutions' highest governing body, loss of public servant status for both academic and non-academic staff and non-applicability of public accountancy rules to the institutions.

The OECD (2006) was, however, far more influential as regards other proposals, included in the 2007 Act: the loss of influence by collegial bodies, which mostly took on an advisory role; rejection of the principle of parity in the representation of academics and students (except on the Pedagogic Council); concentration of executive power in the Rector or President; external recruitment of the Chair of the General Council; strengthening individual leadership in units and subunits; a reduction in the number of governance and deliberative bodies; a decrease in the number of academics on governance bodies. In general, the reform adopted various dimensions both of the managerialist canon that have been examined here as well as the 'entrepreneurial' construct of higher education institutions. The 2007 Law also adopted a new governance and management paradigm, recommended by the OECD: the public foundation under private law with its much commented Board of Trustees. However, the Government chose to see the 'foundation university' as an alternative for those institutions that met certain requirements in terms of self-financing. This solution gained the support of various Portuguese politicians over the past few years, mainly because the collegial model was seen as a stumbling block both to effective management by the individual leader (Crespo 2003: 71–80) and to 'strong leadership, almost always based on the characteristics of the leader' (Grilo 2005: X–XI). This faith in the 'effective executive leader' draws on a long-standing and consensual school of thought in management theory, which ranges from the Human Relations Theory developed by Chester Barnard (Barnard 1938) in the 1930s to Management by Objectives, elaborated in the work of Peter Drucker (Drucker 1967). In various countries, it reduced the importance of academic governance, collegiality and democratic management, as well as the importance of subunits or departments in which academic staff are organised (El-Khawas 2003; Maassen 2002; Reed 2002).

Foundation Universities, Leveraging Change

To the legislator's mind, the new system of institutional governance anticipates transforming universities and polytechnic institutes into foundations, and as such is a sign of *distinction*, awarded by the Government, upon signing an individual agreement between the Government and institution of higher education. Foundations are governed by private law in respect of financial, patrimonial and personnel management. Funding is established through contracts passed with the Government and which last for a minimum of 3 years. The 'foundation model' – currently taken up by only three institutions – sets up a Board of Trustees comprised of five public figures who have no employment ties with the institution. Their names are put forward by the institution for appointment by the Government. The Board of Trustees approves the statutes and ratifies the General Council's deliberations. It also ratifies the appointment of Rectors and Presidents, who, in the case of the foundations, need not be elected.

The General Council is the highest body, although in terms of democratic participation and representation much curtailed compared to the previous University Senate.

It is composed of between 15 and 35 members, including professors and researchers, who mandatory make up more than half of its membership, students and, possibly (but not necessarily), non-academic staff. At least 30% of members are required to be external, one of whom being the Chairman (Article 81). As the highest governance body, the General Council elects the Rector, approves amendments to the statutes, scrutinises the Rector's or President's management as well as that of the Executive Board and makes recommendations to ensure the institution functions well. It does not, however, interfere in day-to-day governance and management, which are assigned to the Rector (university subsystem) or the President (polytechnic subsystem). These are the institutions' true leaders. They command a vast array of competences (Article 92), some of which, under the previous legislation, were exercised by the University Senate. The Academic Senate, whose existence is optional, is now an advisory body, whilst the previous deliberative Assembly has been excised from the organisational chart.

Thus, individual leadership in terms of governance has acquired new weight and substance. This holds good even for the remit exercised by the General Council, which approves the institutions' major strategic plans and documents. These documents are always presented by the Rector or President, whose competence is to 'conduct the institution's policy' (Article 85, para. 2) as well as to appoint the members of the Executive Board during his – or her – presidency.

Participation in the 'democratic management of the schools' is ensured – though minimally. However, this activity received no mention in the Act of 2007, which comes down heavily in favour of concepts such as management autonomy, self-governance, consortium, foundation and quality, amongst others. In addition, the Act does not underwrite the election of heads of units or subunits, nor does it require collegial bodies representing faculties, departments and research centres. The law merely recognises that they *may* exist in which case they have the power to elect the head. However, faculty or department heads are no longer chair collegial bodies. The latter have been replaced by a single-member body with reinforced responsibilities, but no longer elected by all academic and non-academic staff of the particular unit or subunit.

New Patterns of Governance

Contrary to what is stated in the 2007 Act, this formal structure is not greatly flexible. Institutions are merely given the opportunity to opt for small morphological variations in their governance bodies. They have more leeway in respect of Advisory Councils. The degree of institutional freedom and the choices of management structure are broader once the institution opts for foundation status. However, collegiality is not ensured, nor is the democratic management or the election leadership at middle management level. Whilst these issues are not legally ruled out, the legislator did not regard them as a priority, and as such, they are not mandatory.

An examination of the statutes put in place by the 15 public universities and by a third of the public polytechnic institutes currently existing in Portugal gives some indication of the impact the new pattern of governance has had as well as its consequences for the structure of management. Despite the distinct institutional responses to the 2007 Act, especially the option for foundation status (at present, only three institutions have exercised it), the structures chosen were quite similar. Composition of the General Council varies between a minimum of 15 members in one university and a maximum of 35 in two. Two-thirds of the universities opted for General Councils of 20–29 members, with an average of 25. Only two universities opted not to include representatives of non-academic staff on the General Council. In 12 out of a total of 13 universities, one single member represents non-academic staff. Up till now, foundation status correlates with neither a low number of members on General Council (between 19 and 33) nor with an absence of representation of non-academic staff, contrary to what might theoretically be expected. However, in the three foundation universities, more units (faculties or departments) are bereft of their own management bodies. Their heads were appointed or selected by means other than election, in contrast to what happens in most of the remaining institutions. On the other hand, the majority of faculties and schools, despite the presence of self-governing bodies, do not enjoy financial autonomy. Significantly, these units adopted collegial bodies, which in most cases are responsible for electing heads of unit. Only in three cases did this not happen. Similarly, the Scientific and Pedagogic Councils are filled by means of electoral processes and, in most cases, are chaired by elected members.

On the whole, the structural differences between universities tend to be more pronounced than between the polytechnics. In the latter case, the structural model is more stable. The units do not have financial autonomy. However, when the analysis focuses on the advisory boards created, the diversity of choice stands out. Although the Academic Senate is an optional feature, 11 of the 15 universities opted to create one. Composition varies, however. In general, most members of the Academic Senate are not directly elected. Rather, they are representatives of the middle management bodies. In five universities, an Academic Senate coexists with other advisory bodies. More than ten such bodies were identified, sporting a variety of names and goals. A similar situation occurs in polytechnic institutes.

A study of these organisations in action, and in particular, a study of their governance and management practices, is now possible. It is also both vital and necessary if the impact the reform has produced is to be taken further and, not least, to see whether these preliminary findings are born out.

Envoi

One of the supporters of the recent higher education reforms, after drawing heavily upon the rationale of New Public Management – which was also noted in 2008 by the National Education Council (CNE) (2008) and also more critically by Amaral (2008), – aptly summed up the current situation: '(…) I would say we have fewer bodies, fewer elections, less collegiality, more external participation, more accountability to external stakeholders. If anything is to undergo profound change with this reform, it is clearly the system of governance' (Moreira 2008: 131).

From a formal point of view, this situation had been unveiled by analysing the institutions' statutes. Organisational and management structures show a clear thrust towards increased internal centralisation, as well as a concentration of power in the person of Rectors and Presidents. Though doubtless unprecedented in the history of Portuguese higher education, this reform follows a broad, general trend ranging from France (Le Gall and Soulié 2007) to Japan (Galan 2007). In this sense, higher education in Portugal seems definitely to be part of a wider framework of reforms (Schultheis et al. 2008), spearheaded by the managerialist canon and moving towards a hyper-bureaucratic form of institutional management: centralisation, vertical power structures, standardisation, technical rationality, technical competence and meritocracy, technostructure power, measurement, internal, national and international competitiveness. A new and more powerful species of institutional manager is emerging. And though still recruited from amongst national and international academics, the political climate encourages them to put a distance between themselves and academic culture. The managerial calculus breaks away from the traditional values of collegiality and academic power in favour of a managerialist *ethos,* which, at least during its first phase, combines minimum academic representation (*democratic legitimation*) with the increasingly enhanced power of the technostructure (*technical legitimation*), itself made up of highly specialised and professional managers. In any event, it seeks to ensure that academic culture and influence have no bearing on institutional management.

A new role is now assigned to Rectors and Presidents, often presented nowadays as Chief Executive Officers (CEO). This role is one of intermediation between the State and the market, between the demands of stakeholders and the demands of academic and non-academic staff. Rectors and Presidents are a kind of new 'linking pin' (Likert 1961) between academia and management, between the General Council and management units and subunits.

With the Portuguese reform, the managerialist canon did not reach the heights it has scaled elsewhere in Europe. The more mercantile features connected with neoliberal reform of the State were absent. However, one cannot but notice neoliberalism's increasing influence. Nor can one ignore the various signs that point to its presence over the past decade. Managerialist ideology currently bolsters a complex process of *hybridisation*, already observed in other countries (Reed 2002). This process derives from the concurrent presence of democratic features (losing influence but still a form of resistance within institutions) and from others associated with *expertise*, itself on the rise in universities and polytechnics. In Portugal, the forces at play are threefold. Alongside the influence of collegiality and democratic management, the legacy of the 1974 Revolution (*the University of the Constitution*) flows the recent ascendancy of the managerialist canon and of corporate culture (*the Managerial University*). The third of these shaping forces is to be found in the weight and power wielded by a centralised and hierarchical state bureaucracy built up *de longue durée (the Governmentalised University)*.

Only future research will be able to ascertain how the current period of transition will coalesce and, in doing so, determine how tensions between collegiality and democratic management, on the one hand and professional management and hyper-bureaucracy, on the other, will play out. What the new syntheses will eventually turn out to be is a question better left to a future research agenda. What is clear in Portugal's reform is that never before have the values of democratic collegiality and academia been so questioned nor so ferociously put to the challenge as they have at present by managerial rationality, and by the agendas of modernisation and *Europeanisation*. The Salazar-Caetano regime heartily distrusted these values and fought tooth and nail against academic freedom and democratic management. It did so, however, on the basis of a non-democratic political ideology.

The current strengthening of institutional autonomy, much discussed as it is, may paradoxically lead to reinforcing the power of managers and the technostructures that support them without ensuring more freedom, either for academics or for students. On the contrary, institutional autonomy reinforced in this manner may in effect ensure that managers have control over academic work, which in varying degrees, becomes alienated or subordinated. It would, however, be a mistake to underestimate academic power and its ability to mount resistance in depth, still less to discount its capacity to show normative unfaithfulness, even outside the framework of major social struggles. Recently, there have been significant incidents in other systems.

It remains to be seen whether the option of foundation status will become widespread over the next few years, intensifying thereby inter-institutional competitiveness and reinforcing the managerialist nexus. Will the 'foundation university' remain an exception – its current condition – or, as a final possibility, will it, in its turn, face a crisis of legitimacy and effectiveness in the event that the State proves unable to honour its financial commitments?

References

Amaral, A. (2008). A reforma do ensino superior português. In A. Amaral (Ed.), *Políticas de ensino superior. Quatro temas em debate* (pp. 17–37). Lisboa: Conselho Nacional de Educação.

Amaral, A., & Magalhães, A. M. (2001). On markets, autonomy and regulation: The Janus-head revisited. *Higher Education Policy, 14*, 7–20.

Amaral, A., Magalhães, A. M., & Santiago, R. (2003). The rise of academic managerialism in Portugal. In A. Amaral, V. L. Meek, & I. M. Larsen (Eds.), *The higher education managerial revolution?* (pp. 131–153). Dordrecht: Kluwer Academic Publishers.

Bacharach, S. B., & Mundell, B. (1993). Organisational politics in schools: Micro, macro, and logics of action. *Educational Administration Quarterly, 29*, 423–452.

Baldridge, J. V. (1971). *Power and conflict in the university. Research in the sociology of complex organisations*. New York: Wiley.

Baldridge, J. V., Curtis, D. V., Ecker, G., & Riley, G. L. (1978). *Policy making and effective leadership. A national study of academic management*. San Francisco: Jossey-Bass.

Ball, S. (1987). *The Micropolitics of the school: Towards a theory of school organisation.* London: Methuen.
Barnard, C. I. (1938). *The functions of the executive.* Cambridge: Harvard University Press.
Brunsson, N., & Olsen, J. P. (1993). *The reforming organisation.* London: Routledge.
Bush, T. (1995). *Theories of educational management* (2nd ed.). London: Paul Chapman.
Clarke, J., & Newman, J. (1997). *The managerial state. Power, politics and ideology in the remaking of social welfare.* London: Sage.
CNE. Conselho Nacional de Educação. (2008). Parecer sobre as alterações introduzidas no ensino superior (Parecer n° 7/2008). *Diário da República, 2ª série, N. 227,* 21 de Novembro de 2008.
Cohen, M. D., & March, J. G. (1974). *Leadership and ambiguity. The American college president.* New York: McGraw-Hill.
Cohen, M. D., March, J. G., & Olsen, J. P. (1972). A garbage can model of organisational choice. *Administrative Science Quarterly, 17*(1), 1–25.
Crespo, V. (2003). *Ganhar Bolonha, ganhar o futuro. O ensino superior no espaço europeu.* Lisboa: Gradiva.
De Boer, H. (2003). Who's afraid of red, yellow and blue? The colourful world of management reforms? In A. Amaral, V. L. Meek, & I. M. Larsen (Eds.), *The higher education managerial revolution?* (pp. 89–108). Dordrecht: Kluwer Academic Publishers.
Drucker, P. F. (1967). *The effective executive.* London: William Heinemann.
El-Khawas, E. (2003). Governance in US universities. Aligning internal dynamics with today's needs. In A. Amaral, G. A. Jones, & B. Karseth (Eds.), *Governing higher education: National perspectives on institutional governance* (pp. 261–278). Dordrecht: Kluwer Academic Publishers.
Ellström, P.-E. (1983). Four faces of educational organisations. *Higher Education, 12,* 231–241.
ENQA. (2006). *Quality assurance of higher education in Portugal. An assessment of the existing system and recommendations for a future system.* Occasional papers, 10. Helsinki: European Association for Quality Assurance in Higher Education.
Fergusson, R. (1994). Managerialism in education. In J. Clarke, A. Cochrane, & E. McLaughlin (Eds.), *Managing social policy* (pp. 93–114). London: Sage.
Galan, C. (2007). La liberalisation de l´enseignement supérieur au Japon. In C. Charle & C. Soulié (Eds.), *Les ravages de la "modernisation" universitaire en Europe* (pp. 231–249). Paris: Éditions Syllepse.
Grilo, E. M. (2005). Prefácio. In J. Pedrosa & J. F. Queiró (Eds.), *Governar a universidade portuguesa. Missão, organização, funcionamento e autonomia* (pp. VII–XIV). Lisboa: Fundação Calouste Gulbenkian.
Le Gall, B., & Soulié, C. (2007). Massification, professionnalisation, réforme du gouvernement des universitiés et actualisation du conflit des facultés en France. In C. Charle & C. Soulié (Eds.), *Les ravages de la "modernisation" universitaire en Europe* (pp. 163–208). Paris: Éditions Syllepse.
Likert, R. (1961). *New patterns of management.* New York: McGraw-Hill.
Lima, L. C. (1992). *A escola como organização e a participação na organização escolar. Um estudo da escola secundária portuguesa (1974–1988).* Braga: Instituto de Educação da Universidade do Minho.
Lima, L. C. (1997). O paradigma da educação contábil: políticas educativas e perspectivas gerencialistas no ensino superior em Portugal. *Revista Brasileira de Educação, 4,* 43–59.
Lima, L. C. (2006). Concepções de escola: para uma hermenêutica organizacional. In L. C. Lima (Ed.), *Compreender a escola. Perspectivas de análise organizacional* (pp. ed17–69). Porto: ASA.
Maassen, P. (2002). Organisational strategies and governance structures in Dutch universities. In A. Amaral, G. A. Jones, & B. Karseth (Eds.), *Governing higher education: National perspectives on institutional governance* (pp. 23–41). Dordrecht: Kluwer Academic Publishers.
Magalhães, A. M. (2004). *A identidade do ensino superior. Política, conhecimento e educação numa época de transição.* Lisboa: FCG/FCT.

Meyer, J., & Rowan, B. (1977). Institutionalised organisations: Formal structure as myth and ceremony. *American Journal of Sociology, 83*(2), 340–363.
Mintzberg, H. (1985). The organisation as political arena. *Journal of Management Studies, 22*(2), 133–154.
Miranda, J. (2008). Estatuto legal das instituições de ensino superior. In A. Amaral (Ed.), *Políticas de ensino superior. Quatro temas em debate* (pp. 107–121). Lisboa: Conselho Nacional de Educação.
Moreira, V. (2008). Estatuto legal das instituições de ensino superior. In A. Amaral (Ed.), *Políticas de ensino superior. Quatro temas em debate* (pp. 123–139). Lisboa: Conselho Nacional de Educação.
Morgan, G. (1980). Paradigms, metaphors and puzzle solving in organisation theory. *Administrative Science Quarterly, 25*(4), 605–622.
Morgan, G. (1986). *Images of organisation*. London: Sage.
Neave, G. (1992). War and educational reconstruction in Belgium, France and the Netherlands, 1940–1947. In Roy Lowe (Ed.), *Education and the second world war*. London: Falmer Press.
Newman, J., & Clarke, J. (1994). Going about our business? The managerialisation of public services. In J. Clarke, A. Cochrane, & E. McLaughlin (Eds.), *Managing social policy* (pp. 13–31). London: Sage.
OECD. (2006). *Reviews of national politics for education. Tertiary education in Portugal*. http://.mctes.pt/docs/ficheiros/OECD_124_paginas_pdf.
Partido Socialista (PS). (2005). *Compromisso de governo para Portugal*. http://inet.sitepac.pt/PSProgramaEleitoral2005.pdf
Reed, M. I. (2002). New managerialism, professional power and organisational governance in UK universities: A review and assessment. In A. Amaral, G. A. Jones, & B. Karseth (Eds.), *Governing higher education: National perspectives on institutional governance* (pp. 163–211). Dordrecht: Kluwer Academic Publishers.
Ruegg, W. (2011). Themes. In W. Ruegg (Ed.), *A history of the university in Europe, vol.4 Universities since 1945* (pp. 3–30). Cambridge: Cambridge University Press.
Santiago, R., Magalhães, A. M., & Carvalho, T. (2005). *O surgimento do managerialismo no sistema de ensino superior português*. Lisboa: Fundação das Universidades Portuguesas/CIPES.
Santos, S. M. (1999). Contributos para o estudo do desenvolvimento da autonomia universitária em Portugal desde o 25 de Abril. *Revista Portuguesa de Educação, 12*(1), 7–29.
Schultheis, F., Roca i Escoda, M., & Cousin, P. F. (Eds.). (2008). *Le cauchemar de Humboldt. Les reformes de l'enseignement supérieur européen*. Paris: Raisons d'Agir.
Seixas, A. M. (2003). *Políticas educativas e ensino superior em Portugal*. Coimbra: Quarteto.
Silva, E. A. (2006). As perspectivas de análise burocrática e política. In L. C. Lima (Ed.), *Compreender a escola. Perspectivas de análise organisacional* (pp. 73–132). Porto: ASA.
Smyth, J. (Ed.). (1993). *A socially critical view of the self-managing school*. London: The Falmer Press.
Stoer, S. R. (1986). *Educação e mudança social em Portugal. 1970–1980, uma década de transição*. Porto: Afrontamento.
Tyler, W. (1988). *School organisation: A sociological perspective*. Kent: Croom Helm.
Weber, M. (1964). *The theory of social and economic organisation*. New York: The Free Press.
Weick, K. E. (1976). Educational organisations as loosely coupled systems. *Administrative Science Quarterly, 21*(1), 1–19.
Whitty, G., Power, S., & Halpin, D. (1998). *Devolution & choice in education*. Buckingham: Open University Press.

Chapter 13
The Changing Public–Private Mix in Higher Education: Analysing Portugal's Apparent Exceptionalism

Pedro N. Teixeira

Introduction

Until recently, higher education systems remained, in general, subject to strong public hegemony and regulation (Neave and Vught 1991). Thus, the existence of private institutions remained minimal in most. In recent decades, however, the relevance of private higher education has grown significantly (Altbach 1999). A large part of the explanation for this development has to do with persistent pressures for expansion, which led to the emergence of mass higher education. Higher education has been asked to cater for a growing and increasingly diverse population and to do so in a more economic and efficient way (Barr 2004). Higher education institutions have also been asked to strengthen their responsiveness to the demands of the economic and social environment.

At the same time, due to a variety of complex factors, there were important changes in the traditional role of Government, notably as sole provider of funding and regulation for higher education institutions. Market-like mechanisms have been increasingly employed to raise internal and external efficiency of higher education systems and to improve the responsiveness of universities and polytechnics to economic and societal demands (Teixeira et al. 2004). A major response to these challenges turned around the adoption of market elements in higher education systems, in particular through increased privatisation. The ways this privatisation trend has pervaded higher education systems are various and often latent, though particularly visible in aspects such as the development of private providers concurrently with public provision, the diversification of funding mechanisms and the use of private management in public organisations (Williams 1991).

P.N. Teixeira (✉)
CIPES, University of Porto, Rua Primeiro de Dezembro 399, 4450-227 Matosinhos, Portugal
e-mail: Pedro@cipes.up.pt

This chapter analyses one of the main dimensions in that trend towards privatisation, namely the development of a strong private sector in the Portuguese setting. Portugal is often presented as the only significant exception to the Western European pattern of public hegemony due to the development of a very large private sub-sector over the last two decades (Amaral and Teixeira 2000). This chapter analyses how the private sector came to play a major role in Portuguese higher education. It starts with an overview of the main trends in the system, in particular how in recent decades Portugal moved rapidly from an elite to a mass system, and the process that brought about the development of a significant private system. The major factors that stimulated the rapid development of the private sector, which had its heyday between the mid-1980s and the mid-1990s, and the reasons underlying private sector's present difficulties (Teixeira and Amaral 2007) are then examined.

In order to understand these developments better, the Portuguese experience will be discussed against the broader international background of increasing marketisation and privatisation in higher education and the major characteristics associated with recent waves of privatisation (Levy 2006). This essay will conclude by discussing how far Portuguese higher education has followed a peculiar path in this respect and/or shares with other systems a similar pattern of development.

The Decline of Government Hegemony in Higher Education

Higher education has been facing significant and persistent pressures for expansion in recent decades, which have led to the emergence of mass higher education, even in countries that until recently enrolled very small portions of their younger age groups. This trend has raised significant economic and academic challenges both for higher education institutions and for Governments. Higher education was asked to cater for a growing and increasingly diverse population and to do so at less cost and with greater efficiency. Higher education institutions were also required to strengthen their responsiveness to the external demands of the economy and society.

In recent years, an important aspect in the response to these challenges has been the promotion of market elements in higher education systems, in particular through increased privatisation.[1] Private higher education is at times both an old and a new reality. On the one hand, many of the earliest universities were a product of non-governmental initiatives that took place in Europe during the latter half of the Middle Ages. Even when founded by royal or papal decree, they were normally created as autonomous institutions from a material and organisational point of view. On the other hand, these same universities were not private in the way the term is understood nowadays. Their public orientation made them accountable to religious and secular authorities in a way that would not correspond to what today is held to be the norm in private higher education.[2]

The more we move into the history of higher education, the more pronounced the role of public authorities becomes (Hammerstein 1996; Gerbod 2004). This was increasingly visible throughout the nineteenth and twentieth centuries when the modern State explicitly expanded its functions to include higher education under its wings, in what Neave (Neave 2000) calls the 'nationalisation' of higher education. This process reached its apogee in the post-war decades, which saw the creation in one form of another of about half the universities in existence in Europe by mid-1980s. By the mid-twentieth century, private institutions were absent from most countries worldwide, and even when they existed, their relative size was small in comparison to the public sector. In fact, private higher education institutions today are more accountable to public powers. They tend to face the same regulation and regulatory bodies as public ones – and sometimes on terms stricter still.

The new type of relationship between universities and the State, which emerged in the nineteenth century and largely persisted throughout most of the twentieth century, forged a new and strong state of dependence of universities on secular authorities (Wittrock 1993). This dependence was visible at the financial, administrative, educational and political levels. The growing role of Governments in funding universities was accompanied by a much greater administrative oversight of the former. Universities became increasingly accountable to State authorities and had to obtain governmental authorisation for a wide range of organisational procedures, which by the mid-twentieth century became the so-called model of rational planning and control (Van Vught 1989). This model reached its height in the post-war decades in the shape of the so-called legal homogeneity principle (Neave and Van Vught 1991), that is, Governments defined a standard curriculum and syllabus for each institution which provided higher training in a specific field. These developments were particularly pronounced in Continental Europe.

In addition to national equality, strong governmental regulation of higher education sought to ensure that universities provided the training that officials deemed more appropriate, especially when bearing in mind the future role of university graduates within public administration (Neave 2000). This growing influence of Governments in higher education was significantly shaped by the development of modern administrative and political structures (Middleton 1997). The expansion of government, economic and social policies, especially after World War II, created significant needs for qualified personnel that would be provided by higher education.[3] Thus, the Government became the major employment outlet for many academic programmes and became increasingly involved in 'fine-tuning' the type of training provided by higher education institutions to the increasingly expanding manpower needs of the public sector, not least.

Growth in the role of Governments in higher education was itself part and parcel of that aforementioned post-war expansion of the State. Expanding government expenditure on public education clearly went beyond simply raising the number of students. It reflected a readiness to support education, turning it eventually into a political and budgetary priority (Gosden 1983). In many respects, World War II was a turning point. It showed the importance of a pool of skilled labour and the potential achievements of scientific research for military, economic and social life. Higher education therefore became a major concern for many Governments (Wittrock 1993). This would be enhanced by the Cold War environment and by particular events such as the so-called Sputnik shock which gave increasing political visibility to higher education and science. These expectations, multiple and complex, fuelled a steady and rapid expansion of public higher education in the second half of the twentieth century. It led to the emergence of mass higher education in North America (particularly with the so-called GI Bill of Rights of 1945), Japan and subsequently in Western Europe.

Both in Europe and beyond, the most ancient universities came increasingly under the influence of Governments, though many were originally established as autonomous institutions. This was certainly the case of many religiously affiliated institutions, particularly prominent in Southern Europe and Latin America. These institutions came to be supervised by secular authorities, either as part of the growing share of public funding or by dint of their effective transfer to the public domain. By the early twentieth century, not only was the number of universities still small, especially outside Europe and North America, the number of private institutions was even less significant.

The Rise of Private Higher Education

In the early twentieth century, whilst the existence of private higher education institutions was rather uncommon, they became increasingly part of the higher education landscape during the last decades of the century.[4] For a significant number of countries, the first private institutions to emerge were still nurtured by the traditional role that religion had played in higher education. Although secularisation and the growth of the modern State since the eighteenth century gave rise to a far less favourable environment for religiously affiliated institutions, in many countries the first private institutions were established by Churches, especially by the Catholic Faith, in the late nineteenth and early twentieth centuries. The role of religion was particularly important in the Americas. In other parts of the world, private higher education was clearly a twentieth century phenomenon, following a somewhat later development of higher education as a whole.

For a long time, Europe remained a bastion of public dominance in higher education with a large majority of students in higher education still being enrolled in public higher education institutions, which tends to be the case in most European countries even today. Even those denominational establishments that survived until modern times in Europe came to be assimilated into the public sector during the twentieth century, often through financial mechanisms (Geiger 1986). Although nominally private, these establishments were funded and supervised as any other public universities in the same system and were considered mainly as government-dependent private institutions. Thus, the existence of private institutions remained minimal in most of the Western European higher education systems, despite the increasing willingness of Governments to adopt market-like mechanisms (Teixeira et al. 2004).

One of the major factors in promoting the role of private higher education has been its overall, continuous and marked expansion, even in countries and regions where, until recently, access to higher education was limited to a very small minority. Such expansion of higher education was driven onwards by both societal and individual forces. At the policy level, Governments saw in the advanced qualification of human resources a key factor to advance national economic competitiveness. Recent economic discourse, based on models of endogenous growth, served to strengthen this view that accumulation of human capital can improve the economic prospects of a given community (Romer 1986). In times of growing globalisation, improving the qualification of human resources has become one of the few factors through which Governments may effectively contribute to raising national economic performance (Blöndal et al. 2002).

Expansion of higher education has also been significantly driven onwards by the behaviour of individuals. A higher education degree remains an attractive personal investment, as persistently high private rates of return, observable in many countries, have shown. For several decades, this 'dividend' has nurtured the view amongst the public that graduates of higher education may count on enviable prospects in such matters as long-term income and employability, especially when compared with those holding much lower levels of formal qualification (Mincer 1993).

Such persistent high demand led to the so-called *massification* of higher education, which involved not only growing rates of enrolment but also more differentiated and complex higher education systems. To respond adequately to an increasingly diverse demand, higher education systems developed new and diverse programmes and institutions (Teichler 1988). On the other hand, massification also meant it was no longer possible, or at least advisable, for most Governments to maintain a pattern of detailed regulation over higher education institutions (Neave and van Vught 1991). Hence, Governments set about exploring new and more effective forms of steering within the new condition mass higher education gave rise to (Chap. 6).

Another critical factor, critical to understanding the relative decline in the dominance of public higher education, is that its recent expansion coincided with a period of growing constraint on public expenditure, which affected higher education as well. The difficulties in funding the continuous expansion of higher education posed a problem for both richer and poorer countries alike. In the case of the former, the so-called crisis of the Welfare State challenged the sustainability of higher education's traditional financial dependence on public funding (see Barr 2004). In the case of countries with lower levels of income, the financial reductions associated with a lower level of taxation have been seen as a significant obstacle to the ambition of expanding higher education through public funding.

Changes to the funding base of higher education were also influenced by the change in political climate that affected Western countries from the early 1980s and then progressively moved out to other parts of the world. In the aftermath of the economic turmoil of the 1970s, both the nature and degree of government intervention were hotly debated, with the ideological pendulum swinging towards a marked liberalisation, market regulation and reduced regulation by the Government. (Middleton 1997). Initially, this programme was more visible in macroeconomic policy but subsequently began to permeate social policy in general and educational policy in particular (Barr 2004). Discourse on the public services became filled with managerial jargon and the phraseology of consumerdom.

Arguments in favour of developing private higher education were not related to issues of internal efficiency alone. They also tied in with debates about the degree of external efficiency of the higher education system (Levy 2002). The private sector was supposed to demonstrate an increased capacity for exploring new market opportunities and for occupying market niches, by dint of its greater administrative flexibility and financial acumen. Private and private-like institutions – that is, higher education establishments treated as if they were privately owned – were to promote a supply of higher education better balanced from both a geographical and disciplinary perspective. A similar rationale applied to labour market demands since the anticipated greater responsiveness by private-type higher education institutions was held to be a powerful force in driving institutions to provide qualifications more suited to labour market needs. Changes intended to strengthen market forces and to assign a greater role to private initiative in higher education would, it was confidently expected, generate innovative behaviour (Geiger 1986).

Whether due to a change in the ideological and political context or to pressing financial constraints – or both – the privatisation of higher education has become a rapidly growing reality in many countries worldwide since the 1980s. In most higher education systems in Western Europe, the trend towards privatisation advanced mainly by increasing the private-like aspects within the dominant public system, through stimulating competition for students and for funds, rather than by promoting or even permitting the emergence of a significant sub-sector of private higher education (see, for example Vincent-Lancrin 2007). In other regions, impressive increases in enrolments have become common worldwide, partly as a result of an expanding private higher education sector (Altbach 1999). For some systems, for instance, in Eastern Europe, this entailed a completely new profile in provision. In other cases, this new wave of privatisation enveloped earlier arrangements, consisting in the main of religiously affiliated institutions. It elevated the almost insignificant presence of private higher education into a sizeable part of the system.

During the last two decades, private higher education has become a substantial force in higher education worldwide. Interestingly, the role of religion, so important in earlier years, played a less prominent part in the recent drive towards privatisation. This is not to say there was no growth of religiously affiliated higher education institutions. Rather the denominations lost the dominant role they had in most of the countries where the private sector had deeper roots (Levy 1986, 2006). The process of secularisation in society meant that, despite some religious revival, most members no longer saw higher education as the sole province of the Churches. Moreover, the highly aggressive commercial approach by many of the new private establishments clearly outstripped the growth of the church-affiliated institutions, which often preferred to model themselves on their more established and respected public counterparts.

The Development of Private Higher Education in Portugal

As in many European countries, Portuguese higher education in modern times has been overwhelmingly dominated by public provision. Until the early 1970s of the twentieth century, private provision was very small and characterised by a few small and specialised institutions, often affiliated with the Catholic Church. The initial development of private higher education in Portugal was favoured by the public institutions' involvement in deep political and social turmoil that followed the 1974 Revolution. Many professors were expelled from public institutions because they were held to be too close to the former authoritarian regime. Others left, frustrated by student unrest that paralysed many institutions (Chaps. 7 and 9). At the time, private institutions emerged as a more tranquil alternative where quality and traditional academic values could be preserved.

Private institutions developed slowly. In 1971, the Portuguese Catholic University was founded as part of the agreement between Portugal and the Vatican. Although this institution can be largely seen as a private institution, it enjoyed some special conditions. The subsequent development of the private sector, however, eroded much of that special treatment. Today, very little remains of that early privileged status. In early 1979, the Minister of Education authorised the creation of the first fully private university by granting the 'Free University Cooperative for Education' (*Universidade Livre*) temporary permission to start up. In the early 1980s, the institution was allowed to offer study programmes in the two main cities of Lisbon and Porto.[5]

Until the early 1980s, the size of the private sector was very small. The pace of implementation accelerated after the mid-1980s. Enrolments in private institutions in 1982–1983 amounted to some 11% of total enrolments. In 1986, the Ministry recognised two new private universities – Lusíada and International – together with several polytechnic-type institutions, some of which had been upgraded from already existing medium-level institutions, which until then were not allowed to award higher education degrees. The new institutions concentrated their study programmes in areas of low investment/low running costs – languages and administration, management, journalism, training of secretaries and interpreters, and informatics.

In the mid-1980s, the idea of significantly increasing the role of the private sector received strong political support in Portugal. Certain protagonists presented private higher education as a powerful solution to some of the most important problems of Portuguese higher education, such as meeting regional demand by decreasing regional disparities of access and even absorbing social demand (Chaps. 4 and 16) (Franco 1994). The main motivations for developing the private sector were both pragmatic and ideological. On the one hand, private higher education was heralded as an instrument to solve the dramatic problem of spiralling demand for higher education, demand that could not be met by the public sector, especially in the years of severe economic difficulties following the Revolution. On the other hand, some political actors clearly regarded private higher education as an important ideological instrument for strengthening Portuguese democracy and as a tool for social and economic development (Carneiro et al. 1994). Thus, from the mid-1980s to the mid-1990s, private higher education became the fastest-growing sub-sector in a system that was itself expanding extremely fast (Table 13.1).

Table 13.1 Growth of enrolments

	1971		1981		1991		1996		2001		2007	
	No.	%	No.	%	No.	%	No.	%	No.	%	No.	%
Public universities	43,191	87.3	64,659	76.8	103,999	55.7	147,340	44.1	176,303	44.4	175,998	46.7
Public polytechnics	2,981	6.0	12,195	14.5	31,351	16.8	65,377	19.6	108,486	27.4	108,335	28.7
Private institutions	3,289	6.7	7,319	8.7	51,430	27.5	121,399	36.3	111,812	28.2	92,584	24.6
Total	49,461	100.0	84,173	100.0	186,780	100.0	334,868	100.0	396,601	100.0	376,917	100.0
Gross enrolment rate (%)	7.9%		11.0%		24.4%		44.3%		50.2%	NA	(20–24 years)	

Source: Barreto (1996), Simão et al. (2002), GPEARI

During the past few decades, Portuguese higher education underwent massive expansion. The private sector played a significant role in that process. Most private institutions reached their highest enrolment level by mid-1990s, but then suffered a rapid drop, in some cases more than 50% of their highest level of enrolment. Despite the decline, the private sector still caters for an important part of the higher education population. Only recently has the private sector been overtaken by the public polytechnic sector. Thus, and in contrast to most European countries, private higher education in recent decades has become an important feature in the higher education landscape of Portugal. One of the most striking aspects of Portuguese private higher education is that its rise and its apparent decline both took place in a relatively short period. In the sections that follow, the reasons for such a rapid and eventful evolution during the last three decades will be analysed.

When Social Aspiration Meets Political Will

As other chapters in this volume point out (Chaps. 4 and 12), Portugal traditionally had very low levels of literacy and a poorly qualified labour force. At the turn of the twentieth century, when Northern Europe had largely achieved universal basic literacy, around 90% of the Portuguese population was illiterate (Reis 1993). This was a poor result even when one considers the Nation's southern European counterparts. The twentieth century did not bring a rapid change of this situation. During the post-war decades, when most European countries had embarked on developing mass secondary – and later higher education – systems, Portugal still struggled to achieve a reasonable level of basic literacy. From the 1960s onwards, the situation began to acquire a new momentum. The country recovered part of its qualification backlog. By 1960, though the level of illiteracy remained very high and, although it declined sharply thereafter, a large percentage of the population still today has only basic formal education or no literacy at all.

Given the paucity of qualifications, it is not surprising that the Portuguese system of higher education should traditionally have been elitist, with very limited access. The early 1970s brought important changes to Portuguese higher education, with major reforms, inter alia, to improve access by multiplying the number of public institutions and by diversifying the system by setting up a binary model that mirrored European trends (Teichler 1988).

Pressures for rapid expansion accelerated after the democratic Revolution of 1974. In the wake of the Revolution, the promise of a more egalitarian society engendered an explosive demand for higher education. It also placed a severe strain on the working conditions in many institutions, which led eventually to the Ministry of Education introducing a numerus clausus system to control growth, which today still remains in place. The numerus clausus, by keeping an increasing number of candidates out of higher education but without any acceptable alternative, threw up very strong political and social pressures for enlarging access to higher education.

Table 13.2 Private rates of return to education in Portugal

Study	Period	Estimation technique	Rate of return
Kiker and Santos (1991)	1985	OLS	9.4–10.4%
Vieira (1999)	1986/1992	OLS & IV	7.5–8.2% (OLS)
Martins and Pereira (2004)	1995	OLS & quantile R	OLS – 12.6% QR – 6.7–15.6%
Machado and Mata (2001)	1982/1994	OLS & quantile R	OLS – 1.3–9.2%/0.4–11.3% QR – 0.5–10.1%/0.3–13.8%
Hartog et al. (2001)	1982/1986/1992	OLS & quantile R	OLS – 5.3%/5.5%/6.4% QR – 3.1–6.6%/3.4–7.0%/3.6–8.0%

Source: Teixeira (2008)

Social pressure for expanding higher education since the 1980s may, in large measure, be explained by the view widely held that a higher education degree carried with it a potentially high rate of return on time and money invested, as we noted earlier. Such views have been confirmed by subsequent research that revealed very high rates of return to education in Portugal. In most cases, the *average* return on an additional year of schooling has remained around 10%, which suggests that the *private* return is significant. These results appear to be quite robust and have been confirmed by a variety of samples, periods and different techniques of calculation (Table 13.2).

The average rate of return for education has not only remained significant. It has even increased. Moreover, some of the findings also showed that private rates of return increased when one moves into the higher levels of the educational system (Hartog et al. 2001). This was especially noticeable since the mid-1980s, exactly the moment of substantial growth in the higher education system. In addition, it should be noted that despite the massive expansion of recent decades, rates of return to education have remained the highest in the Europe of the 15 (Pereira and Martins 2004).[6]

Good prospects for university graduates were also evident in terms of employment opportunity. In the 1980s and 1990s, levels of unemployment by educational category converged, with a significant reduction for the lowest qualified groups and a slight increase in the number of unemployed with higher education qualifications, from below 2% to around 4%, though still the lowest amongst all groups. A careful analysis of the patterns of job creation shows that the Portuguese labour market is characterised by high job rotation, with high job creation/destruction occurring for all groups of workers irrespective of their level of schooling (Cardoso and Ferreira 2001). However, both the raw and net rates of job creation were persistently higher for employees with higher education degrees than for those with lower schooling between the mid-1980s and the late 1990s, the very period of greatest expansion in higher education. Hence, the slight increase in graduate unemployment was not due to a fall-off in the willingness of companies to recruit higher education graduates, but rather to the labour market's incapacity to absorb the massive inflow of graduates (Chap. 6).

Such good prospects to be had from high rates of return to education and employability are significant. They explain the persistent and robust demand for higher education throughout the 1980s and 1990s. At the time, most policy-makers considered that the Government had neither the time nor the means to fulfil the promised goal of increasing the numerus clausus to a level capable of meeting the growing demand for higher education. Such pessimism created a golden opportunity for private institutions to take off. Governments took the decision to give the private sector a decisive role in expanding higher education provision.

The political climate of the 1980s also explains the readiness of governments to give increasing leverage to the private sector. Already, the post-revolutionary Constitution of 1976 recognised the freedom to teach and to learn under articles 43 and 74. The Constitution also guaranteed the right to establish private and cooperative institutions under article 43, though under State supervision in accordance with article 74 (Chap. 7). The post-revolutionary environment with its strong leftist leanings looked on the development of the private sector, with a considerable degree of suspicion, which was not confined exclusively to Education. However, by the mid-1980s, the political atmosphere had changed beyond recognition. In 1986, Portugal joined the European Union – then the European Communities – after a series of complex political, constitutional and economic reforms, which in turn speeded up the country's economic and social modernisation.

The Minister of Education at that time (1987–1991), Roberto Carneiro, epitomised the changing political stance vis-à-vis private education. A few years later, he clearly explained his defence of private higher education in an essay entitled 'Manifesto Against State Hegemony'. Strongly influenced by Catholic Social Thought, Carneiro backed the principle of subsidiarity. He argued strongly for a less interventionist role for the State in education in general and in higher education in particular. Carneiro was not alone. Several other prominent political figures saw private initiative as a solution for several problems in Portuguese higher education, amongst which were a limited measure of regionalisation and socioeconomic diversification. Thus, private higher education was clearly identified by leading politicians as an important instrument for strengthening Portuguese democracy as well as being a lever for the country's social and economic development.

The decade following, successive governments created very favourable conditions for the speedy development of private higher education. The first element in the new policy was the outcome of several policy measures, designed to increase significantly the demand for higher education. In 1988, the Ministry of Education changed the regulations for access to higher education by easing entry requirements. National entrance examinations, for instance, were to be used only for ranking students in the national competition for places, without requiring any minimum levels. As Fig. 13.1 shows, the result almost doubled the number of candidates and did so very quickly. Since it was all too obvious that public institutions could not meet this jump in demand, many candidates had perforce to find a place in private institutions. Figure 13.1 also shows another anomalous increase of demand in 1994 and 1995.

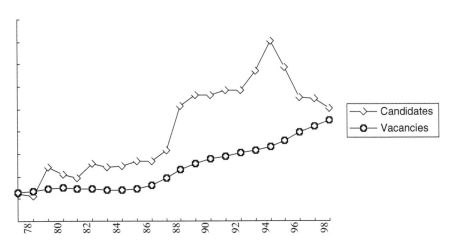

Fig. 13.1 Number of candidates and places in public institutions

This reflected administrative action taken by another Minister with the idea to make the conclusion of secondary education easier for students, whose numbers had significantly risen over the years. Indirectly, both changes created an important market for higher education that allowed private institutions to flourish and to multiply.

The second element in the Government's influence upon the pattern of development in the private sector had to do with regulation – or rather lack of it. From the mid-1980s onwards, Governments did very little to control the quality either of the institutions or of the programmes offered. Moreover, they made it easier for the private sector to take advantage of academics in public sector higher education by having them 'moonlight' – that is, taking on paid teaching in the private sector in addition to their responsibilities as teachers in public sector establishments. 'Moonlighting' was made easier by relaxing the formal restrictions on academic staff against 'double dipping' in both public and private institutions. This policy had a long-term negative effect on the reputation of the emerging private sector (see below), let alone an obvious and clearly negative impact upon teaching and research in the public sector, though in the short-term it ensured a development of the private sector far faster – and much cheaper! Indeed, the development of the private sector was so fast that in the academic year 1991–1992, the number of vacancies at private institutions surpassed those at public institutions despite the fact that the network of public institutions was older and very certainly better endowed in terms of both equipment and staff than the private sector.

Strong social demand and political willingness combined contributed to the fact that from the mid-1980s to the mid-1990s private higher education became the most rapidly growing sub-sector. Already by the mid-1990s, private institutions enrolled more than one third of all students in higher education. Yet, after an explosive start, the private sector faced a very different situation. Stabilisation and then a slight decline in the number of applications to higher education, plus the steady expansion of public higher education, shrank the pool of potential candidates to private HEIs and put their resilience to severe test.

Changing Conditions, Weaknesses Revealed

Pointers to change from the previously flourishing patterns of demand became evident during the latter half of the 1990s. Yet, experience of several decades of sustained growth in demand for higher education convinced many, not the least universities and polytechnics themselves, that it was mostly a temporary down-turn within the pattern of long-term expansion. The 10 years following, however, were to show that the change was more enduring and the difficulties more acute.

An easy scapegoat for changing patterns of demand that affected private higher education so adversely was demography. As was the case in many European countries, Portugal in recent decades underwent significant shifts in its demographic profile, mainly due to an ageing population. Although this phenomenon was delayed by the late phasing of economic and social modernisation, in recent decades the country faced a sharp decline of fertility rates, which had a major impact on population dynamics (Chaps. 4 and 12). Rising income, changes in family life, the growing feminisation of the labour force (for academia see Chap. 14) and the rising qualification level amongst women all contributed to raising the opportunity cost of children and to change families' preferences in the matter of offspring from quantity to quality (Becker and Lewis 1973).

The impact these demographic changes had on enrolment was not only delayed by the late modernisation of the Portuguese economy. It was also compounded in the Portuguese case by the peculiarities of mass education. Expansion of compulsory education and the tardy democratisation of secondary schooling for many years masked the decline in fertility patterns. In addition, similar delay in expanding higher education excluded many from attending higher education and gave rise to a backlog of unmet demand. Many individuals in such a situation decided to take a second chance when the system started to expand by the mid-1980s, especially in less demanding and recently established private institutions.

Although the winds of change blew strongly by the late 1990s (Amaral and Teixeira 2000), most observers either ignored or underestimated the impact demographic change would have on the demand for higher education. At that juncture, forecasts indicated that the decline, which had meanwhile filtered upwards to higher education, would continue and deepen in the course of the following decade and a half. Not a few comforted themselves with the hope that improvements in the effectiveness of secondary education would reduce its high drop-out rates and would thus, at very least, offset demographic decline. This belief was particularly prevalent in the private sector, seen as the most vulnerable to changes in demand, changes due to higher cost and lower prestige with which that sector was associated in student opinion. Reality has been far harsher than those wishful thoughts warranted. The fall in fertility rates largely out-distanced any small improvements the secondary system could accomplish (Chap. 6).

The late 1990s also brought with them another important change to the situation confronting the Portuguese private sector. Whereas the previous decade had been characterised by a very favourable political environment which supported its development and tolerated even the least reputable of institutions, by the late 1990s policy-makers became far less benign towards private institutions. Changes in the political constellation were perhaps more telling because of a traditional and very specific relationship with policy-makers. Although Governments urged the rapid development of the private sector forwards, they retained administrative control over private institutions, which already enjoyed less pedagogical autonomy than public universities. Added to this, the Government by the mid-1990s decided to put a greater emphasis on quality issues, now that quantitative expansion was less of a priority (Chap. 10).

Once again, the lever of access was used to steer the system, but in a way more difficult for private institutions to accommodate. New legislation re-introduced national examinations at the end of secondary education. It authorised institutions to set minimum marks in the examinations, giving access to higher education. Whilst the best institutions did so, such a practice was sedulously avoided by the less reputable, which busied themselves with filling as many vacancies as possible by dropping entrance standards. The upshot was that by the mid-1990s private institutions faced not only a fall-off in student demand but also a far more rigorous stance on the part of policy-makers.

Even so, by no means all the current tribulations most private institutions faced may be explained with reference to these contextual factors alone. An important part of the explanation lay with both the profile and the evident weaknesses of the private sector itself. Growth in Portuguese private higher education corresponded to what is sometimes termed 'demand-absorption' (Levy 2002, 2006). In this particular setting, private higher education is oriented to meet objectives involved in securing higher levels of enrolment, usually the outcome of strong social demand and lax regulation by political decision-makers. The forces of flaccid regulation often stimulate opportunistic behaviour of many newly established institutions by lowering entry requirements or simply by not upholding regulation already laid down (Teixeira and Amaral 2007). This form of evolution may also be the outcome of a strategy that gives priority to quantity rather than quality as the propellant of private higher education establishments.

One feature of the demand-absorption pattern saw Portugal's private higher education developing a very strong programmatic, geographical and disciplinary concentration and focus. Nor, for that matter, is this unique to Portugal. There are, on the contrary, many international examples (Teixeira and Amaral 2002). One of the dimensions involved in this pattern of concentration involved the type of programmes on offer. Private higher education in Portugal remained focused almost entirely on the first cycle, even after that market showed clear signs of stagnation (Table 13.3).

At the initial levels of training, this pattern of concentration is difficult to alter. Academic staffs in most private institutions are less well qualified than their public equivalents. This has become even more evident since qualified staff tends to be more expensive and normally teach fewer hours. In these days of funding constraint, the issue of hiring permanent and qualified staff becomes more problematic by far. From this it follows that most private institutions had a very limited capacity, in respect of their human resources, to develop second and third cycle programmes,

Table 13.3 Distribution of graduates by cycle of studies

Sub-sector	Public			Private		
Year	1996/1997	2001/2002	2005/2006	1996/1997	2001/2002	2005/2006
1st cycle	21,576	25,504	32,672	13,847	15,717	16,210
2nd cycle	1,655	2,207	4,248	229	331	571
3rd cycle	231	585	1,094	1	9	30
Total	23,462	28,296	38,014	14,077	16,057	16,811

Source: Ministry of Science and Higher Education – GPEARI

Table 13.4 Distribution of enrolments by disciplinary area (%)

Area	1971	1981	1991	2001 Public	Private	Total
Natural/hard sciences	12.6	6.8	8.1	7.0	3.2	5.9
Engineering	10.1	19.4	18.8	26.2	11.7	22.0
Health sciences	16.3	12.8	6.2	8.3	8.6	8.4
Agriculture	1.8	2.7	2.1	5.0	0.3	3.6
Social sciences	26.2	32.9	35.2	26.0	45.3	31.6
Humanities	24.7	18.6	10.5	7.4	6.3	7.1
Artsa[a]	3.4	3.3	3.4	2.5	4.2	3.0
Religious studies	2.2	0.7	0.4	0.0	0.7	0.2
Education	na	na	11.1	12.8	13.9	13.1
Other	1.6	2.8	4.3	4.8	5.9	5.3

Source: Ministry of Education various years, Simão et al. (2002)
[a]Arts includes Architecture

which are far more rigorous in terms of their academic and legal demands than first cycle studies.

Concentration in the private sector is equally significant when the distribution of its programmes is analysed according to large disciplinary groupings. As often happens with recent trends emerging from privatisation, almost two-thirds of students enrolled in private HEIs are concentrated around the social sciences, law, economics and business. In contrast, distribution across more technical and costlier subject areas tends to be lower than in the public sector (Wells et al. 2007).[7] The costs of running programmes in those areas make for very high tuition fees. In many cases, this option is hardly viable in terms of attracting large numbers of students. Furthermore, the technical, medical and engineering fields tend to be more closely regulated by both Government and professional associations. Obtaining public and professional recognition for their degrees is a lengthy process for higher education's private sector (Table 13.4).

Concentration is reinforced further by the geographic location of private higher education. Analysis of recent waves of private institutions shows that Portuguese is not exceptional. The private sector tends to be strongly concentrated in the region around the capital. And whilst private HE is often highly concentrated in the wealthiest and most highly populated regions (Geiger 1986; Altbach 1999), in Portugal, both public and private sectors are present in all major regions of the country, though

Table 13.5 Distribution of enrolments by region (%)

Region	1967	1991	2002 Public	2002 Private	2002 Total	Population 15–24 years
North	18.5	26.8	27.0	37.6	30.0	38
Centre	24.6	18.0	25.7	7.7	20.6	22
Lisbon	56.9	49.6	36.0	52.3	40.6	24
South		4.2	9.2	1.9	7.1	11
Islands		1.4	2.1	0.4	1.7	6

Source: INE various years, GPEARI – MCTES

in the case of the second, its presence in some regions is minimal. The private sector concentrates more than half its places around the capital, whilst the same region accounts for only one-thirds of places in the public sector. Such a high degree of concentration by the private sector is reinforced by a high-density pattern in the second main region of activity. By contrast, the public sector, from a regional point of view, is far more diversified, not only as regards the capital but also amongst regions with fewer students (Table 13.5).

The high degree of density of Portuguese private higher education across all three dimensions is significant not only because it runs counter to many of the expectations voiced prior to its development but also because such concentration works against its resilience when the context changed. Concentrated as regards type of programmes, disciplines and geographical location, private universities and polytechnics could not diversify their risks. Many of them could scarcely manage to offset the fall-off in the demand for their traditional programmes.

In addition, the same phenomenon made for a high degree of similarity between private institutions. Hence, when expansion ebbed away, institutions were driven to poaching each other's market – in effect, a zero-sum game. Their behaviour betrayed strong isomorphic tendencies. When one institution started a new programme that drew students in, others leapt on the same bandwagon as a short-term solution and launched new programmes irrespective of whether they had sufficient staffing resources, adequate facilities or libraries.

The limited capacity of private universities and polytechnics to face competition and to diversify their supply stems from the fact that during their expansion phase, they positioned themselves mainly as teaching institutions. We have already touched upon one of these aspects, namely the limitations of their academic staff. As in other countries, many private institutions rely considerably on part-time staff. This quandary tends to be particularly pronounced during the early phases in the development of the private sector. Newly founded institutions often find it difficult to recruit new staff and tend therefore to rely on staff already engaged by other institutions, often public. By so doing, they merely feed tensions between private and public HE (Altbach 1999). On the other hand, some parts of the private sector may recruit part of their academic staff from professional practitioners with skills corresponding to their academic programmes. As a result, the private sector tends to have a higher percentage of part-time academic staff – clearly higher than that observed in the

Table 13.6 Qualification of the academic staff (ETI) – private universities (2005)

	PhD	Master's	No PG	Total	% PhD
Total	551.82	707.04	822.00	2080.86	26.52%
Smallest private university	5.27	6.95	7.23	19.45	27.10%
Largest private university	147.90	181.90	241.10	570.90	25.91%

Source: GPEARI

public sector (Levy 2006) – even in countries where privatisation has attained a more advanced state of maturity. The main rationale for this trait is the advantage of cost saving. Not only does part-time staff cost less, they also permit a more flexible cost structure that may help the institution adapt to changes in student demand (Wells et al. 2007; Altbach 1999) (Table 13.6).

Strictures about the qualification of academic staff are common to all private institutions, regardless of their size, age, disciplinary profile or make-up. They have considerable bearing on another important issue – the balance between teaching and research. Most institutions have but a very limited capacity to develop research, mainly on account of the proportion of non-permanent staff, a necessity if costs are to be held down. Furthermore, many private institutions prefer to recruit faculty with lower academic credentials but possessing significant practical expertise, both because they are cheaper and because it is believed such practitioners enhance the institution's attractiveness to students and employers. The upshot of this choice is that most private institutions have a very limited scope for research, as may be seen from the number of research units accredited by the Portuguese National Science Foundation (FCT) (Teixeira and Amaral 2008).[8]

These intrinsic weaknesses do not help private institutions to develop alternative strategies that may re-adjust their profile. Forged in times of rapid expansion, Portuguese private institutions seem to persist in a pattern of development, which may have been successful in times of accelerated growth in higher education but which seems all too inadequate in helping them face the adversities born from falling demand.[9]

Private Higher Education in Portugal: A Provisional Balance

Although private higher education has long enjoyed historical importance, its role was, until recently, rather small in many higher education systems. Over the last few decades, this situation has changed dramatically with the massive and continuous expansion of higher education worldwide. The evolution of the Portuguese higher education is not dissimilar to this general trend.

As in many other countries, the issue of privatisation in Portugal became inseparable from the development of mass higher education. Historically, the Nation rested on a very low level of educational qualification. Higher education grew slowly until the late twentieth century, though the 1974 Revolution brought about dramatic change and accelerated the pressures expanding higher education.

These pressures were propelled onwards by the speed-up of modernisation during the 1960s and 1970s, which in turn amplified the demand, both social and economic, for more education. However, instability and financial constraint held back the rapid development of a large public system of higher education. By the mid-1980s, higher education in Portugal was still very much an elite affair. The setting became favourable for the development of the private sector as a major vehicle in the drive towards massification.

Squeezed between rising social demand and a potentially heavy bill that massive growth in higher education might present, Governments searched for ways to deal with this paradoxical situation. Urged on by the Zeitgeist of liberalisation and privatisation, policy-makers espoused the view that promoting private higher education was a plausible policy alternative to the historically dominant public sector. Thus, by the mid-1980s the idea of boosting the role of the private sector came to command strong political support in Portugal. The private sector was held out as a way to secure a supply of study programmes, better balanced, from a standpoint both of geographical location and the disciplinary fields covered, and for that reason were better suited to the demands of the labour market.

Up to the early 1980s, the size of the private sector in Portugal was very small. The pace of implementation accelerated after the mid-1980s, however, with the result that this sector showed the fastest growth rate in a system already in the throes of accelerated expansion. Various forces converged around that development. The political climate was clearly favourable. Social pressure was irresistible. Developing the private sector did not, however, make additional demands on the public budget, itself very tightly contained. Social demand was strong, driven onwards by persistently high rates of return and by highly attractive openings on the labour market for most university graduates. An additional factor was the pent up demand that delays in opening up secondary education had held back and which in effect held off the decline in student enrolments and, for more than a decade, kept demand for higher education buoyant.

Having benefited from the explosion in student numbers, the private sector faced an all-too-evident retrenchment. Stabilisation, followed by a slight decline in the numbers applying to higher education, plus steady growth in the public sector, caused the pool of potential candidates to private HEIs to shrink. The speedy and uneven development of the private sector began to work against it, above all as demand spiralled downwards in part because of the widespread mistrust, as much in the political domain as in society itself, which the private sector had gathered around it.

Yet, the advent of the private sector had brought with it high expectations about the role it would fulfil within the Portuguese higher education system, a role conceived mainly in terms of its potential for external efficiency and responsiveness. Two decades later, few of these expectations have been met and then barely so. The private sector was an important instrument in the massification of the system, but only to the extent that the public sector was not yet capable of absorbing demand fully. Once the public sector developed sufficiently, the life of the private sector became increasingly complicated, in part because of its lack of standing and its cost when compared with the public sector. The private sector, in point of fact, contributed little to the expected disciplinary and regional diversification of the system, not least because most institutions were over-eager to capture large parts of the student market. Such eagerness was not devoid of problems, and especially so for some fields of study in relation to the transition from higher education to work of their graduates. Such fragilities were compounded in the area of post-graduate education and in research capacity where the private sector was weak in respect of the former and virtually non-existent in the case of the latter.

As elsewhere, so too with the Portuguese experience: the fate of the private sector is seemingly either to duplicate what public institutions are doing or to expand through low-cost courses into areas with strong demand. The private sector tends to offer a low-quality, low-cost product that maximises short-term benefits instead of a product that in the long run would offer better prospects of survival to these self-same institutions. Even when they achieve some measure of credibility, they skirt around certain study fields and leave certain students aside. They are, in effect, replicating a narrow vision of public sector supply as opposed to complementing it. They leave aside more costly or more risky areas for the public sector to cover. Clearly, Governments may count on the private sector to expand the system but not to increase diversity.

Yet system expansion is no trivial feat, neither from the standpoint of efficiency and still less from that of equity. The rise of private higher education provided an appreciable opportunity for many individuals, and with apparent benefit to society. It is precisely because private higher education has attained so important a role in the development of Portuguese higher education that the weaknesses discussed above resonate so strongly. Over the coming decades, what its current situation requires of the private sector is that it should attend not only to maximising private returns and institutional benefits but that it should do so in a way that contributes to the coherence and effectiveness of higher education and thus to the well-being of Portuguese society.

Notes

1. Even though the concept of privatisation is often used to mean the transfer of ownership and/or financial responsibilities from the public to the private sphere, this is only one of the possible meanings when referring to higher education (see Williams 1991). Others include the development of private providers concurrently with public provision, the diversification of funding mechanisms and the use of private management in public organisations. In this chapter, we concentrate on exploring the development of private sector provision as part of higher education systems (Geiger 1986; Altbach 1999), which is one of the main dimensions of the trend towards privatisation.
2. Separation between the public and private spheres was far less clear-cut at that time, especially between the European monarchies and the Catholic Church; thus, in some respects there was a less clear dichotomy between public and private, a situation no less complex in those countries having a State Church.
3. Although this demand for some types of qualified individuals was already present in the nineteenth century, especially as regards those with some type of legal training and also technical expertise required for infrastructure building, the post-war expansion of the State, especially

with the construction of the so-called Welfare State, required that it had to hire an enormous amount of highly qualified people such as teachers, social workers, doctors, nurses and accountants. The post-war times of macroeconomic demand management also enhanced the governmental demand of individuals with economic training.
4. For more detail on this, see Kim et al. (2007).
5. However, the existence of the university was short. There was an internal strife that eventually led the Government to intervene. In mid-1986, the Minister of Education recognised two new private institutions, one in Lisbon (Universidade Autónoma Luís de Camões) and the other in Porto (Universidade Portucalense), which were established by dissidents from the Universidade Livre. Later in the same year, the Minister withdrew formal recognition from the Universidade Livre.
6. However, in the Portuguese case, data also suggest that the economic return of education seems to vary significantly. The same study analysed the economic return at the same level of education for those in the top and bottom income groups. According to the data, the economic return in Portugal for a similar educational qualification is not only very heterogeneous. It also seems to have increased during the system's substantial expansion. Wage benefits from educational qualifications have decreased for those earning lower wages and increased for those well paid. This suggests that the economic benefit of education has been declining during the last two decades for those at the lower end of the pay scale.
7. The only exception is the case of Health, which includes mainly Nursing Schools, which have a substantial private participation and largely antedate the recent boom in private higher education. Frequently, these are also programmes linked to religious institutions which set a lower priority on market demands and profitability.
8. Moreover, that the number of accredited units is very small poses significant limitations on future development. Only accredited centres and researchers associated with them are eligible for public research funds. That private institutions are significantly concentrated in social sciences and humanities. Their research output is far less visible – especially in respect of bibliometric indicators. This limits their potential to attract significant external resources to develop those activities further. Thus, the situation in research is not likely to change significantly over the next few years.
9. In effect, the main change in recent years in the private higher education landscape is the decline in the number of institutions. On the one hand, this is due to the closure of some institutions unable to hold out against difficult conditions (Teixeira and Amaral 2007). On the other hand, some attempts have been made recently to merge with or to take over other establishments. The merger strategy is far more complex than a takeover. This development has increased the degree of concentration, and seen the emergence of some large players, in a traditionally atomistic sector.

References

Altbach, P. G. (Ed.). (1999). *Private Prometheus: Private higher education and development in the 21st century*. Westport: Greenwood.
Amaral, A., & Teixeira, P. (2000). The rise and fall of the private sector in Portuguese higher education? *Higher Education Policy, 13*(3), 245–266.
Barr, N. (2004). *The economics of the welfare state*. Oxford: Oxford University Press.
Barreto, A. (Ed.). (1996). *A Situação Social em Portugal*. Lisboa: ICS.
Becker, G., & Gregg Lewis, H. (1973). On the Interaction between the quantity and quality of children. *The Journal of Political Economy, 81*, S279–S288.
Blöndal, S., Field, S., Girouard, N. (2002). *Investment In human capital through post-compulsory education and training: Selected efficiency and equity aspects* (OECD Economics Department Working Paper No. 333).

Cardoso, A. R., & Ferreira, P. (2001). *The dynamics of job creation and destruction for university graduates: Why a rising unemployment rate can be misleading* (NIMA Working Paper Series No. 10).
Carneiro, R. (1994). Manifesto contra o Estado hegemónico. In R. Carneiro (Ed.), *Ensino Livre: Uma Fronteira da Hegemonia Estatal*. Lisbon: Edições Asa.
Franco, A. S. (1994). A Liberdade de Aprender e de Ensinar no Âmbito das Liberdades Fundamentais: Fundamentação da Liberdade de Ensino. In R. Carneiro (Ed.), *Ensino Livre: Uma Fronteira da Hegemonia Estatal* (pp. 17–42). Lisbon: Edições Asa.
Geiger, R. (1986). *Private sectors in higher education*. Ann Arbor: The University of Michigan Press.
Gerbod, P. (2004). Relations with authority. In W. Rüegg (Ed.), *A history of the university in Europe* (Vol. III). Cambridge: Cambridge University Press.
Gosden, P. (1983). *The education system since 1944*. Oxford: Martin Robertson.
Hammerstein, N. (1996). Relations with authority. In W. de Rüegg & H. Ridder-Symoens (Eds.), *A history of the university in Europe* (Vol. II). Cambridge: Cambridge University Press.
Hartog, J., Pereira, P. T., & e José C. Vieira. (2001). Changing returns to education in Portugal during the 1980s and early 1990s: OLS and quantile regression estimators. *Applied Economics, 33*, 1021–1037.
Kiker, B. F., & Santos, M. C. (1991). Human capital and earnings in Portugal. *Economics of Education Review, 10*(3), 187–203.
Kim, S., Gilani, Z., Landoni, P., Musisi, N., Teixeira, P. (2007). Rethinking public-private mix in higher education: Global trends and national policy challenges. In P. Altbach & P. Peterson (Eds.), *Higher education in the new century – Global challenges and innovative ideas* (pp. 79–108). Center for International Higher Education – Boston College and UNESCO. Sense Publishers, Rotterdam.
Levy, D. C. (1986). *Higher education and the state in Latin America: Private challenges to public dominance*. Chicago: University of Chicago Press.
Levy, D. C. (2002). *Unanticipated development: Perspectives on private higher education's emerging roles* (PROPHE (Program for Research on Private Higher Education) Working Paper No. 1).
Levy, D. C. (2006). *An introductory global overview: The private fit to salient higher education tendencies* (PROPHE Working Paper No. 7).
Machado, José e José Mata. (2001). Earnings functions in Portugal 1982–1994: Evidence from quantile regressions. *Empirical Economics, 26*, 115–134.
Martins, Pedro e Pereira, P. (2004). Does education reduce wage inequality? Quantile regression evidence from 16 countries. *Labour Economics, 11*, 355–371.
Middleton, R. (1997). *Versus the market: The growth of the public sector, economic management and British economic performance*. Aldershot: Edward Elgar.
Mincer, J. (1993). *Studies in human capital*. Cheltenham: Edward Elgar.
Neave, G. (2000). Universities' responsibilities to society: An historical exploration of an enduring issue. In G. Neave (Ed.), *The universities' responsibilities to society – International perspectives* (pp. 1–28). Oxford: Elsevier.
Neave, G., & Van Vught, F. (Eds.). (1991). *Prometheus bound: The changing relationship between and higher education in Western Europe*. Oxford: Pergamon Press.
Pereira, P. T., & Silva Martins, P. (2004). Does education reduce wage inequality? Quantile evidence from 16 countries. *Labour Economics, 11*, 355–371.
Reis, J. (1993). *O Atraso Económico Português 1850–1930*. Lisboa: INCM.
Romer, P. (1986). Increasing returns and long-run growth. *Journal of Political Economy, 94*(5), 1002–1037.
Simão, J. V., Machado Santos, S., & de Almeida Costa, A. (2002). *Ensino Superior: Uma Visão para a Próxima Década*. Lisboa: Gradiva.
Teichler, U. (1988). *Changing patterns of the higher education system: The experience of three decades*. London: Jessica Kingsley.
Teixeira, P. (2008). A Evidência Mitificada? Educação, Economia e Capital Humano em Portugal. In *Successo e insuccesso: escola, Economia e Sociadade*. Lisboa: Fundação Calouste Gulbenkian.

Teixeira, P., & Amaral, A. (2002). Private higher education and diversity: An exploratory survey. *Higher Education Quarterly, 55*(4), 359–395.

Teixeira, P., & Amaral, A. (2007). Waiting for the tide to change? Strategies for survival of Portuguese private HEIs. *Higher Education Quarterly, 61*(2), 208–222.

Teixeira, P., & Amaral, A. (2008). Can private institutions learn from mistakes? – Some reflections based on the Portuguese experience. *Die Hochschule, 2*(2008), 113–125.

Teixeira, P., Dill, D., Jongbloed, B., & Amaral, A. (Eds.). (2004). *The rising strength of markets in higher education*. Dordrecht: Kluwer.

Van Vught, F. (Ed.). (1989). *Governmental strategies and innovations in higher education*. London: Jessica Kingsley.

Vincent-Lancrin, S. (2007). *The "Crisis" of public higher education: A comparative perspective* (Research & Occasional Paper Series: 18.07). Berkeley: CSHE-UC.

Wells, P. J., Sadlak, J., & Vlăsceanu, L. (Eds.). (2007). *The rising role and relevance of private higher education in Europe*. Bucharest: UNESCO – CEPES.

Williams, G. (1991). The many faces of privatisation. *Higher Education Management, 8*, 39–56.

Wittrock, B. (1993). The modern university: The three transformations. In S. Rothblatt & B. Wittrock (Eds.), *The European and American university since 1800 – Historical and sociological essays* (pp. 303–362). Cambridge: Cambridge University Press.

Chapter 14
Shaping the 'New' Academic Profession

Tensions and Contradictions in the Professionalisation of Academics

Teresa Carvalho

Introduction

Over the past 35 years deep changes have occurred in Portuguese higher education. The Democratic Revolution of 1974 opened the way for both institutions and students to increase. The path to mass higher education beckoned. At the same time, other challenges emerged. System diversification with new institutional types and variety, different actors and even new curricular assumptions appeared in higher education field. Changes in system steering brought major revision to the traditional role of the State, moving it from a Weberian remit of direct control towards a 'panopticon' function of remote steering. An alternative account used slightly different terms, moving from rational planning and state control to a model of state supervision (Neave and van Vught 1994; van Vught 1997).

These changes are not unique to Portugal. They are visible in many Western countries. For Altbach et al. (2009), they amounted to an 'academic revolution', the impact of which ranged from the policy level down to the institutional level and on into the everyday lives of higher education institutions, administrators, academics and students.

Many different perspectives have been brought to bear in exploring these major developments. In Portugal, analysis tends to concentrate on the system level with particular weight on governance, governing and management as key points of inquiry (Magalhães 2004; Amaral and Magalhães 2007; Amaral et al. 2003; Magalhães and Amaral 2007; Santiago et al. 2005, 2006; Santiago and Carvalho 2004). Less attention has been paid to internal dynamics and actors, and very little indeed, to academics.

T. Carvalho (✉)
Departamento de Ciências Sociais, Políticas e do Território, University of Aveiro,
CIPES Rua Primeiro de Dezembro 399, 4450-228 Matosinhos, Portugal
e-mail: teresa.carvalho@csjp.ua.pt

Whilst this lacuna has been addressed recently (Carvalho and Santiago 2008, 2010a; Santiago and Carvalho 2008), tracing the development of the academic profession over the years since the Democratic Revolution of 1974 is a road still largely untrodden.

This chapter sets out to rectify the apparent oversight. It begins by reviewing the concept of 'a profession'. It asks whether use of this term is appropriate for academia. Second, it examines the literature of the sociology of professions as a possible framework to interpret the changes, historical and sociological that affected teachers in Portuguese higher education over the past few years. Three major processes of change are identified: segmentation, feminisation and commodification. The prospects this group of academic actors now face are scrutinised, as are the potential consequences for the standing of this particular group inside academia and in society.

Academics as a Professional Group

Any inquiry into the 'academic profession' must begin by reflecting on the general concept of what it is to be a 'profession'. This conundrum has occupied sociologists for a long time. The first answers to this question emerged during the first half of the twentieth century and rested on frameworks that derived from functionalist and interactionist theory. The functionalist perspective (Parsons 1958, 1972) sought to identify and classify the attributes of an ideal type of profession by isolating professions from other occupational groupings. Symbolic interactionism (Hughes 1958, 1963) focused on how professions constructed their status and privileges through day-to-day negotiation.

During the 1970s, at a time of economic crisis, further critical perspectives developed. Amongst the then contemporary literature, Johnson (1972), Larson (1977) and Freidson (1977, 1978) introduced the dimension of power into the analysis. Johnson (1972) concentrated on power relations between professionals and clients. Differences between the two parties, he argued, are legitimated by the specialised knowledge professionals possess. Larson (1977) interpreted professions as relying on historical processes. Larson proposed that professionals obtain a legal monopoly over certain activities by constructing specific professional markets. To these markets, state protection is added through legal recognition of the professional group, a step that allows it to gain material and symbolic privileges. The monopoly a profession exercised over the market was consolidated by its monopoly over knowledge and over professional qualifications obtained through higher education. Professional monopoly over a specific market and its cultural closure gave rise to 'social closure'. This latter notion, taken up by Parkin (1979) and Murphy (1988), interpreted professionalisation as a closure strategy based on credentialism. To Freidson (1978, 1986) a profession was associated with the organisation of the labour market. Professionals legitimated their power through three different elements: technical autonomy based on control over the way work is done (the professional as expert), monopoly over a specialised and institutionalised area of knowledge and, finally, credentialism which represented a form of gatekeeping. By contrast to Johnson and Larson, Freidson defined the notion of professionals and professionalism positively. In a recent study, Freidson (2001) represented professionalism as a third form of logic in society over the market or the bureaucracy. Professionalism's positive consequences for society derived from its counterbalancing both administrative and bureaucratic power. The professional, based on specialised knowledge, was thus the only protection possible for the organisation of work and to protect the particular interests of clients (Evetts 2003).

At that time, debate over the importance of professionals and of professions in society unfolded along two different lines. Some analysts of post-industrialism argued that the ability professions marshalled would increase their social and political power (Bell 1976). The contending thesis was that of proletarianisation (Oppenheimer 1973; Derber 1983) and de-professionalisation (Hall 1975) – in short, the shrinking importance of professionals, their power, status and autonomy in society.

These analyses of professions as privileged groups with ethical values and norms, ideologies and formal knowledge supporting their control over the organisation of their work – and professionalism, which is a specific system of values and norms – were conducted at a time when capitalism developed under strong economic and financial constraints.

During the 1980s, Abbott (1988) introduced a more systemic and complex perspective. Relying on the concept of a '*system* of professions', he argued that different professions contended for a specific jurisdictional field. In this struggle, knowledge was the first and most important resource which professions used against each other. However, Abbott (1988) also pointed out that professions were not homogeneous. Internally, they split into distinct groups, each with different working situations. Changes to which professions are prone were created by both external and internal forces. Such forces dissolved the profession's hold over the jurisdictional field it previously controlled.

These studies, however, were set in Anglo-Saxon practice. Important differences exist between the concept of a 'profession' in the USA and the United Kingdom and in other states. In Continental Europe, the term profession is applied broadly, though hiding many meanings. Taking the French case as illustration, Dubar and Tripier (1998) identified four dimensions behind the concept: profession as a statement (professional identity), profession as a '*métier*' (vocational specialisation), profession as employment (professional classification) and profession as a role (professional position inside the institution). More recently, Dubar proposed replacing the term 'profession' by 'professional group', and defined it as:

> (…) a fluid set, segmented, in a permanent evolution, reassembling people who share one activity with the same name with social visibility and enough political legitimacy during a significant time period. (Dubar 2003: 51)

Against this backdrop, the academic profession is a most interesting group to examine. Rapid reflection on the 'academic profession' in Portugal reveals that it never faced the need to contend with other professional groups in the same jurisdictional space. Since its origins with the medieval schoolmen, the 'academic profession' always enjoyed a privileged status in the 'system of professions' (Abbott 1988). More than with other professional groups, power relations with the State seem to be the main pillar, upholding its material and symbolic power in society. Thus, the relationship between the academic 'professional group' and the State is specific and unique. Under different political regimes and forms of states, academics – at least in the Western countries – have always benefited from strong state protection. This protection applied not only vis-à-vis the market and religious power but even applied to political, economic and bureaucratic interference (Bourdieu 1996). It is the specificity of this relationship that had Neave and Rhoades argue:

> In mainland Western Europe, academia is not a profession. It is an estate, whose power, privileges, and conditions of employment are protected by constitutional and administrative law.[1] (Neave and Rhoades 1987: 213)

State protection is particularly relevant under the welfare state, especially in view of the alliance professionalism forged with state bureaucracy (Larson 1977; Freidson 2001). Yet, academics exercise monopoly not only over their own knowledge but also over the production and dissemination of other groups' professional knowledge. They exert an important role through the so-called monopoly over credentialism (Slaughter and Leslie 1997; Perkin 1987, 1990).

Whilst recognising these specificities, it is appropriate to bring in other, more-contemporary, theoretical developments from Europe (Evetts 2002, 2003; Wrede 2008; Kuhlmann 2006). Recent studies on professionalism have returned to the ideas of the Italian political theorist, Antoni Gramsci (2000), and those of the French social philosopher, Michel Foucault (1991a, b, 2004, 2006). Gramsci argued that the struggle between different groups to engage in society does not involve economic distribution but, rather, a quest for 'consent' or 'cultural hegemony'. Hegemony entails acquiring more influence, leadership and consent than domination. It relates to how a given social group, by negotiation and compromise, influences other groups with the view of obtaining consent to its leadership in society (Gramsci 2000). Of these groups, the most effective is the one best able to spread its ideas amongst others, even if the latter do not share its economic interests. For Gramsci, civil society was the terrain where groups both build up, but also contest, those hegemonic, normative identities that subordinate them (Gramsci 2000). Hegemony was based not on mechanical so much as on organic, relationships. Individuals form part of social organisms, from the more simple to the more complex. Hence, their interactions are always organic (Gramsci 2000; Jones 2006). Each social group can create, inside itself, in an organic way, one or more intellectual *strata* – organic intellectuals – that ensure homogeneity and an awareness of their own function both in the economic, but also in the political, field (Gramsci 2000; Jones 2006).

The links Gramsci (2000) established between 'organic intellectuals' and the transmutation of 'technical/specialised' knowledge into political knowledge (Jones 2006) opens the possibility of combining Gramscian concepts with Foucault's theories (Foucault 1991a, b, 2004, 2006). For Foucault, expertise had a crucial role in providing solutions to social problems, that is to say, control of the social order and morality (Foucault 1991a, b, 2004, 2006). Academics are part of this 'cohort of experts'. They are also key actors, providing other professional groups with knowledge and techniques, and thus the opportunity to build up skills and capacities to apply scientific and technical knowledge in the control and regulation of social life.

These conceptual approaches open important and additional perspectives for analysing systematically the overall *problématique* in the process of the professionalisation of academics. Furthermore, account has also to be taken of Abbott's (1988) concept of the internal diversity within professional groups.

The academic profession in Portugal has always enjoyed strong support from the State and has been able up to now to cast themselves as 'organic intellectuals'. It is our view, however, that the ability to remain so is related, in the main, to the internal dynamics endemic to this professional group. The academic profession consists of many different groups (Becher and Trowler 2001). Each entertains distinct ideas about academia, the State and society, and is thus engaged in constructing different normative and professional identities.

In this chapter, Gramsci's concepts serve not only to explore the struggle between different professional groups but, primarily, to analyse how struggles and contradictions developed inside a particular group, as well as how a hegemonic normative and professional identity was institutionalised, which in turn upheld its status as 'organic intellectuals'. Likewise, Foucault's insights may be used to show how dominant ideas are transformed into day-to-day practice.

We start from the notion that a historical and sociological interpretation of the academic profession in Portugal can be developed by the way different groups inside it elaborate and impose their interpretative scheme and normative identity. Later, the chapter will examine how this long-term process of internal segmentation unfolded within Portugal's academic profession.

The Long-Term Process of Segmentation

The Pre-democratic Era

As a professional group, academia has never been homogeneous. However, since the Revolution of 1974, a clear tendency developed to increase segmentation and internal diversification.

Under the Dictatorship, academia could be classified as an elite profession. Three main characteristics bear this descriptor out:

1. *Social prestige* – In a study of the Portuguese industrial elite dating from the 1960s, Makler (1968) concluded that academic professionals were amongst the most prestigious in the country.[2]
2. *Small numbers* – Selection for academic positions was so rigorous that only a small minority, shaped into privileged elite, was permitted to acquire this status.

3. *Government involvement* – in his study of political elites during the 'Estado Novo' period, António Costa Pinto (2000) concluded that from 1933 to 1944, a considerable number of ministers – some 40% – had previously served as university professors. The number of ministers who previously held professorial posts was a particularly pronounced feature in Portugal's political elites under the Dictatorship, a situation that Gallagher (1981) qualified as '*catedratocracia*' – an autocracy of full professors.

During the Estado Novo, academics formed a 'profession of the elite', wielding great influence over national policy. Such elitism, to a large degree, derived from an intellectual hegemony born out of a balance between power exerted by the coercive State and the consent of a large fraction of academics (Gramsci 2000). It was directly linked to the expert knowledge academics possessed, which allowed the state to exercise control over civil society and to make it operational (Foucault 1991a, b, 2004, 2006). Cultural hegemony, however, was not merely the consequence of coercive state power. It was also the outcome of authority conceded by the State to 'autonomous' professionals, through degree granting and bureaucratisation. Such authority was granted by the State, confident that expert academic knowledge could, in a Foucaultian perspective (Foucault 2004, 2006), exercise a major role in social and ideological control.

However, within this privileged elite, a distinction should be drawn between what Gramsci (2000) termed 'the consenting' and the 'non-consenting'. The 'consenting elite' had the opportunity to support a specific normative identity for academics, together with the cultural hegemony of the 'Estado Novo'. The 'non-consenting elite', by contrast, rested on a minority of academics who sought to hold out against this hegemony. Furthermore, the presence of a chair holder system marked out a primary fault line between junior and senior staff, which broadly marked the frontier between the 'consenting' and 'non-consenting'. In fact, junior staff was highly dependent on their senior colleagues.

Highly dependent on the good graces of full professors as they were, young academics could count on gaining a measure of academic or teaching autonomy only after their doctorate degree. This demanded several years, for only at that point could young academics aspire to the mantle of academic or pedagogical autonomy to the extent it was available at that epoch (Tavares 1999).

In effect, institutions enjoyed autonomy only insofar as it was defined according to the tenets of 'corporatist logic' that had the Rector as a government appointee and deemed to be the 'representative of the Ministry of Public Instruction in the university' (*Estatuto da Instrução Universitária*, 2 of August of 1930, Article 8). If the truth were out, even full professors possessed little autonomy. They were obliged to develop teaching and research within the ideological framework the Dictatorship set. Some scholarly fields were virtually inexistent – the social sciences, for instance (Pinto 2004). Academic work was subject to strict and direct control. A large number of academics were dismissed on suspicion of working against state ideology.[3] Others were exiled or were forced to return to private life to survive (Marques 1981). Portugal's colonial wars also contributed to 'academic flight', with substantial numbers of academics leaving for other countries, mainly to the United States but also to Europe. They came to play an important role in developing academic communities within the Portuguese Diaspora and were instrumental in fostering resistance abroad to the political regime at home.

From a broad perspective, the Portuguese higher education system at that time was not greatly dissimilar to the profile Clark (1977) assigned to Italian higher education. University governance was grounded on a high degree of hierarchical and central control, both ideological and bureaucratic, a species of hybrid combining features of a pre-Weberian mandate with elements of the Weberian structure (Chaps. 9 and 12). The former involved Rectors and other major administrative actors being incorporated with their 'consent' into the ideological thralls of the 'Estado Novo'. That latter took form around rationalising organisation, structures and processes of decision-making.

The Ministry of Public Instruction exercised a close and unremitting control over university life from the status of teaching staff, over salaries, curricula, courses, budgets and on to the validation of academic degrees, titles and qualifications. Such control was grounded in an oligarchy of full professors, arrayed around a 'chair-holder' system. Here, it is important to note that Antonio Salazar – then Portugal's dictator – was himself an academic and as such well able to defend both dictatorship and academic oligarchy. As Moscati (2002) pointed out for Italy, so for Portugal:

> (The system) operated according to the principles of a centralised administrative system (the French model) with academic power channelled through chair holders (the German model) in the pursuit of the traditional task of the reproduction of elites. (Moscati 2002: 4)

Segmentation Under a Democratic Regime

The Democratic Revolution of 1974 ushered in profound change to the architecture of academic power inside the university. The specific conditions of the state's structure drove in favour of a particular form of academic professionalism. Thus, the way stood open for those groups, previously excluded from an academic career – junior staff without power and academics in exile – to present an agenda that was both counter-hegemonic and professional. The elite of the 'non-consenting', acting as a counter-hegemonic group, saw the opportunity to back and to develop new normative identities. The shift in the nexus of power inside academia was all the more marked because an important number of academics had been purged from public universities thereby paying the price of their previous and close ties with the Ancien Régime (Amaral and Teixeira 2000).

The Democratic Revolution laid down a new basis for the State, rooted in the ideals of the Welfare State, a fundamental redefinition to the role of the state and to state professionalism. Education, and higher education most certainly, was held to form one of the fundamental pillars of democracy and to be essential to social equity.

In these circumstances, the professional group of academics was able to retain its status as 'organic intellectuals'. This it could do by dint of changing its dominant normative identity, by presenting itself as the guarantor of democracy. As Kuhlmann (2006) noted, though in a very different setting, academics appeared to incorporate the image of the professional as a blueprint for the 'ideal citizen'. Two developments were fundamental for consolidating the 'new' hegemonic process of the academic profession: the internal organisation of universities and polytechnics and the legal framework defining the profession.

The new organisational principles for higher education institutions introduced the freedoms to teach and to learn. Under the new Constitution of 1976, the law upheld the principles of university autonomy, though these became effective only in 1988 (Amaral and Carvalho 2003). Earlier patterns of organisation and their structures, grounded in a non-democratic model, made up of elements drawing upon collegiality/hierarchy/corporatism (Lima 2002), were hotly contested by academics, by teachers' associations and by students' unions. All pressed for democracy representative and participative at the level of both central administration and in the basic units. Universities and polytechnics adjusted internal governance around the principles of collegiality and democracy, with full participation of academics, students and non-academic staff. Election became the main legitimation for power (Amaral 2003). Thus, two features were set into Portuguese higher education – 'bottom-up' decision-making (Clark 1983) or what others have described as the model of organised anarchy (Cohen et al. 1972) (Chap. 12).

The democratisation of higher education's governance structure stood as the simultaneous outcome of the radical overhaul of political and social outer frameworks together with an internal redefinition of power. One-time members of junior staff and exiled academics imposed their own counter-hegemonic professional agenda. They injected new cultural symbols, beliefs and values, which concentrated around the ideas of democracy, autonomy and merit. In short, academics saw their level of professionalism rise through increased control they wielded over the organisation of work and over their own careers (Larson 1977).

Thus, the bureaucratic/collegial/political model of governance largely upheld the new occupational ideology of the academic body and was perceived politically as an important technology of governmentality (Foucault 1991a, b) in 'normalising' higher education and Portuguese society.

In reality, the collegial mode of governing granted the academic profession a degree of autonomy virtually without parallel, when compared with other professions in the public sectors. As in many other systems in Western Europe, collegial decision-making, as it developed in the newly democratic higher education institutions, rests upon a highly hierarchical professional structure that largely preserved the earlier characteristics of chair-holder supremacy (Neave and Rhoades 1987).

At the end of the 1970s, the legal outline for university careers was promulgated (Decree-Law 448/79), and at the start of the 1980s, its polytechnic counterpart (Decree-Law 185/81). Laying down the legal framework for careers in both sectors may be seen in terms of a 'strategy of closure' (Larson 1977; Parkin 1979; Murphy 1988). Save for a few minor changes, these enactments remained in place for almost three decades, which seemed to endow them with a *quasi-constitutional* status.

Defining the university career drew on Humboldtian values with academics assuming three forms of responsibility: teaching, research and services to society. The university career covered 5 ranks and four academic degrees: full professor – *agregação*; associate professor – a*gregação*; auxiliary professor – doctor; assistant – master; and assistant trainee – bachelor. Entry was strictly regulated by the Government to avoid irregularities in recruitment. Selection required the setting up of an internal commission, comprising at least three senior academics, to evaluate the *curriculum vitae* of applicants and to select the best on the grounds of merit (Meira Soares 2001; Santiago and Carvalho 2008). The principles defining merit upheld equality in access whilst maintaining the control of professionals over entry to the profession. The importance of limiting the selection of new members to professionals is acknowledged in the literature as a key element in the profession's exercising control over itself (Larson 1977; Parkin 1979; Murphy 1988).

Promotion was automatic, except to senior posts (full and associate professor) that were filled as a vacancy occurred. The tenure position could be granted 5 years after obtaining the PhD – in effect, 5 years at the level of auxiliary professor – based solely on merit. A selection committee of senior level academic staff decide whether the applicant's record of achievement entitles him to a tenured position (Santiago and Carvalho 2008; Meira Soares 2001).

By dint of this legal framework, the academic profession in Portuguese universities was, as Clark noted of Italy, 'an arm of the state bureaucracy (…), wholly supported by the Government and protected (…) by a well-understood Humboldtian tradition' (Clark 1987: 44).

The structure of careers in polytechnics, though also hierarchical, enshrined different principles, stemming from its vocational nature. It too covered five different levels: coordinating professor with the *agregação*, coordinating professor, adjunct professor, assistant (second 3-year period) and assistant (first 3-year period). Additional qualifications did not ensure automatic advancement to a higher rank, however. Academic staff at all levels have to wait for a vacancy to occur (Santiago and Carvalho 2008). Moreover, the PhD did not play so crucial a role in career progress. Academic staff in polytechnics could apply for tenure 3 years after their appointment as adjunct professor, which demanded only a master's degree.

Linkage and cross flow between the two careers was absent. The possibility existed to invite individuals whose main commitments lay outside academia. They formed part of 'specially contracted personnel', non-academics whose curriculum upheld their expertise in a specific domain. With similar working conditions, this category of personnel was not eligible for tenure track appointments. Traditionally, this category was only used in exceptional situations to invite people with 'special skills' to develop teaching (Santiago and Carvalho 2008).

Traditionally, both career paths were considered highly secure and strongly embedded in the idea of full-time permanent academic status. Turning down a tenured post was virtually unknown. Between 1988 and 1997 only 4 cases in polytechnics and 14 in universities took this decision, though between 1997 and 2004, refusals increased to 16 in polytechnics and 45 bold spirits in universities (GPEARI 2004).

Even these academics were covered by the legal framework of careers, which underwrote employment in public sector higher education even for the non-tenured – a clear illustration of academia's unique and privileged status that substantiates both Neave and Rhoades' portrayal of academics as an 'estate' (Neave and Rhoades 1987) as it does Altbach's argument that academics have always been a highly esteemed professional group, 'somehow standing apart from society, with special privileges and responsibilities' (Altbach 2000: 12).

Interestingly, the academic profession in Portugal secured the best working conditions for itself at a time when some European countries, the British not least, embarked on managerialism. Not only did this initiative threaten the main principles of the welfare state, a situation, generated *inter alia*, by the world recession that followed the oil shock of the 1970s. It assumed a new dimension with the emergence of neoliberal ideology and market assumptions (Perkin 1987; Deem 1998; Reed 2002).

Even if the granting of special privileges could not be gainsaid, the launching of a binary system was an important development. Two distinct career modes were established, marking a further step in professional segmentation. As with other European countries (Perkin 1987), universities command a higher social status than polytechnics (Perkin 1987; Taylor et al. 2008), with direct consequences for the working conditions of academics.

If academics may no longer be seen as an elite, they remained nevertheless a key profession. With the advent of a polytechnic subsystem, new training courses emerged as did different occupational groups striving to derive legitimation from scientific knowledge and credentialism (Larson 1977), in short to become a profession in their turn. As the English social historian, Harold Perkin pointed out:

(…) university teaching was the key profession because academics had become the educators and selectors of the other professions. (Perkin 1987: 13)

To sum up, the Democratic Revolution saw a new professionalism emerge within the professional academic group, a professionalism born up by democratic principles, which gave further weight to its position as 'organic intellectuals'. Yet, with a binary system, the academic profession faced rising internal segmentation and stratification. To those devoted to research and training in fields linked to the legitimacy and credentialism of 'traditional' professions, a new constellation of 'knowledge experts' had surfaced, devoted mainly to training for new occupations. Despite the well-documented phenomena of 'academic drift' and 'professional drift' as forms of common identity, different types of higher education establishments, with very different social status, meant different sources of legitimacy, terms of employment and social standing.

The application of democratic and egalitarian principles to higher education had other consequences, not least opening up participation to women, a development that increased both diversification and segmentation inside the academic profession. What the implications may be will be dealt with later.

The Emergence of a Private Subsystem

In the course of the 1980s, the consensus that focused on implementing the welfare state began to unravel. According to sociologist Boaventura Sousa Santos (1993), the 1989 constitutional revision eliminated the last vestiges of the socialist programme proclaimed by the Democratic Revolution of 1974. This 'about turn' in the 1980s was especially visible in the health sector (Simões and Lourenço 1999; Carvalho 2009). Nor was higher education spared.

Certain minority groups, deprived of power and influence by the Democratic Revolution, saw an opportunity to regain both by pressing for a private sector of higher education in Portugal. Once more, a counter-hegemonic group inside academia set out to impose an alternative normative identity. Expanding private higher education rallied political support. Urged on by the former Minister of Education Roberto Carneiro, private higher education experienced 'explosive' growth (Amaral and Teixeira 2000) (Chap. 13). However, it lacked resources, and especially well-qualified academic staff. The Government, bent on expanding market forces in higher education, therefore decided:

> (…) to ease the restrictions to teachers accumulating teaching activities in both public and private institutions in order to allow for the fast development of the latter. (Amaral and Teixeira 2000: 252)

Responding to such encouragement, many academic staff in public HEIs began working with private establishments. The number of hours these stalwarts claimed to spend teaching in both public and private institutions was so spectacular that the media dubbed them '*turbo-professors*'. In reality, some did not teach at all, but rather allowed their names to go forwards as part of private universities' marketing strategy of drawing in more students. As Meira Soares noted: '(…) private institutions went their way, often illegally using professors of the public sector with the complacency of the state authorities' (Meira Soares 2001: 234). Thus, higher education's teaching body, with state support, played an important role in undermining the very social prestige that profession once possessed.

Though little is known about academic staff in Portugal's private sector higher education, an impression, widely shared, exists that by far the larger part are neither permanent nor well qualified. Other differences are to be seen in the status of academia in the two sectors. Whilst public sector teaching staffs have civil servant status, their fellows in private HEIs are contract personnel and their contracts are governed by national labour legislation as it applies to the private sector. The private sector is devoid of career regulations.

The absence of a clearly defined career structure left the way open for private higher education institutions to '(…) use the general law according to their interests' (Meira Soares 2001: 245). It also provides another example of segmentation in academic careers.

Across the 1990s, the academic profession in Portugal faced a high degree of segmentation in the shape of increasing numbers of professionals in the private subsystem whose working conditions were more akin to those of service workers. Added to this, the profession itself saw its profile change with the rise in the number of women.

A Profession Feminised? The Broad Perspective on Structure and Gender

Hegemonic concepts of professionalism were equated at first with the notion of 'hegemonic masculinity' (Davies 1996). Welfare professionalism had a crucial place in the advent of egalitarian policies. As it had in other sectors, the legitimating discourses of the state shifted. A new discourse arose which emphasised the 'sameness' of interests between workers, women and men. No longer were women cast as 'citizen-mothers' (Wrede 2008).

The ideology of egalitarianism (Henriksson et al. 2006) went hand in glove with the rise in the numbers of women employed in the Portuguese system of higher education. Since the foundation of the Portuguese Republic in 1910, women had been authorised to profess in university. Still, the university profession's elitism, combined with the Dictatorship's deeply traditional stance on gender, did not admit women to a visible role in academia. Only in the aftermath of the Democratic Revolution were the same rights granted to women as they were to men, set into the Constitution.

Massification drew an increasing number of women into higher education, first as students but also as teaching staff. Indeed, to a great degree, massification was a function of the rise in the number of women students (Amâncio and Ávila 1995). This trend, well documented in other countries, gave institutional expression to the notion of a 'feminised future' (Leathwood and Read 2009).

This is a construct especially relevant in Portugal where female participation in HE is amongst the highest in Europe (EC 2009; OECD 2006; Rees 2001). By 2007, women formed the majority of students in HE and 41.3% of its teaching body. However, this trend is understandable only against the specific backdrop of gender relations in Portugal. Traditionally, female participation in the labour market was high: In 2006, for example, it topped 62% – well above the average of 57.3% for Europe of the 25. Male participation rates stood at 73.9% (MTSS 2009).

Such a situation reflected a long-term presence of women in the formal economy primarily, as wage earners in agriculture and in subsistence farming and later, under the impetus of political, economic and social change, increasingly in the service sector. The cultural and economic values the Dictatorship upheld played an important part in bringing women onto the labour market. At the very moment when most developed countries saw the rise of movements for women's rights, Portugal was waging a colonial war in Angola, Guinea-Bissau and Mozambique. War, cultural stagnation and economic underdevelopment gave rise to flights both from the countryside and from Portugal itself towards other European countries. The shortage of men thus made women the main source of labour in the economy (Nogueira et al. 1995). Here was a condition compounded by political initiatives intended to uphold traditional gender roles which, paradoxically, increased feminisation of certain professions in the service sector, amongst which were nurses in the health sector (Carvalho 2009; Escobar 2004) and teachers in education (Araújo 1990, 1991). In the latter instance, by 1993 the number of women teachers placed Portugal as the lead country with the highest percentage of women in the teaching body in the whole of Europe (Nogueira et al. 1995).

This trend has continued, though with certain disparities across different levels of the education system. According to the World Economic Forum's report *Global Gender Gap Report* (2009), the percentage of women in primary education was 82%; in secondary schools, 69%; and in tertiary education, 43%. Whilst women's participation in academia has most assuredly advanced in the course of the past three decades, it is not possible – yet – to speak of a feminised profession. True, the formal barriers against women entering academia have given way. But other obstacles to equality of participation at different levels of academic ranking and access to senior posts have yet to be resolved (Sagaria and Agans 2006).

Women in Portuguese Academia

In 2005, academics in public higher education in Portugal numbered 24,280. Of these, 14,063 (58%) were men and 10,217 (42%) were women. Compared to other European countries, Portugal has a higher participation of women in higher education (European Commission 2006). Nevertheless the high proportion hides a certain variability. Whilst men formed the majority of academic staff in both subsystems, the participation of women was higher in polytechnics (4,713; 46.6%) than in universities (5,504; 38.9%) (Carvalho and Santiago 2010a).

That women concentrate in less prestigious institutions is evident from other countries (Bagilhole 2000; Metcalfe and Slaughter 2011). In Portugal, the reasons for these differences draw on four distinct factors. First, polytechnics are recent developments. It is, then, less difficult to recruit female academic staff, given their rise in participation as students in higher education. Second, polytechnics dispense undergraduate programmes in areas traditionally more 'feminised' – the social sciences, education and more recently, nursing. Third, polytechnics focus more on teaching than on research, though conditions of employment tend to be less stable and less secure (Santiago and Carvalho 2008). Finally, since polytechnics are relative 'newcomers', their social and symbolic capital is weaker and less prestigious than universities.

Though Portugal can boast of having a stronger presence of women in academia, the processes of horizontal and vertical segregation, identified elsewhere, are no less evident (Bagilhole 2000; Benschop and Brows 2003; Knights and Richards 2003; Bailyn 2003; O'Connor 2009; Stromquist et al. 2007).

In 2005, horizontal segregation was to be found in teacher education and training (63% women), the humanities (54% women) and engineering (77% men) (Carvalho and Santiago 2010b).

Official data from 2001 to 2005 show that, despite a small rise in the number of women teaching in public sector higher education, no visible impact had followed on for gender distribution by disciplinary field. Women's participation across all appointment levels was similar in education/teacher training – 62% in 2000 and 63% in 2005. It had increased in social sciences – 38% in 2000 and 44% in 2005 – and in the natural sciences – 45%, in 2000 and 48% by 2005. By contrast, it decreased in arts and humanities – 62% in 2000 and only 54% by 2005 (OCES 2004, 2005; Carvalho and Santiago 2010b).

In addition to horizontal segregation in Portuguese higher education career patterns, vertical segregation emerged in the gender distribution across academia's rank hierarchy. Men are more numerous in all academic ranks, with differences more pronounced at the top where women account for only 32% and 22% amongst associate and full professors.

The scarcity of women in senior management is a well-documented and universal tendency (Marshall 1984; Burke and Vinnicombe 2005; Davidson and Burke 2004). It suggests that HEIs, despite their meritocratic principles, are not neutral. It replicates the same 'glass ceiling' as does society itself (Bain and Cummings 2000; Leathwood and Read 2009; Jackson and O'Callaghan 2009; Machado-Taylor et al. 2007; Doherty and Manfredi 2006). The metaphor of the glass ceiling is 'generally viewed as a set of impediments and/or barriers to career advancement for women and peoples of colour' (Jackson and O'Callaghan 2009: 460).

The under-representation of women at the higher levels of responsibility in Portugal may also reflect at all levels a 'creeping' gender discrimination in procedures of promotion and recruitment. Unlike other European countries such as Finland, which has a high percentage of women in higher education, no national committees promote gender equality in academia (Husu 2000). Not dissimilar to the conclusions of van der Brink et al. (2006) for the Netherlands, Portugal would appear to show that the opportunity for equal representation of women in academia is undermined by a clear and lasting 'leak in the pipeline' (Schiebinger 1999; Stolte-Heiskanen 1991; van der Brink et al. 2006).

Be that as it may, both women as indeed the academic profession in general are faced with new issues. Portugal has not remained unscathed or unaffected by the 'crisis of the welfare state' on the one hand and by the onset of neoliberal economic doctrines, on the other. Whilst the new political framework may be sustainable, nevertheless, at the same time it generates a new counter-hegemonic tendency inside the academic profession.

Market Tendencies and/or Commercialisation Inside the Academic Profession

The Portuguese strain of neoliberalism in reconfiguring the State took root at the end of the 1990s. As elsewhere (Wrede 2008; Kuhlmann 2006), both its justification and its rationale were deeply critical of welfare professionalism. As Sprida Wrede noted in the Finnish case:

> welfare state professionalism was portrayed as bureaucratic, self-interested, and narrow, as well as obsolete in face of the complex problems of late modern societies. On the other hand, professionalism was discussed in technocratic terms. (Wrede 2008: 29)

Pressured by this normative and ideological onslaught, academics, as the 'organic intellectuals' of welfare professionalism, saw the terms and conditions of their work undergo a well-nigh universal change (Musselin 2004, 2008; Enders 2001). In its most visible form, change entailed terminating the figure of academic as civil servant and its replacement by a status akin to that of service workers (Musselin 2008).

The drive towards neoliberalism in Portugal did not immediately bring forth legal change in the status of the academic profession. Rather, two tactics were brought to bear. The first saw the exploitation of 'gaps' in earlier legislation. The second entailed modifying the financing both in science policy and in higher education (Chap. 8). Yet, the prevailing discourse about science policy certainly shifted both in perspective and in purpose. In doing so, it also introduced a new hegemonic discourse that applied to academic professionalism.

Amongst the 'gaps' the new discourse exploited was the opening earlier legal provision made for contracting individuals outside academia to act as invited lecturers. This device served to put in place a parallel – or even 'virtual' – career structure based on sheer numbers and flexible availability (Santiago and Carvalho 2008) (Chap. 13). By this means, changes to the conditions of appointment were injected. Some academics were engaged part-time. Full-time academics were assigned positions that did not carry permanent status. The birth of a precarious profession, its terms and conditions of employment deteriorating, was easily to be seen in polytechnics (Santiago and Carvalho 2008).

Changes were no less evident in the key areas of knowledge production and dissemination. At the European level, the European Commission opted for higher education and research as the main vehicles for innovation and economic development in the drive towards a knowledge society and a knowledge economy (Chap. 8). Of no less significance, and within the same general setting, a sizeable part of knowledge production began to take on board new exogenous norms, epistemological, social and economic. Such norms had direct operational and organisational consequences of the highest importance for academia and for academic work. Both involved a complex and radical overhaul in modes of knowledge production. This shift in the basic organisation of academic work, reduced to a snappy slogan, is often presented as substituting mode 1 in academic production for various new forms, described as mode 2. In a mode 1 setting, knowledge production takes place within disciplinary communities and is determined therefore by institutional standards and academic values. In this context, knowledge is produced 'for its own sake'. In mode 2, by contrast, knowledge production is closely aligned with problem solving and is developed to be applicable and transferable to business and to the economy. In this second setting, knowledge is perceived as a crucial means for raising levels of economic development (Olssen and Peters 2005; Ziman 1996, 2000; Santiago and Carvalho 2008).

Falling in with the priorities of the European Commission, the Portuguese Government actively took up the human resources perspective on higher education qualifications. States have always backed the acquisition of further qualifications by academics as an inseparable part of the academic career in public universities. From the 1990s, and drawing on financial support from Europe, the Government embarked on the direct financing of *individuals* to improve their qualifications by individual scholarships and grants rather than, as had earlier been the case, by financing *institutions* through the national budget. Thus, from 1994 to 1999, 8,375 scholarships were awarded through one specific programme – PRAXIS XXI. Of these, 3,486 supported studies at the PhD level, a massive increase compared to the years 1990 to 1993 when the corresponding statistic was 1,572 awards (OCES 2003); 851 to undertake research and 728 to engage in technical research (OCES 2006b). Follow-up evaluation of the jobs taken up by scholarship holders revealed that 55% found employment as academics in higher education, 14% were researchers and 12% held postdoctoral scholarships (OCES 2006a). In effect, this strategy did not raise private investment in R&D. Nor did it boost the private sector's employment of highly qualified human resources. Data from 1999 showed that the overwhelming majority – 74.2% – amongst the highly qualified working in R&D were concentrated in higher education or in other state organisations. A mere 12.7% found employment in private sector industry (Chap. 8).

Change in public policy for generating highly qualified human resources created a new professional group inside higher education – researchers. Research staff lay important issues before academia as a profession. Not only do they extend internal segmentation. They introduce a further degree of internal fragmentation for whilst they work in universities and polytechnics, they research but do not have responsibility for teaching – hitherto one of the major items in the organisation of academic work. Furthermore, researchers personify the split between production and dissemination of knowledge. The advent of this new species of academics may well sunder the profession's control over knowledge production and, by the same token, undermine one of the most important pillars in the professionalism of academics (Johnson 1972; Larson 1977; Freidson 2001). The profession of the researcher accentuates the internal fragmentation of the professional. In turn, fragmentation thrusts a new group into the academics' jurisdictional field (Abbott 1988) with all the potential, for the first time, to challenge the definition of their jurisdictional area.

By stimulating demand for postgraduate programmes, the Government created a 'reserve army' with the ability to replace 'traditional' professional academics and thus giving up the traditional support the State granted to academia in the shape of that condition, known in the literature as 'social closure' (Parkin 1979; Murphy 1988).

The onset of the recent economic recession converted the neoliberal doctrine into a new hegemony that changed the legal framework regulating the institutions of higher education (Law 62/2007) and of professionals (Decree-Law 205/2009 and Decree-Law 207/2009). The Juridical Regime of Higher Education Institutions (Law 62/2007) laid out new patterns for governance and management. It stands as a breakpoint from earlier legislation, grounded in collegiality. It brings important changes to the campus: the choice for institutions to opt for a status under public law or as a foundation regulated by private law. The establishment of a General Council, the axing of existing collegial bodies, namely Senates, the injection of external 'stakeholders' having an extended political and strategic power base, assigning an executive responsibility to the University Rector and to the Polytechnic President are clear examples of drive towards radical reform.

By strengthening accountability, together with the participation of external stakeholders, the State gave another professional group access to the hidden garden of academia's jurisdictional area. Thus, for the first time, academic professionals found themselves facing another counter-hegemonic profession – managers. Whether academics are on the point of losing their status of 'organic intellectuals' in society cannot entirely be dismissed.

For some scholars, changes such as these in the higher education world shift the paradigm of the modern university towards becoming a 'market-oriented university' (Buchbinder 1993: 335), or a 'corporatised' university (Currie et al. 2002: 14). Both downplay and downgrade collegiality, and, subsequently, weaken academic professionalism through loss of liberty and close institutional control over research and teaching. However, the long-lasting impact of these changes is as yet unknown. Empirical studies divide between endorsing the thesis of 'de-professionalisation' (Fulton 2003; Askling 2001; Slaughter and Leslie 1997; Reed 2002; Harley et al. 2003) and the glorious resurgence of a new professionalism born up by strategies professions develop to ensure their survival (De Boer 2002; Henkel 2000; Kogan et al. 2000; Carvalho and Santiago 2009; Enders 1999).

In the logic of the latter prospect, Wrede (Wrede 2008) and Henriksson (Henriksson et al. 2006), given the changes in health sector, argue that what is happening amounts to reframing state professionalism so that it is now aligned upon groups held to be technical experts. In short, the profession is not homogeneous, and in keeping with the same logic that shaped the previous moments of historical change, all one may look forward to is the redefinition of the dominant subgroup inside academia. As with other professional groups, medical doctors (Ferlie et al. 1996; Wrede 2008; Henriksson et al. 2006) and nurses, for instance (Carvalho 2009), whose identity is more akin to technocratic expertise, we may see new opportunities emerging, and with them, new 'organic intellectuals' within the group which, once again, may negotiate new normative identities into hegemony.

Conclusion

This chapter has argued that the academic profession is not homogeneous. On the contrary, internal diversity is one of the main determinants in sustaining the process of professionalisation within a group that faced no competition in or over its jurisdictional field.

Following a line of argument inspired by Gramsci (1971), the directions academic profession in Portugal has taken derive from a 'series of unstable equilibriums'. Status, power and autonomy in the academic profession are generated by a series of temporary alignments in a set of social forces, which include Government, stakeholders but also different subgroups of academics. Concentrating on the internal struggles of academics to legitimate a hegemonic normative identity does not deny the influence of external factors, still less of institutions and state power. Rather, such concentration clarifies the internal equilibrium between different forces and how close is the interplay between them. The dominant notion of academic professionalism is always the outcome of political struggle – internal and external.

The trend towards segmentation within the group has been pronounced and sustained. It assumed at least four forms: first, in the shape of the polytechnics; second, with setting up private higher education; third, through feminisation of the academic profession; and finally, in the rise of the group of professional researchers and managers. Inevitably, an increase in internal differences may interfere with the established equilibrium dominant, with different groups contesting their hegemonic identity. Such internal cohesion is, as Filc suggested (Filc 2006), a precondition to be recognised by the society as 'traditional intellectuals', or following Gramsci's line of argument (Gramsci 1971), ideas are transformed into 'organic intellectuals' by the acknowledgement of their expertise by civil society.

At different times, different hegemonic ideologies break surface in the academic profession as the result of internal contradictions and contentions. These struggles are not confined to internal relations. They embrace sociocultural frames as well as the ability of other groups to assert their own agenda within society.

For a very long time indeed, hegemonic ideology identified the academic profession with men. Even when the participation of women in academia became an undeniable reality, dominant notions of masculinity still hung out, concentrating women in 'soft' subject areas and holding them to mid-level careers.

Other professional groups coalesced and attempted to oust academics as 'organic intellectuals'. The counter-hegemonic agenda of managers seems to be successful in projecting themselves as the primary competitive group in the jurisdictional field (Chap. 15). The instrumentalisation of higher education around the social and economic ends of forwarding the knowledge society and the knowledge economy, in its Foucaultian interpretation, divides the academy into a plethora of experts, a condition which accentuates the academic profession's internal fragmentations still further. Academics as experts are assigned new responsibilities in relation to external demands. Thus, their own criteria of professionalism – truth and competence – yield before external criteria defined by the choices by stakeholders and 'consumers' (Rose 1996).

This sociological and historical analysis of the academic profession in Portugal shows that the shaping of the professional group's cognitive and normative framework cannot today be explained in terms of a simplistic relation between profession and State. Rather, constructing the profession is a political process in which professionals, along with other and different actors and agents, all have an important part to play.

Notes

1. Even if we agree with this definition, in this chapter we abide by the notion of profession. It seems to us that 'profession' is a more dynamic concept. It is more accommodating to the different steps and different strategies an occupational group takes to define or sustain its position in the professional field.

2. With more standing than those exercising top management responsibilities in private firms.
3. Some of them were effectively engaged in political activities against the regime.
4. In 1911 for the first time, a woman – Carolina Michaëlis de Vasconcelos – was authorised to teach an academic subject at professorial level (*cátedra universitária*) (Silva and Vicente 1991).

References

Abbott, A. (1988). *The system of professions. An essay on the division of expert labour.* London: The University of Chicago Press.
Altbach, P. (Ed.). (2000). *The changing academic workplace: Comparative perspectives.* Boston: Centre for International Higher Education.
Altbach, P., Reisberg, L., & Rumbley, L. (2009). *Trends in global higher education: Tracking an academic revolution: A report.* UNESCO 2009 World Conference on Higher Education. Paris: UNESCO.
Amâncio, L., & Ávila, P. (1995). O género na ciência. In J. Jesuino (Ed.), *A Comunidade Científica Portuguesa nos Finais do Séc* (XIX, pp. 47–71). Oeiras: Celta Editora.
Amaral, A. (2003). Consolidation of higher education's legislation. In A. Barblan (Ed.), *Academic freedom and university institutional responsibility in Portugal* (pp. 17–34). Bologna: Bononia University Press.
Amaral, A., & Carvalho, T. (2003). Autonomy and change in Portuguese higher education. In A. Barblan (Ed.), *Academic freedom and university institutional responsibility in Portugal* (pp. 35–46). Bologna: Bononia University Press.
Amaral, A., & Magalhães, A. (2007). Market competition, public good and state interference. In J. Enders & B. Jongbloed (Eds.), *Public-private dynamics in higher education. Expectations, developments and outcomes* (pp. 89–110). Bielefeld: Transcript Verlag.
Amaral, A., & Teixeira, P. (2000). The rise and fall of the private sector in Portuguese higher education. *Higher Education Policy, 13*(3), 245–266.
Amaral, A., Magalhães, A., & Santiago, R. (2003). The rise of academic managerialism in Portugal. In A. Amaral, V. L. Meek, & M. I. Larsen (Eds.), *The higher education managerial revolution?* Dordrecht: Kluwer Academic Publishers.
Araújo, H. (1990). As mulheres professoras e o ensino estatal. *Revista Crítica de Ciências Sociais, 29*, 81–103.
Araújo, H. (1991). As professoras primárias na viragem do século: Uma contribuição para a história da sua emergência no Estado. *Organizações & Trabalho, 5*(6), 127–146.
Askling, B. (2001). Higher education and academic staff in a period of policy and system change. *Higher Education, 41*, 157–181.
Bagilhole, B. (2000). Too little too late? An assessment of national initiatives for women academics in the British university system. *Higher Education in Europe., 23*(2), 139–145.
Bailyn, L. (2003). Academic careers and gender equity: Lessons learned from MIT. *Gender Work and Organisation., 10*(2), 137–153.
Bain, O., & Cummings, W. (2000). Academe's glass ceiling: Societal, professional-organizational and institutional barriers to the career advancement of academic women. *Comparative Education Review, 44*(4), 493–514.
Becher, T., & Trowler, P. (2001). *Academic tribes and territories. Intellectual enquiry and the culture of disciplines* (2nd ed.). Buckingham: Open University Press.
Bell, D. (1976). *Vers La Société post-industrielle.* Paris: Laffont.
Benschop, Y., & Brows, M. (2003). Crumbling ivory tower: Academic organizing and its gender effects. *Gender Work and Organisation., 10*(2), 194–212.
Bourdieu, P. (1996). *Homo Academicus.* Cambridge: Polity Press.
Buchbinder, H. (1993). The market oriented university and the changing role of knowledge. *Higher Education, 26*, 331–347.

Burke, R., & Vinnicombe, S. (2005). Advancing women's careers. *Career Development International, 10*(3), 165–167.

Carvalho, T. (2009). *Nova Gestão Pública e Reformas da Saúde. O profissionalismo numa encruzilhada.* Lisboa: Edições Sílabo.

Carvalho, T., & Santiago, R. (2008). Gender differences on research: Perceptions and use of academic time. *Tertiary Education and Management, 14*(4), 317–330.

Carvalho, T., & Santiago, R. (2009). Gender as a 'strategic action': New public management and the professionalisation of nursing in Portugal. *Equal Opportunities International, 28*(7), 609–622.

Carvalho, T., & Santiago, R. (2010a). New public management and 'middle-management': How do deans influence institutional policies? In L. Meek, L. Goedegebuure, R. Santiago, & T. Carvalho (Eds.), *The changing dynamics of higher education middle management.* Heidelberg/London: Springer.

Carvalho, T., & Santiago, R. (2010b). New challenges for women seeking an academic career: The hiring process in Portuguese higher education institutions. *Journal of Higher Education Policy and Management, 32*(3), 239–249.

Clark, B. (1977). *Academic power in Italy: Bureaucracy and oligarchy in a national university system.* Chicago: University of Chicago Press.

Clark, B. (1983). *The higher education system: Academic organization in cross-national perspective.* Berkeley/Los Angeles/London: University of California Press.

Clark, B. (1987). Introduction. In B. Clark (Ed.), *The academic profession. National, disciplinary & institutional settings.* Berkeley/Los Angeles/London: University of California Press.

Cohen, M., March, J., & Olsen, J. (1972). A garbage can model of organisational choice. *Administrative Science Quarterly, 17*(1), 1–25.

Currie, J., Thiele, B., & Harris, P. (2002). *Gendered universities in globalised economies. Power, career and sacrifices.* Oxford: Lexington Books.

Davidson, M., & Burke, R. (2004). Women in management worldwide: Facts, figures and analysis – An overview. In D. Marilyn & B. Ronald (Eds.), *Women in management worldwide: Facts, figures and analysis – An overview* (pp. 1–18). Aldershot: Ashgate Publishing Limited.

Davies, C. (1996). The sociology of professions and the profession of gender. *Sociology, 30*(4), 661–678.

De Boer, H. (2002). Trust, the essence of governance? In A. Amaral, G. Jones, & B. Karseth (Eds.), *Governing higher education: National perspectives on institutional governance* (pp. 43–62). Dordrecht: Kluwer Academic Publishers.

Deem, R. (1998). New managerialism' and higher education: the management of performances and cultures in universities in the United Kingdom. *International Studies in Sociology of Education, 8*(1), 47–70.

Derber, C. (1983). Ideological proletianization and post-industrial labour. *Theory and Society, 12*, 281–308.

Doherty, L., & Manfredi, S. (2006). Women's progression to senior positions in English Universities. *Employee Relations, 28*(6), 553–572.

Dubar, C. (2003). Sociologie des groupes professionnels en France: Un bilan prospectif. In P. M. Menger (Ed.), *Les Professions et leurs Sociologues* (pp. 51–59). Paris: Éditions de la Maison des Sciences de l'Homme.

Dubar, C., & Tripier, P. (1998). *Sociologie des Professions.* Paris: Armand Colin.

Enders, J. (1999). Crisis? What crisis? The academic profession in 'knowledge' society. *Higher Education, 38*(1), 71–81.

Enders, J. (2001). Between state control and academic capitalism: A comparative perspective on academic staff in Europe. In J. Enders (Ed.), *Academic staff in Europe: Changing contexts and conditions.* Westport: CT Greenwood Press.

Escobar, L. (2004). *O sexo das profissões. Género e identidade socioprofissional em enfermagem.* Porto: Edições Afrontamento.

EU European Commission. (2006). *She figures 2006. Women and science: Statistics and indicators.* Brussels: European Commission.

EU European Commission. (2009). *She figures. Statistics and indicators on gender equality in science*. Brussels: European Commission.
Evetts, J. (2002). New directions in state and international professional occupations: Discretionary decision-making and acquired regulation. *Work Employment and Society, 16*(2), 341–353.
Evetts, J. (2003). The sociological analysis of professionalism. *International Sociology, 18*(2), 395–415.
Ferlie, E., Ashburner, L., Fitzgerald, L., & Pettigrew, A. (1996). *The new public management in action*. Oxford: OUP.
Filc, D. (2006). Physicians as 'organic intelectuals'. A contribution to the stratification versus deprofessionalization debate. *Acta Sociologica, 49*(3), 273–285.
Foucault, M. (1991a). Politics and the study of discourse. In G. Burchel, C. Gordon, & P. Miller (Eds.), *The Foucault effect, studies in governmentality* (pp. 53–72). Chicago: University of Chicago Press.
Foucault, M. (1991b). Governmentality. In G. Burchel, C. Gordon, & P. Miller (Eds.), *The Foucault effect, studies in governmentality* (pp. 87–104). Chicago: University of Chicago Press.
Foucault, M. (2004). *Vigiar E Punir* (29th ed.). Petrópolis: Editora Vozes.
Foucault, M. (2006). *Vigiar E Punir*. Petrópolis: Editora Vozes.
Freidson, E. (1977). The futures of professionalisation. In M. Stacey, M. Reid, C. Heath, & R. Dingwall (Eds.), *Health and the division of labour* (pp. 14–38). London: Croom Helm.
Freidson, E. (1978). *La Profesión Médica*. Barcelona: Ediciones Península.
Freidson, E. (1986). *Professional powers*. Chicago: The University Of Chicago Press.
Freidson, E. (2001). *Professionalism. The third logic*. Chicago: The University Of Chicago Press.
Fulton, O. (2003). Managerialism in UK universities: unstable hybridity and the complications of implementation. In A. Amaral, V. L. Meek, & I. M. Larsen (Eds.), *The higher education managerial revolution?* (pp. 205–229). Dordrecht: Kluwer Academic Publishers.
Gallagher, T. (1981). Os oitenta e sete ministros do Estado Novo de Salazar. *História, 28*, 7.
GPEARI. (2004). *Recusa De Provimento Definitivo – Carreira Docente Do Ensino Universitário E Politécnico – 1988–1989 A 2003–2004*. Lisbon: MSTHE.
Gramsci, A. (1971). *Selections from the prison notebooks*. London: Lawrence and Wishart.
Gramsci, A. (2000). Cadernos do Cárcere. In C. N. Coutinho, L. S. Henriques, & M. A. Nogueira (Eds.), *Vol. 3: Maquiavel. Notas sobre o Estado e a política; edição e tradução*. Rio de Janeiro: Civilização Brasileira.
Hall, R. (1975). *Occupations and the social structure*. Princeton: Prentice-Hall.
Harley, S., Muller-Camen, M., & Collin, A. (2003). From academic communities to managed organisations: The implications for academic careers in UK and German universities. *Journal of Vocational Behavior, 64*(2), 329–345.
Henkel, M. (2000). *Academic identities and policy change in higher education*. London: Jessica Kingsley Publishers.
Henriksson, L., Wrede, S., & Burau, V. (2006). Understanding professional projects in welfare service work: Revival of old professionalism? *Gender Work and Organization, 13*(2), 174–192.
Hughes, E. (1958). *Men and their work*. Westport: Greenwood.
Hughes, E. (1963). Professions. *Daedalus, 92*(4), 655–668.
Husu, L. (2000). Gender discrimination in the promised land of gender equality. *Higher Education in Europe., 25*(2), 221–228.
Jackson, J., & O'Callaghan, M. (2009). What do we known about glass ceiling effects? A taxonomy and critical review to inform higher education research. *Research in Higher Education, 50*(5), 460–482.
Johnson, T. (1972). *Professions and power*. London: Macmillan.
Jones, S. (2006). *António Gramsci*. London: Routledge.
Knights, D., & Richards, W. (2003). Sex discrimination in UK academia. *Gender Work and Organisation., 10*(2), 213–237.
Kogan, M., Bauer, M., Bleiklie, I., & Henkel, M. (2000). *Transforming higher education: A comparative study*. London: Jessica Kingsley.

Kuhlmann, E. (2006). *Modernising health care. Reinventing professions, the state and the public*. Bristol: The Policy Press.

Larson, M. (1977). *The rise of professionalism: A sociological analysis*. Berkeley/Los Angeles/London: University of California Press.

Leathwood, C., & Read, B. (2009). *Gender and the changing face of higher education. A feminised future?* Milton Keynes: Society for Research into Higher Education.

Lima, L. (2002). O Paradigma da Educação Contábil: Políticas Educativas e Perspectivas Gerencialistas no Ensino Superior. In L. C. Lima & A. J. Afonso (Eds.), *Reformas Da Educação Pública, Democratização, Modernização, Neoliberalismo* (pp. 91–110). Porto: Edições Afrontamento.

Machado-Taylor, M. Ozkanli, O. White, K., & Bagilhole, B. (2007). Breaking the barriers to women achieving seniority in universities. Paper presented to EAIR forum, Innsbruck.

Magalhães, A. (2004). *A Identidade Do Ensino Superior: Política, Conhecimento E Educação Numa Época De Transição*. Lisboa: Fundação Calouste Gulbenkian/Fundação Para A Ciência E Tecnologia.

Magalhães, A., & Amaral, A. (2007). Changing values and norms in the concept of governance in Portuguese higher education. *Higher Education Policy, 20*, 315–338.

Makler, H. (1968). *The Portuguese industrial elite*. Lisboa: Fundação Calouste Gulbenkian.

Marques, O. (1981). *História De Portugal* (Vol. III). Lisboa: Palas Editores.

Marshall, J. (1984). *Women managers: Travellers in a male world*. Chichester: Wiley.

Meira Soares, V. (2001). The academic profession in a massifying system: The Portuguese case. In J. Enders (Ed.), *Academic staff in Europe changing contexts and conditions*. Westport: Greenwood Press.

Metcalfe, A., & Slaughter, S. (2011). Academic capitalism. In B. Banks (Ed.), *Gender and higher education* (pp. 13–20). Baltimore: The Johns Hopkins University Press.

Moscati, R. (2002). Italy: A hard implementation of a comprehensive reform. *International Higher Education, 26*, 3–4.

MTSS. (2009). Statistics indicators of women and men in labour market. Retrieved from http://www.mtss.gov.pt/.

Murphy, R. (1988). *Social closure. The theory of monopolisation and exclusion*. Oxford: OUP.

Musselin, C. (2004). Towards a European labour market? Some lessons drawn from empirical studies on academic mobility. *Higher Education, 48*(1), 55–78.

Musselin, C. (2008). Towards a sociology of academic work. In A. Amaral, C. Musselin, & I. Bleikie (Eds.), *From governance to identity. A festschrift for Mary Henkel* (pp. 47–56). Dordrecht: Springer.

Neave, G., & Rhoades, G. (1987). The academic estate in Western Europe. In B. Clark (Ed.), *The academic profession: National, disciplinary, and institutional settings* (pp. 211–270). Berkeley/Los Angeles/London. University of California Press.

Neave, G., & van Vught, F. (1994). *Changing relationship between Government and higher education in Western Europe*. Oxford: Pergamon Press.

Nogueira, C., Constança, P., & Amâncio, L. (1995). Women in management in Portugal. A demographic overview. *Gender, Management and Science* (pp. 207–218). University of Minho: Braga.

O'Connor, P. (2009). Are universities really male dominated? Limits and possibilities for change. Paper presented at International Women's Day conference University of Limerick, 3rd March 2009.

OCES. (2003). *Programa De Formação Avançada Recursos Humanos Em C&T (1990–1993)*. Lisboa: MSTHE.

OCES. (2004). *O Sistema De Ensino Superior Em Portugal: 1993–2003*. Lisboa: MCIES.

OCES. (2005). *Evolução Da Qualificação Do Pessoal Docente No Ensino Superior Universitário Público: 1993–2004*. Lisboa: MCTES.

OCES. (2006a). *A Situação Profissional Dos Ex-Bolseiros de Doutoramento*. Lisboa: MSTHE.

OCES. (2006b). *Programas De Formação Avançada de Recursos Humanos Em C&T (2000–2004)*. Lisboa: MSTHE.

OECD. (2006). *Women in scientific careers: Understanding the potential*. Paris: OECD.

Olssen, M., & Peters, M. (2005). Neo-liberalism, higher education and the knowledge economy: From the free market to knowledge capitalism. *Journal of Educational Policy, 20*(3), 313–345.
Oppenheimer, M. (1973). The proletarianisation of the professional. *Sociological Review Monographs, 20*, 213–227.
Parkin, F. (1979). *Marxism and class theory*. London: Tavistock Publications.
Parsons, T. (1958). The professions and social structure, In *Essays in sociological theory* (pp. 3450). Glencoe: The Free Press, (1ª Edição De 1939).
Parsons, T. (1972). Professions. In *International encyclopedia of the social sciences* (Vol. 12, pp. 536–546). London: Macmillan Company.
Perkin, H. (1987). Academic profession in the United Kingdom. In B. Clark (Ed.), *The academic profession* (pp. 13–59). Berkeley/Los Angeles/London: The University of California Press.
Perkin, H. (1990). *The rise of professional society*. London: Routledge.
Pinto, A. (2000). O Império do professor: Salazar e a elite ministerial do estado Novo (1933–1945). *Análise Social, XXXXV*(157), 1–22.
Pinto, J. (2004). Formação, Tendências recentes e perspectivas de desenvolvimento da sociologia em Portugal. *Sociologia Problemas e Práticas, 46*, 11–31.
Reed, M. (2002). New managerialism, professional power and organisational governance in UK universities: A review and assessment. In A. Amaral, G. Jones, & B. Karseth (Eds.), *Governing higher education: National perspectives on institutional governance* (pp. 163–185). Dordrecht: Kluwer Academic Publishers.
Rees, T. (2001). Mainstreaming gender equality in science in the European union: The ETAN report. *Gender and Education, 13*(3), 243–260.
Rose, N. (1996). Governing "advanced" liberal democracies. In A. Barry, T. Osborne, & N. Rose (Eds.), *Foucault and political reasonal liberalism, neo-liberalism and rationalities of government* (pp. 37–64). Chicago: The University Of Chicago Press.
Sagaria, M., & Agans, L. (2006). Gender equality in U.S. higher education: International framing and institutional realities. In K. Yokoyama (Ed.), *Gender and higher education: Australia, Japan, the UK and USA* (pp. 47–68). Hiroshima: Higher Education Institute Press.
Santiago, R., & Carvalho, T. (2004). Effects of managerialism on the perceptions of higher education in Portugal. *Higher Education Policy, 17*(4), 427–444.
Santiago, R., & Carvalho, T. (2008). Academics in a new work environment: The impact of new public management on work conditions. *Higher Education Quarterly, 62*(3), 204–223.
Santiago, R., Magalhães, A., & Carvalho, T. (2005). *O Surgimento Do Managerialismo No Sistema Do Ensino Superior Português*. Matosinhos: Cipes.
Santiago, R., Carvalho, T., Amaral, A., & Meek, V. L. (2006). Changing patterns in the middle management of higher education institutions: The case of Portugal. *Higher Education, 52*(2), 215–250.
Santos, B. (1993). O Estado, as relações salariais e o bem-estar social na semiperiferia: O caso português. In B. Santos (Ed.), *Portugal: Um retrato singular* (pp. 16–56). Porto: Afrontamento.
Schiebinger, L. (1999). *Has feminism changed science?* Cambridge: Harvard University Press.
Silva, M., & Vicente, A. (1991). *Mulheres portuguesas: vidas e obras celebradas, vidas e obras ignoradas*. Lisboa: Comissão para a Igualdade de Direitos das Mulheres (CIDM).
Simões, J., & Lourenço, O. (1999). As políticas públicas de saúde em Portugal nos últimos 25 anos. In P. P. Barros & J. Simões (Eds.), *Homenagem a Augusto Mantas* (pp. 99–134). Lisboa: APES.
Slaughter, S., & Leslie, L. (1997). *Academic capitalism: Politics, policies, and the entrepreneurial university*. Bristol: The Policy Press.
Stolte-Heiskanen, V. (1991). *Women in science: Token Women or gender equality?* Oxford: Berg Publishers.
Stromquist, N., Gil-Antón, M., Balbachevsky, E., Mabokela, R., Smolentseva, A., & Colatrella, C. (2007). The academic profession in the globalisation age: Key trends, challenges, and possibilities. In P. Altbach & P. Peterson (Eds.), *Higher education in the new century. Global challenges and innovative ideas*. Boston: Center for International Higher Education: Boston College.

Tavares, J. (1999). Formação do professor universitário em Portugal. *Revista Interuniversitária de Formación del Profesorado, 34*, 209–218.

Taylor, J., Ferreira, J., Machado, M., & Santiago, R. (Eds.). (2008). *Non-university higher education in Europe* (Vol. XV, 23, 260 pp). Dordrecht: Springer.

Van der Brink, M., Browns, M., & Waslander, S. (2006). Does excellence have a gender? A national research study on recruitment and selection procedures for professoriat appointments in The Netherlands. *Employee Relations, 28*(6), 523–539.

van Vught, F. (1997). The effects of alternative governance structures. In B. Steunenberg & F. van Vught (Eds.), *Political institutions and public policy* (pp. 115–137). Dordrecht: Kluwer.

World Economic Forum. (2009). *Global gender gap report*. Geneva.

Wrede, S. (2008). Unpacking gendered professional power in the welfare state. *Equal Opportunities International, 27*(1), 19–33.

Ziman, J. (1996). 'Post-academic science': Constructing knowledge with networks and norms. *Science Studies, 9*(1), 67–80.

Ziman, J. (2000). *Real science: What it is and it means*. Cambridge: Cambridge University Press.

Chapter 15
The Rise of the Administrative Estate in Portuguese Higher Education

Maria de Lourdes Machado and Luisa Cerdeira

Introduction

This chapter sets out to undertake a differentiated and analytical view of the development of the 'Administrative Estate' in Portugal's higher education institutions (HEIs) over the years from 1974 to the present. It traces the rise in both number and diversity of universities and polytechnics (Chap. 6); the implementation of policies (Chaps. 7 and 9); the growth in student numbers (Chap. 16); the press for accountability, efficiency, effectiveness and, finally the impact Europeanisation had upon the 'Administrative Estate' during these years (Chap. 11).

Higher education in Portugal changed significantly over the past three and a half decades. Numbers and types of institutions increased. The 1970s saw four public universities and the Catholic University. The 1980s ushered in significant expansion to public higher education, the creation of polytechnics and the emergence of the private sector (Chap. 13). Institutional patterns across public universities and public polytechnics varied as they did in private institutions. Public universities enjoyed a greater degree of institutional autonomy than public polytechnics and private institutions – universities and polytechnics alike (Machado et al. 2008). Whilst there are functional differences between universities and non-university institutions, public and private, there are also similarities. Thus, the weight and focus on administrative issues varied in keeping with the specific profile and status of one higher education institution compared to another.

M. de Lourdes Machado (✉)
CIPES, Rua Primeiro de Dezembro 399, 4450-227 Matosinhos, Portugal
e-mail: lmachado@cipes.up.pt

L. Cerdeira
Rectorate, University of Lisbon, Alameda da Universidade, 1600 Lisbon, Portugal
e-mail: lcerdeira@reitoria.ul.pt

Massification of higher education, the need to cater for larger numbers of students and therefore the growth in the functions higher education establishments were called upon to assume, all contributed to the growth in the structures of administration. Furthermore, the demand for greater accountability by higher education to the public conferred a correspondingly greater responsibility and centrality upon administration in the husbandry and business of higher education (Altbach 1999, 2008). Some researchers of higher education – Magalhães et al. (2005) and Neave (1997), for instance – argued that administrators today are not only under press from accountability but also from the rise of new managerialism. Whilst this may well be so, there are others who, in Portugal, asserted that: '(…) if managerialism exists, it is present at a rhetorical level' (Amaral et al. 2003: 150) (Chaps. 9 and 12).

One of the features that the American comparative educationist Philip Altbach (1999) equated with the drive towards mass higher education was, in universities, the managerialisation of the 'Administrative Estate', a feature compounded by the dynamic the 'Administrative Estate' itself took on board in order to discharge the basic functions a more complex environment demands.

Others upheld the view that in universities and polytechnics, the phenomenon of bureaucratisation, whilst very certainly a response to a more demanding interpretation of accountability, was nevertheless achieved at the price of weakening the bounds of autonomy (Altbach 1999; Kogan 1999). Added to this, the bureaucratisation of higher education institutions gave rise to an administration more assertive, more pro-active and, for those reasons, more central in determining the fate or fortune of the individual university or polytechnic (Bleiklie 1998).

As institutions took on the formal trappings of bureaucratisation, so the power of Faculty diminished. Indeed, the power of academic staff was being worn down in proportion to the rise of an administrative class, just as it was eroded by increased demands that bore down on academe itself to be seen to be more accountable (Altbach 1998, 1999; Henkel 2000). Similar trends are present in Portugal, and academia there too holds that growing bureaucratisation has brought about a loss of influence (Machado 2005; Taylor et al. 2007a, b).

In present-day Portuguese universities and polytechnics, a new balance of power is emerging. The administrator's role is itself under re-definition, just as the demand for management expertise is also growing (Correia et al. 2000; Machado 2005; Taylor et al. 2008) to such an extent that some public HEIs have recruited senior administrators from the business sector.[1]

Within HEIs, administrators have become a new and powerful 'Estate' and a body central to their operation (Altbach 1999, 2008). However, its present condition in Portugal suggests that administration has not yet attained the status of a profession, along lines similar elsewhere, for example in Finland and the United States (Hölttä 2008). Higher education administration is not as yet a career (Correia et al. 2000). Once their moment of glory is past, Rectors or Vice-Rectors in universities, alternatively, Presidents and Vice-Presidents in polytechnics – and Deans in both – finish their mandate, typically they go back whence they came – namely back to their faculty of origin.

As functions expand and diversify, so the numbers of those servicing and engaged in them also multiply. Thus, one of the 'growth sectors' in higher education establishments is to be seen in administrative staff (MSTHE 2006). Analyses were undertaken in order to ascertain the growth rate of administrative staff compared to its equivalent in the numbers of students and of academic staff (Neave 1997).

Altbach (Altbach 1999, 2008) set out a number of perspectives from which the rise of the 'Administrative Estate' could be examined. One of these turned around what he termed the 'dual administrative structure', that is, on the one hand, senior administrators who exercise responsibility within the purely administrative dimension to an establishment's affairs, and on the other, the administrative structure that embraces administrative staff as a whole. 'Senior administrators' have management responsibility but not an academic contract. Their duties range over financing, human resources and estates, student services (enrolments) and student affairs (Whitchurch 2008b, 2009).[2] Administrative staff are all those located in these functional areas in university central administration as well as individual administrators in faculties, schools and departments, who carry out administrative duties involving procedural tasks.

That said, we will address the following issues: What was the developmental 'trajectory' of the 'Administrative Estate' across the four phases that together spanned the three and a half decades of the years of revolution, the period of normalisation, the drive to massification and the period of consolidation? How did the implementation of national policies (Amaral and Magalhães 2005) impinge on the development of the 'Administrative Estate'? In what way was the 'Administrative Estate' shaped by Europeanisation? And, finally, what was then and what is today the reach of power wielded by the 'Administrative Estate'? (Neave 2002) As academic institutions become larger and more complex, the traditional forms of academic governance come under increasing pressure (Chaps. 9 and 12). As sheer demands for accountability increased, as did regular demands for information, and as public expectations of higher education proliferated, so did the growth in, and the basic tasks to be taken on by, an 'Administrative Estate' assume greater complexity and thus formal organisation and rationalisation. Expansion in, and the significant increase of, the weight accruing to the 'Administrative Estate' are the leitmotifs in this saga.

Looking Back to 1974

Growth and Expansion of the Administrative Estate: The Aftermath of the 1974 Revolution

The drive onwards to mass higher education and lifelong learning, the growth of higher education institutions as well as the number of students enrolled since the 1980s (Chaps. 6 and 13), stand as both an achievement and a challenge. Workloads in HEIs have risen as higher education took on new and more complex functions. To deal with this situation, HEIs hired personnel with special skills to develop international relations, informatics and university-business networking. Functions such as materials and facilities planning, human resources hiring and contracting, previously under the supervision of the central services of the Ministry, today come under the direct control of the individual university or polytechnic.[3]

Moreover, there is a changing understanding of the function of higher education institutions (Paradeise et al. 2009) and 'multiple agendas in complex environments' (Gordon and Whitchurch 2007: 136).[4] As functions and formal responsibilities expand and diversify, universities and polytechnics add more administrative staff to deal with a volatile environment, increasing number of students and adding to the range activities Administration must cover,[5] a general trend noted by such specialists as Altbach (Altbach 1999; Fägerlind and Strömqvist 2004; Gordon and Whitchurch 2007). More – and different – expertise is required as Neave pointed out more than a decade ago:

> Society is demanding more of the university, asking it to render – in more precise and assuredly more complex ways – accounts of how it has done with what society has given it. And this trend, as constituencies multiply (as multiply they have done and will continue to do), will demand more expertise to respond to such demands. (…)
>
> If higher education is to be accountable in ways that require the gathering of complex information, it requires either a shift in expertise – an administrative version of recycling – an increase in the personnel to carry out these seemingly vital functions, or it will demand academics spending less time teaching and researching and more time project-hunting, services-selling or sub-contracting on a short-term basis to firms and industry. (Neave 1997: 80)

New challenges on higher education, in particular its place in the cycle of innovation, in stimulating economic growth, in raising levels of qualification to meet the demands of a post-modern labour market, in the strengthening of managerial control (Chap. 12), all drove towards an increase in the number of staff (Altbach 1999; Hazelkorn 2005). In addition, reforms in higher education institutions have also bolstered 'the Administrative Estate' (Lane 1987). In the Portuguese major reform – the University Autonomy Act (Law 108/88), its polytechnics counterpart (Law 54/90) and in 2007, the *RJIES* – the Juridical Regime of Higher Education Institutions – (Law 62/2007) – which laid down the organisational principles for higher education, for autonomy and for institutional accountability, worked to similar effect (see Fig. 15.1).

One of the growing sectors in HEIs, apart from academic staff, is non-academic staff. The growth in the 'Administrative Estate' in Portuguese higher education since the April 1974 Revolution has been significant. In the 1970s, administrative staff was small in number and mostly confined to routine tasks. No data is available on non-academic personnel in Portuguese HEIS prior to 1987, however, and after that date only for the public sector.[6] In effect, collecting data on this category of personnel in higher education was not considered relevant. Furthermore, contemporary sources were equally unrevealing as to statistics or, for that matter, any reference to non-academic staff, though precisely why so little attention was paid to the 'Administrative Estate' may be the subject of scholarly surmise.

15 The Rise of the Administrative Estate in Portuguese Higher Education

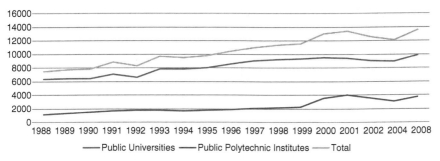

Fig. 15.1 Staff in public universities and public polytechnics, evolution 1988–2008 (Source: Created by the authors based on data from Direcção Geral do Ensino Superior and GPEARI)

Despite the absence of comprehensive data for all sectors of higher education and across the full four decades to plot the rise of the 'Administrative Estate' to a position of strategic centrality in Portugal, the dynamic that drove it along this path is clear. Altbach's account of the components of this dynamic in the North American setting was not greatly different from Neave's examination of it in Western European systems of higher education.

> The new functions are usually too complex for faculty members to handle on a part-time and non-expert basis. They require full-time attention and specialised expertise in accountancy, law, management, health services, statistics, and the many other fields required by the contemporary university. The demands for accountability, have also added to the number of administrators to generate the statistics, reports, financial documentation and other data for government authorities, trustees, and accrediting bodies. (Altbach 1999: 118)

For his part, Swedish political scientist Jan-Erik Lane examined the impact of increasing administrative professionalisation on academia:

> The extensive higher education reforms resulted in a growth of the administrative estate, as various reforms attempted to regulate each and every aspect of academic life. ... An elaborate decision-making systems and schemes of participation were introduced in order to abolish full professorial power and inherited academic excellence. The outcome was an expansion of administrative functions at the expense of professionalism. (Lane 1987: 259)

The rise in recent decades of the 'Administrative Estate' in Portuguese HEIs was marked and particularly so when set against growth of administration in the public sector. In effect, between 1988 and 2008, the Administrative Estate in higher education grew faster than the national civil service itself. Between 1979 and 2005, the number of civil servants in state employ doubled (see Table A.1 in Annexe). Whilst there is no available data covering exactly the same period for higher education institutions, administrative staff in public universities between 1988 and 2008 rose by 2.6 times and in polytechnics for the same period, more than tripled, as Fig. 15.1 shows.

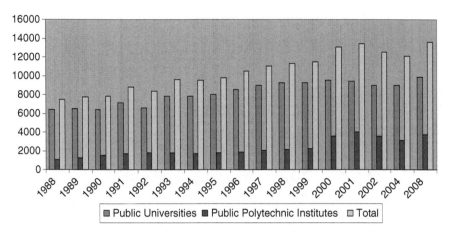

Fig. 15.2 Evolution of the administrative estate by institutional type (Source: Created by the authors based on data from Direcção Geral do Ensino Superior and GPEARI)

Furthermore, in addition to the numbers of State civil servants shown in Fig. 15.1, hiring policy changed and brought in numbers of employees on temporary contract. Despite being a widespread practice extending across all types of public sector higher education, this trend remains bereft of statistical information.

Between 1988 and 2008, the Administrative Estate grew in both universities and polytechnics, to reach a peak in 2001, falling the year after in 2002 and resuming an upwards path in 2008. Clearly, mass higher education not only boosted the development of academic careers across Western Europe (Neave 1983). In Portuguese higher education, it also swelled the ranks of non-academic staff.

Were there any differences in the timing of the Administrative Estate's ascent? Figure 15.2 plots out the total size of the Administrative Estate, controlling for type of institution, whether public university or public sector polytechnic. As was pointed out earlier, the years which saw the Administrative Estate at its most numerous – 2001 and 2008 – also show a slight de-synchronisation in the fortunes of the Administrative Estate depending on whether it had its being in university or polytechnic. For in effect, its continuing growth over the two years 2000 and 2001 was due largely to the rise in the ranks of polytechnic administrators. From 2000, the Administrative Estate in universities appears to decline, whereas in polytechnics, growth went on another year.

Paradoxically, as the numbers of non-academic staff rose, so administrative duties and responsibilities filtered across and were assigned to academic staff (Taylor et al. 2007a, b). The penetration of 'routine administration', the demand for statistics, reports and other information of an evaluative nature was perceived by the Academic Estate as an additional burden and as such a very real form not of rationalisation so much as extending the boundaries of bureaucracy. Thus, the rise of the Administrative Estate from the standpoint of that other constituent order in higher education – the

Academic Estate – was seen as having two faces like Janus, the Roman god of gates and doorways: on the one hand, the growth in the ranks and number of non-academic staff, and on the other, the growing weight of proceduralism and formal process that rapidly replaced an academic community once conceived as functioning 'organically'. Bureaucratisation possessed both features (Altbach 1999; Lane 1987). This growing 'bureaucratisation' of academia led to a loss of influence by academics (Bleiklie 1998; Fägerlind and Strömqvist 2004).

This scenario is consistent with Bleiklie and Kogan's research, which highlighted a tendency in European universities to create *powerful managerial infrastructures* around the academics and therefore a diminished participation by the latter in the decision-making process (Magalhães and Santiago 2011).[7]

In Lane's view, bureaucratisation altered fundamentally the dynamic within higher education. 'Administration in the higher education system is to be a support for the basic functions of academia, teaching and research, but the process of bureaucratisation involves a risk that means and ends are reversed' (Lane 1987: 260). Succinctly stated, the process of bureaucratisation sees the functions of teaching and learning as the means for upholding administrative goals and ends.

Looking to the growth and expansion of the Portuguese 'Administrative Estate', Lane's (1987) observations of the Swedish higher education and the risk of bureaucratisation are applicable to the Portuguese higher education. In recent years, the redrawing of institutional autonomy for universities (Law 108/88) and polytechnics (54/90), changes to the Basic Law for the Funding of Higher Education (Law 9/2005), the framework of quality evaluation (Law 38/2007), the legal framework for higher education system and institutions placed a substantial weight upon the administrative and managerial structures of HEIs.[8]

Key Issues for of the 'Administrative Estate'

Terms of Contract

Most non-academic staff in university and polytechnic, with a few exceptions, are State civil servants.[9] This formal status pertains in many European countries (Maassen 2006).[10] As public servants, their salaries and career advancement were – and still are – set out in national legislation and underpinned by national pay scales.

Managing non-academic staff is not dissimilar to managing the Academic Estate, despite different career paths (Taylor et al. 2007a, b). Oversight is highly centralised and vested in the Ministry of Science, Technology and Higher Education, with the Ministry of Finance controlling the number of posts (Santiago et. al. 2008). This situation is changing, however. The Juridical Regime of Higher Education Institutions of 2007 (Chap. 7) opened the option for universities to change their status and become foundation universities, governed under private rather than administrative law. Amongst the responsibilities transferred directly to the individual university are the raising of at least half its annual budget from non-public sources and, more important from the standpoint of the formal conditions of pay and service, makes the university responsible for the management of human resources.

Though to date, only three out of Portugal's 13 public universities have chosen foundation status, it is an option that in all sobriety cannot be seen as anything less than a radical re-alignment of the formal status the Administrative Estate has enjoyed hitherto. Certainly, administrative staff, already in place, retain their civil servant status. This most certainly is not the case for new appointees. The individual foundation university now has the power to set its own salary scales and to replace permanent contracts of employment with fixed-term agreements. It remains to be seen, however, whether as in Britain for example, Portugal will see the emergence of short-term, temporary appointments (Gordon and Whitchurch 2007) or whether it will not be tempted by the equivalent of what in France is known as the *'regime de vacataire'*, contracts issued on a year-by-year basis with no guarantee of renewal at year's end.

Irrespective of whether the potential becomes actual – or for that matter, when – this particular provision in the Juridical Regime of Higher Education Institutions of 2007 stands as a break point in the collective status of the Administrative Estate within the public sector of Portuguese higher education. For effectively, public oversight for conditions of employment, career advancement and promotion obeyed the principle of 'Legal homogeneity', that is, it applied across all public sector institutions in a similar manner (Neave and van Vught 1991). In the case of Portugal, legal homogeneity laid out a standard template for career development across all public sectors and had in consequence national validity and application. There are, in the matter of career development, no differences between universities and polytechnics.[11] To be sure, vestigial exceptions exist. One of these, shared by both the Universities of Coimbra and Lisbon, is to be seen in the office of *'archeiro'*, today a largely symbolic and honorific function of bearing aloft the seals, coats of arms and trappings of university authority on official occasions and events. Such a relatively minor exception serves merely to reinforce the validity of the general rule that legal homogeneity embodies, however.

The advent of the foundation university, inasmuch as it concerns the collective status of the Administrative Estate, drives a coach and four through the principle of legal homogeneity in public sector higher education. In theory, though how far and how fast are issues only the future will resolve, it confronts the Administrative Estate with the prospect of fragmentation and differentiation, a prospect all the more redoubtable for being anticipated *de jure*. An alternative perspective on this same development would merely note that however homogeneous the conditions of career, advancement and promotion in public sector higher education, they were already being eroded *de facto* in the terms offered by private sector establishments of higher education (Chap. 13).

Interestingly, the past two decades have seen a number of attempts to develop specific administrative career tracks in higher education. The prime motive behind these proposals was to raise the professional skills of non-academic staff and thus to improve the quality of service they dispensed.[12] However, the proposal did not see the light of day. The employment conditions for non-academic staff are still regulated in keeping with other public sector employment.

Growth of the 'Administrative Estate' Compared with Other Estates

The Administrative Estate in higher education grew faster than the public sector as a whole. Here, however, the question is whether growth in the numbers of non-academic staff outstripped the annual percentage growth rate that the two remaining constituent orders – the Academic Estate or the Student Estate – displayed over the same period (Neave 1997). Over the period from 1987 to 2008, growth proceeded at a different rate for universities and for polytechnics.

Over these 20 years, in Portuguese higher education, academic staff outnumbered their administrative counterparts. But growth in the ranks of non-academic staff in polytechnics was greater still. Polytechnics took their first student intake in 1986. Since 1987, academic staff multiplied almost five times over in polytechnics – to be precise, 4.8 times – whereas administrative staff rose by a factor of 3.5. Over the same period, public universities saw their academic staff numbers grow 1.5 times. Their Administrative Estate flourished and saw numbers rise by 2.6 times.

As elsewhere in Europe, growth in student enrolments in Portuguese higher education during the last few decades has been pleasingly substantial (Chaps. 6 and 14). Comparing the growth in student numbers over the years from 1987 to 2008 – the same period for which data on non-teaching staff were available – a significant increase in the number of polytechnic students stands out. Student numbers multiplied 7.0 times over as against a rise of 3.5 times for non-academic staff. In public universities, the number of students increased 2.08 times, whereas non-academic staff expanded 2.6 times over (GPEARI 2010). Whilst there has been growth of non-academic staff, the overall student to staff ratio did not increase significantly since 1987. However, there are significant differences when comparing ratios between institutional types. For instance, the ratio at polytechnic institutes is much higher and is less favourable, as Fig. 15.3 shows.[13]

Growth between 1987 and 1988 was exceptional and coincided with the opening of the new polytechnics. Comparing the annual percentage growth rates for all three Estates for the period from 1987 to 2008 shows non-academic staff peaking in 1991, 1993 and 2000. The explanation, we believe, is to be found in the *desconge-lamentos* 'unfreezing' of the annual *quotas*, fixed by the Ministry of Finance, on hiring new personnel by polytechnics.[14] With the exception of the three 'peak years', growth in non-academic staff did not follow growth in the Student Estate: the *administrative* staff to student ratio fluctuated, not even keeping pace with the growth in student numbers. The declining numbers of academic staff in the latter

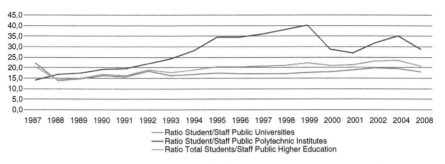

Fig. 15.3 Staff to student ratio in public HEIs, 1987–2008 (Source: Created by the authors based on data from Direcção Geral do Ensino Superior and GPEARI)

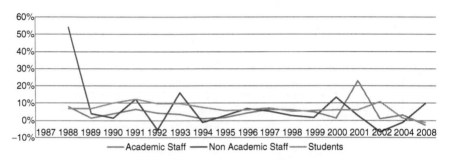

Fig. 15.4 Annual percentage growth rates for all three Estates, 1987 to 2008 (Source: Created by the authors based on data from Direcção Geral do Ensino Superior and GPEARI)

year reflected changes in retirement legislation.[15] Also evident is a significant growth between 2004 and 2008 in contrast to the decline in the numbers of students and academic staff. This, in our opinion, reflects efforts made to give public servant status and thus permanent employment to personnel hitherto under temporary contract (Fig. 15.4).

Changing Roles

The Administrative Estate has grown. Its roles and responsibilities have changed over time. The traditional roles assigned to non-academics have evolved, and increasingly new functions and additional skills are required amongst which languages, the proven ability to negotiate with interests both external and internal, costing and cost control, fund raising, publicity and computer skills, seeking out local, national and international 'markets'; strategic planning, monitoring performance, developing performance incentive schemes are not the least amongst the virtues the Administrative Estate is expected to possess today. As Whitchurch pointed out in connection with developments in the United Kingdom:

> (…) as the capacity of staff expands and diversifies to cope with the ongoing demands on institutions, professional roles and identities are subject to continual revision. The situation is, therefore, more dynamic and complex than organisation charts and jobs description would suggest. (Whitchurch 2008a: 2)

As institutions set out to respond to competitive markets, national requirements, generated by the Government, external demands – for instance, the international flow of students both within Europe and with Portugal's one-time colonies – evaluation and quality, output and 'academic productivity' issues, so new tasks fall to non-academic staff, new services are set up and new lines of responsibility laid down. Moreover, the calls for higher education institutions to change and to respond to challenges coming from within the world of higher education as well as from broader sectors of the economy (Chap. 5) have not only grown. They have taken on a new urgency. The pressures for non-academic staff to achieve objectives and monitor quality procedures, both are incessant, though it is rare for either universities or polytechnics to have a 'formal quality culture' other than that which applies to the academic enterprise. As yet, administrative quality is rarely accorded the same degree of well-publicised priority in institutional standing as the academic output, which it is entrusted to oversee.

Feminisation of the Administrative Estate

Yet, the Administrative Estate is marked by another important feature, one that is present in both universities and polytechnics. This feature emerges in its gender composition. Whilst statistics that break out the gender distribution within the Administrative Estate over the past 30 years sparkle by their absence, data for 2008 are available. What they show is that the feminine presence is even more pronounced amongst non-teaching staff in polytechnics than it is in universities. Table 15.1 makes

Table 15.1 Feminisation of the Administrative Estate by institutional type, 2008

	Female	Male	Grand total
Distribution by gender of non-teaching staff – Universities			
University	6,551	3,278	9,829
Polytechnic	161	52	213
Grand total	6,712	3,330	10,042
Distribution by gender of non-teaching staff – Polytechnic and non-integrated schools			
Schools	275	66	341
Polytechnic	2,123	1,054	3,177
Grand total	2,398	1,120	3,518

Source: Created by the authors based on data from Direcção Geral do Ensino Superior and GPEARI

this very plain. Three members of the polytechnic Administrative Estate out of four – 75% – are women compared with slightly over two out of three – 68% – of their university-based colleagues. Interestingly, the pronounced feminine presence is not confined to the Administrative Estate. It is equally evident in the Academic Estate as well (Chap. 14). Whilst a similar trait characterised the Student Estate as well, very recent data suggest the gender distribution over the past half decade is moving back to a state of relative equilibrium (Chap. 16).

Qualifications of Non-academic Staff

In the past, the 'Administrative Estate' was not held to be highly qualified. The majority had not gone beyond completing elementary or secondary school. This is rapidly changing, and the rise in qualification level is now striking with a much higher proportion of staff being graduates.

Certainly, the level of qualification in the Administrative Estate is not as marked as in Australia or the US where a high proportion of staff hold a master's degree and even a doctorate (Whitchurch 2009). Nevertheless, there are significant indications that non-academic staff in Portugal have a foot on the same ladder, some holding a bachelor's degree, with a few having successfully pursued their studies up to an earned PhD degree, as Table 15.2 shows.

The Greying of the Administrative Estate

Even though polytechnic institutes are relatively recent in their foundation, no significant differences emerge in the age distribution of non-teaching staff. In universities, non-teaching staff over the age of 46 years account for 46% of the Administrative Estate in its totality and 42% of their polytechnic counterparts (see Table 15.3). The age profile of non-academic staff in higher education seemingly reflects the trend in the age distribution of staff in other areas of the public sector (Rosa and Chitas 2010).

Other Issues

Whilst both the Academic Estate and the Administrative Estate over the past three decades have seen the range of activities for which they are held formally responsible and answerable to Government, to the public and to external stakeholders proliferate and multiply and whilst many of these developments blur the boundaries between the academic and the administrative spheres, nevertheless the gap between

Table 15.2 Qualifications of non-academic staff, 2008

	A - 12 or fewer years	B - STC	C - Bac.	D - Lic.	E - Grad	F - Mast	G - PhD	H - Qualification ignored	Total
Qualifications of non-teaching staff in 2008 – Universities									
Number of non-teaching staff	5,813	9	231	2,838	82	318	735	16	10,042
Qualifications of non-teaching staff in 2008 – Polytechnic and integrated schools									
Schools	271	0	3	62	2	3	0	0	341
Polytechnic	2,009	3	106	901	34	96	17	11	3,177
Grand Total	2,280	3	109	963	36	99	17	11	3,518

Source: Created by the authors based on data from Direcção Geral do Ensino Superior and GPEARI
Key: *STC* Specialised Technology Course; *Bac.* Bachelor; *Lic* Licenciado; *Grad* Graduate; *Mast* Master

Table 15.3 Age distribution of the Administrative Estate

	>25	[25 e 35]	[36 e 45]	[46 e 55]	[56 e 65]	>65	Unwritten	Total
Distribution of non-teaching staff in 2008 by age group – Universities								
Total	58	2,209	3,207	2,746	1,699	123	0	10,042
Distribution of non-teaching staff in 2008 by age group – Polytechnic and integrated schools								
Schools	6	73	73	127	56	3	3	341
Polytechnic	20	857	1,007	913	343	36	1	3,177
Grand Total	26	930	1,080	1,040	399	39	4	3,518

Source: Created by the authors based on data from Direcção Geral do Ensino Superior and GPEARI

both Estates remains wide. And some would wish to it remain so (Santiago et al. 2006: 215–250). The prime and obvious feature, important as much in its symbolism as in the operational consequences that flow from the various ways in which it is interpreted, is the credo of academic or positional autonomy (Chap. 7). That autonomy stands as the essential value and ethic of the Academic Estate, springs from the latter's essential nature and purpose and stands as the unconditional construct on which the freedom to teach and to learn was once both held to rest (Thorens 2006). In Portugal, this fundamental condition is formally enshrined in the 1976 Constitution and confirmed in the Law on Pedagogical Autonomy of 1988 (Chap. 7).

Recognising academic autonomy as a fundamental principle is one thing. Determining its extent and its boundaries is a very different matter indeed. Some scholars have seen academic autonomy as 'the private life of higher education' (Trow 1975), which, for that very reason, separates as well as distinguishes the Academic Estate from its Administrative fellow. The Administrative Estate does not of necessity require either *Lehr* or *Lern freiheit* for the pursuit of its purposes because those purposes do not engage freedom of the mind or of opinion, though the consequences of decisions made by the Administrative Estate may indeed be dire for the institution. They may also serve, maintain and uphold academic freedom. But, under the classic dichotomy between Academia with Administration acting as its handmaiden, this is a second-order function of servicing, vital to be sure, but not the central function itself.

Inasmuch as *academic* autonomy is precisely that – it is engaged by dint of the intellectual nature of the task undertaken – it could be argued that the Administrative Estate is relatively marginalised. It does not enjoy this distinctive and identifying characteristic of higher education, research and scholarship (Taylor et al. 2007a, b). However, just as it is arguable that academia once occupied a 'private sphere', so today it is no less evident that by the same token, the Administrative Estate occupies what may be termed 'the public sphere' between the inner private life of academia and the external world of Government, stakeholders, founders, contractors and those who see in the knowledge the university creates a vital condition of their own fortunes or interests. Irrespective of whether the particular paradigm engaged is that of a 'Knowledge Society', a 'Knowledge Economy' or of the university itself cast as an agency of 'service'. The fundamental feature of these representations is the tension they create in defining the boundaries between not one species of autonomy – the 'private life' of academia – so much as two very different concepts of autonomy which, if conceptually clear and complementary, in reality are very far indeed from this enviable state. Just as the identifying feature of the Academic Estate turned around academic or positional autonomy (Neave, forthcoming) so today the Administrative Estate – whether deliberately or whether driven by external circumstances is beside the point – exercises a powerful countervailing claim to a parallel ethic in the shape of institutional – others have called it, 'managerial' – autonomy (OECD 2007). Put succinctly, the Administrative Estate today sees its task as upholding the autonomy of the *institution* in its dealings with the world outside the campus – that is to say, the public sphere which, paradoxically, in this age when the virtues of privatisation are shouted from the rooftops, is now regarded as conditioning and defining the boundaries of the 'private sphere' in which academia exercises those tasks, under conditions and according to the priorities defined, permitted or subject to benign neglect by the public sphere (For another perspective on this issue see Chaps. 9 and 12).

To be sure, the Academic Estate can still claim formally to be far and away better qualified than its Administrative fellow, despite the latter's significant improvement over the past few years. But satisfying though this might be to both parties, it is largely irrelevant beside the undeniable fact that the Administrative Estate, perhaps for the first time in its history, now possesses an immensely powerful countervailing ethic that encapsulates not only its *raison d'être* but also exercises the most potent of all leverages – namely, to define, shape, operationalise and – last but very far from least – to evaluate the performance of the Academic Estate as functions integral to the strategic role the Administrative Estate is seen as upholding, to wit *institutional* autonomy. What this signifies is clear indeed. Once seen as the quintessential condition for the advancement of science and scholarship, the relationship between Academic and Administrative Estates is evolving very rapidly. It is no coincidence that the rise to prominence of the Administrative Estate was born aloft on the wings of institutional accountability. What remains unclear for the moment is whether the two ethics – some might grace them with the descriptor of 'ideologies' – will coexist in relative balance or whether, as indications seem to suggest elsewhere in Europe, academic autonomy, like the Estate it defines, will not become a sub-set of institutional autonomy that likewise defines the Estate that subscribes to it.

Centralisation of Governance

Key to the issue just broached is the question of the centralisation of governance. The Ministry of Science, Technology and Higher Education exercises overall responsibility for higher education (Chap. 2). Portuguese higher education institutions are for the most part public- and state-funded, a pattern found in most European systems (Paradeise et al. 2009) (Chap. 6).

Governance of all public higher education institutions comes under the purlieu of the Ministry of Education and Research and is laid down in law and regulations. Moreover, public higher education had a tradition of strict centralisation, with tight control over funding (Cerdeira 2009a, b).

Governance at the institutional level has, not surprisingly, inspired several scholars to see autonomy as a crucial issue (Amaral et al. 1996; Brites et al. 2004; Taylor et al. 2007a, b). The basic framework of the Administrative Estate is established by the State through law and regulations. Though universities and polytechnics have pedagogical and scholarly autonomy, nevertheless they depend on the State for financing, and this in turn engages the question of human resources management.

As has been argued, an optimal relationship between State, university or polytechnic is no easy matter, and for higher education, the balance between autonomy and accountability is itself a matter of enduring preoccupation. Over a decade ago, Amaral et al. (2002: 89) noted:

(…) in Portugal, despite the autonomy laws for public universities and public polytechnics, and despite the favourable attitude towards the market, it looks without controversy that the State keeps its role as the most important regulator of the system of higher education.

More recently – and though State control continues to be exercised through formula funding as opposed to funding by increments – institutional autonomy exercised in the management of human resources has been strengthened. However, decentralisation, whilst consolidating institutional management and governance, also called for both rigorous quality procedures and for effective accountability (Heitor 2008)[16] (Chap. 10).

The 'Dual Administrative Structure'

What contemporary jargon often describes as a 'full-time chief executive' – the Rector in universities or the President in polytechnics – exercises overall responsibility for the establishment in the public sector of higher education. Vice-Rectors, alternatively Vice-Presidents, support these positions. Within each public institution, the *academic* community elects its own officers amongst whom are deans and department chairs. In the election of Rector, or President, academia is only one constituency amongst others represented on the Governing Board. Whilst Rectors, Presidents and Deans carry formal legal powers, such power is crosscut by power vested in other collegial bodies and in academic staff. Formally, in the public sector, University Rectors and Polytechnic Presidents chair the governing bodies and oversee their institution. However, the provision exists both in the basic law governing higher education and in the statutes and byelaws of each institution that allows for rectoral or presidential authority to be delegated.

The other side of this bi-cephalous arrangement rests on senior administrators – heads of administration – with institution-wide responsibility for the budget, for the management of human resources and the other administrative functions.

From the 1980s onwards, duties assigned to administrators multiplied significantly. Depending on institutional type – whether universities or polytechnics – administrative tasks were extended to include academic services, student enrolments, external relations and the planning of equipment, materials and other facilities including buildings. Interestingly, as the economic imperative took on increasing weight in university affairs (Huisman and van der Wende 1999), some establishments in Portugal began to buy in administrative know-how from the business sector.[17]

As tends to be the case elsewhere, senior administrators are regarded as 'men having authority' and influence – a strange obverse to the usual administrative medal which deems administrative staff generally to be layered in bureaucracy and confined to operational duties (Paradeise et al. 2009). As a descriptor, the designation 'administrator' is not greatly cherished. Indeed, Rectors and Presidents in Portugal's universities and polytechnics perceive both their functions and their title as defining them as 'academics'[18] – a situation different indeed from their fellows in the US where Presidents are referred to as 'academic administrators' (Birnbaum 1992; Kerr and Gade 1986). Whilst 'professional staff … appear to have a greater equivalence vis-à-vis their academic counterparts'. In effect, it would appear that as far as perceptions are concerned, associations current in Portugal might be more akin to the UK where '"administration" has tended to become devalued in that it is often used to refer to procedural and even clerical tasks' (Whitchurch 2009: 411).

Legal Framework: Evolution and Vicissitudes

Since 1974, the Administrative Estate has been shaped and reshaped by successive bouts of regulation[19] (Chap. 7).

Two enactments, Law 108/88 – the University Autonomy Act – and Law 54/90 – the Law of Organisation and Management of Polytechnic Institutes – conferred some degree of autonomy on public higher education. Prior to 1988, creating new posts and hiring non-academic staff in universities and polytechnics were formally decisions made at ministerial level. Seen within this perspective, the Portuguese Administrative Estate in its historic configuration could be regarded as a sub-sector of national administration reaching down into the individual university and polytechnic, even though the authority to hire new non-academic staff was delegated by the ministries in charge of higher education to the Directorate General of Higher Education (DGES). After 1988, this responsibility was handed off to the individual HEI, though remaining subject to the availability of funds and provided certain formal criteria were met. Following the decentralisation of higher education, decisions on hiring are made in the light of funding and budgeting at the institutional level. In theory, such provision constituted a watershed in the development of the Administrative Estate and, formally at least, changed its status, though not its servicing function, to become an integral part of the institution. Each individual higher education institution may, in effect, decide which posts are to be filled, subject to certain budgetary rules (Cerdeira 2009a, b).[20] Nevertheless, whilst this 'act of restitution' in shaping and hiring the Administrative Estate according to perceived institutional rather than State priorities was a marker point in the history of that Estate, the State continued to play an important part in institutional policy-making through its budgetary policies (Bleiklie 1998; Cerdeira 2009a).

Yet, growth in the numbers of administrative staff relative to academic staff was not without its tensions. Growth in the ranks of administration meant a corresponding increase in the expenditure required to support it. And this, in its turn, gave rise to the fear amongst both politicians and administrators that the cost of higher education would itself escalate further. In the course of the last decade, HEIs faced a budget squeeze (Cerdeira 2009a) and were forced to introduce cuts. Non-academic staff are not considered essential for the functioning of a higher education institution, so all pointers are that new recruitment will not proceed in the immediately foreseeable future.[21]

Managerialising the 'Administrative Estate'

Times change. So too do the methods, instruments and levers that bear upon higher education. Institutional evaluation (Chap. 10) and public accountability (Chaps. 9 and 12); costs, cost-benefit analyses and cost-sharing; the rise of private HEIs and for-profit providers (Chap. 13); the exponential growth of information technology; internationalisation and student mobility; managerialism and the emphasis placed on a more corporate mental set as models for HEI management and leadership (Kwiek 2003; Machado 2005; Taylor et al. 2008) all struggle to have their place in a post-modern world just as they do in a system of higher education, which finds itself in such a turmoil.

Increased student participation (Chap. 6), insistent demands for external accountability and equally insistent calls for better internal efficiency, raise all manner of questions, not least of which the quality of human resources present, available or required. The clamour for accountability is deafening. As Magalhães points out, somewhat testily:

Accountability is increasingly becoming the 'data display' of institutions, for it supposedly translates the worth of the institution or system into economic and financial terms. (Magalhães 2001: 114)

For Altbach (Altbach 1999) and Lane (Lane 1987), the pressing demands for accountability to be demonstrated – and to be seen to be demonstrated – were themselves a direct cause of the growth in the 'Administrative Estate'. The rise of the Administrative Estate, in Lane's opinion, owed much to the belief that '…more of administration is a means to efficiency' (Lane 1987: 260), a point Bleiklie took further:

Together with the conviction that greater efficiency can be achieved by means of performance indicators, these notions imply that the administrative aspect of university governance should be strengthened to ensure a standardised and controllable treatment of the growing burden of teaching and research. (Bleiklie 1998: 307)

In parallel to calls for more accountability and efficiency, both Magalhães et al. (Magalhães et al. 2005) and Neave (1997) suggest that administrators too faced the onrush of 'new managerialism' as well as acting as the principle channel through which it was conveyed. Paradeise et al. (2009: 199) pursued a slightly different line of argument. For them, the origins of 'new managerialism' lay in the public sector and in the faith that raising both quality and productivity '... was to transform public *bureaucracy* by means of public *management*'.

In Portugal, however, the situation was less clear-cut. Amaral and his colleagues, writing more than a half decade ago, took the view that '(...) if managerialism exists, it is present at rhetorical level' (Amaral et al. 2003:150), a view endorsed more recently by Rectors of public universities.[22] The new legal framework for public higher education passed in 2007 (RJIES 2007, the Juridical Regime of Higher Education Institutions – Law 62/2007) – (Chaps. 7 and 9) cuts in state funding, the drive for further accountability to meet the Government's priorities and align Portugal's higher education with guidelines of quality and accreditation established at European level – all bolstered the managerialist perspective on, and in, higher education. As Bleiklie anticipated a decade gone, this thrust,

(...) would lead individual institutions in new directions. (...) administrative structures are strengthened both in extent and in the formal competence of administrators and their authority as decision makers. (Bleiklie 1998: 307–308)

Managerialisation may well lead to further growth in the 'Administrative Estate'. Indeed, precisely this happened in the Nordic countries according to the analysis undertaken by Fägerlind and Strömqvist (Fägerlind and Strömqvist 2004: 119): 'The managerialisation of higher education and the rise of the evaluative state, they noted, have led to the strengthening of administration in the field of Finnish higher education'. And whilst in the near future as new legislative guidelines[23] begin to bite in Portugal, managerialism may indeed have an even greater impact on the 'Administrative Estate' than on the Academic Estate. The real issue at stake is neither size nor the former's numbers. Rather the central issue is – and will remain – by whom the new instrumentality of managerialism, the interpretation and the operational definitions of the criteria of efficiency and performance that managerialism brings in its train are to be drawn up, by whom they are to be determined and who will have the duty to mete out the consequences for performances that are sparkling just as it will for those whose performance is lack-lustre? So, depending on the answers given to these burning issues at institutional level, the relationships between Administrative and Academic Estates will be set in the unyielding granite of subordination of the latter to the former or on the basis of a creative coexistence and mutual confidence that links one with the other.

The Influence of Europeanisation and Globalisation

If the Administrative Estate today serves as a two-way channel between university and the society at its gates, it is clear that external demands and entreaties do not stop at the nation's political and geographical frontiers. For the past two decades, higher education in Europe has been required to accommodate to developments that lie beyond the Nation, in Europe (Chap. 11) and, as some would argue (see Chap. 5), to others yet further afield still. These 'spheres of action' have very certainly shaped both the responsibilities and services the Administrative Estate is called upon to facilitate, if not provide, international student exchange, certification, trans-national research collaboration being amongst the most visible.

It is appropriate then to consider how far the processes of globalisation, internationalisation and 'Europeanisation' influenced developments in the 'Administrative Estate' (Neave 2002). The forces of 'Europeanisation' and globalisation are changing – some would say threatening – the established role of the nation state by imposing externally devised policies on national systems (Machado 2005; Taylor et al. 2008). Huisman and van der Wende inclined to the view that:

> The (short) overview of ... developments in some European countries (Austria, Germany, the Netherlands, Portugal, Greece, UK and Norway) shows that Governments have developed policies that fit the European agenda towards converging systems of higher education. (Huisman and van der Wende 1999: 355)

Neave, examining the issue from the standpoint of the political historian, argued that the European Nation State found itself under attack from two directions:

> It is precisely this historic European construct of the national community as the highest level of aggregation and decision making in higher education (Clark 1983) that stands under duress from two directions: from the emerging supranational level represented by the European Union and from a development ... more advanced than the European Union in shaping higher education policy within individual member states- namely, regionalisation. (Neave 2005: 4)

Research works by Amaral, Magalhães, Veiga, to name but a few, are full of examples of alignment of national policies[24] in higher education implemented by Portugal but influenced by developments in other European countries. Very often, implementation itself depends on the aura of legitimation that surrounds such measures coming as they do from the EU or from international agencies (Huisman and van der Wende 1999).[25] Indeed, Amaral and Magalhães (2005) argued that implementing higher education policies in Portugal was influenced to a significant degree by such external factors. However, it is only fair to note whilst such initiatives were rarely designed for direct application to the 'Administrative Estate', their indirect 'fall out' most certainly had such an impact (Chap. 11).

Dissecting the Rise and the Growth of the 'Administrative Estate'

The Administrative Estate has grown and, as current statistics show (see Fig. 15.1, p. 357), has resumed growth after a short plateauing out during the first half decade of the twenty-first century. Whilst some in academia might take the same view on Administration's growth as the eighteenth century British Parliamentarian, George Dunning, entertained about the power of King George III, 'it has grown, is growing and ought to be diminished', the latter is an unlikely scenario. Many developments account for the rise of the Administrative Estate. They may be summarised as follows:

- *The setting up of new public institutions and institutional diversity*: Growth in the scale of the system of higher education requires the provision of human resources – both academic and administrative to maintain the range, type of services and their levels of performance at very least on a level similar to those previously in place. Failure to do so risks equating mass higher education with deterioration in performance and quality, and thus undermines its standing with the public.
- *Growth in the Student Estate*: A significant increase in the number of students enrolled in all types of higher education institutions was marked indeed.[26]
- *The expected role of higher education institutions*: Higher education institutions have been called upon not only to provide teaching and research but also an expanding range of services to society, often represented nowadays as the 'Third Task'. These can range from specialised contract teaching and firm training services, adult education, through to R&D for small- and medium-sized industry within the region. These latter tasks often require new skills and support structures to sustain them, quite apart from the capacity of the university or polytechnic to seek out and negotiate with external 'clients' of a highly heterogeneous nature. Such activities call for special skills and doubtless, an appropriate organisational frame to develop and to maintain them. This in turn generates
- *New functions*: The development and organisation of new 'support' services, offices of international relations, legal services, computer services, updating personnel in techniques, generating new skills, enhancing those already utilised, student financial assistance and other administrative tasks, all drive towards a corresponding growth in the levels of expenditure levels in administration.
- *Accountability, Efficiency:* Demands for accountability and efficiency are growing. These were principally to be seen in changes introduced with the Law on Funding (Law 37/2003) which injected objective criteria, performance indicators to assess the quality of teaching, rationalisation, efficiency and a new framework for evaluating quality (Law 38/2007) all of which added to the administrative burden on HEIs. As Magalhães and Santiago (2011: 6) also pointed out:

  In the last decades of policy making in higher education autonomy, accountability and quality assessment were transformed into key-words and cornerstones of higher education reform.

- 'More elaborate mechanisms of accountability' are also noted by Amaral and Magalhães (Amaral and Magalhães 2002).[27]
- *New services inside the establishment*: The rise of what some scholars term 'The Stakeholder Society' has immense significance for the responsibilities that may be assigned to the Administrative Estate. It remains to be seen whether the Stakeholder Society strengthens the Administrative Estate as the site of central coordination through centralising those functions hitherto reserved for its Academic counterpart – project management, contract negotiation and

bargaining for instance. Or whether the impact of the Stakeholder relationship is less direct and takes the form of additional administrative support staff to bolster the scholarly productivity of Faculty. Amongst the latter, for instance, are computing, grant writing assistance, the assignment and hiring of administrative staff specialised in communications and publicity to polish up the institutional image and to 'market' the university. The development of personal services to students to raise student satisfaction, performance and development, amongst which professional advisors, careers counsellors, or sport or recreational staff, though important *per se*, are in reality a form of sub-agenda to those services crucial to academic efficiency and productivity.

- *Capacity for Innovation*: Many of these issues have taken on a new significance with the creation by the Juridical Regime of Higher Education Institutions of 2007 of so-called foundation universities. So far, three public universities have exercised this option (Chaps. 2 and 7). Central to this new status, which places establishments previously public under private law, is the requirement to generate at least 50% of the institutional budget from non-state funding sources.

Earlier, the question of the relationship between the two was posed, largely in a theoretical setting. Seen from the perspective this chapter has developed, it is a point of second-order importance whether the new economic and entrepreneurial functions will allow each Estate to sell its research-related products and knowledge-intensive services (Clark 1998). And whilst some may indeed seek to trace how far foundation universities move down the path the American sociologist, Burton Clark, detected amongst certain pioneer universities in Western Europe, far more important is at what price and on what type of relationship between 'innovative periphery' and 'strong steering core' the Administrative Estate will come to occupy vis-á-vis the Academic Estate. Put crudely, and within the perspective this chapter follows, it is not the entrepreneurial nature *per se* of these establishments that merits the closest of attention. Rather, is whether the balance of power between the two Estates is to be complementary, on a footing of equality or to be welded into what many in academia and administration see as 'business-like' line management models that all too often derived from the business world of yesteryear but give the illusion of clarity because tied to the principle of subordination.

ENVOI

This chapter traced the growth and expansion of the 'Administrative Estate' in the public sector of Portugal's higher education system.

Looking back at the way the Administrative State has evolved over the past three decades, it has most certainly grown. It has also become better qualified just as it has also become a largely feminised domain. The Administrative Estate has been detached from the central services of the State, and though this is far from being unique to Portugal, it is equally clear that it is moving towards a status and standing that bear closer parallels with the Anglo Saxon vision of that body. Moving towards what is perceived to be a desirable model for emulation does not mean either that one has reached that felicitous condition or that the route to be taken inevitably sees Portugal trudging down exactly the same weary path. And still less, that progress along it will assume the same bustling gait. If there is one thing that the comparative study of higher education policy tells us, it is that shared objectives mean neither shared capacity to attain them and still less the ability to do so with equal expedition. That is precisely why amongst other reasons, we study individual national systems of higher education – above all in an epoch that prides itself on its Europeanization.

Like its counterparts elsewhere in Europe, the rise of the Administrative Estate in Portugal has been driven onwards by several powerful forces in society. We have summarised them above. But there are a number of points still to be made. The first of these must surely be that whilst student numbers sired a more numerous Administrative Estate, they did so as a second-order variable – that is, as an indirect consequence of growth. The prime and direct impact fell foursquare on the Academic Estate. The second point has to do with the all-pervasive notion of accountability and, more particularly, its timing in the Portuguese setting.

In its classic meaning, accountability involves the moral obligation to render an account of what one has done as a condition of receiving the means – whether legislative, financial or in terms of human resources – to accomplish a purpose agreed upon beforehand (Neave 1984; Becher et al. 1981). Accountability in its current meaning is very different from the legal obligation to prove that public monies are spent according to the terms current legislation sets down. From this latter standpoint, accountability has always been present as an integral function of what some students of higher education have called the 'State control' relationship between Government and higher education (Neave and van Vught 1991). The current interpretation is different because, like the systems in which it largely originated – the United Kingdom and the United States – it rests upon the assumption that universities and polytechnics are not direct emanations of State authority. They are, on the contrary, largely self-administering in a relationship, which, in theory, held the role of the State at a distance, an interpretation that derived from nineteenth century Liberalism that shaped higher education in those two lands.

Arguably, the first moves in this direction in Portugal emerged in the legislation on Pedagogical Autonomy of 1988 and 1990, respectively, for universities and polytechnics. With it came the change in status of the Administrative Estate itself, as we have noted. The contemporary interpretation of accountability builds out simultaneously from the drive to 'offload' such responsibilities as administrative appointment from central ministry to institution. This, when set against the onset of managerialism in Portuguese higher education (see Chap. 9), suggests a certain 'lagged response' by Government to the supposed benefits of its ideological overlay contained in neoliberal policies for higher education. For whilst the neoliberal ethic and its operational consequences in the form of the new interpretation of accountability and its modus operandi, 'managerialism', took on legal weight in the early years of the current decade, other systems of higher education – amongst which one may cite the Dutch, the Danish, the Swedish and the British, to mention but the most obvious – were already firmly embarked on this course which had evolved from national policy to institutional practice.

In short, as far as shaping the Administrative Estate is concerned, we would take the view that as of 2010 that Estate is in the midst of a further transition. New Managerialism, if present, and in certain instances active, has still to work its way into the institutional fabric. Whether the Law of 2007 has served to speed the process up remains as yet to be seen. What cannot be doubted is the further elaboration of the Administrative Estate. Indeed, that Estate may well see a period of root and branch restructuring and with it a new distribution of authority between Estates Administrative and Academic as institutional autonomy is increasingly held out as the price of survival for both university and polytechnic in Portugal.

Notes

1. One of the authors was a member of the Council of University Administrators and has personal knowledge of university administrators.
2. Public sector higher education institutions have two administrators: one for the institution itself, the *Administrador (a)*, and another for student affairs called *Administrador (a) dos Serviços Sociais*. *Administradores apart*, each Faculty and School usually has a Secretary-*Secretário (a)*. Secretary duties include financing, human resources and student services on the faculty or school level.
3. Before the Law on University Autonomy (1988) and similar legislation that applied to polytechnics (1990), those functions were centralised at national level.
4. Hazelkorn (2005: 18) pointed out 'It is widely accepted that higher education in the twenty-first century across the OECD is operating in a changed and challenging environment. The emergence of a global knowledge-based or information society is dramatically transforming the modes of production and social organisation of advanced societies. […] There is a more clear understanding of the innovation process with its dynamic links between the production of new knowledge, knowledge transfer and economic performance; knowledge has become a commodity. […] This changed perception of the role and importance of higher education has gone hand-in-hand with calls for greater institutional accountability and responsibility. Once perceived as 'the training ground for professionals', universities are increasingly being 'treated more like other organisations and professionals more like workers' (Slaughter and Leslie 1997).
5. See Magalhães and Santiago (2011) chapter 'Public Management, New Governance Models and Changing Environments in Portuguese Higher Education'.
6. An exhaustive effort was made to obtain statistical information on non-academic staff in higher education. Amongst the sources contacted were the central services of the Ministry of Science, Technology, the National Institute of Statistics, the *Tribunal de Contas* (the Audit Court to which all public institutions report their annual budgets and the hiring of new posts) and former vice-directors in charge of the Directorate of Higher Education. Despite extensive inquiries, the general conclusion reached was that no statistical information was available. The data provided for the years 1980s and 1990s was possible only because one of the authors is responsible for financial services and human resources at the Directorate of Higher Education.
7. 'They underline (Bleiklie and Kogan 2007) that the decision-making processes by academics have become integrated into the administrative line of the organisation and therefore academics appear less and less as such and increasingly as part of the institutional decision-making processes. This corresponds to a move from the idea of collegial and institutional governance to another that emphasises the organisation rationales as opposed to the occupational or professional

codes, and the organisational rationalism as opposed to the occupational rationalism with regard to the regulation of higher education institutions internal life. The claims for more professional management ultimately aim at replacing the professionals/academic control over higher education internal life by the managerial power'. (Magalhães and Santiago 2011: 13)

8. Magalhães and Santiago (2011: 2) clarified this point: 'It will be suggested that the emergence of new policy instruments, organisational arrangements, processes and structures is substantially changing higher education institutional environments and are moulding higher education institutions choices which regard to their legal status (e.g. the foundation model versus public universities model), administrative and managerial structures and their "internal life", i.e., education and research'.

9. By far the greater majority of non-academic staff are public servants with a few exceptions. These are:

   1. Students affairs can, since the 1980s, hire personnel ruled by private law for cafeterias and residence halls.
   2. HEIs hire for research activities personnel on a temporary basis (ruled by Decree–Law 225/97). Those contracts end when the research project is finished.
   3. For some specific functions such as lawyers, computer personnel and media consultant, usually HEIs contract on a negotiated monthly or year amount named *avença*.

10. For instance (Maassen 2006: 34) stated: '(…) academic and administrative members of European HEIs are still in many countries civil servants, with relatively little room to manoeuvre for the institutional management in their personnel policies'.
11. Even career development in HEIs followed the same path laid down for all public services. The universities have a greater flexibility, however. For instance, during the 1990s, universities could hire new personnel without prior authorisation from the Ministry of Finance. This was not the case for polytechnics. The Constitution and Law 108/88 both endowed universities with greater autonomy over their internal organisation.
12. This is based on the authors' personal knowledge as part of a project for professionalising non-academic staff. The authors take the view that HEIs have specialised functions and needs that have much to gain from enhancing the professional skills and competence of administrative staff. The project began in 1988 (*Boletim Informativo, N° 11, Maio 1998*) and renewed in 2001 (*X Encontro Nacional da ANFUP- Associação Nacional dos Funcionários das Universidades Públicas, Coimbra, 30 de Junho de 2001*).
13. During the 1980s and 1990s, universities had greater discretion for hiring non-academic staff. This, in all likelihood, is reflected in the number of non-academic staff in polytechnics. Furthermore, polytechnics are compared generally to universities, even the new ones, more recent foundations.
14. As was pointed out earlier, polytechnics did not have the same flexibility to hire new personnel. Polytechnics grew significantly in the 1980s and 1990s.
15. Academic staff usually remained in post until their 70th year, then the limit for retirement. Now, with changes in the retirement legislation, academics start to retire at age 60. It is a particularly obvious development over the past 2 years.
16. The following is an extract from a presentation made by the Secretary of State for Higher Education: '(…) there is a consensus about the need, and opportunity, to *accelerate reform* of HEIs in order not only to stimulate progress across the whole tertiary education system, but also to foster the emergence and strengthening of our institutions which can demonstrate their excellence at international level. But accelerating reform requires the need to concentrate tertiary education reform on a myriad of issues that will ultimately open the "Black Box" associated with all type of institutions, preserving autonomy whilst building up a new set of relationships with society at large and introducing an "intelligent accountability" associated with a renewed structure of incentives' (Heitor 2008: 20).
17. To our knowledge, at least two public universities hired administrators from the business sector, one an old university, the other being established in 1973.

18. On this matter, Santiago et al. (2006: 242) in a CIPES research project noted 'This group of Portuguese academic managers appear to be at best, reluctant managers, experiencing a number of conflicting expectations and often desiring more time (to be spent) on things other than managerial'. More recently (2008–2009), one of the authors is researching on an international and comparative research project on Women in Higher Education Management (WHEM). In interviews conducted in Portugal with Rectors, both men and women saw themselves as 'academics'. They were greatly reluctant to cast themselves as managers.
19. See Annexes Table A.2, which sets out the most important regulations and events since 1974 that bore upon the Administrative Estate.
20. To summarise, at the beginning of its application, the funding formula included the following variables:

    - Number of students per type of programme in the higher education institution.
    - Definition of the staff: student ratios per type of course (for example, in the field of Engineering, 1 FTE teacher for 11 students; in the field of Medical Sciences, 1 teacher for 6 students; in Humanities, 1 teacher for 20 students, etc.).
    - Definition of non-teaching staff by means of the 'standard' teaching staff per type of course, added to the remaining staff in the rectorate and central services (Engineering, 1 FTE standard teacher →0.75 Non teaching; Medical Sciences, 1 teacher →0.85 Non Teaching; Humanities, 1 teacher →0.35 Non Teaching).
    - Calculation of the 'standard' staff for each institution, which portrayed a certain percentage of the institution's overall budget.
    - If the real situation of the institutions deviated from the 'virtual' budget, a period of adjustment would be set, with the definition of annual convergence levels proxy to that goal, in a 4- to 5-year period.
    - The calculation also included allocations for staff promotions (2%), research allocations (+2% for universities, 0.8% for polytechnics) (Cerdeira 2009a, b).

21. In the year 2010, hints made during the preparation of the upcoming budget suggest that public institutions (including HEIs) will not be allowed to hire new personnel.
22. One of the authors, in interviews with Rectors for the Women in Higher Education Management (WHEM) project, found that they rejected both the idea of managerialism in universities as too the notion they themselves were managers.
23. The new legal framework (Law 62/2007 – RJIES – *Regime Juridico das Instituições de Ensino Superior* of 2007) opens the possibility for HEIs to become foundations governed by private law.
24. Examples of national policies aligning Portuguese higher education with such outside agencies as EU, OECD, World Bank may be seen in the creation of the polytechnic and the implementation of the Bologna Process.
25. Huisman and van der Wende (1999: 351) noted that national systems '... often had an open eye for what was happening in the higher education systems of neighbouring countries or in Europe in general. Fuelled both by the general expectations of The European Commission pleading for a European dimension in higher education, and maybe even more by the OECD education policy reviews, national Governments realised (albeit subjectively) whether their national higher education system was still sufficiently in line with a certain (European) model, even if this ideal model might never be attained nor exist in practice'.
26. The expansion in the Student Estate allowed the expansion of non-academic staff, as the figures above show. Student numbers expanded significantly in the 1980s and on into the 1990s. Furthermore, new constituencies of learners – 'mature students' – began to make their way to higher education. (For this, see Amaral and Magalhães 2009, and the Chap. 16)
27. 'Outside pressure on universities to become more relevant and responsive, more elaborate mechanisms of accountability – even when these mechanisms assume more civilised form as the by-product of quality improvement – and the emergence of practices imported from business world (managerialism) are all assuming an increasing role in higher education' (Amaral and Magalhães 2002: 18–19).

Annexes

Table A.1 Evolution of the civil servants in Portugal from 1979 to 2005

Evolução donº de Efectivos na Administração Pública							
1979	1983	1986	1988	1991	1996	1999	2005
372 086	435 795	464 321	485 368	509 732	619 399	716 418	747 880

Source: Ministério das Finanças e da Administração Pública

References

Altbach, P. (1998). *Comparative higher education: Knowledge, the university and development.* Hong Kong: Comparative Education Research Centre, The University of Hong Kong.

Altbach, P. (1999). The logic of mass higher education. *Tertiary Education and Management, 5*(2), 107–124.

Altbach, P. (2008). The changing nature of HE institutions, HE Systems and their governance. *Seminar Series on Mass Higher Education in UK and International Contexts*, Slough: England.

Amaral, A., & Magalhães, A. (2002). The emergent role of external stakeholders in European higher education governance. In A. Amaral, G. Jones, & B. Karseth (Eds.), *Governing higher education: National perspectives and institutional governance.* Dordrecht: Kluwer Academic Publishers. http://cipes/docs/doc_pdf/abst36.pdf.

Amaral, A., Correia. F., Magalhães, A., Rosa, M. J., Santiago, R., & Teixeira, P. (2002). *O ensino superior pela mão da economia.* Coimbra: Fundação das Universidades Portuguesas - CIPES.

Amaral, A., & Magalhães, A. (2005). Implementation of higher education policies: A Portuguese example. In A. Gornitzka, M. Kogan, & A. Amaral (Eds.), *Reform and change in higher education.* Dordrecht: Springer.

Amaral, A., & Magalhães, A. (2009). Between institutional competition and the search for equality of opportunities: Access of mature students. *Higher Education Policy, 22*(4), 505–521.

Amaral, A., Magalhães, A., & Teixeira, P. (1996). *Management structure in the European Union and South African higher education systems – The Portuguese case.* South Africa: CHEPS.

Amaral, A., Magalhães, A., & Santiago, R. (2003). The rise of academic managerialism in Portugal. In A. Amaral, V. L. Meek, & I. M. Larsen (Eds.), *The higher education managerial revolution?* Dordrecht: Kluwer.

Becher, T., Eraut, M., & Knight, J. (1981). *Policies for educational accountability.* London: Heinemann Educational Books.

Birnbaum, R. (1992). *How academic leadership works.* San Francisco: Jossey-Bass Publishers.

Bleiklie, I. (1998). Justifying the evaluative state: New public management ideals in higher education. *European Journal of Education, 33*(3), 299–316.

Bleiklie, I., & Kogan, M. (2007). Organization and governance of universities. *Higher Education Policy, 20*, 477–493. doi:10.1057/palgrave.hep.8300167.

Brites, J., Machado, M. L., & Santiago. R. (2004). *O ensino superior politécnico em Portugal.* Paper presented at the conference análise comparativa do ensino superior politécnico. Leiria, Portugal.

Cerdeira, L. (2009a). *O Financiamento do Ensino Superior Português: a partilha de custos.* Coimbra: Almedina. CDU 378, 37. ISBN 978–972–40–3978–7.

Cerdeira, L. (2009b). Cost-sharing policy in the European higher education: A comparative perspective. *PEC, 15*(15), 60–77, ICID: 899677, IC™ Value: 5.38

Clark, B. R. (1983). *The higher education system: Academic organisation in cross-national perspective.* Berkeley/London/Los Angeles: University of California Press.

Clark, B. R. (1998). *Creating entrepreneurial universities: Organisational pathways of transformation*. Oxford: IAU Press/Pergamon.

Correia, J. M., Mano, M., Freitas, M. J., & Lopes, J. B. (2000). *Contributos para um modelo de estrutura dirigente nas Universidades Públicas*. Lisboa: ANGUP – Associação de Gestores das Universidades Portuguesas.

Fägerlind, I., & Strömqvist, G. (Eds.). (2004). *New trends in higher education: Reforming higher education in the Nordic countries – studies of change in Denmark, Finland, Iceland, Norway and Sweden*. Paris: UNESCO.

Gordon, G., & Whitchurch, C. (2007). Managing human resources in higher education: The implications of a diversifying workforce. *Higher Education Management and Policy, 19*(2), 135–155.

GPEARI/MCTES. (2010). *Docentes do Ensino Superior [2001 a 2008] – Inquérito ao Registo Biográfico de Docentes do Ensino Superior*. Lisboa: Gabinete de Planeamento, Estratégia, Avaliação e Relações Internacionais.

Hazelkorn, E. (2005). *University research management: Developing research in new institutions*. Paris: OECD.

Heitor, M. (2008). *Which tertiary institutions in times of accelerated technical change? A system approach towards knowledge networks and enhanced societal trust*. Presented at the 2008 Kauffman-Max Planck annual summit on Rethinking the role of the University and public research for the entrepreneurial age.

Henkel, M. (2000). *Academic identities and policy change in higher education*. London/Philadelphia: Jessica Kingsley Publishers.

Hölttä, S. (2008). Funding of universities in Finland. In T. Aarrevaara & F. Maruyama (Eds.), *University reform in Finland and Japan* (pp. 104–116). Tampere: Higher Education Group, Tampere University Press.

Kerr, C., & Gade, M. L. (1986). *The many lives of American presidents: Time, place and character*. Washington, DC: Association of Governing Boards of Universities.

Kogan, M. (1999). Academic and administrative interface. In M. Henkel & B. Little (Eds.), *Changing relationships between higher education and the state* (pp. 263–279). London/Philadelphia: Jessica Kingsley Publishers.

Kwiek, M. (2003). The state, the market and higher education: Challenges for the new century. In M. Kwiek (Ed.), *The university, globalisation, Central Europe*. New York: Peter Lange.

Lane, J. (1987). Against administration. *Studies in Higher Education, 12*(3), 249–260.

Maassen, P. (2006). *The Modernisation of European Higher Education – A multi-level analysis*. Paper presented at the directors general meeting for higher education, Helsinki.

Machado, M. L. (2005). Strategic planning in portuguese higher education institutions (PhD dissertation, Minho University, Portugal).

Machado, M. L., Brites Ferreira, J., Santiago, R., & Taylor, J. S. (2008). Reframing the non-university sector in Europe: Convergence or diversity. In J. S. Taylor, J. Brites Ferreira, M. L. Machado, & R. Santiago (Eds.), *The non-university higher education in Europe* (Higher Education Dynamics Series). Dordrecht: Springer.

Magalhães, A. (2001). Higher education dilemmas and the quest for identity: Politics, knowledge and education in an era of transition. (PhD dissertation, University of Twente, Enschede).

Magalhães, A., & Santiago, R. (2011). Public management, new governance models and changing environments in portuguese higher education. In P. Teixeira & e D. Dill (orgs.), *Public vices, private virtues? Assessing the effects of marketization in higher education* (pp. 177–192). Roterdão: Sense Publishers.

Magalhães, A., Santiago, R., & Carvalho, T. (2005). *O Surgimento do Managerialismo no sistema de Ensino Superior Português*. Matosinhos: CIPES.

MSTHE – Ministry of Science, Technology and Higher Education. (2006.) *Tertiary education in Portugal. Background report: A working document*, Version 1.1. Lisbon: Ministry of Science, Technology and Higher Education.

Neave, G. (1983). The changing face of the academic profession in Western Europe. *European Journal of Education, 18*(3), 217–227.

Neave, G. (1984). Accountability in education. In T. Husén & T. Neville Postlethwaite (Eds.), *International encyclopedia for education, research and studies*. Oxford: Pergamon Press.

Neave, G. (1997). Back to the future: Or, a view on likely brain teasers with which university management is likely to be faced in a Fin de Siècle world. *Tertiary Education and Management, 3*(4), 275–283.

Neave, G. (2002). The stakeholder perspective historically explored. In J. Enders & O. Fulton (Eds.), *Higher education in a globalizing world*. Dordrecht: Kluwer.

Neave, G. (2005). *On snowballs, slopes and the process of Bologna: Some testy reflections on the advance of higher education in Europe*. Paper presentation at ARENA 31, Oslo University.

Neave, G., & van Vught, F. A. (1991). *Prometheus bound: the changing relationship between Government and higher education in Western Europe* (253 pp). Oxford: Pergamon Press.

Neave, G. (forthcoming). *Institutional autonomy, the evaluative state and re-engineering higher education in Western Europe: The prince and his pleasure*. New York/Basingstoke: Palgrave.

OECD. (2007). *Review of the Portuguese higher education system*. Paris: OECD.

Paradeise, C., Reale, E., & Goastellec, G. (2009). A comparative approach to higher education reforms in Western European countries. In C. Paradeise, E. Reale, I. Bleiklie, & E. Ferlie (Eds.), *University governance: Western European comparative perspectives* (pp. 97–225). Heidelberg/London/Dordrecht: Springer.

Rosa, M. J. V., & Chitas, P. (2010). *Portugal: os Números*. Lisboa: Fundação Francisco Manuel dos Santos.

Santiago, R., Carvalho, T., Amaral, A., & Meek, V. L. (2006). Changing patterns in the middle management of higher education institutions: The case of Portugal. *Higher Education, 52*, 215–250.

Santiago, P., Tremblay, K. E., Basri, E., & Arnal, E. (2008). *Tertiary education for the knowledge society. Special features: Equity, innovation, labour market, internationalisation* (Vol. 2). Paris: OECD.

Slaughter, S., & Leslie, L. L. (1997). *Academic capitalism: Politics, policies, and the entrepreneurial university*. Baltimore: The Johns Hopkins University Press.

Taylor, J. S., Amaral, A., & Machado, M. L. (2007a). Strategic planning in U.S. higher education: Can it succeed in Europe? *Planning for Higher Education, 35*(2), 5–17. Ann Arbor: The Society for College and University Planning

Taylor, J. S. Graça, M. Machado, M. L., & Sousa, S. (2007b). Adapting in order to promote change. In W. Locke, & U. Teichler (Eds.), *The changing conditions for academic work and careers in select countries* (pp. 211–227). Kassel: International Centre for Higher Education Research.

Taylor, J. S., Machado, M. L., & Peterson, M. (2008). Leadership and strategic management: Keys to institutional priorities and planning. *European Journal of Education, 43*(3), 369–386.

Thorens, J. (2006). Liberties, freedom and autonomy: A few reflections on academia's estate. *Higher Education Policy, 19*(1), 87–110.

Trow, M. (1975, November). The public and private lives of higher education. *Daedalus, 104*, 113–127.

Whitchurch, C. (2008a.) Shifting identities, Blurring Boundaries: The Changing Roles of Professional Managers in Higher Education. *UC Berkeley: Center for Studies in Higher Education. Research and Occasional Paper Series* CSHE.10.2008 http://escholarship.org/uc/item/3xk701cnpage-1

Whitchurch, C. (2008b). Shifting identities and blurring boundaries: The emergence of third space professionals in UK education. *Higher Education Quarterly, 62*(4), 377–396.

Whitchurch, C. (2009). The rise of the blended professional in higher education: A comparison between the United Kingdom, Australia and the United States. *Higher Education, 58*(3), 407–418.

Chapter 16
The Student Estate

Madalena Fonseca

Introduction

In the 35 years since the 1974 Revolution, which overthrew the Dictatorship, the number of students in Portugal's higher education system rose more than sixfold, from 57,000 to 373,000 between 1974 and 2008, having peaked at over 400,000 in 2002. The largest increases took place between 1980 and 2000, when the decade 1985 to 1995 saw the number of students triple from 106,000 to 313,000. Over the same period, Portugal's population grew by less than 20%, from 8.9 million in 1975 to 10.6 million in 2008. Clearly, the enormous significance of the number of students driving into the country's higher education system cannot be doubted (Fig. 16.1).

In terms of student numbers, it was indeed the most extraordinary period of growth in higher education. Despite this, the highest level of education attained by the active population aged 15+ is considerably lower than the European Union average, and is still far from the utopian ideal of *Education for All* (Fig. 16.2).[1]

Students are at the core of higher education. They are its business. For that reason, they merit close scrutiny and particularly so over the past four decades in view of their spiralling numbers. Together with academics and university administration, students constitute one of the 'Estates' of higher education (Chap. 14). They are, however, very much a Third Estate, visible on account of their numbers but, today, with little effective participation in the system. The Student Estate has naturally the enthusiasm and generosity of the young and, at certain special moments, has the potential, always remembered, but never mentioned, to galvanise society, if not always to change it (Chaps. 2, 3 and 9).

M. Fonseca (✉)
A3ES, Praça de Avaladade 6 – 5 Frente, 1700-36 Lisbon, Portugal
e-mail: madalena.fonseca@a3es.pt

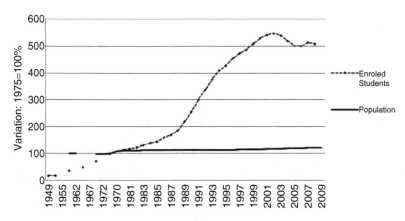

Fig. 16.1 Enrolled students in higher education in Portugal

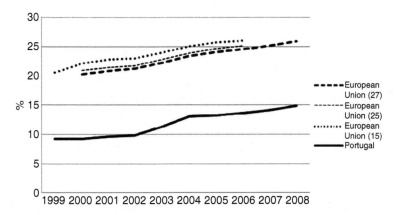

Fig. 16.2 Economically active population by highest level of education attained terciary education levels 5–6 ISCED

In the late 1950s, higher education began to expand all over Europe, giving rise to a process later known as 'massification'. Growth in student numbers was not at first accompanied by democratisation and modernisation of higher education, save in a very particular sense namely, opening up of access to a wider social spectrum. This was certainly the explicit aim of education policy. But it did not entail immediate changes in power and participation in the internal governance of universities and polytechnics. Certainly, higher education became more diversified and more complex, both with regard to its formal structure increasingly differentiated and segmented, as was the background of those entering it (Trow 2000; Neave 1976; Amaral et al. 2000; Amaral 2008a; Maassen 2008b; Magalhães et al. 2009). New and different types of institutions were set up. Different fields of teaching and research emerged which, in turn, drew in more and different types of students. The traditional recruitment of students from the social elite extended to sections of the population hitherto less represented – particularly women, who today form the majority in the Student Estate – as well as students from lower socioeconomic backgrounds, older students, many of them currently employed, and those entering higher education, not directly from secondary school, but on the basis of skills acquired in the labour market or in professional training (Amaral et al. 2000; Amaral 2008a, b; Santiago et al. 2008), and finally, but no less important, students from peripheral areas beyond the main urban centres (Chaps. 4 and 6).

This chapter focuses on the students themselves. Over and above studying the Student Estate *as an institution*, it sets out to understand the cultures of students and their families as part of the major secular changes that unfolded across Portugal over the last 35 years. Massification in higher education brought with it more students but also more first-generation students.[2] This, coupled with society's overall development, changed profoundly the way higher education system socialised students. In the past, the *university* (Readings 1997: 64)[3] provided a significant element of socialisation in the lives of students (Brennan and Patel 2008: 23). Today, this initiation is neither so intense nor so generalised. The *campus* as a rite of passage between the family into which students are born and the attainment of personal independence is no longer necessarily a central part of the student experience. Growth in size and diversity generated different types of segmentation and stratification, thereby bringing into higher education many of the conflicts and contradictions that once flourished in society beyond university and in the world outside. More diversified, seemingly more stratified and more polarised, the ways in which higher education perceives students today and, for that matter, the way the students perceive higher education are more varied by far.

The place of the student seems to have shifted from the centre of higher education to become a secondary order variable (Trow 1996). True, the *university* no longer absorbs the whole social agenda of students as it used to. Today, the lives of students are more complex, have other interests, including work and/or family commitments (Brennan and Patel 2008) (Chaps. 6 and 10). Higher education has changed. '(Politically) it has become more important but at the same time less special' (Maassen 2008a: 74). Though not necessarily in ruins (Readings 1997), nor devoid of either mission or soul, still much of it is strangely *low cost* (Gaggi and Nardzulli 2006), dominated less by the middle classes, who are themselves being ground down. Portugal's university students have changed in a world that is also changing, with pathways sometimes converging, sometimes diverging.

The second part of this chapter focuses on the student universe in higher education in Portugal, with a brief description of their numbers, characteristics and geographic location. Their recent evolution is described, with 2002 – the apogee in the volume of students – as a reference point. Part Three explores likely trends in the future in the light of the 35 years since the Revolution of 1974 – years that saw the real campus transformed into the virtual and invisible campus of our time (Rothblatt 2007). Part Four, more an evaluation than a conclusion, looks at the prospects in the short term for students in Portugal. It seeks to shed light on changes not only in the volume of the Student Estate but also in its attitudes and how the system of higher education in its turn adapted to the culture of the young.

The chapter draws on earlier studies and on statistics from the *Ministérios da Educação e da Ciência, Tecnologia e Ensino Superior*, Eurostudent, *Instituto Nacional Estatistica*, from the *Agência de Avaliação e Acreditação do Ensino Superior*, Eurydice and Eurostat.

The Student Estate in Graphs and Figures

In the academic year 2008/2009, 373,000 students were registered as following higher education courses in Portugal. Of these, 75% were enrolled in state institutions and 25% in private institutions. State universities accounted for 175,000 students, almost half the total, followed in descending order by state polytechnics with 106,000 students, private universities with around 61,000 and private polytechnics with almost 30,000. Since 2002, the year that marked the historic maximum of almost 401,000, overall student numbers fell by 7%, with both losses followed by gains, and thus with no clear trend emerging (Table A.1 – Appendix). Private institutions lost the most, with a fall of around 18%. Relatively speaking, since 2002, the most marked rise involved male students at public universities and to a lesser extent at private polytechnics. Apart from these two sub-groups, since then all others have decreased. The most significant internal shifts resulting from these losses are the rise in the relative importance of state education and the increased relative weight of male students whose numbers are approaching those of women.

The provision of higher education in Portugal currently stands at 13 state universities, one state university institute, one state distance-learning university, 15 state polytechnics, five specialised higher education institutions, four military institutions (state), around 80 private entities administering both universities and polytechnics, which in some instances offer both types of courses. In all, there are over 100 private faculties and other higher education schools and one Catholic university.

Currently, 4,376 study programmes are managed, 70% by the state, almost half of which are university courses. Bachelor degrees (*Licenciatura* in Portugal) account for 38%. Master's degrees represent the largest segment, which, when combined with Integrated Master's courses, made up almost half of the higher education courses on offer (Table 16.1).

The number of first-time enrolments raised over the past few years, to reach its highest level in the academic year 2008/2009, with 115,000 students, almost one-third of all students in higher education.[4] The public system saw the largest increases, whilst student numbers entering private institutions remained more or less stable. First-time enrolments amongst men rose more than for women (respectively 42% and 12% between 2000/2001 and 2008/2009). First-time enrolments for women have even declined 30% in private polytechnics. Master's or specialisation courses and other, non-degree courses account for a very significant number of first-time enrolments in the first year. Indeed, about 20% of all new students registered for second cycle courses and master's degrees, and almost 10% for integrated master's (Table 16.2).

Table 16.1 Higher education in Portugal: study programmes 2009/2010

		Bachelor's	Master's	Integrated master's	Doctorate	Total No.	%
State	Universities	463	1,085	111	478	2,137	48.83
	Polytechnics	591	372			963	22.01
	Total	1,054	1,457	111	478	3,100	70.84
Private	Universities	367	391	27	66	851	19.45
	Polytechnics	246	129			375	8.57
	Total	613	520	27	66	1,226	28.02
Associations		0	26		24	50	1.14
Total	No.	1,667	2,003	138	568	4,376	100
	%	38.09	45.77	3.15	12.98		100

Source: A3ES: Agência de Avaliação e Acreditação do Ensino Superior (Agency for Assessment and Accreditation of Higher Education – April 2010)

Table 16.2 Access to higher education: first-time first-year enrolments 2008/2009

Degree type	Enrolled students	(%)
First cycle (Bachelor's)	73,444	63.66
Integrated master's	10,857	9.41
Second cycle (Master's)	22,968	19.91
Third cycle (PhD)	3,340	2.89
Without grade	4,763	4.13
Total	115,372	100

At present, undergraduate courses account for only 64% of new enrolments in higher education in Portugal. This new distribution of students across degree types began to develop in 2005/2006, following the end of the first Bologna round (Fig. 16.3) (Chap. 11). New students registering for doctorates and other postgraduate cycles are a smaller, but nonetheless significant group, and their numbers may rise in the future.

Currently, higher education in Portugal counts more females than males – 53.4% females and 46.6% males in 2008/2009 – itself the outcome of admitting in recent times large numbers of girls and women which overturned an earlier male predominance. This pattern is evident in all European countries (Eurostudent 2005) and in the majority of OECD countries (Santiago et al. 2008), although a trend of convergence is evident (Fig. 16.4).

In some subject domains of higher education in Portugal, as is the case elsewhere (Santiago et al. 2008: 27, vol. 2), the gender gap in Science, Maths and Information Technologies, Engineering, Manufacturing, Construction and Services, has tended to widen. Today's Engineering courses still have three men to every woman. Men also predominate considerably amongst mature students, students currently working and those on non-degree courses. In the early years of the twenty-first century, a higher proportion of males registered for Doctoral courses, but the situation is

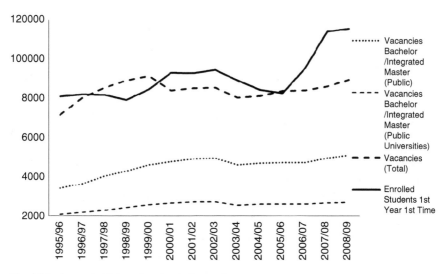

Fig. 16.3 Access in higher education in Portugal

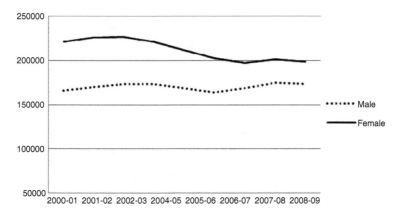

Fig. 16.4 Enrolled students in higher education in Portugal by gender

changing with a larger proportion of women, a situation similar to other course levels (For the implications of this for the Academic Estate see Chap. 14). A clear predominance of men pertains only in Integrated Master's courses, probably because most of these courses are found precisely in areas, such as Engineering, where the percentage of men was already higher. In the academic year 2008/2009, the gender distribution across the whole system was 87 males for every 100 females, the highest being in state universities, with 95.6 males for every 100 females, and the lowest being at private polytechnics with 49 males to every 100 females (GPEARI/MCTES 2009). Over-representation of women at private polytechnics can chiefly

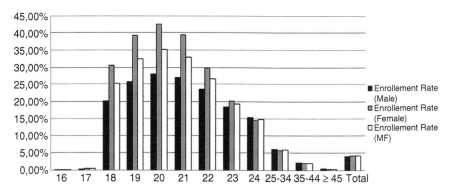

Fig. 16.5 Enrollement rate (%)

be explained by the increased supply of places in these institutions for Nursing, and other health-related areas, apart from Medicine, in the hope of attracting applicants who were not admitted to Medicine, Veterinary Science and Pharmaceutical Sciences, and other applicants turned down by state institutions (Fonseca et al. 2011).

Student age distribution shows a clear difference between men and women, less visible among older students however, than among the younger, which points towards social inequity in access to higher education (Fig. 16.5). A large number of males enter the labour market earlier, putting off higher education, a situation borne out by some case studies. The difference between genders according to social class yielded the highest values, with a higher presence of women, among the children of unqualified working class parents at the University of Coimbra, according to a study by Estanque and Nunes (2003: 21). Portuguese students, however, take the view that gender does not condition access or choice of institution (Cerdeira 2009: 428). Such a view supports the hypothesis that obstacles are not direct but take the form of socioeconomic factors, which lead to the imbalance between the genders that becomes more evident when the indicators are analysed for subsystems.

Indeed, when access routes[5] for first-year first-time enrolments in 2008/2009 are examined, clearly different trends are present (Table 16.3). In public higher education, differences between the genders are less significant. Almost 75% of students enter through the general route or regime, and about 10% enter as holders of higher qualifications. In both cases, there are no significant differences between genders. The over 23 access regime is very significant in public polytechnics among males. Change of course accounted for over 10% of registrations of males at private institutions, as did and with the same percentage for females restarting their education at polytechnics. The over 23 access regime was important in both genders, being 15.5% for females and 31.7% for males at private polytechnics. Indeed, in the subsystem of private polytechnics for males, the general access regime showed the lowest values at 40.9%. Clearly, stratification starts with the access routes themselves. Public universities stand out at this point, for despite internal differences,

Table 16.3 Access regimes/routes first-year first-time enrolments 2008/2009 (% > 10%)

Higher education institutions and gender			General regime	Restarting	Change of course	Holders of previous degree	Over 23 access regime	Total
Public	Universities	M	71.73		6.66	10.84	6.04	100
		F	77.29		4.65	10.44	4.46	100
	Polytechnic institutes	M	66.13	2.18	6.88	2.83	13.93	100
		F	73.93	5.35	4.21	3.63	9.32	100
Private	Universities	M	52.92	0.08	11.07	2.81	25.45	100
		F	63.27	0.06	8.03	4.71	18.45	100
	Polytechnic institutes	M	40.87	9.97	12.51	1.62	31.68	100
		F	57.03	15.94	6.29	2.80	15.46	100
Total	Private	MF	55.77	4.85	9.17	3.29	21.67	100
	Public	MF	72.85	1.68	5.52	7.48	7.85	100
	Total	MF	68.77	2.44	6.39	6.48	11.16	100

M male, *F* female

they recruit from the outset the *best* applicants – those with the highest final grades at secondary school; they attract the highest number of students having intermediate- or higher-level qualifications, and the gender distribution is more balanced.

Subject areas drawing in the highest number of students are, in descending order, Social Sciences, Business and Law, with almost one-third of the total, Engineering, Manufacturing and Construction with slightly over 22% of the total, followed by Health and Welfare with 17% (Table A.1 – Appendix). Changes, since 2002, and the trends emerging from the number of first-time registrations for the first year show that subject choice is changing. The only study areas not to lose students after the peak of 2002 were Health and Welfare and Services – precisely the subjects highly attractive to new students. The Service area[6] saw the greatest rise in student numbers.

By contrast, teacher training not only faced a haemorrhage in student numbers, it was also less in demand. The rise in the number of new students involved more men than women. Furthermore, men increasingly apply to Arts and Humanities – which previously was not the case – Social Sciences, Business and Law and Services.

The most recent application statistics for the public sector in 2009/2010[7] show 52,557 students applied for 51,352 places. Of these applicants, 40,067 registered in the first phase,[8] that is a 78% enrolment rate. With 23,149 taking up their first choice, effectively 44% of students were able to start on subjects and institutions of their first preference. Subject areas with the highest number of candidates choosing them first were in order of importance, Management, Electronics (Informatics), Medicine, and Law[9], which falls in with the general tendency in recent years.

The age distribution of registered students suggests a clear move towards diversification and expansion in the intake age. A large group of 'mature' students, older than those usually recruited in the past is evident – whilst the number of younger first-time enrolments in the first year has also increased (Fig. 16.6).

Data do not always permit an assessment of the social background of students entering higher education. Approximately 40% of those registering for the first time and 70% of all those registered in 2008/2009 were unaware of – or were unwilling

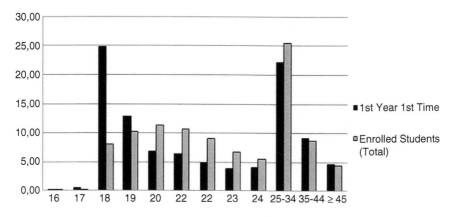

Fig.16.6 Enrolled students by age (%)

Table 16.4 Social indicators 2008/2009

Percentage of students	Enrolled students first year first time	Total enrolled students
Part-time (%)	1.11	1.48
In evening courses (%)	11.96	9.87
With working student status (%)	12.07	11.76
Applicants for grants and other social support (%)	16.87	13.15
With no other professional activity (only students)	26.53	19.66
Workers (not self-employed) (%)	12.82	7.11

Source: GPEARI. MCTES

to disclose – their parents' educational level. Over half the first-time enrolees and overall, almost 80% were unaware of – or refused to disclose – their parents' current occupational status. Fifty-six percent of those registered for the first time in the first year and 71% of the student population gave no indication as to their own occupational status. While 19.6% of the latter claimed only student status, 26.5% of the former stated they were simply students (Chap. 6). Thirteen percent of students registering in the first year for the first time were employed. For the whole student population, those employed amounted to 7%.[10] Whilst this might point to a rise in the number of students working who embarked on higher education, and thus confirms the trend towards non-traditional students in higher education, the non-response rate suggests caution is not misplaced (Table 16.4).[11]

Case studies drawing on questionnaire-based enquiry confirm the enduring social disparity in students' socioeconomic origin, despite a steady increase in the participation of students from lower income families and from families with less advantaged backgrounds (Gonçalves et al. 2009; Cerdeira 2009; Justino 2010; Tavares 2008; Costa and Lopes 2008). In their study of Coimbra University in 2003, Elísio Estanque and João Nunes were categorical: 'These data reveal recent tendencies for the opening up and democratisation of (the) University (in Portugal) making it easier for children from the working classes to enter higher education'

(Estanque and Nunes 2003: 17).[12] Systematic studies for England between 1994 and 2000 confirmed the persistence of social imbalances in recruitment for higher education, largely because the socially and culturally less well-off often believe certain institutions are 'not for them' (Christie 2007: 2446–2453).[13]

Students elsewhere in Europe have also been critical of recent changes. In their view, the social dimension in the Bologna Process remains unmet. Nor has any genuine democratisation been achieved in the matter of socioeconomic background of students, still less done for students with families, those handicapped or working (Carapinha 2009).

Amongst the more developed European countries, Ireland stands out with the highest participation rates in higher education by students with working class parents – a participation rate which is almost in keeping with their distribution in the population at large. Germany, Portugal, Austria and France, however, have the lowest rate with a ratio between the two percentages of approximately 0.5 (Eurostudent 2005: 61).[14] When turning to the educational level of students' mothers, the highest scores on this indicator across Europe are to be found in Spain, the Netherlands and Ireland (Eurostudent 2005: 63), and Portugal still remains in that group of countries with the lowest participation rates for this group of students (Chap. 6). Such inequalities are confirmed when the participation rate of students with parents who themselves had attended higher education is examined. Compared to their part in the overall population, students with degree-holding parents are over-represented in higher education. Whilst this phenomenon holds good for all European countries, it is particularly marked in Portugal, though to a lesser extent in Ireland (Santiago et al. 2008: 23, Vol. 2). Yet, changes to the social economic origins of the Student Estate do not depend on policy alone (HEFCE 2009). They are also shaped by lower levels of education and attainment, by a country's economic progress and by the integration and articulation between policies applied to school and to higher education (Santiago et al. 2008).

Equity is not just a matter of fairness and transparency in access. It engages the broader question of equality of opportunity and social inclusion as well (Woessmann 2004). And here, equity ought not to be divorced from funding. Changes in funding higher education are well-nigh universal. Once entirely born by governments, costs are today shared by families and students. The debate over cost sharing and increased private funding has grown, as has higher education, though self-evidently funding remains a key to massification and democratisation in higher education (Santiago et al. 2008; Teixeira et al. 2006; Cerdeira 2009). Student status has moved on from being a 'student-citizen' to become a 'student-client' or a 'shopper' (Brennan and Patel 2009) – a consumer who pays. In Portugal, fees were *increased*[15] in 1992 and, after a short interlude, rose from 1996 to the present (Chap. 3). Currently, students in state higher education are charged 1,000€ per annum[16] for a first-degree course (*Licenciatura*), around 1,250€ for second-cycle courses (Master's) and around 3,000€ for third-cycle courses (Doctorate's). The aim to broaden access to higher education, which is one meaning of democratisation – and cost sharing – appears paradoxical, if not contradictory. If the task of education is to reduce social inequity, then making families bear the costs, however implemented, creates very real barriers to all social classes participating in higher education (Le Chaperain 2008).

Students bear not only fees and other direct outlays but also opportunity cost, that is the price paid for delaying the acquisition of other goods and services in the hope of a return on the *investment* students make in their education. Perceived opportunity cost varies according to social strata and cultural level, and, for some, is itself an obstacle to equality of access (Le Chaperain 2008: 17). Moreover, higher education is a positional good. It confers a competitive advantage on students, the prospect of higher status when competing later for jobs (Marginson 1998) (Chap. 13). Although different from what was identified by Roger Geiger, in the USA, as the bifurcation of American higher education, with a selective sector contrasting with an open (non-selective) sector (Geiger 2009), there is, in Portugal, increasing competition for places in more prestigious universities and study programmes, which are quasi-monopolised by the upper classes given that attendance at a selective institution enhances career prospects and earnings.

The Spatial and Locational Dimensions in Equity

In present-day Portugal, spatial and locational aspects of equity are no longer relevant. The nation's higher education network closely ties in with its urban system, with a concentration of the largest number of institutions and study places in the two major metropolitan areas of Lisbon and Porto, with a more or less balanced spread in second- and third-tier urban centres, directly related to their functional importance and to the demographic characteristics of their region.

From the mid-1970s onwards, the network's coverage, with the creation of new universities and the establishment of polytechnics throughout the country in the decade following, saw supply brought close to the potential demand. The current network of state higher education has remained practically unaltered since 1994, when the last polytechnic was founded. Contrary to government expectations, private higher education never spread all over the country. It remained highly concentrated in the metropolitan areas (Amaral et al. 2008) (Fig. 16.7a, b). In recent years, private provision did not grow. On the contrary, it shrank.

Despite the availability of higher education, a clear imbalance persisted in the state sector between supply and demand (Teixeira et al. 2009) (Fig. 16.8). The state has difficulty meeting the objectives of efficiency and equity both in supporting regional development and in boosting human capital in more remote areas. As has already been pointed out, in 2009 students in their first choice filled only 44% of all places available in the public sector, though the number of applying exceeded the number of places. Mismatch is evident both in respect of study fields and region. In effect, taking into account similar access data for the last years (Amaral et al. 2008), students move mainly into the two metropolitan areas of Lisbon and Porto. The reverse flow out of the metropolitan areas to smaller inland towns is less visible (Chap. 4).

With one public sector Open University, distance learning in Portugal is moving ahead. Some take the view that for certain fields of study, and given the appropriate equipment and infrastructure, information and communication technologies might

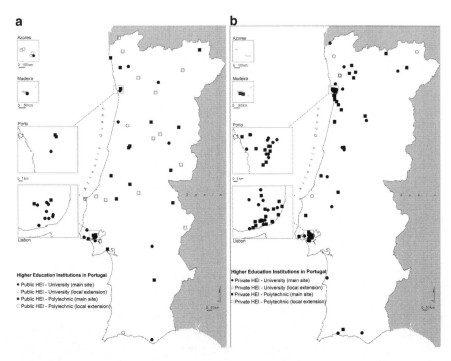

Fig. 16.7 (**a**) Public higher education institutions and (**b**) Private higher education institutions

extend higher education access to remote areas of the country. However, it is by no means sure that distance learning might not accentuate their marginalisation further. Learning is still a social activity in which physical proximity retains its importance, and, last but not the least, life in the multi-function urban centre may well provide value added to both teaching and learning.

Student Mobility: A Sociological Phenomenon

Paradoxically, the social and spatial extension of higher education has seen student mobility decline not only because of the greater availability of courses across the country, which brings supply closer to students, but also because the socially less favoured and non-traditional student tends to be less mobile. Mobility concerns not only the individual but also the family. Nor is finance the only consideration though obviously highly significant. Leaving home to study at a university is an idea fast disappearing, in part because of improvement in access and also because of the decline in social standing associated with higher education. For those commanding less social and cultural capital, staying at home is no disadvantage. On the contrary, all too often they cannot afford to study on their own which, seen in this light, is itself a very real handicap. For reasons as much emotional as of personal choice and lifestyle, students prefer to remain in contact with the local network of family and

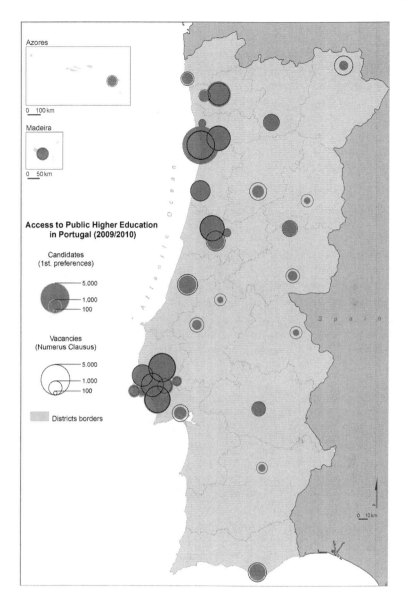

Fig. 16.8 Access to Public HEI 2009/2010: Candidates and Vacancies

friends. Moving out elsewhere is seen as a threat. This is not unique to Portugal. In England, for instance, 8 students out of 12 did not even consider leaving the parental nest (Christie 2007: 2446).[17]

Certainly, by tradition, working class families urged their children to leave home the better to follow in the fortunes of middle class youngsters who tend in general to be more adventuresome (Patiniotis and Holdsworth 2005: 92). Young people from disadvantaged homes, however, need a strong will to break the ties with local and family networks. For them, entering higher education is not just a financial risk. It is a threat to their identity (Patiniotis and Holdsworth 2005: 92). Naturally, for students older or actively employed, the difficulties of moving out are more complex still. Leaving home, hearth and family to study is a concept associated with the middle classes (Patiniotis and Holdsworth 2005), with social and economic elites, whose contact networks reach farther and are denser.

Home, Family and Friends

In Portugal, more than half the students in higher education live with parents or other relatives – between 55% and 58% according to Eurostudent (2005: 70; Cerdeira 2009: 432). Each sector of higher education shows significant variations. The highest proportions of the 'non-mobile' are found in private universities, where over 80% of students live at home (Cerdeira 2009: 435). By contrast, students at public universities are amongst the least likely to be 'home based' (Chap. 6). Research undertaken in 2005 by Luísa Cerdeira, based on a major survey of university students, showed the most significant factor in the choice of institution to be entry grades, followed by location. Clearly, mobility is strongly influenced by type of course and possibly by the institution's standing (Cerdeira 2009: 422), as the analysis of entry data revealed (Amaral et al. 2008). Apparently, students are ready to leave home and move elsewhere if this means they can embark on the study programme of their first choice at a state university. If faced with having to register at a private university, whether by choice or perforce, they tend to stay at home. Mobility, in the case of private universities, involves a hefty rise in costs, quite apart from enrolment fees, which outstrip by far those levied by state universities.

The phenomenon of differential mobility is particularly evident in Medicine, Veterinary Science, Pharmacy and Dentistry (Fonseca et al. 2011). In contrast to growing immobility of new students in higher education stands the rise in international student mobility associated with European exchange programmes and with *Erasmus* in particular. The 1999 Bologna declaration and the process of re-contouring higher education around the mutual recognition of qualifications were launched. It arose not only as a response to this increasing mobility but at the same time to facilitate it, with the creation of better conditions for global mobility of Europeans with regard to the labour market.

Dropout and Survival

In the past, policies for higher education concentrated more on access than on outcomes. In their contemporary form, however, priority is now placed on the end result. Analysing 'learning outcomes' is a means to make higher education more efficient and effective. By reducing failure and dropout, such leverage ensures that as many students as possible successfully complete their studies.

An examination of 'survival rates' in higher education, based on OECD data for Portugal in the year 2000, showed them to be very similar to the majority of European countries at ISCED level 5-A and well below average for a small group of countries at level ISCED 5-B (MCTES 2006: 87–88).[18] The OECD report of 2006, *Thematic Review of Tertiary Education: Portugal* (*idem*), suggested that lower efficiency at the ISCED level 5-B was influenced by the system of assigning students places together with the effects of the *numerus clausus*, which caused applicants for some courses and institutions to enrol in courses and at institutions which were not their first choice (*idem*: 89). The same report compared the proportion of students registered who failed either to complete their courses or to obtain degrees against all students registered as entering the same year. Whilst dropout rates rose for the years 2002–2004, this might suggest either less rigorous admission standards or the absence of effective teaching save in Arts, Health and Education Sciences apparently more efficient.

No precise details are to hand in Portugal on current dropout rates in higher education. Information exists on the number of years the individual student takes to complete a course. This does not, however, permit a detailed analysis to be made. Comparable data lacks and constructing time series data over a suitable period is not thought possible! At the University of Porto, however, student performance saw a marked improvement in study duration – more students took a shorter time to complete their studies, particularly after the Bologna Process was introduced (Universidade do Porto 2010). Since Porto is the largest public sector university with a correspondingly broad subject offering, it could, with a certain latitude, be seen as giving some hints as to the possible general trend at system level.

Official statistics on graduate unemployment do not allow any more precise diagnostic than the general statement that graduates are less likely to find themselves unemployed than non-graduates (Fig. 16.9) (Chap. 13).

There is, however, a significant disparity in unemployment rates between men and women graduates to the detriment of the latter, as Table 16.5 shows.

Institutions that enjoy high prestige and draw on potentially *excellent* students seek to set themselves apart from the rest, by reinforcing their links with networks of excellence nationally and internationally, in new patterns of elitism. Universal higher education, seen by Martin Trow in the 1970s as the third stage in the development of higher education following on the stages of elitism and massification (Trow 1973), is universal only in respect of external intake. The inner dimensions of higher education and their accompanying dynamic drive, however, towards accentuating difference, which bids fair to take on the characteristics of a highly complex geometry of segregation.

Portuguese Students on the Eve of the Revolution

In the run-up to the Revolution of 25 April 1974, higher education in Portugal, like most other systems in Europe, was highly elitist. By contrast, however, with other systems of higher education in Western Europe, growth and institutional expansion

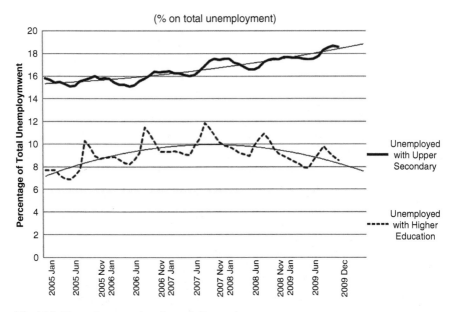

Fig. 16.9 Unemployment of graduates in Portugal

Table 16.5 Unemployed graduated by gender

	Unemployed		Unemployed high education graduated	
	Nr	%	Nr	%
M	236,791	46.9	15,007	34.3
F	267,984	53.1	28,748	65.7
Total	504,775	100.0	43,755	100.0

in Portugal, timid at best, had only begun to be considered (Chaps. 2 and 3). There were 4 universities in 3 cities – Lisbon, Porto and Coimbra, and degree courses lasted from 5 to 6 years. Higher education was still home to an elite, social and economic but also cultural and educational, which embraced both students and teachers, an elite far better informed than the average citizen and, to a limited degree, part of broader international networks. These elites were to be the driving force in opening up and modernising higher education, though striking inequalities remained (Chaps. 2, 3, 9 and 12). Traditionally turbulent, against authority and then influenced by the heady days of May 1968, Portuguese students injected into the university both a spirit of confrontation and a determination to break with the past.

Prior to the demise of the Dictatorship, university student activism in Portugal had begun to impinge on the political life of the country both from within and from without higher education. The most evident signs of this tension, which often mirrored the broader problems in Portuguese society of the day, took the form of pronounced mobilisation amongst the Student Estate. A strong associative movement led on to confrontation in different forms (Estanque 2008).

Student associations, the oldest of which were founded in the nineteenth century and at the start of the twentieth century, especially during the First Republic, had become centres of political activism. From the 1960s – apart from the routine issues of academic life and student high spirits – they became increasingly involved in the political life of the country, opposing the Dictatorship and supporting ideals of democracy, human rights, freedom of expression and, in particular, the fight against colonialism and colonial wars (Chaps. 2 and 3).

Earlier, student associations had been viewed as a threat to the regime. In 1956, an attempt was made to rein in their activity through the promulgation of Decree-Law 40900: 'This measure permitted the appointment of association leaders only after authorisation by the Ministry, (it) established the participation of a "permanent representative of the director of the faculty" in all associative meetings and gave the Minister the power to replace elected committees with "administrative committees", nominated by the Minister who could suspend their activity or even ban them permanently' (Grilo 1999).

From this point on, student activism intensified (Torgal 1999, 2008). It moved outside the university. Students became more engaged in the struggle against Fascism. Demonstrations, government bans, crackdowns, police baton charges and imprisonment, strikes and other measures fell thick and fast which served to draw more and more students into the fray. In 1962, the so-called 'Academic Crisis' erupted. Its epicentre lay in Lisbon, followed by Coimbra and, to a lesser extent, Porto.[19] The government responded with Draconian measures, outlawed student associations and forbade the ritual of *luto académico*[20] (student mourning). Try though it might to control student associations by placing their running in the hands of those known to be favourable to the regime, the government did not succeed in muzzling the Student Estate. Rather the contrary, it added further fuel to feed the flames. One of the most marked student demonstrations occurred in 1969 at Coimbra. An official ceremony, attended by the Head of State,[21] was singled out for boycott by students, an action that brought swift retribution and all due repression from both police and military. A large number of students were arrested and many wounded. The reasons behind the student protest were many, and political protest spread far beyond the university. In 1971, for example, the Coimbra Academic Association (*Associação Académica de Coimbra*) was closed down, which sparked off another round of repression and harassment of students opposed to the regime. Amongst the instruments of suasion the government brought to bear was immediate and forcible induction of student protesters into the armed forces. They were then dispatched to fight the colonial wars in Portuguese Africa.

In short, on the eve of the Revolution, student protest had become so pervasive and had acquired such a level of organisation that with the abandonment of punitive measures by the government, the student body became an important driving force for reshaping higher education in Portugal.

Politically more active than the rest of the population, students played an important role in the Revolution. They allied with the *MFA – Movimento das Forças Armadas* (Armed Forces Movement), which spearheaded the coup of April 25 – and with 'the people'. In effect, students were an active component in the Revolution.

Student Participation in Higher Education: Merely Numbers or an 'Estate'?

Political experience accumulated by students and their organisations gave both a privileged position as leading players in the revolutionary period – PREC[22] – between 1974 and 1977 (Chap. 3). The RGAs[23] – General Assemblies of Students, which mobilised almost the whole student body – were hotbeds where issues of politics and education were thrashed out. Decisions on many aspects of institutional life were made. Teachers were purged. New teachers were awarded contracts. Governing bodies were elected. Assessment criteria were hammered out and set in place.[24] In the deliberations these meetings unleashed, students expressed most intensely – and acted out to the full – their role as a Third Estate. They moved onto and began to participate in university governing boards. They set up and organised faculty assemblies and management committees on which students and teachers were represented in equal numbers. In universities, the language of revolution, welded together by a mixture of traditional Marxism and military jargon, became the dialogue of the moment. *Comités* were set up. Situations were defused and disarmed (*despoletadas*[25]).

> ...the Revolution naturally brought with it claims for the 'democratisation' and 'socialisation' of education. These statements followed the student struggles of the 60's, with after-effects in the 70's. As a result, a climate of confusion in education in general, and in higher education in particular, by the revolutionary measures adopted, with administrative pass[26], removal of teachers, changes to the curricula in accordance with Marxist principles, mass entry of students into higher education, preceded by the experiment of 'civic service', with no regard for the criteria hitherto adopted for selection of students or any other, etc. (Torgal 2000: 20) (See also Chap. 3 and 9)

Parity in elected bodies between students and teachers was confirmed. It was to remain in place over the decades that followed. In 1988, the law granting university autonomy[27] confirmed this principle in University Assemblies, in Senates and in the Assembly of Representatives at Faculty level. Only in 2007 with the new Higher Education Framework Law – RJIES[28] – was parity, in its turn, done away with as a legacy of the Revolution and the rebirth of democracy (Chap. 7).

The 'Cooling Out' of the Student Estate

Since the high noon of the Revolution, social and political activism amongst university students has cooled. The collectivist mental set is less apparent. Today, students tend to be more individualistic in their behaviour (Estanque 2008: 26), a feature which reflects a more marked individualism in social relations generally. They display closer affinity with those tendencies generally abroad in Portugal, tendencies that one scholar interpreted as part of 'a growing divorce between politics and the population' (Estanque 2008: 35). One instance of this broader phenomenon of 'privatisation in politics' emerged from a survey in 2006/2007 of students at the University of Porto.

Those polled held the family to be the most important thing in their lives, followed respectively by friends, work and leisure. Their participation in the life of the community was no longer strongly tied in with party politics (Gonçalves et al. 2009: 44).

Effectively, behaviour of students in higher education reflects nowadays the segments of society from which they hail. The growing place of women as students, the presence of mature students, of children from working class homes, increasingly given over to academic success, to getting a degree as quickly as possible, uninvolved in, and detached from student associations and movements, all contributed to a decline in student participation and engagement which were so marked and so important in the period leading up to and after the Revolution. Once, different academic subject fields and their attendant 'cultures' (Becher and Trowler 2001; Becher 1992) played an important part in defining both personal and potentially professional identity (Brennan and Patel 2008). Now, with increased flexibility in the labour market, plus the reorganisation of higher education around new subject fields and specialities, such ties no longer hold together. To a considerable degree, the unravelling of the ties of identity between the subject studied and its often very specific 'culture' sees that feeling of unity and bonding between students across different courses itself dissolving, a powerful hindrance to the ability to rally and mobilise around a cause.

The Anatomy of the Student Estate Demobilised

Political demobilisation is not the only feature to evolve in the Student Estate. Nor for that matter is de-mobilisation unrelated to that phenomenon already touched upon earlier – namely, physical and personal mobility. Student mobility has mutated, not only by dint of greater numbers of higher education institutions available across the nation but also by easier accessibility to higher education within regions. Physical access, particularly following Portugal's entry to the European Union in the 1980s, has improved beyond measure. A motorway network has been built. Rapid rail services have improved. Ease of physical access has several consequences, not least of which, that it compounds, though across a very different dimension, the dissolving ties between subject culture, student solidarity and political socialisation. Paradoxically, political de-mobilisation is itself extended by what we alluded to earlier as the 'non-mobility' of the new student generation.[29] By staying at home, students retain their social, political and civic points of reference while studying at university. Often, their friendship networks remain constant and unchanged. Whilst even those studying away from home can return at weekends to the circles of family and friends with which they identify.

Physical mobility has immense significance for that function, which historically, has always been laid upon the University, namely to act as an agent of socialisation of young people into the values, ethics and professional *déontologie* in addition to the technical and cognitive mastery of a subject in preparation to the young person assuming his or her place in society and in the nation. Taken in its broadest meaning, socialisation into the role of adult, as citizen and often incidentally as salary earner, have been the explicit, central and abiding task of the University. It is precisely this function that faces dilution – or worse still, is perceived as irrelevant – precisely because life in academia as a full-time activity sufficient unto itself has, for many students, lost all centrality and significance. For broad swathes of students, what was once known as 'the university experience' is no longer central to their lives. They attend lectures and seminars at the university and then return to their daily round, which is seen as the normative referential setting. The 'university experience', central though it once was, has today become peripheral, literally extra-ordinary, outside the usual. Thus, sheer physical accessibility serves precisely its opposite: It guarantees one can leave the groves of academe aside just as soon as one wants. Higher education is, literally, marginalised.

The Campus University, conceived expressly as an area wholly given over to providing an appropriate, judicious, deliberately designed and total environment for learning and scholarship, with the best that nature had to offer, utopian and set apart from the rest of the world (Rothblatt 2007: 49), never took a firm hold in Portugal. In fact, it developed only in the aftermath of the Revolution, though the first Campus had been planned a few years beforehand.[30] Though elsewhere the Campus model has today lost ground, not least because of the expense involved, in truth Portugal never experienced a *Golden Age of the University Campus*.

Even so, as Scott noted '…the University still has a very strong sense of place. It is a place to which students come (and from which others are excluded)…' (Scott 1998: 128). The University is, even today, more than a mere site. It is still an autonomous, free and protected domain, the symbolism and rituals of which continue to exert a hold – though how deep is a matter for discussion – over the student imagination. Leaving aside whether the appeal of university rituals and symbolism to students is substantial or merely vestigial, signs, here and there, still testify to its persistent reality. Thus, for instance, formal academic dress, the black cape and student gown, rapidly cast aside during the heady days of 1974 as trappings of an older order, did a comeback. In itself, this is an interesting development. It suggests that even in today's world of the virtual, invisible and de facto part-time campus, the university still provides – and more to the point – meets a need amongst students to assert a form, more limited to be sure, of collective and personal identity over and above the familial and local that personal networks sustain.

Just as the outward signs of student identity wax, wane and change, so student associations have also changed. They no longer serve as the active agents for mobilising the Student Estate. Rather they have, as much else in higher education, mutated into a role as providers of services – from computers to photocopying, organising events more festive in nature and serving individual and personal needs rather than political engagement in shaping higher education's agenda or policy. Indeed, students are the first to recognise their weak participation in both student associations and in running the institution. What participation there is driven more by a sense of duty and obligation than by the sure and certain conviction that student opinion counts or that theirs is a contribution of real weight and consequence to managing either university or polytechnic (Carapinha 2009). Whether so marked a 'de-mobilisation' of the Student Estate has accelerated with the rise of managerialism or by growth in the range of tasks that national policy has laid upon the Administrative Estate is a question well worth the asking (Chaps. 9 and 12).

Democratisation and Massification – The Early Days of Democracy in Portugal

So far, we have examined the changes and shifts in condition and role of the Student Estate from what may be seen as an 'internalist' perspective – that is to say, we have presented it in terms of the stances taken *within* the Student Estate to what were essentially *external* developments in the political sphere. But the Student Estate cannot be viewed, nor for that matter fully understood, if it is seen simply as a self-standing body, however much its rights, duties, privileges and responsibilities may be formally recognised and enshrined in legislation. Though the Student Estate may determine its degree of mobilisation or bow to the broader influences in society that make for demobilisation and dampen interest in participating as one of the three constituted orders in higher education, along with the Academic and the Administrative Estates, the weight and consequence of the Student Estate are not, in first instance, self-determined. They are, however, most assuredly determined by the polity. From this it follows that the basic condition of the Student Estate cannot be sundered from national policy and very particularly from policies of access, nor from the priorities governments attach to that policy. Militant or torpid though, the Student Estate may be in its inner agitation or quiescence; it is also most definitely shaped by external forces. To put no finer point on the matter, what is presented as phases in the evolution of the higher education *system* – elite, mass and universal – are also descriptors of the status of the *Student Estate.*

Yet – and it is a curious feature in the broader study of higher education – access is all too rarely and explicitly related to the status and condition of the Student Estate as such. Rather, access policies are examined either as a self-contained issue or, as has been shown earlier in this chapter, as a sub-set of policies involving equality of opportunity, social justice, the maximisation of human capital, raising national levels of productivity or enhancing the nation's ability successfully to innovate. Seen within these perspectives, the Student Estate, whatever stance it is pleased to take up, is simply a transitional condition, an intermediary stage through which such strategies are brought to fruition or their failure noted.

With this re-interpretation of the relationship between access and the Student Estate, we will now turn our attention briefly to the broad developments that bore down on these two constructs in the aftermath of the Revolution. The overriding priority, more important even than extending the network of higher education across the country, lay in broadening access, a priority set out explicitly in the 1976 Constitution, to open higher education to members of the working class and students from working class homes. So important was access that it brought to a halt moves towards a binary system, already in hand before the Ancien Regime was overthrown,

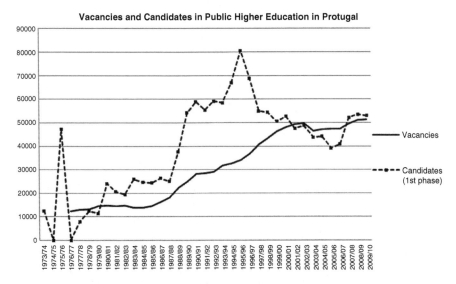

Fig. 16.10 Vacancies and candidates in public higher education in Portugal

a delay justified on the grounds that a two-tier system would serve merely to perpetuate existing social divisions (Amaral et al. 2008) (Chaps. 3, 9 and 12).

A close scrutiny of access policies *stricto sensu* shows that whilst they were also driven by considerations external to higher education, raising efficiency and quality were not always evident. In their examination of access policy and the particular issues it sought to tackle, Amaral and Magalhães (2009) distinguished three periods. The first, in the immediate aftermath of the Revolution, turned around expanded place provision and the corresponding social ethic of democratising access, in effect broadening the social basis of the Student Estate. 'More means better' was the watchword of the day. Second thoughts, not inappropriately, accompanied the second phase, fuelled by what many saw as a lowering of standards in higher education and with it a loss of confidence in the policy-making milieux. The slogan of the hour changed to read, 'More means a problem.' The third phase, current today, saw place provision rise and with it both diversification and stratification across institutions and sectors with the subsequent revision in the catch phase, now cast as 'More, but different' (Amaral and Magalhães 2009).

The three phases, which spanned the years 1973/1974 to 2009/2010, saw an unprecedented growth in the Student Estate. It also experienced four 'leaps' in the flow of social demand, episodes all closely aligned with substantial shifts in policy, that, in turn, owed much to party politics. The 'leaps' in student applications were themselves the outcome of short-term measures that required other measures to correct them – higher education's equivalent of a 'Stop/go' policy in which hasty back-pedalling followed the equally hasty initiative (Fig. 16.10).

The first sudden increase in applications followed in the wake of the Revolution in 1975/1976, and was a direct consequence of the commitment to democracy in general and to opening up higher education in particular. Upper secondary school leaving examinations were made less demanding. The torrent of new students this measure unleashed overwhelmed higher education's ability to cope. Two measures were rapidly introduced – a propaedeutic year – later to be moved back into secondary education as a 12th year of schooling, together with a subject-based national quota in the form of the *numerus clausus*. The second and third increases took place in the late 1980s and the mid 1990s. They too were products of radical changes to the terms of access (MCTES 2006) (Chaps. 6, 12 and 13). In the course of the 1990s, they served to ensure a sustained flow of students into the then nascent private sector of Portugal's higher education (Chap. 13).

The Anatomy of Increase and Decrease

Paradoxically, some scholars see the regulation of access to higher education, which clearly determines both the pace and the scale of massification as much for the system as it does for the Student Estate, as part of a tendency worldwide to move higher education from being state-controlled to becoming market-driven (Maassen 2008a). The paradox lies in the fact that market-driven systems apparently require closer regulation of access than their state-controlled predecessors. Portugal's move down the path to liberalisation completed by the 1990s with higher education taking on board private universities and private polytechnics. Effectively, however, policies that drove towards a market-driven system went through two clear phases: demand-driven and supply-driven.

During the demand-driven phase, expansion was urged forward by spiralling demand. In its turn, spiralling demand justified summoning up a private sector to handle it. During the supply-driven phase, as its name implies, both system development as too the policies that shaped it, were determined by supply – or to be more accurate – by a wavering demand as rates of growth in student numbers began to taper off. Faced with this unwelcome prospect and to attract new students whilst retaining those they already had, universities and polytechnics began frantically to diversify programmes and courses.

Policy Demand-Driven

The origins of demand-driven policies go back to the 1980s, when an extraordinary rise in demand overwhelmed the provision of higher education to meet it. As with the earlier 'leap', which revolutionary fervour had generated, the second 'demand leap' owed much to changes introduced in upper secondary education. This time, however, different motivations were involved. Prime amongst them was the wish to bring education in Portugal up to a level comparable with the rest of Europe, an ambition spurred on as part of the process of adjustment that both pre-conditioned and followed from Portugal's accession to the European Union. It was, in short, a policy based on statistical emulation.

Thus, for instance in 1980, an unusual number of students passed the preparatory year (*ano propedêutico*), whilst 3 years later, 12th-year examinations were abolished (Ministério da Educação 1984: 71). The steady loosening in the conditions of access continued the strategy of 'statistical emulation'. In 1988, the minimum mark in the upper secondary school leaving examination, which previously demanded a minimum of 10 points out of 20 to enter higher education, was terminated. Grades achieved in that examination were henceforth to serve only to rank students with the result that it was even possible, provided places were available, to embark on higher education with negative grades (Amaral and Teixeira 2000: 252). Thanks to such accommodating requirements, the number of students doubled overnight.[31]

The second sudden increase in demand gave way to a short period of respite only to be followed in 1994 and 1995 by a third 'leap' in applicants, which, once again owed much to changes in years 11 and 12 of secondary school, where successful completion of this stage was 'freed up' further (Amaral and Teixeira 2000: 252) (Chaps. 13 and role of Roberto Carneiro). Taken together, the strategy of demand control is of more than passing interest. Clearly, the strategy did not seek to engage other approaches to deal with social demand for higher education. Rather, it confined itself to regulating – in the sense of turning the tap of demand on further, rather than turning it off. In this somewhat mechanistic approach, the underlying motives are very far from evident. Moreover, when placed against this backdrop, founding new establishments of higher education beyond the two major metropolitan areas (Chap. 12), which culminated in opening higher education up to the private sector (Chap. 13), cannot be explained simply in terms of 'meeting demand'. On the contrary, such initiatives did not so much 'meet demand'. They fuelled it further.

Beneath the oscillations in student demand, higher education continued to expand, eventually to cover the whole country (Chaps. 6 and 12). A number of polytechnics – some of which had been planned since 1973 – were created. Existing institutes and other higher schools were merged. Some university institutes, created by the reform of 1973, were elevated to full university status – Évora, Universidade de Trás-os-Montes e Alto Douro (UTAD) and Universidade da Beira Interior (UBI). In the Autonomous Regions of the Azores and Madeira, and as in the Algarve, new universities were established in 1976, 1979 and 1988, respectively. Thus, the network of higher education came to cover the whole territory and to some extent dispersing supply away from the main urban areas.

Expansion reinforced and set the binary system firmly in place. It also and by the same token gave expression to a number of pre-conceived notions about the diverse nature of the Student Estate. Widening opportunities ought to have supported greater variation in institutional type as too in the courses offered, so that supply and provision met the demands of the new social and occupational strata moving into higher education, thereby matching content of provision with statistical and quantitative massification, which as has already been noted, accelerated further during the mid-1980s. Certainly, the rise in demand went hand in hand with a similar rise in course offering. Substantial diversification in course offering, so it was believed, would simply on its own account ensure a 'better fit'. It would of itself improve higher education's adaptability to both student demand, on one hand, and to the needs of the labour market, on the other.

It was not to be. The mid-1990s saw the first doubts voiced as to whether the rise in supply and provision could be sustained. Other questions, no less delicate, broke surface. Could it be that policies of expanding and diversifying higher education were driven primarily by institutional considerations rather by than the needs of those applying? Broader access and rapid growth of the Student Estate – the three 'demand leaps' which began in the 1970s and were replicated in the 1980s and mid-1990s – had unfolded independently from any parallel strategy for the development of human resources and equipment needs in the institutions themselves. In short, massification had most assuredly fulfilled its goal as regards quantity. What remained unclear was whether quantity had been fulfilled at the price of quality. For one noted historian who drew a comparison between the 'policy style' of governments of the day and those of an older order, the verdict was clear:

> With the *Estado Novo* (Old Regime) [Portuguese universities] fluctuated between a centralist organic corporative arrangement and a spontaneous or political statement of student autonomy, which is always very difficult to put into practice. After April 25th, the door was opened to democracy but democracy wavered between centralism and neo-liberalism which caused the gradual loss of prestige for state universities (together with the loss of identity for public polytechnics) the proliferation of private universities and cooperatives, which in the main did not have the necessary conditions for independence or quality assurance. (Torgal 2000: 9) (Chaps. 3, 10 and 13)

Policy as Supply-Driven or the Question of Institutional Survival

No one in the mid-1990s could have foreseen the demand for higher education shrinking (Gago 1994: 17). By 2001/2002, the number of applicants on courses in state higher education was less than the number of places available, a dismal state of affairs, which persisted until 2007/2008, when once again applicants exceeded the number of places (Fig. 16.10). The licentious increase in the number of places on offer[32] plus considerable variation in supply between different study cycles and across different subject areas spurred universities and polytechnics to new heights to draw in students and to ensure the establishment's survival. Many, above all establishments facing financial and other difficulties, rushed into policies of diversifying their subject coverage in a way neither viable nor tenable. Some even announced courses for which there was not the slightest applicant. Frenzied competition between institutions generated tremendous and unceasing agitation, which served to convert whole swathes of higher education into a vast vocational training firm, as had already happened in other countries (Richter 2008). Geiger identified a similar trend on the 'open (non-selective) sector' in higher education in the USA, which evolved towards increasing emphasis on vocational programmes (Geiger 2009: 9).

Year 2002 was a watershed. Not only did it see the highest number of students ever to be enrolled in Portugal's higher education. It saw government regulation strengthened. This time, however, regulation went beyond laying down the number of places. It addressed the issue of quality (Chap. 10). The larger and more diversified the system had became, the more its credibility – among students, families, employers and society in general – seeped away. Not surprisingly, the government's measures for closer oversight and more accountability in higher education received wide support. Some of these measures formed part of Portugal's response to the Bologna Process (Chap. 11). Over the ensuing 5 years, the extension of public oversight in the areas of quality assurance, institutional evaluation, assessment and accreditation were signally strengthened and a new framework law for higher education (Law 62/2007 of 10 September) enacted. As a final step in maintaining a continuous, regular and formal oversight for both quality and accreditation, an independent Agency for Assessment and Accreditation of Higher Education (A3ES) was set in place (Decree-Law 369/2007 of 5 November) (Chaps. 7 and 11).

Conclusion

From a student's standpoint, what has changed in Portugal's higher education since 25 April 1974? In a word: Everything. The Student Estate today is 6.5 times more numerous than it was in 1974. It draws upon a greater range in socio-economic backgrounds, is more varied in age with non-traditional students – students mature, students working even, and already retired – but increasing by leaps and bounds.

Today's Student Estate is, in the majority, female, though the tendency is towards a balance between the genders. Although concentrated in the two metropolitan regions (Chap. 12), there are students all over the country. It is now possible to attend a higher education institution in virtually all cities, even the smaller ones where some establishments have local extensions. Students today pay fees. They apply to the university or polytechnic nearest home or, for older students, nearest their family or job. Those who cannot find a place near home maintain strong links with their hometowns. Thanks to improvements in road and rail, they go home at weekend to meet friends, their family group and those with whom they most identify. Today's student, if *in* the Student Estate, is not *of* it. She – or he – does not identify with, or become involved in, student movements, as once was the case. Indeed, if we consider student celebrations and events, they are akin more to commercial shows, similar to those attended by students and non-students alike. In short, the Student Estate, which once enjoyed a particular status, seems to have undergone a certain shift in social location. It is now a fluctuating sub-set of youth culture.

Yet, massification does not inevitably mean democratisation, universal access, or even homogenisation for that matter (Chap. 3), for massification brings new forms of stratification in its train, a dynamic evident first of all amongst universities and polytechnics and then subsequently amongst students themselves. Massification is not the end of elites. It is, on the contrary, the rise of new elites.

Competition is today held to be the most potent force in shaping institutions and in motivating large numbers of students. The most prestigious universities seek to stand out from their national counterparts. They seek actively to emulate their international peers.

Taking into account the most recent trends, Portugal's new elites will be predominantly male and urban. The relative weight of male students is increasing, and for the first time, enrolments amongst men rose faster than for women. The future elite of Portuguese higher education will be concentrated in the metropolitan areas of Lisbon and Porto. It will be internationally mobile. It will contend for places in programmes such as Health and Welfare, Medicine included. Its members will push themselves forward for places on Management courses (including Services), Electronics and in Law.

In the long run, the outcome for Portuguese universities may well be to follow the path Scott described more than a decade ago: 'The most likely outcome is a highly differentiated development of a few world universities (or, more probably of world-class elements within them)' (Scott 1998: 129).

Appendix

Table A.1 Higher Education in Portugal: Enrolled students by fields of education and training

Higher education in Portugal: enrolled students by fields of education and gender

Field of education and training (EUROSTAT)	Gender	2002–2003	2008–2009	2008–2009 (%)	Variation 2002–2003/2008–2009 (%)
Education	M	7,966	2,886	0.77	−63.77
	F	39,371	15,667	4.20	−60.21
	MF	47,337	18,553	4.97	−60.81
Humanities and arts	M	12,229	13,551	3.74	14.08
	F	22,027	18,219	4.88	−17.29
	MF	34,256	32,170	8.62	−6.09
Social sciences, business and law	M	50,770	50,120	13.44	−1.28
	F	75,930	69,183	18.55	−8.89
	MF	126,700	119,303	31.98	−5.84
Science, mathematics and computing	M	16,039	14,624	3.92	−8.82
	F	15,989	12,787	3.43	−20.03
	MF	32,028	27,411	7.35	−14.42
Engineering, manufacturing and construction	M	61,922	61,699	16.54	−0.36
	F	22,783	20,946	5.62	−8.06
	MF	84,705	82,645	22.16	−2.43
Agriculture and veterinary	M	4,134	3,218	0.86	−22.16
	F	5,125	3,864	1.04	−24.60
	MF	9,259	7,082	1.90	−23.51

Access to higher education in Portugal: 1st time 1st year enrolments by fields of education and gender

Field of education and training (EUROSTAT)	Gender	2000–2001	2008–2009	2008–2009 (%)	Variation 2000–2001/2008–2009 (%)
Education	M	2,495	1,206	1.05	−51.66
	F	13,509	5,937	5.15	−56.05
	MF	16,004	7,143	6.19	−55.37
Humanities and arts	M	3,012	4,914	4.26	63.15
	F	5,572	6,412	5.56	15.08
	MF	8,584	11,326	9.82	31.94
Social sciences, business and law	M	10,828	16,646	14.43	53.73
	F	16,485	23,341	20.23	41.59
	MF	27,313	39,987	34.66	46.40
Science, mathematics and computing	M	3,716	5,068	4.39	36.38
	F	3,841	4,363	3.78	13.59
	MF	7,557	9,431	8.17	24.80
Engineering, manufacturing and construction	M	10,889	15,184	13.16	39.44
	F	4,303	5,553	4.81	29.05
	MF	15,192	20,737	17.97	36.50
Agriculture and veterinary	M	718	895	0.78	24.65
	F	996	942	0.82	−5.42
	MF	1,714	1,837	1.59	7.18

Health and welfare	M	10,719	14,372	3.85	34.08
	F	34,924	48,037	12.88	37.55
	MF	45,643	62,409	16.73	36.73
Services	M	10,192	13,130	3.52	28.83
	F	10,711	10,299	2.76	−3.85
	MF	20,903	23,429	6.28	12.08
Total	M	173,971	174,000	46.65	0.02
	F	226,860	199,002	53.35	−12.28
	MF	400,831	373,002	100.00	−6.94

Health and welfare	M	2,448	3,605	3.12	47.26
	F	9,476	13,288	11.52	40.23
	MF	11,924	16,893	14.64	41.67
Services	M	2,381	4,429	3.84	86.01
	F	2,580	3,589	3.11	39.11
	MF	4,961	8,018	6.95	61.62
Total	M	36,487	51,947	45.03	42.37
	F	56,762	63,425	54.97	11.74
	MF	93,249	115,372	100.00	23.72

Source: Portugal – GPEARI/MCTES
M male; *F* female

Notes

1. *Education for All* is a UNESCO programme launched in 1990, the title of which is used as a synonym for the democratisation of education.
2. Students whose parents did not attend higher education.
3. An idea developed by Readings with reference to Humboldt's concept of University of Culture.
4. In Portugal, unlike most European countries (European Commission 2007), access to higher education is centrally controlled by the government. For state institutions, the government stipulates the number of places for each course – *numerus clausus* – with a national applications process including all students who apply for places. Each student indicates six combinations of institutions/courses by order of preference (Fonseca et al. 2011). The government also authorises the number of places to be offered by private institutions, but they are responsible for recruiting their own students.
5. There are 17 different access regimes; the most relevant is the general regime for candidates having accomplished the secondary school; other regimes are for candidates in special conditions, like handicaps, children of diplomats, athletes, etc., and have some restrictions or quotas.
6. According to Eurostat and The Fields of Education and Training, the broad field of Services includes the narrow fields of personal services, transport services, environmental protection and security services as well as the correspondents detailed fields of hotel, restaurant and catering, travel, tourism and leisure, sports, domestic services, hair and beauty services, environmental protection technology, natural environments and wildlife, community sanitation services, protection of persons and property, occupational health and safety, military and defence.
7. Source: DGES. Database for the Higher Education Applications Process 2009/2010.
8. Access to higher education first-cycle programmes in the first year has two phases, the first one in July and the second one for the remaining vacancies, in September.
9. According to Fields of Education and Training. ISCED 97.
10. Source: GPEARI. MCTES.
11. The questionnaire on family socioeconomic conditions is filled in when students first register, and it is not compulsory to complete these fields.
12. The authors make clear that the study was based on students who were already 'inside' the system. Rather than democratisation of access, the study measures social inclusion within universities.
13. Based on HEFC Higher Education Funding Council for England and on the UCAS Statistical Bulletin.
14. The census categories of the different countries may be different. Eurostudent does not clarify the census categories.
15. Law 20/92 14 August 1992. It is usually thought that fees were introduced in 1992, when they were in fact introduced in the 1940s. Set at 1,200 Escudos (approximately. 6.5 Euros), they were not increased until 1992, when they were raised to 200 Euros, and in 1995 to 300, and in 2005 to around 900 Euros.
16. The national minimum salary was set at 475 Euros in 2010.
17. Based on HEFCE Higher Education Funding Council For England and on the Statistical Bulletin of UCAS.
18. International Standard Classification of Education (ISCED): ISCED 5 Tertiary Education. Tertiary-type A programmes (ISCED 5A) are largely theory-based and are designed to provide sufficient qualifications for entry to advanced research programmes and professions with high skill requirements, such as medicine, dentistry or architecture. They require a minimum cumulative theoretical duration (at tertiary level) of 3 years' full-time equivalent, although they typically last four or more years. Tertiary-type B programmes (ISCED 5B) are typically shorter than those of tertiary-type A and focus on practical, technical or occupational skills for direct

entry into the labour market, although some theoretical foundations may be covered in the respective programmes. They have a minimum duration of 2 ears full-time equivalent at the tertiary level.
19. Jorge Sampaio, former President of the Portuguese Republic between 1996 and 2006, was the President of the Academic Association of the Students of the Law Faculty in Lisbon, in 1961 and the general secretary of the Federation of the Students Associations in 1962; he was one of the leaders of the students' protests against the Dictatorship.
20. *Luto académico* is literally student mourning and takes place when a student or a professor dies. Students wear their clothes in a special fashion and do not exhibit any pins or colours. Student mourning was however used as a protest against government or academic administration.
21. The students' association – Coimbra Academic Association – was invited to the ceremony of 17 April 1969, and wanted to do a speech but was not allowed. The president of the students' association (Alberto Martins) started to speak anyhow and the ceremony was suddenly terminated; Alberto Martins was imprisoned; the University was closed until the examinations started, and a group of students were send to the armed forces (http://praxe.org). Alberto Martins has a Law Degree, has been a lawyer and is currently – 2010 – the Portuguese Justice Minister.
22. PREC: *Processo Revolucionário em Curso* (The Revolutionary Process Unfolding).
23. RGA: *Reunião Geral de Alunos*. General Assembly of Students.
24. One example was the abolition of the 20-point marking system, which was replaced by the democratic, egalitarian and binary two-point assessment: 'apto' or 'não apto' – pass or fail.
25. Paradoxically, this military expression became highly fashionable during the Revolution but changed its meaning from *defusing* or *disarming* to *triggering*.
26. Students were approved by administrative decisions (*pass*) and not through examinations!
27. Law 108/88, 24 September 1988.
28. Law 62/2007, of 10 September – RJIES: *Regime Jurídico das Instituições de Ensino Superior*.
29. For this, see above, p. 363.
30. Veiga Simão, Minister of Education during the latter days of the New State created the University of Mozambique. It is now the Universidade Eduardo Mondlane, in Maputo, formerly Lourenço Marques. There, he experimented with the idea of a university along lines that were unfolding in Europe and founded a campus very similar to those planned, but only later built, for the New University of Lisbon and the University of Aveiro.
31. 25,047 applicants in 1987 and 54,141 in 1989!
32. Since the introduction of the *numerus clausus*, the distribution of places in higher education has always been the responsibility of the government; rapid expansion in the private sector was reflected in the authorisation of government for places in that sector.

References

Amaral, A. (2008a). Transforming higher education. In A. Amaral, I. Bleiklie, & C. Musselin (Eds.), *From governance to identity. A Festschrift for Mary Henkel, Higher education dynamics*, vol. 24 (pp. 81–94). London: Springer.
Amaral, A. (2008b). *A Reforma do Ensino Superior Português*. Lisboa: CNE.
Amaral, A., & Magalhães, A. (2009). Between institutional competition and the search for equity of opportunities: Access of mature students. *Higher Education Policy, 22*, 505–521.
Amaral, A., & Teixeira, P. (2000). The rise and fall of the private sector in Portuguese higher education. *Higher Education Policy, 13*, 245–266.
Amaral, A., Correia, F., Magalhães, A., Rosa, M. J., Santiago, R., & Teixeira, P. (2000). *O Ensino Superior pela Mão da Economia*. Porto: CIPES.

Amaral, A., Fonseca, M., Tavares, D., & Sá, C. (2008). *A Rede Pública do Ensino Superior em Portugal. Um Olhar sobre o Acesso 2006/2007*. Porto: CIPES.
Becher, R.A. (1992). Disciplinary perspectives on higher education. In B. R. Clark, & G. Neave (Eds.), *Encyclopedia of higher education. Vol. 3. Disciplinary perspectives on higher education* (4 vols., pp. 1763–1776). Oxford: Pergamon Press.
Becher, R. A., & Trowler, P. R. (2001). *Academic tribes and territories: Intellectual enquiry and the culture of disciplines* (2nd ed.). Milton Keynes: Open n Press/SRHE.
Brennan, J., & Patel, K. (2008). Student identities in mass higher education. In À. Amaral, I. Bleiklie, & C. Musselin (Eds.), *From governance to identity. A Festschrift for Mary Henkel* (pp. 19–30). Dordrecht/Heidelberg/London: Springer.
Brennan, J., & Patel, K. (2009). 'Up-market' or 'Down-market': Shopping for higher education in the UK. *CHER annual conference*. Porto: CHER.
Carapinha, B. (2009). *Bologna with students eyes 2009*. Leuven: EC Education and Culture DG. Lifelong Learning Programme.
Cerdeira, M. L. (2009). *O Financiamento do Ensino Superior Português*. Coimbra: Edições Almedina.
Christie, H. (2007). Higher education and spatial (im)mobility: Nontraditional students and living at home. *Environment and Planning A, 39*(10), 2445–2463.
European Commission. (2007). *Key data on higher education in Europe* (2007th ed.). Brussels: EC.
Costa, A. F., & Lopes, J. T. (2008). *Os Estudantes e os seus Trajectos no Ensino Superior: Sucesso e Insucesso, Factores e Processos, Promoção de Boas Práticas*. Lisboa: CIES-ISCTE, IS-FLUP.
Estanque, E. (2008). Jovens, estudantes e 'repúblicos': culturas estudantis e crise do associativismo em Coimbra. *Revista Crítica de Ciências Sociais, 81*, 9–41.
Estanque, E., & Nunes, J. A. (2003). Dilemas e desafios da Universidade. Recomposição social e expectativas dos estudantes da Universidade de Coimbra. *Revista Crítica de Ciências Sociais, 66*, 5–44.
EUROSTUDENT. (2005). *Eurostudent 2005 social and economic conditions of student life in Europe 2005*. Hannover: HIS Hochschul-Informations-System.
Fonseca, M., Tavares, D., Sá, C., & Amaral, A. (2011). *Waves of (dis)satisfaction*. (forthcoming)
Gaggi, M., & Nardzulli, E. (2006). *Low cost. O fim da Classe Média*. Lisboa: Editorial Teorema.
Gago, J. M. (1994). *Prospectiva do Ensino Superior em Portugal*. Lisboa: Departamento de Programação e Gestão Financeira. Ministério da Educação.
Geiger, R. L. (2009). Markets and the end of the current era in U.S. Higher Education. *CHER 22nd annual conference*. Porto: CHER.
Gonçalves, C., Menezes, I., & Martins, M. C. (2009, Setembro). *Transição para o Trabalho dos Licenciados da Universidade do Porto (2006–2007)*. Accessed on May 17th 2010, Universidade do Porto – Observatório do Emprego: www.up.pt.
GPEARI/MCTES. (2009). *Inquérito ao Registo de Alunos Inscritos e Diplomados do Ensino Superior*. Lisboa: GPEARI/MCTES.
Grilo, R. (1999). As origens do actual Dia do Estudante A Crise Académica de 1962. *Jornal da Universidade de Évora*. Abril, 1999. Évora: Universidade de Évora.
HEFCE Higher Education Funding Council For England. (2009). *Report of the sub-committee for teaching quality, and the student experience*. Bristol: HEFCE.
Justino, E. R. (2010). *A Procura do Ensino Superior – A Influência da Condição Socioeconómica dos Estudantes na Escolha de uma Instituição*. Lisboa: Universidade Católica Portuguesa (Tese de Mestrado. Policopiado).
Le Chaperain, C. (2008). Fair access to higher education: Analysis of a target incentive education policy. *Higher Education Management and Policy, 20*, 9–23.
Maassen, P. (2008a). The modernisation of higher education governance in Europe. In C. N. Educação (Ed.), *Políticas do Ensino Superior. Quatro Temas em Debate* (pp. 71–106). Lisboa: Conselho Nacional de Educação.
Maassen, P. (2008b). The modernisation of European higher education. National policy dynamics. In A. Amaral, I. Bleiklie, & C. Musselin (Eds.), *From governance to identity. A Festschrift for Mary Henkel* (pp. 95–112). Dordrecht/Heidelberg/London: Springer Verlag.

Magalhães, A., Amaral, A., & Tavares, O. (2009). Equity, access and institutional competition. *Terciary Education and Management, 15*(1), 35–48.
Marginson, S. (1998). Competition and diversity in the reformed Australian higher education system. In L. Meek & F. Q. Wood (Eds.), *Managing higher education diversity in a climate of public sector reform* (pp. 81–96). Canberra: Department of Employment, Education, Training and Youth Affairs.
MCTES. (2006). *OECD thematic review of tertiary education – Country background report: Portugal*. Lisboa: MCTES.
Ministério da Educação. (1984). *Análise Conjuntural*. Lisboa: Ministério da Educação.
Neave, G. R. (1976). *Patterns of equality: the influence of new structures in European higher education upon the equality of educational opportunity*. Windsor: National Foundation for Educational Research.
Patiniotis, Jackie, & Holdsworth, C. (2005). Seize that chance!' leaving home and transition to higher education. *Journal of Youth Studies, 8*(1), 81–95.
Readings, B. (1997). *The University in Ruins*. Cambridge/London: Harvard University Press.
Richter, S. (2008). Vorbild in der Krise. *Die Zeit*: 63. 19. Juni.
Rothblatt, S. (2007). Prolegomena to an inquiry into the campus invisible. In J. Enders & F. V. Vught (Eds.), *Towards a cartography of higher education policy change. A Festschrift in honour of Guy Neave* (pp. 45–52). Twente: CHEPS.
Santiago, P., Tremblay, K., Basri, E., & Arnal, E. (2008). *Terciary education for the knowledge society (vol 1, vol 2)*. Paris: OECD.
Scott, P. (1998). Massification, internationalisation and globalisation. In P. Scott (Ed.), *The Globalisation of Higher Education. Proceedings of the 1998 Annual Conference of the Society for Research into Higher Education at Lancaster University,* (pp. 108–129). Buckingham/Philadelphia, PA: Society for Research into Higher Education and Open University Press.
Tavares, D. A. (2008). *O Superior Ofício de Ser Aluno. Manual de Sobrevivência do Caloiro*. Lisboa: Edições Sílabo.
Teixeira, P., Johnstone, B., Rosa, M., & Vossensteyn, H. (2006). *Cost-sharing and accessibility in higher education: A fairer deal?* Dordrecht/Heidelberg/London: Springer.
Teixeira, P., Fonseca, M., Amado, D., Sá, C., & Amaral, A. (2009). A regional mismatch? Student applications and institutional responses in the Portuguese higher education system. In K. Morhman, J. Shi, S. E. Feinblatt, & K. W. Chow (Eds.), *Public universities and regional development*. Chengdu: Sichuan University Press.
Torgal, L. R. (1999). *A Universidade e o Estado Novo*. Coimbra: Minerva.
Torgal, L. R. (2000). *Caminhos e contadições da(s)universidade(s) portuguesa(s)*. CEIS 20. Coimbra: Universidade de Coimbra.
Torgal, L. R. (2008). *A Universidade e as Condições da Imaginação*. Coimbra: CEIAS.
Trow, M. (1973). *Problems in the transition from elite to mass higher education*. Berkeley: Carnegie Commission on Higher Education.
Trow, M. (1996). *Trust, markets and accountability in higher education: A comparative perspective*. Berkeley: CSHE – University of California.
Trow, M. (2000). *From Mass Higher Education to Universal Access: The American Advantage*. Research and occasional paper series: CSHE.1.10. Berkeley, CA: CSHE.
Universidade do Porto. Serviço de Melhoria Contínua. (2010). *Universidade do Porto*. 17 de May de 2010, de www.up.pt.
Woessmann, L. (2004). *How Equal are educational opportunities? Family Background and Student Achievement in Europe and the US*. CESIFO working paper no.1162 category 4: Labour Markets.

Index

A
Access to higher education
  access as an external instrument
    of policy, 403
  in the 1976 Constitution, 22, 403
  defining the Student Estate (*see* below)
  growth rates in, 140
    and the Bologna process, 269
    as lever to 'steer' national
      policy, 320
    and the Lisbon Agenda, 271
  policy, three phases in, 404
  role of private sector HE
    and economic progress, 392
    and equity, 392
    social class disparities in Portugal,
      25, 389, 391
    and age differences, 389–390
    compared with Europe, 392
    and institutional differences, 389
Accountability, 345
  an Anglo American construct, 375
  balanced by autonomy, 367, 375
  and the Bologna process, 408
  and 'institutional worth', 370
  reinforced, 408
  and rise of the Administrative Estate,
    353, 367
Accreditation, 36
  as political 'fashion', 257
  set up under Law 1/2003, 241, 251
ADISPOR (Association of Portuguese Public
  Polytechnics), 255
Agency for the Evaluation and Accreditation
  of Higher Education (A3ES)
  its creation in 2007, 251, 258, 408

  its mandate, structure and programme,
    82, 259, 271
Altbach, P.A., 355, 357
Amaral, A., 132, 255, 335, 339, 372,
  387, 404
APESP (Portuguese Association of Private
  Higher Education)
  its role in evaluation, 70, 255
Associated Laboratories
  regular evaluation of, 213
  strengthening academic research, 213
Autonomy
  latitude granted to Public
    Universities, 237
  and reaction of HE to 1988 reforms, 236
Aveiro University founded 1973, 69

B
Backwardness
  in economic development, 110
  in educational development, 60, 63
Barro, R.J., 129, 130
Basic education
  and regional disparities, 97–98
  and quality of life, 101
Becher, T., 19
Binary HE
  its creation, 31, 233, 406
  its origins under Estado Novo, 63
  its re-affirmation through Decree
    Law 74/2006, 270
Bologna (Italy)
  University of, 2
Bologna Follow Up Group, 271
  Lourtie, Pedro, President of, 78

Bologna process, 11, 36, 265–283
  exceptionalism re-defined, 13
  the future of, 78
  its critics, 77–78, 392
  its impact in Portugal, 276–283
    form or substance, 266
    and 'over-teaching', 77
    its scope as a multi-level
      policy process, 267
    'Soft Law', 265
    its historical significance, 16
  implications for academic staff training,
    281, 387
  and the logic of neo-liberalism, 78
  Portugal's performance, 274
  Portuguese HE's perceptions of Bologna
    priorities, 279
  professionalisation *vs.* employability, 269
  rise in post-graduate numbers,
    143, 261
  role of Bologna Process in rise
    of managerialism, 295
  'Stocktaking Reports' and monitoring
    progress, 271–276
  'Bologna type' degree structures Decree
    Law 74/2006, 276
  and doctoral level registration, 387
Bleiklie, I., 280, 354, 359, 370
Bourdieu, P., 51, 83
Bureaucratisation in HE, 359
  an ends/means reversal, 359
Business Expenditure on Research and
  Development (BERD)
  compared to other EU States, 197
  in Portugal 181, 191
Business Sector
  universities 'buying in' management
    techniques from, 368

C
Caetano, M., 63
Catholic University, 233, 253, 313, 353
Carvalho, Rómulo de, (Portuguese historian of
  Education) 15, 52, 55, 57, 59–61
Charle, Christophe and Soulié, Charles
  (French historians)
  and modernisation of the university, 79
Christie, H., 392
'Civic service for students', 138, 400
Clark, B.R.
  and the 'system' perspective, 17, 374
Class structure
  and educational change, 385

Conselho Nacional de Avaliação do Ensino
  Superior (CNAVES) National
  Council for Evaluating higher
  Education, 253
  internal tensions in, 254
  mandate, 253
Constituent Orders of Higher Education,
  17, 37, 39
  Academic Estate, 329–347 (*see also*
    Professions) academic career and
    Humboldtian values, 337
  condition of Academia under the
    dictatorship, 39, 333
  its powers of resistance, 292, 334
  democratic revolution and stratification
    of status, 338
  emergence of managerial 'counter
    hegemony', 344, 346
  emergence of private sector HE, 339
  dependency on public sector staff, 339
  different working conditions, 339
  feminisation of, 341–342
  and disciplinary differences, 341
  human resource policy and researcher
    expansion, 344
  of 'managerial autonomy', 367
  new normative identities, 345
  the role of 'organic intellectuals',
    39, 333
  Administrative Estate 353–379
    the 'centrality' of new managerialism,
      292, 354, 356
    controlled by law and regulations,
      368, 369
    its 'counter hegemonism', 39
    feminisation in, 363, 374
    women in senior management, 341
    formal Status of, and 2007 Higher
      Education Guideline Law, 362
    as the handmaiden of evaluation and
      performance, 367
    massification of HE and growth in,
      354, 358
    multiplication of administrative
      functions, 355, 363
    its growth compared to the national
      civil service, 357
    in public sector universities and
      polytechnics, 361–362
    and new managerialism, 40
    seven factors in the dynamics of the
      Administrative Estate, 372–374
  Student Estate, 383–413
    changing student identity, 401

cultural change and demobilisation, 41, 392, 401
dissolving ties between subject 'culture', solidarity and political socialisation, 401
drop out rates in, 396–397
on the eve of revolution, 397–399
family financing and its consequences, 151
feminisation of, 137, 153–154, 340, 387
at doctoral level, 387
its growth, 20, 40, 383, 408
relationship with Armed Forces Movement, 399
socialisation, family, friends and mobility, 394–396
student 'experience' mutating, 402
as subset of 'Youth Culture', 408
the Third Estate, 9, 383
shaped by the polity, 402
work experience in, 385
compared to other EU States, 151
and mature students, 390
Constitution of 1822 and Portuguese Liberalism, 58
higher education reform, 59
state sovereignty redefined, 58
Constitution of 1976, 29, 69
and curriculum reform, 69
and principle of participant democracy, 22,
and principle of quality assessment, 250
and principle of University Autonomy, 171
Corporative State, 67. See also Estado Novo
Corporative University, 287
Council of Rectors of the Portuguese Universities (CRUP), 236
in piloting quality evaluation, 238, 252
and role in creating self-regulatory model of governance, 236, 293
Crespo, V., 184
Critical Mass in S&T policy, 34, 180, 192, 200, 208
in associated laboratories, 213
'Cultural University' 82–85
ideas of Antonio Lobo Vilela, 83

D
Dale, R., 7
de Almeida, A.J., 83
de Boer, H. 299
Democratic management
its introduction in 1976, 291
in 1988 University Autonomy Law, 293

Democratisation of HE, 38. *See also* Massification
Demography
challenge of fecundity rates, 157
changed notions of childhood, 145
fertility rates, 93, 319
its impact on private HE, 319
Portugal: a lagged response, 42, 150
Derrida, J., 78
Dubar, C., 331

E
Economic liberalisation, 109
and accession to EU, 113
Economic perspective, 109–132
transition from agrarian economy since 1950, 110–113
Economy in Portugal, 109–132
convergence towards European income levels, 113
decline explained, 115–120
decline in capital accumulation, 118, 122–124
economic convergence, 109
inequalities economic and poverty, 100
loss of competitiveness, 120–121
Portugal GDP trends, 112
return to democracy, 131
role of human capital as driver of growth, 117
and social vulnerability, 100
total factor productivity as source of growth, 115–118
transition to knowledge economy, 125
and World War I, 113
and World War II, 113
Elite university
participation rates, 139, 304
Entrepreneurial University as symbol of paradigm shift, 81
Estado Novo (1933–1974)
cultural concept of science as expression of opposition to, 84
"democratising higher education", reforms of Veiga Simão, 63
ideology of development, 63
I Plano do Fomento 1953 (First Development Plan), 185
its ideological impact on HE, 62–63
its role in science policy, 35, 184–186
Ministry of Public Instruction and dimensions of control, 335
nationalism during the, 63–64

Estado Novo (1933–1974) (*cont.*)
  public administration during the, 230
  stabilisation plan of 1930's, 113
  strong state, Authoritarian State, 66, 159, 230, 334
  views on education, 184
Estanque, E., 391
Euro, adjustment to, 115, 120–122
European Commission, 2
  and 'creeping competence', 267
  pilot project on evaluation methods 1991, 251
European Council
  and press for convergence, 268
European credit transfer system (ECTS), 37, 270
European dimension in higher education, 3
  its legal basis, 12
  a critique of, 78–80
  redefining exceptionalism, 12–13
European Diploma Supplement
  its token usage in Portugal, 37, 280
European Economic Community, 111, 113
European Free Trade Area (EFTA), 109
European Higher Education Area, 2
  ERASMUS Programme, 72
  ERASMUS MUNDUS, 275
  Lisbon Agenda, 267–268
    Lisbon Scorecard Reports, 275–276
    Portugal's 'villainous' status, 276
  Rise of 'managerialism' and construction of, 295
European Network of Quality Assurance Agencies (ENQA), 11, 32, 241, 250, 257
European Quality Agency Register (EQUAR), 11
European Research Area, 2
  EU Framework Programmes, Portuguese participation in, 218
European Standards and Guidelines, 257
European Union
  and impact on economy, 113
  and impact on rise of managerialism, 295, 371
  and impact on S&T policy, 188
  Portugal's accession to, 161, 201
  and shift in policy paradigm, 71
European University
  in the middle ages, 2
Evaluation
  attempt to define (1997), 70
  extended to polytechnics 1990, 250
  of higher education, 238, 250, 254
  and Law 38/94, 239
  of research units and output (1993), 190
  resistance to, 238
  Role in S&T, 239
  in University Autonomy Act 1988, 250
Evaluative State, 36, 243, 370
Évora University, 406
Exceptionalism
  its 'European' construct, 8, 11
  four dimensions in, 21–22
  its historic dimension, 36
  in Portuguese higher education, 15, 31
External Stakeholders, 243, 344
  and demands for information and accountability, 355

F
Faculties and Schools
  and democratic governance, 232
Family networks
  and attendance patterns in HE, 396
Financial autonomy
  and 1973 Decree Law, 230
  Basic Law for the Financing of Higher Education (Law 113/97), 73
Financial Crisis in Seventies, Eighties, 110
  2008–2009, 72, 79
First Republic (1910–1926)
  and access to higher education, 62
  First Constitutional Government 1976 and political normalisation, 291
  higher education reform, 61, 83, 183, 228
  University Constitution 1911, 228
Foundation University, 75, 170, 288, 300–301
  and autonomy, 173
  balance of power between Academic and Administrative Estates, 374
  and changed status of Administrative Estate, 359
  viewed from S&T perspective, 214
Freedom to teach and to learn
  confirmed in 1988 University Autonomy Act, 366
  in 1976 Constitution, 366
Fundação Luso-Americana para o Desenvolvimento (FLAD), 200
Fundação para a Ciência e a Tecnologia (FCT), Foundation for Science and Technology, 75, 189, 200

Index

competitive funding for doctoral and post doctoral fellowships, 201–203
and reform of State Laboratories 1998, 211
Funding higher education, 172

G

Gago, José Mariano, (Minister MCTES 2005–2011), 78, 180
General Assembly of University
  role and composition under 1911 University Constitution, 229
General Council
  powers under 2007 Higher Education Guideline Law, 241
Generational Perspective
  generation of Reform in Portugal, 23–24
  as a unit of analysis, 24
Giddens, A., 49, 50
Globalisation, 20
  and drive of governments to improve national economic performance, 311
  and internationalisation of the academic career, 144
  and the 'new governance paradigm', 244
  shaping the Administrative Estate, 372
Golden Age in Portugal (1530–1640), 53–55
  and 'national image' 53 (*see also* National Identity)
Governance
  from autocracy to revolutionary change, 288
  in polytechnics, 233
  post revolutionary normalisation, 232–233
  in private sector HE, 236
  and 1974 Revolution, 232
  and 1988 University Autonomy Act, 235
  as a 'competitive market', 298
  and 2007 Higher Education Guideline Law, 34, 241
  and links with quality, 240
  new patterns of, 301–302
  tensions between collegial and managerial governance, 295
  University Constitution 1911, 228
  under the dictatorship, 334
Government and higher education relationships, 34
  the legal perspective on the 2007 Higher Education Guideline Law, 288
Gramsci, Antoni and concept of 'organic intellectuals', 332

Grand Narrative, 17
Grosby, S., 49
Gross Expenditure on Research and Development, (GERD), 195
Guild University, 85
Gulbenkian Institute of Science 1961, 185, 200

H

Hegemonic discourse
  and academic professionalism, 342
Higher education
  driven by institutional considerations, 407
  dual system, 137
    and geographical location, 156
  expansion of provision, 139–141, 397–398
  and privatization, 307–326
  provision in Portugal, 386
  and the regions 138, 385
  as a 'system', 18
Higher Education Guideline Law 2007 (RJIES) (Law 62/2007), 73, 164
  and institutional management, 38, 74, 299, 360, 371
  university autonomy re-defined, 171–173, 296–297
  and reinforcement of evaluation and quality, 408
'Higher Educationism', 7, 21
Higher Education Policy
  and balance of power between Nation State and Europe, 11
  from demand driven to supply driven, 405–407
  as 'lagged response' to modernisation, 25
  rise of private sector HE, 406
  viewed de longue durée, 16
Higher Institute of Work and Entrepreneurial Sciences (ISCTE) Lisbon, founded 1972, 69
Historical Attention Span Deficit Disorder, 21, 32
Huisman, J., 372
Human capital in Portugal, 110
Human resources
  compared to other research systems, 207
  government action to improve qualification levels, 311, 343
  growth of 'researcher pool', 205–207
  impact on private sector industry, 344
  key to viability in S&T development, 222
  management, and state oversight, 368
Hybridisation in HE, 303

I

Illiteracy rates, 95–98, 128, 315
Images of organisation, 288
Implications for the Administrative Estate, 371–372
Incentive programmes for R&D, 219
  tax breaks for firms investing in R&D, 219
Industrialisation, 111
Industry-science links, 218
Institutional autonomy, 38, 234, 288
  and human resources management, 368
  instrumental/operational interpretation of, 296
  and modernisation, 292–294
  and move to 'remote control' relationship, 239
  and quality oversight, 241
Institutional management, 38
  importance of collegial model up to mid 90's, 295
  patterns of, 288
Institutional performance
  linked to funding, 250
Instituto de Cooperação Científica e Tecnológica (Institute of International Cooperation in S&T), 190
Instituto Superior Técnico Lisbon, 182
Instrumentalities of change, 35
Integrated Masters degrees 269, 278
  and gender distribution, 389
International Iberian Nanotechnology Laboratory, 215
  close ties with public policy, 216
  consortia-based research, 219
  creating "thematic networks, 214
  international partnerships and national research capacity, 214
International Monetary Fund (IMF) 18, 102
Investment in S&T, 222
Invisible Campus
  rise of, 385

J

Jorgensen, M.W., 12
Junta Nacional de Investigação Científica et Tecnológica (JNICT) National Board for Scientific and Technological Research, 75, 186, 200
  Plano Integrado de Desenvolvimento, 188
  Programa Mobilizador de Ciência e Tecnologia, 1987, 189, 218

K

Kant, I., 83
Knowledge Economy, 1, 34
  and change in organisation of academic work, 343
  difficulties in transition to, 125, 131
  improvements in technological content of Portuguese exports, 125–127
  knowledge integrated communities, 179
  and Portugal's shortcomings in human capital formation, 130
  rise in public expenditure on education, 128
  and rise of student numbers, 383, 386
    in services sector, 390
  and role of education in, 127–131
  transition of the Administrative Estate to the public sphere, 366
  transition to, 125, 132
Knowledge Society, 1, 282, 366
  and EU role, 343
Kogan, M., 242

L

Labour market
  for undergraduates, 155
Lane, J.E., 357
Laslett, P., 25
Leadership principle
  and tight articulation between governance and management, 298
Learning economy, 1, 35, 179
Learning society, 24
  vulgarisation of S&T to general population, 199
Lee, J.W., 129, 130
Legal codification
  Legal Framework for Research Laboratories Decree 125/99, 213
Legal homogeneity model of state control, 230, 309, 360
  Implications of Foundation Universities, 360
Legal perspective in Portuguese HE, 34, 162–165
  change in University's legal status, 162
  as means to pursue policy goals, 162
Lima, L., 239
Lisbon agenda, 36
  and consequences for access to HE, 280
Loosely coupled systems, 288, 294, 295

M

Maassen, P., 385
Magalhães, A., 371, 373, 404
Management. *See* University management
'Management Revolution' in Portugal, 287
  management and governance democratised, 289
  reassertion of central regulation, 295
Managerialism in Higher Education, 38
  as driver for modernising HE, 298, 370
  as a 'lagged response', 375
  its consequences for the Administrative Estate, 371
  its operational dimensions, 296, 298
    hegemonic shift from the Academic to the Administrative Estate, 344
  The Managerial University, 303
    shifts in student attitude towards participation in, 403
  rise from 1996 to 2009, 228, 239–242
Marçal Grilo, E., 77
Marshall Plan for European Reconstruction
  Training Portuguese Engineers in USA, 185
Massification of HE, 3
  decade of, 1986–1996, 36, 228, 234–239
  and democratisation, 403–405
  driven by quantity, not quality, 407
  and feminisation, 39, 340
  growth of the polytechnic sector, 235, 406
  imbalance of supply and demand, 139
  and its significance for S&T policy, 223
  new patterns of hierarchisation, 143–144, 280
  pressure on public expenditure, 309, 311
  and the rise of private HE, 310–313
  and second cycle studies, 261
  and state supervisory relationship, 236, 317
  Trowian model of, 397
Mass University
  and social reproduction, 143, 144
  and student culture, 385
  working class students, 150, 389
Migration patterns
  between Portugal and Europe, 93
  inside Portugal, 92
Ministry of Finance
  Control over quotas of posts in Administrative Estate, 361
Ministry of Science and Technology, 34, 189
  hived off from Ministry of Education, 76
Ministry of Science, Technology and Higher Education Created 2005, 76, 268, 269, 367
  centralised control over Administrative Estate, 367
  micro interventionism of, 296
Modernity
  and Idealism in Portuguese Higher Education Policy, 150
  as lead up to 2007 Higher Education Guideline Law, 241
Moreira, V., 303
Moscati, R., 335

N

National identity, 32–33
  and higher education, 62
  and nationalism, 58–60
  redefined by the 1974 Revolution of the Carnations, 63
  and religion, 63
  and the state, 50–51
Nation as legitimacy for political power, 50
National Council on Education (Conselho Nacional de Educação), 164, 170
Nationalism and HE reform, 58–60
Nation State
  its historical origins in Portugal, 50
  its weakening from above, 372
  in the world economic order, 4
Neave, G., 332, 338, 354, 371, 372
Neo liberalism
  in East and Central Europe, 22
  and the emergence of a 'political university', 33
  as expression of new Economic Orthodoxy, 26–27
  and the 2007 Higher Education Guideline Law, 26
  its role in shifting policy discourse, 30–31, 303
  and its critique, 78, 80
  as new hegemony in Academia, 344
  in Portugal, 26
  Portuguese perspectives on Neo Liberalism, 27–28, 31
  as driver changing the relationship between government, higher education and society, 26
  possible impact on women in academic profession, 341–342

Netherlands, 151
  evaluation model and influence on Portuguese HE Policy, 252
New elites
  in Portuguese HE, 409
New Public Management, 21, 24, 169, 239
  and 'governance', 240
  and Higher Education Guideline Law of 2007, 32, 241
  its institutional impact, 241
Numerus clausus, 70, 139, 261, 315, 317
Nunes, J.A., 391

O
Open method of coordination, 265
Open University, 69, 393
Organised anarchy model of organisation, 288
  its prevalence in HE during the 70's, 294, 336
Organisation for Economic Cooperation and Development (OECD), 18, 234, 271, 288
  as "Great Spectacle", 82
  its influence in shaping 'Managerialism' in Portugal, 299
  and national review of Portuguese HE (2006), 32, 82, 241, 279
  notion of 'managerial autonomy', 367
  OECD economies, 122, 131
  Pilot Teams in Sciences and Technology 1963, 187
  Programme for International School Assessment (PISA), 128
Ortega y Gasset, Misión de la Universidad (1930), 75, 83

P
Pais, S.
  and national vision of education, 61
Paradigm economic
  and the Entrepreneurial University, 5
  implications for culture, 82–85
  and neo liberalism, 4, 5
Paradigm political, 4–5
Paradigm shift, 69, 71–75, 236
  as aim of the Bologna process, 271
  implications for the vision and values of the University, 80–81, 85
  as vehicle of 'New Values', 80–81
Parity of representation
  and its abolition in 2007 HE Guideline Law, 241
  and University Autonomy Act 1988, 369
Participation
  in basic education, 98
  in the labour force
    by gender, 98
    regional disparities, 98
    by social class, 98–100
Participant democracy, 22, 26, 29, 31
  and 1976 Constitution, 69, 165, 169, 250
  enacted in 1988 University Autonomy Law, 29, 163, 293
  in foundation universities at base unit level, 300–301
  University as public service *vs.* university as market-driven, 173
Participation rates and S&T policy, 223
Pedagogical purpose, 8
Peripheral economies
  Portugal, 89, 109, 110, 112, 114
Perkin, H., 338
PhD. output in 2008, 193
  in science and technology, 193
Philips, L.J., 12
Political model of organisation, 290
  and outcomes of 1988 University Autonomy Act, 293
Political normalisation
  and approval of 1976 Constitution, 291
Political University, 33
  revolutionary intent, 68
  and subordination to political power, 164
  a vision resuscitated by Neo Liberalism, 74–75
Polytechnics
  academic career structure in, 343
  expansion of, 301
    groundwork laid during Estado Novo, 63 (*see also* Veiga Simão) purpose, 63, 188
  and Higher Education Guideline Law 2007, 74
  and Law 54/90 granting limited Autonomy, 234
  social class background of students, 138
Portugal:
  and convergence, 13–14
  and European policy dynamics, 14
  and exceptionalism, 12
Portugal: 1976 Constitution
  Marxism, 28
  and political values, 27
  Social Catholicism, 28
Portugal: revolutionary inheritance, 10, 22
  and drive towards New Public Management, 302
  as political 'value set', 23

Index 425

Portugal: Revolution of the Carnations 1974, 161, 196
  and administration, 227–246
  and governance, 227–246, 384
  and 'normative unfaithfulness', 290
  Reassertion of State power, 334
  Universities as political arena, 289
Post-Weberian model of organisation, 288
Private higher education, 34, 307–326
  additional cost of, 374
    at regional level, 98, 103, 104, 208
    subject provision in, 128, 307, 313, 317
    and 'take up' of, 270
  and competition, 312
  in 1976 Constitution, 317
  decline in applicants, 139, 389
    and demography, 319
  as gauge of democratic pluralism, 313, 317
  geographical concentration, 320, 322
  to improve efficiency, 307
  its creation and relevance, 253, 268, 288, 297, 299
  its role in 'demand absorption', 38, 320,
  limited capacity to face competition, 320
  limited research capacity, 325
  move to market mechanisms in HE policy, 261
  political expectations for, 324
  rapid growth rates in, 110, 113, 207, 407
  role of public regulatory bodies on, 309
Privatisation of HE, 5, 22
  as ideological justification, 32
Productivity, slow-down in, 115
Professional segmentation, 338
Professions
  The Academic 'Profession' in Portugal, 39
  in the Anglo American literature, 39
  their definition, powers, and scope, 309
  in the French literature, 39
  Gramsci's concept of 'organic intellectuals', 39
  and relationship with the State, 162
Public administration
  and its 'normalisation, 232–234
  'Conditional permission' and the 'Parallel State', 233
Public expenditure on R&D, 1986–1995, 128, 189
Public funding of human resources, 190
Public infrastructures, 122
Public sector HE
  geographical concentration, 156
  and governance structures, 233

Q
Quality as political discourse, 234
  as state responsibility, 241
Quality assurance and scientific quality, 241
  CNAVES and erosion of trust, 253
  quality control, 22
    impact on private HE, 321
    and Law 38/94, 238
    pilot projects, 251
    quality control and 'massification', 311
    quality culture within HEIs, 363
    quality drift or drive towards market forces, 31, 207, 231, 312
Quality of life, 33, 89–105
  and welfare provision, 102
Queiró, J.F., 236

R
Rational bureaucratic model of organisation, 288
Readings, B., 72, 78
Rectors as institutional leaders, 36
  appointment procedure under 1911 University Constitution, 228
  disciplinary background of, 82
    powers redefined by 2007 HE Guideline Law (RJES), 26, 32, 342
  election and participant democracy, 231, 291
  under Estado Novo, 229, 334
  powers under 1988 University Autonomy Act, 29
  responsible for quality assurance, 241
  role in Foundation Universities, 274
Regionalisation
  and 'mismatch' of study fields and region, 393
  and student attendance patterns, 95, 96
  weakening the national community from below, 313
Report on Portuguese quality assurance system 2006, 257, 271
Research funding
  competition between HEIs, 243
Return to democracy, 131
Revolution of the Carnations (1974), 10, 33, 63, 180
  and its interpretation, 23
  leading role of students in, 199
  and role of General Assembly of Students, 229
Rhoades, G., 332, 338
Robertson, S. L., 7

Rosa, M.J., 70, 132, 255, 368
Rothblatt, S., 385
Royal School of Surgery of Lisbon, 59
Royal School of Surgery of Porto, 59

S
Salamon, L., 244, 246
Salazar, Antonio de Oliveira, 335
  and stabilisation plan of 1930's, 113
Santos, S.M., 253, 255
Santiago, R., 373
School drop-out rates, 319
Schooling
  average years in secondary, 128, 130
Science and technology policy, 34, 188, 223
  drive towards internationalisation, 194
  and higher education guideline
    law 2007, 241
  international exchange/partnerships,
    194, 211
  and regional development, 163
  late awakening of scientific base
    1986–1995, 188–189
  links between graduate education and
    research, 199
  quality and standing, 34
  reorganisation of research units. Its
    dynamic, 191
Scientific competitiveness
  and impact on institutional autonomy, 289
  Portugal and other EU member states, 218
Scott, P., 409
Senate
  axed under 2007 HE guideline law, 230
  composition under 1911 university
    constitution, 228
  and role under 1988 university
    autonomy act, 162, 165
Sergio, António (Minister of Public Education
    during First Republic), 61
Serrão, J., 180
Soares, M., 72
Sobral, J.M., 49
Social Asymmetries in Portuguese Society,
    105
Social demand for higher education, 22
  and role of private sector HE,
    310–312
Socialisation of students
  role of HE, 373
Social mobilisation in Portuguese Society, 25
  'parental mobilisation', 146
  portugal as a 'semi peripheral' society, 89

Social structure, 33
  agrarian society, 109–132
    transition from, 92, 110
  female employment
    in education, 339
    in health sector, 92, 339
    in service sector, 340
  female research staff in academia,
    192, 341
  social selectivity in HE, 151
Social values and changing attitudes towards
    higher education
  decline in student participation and
    'political privatisation', 400
  towards schooling, 143
Socrates, José Prime Minister, 78
State. *See also* Estado Novo dictatorship
  surveillance of personnel, 223
  in the middle ages, 52–53, 308
  responsibility for HE under 1976
    constitution, 165
  role in constructing national identities, 51
  state laboratories in S&T policy, 77, 203
  'state supervisory' relationship, 236
  new forms of state regulation, 295
  the governmentalised university, 304
State professionalism reframed, 345
  emergence of new 'organic
    intellectuals', 345
Structural change in the economy, 125
Structural weaknesses in economy, 115
Student fees, 73, 268, 393
  and cost sharing, 392
  and mobility, 394–396
Student support and finance, 151
Student unions and associations
  and collegial governance, 242
  their 'demobilisation', 401–403
  role in 1974 revolution, 228,
    355–359
  and links with armed forces
    movement, 399
  role as Third estate in Portuguese
    revolution, 400
Subject differentiation, 397
Subject parturition, 18
System perspective
  in the study of HE in Portugal, 19, 321

T
Teacher training
  and decline in numbers, 390
Technological progress, 113

Teixeira, P., 335, 339
The 18th century enlightenment,
    55–58, 83
    pombalian reforms, 56
Torgal, L.R., 67–85
Trow, M., 20

U
Undergraduate degrees
    rates of return in Portugal, 316
    their value on labour market, 155, 313,
        331, 389
Unemployment, 120
Unit labour costs, 121
United Kingdom, 192
    pioneer in the managerialist
        canon, 287
United States of America
    as a reform model, 286
University Autonomy
    1988 act on university autonomy, 29, 162,
        234, 293, 369, 400
        as belated result of the 1974
            Revolution, 168
        and internal decentralisation, 294
        governing bodies, 162
University Management
    and authoritarianism, 230
    and university as 'service agency,' 231
University Nova de Lisboa, 69
University of Beira Interior, 69, 406
University of Coimbra, 228
University of Lisbon, Founding, 186
University of Madeira, 69

University of Porto, Founding of
    creation of faculty of arts, 83
    social class origins
        of students at, 396
University of the Algarve, 69
University of the Azores, 69, 406
University Constitution, 228
University of Trás os Montes e Alto Douro,
    founded as polytechnics, 406
Urbanisation, 94, 95, 99, 105
Value allocating bodies, 6
Value Systems and Cultural Dynamics,
    103–104
    high culture, 104
    ideological pluralism, 104
    secularisation, 103
Veiga Simão and higher education reform,
    63, 85, 230
    its reception in universities, 63
Veiga, A., 353–355
Vertical Power Structures in Portuguese HE,
    38, 303
Vilela, A.L., 84

W
Wages, 97
Welfare provision in Portugal
    and 1976 Constitution, 102
    and specific features of, 100–102
        current constraints upon, 102
    as symbol of droits acquis, 23
Whitchurch, C., 366
World Bank, 18, 234
Wrede, S., 332